Management Systems

A Viable Approach

Management Systems

A Viable Approach

Maurice Yolles

Liverpool John Moores University

FINANCIAL TIMES
PITMAN PUBLISHING

FINANCIAL TIMES
MANAGEMENT

LONDON · SAN FRANCISCO
KUALA LUMPUR · JOHANNESBURG

Financial Times Management delivers the knowledge,
skills and understanding that enable students,
managers and organisations to achieve their ambitions,
whatever their needs, wherever they are.

London Office:
128 Long Acre, London WC2E 9AN
Tel: +44 (0)171 447 2000
Fax: +44 (0)171 240 5771
Website: www.ftmanagement.com

A Division of Financial Times Professional Limited

———————————————

First published in Great Britain in 1999

© Financial Times Professional Limited 1999

The right of Maurice Yolles to be identified as Author
of this Work has been asserted by him in accordance
with the Copyright, Designs and Patents Act 1988.

ISBN 0 273 62018 5

British Library Cataloguing in Publication Data
A CIP catalogue record for this book can be obtained from the British Library

10 9 8 7 6 5 4 3 2 1

Typeset by Pantek Arts, Maidstone, Kent
Printed and bound in Great Britain by Clays Ltd, St Ives plc

The Publishers' policy is to use paper manufactured from sustainable forests.

CONTENTS

PREFACE

The approach taken in this book may be seen as one of cybernetic-based systems. It is fundamentally pluralistic, and within this context offers a way of extending beyond traditional systemic niches like managerial cybernetics or soft systems, pointing to a way of relating different ways of seeing in systems thinking. It also takes a view that systemic representations of situations are metaphors. In practical situations they generate particular models that must always be validated in order to determine whether that should be seen as apt or over-extended. The validation process can occur from a variety of perspectives determined by the penchant of an inquirer. Thus, a perspective may derive from soft systems thinking when it will be more people-orientated, which tends not to see things as very tangible, or from hard systems thinking when it will be more object directed, which sees things more in tangible terms.

This is a book about managing complexity, and within it we adopt a management systems approach to situations that we see as uncertain and complex, and that involve what many might refer to in the abstract as *purposeful adaptive activity systems*. When purposeful adaptive activity systems are considered in terms of their exogenous behaviour and their interaction with other such systems, we might more simply refer to them as actors. When considered in terms of their endogenous processes, however, we might more usefully think of them as organisations.

Management systems is the use of systems thinking to pursue management activities. It can provide an important way to showing managers and other leaders how they may be able to deal satisfactorily with complexity. Some aspects of management systems provide ways by which complex situations can be described, while others give guidelines that enable us to explain such situations. Our interest will, in addition to this, be to explore the nature of systemic inquiry into complex situations through methods that enable managers to formulate dynamic strategic plans. To do this we will take you on a journey through ideas of management systems. We explore methods that are capable of dealing with complexity by creating conceptualisations that in effect simplify the complexities. The methods generate rules that centre on these conceptualisations, and that the inquirer will adopt to explore the situation of interest. These methods are phenomena that, following Cohen and Stewart (1994), we might refer to as instruments of *complicity* that turn complexity into *simplexity*.

Within this book we shall explore some of these methods, and show the power that they have in helping an inquirer seek intervention strategies in given situations. While all the methods have some broad similarities (since they are both scientifically and system based), they also have differences that come from the distinct perspectives of the people who create and evolve them. These perspectives are embedded in what we can call a cognitive model, and each model that links with each method is unique in itself. This very uniqueness means, according to some people, that there is no way that we can use the different methods together in an assembly that takes advantage of their uniquenesses. One of our interests here will be to show that there are conditions under which methods can be mixed.

Pragmatists have been defined as those people who mix methods without worrying about whether they can do so 'legitimately'. The major problem is that even if their approach is 'legitimate', they rarely make it transparent. In this case it is not possible for *others* to see their logical basis, and thus have the possibility of agreeing or disagreeing with what they have done. The theory here sets up a way for them to work more transparently, and thus enables the possibility of their approach being legitimated.

We have created a view that enables us to mix methods that centres on the notion that inquiry, like any other activity in a purposeful activity system, can be viable. The inquirer, method and situation are all distinct parts of this. In order to explore this further, a number of ideas currently offered in the management systems field have been brought together. We have done this with the novice management systems practitioner in mind by setting the work up in three parts. In the first two parts the purposes are to create a foundation for (a) systems theory and method that explicitly addresses complexity, and (b) viable systems theory and the dynamics of method that implicitly addresses complexity. To help the reader out, chapters are occasionally punctuated with minicases designed to illustrate some of the conceptual points being made.

In the third part of the book five methods are explored, only two of which are probably very well known. For each method an application to a complex situation is illustrated through an exemplar case study. The purpose of the case studies is to illustrate how the methods *can* be used, not how they *should* be used. There will be at least as many ways of using the methods as there are inquirers wishing to do so. The book is intended as a standalone text, and the case studies that it provides enable this to occur. This was seen to be necessary because many of its conceptualisations are either new or expressed in new ways.

This book is directed at a variety of audiences, from undergraduate students on the second level upwards who attend courses involving the modelling of human organisations, such as business information systems or public administration. Many of the concepts presented in this text are already used with intermediate and final year students on business studies, business information systems and public administration courses, as well as for the Master in Business Administration, Master in Public Administration and Master in Information Systems Management. It also works as a basic text for doctoral students in systems or what may be considered to be systems-related topics. Since systems is generalist, it can therefore be argued to cover all areas of academic work that doctoral students may be engaged in. The ideas presented here have, for instance, been applied to the domain of learning theory, developing theory that relates to learning processes and learning auditing. They are also currently being explored for the area of information retrieval in the domain of librarianship.

The book is also suitable for professionals who are interested in exploring management system methods capable of dealing with complexity, or those who simply wish to develop their knowledge of these areas.

The message of this book can address advanced and specialist readers in management systems and management science. It also addresses a wider audience than this. It defines principles of systems that can apply to other subject domains in the same way that these domains may have contributed to systems in the first place. It is a book of its time, its theory centring on complexity. This is because the seemingly popular paradigm of complexity is fundamentally systemic, as illustrated by arguments about the way that chaos is collapsed. It is a paradigm that is influencing most science disciplines, suggesting that they are implicitly adopting systems concepts. This book highlights many of those aspects of systems that are of particular importance to the complexity paradigm. In pursuing this line, the book also hopes to show how to provide an integrative capability for at least some of the fragmentations that make up the subject domain.

Reference

Cohen, J. and Stewart, I. (1994) *The Collapse of Chaos: Discovering simplicity in a complex world*. London: Viking.

ACKNOWLEDGEMENTS

This work has not been undertaken *in vacuo*. It was inspired through my teaching, and I must thank all of my students who helped me develop it through the feedback that they gave me. I must also thank those students whose case study material I have used as a base from which I could illustrate how the methodologies described could be used. These include Terry Ashford, Judy Brough, Nicola Magill, Mark Muirhead, Kathy Ricketts and Raymond Turner.

I would also like to thank my colleagues who, through comments during discussions or on early drafts of various chapters, allowed me to develop my ideas and integrate them. The list of those I would like to mention includes Denis Adams, Bakri Ahmad, David Brown, Noyan Dereli, Agustin Duarte, Roger Harnden, Doug Haynes, Graham Kemp, Paul Iles, Allena Leonard, Chris Mabey, Gerald Midgley, Saundra Middleton, Ann Mulhaney, Terry Murray, John Naylor, Mo Pirani, Eric Schwarz and Jim Sheehan.

Of these people, Gerald Midgley was kind enough to make very useful comments on chapters dealing with the problem of paradigm incommensurability, and David Brown on other aspects relating to the nature of the paradigm. Chris Mabey was very helpful with ideas that related to systems intervention strategy, and he and Paul Iles with organisational development. Allena Leonard provided quite important feedback to me on the viable system model, as did Doug Haynes. Denis Adams was also particularly helpful in this respect, as he was in other more general areas of the book, and I am indebted to him for the time he gave me in general discussion of the concepts I have developed in order to address some theoretical problems in management systems. Saundra Middleton assisted me with comments over soft systems methodology. Ann Mulhaney provided comments on complexity and on systems in general. Jim Sheehan was kind enough to comment on aspects of cybernetics, and Graham Kemp and Mo Pirani on aspects of the conflict modelling cycle. Eric Schwarz gave me important feedback on his ideas relating to his theory of viability, and his work, together with that of Stafford Beer, has provided a foundation for the work here. Roger Harnden was particularly helpful to me early on in the development of my ideas by providing essential support. Also, I am grateful to John Naylor, who acted in a similar capacity, and to Agustin Duarte for some general comments. Without the time these colleagues gave me, this book would have taken much longer to complete. I would also like to thank Shyamal Mukhege, a senior medical practitioner, who was kind enough to comment on the case study on the National Health Service associated with soft systems methodology.

I would also like to thank John Cushion, who worked on behalf of my publisher and who gave me early encouragement after we originally discussed the idea of this book. At least as much as any of these, however, I wish to thank my wife Maria Teresa Ventura, who helped me with this work both intellectually through our discussions, and with her understanding and patience.

INTRODUCTION TO THE BOOK

There is a relationship between management practice and management theory. Management practice mainly still resides in the early 19th century, when linear and mechanical thinking was able to achieve a high level of achievement in the industrial revolution. Managers often manage by the 'seat of their pants' and without a full understanding of what the consequences of their actions will be. They more often than not see problem situations, and establish intervention strategies that inflict results that are to the penalty of the organisation rather than its salvation. The norm of management practice lags behind management theory by many decades, and many practitioners still have not realised the existence of management systems. This book is not a practical guide on how to bring management practice into the modern age, but is a contribution to management systems that will provide readers with exemplars by which to develop their own understanding of how to practice in the new management Age of Aquarius.

Management systems arose as a subject domain in the 1950s and 1960s, and represents more than just seeing management situations in systemic terms. It is also concerned with inquiry into complex problem situations that are seen to have a need to be managed, and from which system views of the situation emerge. The inquiry is systemic, and its intention is to find decision processes or intervention strategies that will satisfy systemic management needs.

Management systems has come after the deterministic and reductionist period of the industrial revolution, during which problem situations were modelled in terms of an arbitrarily defined set of parts. We say arbitrary, but in most cases it was seen that there is a 'best' way of defining the parts, a characteristic of simple rather than complex situations. Another tendency in the modelling of situations that came from this period was the idea that they were naturally in stable equilibrium. This meant that the behaviour of organisations would likely not change over time, or if it did, then the nature of that change would normally be predictable. If the nature of a situation changed, then it was seen that this occurred through a shift from one discrete equilibrium position to another. Basically, the world was seen as an orderly place.

Since the 1960s, it has become clear that this view is beginning to change: that the world is a complex, chaotic place. The idea started to gain acceptance because inquiry into situations did not always generate interventions that resulted in predictable outcomes. To deal with this an explanation was required that differentiated between difficult problems and messy problems, equivalent to distinguishing between simple and complex situations. In difficult problems the traditional management practice approach, which centres on intuition, often worked well if the manager was experienced and outcomes were more or less predictable. In messy problems the situation was seen to be too complex to be dealt with adequately in this way or for the consequences of an intervention to be predicted. This is because complex situations are not easily identifiable in clear-cut ways. As a result, structured approaches to inquiry were developed that could more ably deal with complexity and uncertainty. These methods generally operated from a conceptual model that enabled the situation to be examined in a way that could effectively reduce its complexity.

An idea that began to achieve substantive support in the 1970s and the 1980s is that the complex nature of messes makes them prone to chaos. The concept of chaos has become particularly well supported because it explains so well the changes in a whole variety of complex situations. It became useful in examining the weather system, as well as important in the social context. This was particularly so in management science and the operation of the market economy. Today, organisations rise and fall at a rate that was unimaginable in the 1960s, a birth and death behaviour that appears to have coincided with the Western recession that began in the mid-1970s. There is a lack of stability in markets, and organisations seem unable to maintain their viability.

Explanations about how organisations can better survive are quite forthcoming. For instance in 1985 Drucker espoused his view in the 1960s explaining that organisations should direct themselves towards being innovative and entrepreneurial. He informs us that the view that the market environment is a place of dynamic disequilibrium as opposed to one of equilibrium optimisation was already being postulated in 1911 by Schumpeter. It is suggested that such conditions represent the natural situation for the innovating entrepreneur, who always searches for change and wishes to exploit it as an opportunity.

Tom Peters, in his book *Thriving on Chaos* published in 1988, tells us that the management paradigm is changing. The penchant of organisations for mass production and mass markets based on a relatively predictable environment is being replaced by flexibility and change: it should not be assumed that situations will have long-term stability and predictability, because of the impact of chaos and uncertainty.

Stacey is another advocate of the idea that organisations should be managing chaos. He tells us in his 1993 book that our Western organisations are mostly managed through the false assumption that equilibrium is the normal condition, and that stability comes from equilibrium. This represents the belief that long-term success flows from stability, harmony, regularity, discipline and consensus; that general prescriptive behaviour can thus turn action into successful achievement of objectives. These procedures can be formulated as a method for action.

Stacey advocates that few will question the deterministic logic from which this belief derives. Assumptions are normally that it is cognitive control alone that enables stability and viability to be maintained. It is supposed that either stability is cognitively achieved or maintained, or instability occurs together with death. It is the same belief system that sees the irretrievable loss of cognitive control as a perception of failure. An alternative view is that stability can be achieved without cognitive control, though it may occur in unpredictable or undesirable ways.

We are aware that management systems is directly concerned with these ideas. However, its inquiry methods have developed in a fragmented way, as each pulls in its own direction without compromise. There has been a movement towards rescuing this, led principally by what we shall refer to as the Hull school of thought, through the work of such authors as Jackson, Flood and Midgely.

One perspective in management systems comes from Stafford Beer's work that lies at the basis of his viable system model, which has been built into a method intended to make organisations viable. Recently, new systems theory has been created by Eric Schwarz, which we refer to as Schwarzian viable systems theory, and which is intended to explain how viable systems adapt and change in complex situations. We have linked the two by creating what we refer to as viable systems theory. It explains how viable organisations are able to maintain their viability through self-organisation and thus survive in problematic or chaotic situations. The consequences of this theory can provide a way of looking at the methods of management systems, and enable them to be seen systemically; that is, as a whole rather than as a fragmented set. We refer to this view as viable inquiry theory, and it is the ultimate focus of this book. To reach that point, however, we must first take the reader along a gentle road of discovery.

To do this we have structured the book into three separate parts. Part 1 develops a foundation for a modern perspective of management systems. It is composed of five chapters that take the reader through a variety of fundamental concepts. The first chapter is concerned with providing an appreciation of the nature of management systems, and to do so it explores both management and systems, and their association. Chapter 2 is concerned with how we see and model the world around us through the world views that we all have. We define two classes of world view, weltanschauung and paradigm. The term weltanschauung was introduced into management systems by Checkland in the 1970s, and the term paradigm was made important by Kuhn at about the same time. The two terms differ. Weltanschauung, some would say, is a typically personal and often indescribable world view. We would prefer to call it an *informal* world view that is not fully describable. In contrast, the paradigm is more or less fully describable, and can therefore be referred to as formal. One of the tasks of this chapter is to explore their relationship and some of the problems that they present in using methods, particularly in a mixed mode. These conceptualisations form the basis of the theory that we then build upon in the rest of the book.

Chapter 3 provides an introduction to the nature of complexity and its connection with simplicity. This will provide for us a base from which we can explain how to deal with complexity. In Chapter 4 we explore how management science paradigms have changed in order to deal with complexity. In the following chapter we introduce a core concept for this book, complex adaptable purposeful activity systems – sometimes referred to more succinctly as actor systems. They are autonomous and implicitly unstable, and are frequently seeking ways of achieving behavioural stability. The search for stability occurs through a process of methodological inquiry and intervention into developed problem situations involving these systems. We take this as an opportunity to address a difficulty in the literature in distinguishing between method and methodology, and we provide a new definition that is both consistent with the current usages of the terms, and involves the notion of complexity.

Part 2 is also composed of five chapters. The purpose of these is to define our approach to management systems through the concept of viability. In Chapter 6 we explore the idea that we can model situations as a bounded network of actor systems, and the consequences of this conceptualisation are explored. As part of this we distinguish between an actor system's 'cognitive consciousness' or metasystem, and its behavioural system. In doing this, innovative linkages are made between existing cybernetic and soft systems theory. Chapter 7 explores complex purposeful adaptive activity systems in terms of viability, while Chapter 8 considers how non-equilibrium theory can provide explanations of how they are able to survive and indeed evolve, as they pass through periods of chaos. In exploring this we provide for the first time a linkage between Beer's viable system model and the recent Schwarzian viable systems theory.

In Chapter 9 we think of methodologies as part of a complex adaptable purposeful activity system. This provides us with the possibility of exploring viable systems of inquiry during our search for stable intervention strategies that are able to deal with complex problem situations. Chapter 10 links this back to some of the ideas of Chapter 2, and is concerned with the examination of problem situations that are world-view plural.

It leads us to the notion of how to deal with paradigm incommensurability when trying to mix methods.

Part 3 involves five methodologies suitable for management systems intervention, taking the reader from Chapter 11 through to Chapter 15. In Chapter 11 we introduce systems intervention strategy, originally proposed by Mayon-White. This is designed to offer a straightforward and more familiar approach to the examination of messy and relatively soft situations that novice inquirers can become familiar with quite quickly. In the next chapter, organisational development is introduced as a very well-known soft methodology that is used to explore situations by addressing individual perspectives in an organisational situation. In particular, the approaches of Pugh and Harrison are considered.

In Chapter 13 we introduce soft systems methodology. This is perhaps the most well-known soft methodology in management systems. In developing it, Checkland has needed to develop many new ideas that have contributed to the formulation of a base for management systems theory. The next chapter addresses Beer's viable system model, which has become a powerful way of addressing problem situations that involve control and communication processes. Chapter 15 introduces the conflict modelling cycle, through which all problem situations can be seen in terms of patterns of conflict. It provides a novel way of exploring both organisational and social-scale problem situations.

Finally, Chapter 16 is concerned with providing guidance in the practice of mixing methods. It shows how a framework can be established that enables methods to be mixed, and knowledges from different methods to be applied without confusion. The approach is simple, but holds behind it necessary epistemological theory.

Towards the end of Chapters 11–15 we introduce major case studies that are intended to provide an indication of how the given methodology can be used. At the end of Chapter 11 a problem situation involving Liverpool City Council is explored. The Council is experiencing a budget deficit as well as increasing demands on its services. Government policy has been that local authorities must solve their own problems. As a result Liverpool City Council introduced service charging as a policy in its social service unit, a practice historically alien to it. The study explores some of the difficulties associated with this in terms of systems intervention strategy (SIS). While SIS is capable of exploring the local council situation in terms of its technical and organisational aspects, it is not designed to be particularly sensitive to the cultural feasibility of the proposed intervention. As a consequence, the same case study is further explored through organisational development in Chapter 12.

The case study in Chapter 13 is on the National Health Service (NHS). It has recently passed through a paradigm shift, and the consequences of this are explored. The study also identifies some of the problems that have arisen within the new NHS as a result of the conflicting interests of what we have referred to as financial accounting and medical accounting. It centres on a particular organisation in the NHS, and explores some of the problems that have arisen due to the change.

Another area that has been influenced by Government policy is that of education. We do not explore this from that context, however. Rather, we are interested in the structure of the local provision of further education, and the related 'faults' it appears to have. We apply the viable system model (VSM) (Chapter 14) to the case of the City of Liverpool Community College of Further Education. Further education in Liverpool has passed through a number of restructurings in a very short time. This was partly due to the need for it to become more efficient in its delivery of training courses. The study concentrates on one particular area, that of the School of Transport, and explains how the situation can be explored so that faults in its form can be sought and corrections introduced.

The methodology in Chapter 15, conflict modelling cycle, could with interest have been applied to the Liverpool City Council case of Chapters 11 and 12, or indeed to any of the other case studies. However, in order to explore the specific facilities unique to the methodology, we present for this a problem situation that centres on a two-year-old industrial dispute centring on the Liverpool dockers. A further case examines the fall of the Soviet empire.

PART 1

Management systems: a foundation

INTRODUCTION TO PART 1

The interest in this section is to provide an introduction to some of the basic ideas associated with management systems in its approach to addressing complexity.

Management can be argued as being concerned with inquiry and action, and involving cybernetic processes. Inquiry, the very interest of this book, occurs through planning and by defining organisational mission, goals and manager aims. It also results in action and involves the cybernetic processes of control and communications. The recent tradition of scientific management (which saw situations in terms of a set of mechanistic parts) has at least at a theoretical if not practising level given way to management systems, where management is pursued according to systemic principles. The theoretical shift has occurred with the realisation that there is a distinction between simple and complex situations. The shift in management practice to management systems is in general far from being realised. Managers still do not realise the need for systems modelling, even when it is simply seen as a metaphor for a problem situation that can be used to help them formulate intervention strategies.

All strategies are influenced by world views of individuals and of groups. We are individual in the way we see the world, and how we do so determines how we respond to it. Our world view is determined by the way we were brought up as children, and is affected by our experiences. As our beliefs, values and attitudes change, so does or world view. World views are regarded as informal, when they are called weltanschauungen, and can belong to either an individual or a group. The beliefs, values attitudes and concepts that are part of group world views can be made more or less transparent to others. When this occurs we say that they have been formalised, and turned into paradigms. Contrary to this, weltanschauungen are not transparent to others, and are informal. World views are manifested as behaviour that is a result of the interplay between weltanschauungen and the paradigms of those organisations around us.

Situations that we are involved in are sometimes seen to be problematic when things do not seem to go as we might expect to wish. If a problematic situation can be seen in terms of a set of differentiable problems that are to be dealt with, then it may be referred to as a difficulty. However, if it seen as a complex tangle of undifferentiable problems then it is referred to as a mess. The former type of situation is an example of a 'simple' situation, while the latter is one that is 'complex'. There are other criteria that distinguish simple from complex situations, and that enable us to find strategies for intervention that are intended to create stability.

As we develop our conceptual structures in science, we see that the paradigms that enable us to contextualise these conceptualisations evolve and mature. As they do so they may also become bounded through the very structures that originally made them successful through the exclusion of other conceptual possibilities. The paradigm of complexity is able to conceptualise problem situations in terms of certainty, softness and structure. These conceptualisations can be used to evaluate how different paradigms are able to deal with complex to simple situations.

Our interest in this book is with purposeful activity systems and making inquiry into the complex behaviour that they manifest under the influence of the environment. Purposeful activity systems have dynamic goal-seeking behaviour. If goal seeking becomes unstable, then methods are needed to find intervention strategies that can engineer stability. We can distinguish between simple methods – that is, those that have poor conceptual variety – and complex methods, which have rich conceptual variety. In simple situations with difficult problems, simple methods are satisfactory. In complex situations with messy problems a sufficiently complex method is required. Methodologies can been seen as complex methods. Methods can also be mixed and compared, while maintaining the truth of their paradigm incommensurability.

CHAPTER 1

The nature of management systems

OVERVIEW

One view of management is that it is concerned with inquiry, action and cybernetic processes. Inquiry occurs through planning and by defining organisational mission, goals and manager aims. It also results in action and involves the cybernetic processes of control and communications. The recent tradition of scientific management (which saw situations as mechanisms) has at least at a theoretical if not practising level given way to management systems, where management is pursued according to systemic principles. This shift has occurred with the realisation that there is a distinction between simple and complex situations. In particular, systems models are metaphors for a problem situation that are used by managers to help them formulate intervention strategies.

OBJECTIVES

This chapter will examine:

- how and why management has shifted from a mechanistic to a systemic view of reality;
- the nature of the systems metaphor;
- the nature of management systems.

1.1 Management

The term management can be said to refer to the process of pursuing effective and efficient activities with and through other people. It involves three functions or primary activities:

1 inquiry through analysis that leads to planning, which includes decision making;
2 action through organising and leading;
3 cybernetics through control and communication.

Management can be seen as the process of acquiring and combining human, financial and physical resources to attain the organisation's primary goal of producing a product or service desired by some segment of society, and this is enabled by the aims of the managers who facilitate it. It can also be described as a process whereby individuals within an organisation are required to anticipate activities likely to be necessary in the future. In addition, it concerns carrying out such activities, while always attempting to ensure that 'things don't go wrong' thus creating problems.

A feature of all the functions of management is that they require the manager to practise decision making. There is a perceived need to understand not only how managers tend to behave in performing management practice, but also the logical processes that might best be systematically followed in the process of making decisions. The behavioural process that results from this is often referred to as method, a typical example of which is: investigate the situation; develop alternative decisions; evaluate alternative decisions; select appropriate decision; implement and follow up.

Despite systematic approaches to management presented in the literature, management often fails to be effective. Failure can be related to two causes: the inabilities of individual managers and the complexity of the situations in which managers work.

1.2 Inquiry

A manager must be able to analyse a situation in order to explain it. An early part of this process is planning, consisting of defining a mission, setting goals, establishing key premises or assumptions, setting policies, making strategic decisions, and acting on the plans and decisions. Organisational *mission* defines purpose and can be used to convey such ultimate ends as the basic reason for the organisation's being. Organisational *goals* reflect qualitative or quantitative operational expectations. They are pursued through the aims of managers, who act as agents of decision.

Goals must be set for the organisation as a whole and for each of its subdivisions. They are often prescribed for both the short and the long term, and achievements have to be regularly monitored against expectation. They must be planned and communicated throughout the organisation, and local aims established by individual managers.

Policies are guides to thinking in decision making. They reflect and interpret goals, channel decisions to contribute to goals, thereby establishing the framework to planning programmes, and guide managers' aims. They thus establish limits to plans, as planning premises provide for them an operational background. Decision making – the actual selection from among alternatives of a course of action – is at the core of planning. In the classical view of management inquiry, we assume that the goals are known and that the planning premises are clear. Then the first step in decision making is the development of alternatives. Once appropriate alternatives have been isolated, the next step is to evaluate them and select the one that will best contribute to the organisation's goals. That process of evaluation and selection will be based on experience, on experimentation, or on further research and analysis. When a plan is complete – with proper assignments made and understood – and it enters the phase in which the manager checks on actual execution, the planning function shifts into control. In practice, however, these two functions inevitably blend into a whole, and the shift to control may be imperceptible.

There are some difficulties with this view of management practice, particularly where planning is long term. Goals change, and so planning should be dynamic. Moreover, managers become embroiled in conflicts and power struggles, and this affects the behavioural capacity of a workforce to achieve goals. A long-term planning mentality leads managers to design actions that reinforce what they already know and do best. However, organisations are subject to perturbations from the external environment, and their old strengths may not be appropriate for their new futures. According to Stacey (1993), this 'planning mentality' denies uncertainty, and pursues historical pathways of action that may have little future value. Planning attempts to avoid surprises, and can act as a counter to essential innovation. It is part of a paradigm that lets us see failure as a negative attribute rather than a positive one from which learning occurs. It is against the tradition of entrepreneurship, where innovation, variety and learning processes are linked.

1.3 Action and cybernetics

Action occurs through the process of organising and leadership. Whatever is planned needs to be organised if it is to take effect. Organising encompasses the span of management, basic departmentation, the assignment of activities, line and staff functioning, the decentralisation of authority, and making organising effective.

Leadership is that skill of a manager which enables him or her to persuade *others* being led to apply themselves with zeal and confidence. Leadership also means shaping the 'character' of the organisation so that the execution of policy will be achieved to the 'spirit' as well as to the 'letter'. The leadership function may be classified as directing, responding and representing. Whereas directing is of the essence of leadership, the good leader is responsive to the *others'* felt and expressed needs, and represents them effectively to superiors, and to those in the outside world. Finally, a leader has special traits – especially self-knowledge, empathy towards others and objectivity towards situations. In fact it is impossible to be objective without self-knowledge, and it is impossible to inspire people to follow your lead without empathy for them and their situations.

Action is maintained in a desired way through cybernetic processes that involve control and communications. Good management communication might be defined as the interchange of thought or information to bring about mutual understanding and confidence, as well as good human relations. It is the means whereby organised activity is unified. It is also the means whereby behaviour is modified, change is effected and goals are achieved. In its broadest sense, according to Koontz and O'Donnell (1968), the purpose of communication within the enterprise is to effect change – to influence action in the direction of the corporation's overall interest. They also identify four principles for establishing good communication:

1 the principle of 'clarity': communicate in commonly understood language;
2 the principle of attention: give full attention to receiving communications;

3 the principle of integrity: make communications support organisational objectives;
4 the principle of 'strategic use of informal information'.

Controlling implies measurement of accomplishment against plan, and the correction of deviations to assure attainment of objectives – referred to as homeostasis. Once a plan becomes operational, monitoring and control are necessary to measure progress, to uncover deviations from the plan, and to indicate corrective action. In the conventional organisation, control is thus the function whereby every manager, from chief executive to operations supervisor, makes sure that what is done is what is intended. The basic control process involves three steps:

1 establishing standards
2 measuring performance against these standards
3 correcting deviations from standards and plans.

Standards represent the expression of planning goals in such terms that the actual accomplishment of assigned duties can be measured against them. The measurement of performance against standards should ideally be on a future basis, so that deviations may be detected in advance of their actual occurrence, and corrective action taken. Such corrective action is the point at which control merges with the other management functions.

For Koontz and O'Donnell, there are ten requirements of effective controls: they must reflect the nature and needs of the activity; they should report deviations promptly; they must be forward looking; they should point out exceptions at critical points; they should be objective; they must be flexible; they should reflect the organisational pattern; they should be economical; they must be understandable; and finally, they should indicate where corrective action is required. These ideas will be revisited in due course throughout the book.

Control involves feedback from the outputs of a process that is following a goal, to its input. Control processes are normally thought of as involving negative feedback (homeostasis), where a damping action occurs on the deviations that occur in a process due to perturbations that shift it away from achieving the goal. However, feedback may also be positive when the deviations are amplified in the case that they are seen to be beneficial. In both cases, the processes are well behaved – that is, stable. There is, however, another condition, referred to as bounded instability. Here predefined long-term goals may not be achievable, being independent of the control processes or criteria that are applied. Feedback is nonlinear, and small perturbations can be subject to large amplification, resulting in unpredictable behaviour. When this occurs it is said that the process displays complex behaviour that can be represented by hidden (fractal) patterns. This behaviour is referred to as chaotic.

1.4 Scientific management

What we may now refer to as scientific management has a background of conceptual influences from paradigms in other scientific fields. Thus in biology advocates of the vitalistic paradigm believed that a mysterious vital force inhabited complex organisms. There does not seem to be any equivalent to this in management theory since in those days managers tended to manage idiosyncratically and arbitrarily, with little or no specialist support (Burnes, 1992).

Scientific management derives from the work of the American Frederick Taylor (1856–1915). Its paradigm is mechanistic in that it is believed that everything is predeterminable by that which preceded it. Stakeholders of this paradigm examine things in terms of their parts, leading to a view that they are composed of components that work together like a machine. Scientific management advocates believed that management solutions should be achieved by:

- a scientific analysis of the work done and the development of improved methods by the application, perhaps, of management techniques, or by
- applying certain principles of organisation to create the organisation's structure, and applying certain principles of management.

Taylor was able to introduce considerable increases in productive efficiency by questioning traditional work practices and finding the one 'best way' in which each job should be done. With others he defined what we now refer to as the classical school of management thought. Their contributions were:

1 to introduce technique in order to study the nature of work and solve the problem of how to organise work better (Taylor, Gnatt, Gilbreth);
2 to suggest a theory of organisation and management, based largely on formal structure – that is, clear lines of authority, distinguishing line and staff management, organisation charts (Fayol).

The concept of organisation through this view was essentially a mechanistic one; employees were to be given instructions, and no choice in their method of working. However, the classical school provided theories where none had previously existed, and they provided a basis from which new conceptualisations could emerge.

1.5 The rise of systems thinking in management

The systems paradigm was driven by biology, where biological organisms were found to be too complex to be modelled through the mechanistic paradigm. In order to simplify situations under investigation, tools were used that enabled them to be seen in a conceptually different way. One tool that enables these comparisons to occur is the *simile*, which enables one to say that something is *like* something else. Another is the *metaphor*, which enables one to say that something *is* something else. These devices are usually used in poetry or verse to provide more strength to intended meanings. When we are exploring an object of inquiry, it is through the use of similes and metaphors that we can assume the same characteristics that have been assigned to an analogous object.

One example of a generalised object is the *system* (Weinberg, 1975), the common idea of which is that it is composed of a set of interactive parts that have properties or qualities that can be differentiated from an environment by a boundary. In particular, the parts work together as a whole and have emergent properties. The system is a metaphor because it derives from our experiences of taking physical objects that are part of a situation, and working with them separately. Thus, in most cases of inquiry, when we talk of a system we therefore mean a metaphorical view of a situation, and we should not be confused that the system is the situation. This understanding of the nature of a system is particularly important when we are attempting to intervene in a situation, since real situations will not always comply with our models of analogy. This is because a metaphor may carry inappropriate conceptual baggage for a situation that suggests that the detail of the metaphor that we are using may not be totally applicable to the situation. When this happens it is said to be over-extended.

9

In this text we will either use the concept of a system in an abstract way; or when we as inquirer examine a situation as though it is a system or talk of a system representation of a situation, we will be aware that we are using that description metaphorically and in practical terms. As a consequence of this, if a particular situation is defined as a system we must be aware that (a) the situation is not really a system, and the system model created by an inquirer may break down, and (b) the nature of the system model will vary with the purpose and world view of the inquirer who created it. Inquirers into situations may adopt systems metaphors to clearly understand a changing situation. If the changes are to be guided deterministically, then an intervention strategy will be sought. The belief about the relationship between the inquirer, the system metaphor and the real world will be a factor in the creation and evaluation of this strategy.

From these beginnings, systems thinking was found to be successful where it was applied. It developed significantly from the 1950s, when through authors like Ackoff, Ashby, Beer, von Bertalanffy, Koestler, Weinberg and Simon it became an independent domain of study in management. Several branches of systems arose. One branch related to the use of computers in organisations as the technology was seen to be able to induce more efficiency and effectiveness into organisational situations. Systems techniques were used both to design computer programs and then to introduce computer systems into organisations. The tendency was for inquirers to design systems rather than metaphors, so that the situation is identified as a system. This perspective provides the antecedent for hard systems thinking.

Other approaches developed from the social sciences, through the work of such authors as Nadler, and contributed to a different way of looking at organisations, from a softer systems perspective. The interest of inquirers into the nature of human systems and their management developed through work from Checkland and others in the 1970s and 1980s. One of the distinguishing ideas of soft systems, according to Checkland and Scholes (1990), is that it reaffirmed the view that situations can be seen metaphorically in terms of systems, and these metaphors were capable of being changed. This was in contradistinction, it was claimed, to the hard systems perspective, which saw situations actually as systems that might malfunction.

To highlight this, Checkland and Scholes make the following comment: 'Bertalanffy (1968) clearly regards "system" as an abstract concept, but unfortunately he immediately starts using the word as a label for parts of the world. Now going back to the idea of an "education system", it is perfectly legitimate for an investigator to say "I will treat education as *if it were* a system", but this is very different from declaring that it is a system ... Choosing to think of the world as if it is a system can be helpful. But this is a very different stance from arguing that the world is a system, a position which pretends to knowledge no human being can have' (Checkland and Scholes, 1990, p. 22). Hence the distinction between *attributing* to a situation the properties of a system and *declaring* it to be a system is fundamentally an epistemological one. Checkland and Scholes distinguish between their 'soft' and the von Bertalanffy 'hard' approaches to systems by saying that the 'hard' tradition takes the world to be systemic, while the 'soft' tradition rather creates the process of inquiry as a system (p. 25). Having said this, Checkland and Scholes (like von Bertalanffy) are not immune to labelling parts of the situation as systems that define their world of inquiry. They first describe situations as having social and political attributes, and then commonly use the terms 'social system' and 'political system'. They distinguish their soft approach from a hard one by saying that 'In both cases the phrases within inverted commas are used as in every day language, rather than as technical terms ... [relating] respectively to problem solving, the social process, and the power-based aspects of human affairs' (p. 30).

Stafford Beer created his own approach to dealing with uncertain complex problem situations that also involves soft principles, referred to as managerial cybernetics. Part of its theory involves conceptualisations about *viable* organisations that are purposeful, adaptive and able to maintain their long-term stability. After Habermas some refer to it as a technical approach that centres on control and prediction. We might note that the concept of viability has been picked up by Eric Schwarz in his attempt to apply the dynamic concepts of chaos and complexity to self-organisation systems that change and evolve. We refer to the theory that has been created as Schwarzian viable systems theory.

As a variety of ways of seeing situations developed and found a following, so conflicts began to appear between the stakeholders of the various approaches. The soft systems movement decried the *hard* inquiry approach that saw things as objects that had to be manipulated, saying that it did not take people and their needs into account. Criticism occurred the other way too, indicating for example that soft methodologies were consensus approaches that had their own failings.

A new question arose: is this conflict resolvable? Feyerabend in the 1960s was one of the authors whose work would implicitly advocate that resolution would not be possible. In his book *Against Method* he argued that 'no set of rules can ever be found to guide the scientist in his choice of theories, and to imagine that there is such a set is to impede progress. The only principle that does not impede progress is anything goes' (Casti, 1989, p. 38). The idea of incommensurability was being born, and was adopted by Kuhn in discussing his concept of paradigm. It has encouraged fragmentation in the domain of management systems inquiry approaches.

There is a new movement, however, that is attempting to apply the systems metaphor to the systems domain in order to mend the fragmentation. In management systems this means that we must see methodologies in terms of a totality rather than as parts that cannot be connected. Each methodology should be seen as part of a complex web of approaches that can enable us to inquire into situations from a variety of perspectives.

1.6 Management systems

Management systems can be seen as the process of management through the application of systems metaphors. It has developed with the rise of systems science, and dates from the 1930s with the work of Barnard, where organisations are seen as cooperative systems. All managed organisations are seen as systems that share certain conceptual elements. These include input, process, output and feedback. The inputs in the manufacturing firm, for instance, consist of raw materials, technical knowledge, labour, equipment and financing, all of which are combined under managerial direction into a process that results in a finished output or product. Consumer acceptance of the product results in a financial return (feedback) to the firm, which reactivates the cycle. Low sales, on the other hand, indicate that a change in the input or process is necessary to produce a more acceptable output. Through cycles such as these, organisations maintain their existence. And many organisations outlive by decades or even centuries those human beings who founded them.

Organisational systems are seen to be open to their environment. They import inputs, export outputs and interpret the feedback they receive from the environment. What happens in the environment affects them, and as the environment changes, management must monitor the changes and adapt the organisation to the new situation.

Although all organisations are open to their environment, the degree of openness varies. Some systems are designed to be relatively closed – a maximum security prison, for example – while others are deliberately quite open – a state legislature, for instance. Some managers believe that increasing the openness of their systems can be beneficial. Companies such as IBM and Sperry Corporation, for instance, have established panels of outsiders to evaluate technological trends and assess the potential of new opportunities. Such advisory boards help keep management informed of new developments in the environment and are able to advise without feeling constrained by corporate policy. At a national level, the countries of the European Union maintain a totally open policy to each other. Within this the EU stimulates joint ventures that occur as new associations are able then to generate innovative strategies for development.

Organisational systems may be seen to consist of a number of interrelated subsystems. Major subsystems of a university for example, might be the faculties of economics, engineering and so on. Corporate subsystems include the marketing division, production division, personnel department, and others. Each of these subsystems has a purpose which, if attained, aids the larger system in reaching its overall goals. Each subsystem, in attaining its purpose, must mesh its activities with the activities of the other subsystems. Within a system, there is no provision for a totally independent subsystem.

We often model organisations as structured systems, the parts of which we commonly equate with units, departments or divisions. However, these parts may themselves be seen in terms of goal-directed role players who might alternatively be seen to define the structure of the organisation. To achieve organisational goals, people must perform tasks, using technical knowledge and equipment, and they must work together in structured relationships. However, human beings are not mere robots – they will, and indeed must, enter into social relationships, both formal (job-related) and informal (non-job-related). The task of management is to coordinate all of these parts and plan future activities. It also involves decision making and regulation of the organisational system. Managers are involved in planning, directing and controlling parts of the total organisational system. Consequently, the managerial role should be seen in its relationship to the total organisation.

The thread that binds together the seemingly disparate activities of managers is revealed by this view of the managerial task. Individual managers do not work in isolation, and one function or activity is not performed without reference to another. The planning of Manager A must be harmonised with that of Manager B if organisational goals are to be achieved.

There are two overriding lessons for the manager contained in open systems theory. The first is that no organisation exists in a vacuum. The environment constrains what the manager can do, but it also offers opportunities and potentialities. Managers must be aware of and understand environmental events and trends because the organisation's well-being and even survival depend upon appropriate adaptation to change.

The second lesson of the systems approach is its stress on the interrelatedness of the parts of an organisation. A manager is often tempted to see organisational problems and activities in isolation. In an extreme case, a manager may concentrate upon the efficient functioning of his or her own department and give only secondary attention to its relationships with other parts of the organisation. Any neglect of important relationships results in some degree of inefficiency or ineffectiveness.

1.6.1 Closed systems thinking

Closed systems thinking stems primarily from the physical sciences and is most applicable to mechanistic systems thinking. Early systemic modelling of social situations created closed models because it considered that the system was self-contained. A system is said to have a boundary. The nature of the closure of a system will depend upon the nature of the boundary defined for it. A closed system that has 'no exchanges with its environment' (Jantsch, 1980, p. 32) can also be referred to as *isolated*.

In an example of closed system thinking, consider a management situation in which only the internal operations of the organisation under examination are considered (Kast and Rosenzweig, 1979). To enable such a view to hold, the organisation must be seen to be sufficiently independent to enable problems to be examined in terms of internal structure, tasks and formal relationships. No reference can be made to the external environment.

Closed system thinking is bound up with the idea of equilibrium. Equilibrium systems do not change over time, or if they do their movements are easily determinable: thus, for instance, moving equilibrium occurs when change is a constant. In order to explain how isolated systems can survive, the idea of entropy has been borrowed from the past successes of equilibrium thermodynamic theory in physics (Cohen and Stewart, 1994).

All thermodynamic systems are seen to produce entropy, or disorder. Entropy derives from the idea in physics that part of the total energy (the entropy) of a system is not freely available and cannot be used as directed energy or information flow. In an isolated system, entropy builds up and becomes maximised, destroying all order in the system. If systems are defined in terms of differentiation, the destruction of order means the death of the system. If entropy builds up to a maximum, the behaviour of the system becomes equalised so that any event can be expected with equal likelihood anywhere within the system. This is equivalent to the destruction of order, or the breaking down of purposeful internal organisational boundaries, that leads organisations to run down. Because of the build-up of entropy, isolated systems inherently tend to move towards a condition of (static) equilibrium. Viewing systems as isolated bodies is therefore consistent with their being seen to maintain equilibrium.

This type of thinking was prevalent in the 1950s. Then, Ashby theorised that when systems are subject to perturbations from a changing environment, they shift from one equilibrium to another to ensure their stability. Shifting between equilibria implied that systems change through discontinuous steps in some sort of 'evolutionary progression'. The paradigm that supports these ideas has mostly been abandoned, and replaced by those supporting the concept of bounded non-equilibrium as defined within complexity theory. In this explanation of system behaviour the notion of entropy becomes unnecessary (Cohen and Stewart, 1994, p. 252).

The theory of closed systems is still actively pursued, but not in its traditional sense. Closure can occur in a variety of ways, and most appropriately today systems are seen as isolated bodies in terms of their self-actuation. Examples of self-actuation systems are those that we can describe as being self-influencing, self-regulating, self-sustaining, self-producing, self-referring and self-conscious.

1.6.2 Open systems theory

Open systems theory enables us to model situations that have boundaries that are open to the environment with respect to a given class of interaction. Thus, an open system interacts with its environment. In particular, 'with respect to its *relations with the environment*, a system is called open that maintains exchanges with its environment –

especially exchanges of matter, energy and information – and that is open towards the new and inexperienced (towards novelty...)' (Jantsch, 1980, p. 32).

According to von Bertalanffy (1968) the theory of open systems represents generalisations of physical theory, kinetics and thermodynamics, which led to new principles and insight. Negative feedback is one of these. It occurs when homeostatic maintenance of a characteristic state or goal is desired. It is based on circular causal chains and mechanisms monitoring and feeding back information on deviations from the state to be maintained or the goal to be achieved. Another is the idea of equifinity, where an open system has a tendency to move towards having final states that derive from different initial states and in different ways.

Adaptation is also seen as an important feature of open systems. Open systems theory recognises that systems are in a dynamic relationship with their environment, and receive inputs that they transform in some way to create outputs. The open system is seen to adapt to its environment by responding to perturbations through changes in its form. The open system is supposed to be in continuing interaction with its external environment and maintains homeostasis. Thus, for example, an organisation receives inputs of people, money, materials and information. It transforms these into outputs which constitute products, services and rewards to the organisation that are sufficient to maintain its interest.

A frequent representation of 'open system' organisations is provided in Fig. 1.1. The terms used are explained as follows.

- *Inputs (resources)*: like raw materials, money, people (human resources), equipment, information, knowledge, legal authority from the environment for action.
- *Outputs*: products, services, ideas as an outcome of organisational action; an organisation transfers its main outputs back to the environment and uses others internally.
- *Technology*: tools, machines, techniques for transforming recourses into outputs; techniques can be mental (e.g. exercising judgement), social, chemical, physical, mechanical or electronic.
- *Environment*: the task environment includes all of the external organisations and conditions that are directly related to an organisation's main operations and its technologies.
- *Goals and strategies*: future states sought by the organisation's dominant decision makers. *Goals* are desired end states, while objectives are specified targets and indicators of goal attainment. *Strategies* are overall routes to goals, including ways of dealing with the environment. *Plans* specify courses of action towards an end goal. Goals and strategies are the outcomes of conflict and negotiation among powerful parties within the outside organisation.
- *Behaviour and process*: prevailing patterns of behaviour, interactions, and relations between groups and individuals – including corporations, conflict, coordination, communication, controlling and rewarding behaviour, influence and power relations, goal setting, information gathering, self-criticism, evaluation, group learning.
- *Culture*: shared norms, values, beliefs and assumptions, and the behaviour and artefacts that express these orientations – including symbols, rituals, stories and language; norms and understanding about the nature and identity of the organisation, the way work is done, the value and possibility of changing or innovating, relations between lower and higher ranks, the nature of the environment.
- *Form*: this is composed of *structure* – the enduring relations between individuals, groups and larger units, including role assignments, grouping of positions in divisions/departments – and *process*, such as standard operating procedures and human resource mechanisms.

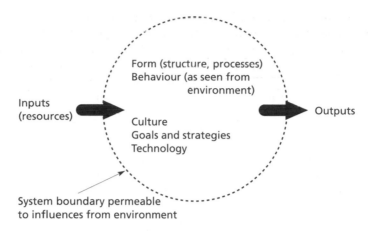

Fig. 1.1 Organisation as an open system
(*Source*: Adapted from Harrison, 1994)

1.7 The system metaphor

A situation can be seen as a *system* if it can be associated with the accomplishment of some purpose. More particularly, the system can be generically defined through the conceptualisation that it has:

1 a set of connected parts
2 a complex whole
3 a materially or immaterially organised body.

While we shall explore these generic attributes shortly, it will be useful to take a moment out to consider them in terms of the system's metaphorical nature. Like all metaphors, systems can be used in the abstract very effectively to characterise (or even caricature) a situation through a set of generic features. They can also be used in the particular, as practical models intended to represent a given situation. However, in this case, since they are metaphors, their use to represent the situation can be over-extended. Consider a specific example of the use of a metaphor. Let us say that 'person P is an elephant'. The feature of metaphorical representation is that P moves in a heavy clumsy way since this is the popular image of an elephant. To over-extend the metaphor would be to take an additional feature associated with the elephant, say a prehensile nose, and attribute it to person P. Examples of such over-extension for practical situations in terms of the above generic attributes are as follows.

- A situation may be described as a set of connected parts (however they are defined), but in any particular case, if some of these parts are not represented in the system model that is seen by others active in the situation, then the model may not be a satisfactory representation of the situation.
- Neither can the system model be a satisfactory model of a situation if it does not represent it as a complex whole because it does not satisfactorily represent the whole (according to some perspective).
- Finally, if a situation that is said to be a system has elements that (according to some view) can be described as disorganised, then once again a system metaphor cannot be a satisfactory representation.

15

Most people who hold to the management systems approach believe that systems can represent situations in a desirable way. Further, the more closely a given situation associated with some organisational purposes can be represented as a system, the more effectively it is believed to be able to operate to affect its purposes. It is therefore the case that during processes of inquiry, when situations are modelled systemically, differences are sought between *how* the situation *should* operate if it were a system and *how* it is *seen* to operate. Attempts are then made to find intervention strategies to make it operate more like a system. However successfully an inquirer has been in making an inquiry, and in finding and implementing intervention strategies that will make the situation look like a system (according to the view of the inquirer), it cannot practically be seen as system because (a) others may not see it as such and (b) over time its close generic description as a system may be lost as the situation changes.

It is clear that adopting the notion that the system is a metaphor is not new, and indeed it is often used in soft systems inquiries. Our interest is to propose that metaphor over-extension is a comparative property of the metaphor and its related situation. Now, evaluating a metaphor against a situation is a cybernetic process, and is called validating the model. The criteria that are used to do this derive from the world view(s) adopted in making an inquiry, and hence the primary manifestation of any given world-view approach is validation. If for instance a hard world view is adopted, then the validation process is hard, while if a soft world view is adopted, then validation will take a soft approach. This will be discussed further in Chapter 10.

1.7.1 A set of connected parts

A situation is often perceived to be divisible into a set of parts that can relate to one another. These parts will:

1 normally be supposed to have distinguishing identity;
2 be connected together in some way, and how this occurs will be determined by the relationship that exists.

An *identity* enables one to distinguish between parts of a situation so that differentiation can occur. It also enables explanations to occur unambiguously. Identity is particularly important if the parts have purposes associated with them that are similar. Relationships are needed in order to understand how different individual components in a situation connect. A systemic model of a situation is one that is composed of a set of parts that relate to one another. The relationship that appears may be close or distant, and the distance can be represented diagramatically by the length of a line, as shown in Fig. 1.2.

The parts may be *richly* or *poorly* interactive. In modelling a situation systemically, an inquirer will make a judgement about what constitutes a rich set of interactions, and distinguish between this group by creating a *boundary* around it (Fig. 1.3) that distinguishes the rich interactions from the set of poor ones. The interactions may be defined in terms of a variety of concepts, such as purposes or properties, and this provides the frame of reference for the boundary.

1.7.2 Purposefulness

Once a boundary has been created, we can refer to the space of rich interactions as the system domain, and that of poor interactions as its external environment. A system may

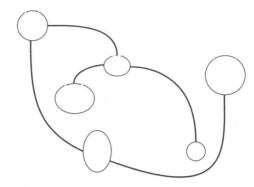

Fig. 1.2 Relationship diagram showing relationship between different defined parts

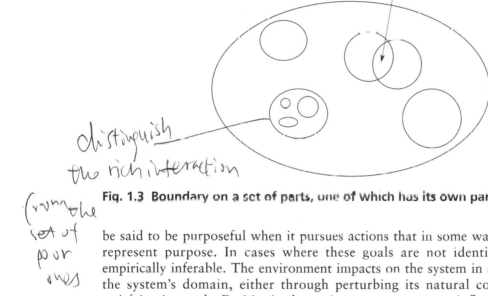

Intersection between
two parts showing
some common attribute
(e.g. purpose)

*distinguish
the rich interaction*

Fig. 1.3 Boundary on a set of parts, one of which has its own parts

*(from the
set of
poor
ones*

be said to be purposeful when it pursues actions that in some way relate to goals that represent purpose. In cases where these goals are not identifiable they must be empirically inferable. The environment impacts on the system in a way that can affect the system's domain, either through perturbing its natural condition, or through satisfying its needs. Entities in the environment are seen to influence the system or its parts. This enables one to draw an influence diagram as given in Fig. 1.4.

The system takes inputs from the external environment, and in return provides it with outputs. It is thus seen as a transformer of inputs to outputs. The processes that occur to enable this are said to be *purposive*. The inputs are resources that may be either material or non-material, and may include raw materials, equipment, people, money, information, knowledge and energy. The outputs may be material (like products) or non-material (like services).

A system can be seen as a whole with a set of parts that may be systems in their own right, when they are called subsystems. Thus the system domain will be part of the environment of the subsystem. This idea is recursive, so that subsystems can themselves have subsystems.

17

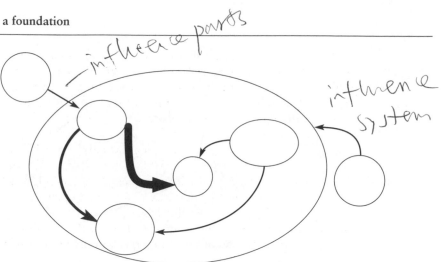

— influence parts

influence system

Fig. 1.4 Influence diagram for a set of interactive parts
Line thickness indicates strength of influence.

*richly
interactive
||
purpose
common*

Within the bounds of a system, the parts form a richly interactive group that has been bounded together holistically through purpose. They are said to be *synergistic*. The concept of *synergy* means that the value of the parts of a system is greater when they work together cooperatively as a whole. As the level of cooperation reduces, so the parts begin to operate for their own independent purposes (in pursuit of their unrelated goals), and this may be contrary to the purposes of the system as a whole.

We can talk not only of purposes, but of *primary* and *secondary* purposes. For example, in dentistry, it will probably be generally agreed that the primary purpose is patient dental health care with a secondary purpose of patient dental education. The definition of a system model with a primary purpose can be referred to as the *relevant* system (Checkland and Scholes, 1990). Now, a relevant purposeful system is *task orientated* through its *actions*. A *primary task* enables the primary purpose to be accomplished. While in dentistry the primary task may be considered to be dental treatment, in a bookshop it will be book sales.

1.7.3 A complex whole

The parts of a system can be complex, and the nature of complexity will be discussed at some length later on. For the moment, however, it will suffice to distinguish between two types of complexity. Technical complexity relates to situations involving a large number of dynamic parts that contribute to the development of the structure of a whole. Emotional complexity occurs when high levels of emotion are invoked in a situation, this in particular relating to softer situations.

The traditional definition of a *part* is something fragmented and incomplete which by itself would have no legitimate existence. A *whole* is considered to be something complete within itself that needs no further explanation. However, such an absolute definition of parts and wholes is not valid (Koestler, 1967). Conceptually, we can distinguish between the whole (referred to as a holon) and its set of constituent parts, which may themselves be sub-wholes (also holons). To distinguish between them, we can talk of different levels of focus in a system hierarchy. We shall discuss this topic further later.

A system is a set of parts, each of which has its own properties, the nature of which will be dependent upon the way in which the part has been modelled. A system as a *whole* has *emergent properties*, determined by the properties of the parts. The concept is meaningless when applied to the individual parts themselves. As examples of this, consider the cases of a clock and a cloud. In the clock the necessary properties of the cogs will be determined by their specific interrelationship, which will in the end enable the clock to have an emergent property. This is its ability to represent the passage of time, which is the only intended function that can be undertaken by the clock as a whole. The emergent properties of the clock (indicating the time) can be used as a point of reference to simply consider the relational changes of its parts. Without this a clock may be seen as computationally complex. Consider now the case of a cloud of gnats. If we suppose that the purpose for the gnats to fly in a cloud is to provide protection for the individual, then we must take it that the properties of the cloud are different from those of each individual gnat. However, there is another way of conceptualising the cloud. Let us suppose that the flight of each gnat can be described statistically (e.g. as a random movement). Let us now arbitrarily divide the cloud up into a set of parts of more or less equal volume. If the parts are sufficiently large, then the properties of each part will be the same as those of the cloud as a whole. In this case, like segments of a hologram, the parts maintain an implicit referencing to the whole.

1.7.4 An organised body

A coherent situation can be modelled to have a form and as such will be seen to be organised. An organised body is something which:

1 has an orderly structure
2 has a working order
3 is organic.

An *orderly structure* occurs if the parts of a whole can be seen to have a relationship that has a meaning for the perceiver. Normally, this means that the structure has a purpose that the order is responsible for. If a coherent situation has a *working order*, then it is engaged in processes that occur according to some progression such that a purpose can be identified. If a coherent situation is *organic*, then it has a set of parts that are constituent of the whole and are coordinated within it. If an organic whole continues to exist, then coordination implies that there will be some control and communications processes at work that contribute to its continuance.

An alternative expression that we shall use for an *organised body* is an *organisation*. When we refer to an organisation we will be referring to a situation that it is involved in, or at least a model of such a situation. This is in keeping with the idea that we can not talk about reality, but only about models of that reality.

It may be worth noting at this point that in the literature there is some difference over the definition of organisation and structure. Our interests are not to debate this here, but rather they are to amplify our own definition through the works of authors such as the social anthropologist Frith. In a book on social structure in 1949, Frith tells us that social *structure* refers to fundamental social relationships seen to apply to *any ordered arrangement of distinguishable wholes* that represent the principles underlying social relations, and not the content. The nature of structures is that they set bounds on, or limit, possible courses of organisational action (Mitchell, 1968, p. 186). Thus, structure can be seen to be devoid of action, but relating to it. Now, action that involves the transformation of something is referred to as process, and we may therefore see that structure and process can be differentiated.

Contrary to this, Frith (1959) sees social *organisation* as being concerned with *choices and decisions involved in actual social relations* (the working arrangements of society). Consequently, organisation is to do with both structures and processes. The organisation of a body can also be seen in terms of *conditionality* (Ashby, 1968). Consider that a situation is seen as a whole with a set of parts. Without constraint, any activities can occur in any of the parts, and each part can be seen as a space of potentially unlimited possible activities. These can become limited through the process of *communication* that occurs between the parts, which enables activities in one part to be related in some way to those of another and vice versa. Communication thus acts as an enabling mechanism for organisation that constrains the potential for activities in the parts so as to facilitate them to work together as whole. A whole is said to be richly connected when the parts are not easily reducible so that separate individual examination can occur without reference to the other parts.

Conversely, poorly connected situations occur where the parts of the whole are highly reducible. In richly connected situations, according to the proposition of Ashby, we would expect to find a great deal of communication. Whether the amount of communication in a situation is an indicator of its richness is not clear. However, if such a proposition were to be made, we would have to talk not of communication, but rather of meaningful communication. This must be a function of the individuals who transmit and receive the communications, their nature and their context.

Ashby also introduces the idea that organisation can have *quality* by distinguishing between good and bad organisation in relativistic terms. What constitutes good and bad varies in terms of the context of the situation, the purpose of an inquiry, the paradigm being used and an inquirer's world view. Clearly, this is necessarily consistent with the argument about an inquirer's relativistic perception of structure referred to above. In defining good and bad, Ashby interprets the idea of Summerhoff (1950), who explains that good and bad organisation is determined through the relationship between (a) the set of perturbations that disturbs the situation in some way and (b) the perceived goals that the organisation is seen to be attempting to achieve. If the nature of the perturbations changes, then the organisation is said to be good if it responds to the changes, and bad if it does not.

Ashby has created a view of what constitutes a good or a bad organisation through a model that has become central to managerial cybernetics, as it has to other fields of management theory. It has done this because it generates a *satisfactory* way of looking at organisations. In particular, it has led to the idea of variety: the environment generates variety that the organisation must respond to through the generation of its own (requisite) variety. This view is consistent with much of the recent management theory literature in that it promotes the idea that it is through the institutionalisation of innovation and entrepreneurship (Drucker, 1985) that organisations are able to respond to an uncertain and unpredictable environment, and the use of innovation (Peters, 1987) in order to promote survivability.

Successful though the notion of variety is, it would be of interest to see if there are other ways of creating judgements about models of situations, and we shall consider this question now within the context of what we shall refer to as a satisfactory view of a situation.

1.8 Generating satisfactory views of reality

We distinguish structures, discover related processes and assign identities. These are our models of reality that must enable us to account for the changes that we perceive in the world around us. It is a process of making our environment meaningful. In doing this we are continually formulating patterns of thought that provide explanations about what we see as reality. How we model the real world is limited by our capacity to generate ideas that we are able to believe. The way that we see the world in which we live is therefore constrained by belief, and this determines how we act. These beliefs often change when they are in some way challenged, either by other different beliefs or by our perception of events in the real world that are unexpected.

belief changes

To help this process we use conceptual tools. We have said that models are built to explain something about our reality. In addition, methods can be developed to enable us to structure our inquiry into perceived situations. These are often ultimately based on a common group belief that the methods derive from sound principles, and exist according to some appropriate logic. Methods often appear as a simple sequential list of activities. More complex and uncertain situations may require the use of methodologies. These are logic based, and have implicit controls built into them in an attempt to validate and schedule the steps of an inquiry process. It may occur that the results of a particular step are seen to be inadequate, according to criteria identified by the inquirer. In this case this step or a previous one may be retaken.

Some situations of perceived reality are simple and some are complex. How we distinguish between whether a situation is simple or complex alters with our perspective. Our ability to explain high levels of complexity in terms of simple dynamics is changing as new qualitative models of explanation emerge. It is because of this that Nicolis and Prigogine (1989) prefer to talk about whether systems are well or ill behaved, rather than whether the systems themselves are simple or complex. If we were to provide a scale of well-behaved to ill-behaved, then the behaviour of a system is determined by whether it is seen as being well-ordered and coherent, or chaotic. The degree of ordering and coherence in a situation is itself dependent upon the mental models that enable us to see form. It is therefore perspective-sensitive.

When we attempt to describe and explain situations that we perceive to occur in the real world, we do so through models that we try to make *satisfactory*. This means that they conform to a set of implicitly or explicitly defined cognitive models that enable a situation to be explained from a view that is satisfying. Cognitive models involve beliefs, values, attitudes, norms, ideology and meanings, and project cognitive purposes. We perceive reality through our cognitive models as we interact with it through them. These models involve concepts that, according to Tiryakian (1963, p. 9), are the name for the members of a class or the name of the class itself. The concepts are precise, may have empirical referents, and are fruitful for the formation of theories to the problem under consideration. They are intended to represent aspects of reality.

To provide a satisfying explanation, we often try to reduce the computational complexity of a situation that is seen to have many parts and even more interrelationships between them. In doing this we often imagine the emergence of characteristics that can be used to describe behaviour in more simple terms.

Perhaps a better way of describing when something is *satisfactory* is to identify a view from which a judgement is made, and we refer to this as a *satisfying view*. According to Weinberg (1975, p. 140), a satisfying view can be defined as follows:

When we see situations that are complex and uncertain, we implicitly attempt to *view* them such that three pragmatic goals are satisfied:

1 the view should be *complete*, meaning broad enough to encompass all phenomena of interest in order to reduce surprise;
2 the view should be *minimal,* meaning to integrate the states of a situation that are unnecessarily discriminated in order to make inquiry easier;
3 the view should be *independent*, meaning decomposing a set of *inquiries* into non-interacting qualities in order to reduce mental effort.

These goals may not be achievable. However, in trying to achieve them we can become *satisfied* with our perspective of the situation and its representation through our models.

Let us consider an example of a satisfactory model with respect to methodology. Checkland and Scholes (1990), in their work in developing soft systems methodology, want to explain how we can judge an intervention strategy to be satisfactory. They identify five criteria (the 5Es):

1 efficacy (do the means work?)
2 efficiency (are minimum resources used?)
3 effectiveness (does the change help the attainment of longer-term goals related to the owner's expectations?)
4 ethicality (is the change a moral thing to do?)
5 elegance (is the change aesthetically pleasing?).

Let us see how the 5Es relate to the Weinberg goals. The 5E criteria provide a view of the proposed strategy of intervention that would seem to be regarded as complete and broad enough to encompass all phenomena of interest in order to reduce surprise. The apparent simplicity of the set of criteria provides an integrated and minimal way of evaluating the situation. These criteria are axiomatically seen as necessary and sufficient. The criteria are also independent in that they are non-interacting qualities. If a judgement is made that the five criteria have been fulfilled, then a satisfying view of the intervention strategy has been achieved.

We have said that the relationship between what is simple and what is complex is relative. We have also said that it is a function of both perspective and knowledge. Thus:

1 Perspectives arise from both experiences and beliefs about the world. It is through experience of past situations that we are able to understand and judge situations in the present, and predict the future through expectations. Assumptions are accepted through faith (Weinberg, 1975), which provides orientation for perspective.
2 Our beliefs determine what we can identify as knowledge. When we perceive that we do not have enough knowledge to be able to satisfactorily describe situations and predict the future, we say that they are unclear or uncertain.

Uncertainty is a major factor responsible for our inability to determine the future, and our perceived lack of knowledge is what critically affects our ability to make predictions (Morgan, 1980). The acquisition of knowledge is central to us. Later we shall explore the question of what we regard as knowledge relative to the acquisitor. Knowledge acquisition has been driven by our curiosity about how we have come about, and how we maintain our ability to survive. It enables us to develop theories about change and about evolution, which have been applied for example to the origins of the universe, and to the evolution of biological life forms. In later chapters they will also be considered with respect to changes in beliefs about change.

An evaluation of the satisfactory nature of any strategic decision can be made, and this is especially easy to do retrospectively. As an example, in Minicase 1.1, we examine the UK Government's policy of privatisation in the 1980s, and explore the possibilities of its success. This process is assisted by observing that the policy can be seen to be directly connected to the failed Darwinian evolutionary theory, its fundamental flaws being highlighted by applying what we shall call the Kauffman caveats, as given in Minicase 1.1 below.

Minicase 1.1

The Darwinian theory of natural selection and social policy

We shall argue that UK Government's policy towards privatisation during the 1980s was Darwinian, and satisfying to the Government of the times because it conformed to ideology. Darwinism is normally associated with biological life forms, but social organisations, too adapt and evolve.

In 1859 Darwin published his *Origin of Species*, in which he presented a theory to account for the manner in which species might have arisen one from another through gradual evolution. The species were seen to compete in a given environment, and adapt according to principles of variation, to develop a slow and continuous process of transformation. Powerful though this work was, it diverted attention away from the way in which *species* originate (Punnett, 1919, p. 11). Mendel was concerned with this through his work on selection in 1865, but its implications tended to be lost because biologists were in the main committed to Darwinian thought. Mendelists saw individuals no longer as a general whole. Rather, they were to be seen to be organisms built up of definite characteristics according to some structure that depends upon variety in some of its components.

More than a generation later, in 1895, Bateson explained that *species* do not grade gradually from one to another as was suggested by Darwinian theory. Rather, their differences are sharp and specific. He advocated empirical studies to verify this. Vries, a few years later, showed empirically in his book *The Mutation Theory* that new varieties arose from older ones by sudden sharp steps or mutations, rather than a gradual accumulation of minute differences. This highlights the idea that changes in species occur discontinuously.

One of the problems with Darwin's work was that it *concentrated* on natural selection. This 'fails to notice, fails to stress, fails to incorporate the possibility that simple and complex systems exhibit order spontaneously' (Kauffman, 1993, p. xiii). Such ideas are strongly supported by Hitching (1982), who explores the inadequacy of Darwinian and neo-Darwinian thought. Kauffman suggests that while Darwinian thought considered natural selection the prime factor of evolution, it would have better taken into account processes of self-organisation. This would enable us, he suggests, to:

1 identify the sources of order, as well as the self-organising properties of both simple and complex systems, which provide the inherent order that evolution is to work with both *ab intio* and always;
2 understand how self-ordered properties *permit, enable* and *limit* the efficacy of natural selection, and that organisms should be seen in terms of balance and collaboration; natural selection then acts on such pre-ordered systems;
3 understand which properties of complex systems confer on the system the capacity to adapt, and the nature of adaptation itself.

We would argue that the pure ideas of Darwinian evolutionary theory have been applied socially in the UK through the concept of *privatisation*. It is not that privatisation is itself Darwinian, but rather that the policy that underpinned it was. Privatisation was introduced into the UK in 1979 by the then new prime minister, Margaret Thatcher. The idea that accompanied it was that private organisations were more efficient and effective than public organisations, due to the competitive nature of a marketplace. The 'best' organisations would emerge because they had gradually evolved the best ways of dealing with the market, while still maintaining their original infrastructural purposes. In this way, our privatised organisations would be able to provide a superior social infrastructure at a lower cost to the public. This idea was so successful during the recessionary period that the Western world was experiencing that to some extent it has influenced virtually the whole of Europe and indeed much of the world.

To explain the notion of Darwinian competition in the context of social organisations, let us imagine that we have a privatised and therefore freely competitive social infrastructure sitting within the boundaries of a system. The organisations that compose it interact together directly, and indirectly through influence. Thus, if one company in a given infrastructural sector reduces or increases a tariff for its service, then according to the laws of commerce, so might the rest. The organisations operate according to commercial pressures and processes, and their relationships change. They are collaborative in situations where there is a perceived return, but collaboration is counteracted by such factors as self-interest, mistrust and suspicion. Collaboration may become unfair trading when the controls that normally limit their level of profitability are lost. It is not unknown for lawsuits to be pursued by Government bodies against a collection of companies believed to be operating as a cartel to form a monopoly for their mutual benefit against the public interest.

The system sits in an environment that includes changing public needs (health, power, communications), new technology, demands from shareholders, and Government reluctance to invest in social provision. It will only survive if it can achieve a shifting balance with its environment. Achieving balance often makes demands that cannot be satisfied, so if it is to survive the system must adapt. Not all of the organisations within the system are capable of the adaptation required, and so will cease to exist. Adaptation requires that the organisations must have self-ordered properties that permit, enable and limit the efficacy of survival through free competition (which we see as a process of natural selection – refer to the Kauffman caveats above). Self-organisation is central to this process, and through the changing environment the system will be forced to evolve if it is to survive. Indeed, even if organisations do survive, then they may change from one 'species' classification to another. In this case, the species analogy will relate to the nature and purposes of the organisation, and creation of a new meaning for the services it provides to the public. If there is no control on the change process then the result may well be to shift the nature of our infrastructure in a way that may now be seen to be undesirable.

The intervention by Government to create a social infrastructure that operates under natural selection draws our attention to the considerations that initiated that intervention. Drawing on the 5Es of Checkland and Scholes (1990), we are able to question this. However, before briefly exploring these, two things should be examined: (a) what are the purposes of privatisation, and (b) who are the stakeholders who will contribute to the context of our inquiry? The purposes are not clear even though Government would have advocated that they are. The basis for the programme of reform was ideological, and seemed to be satisfying for the Government to seek the implementation of this ideology. It was argued that free competition was a mechanism that would ensure that the organisations that survive are efficient and effective. The idea then was to establish a number (at least two if possible) of organisations in each infrastructural domain (water, power, telephone, railways) that could compete with one another. It would not only therefore make our infrastructure more efficient and effective, the argument seems to go, but also presumably less Government-dependent. There was a particular need for this in the health service.

The second question now relates to who the stakeholders are. Stakeholders in this case are those people who in some way hold a stake in the infrastructure. Since it is an infrastructure, one might suppose that the stakeholders are all the people in the social system. However, there are other perceptions. One of these derives from the argument that it is the entrepreneurs and senior managers of our organisations who generate the wealth of a society. They are seen as our steersmen, and if we can encourage them to achieve wealth, then society will also profit secondarily. In this case, the primary stakeholders are the elite who determine, without social obligation, the nature and nurture of the infrastructural services to society. If such a belief is held, then we should be aware of the potential 'collateral' damage to those in society who are increasingly most vulnerable, and the potential impact on society as some of the collaterally damaged respond in kind.

Can we now determine whether the privatisation policy was pursuing a satisfactory model for change? One way of exploring this is to find some criteria that enable us to satisfy the Weinberg goals. We earlier introduced the Checkland and Scholes 5Es criteria for this, and we shall explore the possibilities of applying them to the situation as follows.

- *Efficacy*: our interest here lies in whether privatisation will work. The question must be put, work in what way? To investigate this the goals must be defined and explored within context. Unfortunately, in the case of privatisation it is not clear whether all of the goals are declared, and one must perhaps surmise goals from behaviour. One of these goals probably relates to survivability. Thus, will a privatised infrastructure survive? We know that commercial organisations survive on average, but that they tend not to do so individually over longer periods of time. The failure of an individual organisation is always accompanied by some 'fall out' or 'collateral' damage. Its degree is determined by circumstances. We have historical experience of this, when for instance the UK Government of the last generation nationalised failing infrastructural industries.

- *Efficiency*: it is not clear that minimum resources are used in privatisation. There are arguments about how such resources should be counted and compared, and indeed what exactly we mean by efficiency. We can consider the system only in terms of its parts. This may enable us to minimise the need for resources at the level of only one part. However, it may also make unforeseen demands on other parts that make the system as a whole inefficient. This can very much depend upon the definition of the boundary of the system (i.e. what you define to be included in the system).

- *Effectiveness*: the longer-term goals in the case of privatisation would seem to relate to a reduced demand on the public purse while maintaining the quality of service. This topic is one that requires a great deal of consideration, and cannot be responded to briefly. Central to it is the creation of measures of effectiveness, which has been discussed in general and at length by, for instance, Harrison (1994), and is commented upon in Chapter 12.

- *Ethicality*: are the morals that relate to privatisation consistent with the (stakeholder) expectations of good government? This really demands that we explore the belief of what government is or should be. Many authors have said, for instance, that privatisation leads to self-interest and egocentric attitudes, and this would seem to be in conflict with the public good.

- *Elegance*: to whom do we address the aesthetics of privatisation? Let us take an example of privatisation in the UK, say of British Rail. It would seem a consensus opinion from the mass media in the UK that it is far from aesthetic in its implementation. This leads us to a discussion about the nature of elegance, consensus, and relative perspective. There is a further question: does the mass media reflect the consensus of the stakeholders?

A privatised social infrastructure will not be controlled by Government to ensure control in providing the social good for the benefit of the individual, but will rather independently self-organise, adapt and evolve. This must implicitly develop from the perspective that the people whom it services are its secondary stakeholders. They will be regarded as clients who do not have a significant consultative role in the evolution of the infrastructure. Their demands are therefore to be respected, rather than affective, in decision making. The installation of this form of social infrastructure by Government means that it currently operates according to the principles of natural selection, rather than taking into account the Kauffman caveats above. Such considerations will likely enable us to envisage the possibilities of change. However, they might not be able to permit us to predict:

1 the nature of that change and its impact on the social system;
2 the distribution of infrastructural provision that it makes;
3 the impact on the potential of the individuals in society.

Some of these concerns will be explored again in Part 3.

SUMMARY

Management theory has passed through a process of change. Influences from the mechanical age have moved to influences from the systemic age. This has been accompanied by a new way of viewing the world, from a simple deterministic approach to a more complex view. Systems provide a metaphoric way of seeing situations by imposing systemic conceptualisations on them. Central to this is the idea that systems have associated with them 'wholes' that are not also properties of the parts contained within them. Systems concepts have themselves developed in order to deal more satisfactorily with the complexities that we see around us. The domain of management systems adopts tools of system metaphors. This occurs in order to enable managers to deal with instabilities that occur in situations, and enables them to seek intervention strategies that are able to correct this.

REFERENCES

Ashby, W.R. (1968) 'Principles of self organising systems'. In Buckley, W. (ed.) *Modern Systems Approach for the Behavioural Scientist*. pp. 108–18. Chicago, IL: Aldine.

Burnes, B. (1992) *Managing Change*. London: Pitman.

Casti, J. (1989) *Paradigms Lost*. London: Abacus.

Checkland, P.B. and Scholes, J. (1990) *Soft Systems Methodology in Action*. Chichester: Wiley.

Cohen, J. and Stewart, I. (1994) *The Collapse of Chaos: Discovering simplicity in a complex world*. London: Viking.

Drucker, P.F. (1985) *Innovation and Entrepreneurship: Principles and practice*. London: Heinemann.

Frith, R. (1959) *Social Change in Tikopia*. London: George Allen & Unwin.

Harrison, M.I. (1994) *Diagnosing Organisations*. London: Sage.

Hitching, F. (1982) *The Neck of the Giraffe, or where Darwin went wrong*. London: Pan.

Jantsch, E. (1980) *The Self-Organising Universe: Scientific and human implications of the emerging paradigm of evolution*. New York: Pergamon Press.

Kast, F.E. and Rosenzweig, J.E. (1979) *Organisation and Management: A systems approach*. New York: McGraw-Hill.

Kauffman, S.A. (1993) *The Origins of Order: Self-organisation and selection in evolution*. Oxford: Oxford University Press.

Koestler, A. (1967) *The Ghost in the Machine*. London: Picador.

Koontz, H. and O'Donnell, C. (1968) *Principles of Management*, 4th edn. New York: McGraw-Hill.

Mitchell, G.D. (1968) *A Dictionary of Sociology*. London: Routledge & Kegan Paul.

Morgan, C. (1980) *Future Man*. Newton Abbot: David and Charles.

Nicolis, G. and Prigogine, I. (1989) *Exploring Complexity*. New York: W.H. Freeman.

Peters, T. (1987) *Thriving on Chaos: Handbook for a management revolution*. London: Macmillan.

Punnett, R.C. (1919) *Mendelism*. London: Macmillan.

Summerhoff, G. (1950) *Analytical Biology*. London: Oxford University Press.

Stacey, R. (1993) *Managing Chaos*. London: Kogan Page.

Tiryakian, E.A. (1963) *Sociological Theory, Values, and Sociocultural Change*. New York: Free Press.

von Bertalanffy, L. (1968) *General Systems Theory*. Harmondsworth: Penguin.

Weinberg, G.M. (1975) *An Introduction to General Systems Thinking*. New York: Wiley.

CHAPTER 2

Introduction to the theory of world views

OVERVIEW

We are all individual in the way we see the world, and how we do so determines how we respond to it. Our world view is determined by the way we were brought up as children, and is affected by our experiences. As our beliefs, values and attitudes change, so does our world view. By weltanschauung, we can be referring to the world view of either an individual or a group. Weltanschauungen are not normally described, if indeed those associated with the world view are able to do so. They are therefore referred to as informal world views. Another type of formal world view is the paradigm. World views are manifested as behaviour, and result in the interplay between weltanschauungen and paradigms.

OBJECTIVES

This chapter will:

- explain the idea of world view;
- distinguish between the concepts of weltanschauung and paradigm;
- identify the relationship between weltanschauung and paradigm;
- explore the behavioural context of weltanschauung and paradigm.

2.1 Modelling reality

Reality is a relative phenomenon, and is seen according to the world views of the individuals and groups that define them. It is a 'conjectural model based on the unique human capacity to define experience, anticipate experience (and behaviour), formulate responses, and make corrections according to whatever happens' (Berke, 1989, p. 317). 'Its creation begins with the first tentative steps to locate and conceptualise the source of supply, a task that continues through one's life. Initially reality comprises basic experiences such as warmth and fullness, roughness and tension, as well as the act of experiencing these things. Or it is a part of the mother–baby body, such as the mouth or nipple, and the aptitude to perceive, remember, and appreciate these organs. However, as the one matures, reality grows too and encompasses, for example, material things, human relationships, and physical quantities as well as the contents and functions of the mind' (Berke, 1989, pp. 93–4).

What constitutes a process of maturing may be open to question. One view of this centres on Zen Buddhism that tells us that 'most Westerners view the physical world as the operative reality, while the unseen non-physical world is an abstraction ... reality is the fundamental unity of mind and matter, inner spirit and external world' (Hoover, 1977, p. 7). Our experiences tell us that reality contains dualities, but it should be treated as 'a convenient fiction whose phenomena you honour as though they existed, although you know all the while that they are illusions' (Hoover, 1977, p. 8). It may be argued that very few of us have achieved this Zen idea of a mature view about reality. We are then left to interpret reality through our individual and group models.

Understanding something about the nature of reality is essential for our ability to deal with situations through the models and the modelling processes that we use. We can only model reality; we can rarely say that what we see as reality actually exists.

In science a Buddhism-related view of the nature of reality has developed, as explained by Talbot (1991). He refers to the work on brain processes by Pribram (1977), who developed a holographic view of the way memory worked. We can buy holographic pictures in novelty stores that show a given scene from perspectives that depend upon the direction from which an observer looks at them. A hologram is a virtual image that has no more physical extension in space than does the image you see of yourself when you look in the mirror. Pribram considered that a holographic brain model could lead to the idea that objective reality as such might not exist as we believe it to. 'Was it possible that what the mystics had been saying for centuries was true, that reality was maya, an illusion' (Talbot, 1991, p. 31), and that reality is defined as we know it only after it enters our senses?

These ideas are supported elsewhere, as for instance explained by Hiley and Peat (1987) in their exploration of the quantum ideas of Bohm. He asserts that just as in a holographic image, the tangible reality of our everyday lives is really a kind of illusion. There is seen to be an underlying deeper order of existence that gives birth to all the objects and appearances of our physical world. This deeper level of reality is called the implicate (meaning 'enfolded') order, while our physical level of existence is the explicate, or unfolded, order. Bohm saw the manifestation of all forms in the universe as the result of countless enfoldings and unfoldings between these two orders.

Reality is represented by something that science calls *facts*, which are used in an attempt to validate a view of that reality. The nature of facts, however, very much depends upon the context and framework from which one views them. Stafford Beer has called facts 'fantasies that you can trust'. Now, trust is 'a firm belief in the honesty, veracity, justice, strength, etc., of a person or thing' (*Shorter Oxford English Dictionary*, 1957). Since trust occurs through *belief*, it should be realised that it can vary from individual to individual, from group to group, or from time to time. Beliefs are also culturally based.

2.1.1 Reality and knowledge

A more traditional view of reality has been defined by Berger and Luckman (1966) as 'a quality appertaining to phenomena that we recognise as having a being independent of our own volition (we cannot wish them away)'. In other words, reality is something that is not determinable by our *ad hoc* fancy. In an attempt to be clear that we know that what we see is real, we must have knowledge about that reality. This is in turn determined by our assumptions, which are established through the culture of our social environment. These assumptions form a basis for the interpretation of events as we see them, and thus lead to the building of knowledge.

It is from beliefs that we are able to conceptualise the world, and so generate what we consider to be knowledge about it. Knowledge determines what we are able to do and how we are able to do it. The theoretical study of knowledge and its acquisition and development is called *epistemology*.

This stream of thought has led to the idea of *social realism*, a concept considered by authors like Durkheim (1915) and, in particular, Stark (1962), who discusses whether society is an entity in itself or whether it is merely a composition of many individual persons. Realists would say that it is meaningful to speak of society as having a basic reality of its own.

In explaining the view of social realism, one can talk of common realities – that is, realities that are in some way shared by a group of people. Here, we are not talking about the creation of a single shared reality but rather one in which people retain their own realities and use common models to share meaning (Espejo, 1993, p. 72). Meaning is provided through understanding, and this is determined by what we consider to be knowledge. Shared meaning therefore occurs through sharing knowledge. In order to share meaning between a group of individuals, it is necessary for people to communicate between one another. The development of common models of reality occurs through a communication processes that is manifested through the transmission of symbols (Ackoff, 1981, p. 23). When symbols are used according to a set of commonly accepted rules that are able to convey meaning consistently, they are said to be a language. At this juncture it is sufficient to conceptualise that this is in part the process by which our organisations grow and develop.

While we can talk of common or group knowledge, we can also talk of institutional knowledge. In an institution stable controls of human conduct are created by setting up predefined patterns to which members must conform (Berger and Luckman, 1966). The channel of control occurs in one direction as opposed to any other theoretically possible direction. This mechanism constitutes a system of social control.

While this is a path to the formation of common realities, it is also one towards differentiation. This is because the development of institutional roles enables segmentation to occur between individuals. This enables different perspectives to develop, which themselves act to establish perceptions of reality. This in turn can lead to change in the institution itself.

Humans have always sought knowledge about their reality. Knowledge is institutionally valid in the society in which it appears if it is accepted by the institutions that examine it. Whether it is accepted as valid will depend upon the social culture in which the institutions exist. In the Western European tradition of the past few hundred years, knowledge is institutionally valid if it conforms to the notion of its being scientific. The definition of what constitutes scientific knowledge is determined by sociocultural acceptance. The criteria of acceptance are determined by a set of conventions that must be followed. These are in turn determined by the logic of the sociocultural group that produces the conventions. As the culture changes, so the epistemological logic may change, and new views of science may develop.

The scientific community represents one of the segments of the institutional establishment that is undergoing change. Our understanding of what makes up scientific knowledge has been changing because it has become apparent that the problems we have been perceiving and trying to solve are more complex than we had originally considered. A useful and brief history of this change can be found in Hirschheim (1992).

Evaluation of what constitutes reality is not only an interest of philosophy. It has practical implications for the way in which we behave to each other, and the judgements that we make about others. As an example of this Holsti (1967) discusses culture in respect of political situations, and shows the relativistic way in which people view reality by using ideology as a filter to interpret information.

2.2 Concepts of world view

The concept of world view is an ancient one. It can be found, for instance, in Tibetan Buddhism within the concept of karma. This means 'action', and represents both the power latent within actions, and the results that our actions bring (Rinpoche, 1992, p. 92). While karma can be explained as 'the sum of a person's actions in one of his successive states of existence', it may relate not only to individuals, but to groups, institutions, cities, or even nations. Rinpoche (1992, p. 112) has explained karma in the following terms: 'We each have different upbringings, education, influences and beliefs, and all this conditioning comprises that karma. Each one of us is a complex summation of habits and past actions, and so we cannot but see things in our own uniquely personal way. Human beings look much the same but perceive things utterly differently, and we each live in our own unique and separate individual worlds.' As a result, we are all different and all have our own distinct karmas. The way that we look at the world, the view we take, is karma determined and is referred to as the *karmic view*.

While we could adopt the term karmic view to explain how we build our models of reality, and why people will see reality in different ways, it is more appropriate for our purposes to work through a scientific rather than a Buddhist tradition. The modern scientific tradition has developed its own terminology for a reduced concept that we can refer to as *world view*. Two types of related world view can be identified: *weltanschauung* and *paradigm*. It is our exploration of these terms that will form a foundation for this book.

2.2.1 *Weltanschauung*

Human activity can be viewed in a number of different ways. The way in which it is seen by someone is from a viewpoint that is determined by that person's *beliefs, background, interest* and *environment*. It generates a perspective, a mental picture of the relationships and relative importance of things that is itself a mental model of an activity or situation. Since different people may have different viewpoints, they will also have different perspectives, and consequently different mental models. These mental models

31

may be more or less common to a group of people. In this case they have shared perspectives that directly relate to common understandings.

At the turn of the century Scheler (1947) was concerned with this concept of relativity in respect of knowledge and knowledge acquisition. Within each *individual*, there is an organisation of knowledge, or order. This order is influenced by the sociocultural environment, and appears to the individual as the natural way of looking at the world. Scheler called this the 'relative-natural world view' (*relativnatürlische weltanschauung*) of a society. Mannheim (1964), at about the same time, had interests that lay with the concept of ideology. He used Scheler's ideas, which became referred to as *weltanschauung*, literally translated as 'world view'. Weltanschauungen are relative to the institutions that one is attached to in a given society, and they change as the institutional realities change.

The acquisition of knowledge is important for those people who try to explain what they see about problems that they wish to solve. The process of developing a view of the problem is called modelling it. A person who is in the process of modelling what is conceived to be a reality will have a weltanschauung that will eventually determine how that model is built and operated. The term was later used by Churchman (1979) and by Checkland (Checkland, 1981; Checkland and Davis, 1986) as one of the cornerstones of their systems approaches directed at solving problem situations that involve human activity. The use of the word by Checkland can be defined as 'the world view that makes it [the transformation process] meaningful [in a given context]' (Checkland and Scholes, 1990, p. 35). It has also been defined as 'the perspective of a situation that has been assumed ... i.e. how it is regarded from a particular (explicit) viewpoint; sometimes described as the assumptions made about the system' (Patching, 1990, p. 282).

Individuals who undertake action can be called actors. In the same way, groups have a shared world view and thus common models of reality that are manifested in some way (often as action, when they can be called actors or, more generally, *social actors*). Consequently, when we talk of weltanschauung we will be referring to the *world view* of an *actor* that may be *individual* or *shared*. Shared weltanschauung occurs through a process of socialisation. During this individuals become members of the group when they assign themselves to it, and identify with it, taking on its members' roles, attitudes, generalised perspective or, more broadly, its norms (Berger and Luckman, 1966). Identity is thus 'objectively' defined through the group. However, there is always a distinction between the individual and the group. The two realities correspond to each other, but are not *coextensive* (Berger and Luckman, 1966, p. 153).

We have said that weltanschauung may be seen as a world view that can be individual or shared. We refer to a holder of a given world view as a *viewholder*, and those who share a given world view are its viewholders. This is different from the more usual idea of the *stakeholders,* who may support a given view in some way because they have invested some form of stake in that view. Stakeholders may not be viewholders, but often are. Viewholders do not normally exist alone. They form part of a larger group that altogether is composed of both *the* viewholders and *others* who are not *the* viewholders. Among these others there will be different world views for which we can also distinguish between the viewholder and the other others.

Weltanschauung is seen by some to be a world view that is often personal and indescribable. For us, this means that weltanschauung is *not formally described* such that it can become *visible to others*. Formality occurs through language via a set of explicit statements about its beliefs and other attributes that enables everything that might be expressed about the world view to be expressed. Consistent with this, we refer to weltanschauung as an *informal* world view: that is, the world view being referred to is principally *visible to only its viewholders,* when it is said to be more or less opaque to others.

Our use of the term weltanschauung differs from that of Checkland, whose view may well be unnecessarily complex. For instance, Fairtlough (1982) has explored Checkland's notion of weltanschauung and found that it has been used in 26 different ways. In response to this, Checkland and Davies (1986, p. 110) explored Fairtlough's analysis and confirmed that weltanschauung can be identified in terms of eight attributes that together can be collected into three forms of world view. The attributes that they identified are as follows.

- *Appreciations*: in the sense of the word given by Vickers (1965) these are meant as a somewhat reflective view of a situation, with both cognitive and evaluative aspects. They might also be called attitudes with reflection.
- *Appreciative systems*: these are generalised versions of appreciations, which allow us to give accounts of a variety of situations.
- *Presuppositions*: these are expectations, fairly easily changed by new data.
- *Concepts*: these are theoretical structures which allow us to grasp a situation.
- *Conceptual systems*: these are interlocking sets of concepts, seen to be similar to Kuhn's paradigm.
- *Prejudice*: this is used to mean ill-thought-out evaluations, which can be changed by reflection or wider information unless they are 'ingrained'.
- *Values*: these are seen to be similar to ideologies, and are established in *value systems*.

We find Checkland's understanding that a paradigm is 'similar' to a conceptual system as curious and limiting when Kuhn's work is further explored. We shall also see that Checkland's definition of the word weltanschauung can be simplified when it is linked to the Kuhnian notion of paradigms. We would argue that this is necessary because Checkland's idea of weltanschauung is not a primary one, but involves secondary derivative aspects that unduly complicate the definition. For example in primary terms, the attribute *prejudice* may be better seen as a consequence of such of its attributes as *attitude*. Similarly, the attribute *appreciations* can be seen to be the consequence of such attributes as attitudes and values. There is no difficulty in including such terms as prejudice and appreciations as part of weltanschauung, providing that they are clearly seen to be secondary attributes.

2.2.2 Paradigm

A paradigm is 'the set of views that the members of a ... community share' (Kuhn, 1970, p. 176). Clearly, then, since paradigm is related to the members of a community, all of whom have a weltanschauung, the two concepts must be related, and both can be related to the notion of *social actor*.

Paradigm is more than shared weltanschauung. It is *shared weltanschauung* together with the explicitly defined propositions that contribute to understanding. When weltanschauungen are *formalised* they become paradigms, and transparent to others who are not viewholders. We have said that a formalisation is a language that enables a set of explicit statements (propositions and their corollaries) to be made about the beliefs and other attributes that enable everything that must be expressed to be expressed in a self-consistent way. Formal propositions define a logic that establishes a *framework* of thought and conceptualisation that *enables* organised action to occur and problem situations to be addressed. They also constrain the way in which situations can be described. Formal logic (Kyburg, 1968, p. 20) provides a *standard* of validity and a means of *assessing* validity. While groups may offer behaviour in ways that are consistent with their shared weltanschauung, paradigms emerge when the groups become *coherent* through formalisation.

There may be a notion that defining a paradigm as a formalised shared world view is problematic. This is because it implies the concept of an 'observer' who identifies the degree of 'sharedness' and its formalisation. Viewholders do not normally exist alone in an isolated field of science. They form part of a larger group called the scientific community. Together with the viewholders, it is made up of *others* who are not viewholders. Consistent with the idea in quantum physics of 'observer indeterminism', which we shall consider again later, *others* are participants in situations and replace the positivist idea of passive non-participant 'observers'.

Any formalisation that occurs within the world view is a result of a process internal to the group of viewholders. It is up to the group to determine the degree of sharedness that their paradigm has if this is a factor in defining their world view. If the degree of sharedness is 'too' small because their common understandings are negligible, it is hardly likely that the group will survive long enough to form a paradigm. Whether the world view is 'sufficiently' formalised for it to be classed as a paradigm is a matter of agreement by the viewholders. It is often only accepted by others in the community after a period of conflict with the viewholders, and retrospectively at that.

Like weltanschauung, paradigms are belief based, and beliefs are not susceptible to rational argument. Paradigm stakeholders may thus be unable to release their beliefs easily. While paradigms can evolve, their degree of evolution is bounded by the capacity of a given belief system to change. In concert with this argument, Casti (1989, p. 40) tells us, for instance, that:

> scientists, just like the rest of humanity, carry out their day-to-day affairs within a framework of presuppositions about what constitutes a problem, a solution, and a method. Such a background of shared assumptions makes up a paradigm, and at any given time a particular scientific community will have a prevailing paradigm that shapes and directs work in the field. Since people become so attached to their paradigms, Kuhn claims that scientific revolutions involve bloodshed on the same order of magnitude as that commonly seen in political revolutions, only the difference being that the blood is now intellectual rather than liquid ... the issues are not rational but emotional, and are settled not by logic, syllogism, and appeals to reason, but by irrational factors like group affiliation and majority or 'mob' rule.

According to Kuhn the paradigm involves four dimensions of common thought:

- common *symbolic generalisations*
- shared commitment to *belief* in particular *models* or *views*
- shared *values*
- shared commitments of *exemplars*, that is concrete problem *solutions*.

We shall now argue that the paradigm can equivalently be expressed in terms of:

- a base of propositions that defines a truth system
- culture, including cognitive organisation and normative behaviour
- language
- exemplars.

Propositions

Kuhn's term *symbolic generalisations* can be explained in the following way:

- something *symbolic* is a *representation* of the thing by association;
- a *generalisation* is a general *proposition* that has been abstracted away from the facts and data of a situation, and draws your attention to its principles.

Thus, a set of symbolic generalisations occurs through a base of propositions, and is by its very nature able to represent knowledge and concepts. This involves belief-based assumptions, some of which require no proof (are axiomatic) and others that require proof or demonstration. Both types are referred to as propositions.

The propositions coalesce into a logic that validates the group's reasoning process. They also enable 'technical' terms to be used to describe what is seen or conceptualised. This latter aspect of the paradigm offers a common way to communicate the meaning of situations that the group is exposed to, and is referred to as a *metalanguage* (Koestler, 1975) that provides definition for its epistemology (Checkland and Scholes, 1990). According to Kyberg (1968, p. 7), whenever we talk about something formally defined, we must involve metalanguage.

Beliefs, values and attitudes as cognitive organisation

The paradigm is a group phenomenon, and as such we must recognise that it operates with a *culture* of its own. The concept of culture (Williams *et al.*, 1993, p. 14) involves not only *values and beliefs*, but also *attitudes*, and *behaviours* that are predicated on belief. The definition of a paradigm might usefully be extended from Kuhn to involve culture. To see why, consider the nature of the components of culture.

Beliefs relate to *objects*, which may be other individuals or groups, issues or some manifest thing to which a belief may be attached. They determine paradigms as they do weltanschauung. A belief is any simple proposition, may be either conscious or unconscious, and represents a predisposition to action. A *belief* may be (Rokeach, 1968, p. 113):

- *existential* and thus related to perceived events in a situation;
- *evaluative* and thus related to subjective personal attributes (like taste);
- *prescriptive*, relating, for example, to human conduct.

Beliefs are conceived to have three components:

1 *cognitive*, representing knowledge with degrees of certainty; more generally cognition is 'of the mind, the faculty of knowing, perceiving or conceiving';

2 *affective*, since a belief can arouse an *affect* centred around an *object*;

3 *behavioural*, since the consequence of a belief is *action*.

Beliefs are a determinant for values, attitudes and behaviour. *Values* (Rokeach, 1968, p. 124) are abstract ideas representing a person's beliefs about ideal modes of conduct and ideal terminal goals. *Attitude* (Rokeach, 1968, p. 112) is an enduring organisation of beliefs around an *object* or *situation* predisposing one to respond in some preferential manner. When considering the attitude of an inquirer towards an object or a situation, Rokeach highlights that it is attitude that is related to:

- an *attitude object* – that is, an inquirer's attitude towards an object;
- an *attitude situation* – that is, an inquirer-organised set of interrelated *beliefs* about how to behave in a *situation* consisting of objects and events in interaction.

Thus, *behaviour* relates to a *situation* in which there will be *objects* towards which behaviour is directed. An example of an attitude object held by an individual is the belief that people of *race A* are strongly inferior to another *race B* to which the individual belongs. Suppose that the same individual has always wanted to win an award for having high levels of morality. An example of an attitude situation for that same individual is that the decision maker in the organisation giving awards for high levels of morality is a member of race A.

Beliefs, values and attitudes have a special place together. Beliefs are contained in an attitude, and attitudes occur within a larger assembly of attitudes. The collections of beliefs, attitudes and values are referred to by Rokeach as *cognitive organisation*.

Behaviour and norms

Behaviour can be referred to as social action. Action is social (Mitchell, 1968, p. 2) when the actor behaves in such a manner that his or her action does or is intended to influence the actions of one or more other persons. We may say that it is normative when it adheres to a set of social constraints on behaviour identifying what is acceptable to the group and what is not.

Norms are group phenomena that provide standards defining what people should *do* or *feel* or say in a given situation (Burnes, 1992, p. 155). In particular, norms can be described as being able to (Secord and Backman, 1964, p. 463):

● shape behaviour in the direction of common values or desirable states of affairs;
● vary in the degree to which they are functionally related to important values;
● be enforced by the behaviour of others;
● vary as to how widely common they are, being either socially wide or group specific;
● vary in range of permissible behaviour.

Norms can be seen as part of the paradigm. They define acceptable social behaviour in a way that is belief and attitude dependent (Thomas and Znaniecki, 1918). Behaviour itself is a result of the cognitive interaction between two types of attitude (Rokeach, 1968, p. 127): (a) towards an object and (b) towards the situation. It can thus be seen as a manifestation of attitude differences.

Paradigmatic norms are often manifested as the protocols or behavioural procedures that discernibly exist in coherent groups, and which define how things should be done. Discernible protocols are indicators of patterns of behaviour. The paradigm is concerned with these patterns of behaviour because it 'governs, in the first instance, not a subject matter, but rather a group of practitioners' (Kuhn, 1970, p. 180). The implied orientation towards *practice* by practitioners highlights the idea that actors carry out action and have behaviour. Patterns of behaviour develop, and at some level involve group norms and agreed ordering processes of behaviour.

While normative behaviour imperatives can be thought of as part of the paradigm, this is not the case for behaviour *organising*. This is the process of establishing order in behaviour. It is not part of the paradigm, but derives from it and represents the logical processes from which behaviour develops. Paradigms offer a framework of thought that determines how an organisation should operate, and what it should consider to be important for decision making and activity. They embed any aspects of organised life that can be related directly to cognitive activity.

Exemplars

A paradigm will enable situations to be described in a way that is implicitly understood by the group to which it belongs and from within its common culture. The propositional base is supported through group experience of *exemplars*, which also indirectly reinforces group culture through communications using language. Exemplars can be thought of as exemplary case study representations of the application of the propositions and cognitive organisation to a real-world situation. For us, the real world is actually a viewer perceived behavioural world.

Paradigms and language

Since the paradigm is a cultural phenomenon involving cognitive organisation and normative behaviour, it will also have a language associated with it that enables the ideas of the group to be expressed. There is a body of theory that expounds the relativity between culture and language. For instance, in the study of natural languages within sociocultural environments, the Sapir–Whorf hypothesis (Giglioli, 1972) explains that there is a relativistic relationship between language structure and culture. It relates in particular to the *communication of ideas* between members of the group. This line of thought is also supported, for instance, by Habermas (1979) and Maturana (1988) and by the ideas contained within the subject of *autopoiesis* or self-producing systems (Mingers, 1995, p. 79). Here, language is considered to be an activity embedded in the ongoing flow of actions, rather than a purely descriptive thing. It is a dynamic part of sociocultural change.

Language is epistemological in that it uses words that are defined through knowledge, concepts and propositions, and enables a weltanschauung formalisation to occur. It also operates as an enabling mechanism for the paradigmatic group. Since communication is central to the ability of the group to work, language may be seen as a way of enabling a class of paradigmatic explanations to be generated. The framework of thought that develops within the group is cultural and will therefore be reflected in the language used to transmit those ideas. The propositional base of the paradigm that lies at its foundation will determine the language of the group, just as the language itself develops this base in a mutual development. This determines what can legitimately be described and the terms defined in order to enable those descriptions to be made.

Language is also a formalising element of a paradigm. Language enables a set of explicit statements to be made about the beliefs and propositions (and their corollaries) of a weltanschauung that enable everything that must be expressed to be expressed in a self-consistent way. It is through the formalisation process of language that a weltanschauung can be represented as a paradigm.

The generic form of paradigms

The above ideas are illustrated in the context diagram of Fig. 2.1, which derives from Yolles (1996). There is an alternative way of representing a paradigm, as shown in Fig. 2.2. It is based on a suggestion by David Brown (personal communication, 1996) intended to highlight the ideas that:

1 the paradigm is culture centred;

2 cognitive organisation (beliefs, values and attitudes) are its attributes;

3 there may not seem to be a differentiation between normative and cognitive control of behaviour or action;

4 there may be debate about whether there is a distinction between formal and substantive rationalities.

The cognitive space is seen as a space of concepts, deep knowledge and meaning, and its relationship to culture is underlined. Exemplars form part of the cognitive space. Cognitive space also relates directly to action and communication, which is a prerequisite for organised behaviour.

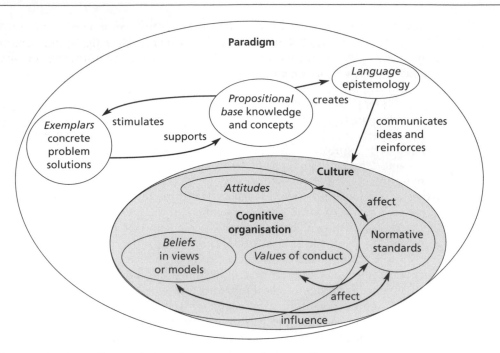

Fig. 2.1 Context diagram showing concept of a paradigm

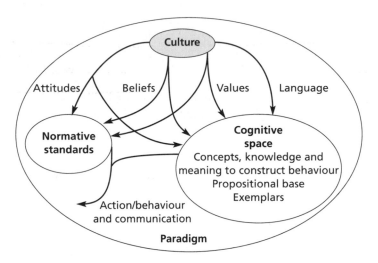

Fig. 2.2 Context diagram for a paradigm

2.2.3 Communications between paradigms

In some instances there will be a set of paradigms that have common language elements that reflect common epistemology. Now, language that belongs specifically to a paradigm can also be referred to as metalanguage, and the common epistemology will often be reflected in the individual metalanguage of paradigms through common semantics and metawords. The commonalties of metalanguage may occur accidentally and have different epistemological identity. More usually, however, this will have occurred because of some degree of direct or indirect inter-paradigm communication, when the epistemological identities can be connected. Such communication will have enabled the development of common areas of epistemology.

Where there are no commonalties between paradigms, meaningful inter-paradigm communications become difficult, if not impossible. This is because there is little common knowledge that enables concepts to be compared, and paradigm viewholders must resort to the use of natural language in order to attempt to convey meaning. This must always be possible since natural language is a common denominator for any paradigm, even though it leaves open the broad possibility of misinterpretation. Different epistemologies may be in conflict such that attempts at intercommunication may have a perturbing action on the paradigms to which they are attached. This is particularly the case if the ideologies of those who are viewholders of these paradigms clash. While this action can be constructive by creating challenge, it can also be destructive and fragmentive.

2.3 Interaction between weltanschauungen and paradigms

2.3.1 The ideas loop

Checkland and Scholes talk of a relationship between the perceived world and ideas. 'We perceive the world through the filter of – or using a framework of – ideas internal to us; but the source of many (most?) of those ideas is the perceived world outside. Thus the world is continually interpreted using ideas whose source is ultimately the perceived world itself, in a process of mutual creation' (Checkland and Scholes, 1990, p. 20). The relationship between the real world and ideas is shown in the influence diagram in Fig. 2.3. For ease of reference, we have called this the *ideas loop*.

The ideas loop can be linked to the paradigm. Now conceptual tools spring from the beliefs that result in a paradigm. We can therefore more clearly define the ideas loop by introducing the paradigm. Second, ideas derive from the individual and so are embedded in weltanschauung. This is the case even though the ideas may find their way into a group with its dominant norms, and thus become part of the paradigm. Necessarily, therefore, this suggests a relationship between weltanschauung and paradigm that must be seen as a development of the ideas loop. While paradigms explicitly provide the

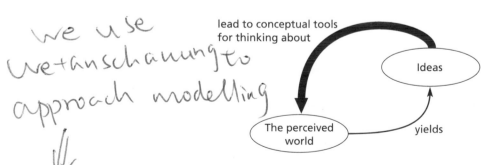

Fig. 2.3 Ideas loop, showing relationship between ideas, methodology and the perceived world
(*Source*: Based on Checkland and Scholes, 1990, p. 21)

formal mechanisms by which inquiry can occur, weltanschauung is important for an understanding of how we approach modelling: with what perspective, set of pre-assumptions and ideas.

2.3.2 The paradigm cycle and inquiry

We have compared weltanschauung with shared weltanschauung, and indicated that the former can never be totally identified with the latter. The same may be argued to be true of the relationship between weltanschauungen paradigms and the perceived real (or behavioural) world, which we refer to as a paradigm cycle (Fig. 2.4) based on Yolles (1996).

Shared weltanschauung acts as a cognitive basis for the paradigm. Within it we develop cognitive models that involve beliefs, values, attitudes, norms, ideology, meanings and concepts. We perceive 'reality' through our cognitive models as we interact with it through them. It is through the process of cognitive formalisation that weltanschauung becomes manifested as a paradigm that itself changes through a process of cognitive challenge. This may involve: a process of conflict that should be resolved; reflection to enhance our understanding of what we perceive; and conciliation enabling world-view boundaries to change. The relationship between the perceived real world and weltanschauung is partly through interpretation. By this we mean that the 'real world' is an interpretation that involves our perceptions, and these are generally influenced by our beliefs. It also involves empirical challenge, which is connected to observation. The real world is represented in the paradigm in a way that conforms with its belief system that defines its cognitive organisation. Action is manifested in the real world through an organising process that is in effect a transformation. This means that the cognitive basis of the paradigm is applied to what is seen as the real world according to some formalised regime which involves a transforming organising process that effectively defines logical relationships that become manifested as structures with associated behaviour in the perceived real world. Another more familiar way of referring to this in the context of inquiry is as method. Methods are used by inquirers according to their weltanschauung, and weltanschauungen and paradigms are connected through cognitive

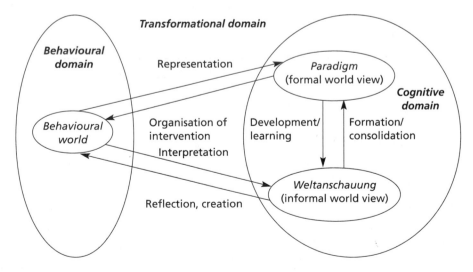

Fig. 2.4 The paradigm cycle

development. The relationship between weltanschauung and the real world is empirical and explains how individuals become involved in perceived real-world creation. Empirical explanations are based on the observation of behaviour.

The very idea of there being an organising process is a consequence of the notion of purposefulness, and results in purposeful behaviour. Purposeful behaviour is said to occur because of cognitive purposes that direct the actions of individuals and groups in a given situation. It is world view determined, and can be expressed in terms of a behavioural mission. Cognitive purposes are interpreted within a domain of action through a knowledge of data processes and structural models, modelling processes that contain data, and procedures or rules of operation and other models relating to the current situation, and a mechanism for structured inquiry.

In his discussion of paradigms, Casti (1989, p. 41) adopts a cartographic metaphor that provides for an interesting illustration of the circumstances for the rise of a new paradigm, and its relationship to weltanschauung. The paradigm is seen as a crude knowledge map. It has major landmarks, but little detail. Suppose that there are a number of knowledge cartographers, each offering distinct maps intended to represent the same terrain. Suppose one map is dominant because it is the oldest and best known. Explorers may use it in order to take on the task of discovering the detail of the terrain, but there is often found to be empirical inconsistency. That is, the map and the terrain do not exactly match. One difficulty that must be highlighted is that each explorer must interpret the map and relate it to the terrain being explored. This interpretation will vary for each explorer, and this may result in a conflict. Close cooperation between the cartographer and the explorers can result in the dominant map being changed, if a common agreement can be achieved. However, the cartographic principles being used may implicitly limit the degree of change possible, and so the explorers may shift to another map with better representation and more flexibility.

The rational view of the paradigm cycle is that the real world is seen first, examined in terms of the weltanschauung, and an appropriate paradigm adopted. It is not often followed, however. The paradigm frequently comes first, and this constrains the way in which the inquirer sees the real world. Since the paradigm is belief based this tends to deny the old adage that 'seeing is believing', and supports the obverse idea that 'believing is seeing'.

Cognitive development occurs in a paradigm when it needs to evolve in order to explain empirical evidence of the real world. Sometimes, however, the empirical evidence provides contradictions or paradoxes that a paradigm is not capable of handling because of the implicit cognitive barriers of its beliefs. In this case a paradigm shift may occur.

2.4 Collapsing the paradigm cycle

In Fig. 2.4 we have collected together the types of world view and called them the cognitive domain. This is differentiated from the behavioural domain which is defined by the 'real' or perceived behavioural world. In order to distinguish between these two domains and the transformations that occur between them, we have also introduced the transformational domain. This conceptualisation can be reformulated into a new tri-domain model. The three domains are placed together to form a deep, surface and transforming relationship. The transforming domain involves an organising process that manifests at the surface whatever is projected from the deep domain. We shall refer to

41

the transformation as transmogrification – which is a transformation that may be subject to surprises. Transmogrification is a mapping from the cognitive to be behavioural domain that manifests a structure with which behaviour is associated. We shall refer to the properties of a transmogrification that enable it to map from the one domain to the other as its morphism. In mathematics (*see* Bachman and Narici, 1966, p. 5 and p. 51), and in particular in the dynamics of complex (ergodic) systems (Arnold and Avez, 1968), two types of morphism can be defined. An isomorphism is a 1:1 transmogrific mapping, while an homeomorphism is a 1:n mapping. This is illustrated in Fig. 2.5 below where in the homeomorphism n = 3.

To use this, let us collapse the types of world view (paradigm and weltanschauung) of Fig. 2.4 into a deep or *cognitive* domain. Transmogrification converts from the cognitive world to that of the physical behavioural manifest world. If this manifest world is seen to be composed of individuals who create organisations that each have a form, then that manifest behavioural form is sensitive to the composition of individuals that defines a possibly innumerable number (n, which may be large) of situations over time. The composition of individuals who make up a situation will potentially influence the nature of that transmogrification. Therefore, a manifested physical form is the result of homeomorphic transmogrification. These forms may each be different, and have associated with them different behaviours. In contrast to this, an isomorphic transmogrification will define a unique manifestation if it has not been subjected to surprises that interfere with meaning. This conceptualisation is illustrated in Fig. 2.6, where we use a closed curve to show the homeomorphic potential of the tri-domain model.

We can use this figure recursively to show how we are able to *attribute* the properties of a system to a behavioural situation rather then *declaring* it to be one. In the same way that we can map from the cognitive to the behavioural domain, so too we can map from the domain of world views to the 'explicitly imagined' behavioural domain. From this we can project a cognitive system model on to the dotted line in Fig. 2.6. This can now be designated as the boundary of a 'new' cognitive domain that can be mapped into the behavioural domain. Alternatively, some may wish to see the dotted line imposed on the behavioural domain, taking it to be a system.

This model connects with the work that has appeared in artificial intelligence and language theory. Chomsky (1975), in his attempts to develop a theory of transformational grammar of language, distinguished between the semantics of a message and its syntax.

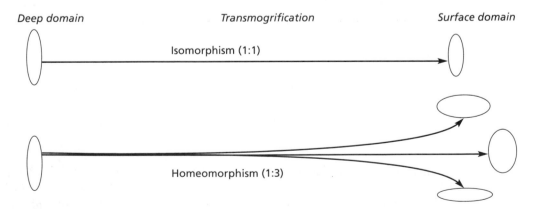

Deep domain *Transmogrification* *Surface domain*

Isomorphism (1:1)

Homeomorphism (1:3)

Fig. 2.5 An isomorphism and a homeomorphism

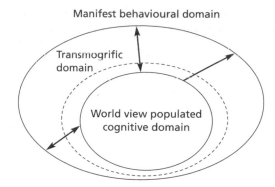

Fig. 2.6 Tri-domain model identifying a relationship between world views and behaviour

Semantics occurs at a 'deep' or cognitive domain of knowledge that carries meaning. Syntax is a manifestation of semantics that is created through the 'surface' that has structure and from which we make utterances. A structurally-similar model is used in the field of artificial intelligence (Clancy and Letsinger, 1981) that distinguishes between deep and surface knowledge.

Deep knowledge is generic, being independent of any particular situation. It adopts first principles and fundamental propositions that can represent individual or shared group beliefs. It is associated with understanding, and develops according to general theories. It is also associated with deep reasoning processes, the purposes of which are (a) to build up or maintain cognitive models perceived to be relevant to the current 'reality', (b) to make generalisations and (c) to formulate models relevant to surface knowledge. Deep knowledge can also be called cognitive knowledge, and is generated by a world view. Surface knowledge can be called situational or behavioural knowledge because it directly relates to a particular situation and its associated procedural behaviour. Its acquisition occurs through the collection of facts, through measures of performance and through the creation of algorithms, procedures or sets of rules. Such knowledge acquisition occurs through a process of learning and experience about the situation. It is related to skill, and can derive from heuristic processes. The two types of knowledge are analytically and empirically distinct.

In a rather different vein, our model would also appear to be consistent with one proposed by Chorpa (1990). His interests lie in merging elements of eastern (Ayurvedic) philosophy with medical science, and his thesis concerns the relationship between biological behaviour in individuals, consciousness and paraconsciousness (beyond-consciousness). As part of his modelling process, a distinction is made between different states, such as conscious thinking, and the body's biological self-organisaing know-how that Chorpa calls its *intelligence*. These states are separated by a 'gap' that he identifies as a 'quantum field' – a space of possibilities that enables the manifestation of events to occur that are related to the two states, and is suggestive of our transmogrific domain with its homeomorphic potential.

Returning now to Fig. 2.6, we note that the cognitive domain is populated by world views that can be seen as a system of 'truths' that rests upon world-view conceptualisations, and is able to generate knowledge as a result of manifest behaviour. For this knowledge to be applied in the behavioural domain, we say that transmogrification occurs – when the morphology is subject to surprises. The transmogrific domain is

43

strategic in nature. It is also a logical domain so that all transformational relationships exist there. Consequently, it is also a cybernetic domain so that it is where control processes are defined. This domain is, however, a construct that derives from the world view itself. This means that the nature of the transmogrification that occurs is determined ultimately by world-view concepts and propositions.

The same basic tri-domain model can be used to represent the relationship between world views and shared world views as illustrated in the paradigm cycle. Let us take the shared world view under consideration to be informal, that is a weltanschauung rather than a paradigm. A shared world view derives from the association of a group of people who through their association together have developed a common cognitive model. Relative to the individual's world view, the shared world view can be seen as a system of semi-formalised 'truths' that involves a production of knowledge that is common and visible to those viewholders involved. These 'truths' will be local to the group that defines the shared world view, and will change as the composition of the group changes in social space. It will also vary with time, since individual perspectives are dynamic experimental phenomena. Referring to Fig. 2.7, the surface of the outer circle represents the existent individual world views, and the innumerable possible individual world views that together form a given shared world view through transmogrification. The nature of that world view will, however, be dependent upon cognitive challenge, that can involve conflict, reflection and conciliation.

Thus, the transmogrific connection between an individual's world view and a shared world view is always a potentially homeomorphic transformational process. This construction suggests that shared world views are a composite manifestation of the world views of individuals. They will alter with group composition, the situation that the group members find themselves in and the way that they deal with the situation.

2.5 Virtual paradigms

Paradigms may be incommensurable, but 'new paradigms are born from old ones' (Kuhn, 1970, p. 149). New paradigms occur through a process of transition from competing incommensurable propositions, standards, norms, tools and techniques. This means that these elements can be in conflict across different paradigms, particularly when differences in language force misunderstanding. Changes in paradigms occur with

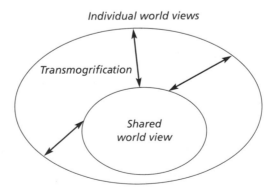

Fig. 2.7 Relationship between shared weltanschauung and paradigms

a 'transition between competing incommensurables; the transition between paradigms cannot be made a step at a time, forced by logic and neutral experience. Like the gestalt switch, it must occur all at once (though not necessarily in an instant) or not at all' (Kuhn, 1970, p. 150).

When new paradigms are born, it is because stakeholder belief develops that the old paradigms do not adequately explain the empirically examined situations. If a critical mass of stakeholders find themselves in this position, then a shift to a new paradigm will occur that can explain the situations. Put another way, paradigm shifts occur when a paradigm moves into a region of instability because a divergence occurs between its ability to explain reality and the events that we perceive to occur in reality. Normally the divergence is seen as the development of paradox or contradiction. Partly, then, our changing perceptions are responsible for the paradigm shifts that are partly responsible for our changing perceptions. Our interest here lies in the gestation period necessary before new paradigms can be born.

If it is possible to formally compare or coordinate two paradigms, then it cannot be done from inside either paradigm unless they converge to a single paradigm (Yolles, 1996). To be able to do so, we must use a new paradigm that is capable of generating a new language that subsumes the others. However, such a paradigm may not exist except in the conceptual eye of an inquirer wishing to undertake a comparative or coordinating approach. However, a paradigm is a group affair that requires norms and formalisms that are visible to others who are not viewholders. We will therefore talk of not a new paradigm, but rather of a new *virtual* paradigm. The virtual paradigm has virtually all of the elements of a paradigm. It may or may not contain exemplars. Also, rather than having a group culture, it has a weltanschauung or shared weltanschauungen that may form into a group culture through the development of normative beliefs. The virtual paradigm may become still born, or it may develop into a healthy vibrant new paradigm. If it survives, then like all natural organic gestations, the final form of the paradigm that develops will be a function of the complexities that impinge on its development.

A virtual paradigm becomes established when there is a reasoned set of propositions (with related epistemology and logic) that provides it with some *formality*, and a weltanschauung that enables a relative paradigmatic view of a situation to occur. In this way a virtual paradigm is a *formalised* weltanschauung. The virtual paradigm may become a new paradigm under the:

1 necessary condition that its coherent beliefs and conceptualisations are adopted by a group;
2 sufficient condition for that group to be of a critical size.

One difficulty is to identify when a group has reached a critical size. This can be recognised through mechanisms of a communications medium, when a 'sufficient' expression of support about the paradigm is made. Negative expressions may influence the virtual paradigm by its evolving to account for them. It may alternatively die. In general, when we speak of paradigms we will include virtual paradigms.

The idea of a virtual paradigm may also be seen as temporary working paradigm that has been created for a specific purpose so long as it is seen as a formalised non-normative or semi-formalised weltanschauung. Its cognitive organisations and conceptualisations tend to be much more visible than occurs in a shared weltanschauung. It is always possible to create a semi-formalised non-normative virtual paradigm. This involves the declaration of at least the most important cultural attributes and propositions of the world view that seem relevant to the viewholder in the pursuit of a purposeful behaviour. Whether the nature of the purposeful behaviour is valid will be determined by others who may refer to the virtual paradigm. In some cases where the virtual paradigm has been seen by others as successful, the formalisation of the virtual paradigm can become extended, and it may become normative. An example of the creation of a semi-formal and perhaps non-normative or at least semi-normative paradigm is offered in Minicase 2.1. Summary attributes of the virtual paradigm are provided in Table 2.1.

Minicase 2.1

The paradigm of community rehousing

In the period of the boom years in Britain in the 1960s, anything was possible. The socio-economic environment enabled some degree of adventure and experimentation to be possible. It was the first time since the Second World War that there was a surplus of money to enable new developments to occur. Social conscience could afford to take a high political profile.

It became politically appropriate to pursue housing policy that enabled housing conditions to be improved for certain less privileged communities. Areas of poor housing were identified, and plans were made to move whole communities to new housing estates. The paradigm for building housing that was in use enabled human space needs to be equated with building designs. Since there had been no experience of moving whole communities before this, the paradigm was blind to other factors that might be involved, like human and sociocultural need.

The perceived reality of a rehousing need was identified in terms of the traditional paradigm. The situation was therefore approached in terms of previous building design experience, introducing the concept of housing efficiency and high-rise housing estates. There was no conceptualisation that the community rehousing projects were about to introduce geographical structures that would have a major impact on the communities. It was to represent a new dimension of sociological understanding that had not been experienced or expected.

It was only some years later that it was discovered that virtually all of the communities that had been rehoused in this way were dying. Vandalism, crime and lack of housing care were all factors that were rampant, and were eventually driving members of the community away. The new estates had not addressed the human and sociocultural needs of the community, for instance by examining lifestyles and processes of communication. The use of high-rise buildings resulted in individual families becoming isolated from the rest of the community because they lived one above the other. Lifts meant that people usually only ever saw their neighbours on either side of their flats. This broke up the community by making it more difficult for normal social intercourse to occur.

It is possible to summarise an interpretation of the modelling process through the use of a method in the above situation (Table 2.1). To do this we shall adopt an arbitrary method composed of three phases: *examination* of the situation, *model* creation for *explanation* and *option selection* to determine how the model options might be chosen.

Table 2.1 Summary of inquiry

Activity	Description
Weltanschauung	There is a need to improve housing conditions of some communities.
Inquirer's mission	To shift communities with 'poor' housing to more satisfactory housing.
Paradigm	Simple organisational model to be used defining relationships between the family needs like average living space requirements per individual, and domestic amenities. Cost effectiveness in the building operations is a prime requirement. Communities not involved in consultation about their future environments.
Method	This applies conceptual tools like methods that derive from the given paradigm. In this case the arbitrary method chosen is simply an examination of the situation, producing a model for this explanation, and identifying how an option can be selected.
Examination	Characteristics of communities in need to be matched in candidate communities. These include housing with lack of modern conveniences like indoor toilet, bathroom, hot running water, effective space heating.
Explanatory model	Cost effectiveness determines replacement housing to be built on relatively low cost land as high-rise apartment building estates. Mechanical model determines building options which include size of the flats and the numbers of blocks required for any community. Estate design requirements require minimum consideration. Community participation in design not a consideration.
Options selection	Option chosen determined by the size of the community being rehoused.

2.6 Paradigm incommensurability

Paradigms are created through cognitive models that involve beliefs, values, attitudes, norms, ideology and meanings and that define mission. They use concepts that form extensions that are logically and analytically distinct.

While different paradigms may be defined as a formalisation of individual weltanschauungen, there is an argument that they cannot legitimately be compared or coordinated (Burrell and Morgan, 1979; Midgley, 1995). This is because paradigms are *incommensurable*. To understand this in the context of the paradigm let us consider the meaning of *commensurability*. Things that are *commensurable* can be described as being (a) coextensive and (b) qualitatively similar. To see this we define the characteristics of paradigms listed in Table 2.2.

Even if two paradigms are coextensive, they are incommensurable if their concepts cannot be measured on the same scale of values, that is if they are qualitatively dissimilar. Since paradigms are formalised world views, we can more broadly talk of world-view incommensurability and maintain the original meaning.

Now paradigms are generators of knowledge that derives from the propositions that make it up. Let us say that associated with each paradigm is a set of knowledge. A

Table 2.2 Characteristics of paradigms

Propositions	Paradigms are formally expressed through propositions. A proposition is a statement of assertion that includes an illustration of its truth, unless that truth is self-evident (axiomatic). The propositions of a paradigm therefore enable it to be described as a 'system of truths'. Propositions are created through the use of concepts and conceptual schemes.
Concepts	Concepts are (Tiryakian, 1963, p. 9) the name for the members of a class or the name of the class itself. Conceptual schemes are groups of concepts used in conjunction for a particular purpose. Concepts are precise, may have empirical referents, and are fruitful for the formation of theories to a situation under consideration. They are intended to represent aspects of reality.
Extension	The extension of a paradigm is defined by the set of concepts that it adopts.
Coextension	Two paradigms are coextensive when they occupy the same spaces of extension and have empirical referents that can be measured on a common platform. This does not necessarily mean that they must have a form of interrelationship, though this is possible.
Similarity	If the measurements of the empirical referents of concepts are qualitatively similar then they can be measured on the same scale of values and are commensurable. However, if they are qualitatively different, then two paradigms are qualitatively dissimilar and therefore incommensurable.

consequence of paradigm incommensurability is therefore that the sets of knowledges that occur across two paradigms can in some way and to some degree be contradictory.

An appreciation of the nature of paradigm incommensurability can be gained by examining two paradigms, and seeing how they differ. An example of this is provided in Minicase 2.2.

Minicase 2.2

The paradigm incommensurability of impressionist and cubist art

Let us consider an example of two incommensurable paradigms. A paradigm exists for cubist paintings, and another different paradigm exists for impressionistic paintings. Both operate from a base of characteristics such as *form, boundary, texture, depth, colour* and *tone*, which are extensions enabling discussion about the paintings. However, the methods defined by each paradigm are different, as is shown in the way the paintings are carried out.

The two paradigms are likely to be coextensive. This is because they can both be discussed in terms of the whole set of characteristics; that is, using all of the extensions of the propositional base like form, boundary, texture and so on. However, the interpretation of each extension in the two paradigms is not measurable with the same set of values. This is because for each paradigm the bounds on every extension are so different that they are qualitatively distinct. This qualitative difference would be expected because the purpose for which each paradigm is being used is different.

Let us discuss this in terms of one of the extensions: *boundary*. Discussion about the boundaries in an impressionist painting would have a different meaning from a similar discussion about a cubist painting because of their different purposes. Impressionism has the intention to enable paintings to give general effect (a) without providing elaborate detail, or (b) with detail so produced as to provide impact rather than realistic correctness. As a consequence, for example, boundaries and texture may be implied rather than stated. This offers harmony between the parts of the painting and a feeling and appreciation of a reality without offering the distraction of detailed representation of a subject matter.

The purpose of cubist paintings is to represent two-dimensional objects within a subject matter in a three-dimensional way. In doing this ideas or messages can easily become highlighted. The objects have very well-defined boundaries and may be placed out of normal context in a subject matter in an attempt to project the quality of it being three-dimensional. The relationship between identifiable objects within a painting thus enables meaning to be inferred that is peculiar to cubist art.

The purposes for each class of composition will thus be different and distinct. It is not usually legitimate to use cubist forms in impressionistic paintings, for such a mix will disturb any meaning or interpretation that a painting might have ascribed to it. However, this is not to say that both forms of painting will not contribute individually to an overall meaning associated with the subject of composition, and enrich the overall interpretation of a subject matter. However, a committed cubist and a committed impressionist may not be able to encounter the belief that the other approach has any coordinating value.

Assignment

Produce a similar argument to that in Minicase 2.2 for the incommensurable paradigms that operate for the written works: novels and biographies.

SUMMARY

The concept of group perception of reality has resulted in the idea that groups have common reality by virtue of sharing the cognitive models that they construct. They do this through relating their world views. Weltanschauung is the world view of an individual or group of individuals that is modelled through a set of assumptions and beliefs manifested in the real world as behaviour. The formalisation of these assumptions and beliefs takes place through statements that can be seen as propositions, when paradigms are born. Both the weltanschauungen and the paradigms are interactive, their relationship being defined through a paradigm cycle.

Paradigms are incommensurable in that they have extensions that are different. Common extensions may be qualitatively different. Thus, paradigms can neither be directly coordinated nor compared. Since paradigms are formalised weltanschauungen, more general than paradigm incommensurability is the conceptualisation of world-view incommensurability.

REFERENCES

Ackoff, R.L. (1981) *Creating a Corporate Future*. New York: Wiley.

Arnold, V.I. and Avez, A. (1968) *Ergodic Problems of Classical Mechanics*. New York: Benjamin Cummings.

Bachman, G. and Narici, L. (1966) *Functional Analysis*. London: Academic Press.

Berger, P. and Luckman, T. (1966) *The Social Construction of Reality*. Harmondsworth: Penguin.

Berke, J.H. (1989) *The Tyranny of Malice: Exploring the dark side of character and culture*. London: Simon & Schuster.

Burnes, B. (1992) *Managing Change*. London: Pitman.

Burrell, G. and Morgan, G. (1979) *Sociological Paradigms and Organisational Analysis*. London: Heinemann.

Casti, J.L. (1989) *Paradigms Lost*. London: Abacus.

Checkland, P. (1981) *Systems Thinking, Systems Practice*. Chichester: Wiley.

Checkland, P.B. and Davies, L. (1986) 'The use of the term weltanschauung in soft systems methodology', *Journal of Applied Systems Analysis*, 13(1), 9–115.

Checkland, P. and Scholes, J. (1990) *Soft Systems Methodology in Action*. Chichester: Wiley.

Chomsky, N. (1975) *Problems of Knowledge and Freedom*. New York: Pantheon.

Chorpa, D. (1990) *Quantum Healing: Exploring the frontiers of mind/body medicine*. New York: Bantam Books.

Churchman, C.W. (1979) *The Systems Approach*, 2nd edn. New York: Dell.

Clancey, W.J. and Letsinger, R. (1981) 'Neomycin: reconfiguring a rule based expert system for application to teaching', *IJCAI*, 7(2).

Durkheim, E. (1915) *Les formes elementaires de la vie religieuse*. New York: Free Press.

Espejo, R. (1993) 'Management of complexity in problem solving'. In Espejo, R. and Schwaninger, M. (eds) *Organisational Fitness: Corporate effectiveness through management cybernetics*. Frankfurt: Campus Verlag.

Fairtlough, G. (1982) 'A note on the use of the term "Weltanschauung" in Checkland's "Systems Thinking, Systems Practice"', *Journal of Applied Systems Analysis*, 9, 131–2.

Giglioli, P.P. (1972) *Language and Social Context*. Harmondsworth: Penguin.

Habermas, J. (1979) *Communication and the Evolution of Society*. London: Heinemann.

Hiley, B.J. and Peat, F.D. (1987) 'The development of David Bohm's ideas from plasma to the implicate order'. In Hiley, B.J. and Peat, F.D. (eds) *Quantum Implications*. London: Routledge & Kegan Paul.

Hirschheim, R.A. (1992) 'Information systems epistemology: an historical perspective'. In Galliers, R. (ed.) *Information Systems Research*. Oxford: Blackwell, pp. 28, 60.

Holsti, K.J. (1967) *International Politics: A framework for analysis*. Englewood Cliffs, NJ: Prentice Hall.

Hoover, T. (1977) *Zen Culture*. New York: Random House.

Koestler, A. (1975) *The Ghost in the Machine*. London: Picador.

Kuhn, S.T. (1970) *The Structure of Scientific Revolutions*, 2nd edn. Chicago, IL: University of Chicago Press.

Kyberg Jr., H.E. (1968) *Philosophy of Science: A formal approach*. London: Collier-Macmillan.

Mannheim, K. (1964) *Wissenssoziologie*. Luchterhand: Nenwied/Rhein.

Maturana, H. (1988) 'Reality: the search for objectivity or the quest for a compelling argument', *Irish Journal of Psychology*, 9, 25–82.

Midgley, G. (1995) 'Mixing methods: developing systemic intervention'. Research Memorandum no. 9, Centre for Systems Studies, University of Hull.

Mingers, J. (1995) *Self Producing Systems*. New York: Academic Press.

Mitchell, G.D. (1968) *A Dictionary of Sociology*. London: Routledge & Kegan Paul.

Patching, D. (1990) *Practical Soft Systems Analysis*. London: Pitman.

Pribram, W.D. (1977) *Languages of the Brain*. Monterey, CA: Wadsworth.

Rinpoche, S. (1992) *The Tibetan Book of Living and Dying*. London: Rider.

Rokeach, M. (1968) *Beliefs, Attitudes, and Values: A theory of organisational change*. San Francisco, CA: Jossey-Bass.

Scheler, M. (1947) *Die Stellung des Menschen im Kosmos*. Munich: Nymphenburger Verlagshandlung.

Secord, P.F. and Backman, C.W. (1964) *Social Psychology*. New York: McGraw-Hill.

Stark, W. (1962) *The Fundamental Forms of Social Thought*. London: Routledge & Kegan Paul.

Talbot, M. (1991) *The Holographic Universe*. London: Grafton Books.

Thomas, W.L. and Znaniecki, F. (1918) *The Polish Peasant in Europe and America*, vol. 1. Boston, MA: Badger.

Tiryakian, E.A. (1963) *Sociological Theory, Values, and Sociocultural Change*. New York: Free Press.

Vickers, G. (1965) *The Art of Judgement*. London: Chapman & Hall.

Williams, A., Dobson, P. and Walters, M. (1993) *Changing Culture: New organisational approaches*. London: Institute of Personnel Management.

Yolles, M.I. (1996) 'Critical systems thinking, paradigms, and the modelling space', *Journal of Systems Practice*, 9(3).

CHAPTER 3

The paradigm of complexity

OVERVIEW

Situations often develop that are problematic, and this must be dealt with for the sake of stability. The problems that occur may be simply differentiable from each other, when they may be referred to as a difficulty, or may be seen as a complex tangle of undifferentiable problems, when they are a mess. The former type of situation is an example of a 'simple' situation, while the latter is one that is 'complex'. There are other criteria that distinguish simple from complex situations, and that better enable us to seek strategies for intervention for stability.

OBJECTIVES

This chapter will examine:

- the distinction between a difficulty and a mess;
- the distinction between simple and complex situations;
- approaches towards dealing with complexity.

3.1 Seeing situations in terms of problems

Systems thinking should be seen as a replacement for mechanistic thinking, which sees situations in terms of a machine metaphor. Mechanistic thinking is also called simple thinking, as opposed to systems thinking, which is able to model situations in a way that can capture many more of its interactive subtleties. It was mid-century that Ackoff said that the machine age – associated with the industrial revolution – began to give way to the systems age. 'The system age is characterised by increasingly rapid changes, interdependence, and complex purposeful systems. It demands that much greater emphasis be put upon learning and adaptation if any kind of stability is to be achieved. This, in turn, requires a radical reorientation of world view' (Jackson, 1992, p. 145). Machine age thinking adopts analysis and reductionism, sees cause–effect relationships and is deterministic. A systems view, however, seeks synthesis after analysis, and in doing so seeks to promote a broad picture. It allows for interactivity and unpredeterminable variation, distinct perspectives and changing views.

In systems, a situation is normally seen in terms of a whole and a set of interactive parts that compose it. In problem situations we sometimes refer to the parts as being the individual problems. When we do this we say that problem situations can be examined in terms of a set of problems for which solutions are to be found. The nature of a set of problems may vary with an inquirer, and we should therefore talk not of problems but of perceived problems. They are normally expressed in terms of perceived deviation from desired goals, and explained in terms of related organising processes. The problems are often clustered together, differentiation being difficult because of 'our tendency to associate similar things and assume that they are caused by the same things' (Kepner and Tregoe, 1965, p. 62). The need, then, is to distinguish the problems.

A first step in doing this is to differentiate between different classes of problem situation. Two classes that we define are *difficulties* and *messes*. The distinction between difficulties and messes can be characterised (Table 3.1) by whether the problems are seen

Table 3.1 Characteristics of difficult and messy problems

Problem characteristics	Difficult problems	Messy problems
Plurality	Are unitary single problem situations	Are pluralistic, with a set of interactive problems which mutually relate
Boundedness	Are bounded	Are unbounded
Definability	Are clearly definable	Are not clearly definable
Knowledge-related	Full knowledge can enable information needs to be determined	Have a lack of knowledge about what information is needed to describe the situation
Participative	Involve few people	Involve more people
Role-related	Participants have clearly definable roles	Unclear who is involved, or what role they play
Context	Problems independently examinable	Indivisible from the context due to problem interdependence

Table 3.1 (continued)

Problem characteristics	Difficult problems	Messy problems
Solutions		
Determinable	Solutions types determinable	Uncertain about whether any solutions are possible
Uniqueness	Assuming that the solution approach is classifiable under a typology	Assuming that the solution approached is unique to the problem situation
Applicability	Have limited determinable applications	Application of determined solutions is uncertain, having broader implications
Predictability of situation outcomes	Expected	Unexpected in the long term

as a simple bundle of difficulties that are individually bounded, or as a complex 'tangle' where each problem is unbounded, which defines a mess.

Whether we class a problem situation to be difficult or messy will be determined when we assign to it the characteristics defined in Fig. 3.1 (based on Mabey, 1995). In this we highlight the notion of content being independent or interdependent. There is a potential problem with the notion of independence, and it is equivalent to the problem of whether we regard a system as autonomous (a question we explore in some detail in Chapter 6). Effectively, independence is judged by degree in connection with the 'richness' of the interactions under consideration.

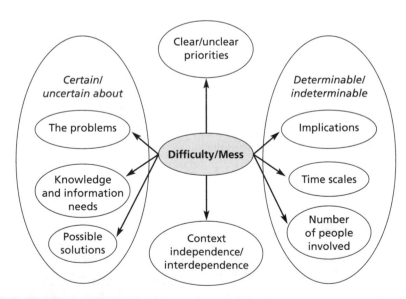

Fig. 3.1 Characteristics of a difficult/messy problem situation

3.2 Messes in a technically emotionally complex field

Problem situations may not only be either simple difficulties or complex messes. There are a variety of states into which they can fall according to our perspective. In Section 1.7.3 we introduced two classes of complexity: emotional and technical. *Emotional complexity* is represented by a 'tangle' of emotional vectors projected into a situation by its participants that itself defines an emotional involvement. *Technical complexity* can also be thought of as cybernetic complexity in that it is represented by a 'tangle' of interactive control processes, a definition that we shall extend shortly. These classes of complexity are analytically independent, but together contribute to the overall complexity of a situation. The states identified in Table 3.2 may be considered to have different degrees of emotional and technical complexity. These states can be placed in the technically complex emotional field (Mabey, 1995) that emerges from a space that defines the relationship between technical complexity and emotional involvement (Fig. 3.2).

Table 3.2 States of possible situation that involve both technical and emotional complexity

Situation types or states	Nature	Explanation
Puzzles	Simple	Direct choice options
Complex projects	Cerebral or mechanistic	Appealing to the faculty of reasoning, knowing or understanding
Complex personal issues	Emotionally charged	Easy to understand, difficult to handle
Messy	Relatively unbounded	Some situations tending towards being computational orientated, others emotional orientated
Intractable	Emotionally and technically complex	Competing cultural and political agents

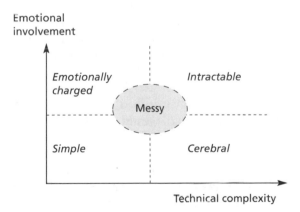

Fig. 3.2 Complex emotional field showing possible problem states
(*Source*: Mabey, 1995)

3.3 Resolving, dissolving and optimally solving problems

Solutions to problem situations are determined implicitly by an adequate definition of the problem itself. That is to say development of a solution is directly related to the way in which the problem is expressed. Typically, a well-defined problem will lead an inquirer to a set of possible solution approaches if they exist. In simple paradigms – that is, those that support simple modelling of situations – problems are perceived to be unitary and have solutions that are perceived to have properties such as optimality, when a single *best* solution exists. However, other paradigms allow for pluralism and much more uncertainty, human value judgement and lack of clear definition in relating its different possible parts.

We remind ourselves here that all situations under examination are first modelled. Without at least a mental model, no perception or view of the situation is possible. Once problems have been identified to exist, attempts may be made to unravel them through *resolution*, *dissolution* or *optimal solution* (Flood and Jackson, 1991, p. 147).

1 *Resolving* problems attempt to settle contradictions, and can be seen as the approach of 'satisficing', where trial and error 'good enough' solutions are sought.

2 *Dissolving* problems assumes that situations are modelled such that the parts are interactive; it involves changing the form of the situation in which the mess or set of interrelated problems is embedded so that problems disappear.

3 *Optimally solving* problems is the approach in which it is assumed that solutions exist and can be found, and, indeed, that one solution or set of solutions may be better than another in that it maximises or minimises something.

The *resolution* of problems is often carried out by 'mature' managers, and is based on experience and common sense. The idea of dissolving problems derives from Wittgenstein. It requires a correct understanding of their nature, so that the contradictions that cause them can be eliminated (Lazerowitz, 1968, p. 159). The *dissolution* of problems is the interactivists' approach, and frequently the problem is idealised rather than satisfied or optimised. Organisational change is part of this process, and development is usually more important than growth or survival. The *optimal solution* of problems often employs formal methods like mathematical techniques. The approach usually develops a model that is 'similar' to the situation being inquired into, which can be solved optimally. This often involves a process of simplification, and it is usually necessary to show that this does not conceptually perturb the problems 'too much'. The closeness of similarity between the problems and their models is determined by the boundaries that define them, and these are world view determined. A colleague, Noyan Direli, once recited the story of the *Khodja*. It refers to the modelling problem of a bird that would appear to come from a Turkish perspective. Modellers in an attempt to model the bird wish first to simplify it. To do this they cut off the wings, the beak and the legs, and still call it a bird. Then they show that it has some remarkable properties that they attribute to the bird rather than the model. However, it can no longer fly, walk or peck. Is it still a bird, and if not, when was it that it lost its valid representation of the bird? Comparison of the boundaries occurs through the definition or appropriate cognitive criteria, and it is up to us to determine whether it is sensible to represent the bird by the model.

3.4 The nature of simple situations

Paradigms change or are replaced as their modelling capabilities are discovered to be limited. This will be shown clearly in the next chapter. What we might now refer to as a simple modelling approach was carried within a paradigm that operated in the early part of the 20th century, when the industrial revolution was at its prime and reflected societies' successes in mass production. The real world was seen to be machine like and created from an assembly of parts. Machine age thinking was based on analysis, reductionism, identification of direct cause–effect relations and determinism.

The reductionist world view sees all objects and events and their properties in terms of their smallest parts that can be examined and evaluated separately. An example of such a view is a clockwork mechanism. Popper (1972, p. 207) used clocks to represent physical organisations that are regular and orderly. They are also highly predictable in their behaviour and thus deterministic. They can be dismantled and each individual part improved (or optimised) to satisfy predetermined needs or objectives. These objectives combine together in order to satisfy overall objectives that would not be possible if each partition did not perform as intended. Later approaches enabled statistical explanations to become an accepted way of evaluating situations, thus providing an extension to determinism.

Simple situations are those that can be defined and modelled according to the methods and tools which enable easy and direct explanation, and confident event prediction to occur. This must be a function of our ability to understand situations, and an ability to find concepts and tools through which explanations can be provided that work. In particular, simple situations are those that can be so modelled that Table 3.3 is satisfied.

Table 3.3 Nature of simple situations

Simple situations:

1   are clearly bounded and can be examined in isolation

2   are populated by a set of entities/events

3   have information needs that are known

4   the roles and purposes of any people, groups or organisations are well known

5   are composed of differentiable problems that are either well known or probabilistically describable

6   have a form that is well known and which can change in predictable ways

7   will have known or probabilistic structural relationships across the set of identifiable parts and cause–effect relationships between events across time

8   each part:
   a   can be examined independently
   b   can be optimised for the benefit of the situation
   c   can have a change that can be measured quantitatively
   d   can have deterministic or probabilistic prediction of change
   e   has a solution to problems that will have an identifiable form

Both Simple

3.5 Clock and cloud modelling

In order to show how both deterministic and probabilistic approaches relate to simple modelling, we can refer to Popper's consideration of a more complex organisation than clocks: clouds of gnats. Clocks are representative of situations that, when analysed, are totally visible and deterministic. Clouds, however, are representative of physical systems that, like gases composed of molecules, have movements that are highly irregular, disorderly, more or less unpredictable and (unlike clocks) indeterministic. Like molecules in a gas, individual gnats fly around together in clusters that make up clouds. While they each move in irregular ways and can be seen individually, it is virtually impossible to pursue a single one by eye since they move so quickly and erratically. For the observer, the cloud is kept together by some indetermined means.

In the case of clocks, the parts can be individual cogs that can each be manipulated by an engineer of clocks and assembled optimally and uniquely into an integral whole that now operates to tell the time. Consider now the case of clouds. Because of the random-like movement of individual gnats in the cloud, clouds can be thought of as statistically examinable within a probabilistic framework. The parts of the cloud can be thought of as arbitrary partitions. They enable a model to be built having certain statistical properties, and allow the application of statistical or quantum mechanics in order to fulfil a possible purpose that we explore in Minicase 3.1.

Minicase 3.1

Simple modelling of a cloud of gnats

Consider the cloud of gnats and assume that they are flying around in their cloud at random. You introduce an object into the cloud and find that gnat flight paths avoid it, thus creating a gnat displacement. This displacement can be seen as the gnats creating a structured pattern of flight within their cloud, otherwise they would simply bump into the object. We wish to inquire whether after removing the object gnat movements would be re-established similar to how they were before. That is, the gnats would return to their original classification of movements: individual gnats having random movement, and there being no overall structure within the cloud.

Asking about the tendency towards disorder is the same as asking about the cloud's entropy, and both represent a single modelling purpose. The idea of entropy is common to the idea of disorder, and so an entropic movement of an organisation is one from order to disorder. The modelling purpose, then, is to see if a cloud of gnats behaves entropically. This purpose has a number of assumptions embedded within it. We are hypothesising that the cloud has the following characteristics:

1 the cloud is made up of the individual gnats;

2 the gnats (appear to) have purpose (flying in a bounded cloud);

3 the gnats have individual properties (e.g. flight, direction, object avoidance);

4 the cloud has properties itself that may be distinct from those of the individual gnats.

We are arguing that it is possible to change our view of the way in which the gnats are seen. It also supposes that the gnat movements relative to the cloud are classifiable, and that all the gnats in their movements conform to a way of flying which is consistent with the classification.

The purpose itself can be better stated. When the gnats are disturbed they fly away from the new boundary that is introduced by the object. When the object is removed, the hole in the space is eventually filled again by gnats. Thinking of the cloud as a single entity, you can say that its entropy (or degree of disorder of the gnats within the boundary of the cloud) has increased because the space has been filled again by random movements of gnats. The modelling purpose, then, is to see under what conditions the cloud of gnats always maximises its entropy.

3.6 Seeing complexity

In contrast to simple situations, a complex situation may be seen to have the characteristics described in Table 3.4.

Table 3.4 Characteristics of complex situations

Complex situations:

1 exist in an environment, though the boundary that distinguishes it from the situation will be unclear or uncertain

2 are populated:
    a by sets of entities/events that may not be sensibly examinable in isolation of the context
    b by individuals, groups or organisations with roles and purposes that may not be well determined

3 have parts:
    a that may themselves be situations (i.e. substitutions) or problems
    b that may not be easily distinguishable from one another (a tangle)
    c that if known may not be related
    d the description and relationship of which may change in time

4 where the parts are seen as (dynamic) events across time, a simple cause–effect relationship between them cannot be identified

5 have a form:
    a determined by the dynamic relationship between the parts
    b that may in some way change in time
    c that may not be easily discernible

6 are world-view determined, since this defines the criteria and knowledge that can be applied to a situation under examination.

In simple paradigms situations can be reduced to a set of parts, and each part can be analysed independently without relating it to the whole assembly that composes the system. This is not the case for complex paradigms. Simple situations involving events across time can be seen in terms of their cause–effect relationships. In complex situations there may be many causes that generate observed effects, and they may not occur in simple relationships. Many people hold the view that complexity begets complexity. Cohen and Stewart (1994) refer to this as the principle of 'conservation of complexity' that occurs when people expect complex situations to have complex causes. This simple cause–effect rule relationship is not often borne out in practice. In certain circumstances systems act as amplifiers so that simple causes can have fall-out consequences that are quite complex and lead to chaos. There is also the idea of antichaos, proposed by Stuart Kauffman. Here, complex causes produce simple effects, indicating that complexity can diminish as well as increase.

Complexity can provide a harbour for chaos, and they are inseparable twins. 'Now that science is looking, chaos seems to be everywhere' (Gleick, 1987, p. 5). Today, we are more frequently talking not of dynamic situations as being simple, but rather as being complex, and when we say this we are implicitly referring to the dynamics of chaos. In complex situations, the dynamics of chaos amplifies tiny differences hidden in the detail of the complexity, and enables the unexpected to become the predominant. The explanation for this is very important, and we shall return to the topic again in due course.

The complexity of a situation can be seen in terms of:

1 its number of parts;

2 its number of interconnections between the parts that must be accounted for;

3 the attributes of the specified parts;

4 its degree of organisation.

The degree of *organisational complexity* that a situation has is determined by the rules guiding the interactions or specifying the attributes. The number of interactions themselves can form what Mabey (1995) would refer to as *computational complexity* since it is concerned with counting. Thus, for instance, a situation for which a large number of parts and many interactions can be identified is more computationally complex than one with fewer of each.

Habermas (1970, 1974) suggests that situations have what we may refer to as technical interests that relate to work situations and the achievement of technical action, which is concerned with control and prediction. This links with the notion of *technical complexity*. We have already referred to this as cybernetic complexity, which occurs when a situation has a 'tangle' of control processes that are difficult to discern because they are numerous and highly interactive. However, it also involves the notion of future and thus predictability. Thus, technically complex situations have limited predictability.

Habermas also defines situations to have practical interests. These are human interaction related, and factors like group cohesion and personal relationships are part of this consideration. Distinguishing between technical and practical situations enables us to differentiate between object- and people-related complexity. This theme is continued by Midgley (1992, p. 153), who tells us that there is an inadequacy with the traditional definition of complexity, given as 'the quantity of relationships between parts in relation to the human capacity to handle an amount of information'. From this definition, a 'simple' situation occurs if all perceived relationships can be *appreciated* by the observer, and 'complex' if they cannot. To arrive at this it concentrates on the relationships between objects (computational, technical or organisational complexity), and excludes the complexities of moral decision making and subjectivity. The concept of complexity (and thus simplicity) is not necessarily only quantifiable and objective, and the evaluation of whether a situation is complex must be seen to be in part world view determined. The term for this is *personal complexity*, and highlights that situations are seen subjectively. They may be complexified through the emotional involvement that we have referred to as emotional complexity.

It might be possible to find some formal support for Midgley's idea that complexity is subjective. If so it may derive from some work in the mathematics of number theory that relates to the domains of cognition and artificial intelligence. David Hilbert believed that all possible mathematical truths could be captured within some formal system, and spent much of his time trying to prove this. In 1931 Kurt Gödel refuted what Hilbert

[handwritten margin note: technical cybernetic complexity]

was trying to do, 'proving that for any formal system $\mathcal{F}$ that can be finitely describable, consistent, and strong enough to prove the basic facts about elementary arithmetic: $\mathcal{F}$ is incomplete, and cannot prove its own consistency' (Casti, 1989, p. 279). This *incompleteness theorem*, as it is called, appears to imply (Casti, 1989, p. 284) that in a formal system there exist truths that may be determinable but cannot be captured.

Gödel's theorem shows that every formal system is subject to inherent limitations on the amount of 'truth' that can be extracted from it, an argument that is differently supported elsewhere in this book. Casti explains that Gödel's theorem can be seen as a special case of the work of Gregory Chaitin on the limitations of formal systems in their ability to deal with complexity. In 1965 Chaitin proved that a finitely describable and consistent formal system $\mathcal{F}$ is limited in its ability to determine the complexity of an arbitrarily selected situation, and in this respect $\mathcal{F}$ is incomplete.

This would seem to support Midgley's view that complexity is necessarily subjective. The argument is as follows. A paradigm is a formalised weltanschauung. It is further a truth system that is seen to be *finitely discernible* (since a given paradigm can only generate its own truths, and not those of a different paradigm) and *consistent*. Its tools of objectivity define its truth system, and if we can apply the ideas of Chaitin and Gödel an objective evaluation of complexity is not possible because the tools cannot be complete.

3.7 Social systems and complexity

Social systems have a socially defined structure, often expressed in terms of roles. In addition they usually have cultural attributes associated with them that explain why people behave socially as they do.

When situations are complex, it is often useful to pull back from the detail of what is happening in order to obtain a broader perspective. In other words, when a microscopic view is not helpful, a macroscopic one may be. This principle is implicit in much of the theorising that occurs about how situations change. For instance, Sorokin (1937) was interested in large-scale social and cultural change, though the theory of dynamic change that he developed would also seem to be applicable to small-scale social and cultural change situations. In Sorokin's view, cultures are highly complex phenomena when seen in terms of the myriad social systems that make them up. 'Since in the total culture of any population there are millions of various cultural systems (and congeries), a study of small systems would give at best, only a knowledge of diverse, infinitesimal fragments of the total cultural universe. It never can give an essential knowledge of the basic structural and dynamic properties of this superorganic reality. As any nomothetic (generalising) science, sociology endeavours to overcome this bewildering diversity of the millions and millions of systems and congeries' (Sorokin, 1937).

Sorokin developed a theory of cultural change that was intended to explain cultural events in terms of a macroscopic pattern. This proposed that cultures should be seen to be composed of a dialectic process between two cultural states, referred to as *ideational* and *sensate*. Any culture is seen as mix of these two states. Thus, during the industrial revolution, the West had a mix of these two, which was referred to as *idealistic* – generating and developing ideas through a balance of ideational creation and sensate constraint. It was thus through an understanding of the properties of cultures in these states and their dynamic relationship that he was able to explain the many seemingly chaotic social events in society.

Both large-scale and small-scale systems need to maintain their stability if they are to survive. We theorise that there are two types of stability, dynamic and structural. Dynamic stability (Berlinski, 1975) is concerned with the achievement of goals in purposeful systems, and couples intention with achievement, quite distinct from that of structural stability.

The concept of structural stability concerns the qualitative condition of a system. Now perturbations from the environment of a system impact on it. These will affect the system in a way that is structure determined – that is, its response will be limited by the capabilities of the structure itself to respond. A system can only respond according to its capability determined by the potential of its structure. In equilibrium circumstance, the structure is 'stable' and responds to perturbation in a way that is expected. Sometimes, however, perturbations may result in surprising ways that are not predeterminable. This is consistent with the idea that they are subject to chaos, a situation where the system is highly sensitive to small random perturbations. We can say that such a system is structurally unstable.

Now structural stability is endangered when small changes in one of the parts of a structured situation can result in a qualitatively distinct change in its form. When form is qualitatively changed, structure and related processes that give it a shape, that define its nature and that determine its behaviour alter in a way that is seen to be qualitatively different. It is therefore with sense that Minorsky (1962, p. 185) prefers to refer to structural instability as a condition of *structural criticality*.

3.8 Dealing with complexity

An example of the needs of complex modelling, and the problems that can arise when a simple approach is taken in such a case, is given in Minicase 3.2. There are ways of dealing with complexity, however, other than just trying to find a more complex model to deal with what is seen as a more complex situation. We have already suggested that we can pull away from the detail of complexity by taking a more macroscopic view of a situation. This idea can be developed further.

Ashby (1956) has suggested that when situations are seen to be complex, it is more useful to explore them in terms of their overall patterns of behaviour. In a similar vein, Ackoff (1981) refers to a problem situation being a mess when it has properties that none of its parts have, and which are lost when the situation is analysed. These properties can be thought of as emerging when a set of interactive parts that can be associated for some purpose come together.

In a complex situation, the idea of emergence can be seen as simplicity emerging from complexity. Emergence can 'collapse chaos' (Cohen and Stewart, 1994, p. 232) and bring order to a system that seems to be in random fluctuation. It is representative of a totality that cannot be disaggregated. The concept is a fundamental proposition of systems theory. It is a function of the whole, and not of the contained parts. If we consider rich formal systems to be those that are computationally and technically complex, then through the work of Gödel discussed earlier it is possible to show (Cohen and Stewart, 1995, p. 439) that they must have emergence.

In discussing complexity and how to deal with it, Cohen and Stewart (1995, pp. 411–19) talk of *simplexity*. In *simplex* situations we have a situation equivalent to that in which emergence has been conceptualised. Large-scale simplicities have developed that can be defined through conceptualisations that we can call *characteristics*. These can be explored through a set of rules that is able to 'explain' a situation in a simple way in terms of these large-scale simplicities. Cohen and Stewart call this *regular* emergence.

They also refer to the notion of *complicity*, which arises when two or more simple systems interact in a way that both changes and erases their dependence on initial conditions. In situations within which complicity is seen to occur, different sets of rules that relate to simplex situations converge so as to exhibit the same large-scale structural patterns. It is a process of emergence on a global scale, and is referred to as *super* emergence. The distinct sets of rules coalesce to form 'meta-rules'. Thus a primary difference between simplexity and complicity is that in the former case our interest lies in emergence within the local system, while in the latter case our interest lies in emergence at a more global level, and concerns the interconnectedness between systems.

Minicase 3.2

Modelling a complex system as a simple set of parts

After it came to office in the late 1970s, the UK Conservative Government under Thatcher introduced policies that affect the way in which public organisations are managed. Like many Governments, some changes were introduced that did not address the complexities of the situations.

One example is the allocation of awards to long-term unemployed persons. A policy has been generated to employ them in temporary jobs. The job allocation process is constrained by geographic mechanisms, and no facility appears to have been established for people in one particular geographic area to be allocated to jobs in another. Efficiency was defined in terms of local cost minimisation. No attempt appears to have been made to have seen the situation as a whole, and no investment has been provided for the establishment of a communications infrastructure for resource and job opportunity sharing. This means that even neighbouring regions do not have an effective approach for matching skills with needs.

Consider now the drive to introduce competitive or privatised mechanisms into all parts of the country's infrastructure. The rationale for this was that when the parts are dealt with independently, they can be made more efficient; consequently the economic system, operating on this premise, can become more efficient. The difficulty is that in such simple thinking, the concept of the whole is lost, which can lead to problematic interventions.

Take one example: privatisation of buses. Originally, most local authorities ran bus services. Here, bus systems operated a variety of routes that we shall model as its parts. These were interactive and operated (passenger) exchanges. Thus, passengers were able to transfer from one route to another. However, with privatisation the different routes became owned by independent operators. It was difficult for the companies to cooperate since some ran routes that were in competition with others. As a result, coordination between the parts suffered, and passenger exchanges between the parts became problematic. This breakdown in the bus system was highlighted by the following situation. Consider the case prior to privatisation. Pensioners with bus passes and passengers with season tickets could take any bus anywhere within the system so long as the tickets represented a journey conjoint with the physical and time boundary of the pass/season ticket. After bus privatisation, it was sometimes quite difficult to find buses that could take such a passenger to the final destination. Reasons included (a) not all bus companies operated all routes and could not offer transfers on their own lines, and (b) it was difficult to make agreements between the competitive companies about ticket validity across the whole bus network. The result could be described as a fragmented bus network.

Assignments

Consider some elements of the initiative for privatisation. Argue your case.

1 Explain why, in your opinion, the approach appears to be one of simple or complex modelling.

2 Identify one infrastructural example, like energy (electricity, gas, coal, oil) or transport (buses, railways), and examine it briefly as a whole to see if it represents a simple situation or a complex one.

3.9 A typology of situations

The foundation principle is that any situation can be seen as a set of parts. If it is seen as a problem situation, then the parts can be taken to be problems. These problems may be simple and thus discernible in all of their attributes, or alternatively tangled and thus indiscernible and uncertain. The problem situation may further be susceptible to change, though the nature of its dynamic change as the relationships between the problems change is not determinable. Furthermore, in a simple situation, behaviour is seen as a manifestation of cognitive processes that is deterministic or expected. However, in complex situations behaviour will additionally be subject to unpredeterminable influences that can disturb cognitive purposes. A simple typology of complex situations is given in Table 3.5, which identifies the two components: the perceived attributes of a problem situation and the attributes of embedded problems.

3.10 Complexity and systems

Like others, Ho and Sculli (1995) hold that complexity is at least closely related, if not embodied, with the idea of the system. Within this context, if systems are said to be defined in terms of a set of elements, then they can be viewed so that (Ackoff, 1981): (a) the behaviour of each element of the system should have an effect on the behaviour of the whole, (b) the behaviour of the elements should be interdependent on the behaviour of the whole and (c) different arbitrarily defined subgroups of the whole should not affect the behaviour of the whole, and none of the subgroups should be completely independent.

Ho and Sculli are interested in describing system complexity in terms or organisational decision making. Their basic perception of this is represented in Fig. 3.3 in terms of an inquirer, rather than a decision maker. The intention of this figure is to show that system complexity can arise from the nature of the system, as well as from how the system is seen from the perspective of an inquirer. We have explored the different dimensions of complexity that relate to this. The type of situation being considered will be interpreted in terms of the goals of an inquirer, and on this basis will be seen to involve different types of complexity. For instance, personal and emotional complexity are conditioned by the interests, knowledge, weltanschauungen and so on of inquirers. The perceived real-world situation will have associated with it resources available to the inquirer, and these will affect his or her capability to inquire into the situation that is being modelled as a system. This will in turn define the nature of the system under consideration for the particular inquirer.

Table 3.5 Summary relationship between simple and complex situations

Characteristic	Simple	Complex
Attributes of situations		
1 Boundary	1 Situations are bounded	1 Situations are unbounded
2 Number of parts	2 Small number	2 Large number
3 Relationships between parts	3 Clearly determinable	3 Indeterminable
4 Interactions between parts	4 Few interactions	4 Many interactions
5 Organisation of interactions	5 Highly organised	5 Loosely organised
6 Governing of behaviour	6 Determinism or expectation	6 Stochastic processes
7 Change in form	7 Unchanging or determinable	7 Indeterminable
8 Change in time	8 Static or equilibrium processes	8 Chaotic processes
9 Change relation of parts to the whole	9 Relationship between change in parts and situation seen as a whole will be clearly visible	9 Relationship between change in parts and situation seen as a whole will not be clear
10 Purposes associated with each part	10 Unitary	10 Pluralistic
11 Dynamic future	11 Predictable	11 Unpredictable
Attributes of situation parts – seen as problems		
1 Definition	1 Clear	1 Unclear and tangled
2 Measurement	2 Quantitative	2 Quantitative and qualitative
3 Timescale	3 Short and determinable/ estimatable	3 Longer and uncertain
4 Problem definition	4 Known	4 Unclear
5 Knowledge	5 Certain	5 Uncertain
6 Problem dependence	6 Independent of context	6 Context related
7 People involved	7 Few (if any) people involved or taken into account	7 People (and there may be many) taken into account
8 Priorities	8 Certain	8 Unclear; questionable
Attributes for problem solutions		
1 Nature	1 Known	1 Unclear
2 Form	2 Predictable or expected	2 Unknown
3 Optimal type	3 Efficiently improves situation	3 None
4 Dissolving type	4 None	4 Restructure situation
5 Resolving type	5 None	5 Find ways out of situation
6 Applicability	6 Limited	6 Uncertain of significance

The inquirer is not divorced from the real-world situation. Goals and perceptions are shaped by his or her own social and cultural conditions. Also, the resources available to him or her to understand and formulate strategies about the situation are context related. This is because the inquirer defines the situation through the interaction between it and him or herself. The complexity of the situation is also subjective, conditioned by what the inquirer considers to be his or her total environment. It is also intersubjective since the complexity of a situation perceived to be problematic is relative to different stakeholders – that is, those people who see that they have a stake in the situation. This reaffirms that complexity cannot be objectively measured, and that there is no absolute bound on complexity that enables it to be empirically evaluated.

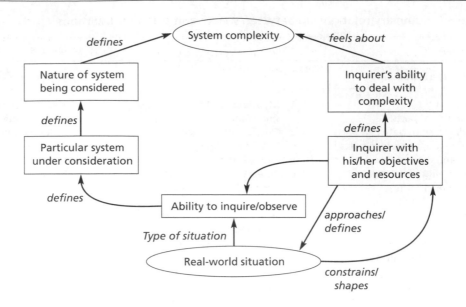

Fig. 3.3 A representation of system complexity

Thus, Fig. 3.3 illustrates that a given situation seen to be problematic will be considered to be simple and manageable by some inquirers, while others will see it very differently, being complex and perhaps unmanageable. Having said this, there are attempts to create paradigms that can clearly distinguish between simple and complex situations (Wafield and Staley, 1996), and so provide indications of how such situations can be dealt with.

SUMMARY

Five types of complexity have been identified:

1 Computational complexity is defined in terms of the (large) number of interactive parts.

2 Technical complexity (also referred to as cybernetic complexity) occurs when a situation has a 'tangle' of control processes that are difficult to discern because they are numerous and highly interactive. It also involves the notion of future and thus predictability, and technically complex situations have limited predictability.

3 Organisational complexity is defined by the rules that guide the interactions between a set of identifiable parts, or specifying the attributes.

4 Personal complexity is defined by the subjective view of a situation.

5 Emotional complexity occurs with a 'tangle' of emotional vectors projected into a situation by its participants (and can be seen as emotional involvement).

Broadly speaking, complex situations involve all these types of complexity to some degree, and tend to be dynamic, uncertain and unclear.

How we think about the meaning of complexity is effectively dependent upon the paradigms that we support (Corning, 1996). Whatever paradigm we adopt, it is also a relative thing that changes with the world views of inquirers. It depends upon how we are able to understand and model the situations that we are examining. It can be defeated through considering situations more macroscopically in terms of emergent properties or patterns of behaviour.

REFERENCES

Ackoff, R.L. (1981) *Creating the Corporate Future*. New York: Wiley.

Ashby, W.R. (1956) *An Introduction to Cybernetics*. London: Methuen.

Berlinski, D. (1975) 'Mathematical models of the world', *Synthese*, 31, 211–27.

Casti, J.L. (1989) *Paradigms Lost*. London: Abacus.

Cohen, J. and Stewart, I. (1994) *The Collapse of Chaos: Discovering simplicity in a complex world*. London: Viking.

Corning, P.A. (1996) 'Synergy and self-organisation in the evolution of complex systems', *Systems Research*, 12(2), 89–122.

Flood, R. and Jackson, M. (1991) *Creative Problem Solving: Total intervention strategy*. Chichester: Wiley.

Gleick, J. (1987) *Chaos*. London: Sphere Books.

Habermas, J. (1970) 'Knowledge and interest'. In Emmet, D. and MacIntyre, A. (eds) *Sociological Theory and Philosophical Analysis*. London: Macmillan, pp. 36–54.

Habermas, J. (1974) *Theory and Practice*. London: Heinemann.

Ho, J.K.K. and Sculli, D. (1995) 'System complexity and the design of decision support systems', *Systems Practice*, 8(5), 505–16.

Jackson, M.C. (1992) *Systems Methodologies for the Management Sciences*. New York: Plenum Press.

Kepner, C.H. and Tregoe, B.B. (1965) *The Rational Decision Maker*. New York: McGraw-Hill.

Lazerowitz, M. (1968) *Philosophy and Illusion*. London: George Allen & Unwin.

Mabey, C. (1995) *Managing Development and Change*, Open Business School course P751. Milton Keynes: Open University Business School.

Midgley, G. (1992) 'Power and language of cooperation: a critical systems perspective'. Paper presented at Sistemica '92, the Primera Conferencia International de Trabajo del Instituto Andino de Systemas (IAS), Lima, Peru.

Minorsky, N. (1962) *Nonlinear Oscillation*. New York: D. Van Nostrand.

Popper, K. (1972) *Objective Knowledge: An evolutionary approach*. Oxford: Oxford University Press.

Sorokin, P.A. (1937) *Social and Cultural Dynamics*. New York: American Book Company.

Wafield, J.N. and Staley, S.M. (1996) 'Structural thinking: organising complexity through disciplined activity', *Systems Research*, 13(1), 47–67.

CHAPTER 4

The dynamic of system paradigms

OVERVIEW

Paradigms can be said to evolve and mature, but during this process they may also become bounded through the very conceptualisations that originally made them successful. The paradigm of complexity is able to conceptualise problem situations in terms of at least three characteristics: certainty, softness and structure. These can be used to evaluate how different paradigms are able to deal with complex to simple situations.

OBJECTIVES

This chapter will show:

- the distinction between difficulties and messes;
- that situations can be seen to be simple or complex;
- that management systems paradigms have been changing towards addressing complexity.

4.1 Inquiry, models of reality and paradigms

Situations develop that are perceived to be problematic because we have desired goals or expected outcomes that do not materialise. It is through an understanding of problem situations that we are able to pose intervention strategies and take action that deals with the problems. Understanding derives from the process of inquiry.

The way in which we see a situation and formulate cognitive purposes for an inquiry is determined by our weltanschauung, and the way in which we formally model it is determined by our paradigms. In the case that we wish to develop intervention strategies for the situation, it is through these models that they can be formulated. Checkland describes the need to ensure that an intervention is sytemically or logically desirable (Patching, 1990, p. 113). This arises because the models of a situation that are intended to represent it (Checkland calls them relevant systems) are also intended to be relevant to the situation. Resulting strategies of intervention are 'systemically desirable if these "relevant systems" are in fact perceived to be truly relevant' (Checkland and Scholes, 1990, p. 52). The question that must be asked is *who* determines whether such a model is 'truly relevant', and *what* criteria do they use? The criteria will derive from the world views involved, and this includes the paradigm from which the situation is being modelled, and the weltanschauung of the evaluating person (the *who*).

Models derive from paradigms that have their own 'truths' that generate knowledge. Since different paradigms are incommensurable, the knowledge that they produce will never be totally reconcilable across their boundaries. The capacity of a paradigm to describe and explain 'real' situations through its models will be related to its *penchant*, which is responsible for the generation of a specialist type of knowledge, and which implicitly determines cognitive purposes. While paradigms operate at the level of belief and conceptualisation and generate cognitive knowledge, cognitive purposes describe the purposes attributable to behaviour in a given situation, and are commonly expressed in a situation through a mission and associated goals or aims.

The conceptual explanations that are provided by a model about a situation should be able to disclose relationships that will be essential to its future stability. If this cannot occur then the capacity of the paradigm from which the model derives is inadequate. Two things may occur in this case: (a) the paradigm will be replaced by another that can be said to represent reality more adequately or (b) the viewholders of the paradigm will learn cognitively, and the paradigm will pass through a change process, thereby evolving.

A new paradigm will provide a new approach to problem situations and pose different classes of questions through its own set of conceptualisations. 'It would pursue its answers with its own set of essential tools, and often evaluates results according to an evolving set of standards and challenges. Thus the new paradigm unearths and explains phenomena that could not have been approached from pre-paradigmatic means. Alternatively, the new paradigm could be shown to provide better, more compact, and more accurate explanations' (Guastello, 1997).

When a virtual paradigm is created, if it survives then it likely does so by passing through a period of incremental or sudden change until it reaches its maturity. A mature paradigm may not have the propositional capacity to explain satisfactorily a given class of situation. As a result it will produce models that are incongruent with perceived behaviour as seen from the perspective of other paradigms, leading to contradiction (and possibly paradox). As an example of this in physics, two classical theories

69

developed that attempted to explain the nature of light and how it passes through space (Hoffman, 1947). These were the *corpuscular* and the *wave* theories, each of which had its own paradigms. In the corpuscular theory, light was seen as particles, and the properties that we might assign to them must satisfy the dynamics of corpuscular bodies. In the wave theory, light was seen to be composed of waves, the properties of which are different from those of particles. Each theory was able to explain the behaviour of light in its own way. Each also predicted the behaviour of light under given circumstances, and formulated experiments that it could point to as exemplars. The difficulty that arose was that each paradigm was able to validate its view for the behaviour of light with respect to its specific experiments, but neither to the exclusion of the other. An eventual result was that a new paradigm of quantum physics arose that regarded light as being able to manifest the properties of both corpuscles and waves.

Systems thinking too has been changing, and indeed passing through its own phases across the decades. It can be argued that prior to the 1970s systems operated under a single paradigm (Jackson, 1992, p. 5). However, new influences were afoot that might today be connected to the developing ideas of complexity. Action research had been gathering support. It was a development of the work of gestalt-field theorists, who believed that successful change requires a process of learning (Burnes, 1992, p. 166). 'It originated from a desire to alter and improve social situations, or to help people in need. Its aim is to not only collect information and arrive at a better understanding, but to do something practical as well. Sometimes, the exponents of action research are dubious about the possibility of making detached and scientific studies of human affairs. They may argue, for example, that an investigator cannot but influence the behaviour of people he is studying, that experimentation is extremely difficult, if not impossible, in the social sciences, that there is the intermediary of the human instrument in measurement, and that all these vitiate the scientific status of social research' (Mitchell, 1968, p. 2). Argyle (1957) argues that action research should:

1 prove that interventional activity is genuinely effective in making change;

2 show the precise conditions under which interventions can result in desirable outcomes.

A further development questioned whether systems thinking could deal with ill-structured and strategic problems. To address this, soft systems thinking and organisational cybernetics arose (Jackson, 1992, p. 5). The paradigmatic basis of the traditional approach adopted a truth system that conflicted with those of the others. For instance, in soft systems thinking the approach to inquiry centres on the weltanschauung principle that in addition is concerned with the cultural attributes of stakeholders. In contrast, traditional 'hard' systems thinking ignores the idea of subjectivity, often by subsuming it within a pattern of behaviour that the situation is perceived to be constrained by. The other approach, organisational cybernetics, is specifically intended to deal with complexity by seeing a purposeful activity system in terms of a dynamic relationship with a metasystem that controls it (the nature of a metasystem will be considered later). This provides a more macroscopic view of the situation, and shifts the focus from the details of the complexity. Some critics of organisational cybernetics regard it as a hard approach to inquiry, while others see it as soft. This is because it is an approach that is very much inquirer determined, and may thus be operated according to a virtual paradigm determined by the inquirer.

4.2 Mapping situations to modelling approaches

In order to be able to distinguish between different inquiry approaches and their ability to handle situations, Harry (1994, p. 255) created a two-dimensional space. The purpose was to map out the relationships between a situation and a modelling approach being adopted. He introduced two variables, softness and structure:

● softness relates to the involvement of people and their mental perspectives;
● structure relates to the relationship between components of a model.

This space is shown in Fig. 4.1, where the vertical axis represents the soft/hard dimension of a situation being modelled, and the horizontal axis of well/ill structure relates to the modelling approach being adopted. Examples of how to interpret plots in this space are given in Minicase 4.1.

Minicase 4.1

Mapping paradigms to situations

The selection of paradigms and their associated methodologies can be related to the situation being examined. As an introduction to this, it is possible to show the relationships between methodologies and problem situations simply by examining different hypothetical combinations and seeing how these have in the past been used.

Consider the four points A, B, C, and D mapped in Fig. 4.1. The following is based on that given interpretation in Harry (1994, p. 256).

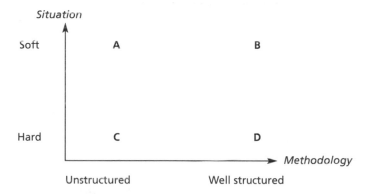

Fig. 4.1 An approach to mapping the relationship between situations and problems

Position A represents the situation where an unstructured approach is applied to a soft situation. An example of this might be found where dispute occurs about the nature of a situation, and people-centred solutions are explored. How such a situation is solved is not predeterminable.

Position B represents a situation where a structured approach is applied to a soft problem. Here one attempts to deal with disputes using approaches like soft systems methodology or organisational development.

71

Position C represents an unstructured approach applied to a hard problem. This occurs, for example, when the problem is clearly defined, and has objectively measurable criteria for success. Such a situation is represented by the use of prototyping applied to the building of a database system.

Position D represents a structured approach being applied to a hard problem. Thus, the system development life cycle and SSADM (Harry, 1994) are examples of methodologies that can be applied to a situation which is apparently very well known.

4.3 Creating a modelling space

Like others in the post-1970s period, Rosenhead (1989) has been concerned with complex situations, and in particular with the development of operational research systems methodologies that can be used for complex situations. In pursuing this interest, he identified three characteristics of complexity:

1 that situations are more complex when they involve people;

2 that complex situations may not be well structured, in particular because cause–effect relationships may not be determinable;

3 that complexity is enhanced when situations are uncertain.

With respect to point 1, when situations are considered in terms of *people and their subjectivities*, the view of the situation is said be soft. On the other hand, if people are seen as *objects* that are to be manipulated, then the view is said to be hard. Considering the second point, if a situation is seen to be well structured, then the parts that are seen to make it up (and their interrelationships) are *well-defined* across space or time. If this is not the case, the situation is said to be ill structured. Finally, in point 3, situations are seen on a scale of certainty to uncertainty that relates to the degree of knowledge about them. A consequence is that this relates to the predictability about the future states of a given situation.

It is feasible to extend the map proposed by Harry to include Rosenhead's ideas. To do this we shall take hardness, structure and uncertainty as three dimensions of consideration. They are seen to be analytically and empirically independent, and establishable in a frame of reference that is indicative of the complexity of a situation. Under these conditions we shall refer to the dimensions as *orthogonalities* in a *modelling space* (*see* Fig. 4.3), an idea originally introduced by Yolles (1996, 1998). All systems paradigms should be susceptible to description through these orthogonalities, and their position in a modelling space will be indicative of how much complexity they are able to deal with. Our task is now to more fully describe these three dimensions, and in so doing illustrate their independence. We do this below under the three subsections hardness, structure and uncertainty. After this, we offer Minicase 4.2 (based on a case provided by Terry Murray, personal communication, 1995) within which we provide an example of how one might wish to argue the case for placing a given situation in a modelling space.

4.3.1 Hardness

Hardness is related to the possible *way* in which the elements of a situation are viewed. In entities that are classed as hard, *tangible things* tend to dominate; that is, they are definite and examinable. Their properties can be objectively defined and measured or assessed in some way that does not depend on personal values. Another way of defining a hard system view of situations (Checkland, 1995, p. 53) is that it supposes a situation to be a complex of systems, some of which may be malfunctioning.

Soft entities, on the other hand, are relative to people and their mental perspective. They have properties that cannot be measured objectively. Personal values, opinions, tastes, ethical views, emotions and weltanschauung are examples. People and their psychological needs dominate. Softness is therefore directly related to *subjective mentality*. The soft approach is said to make no assumptions about the nature of the world, beyond assuming it to be complex. However, the process of inquiry can be seen as a learning system.

Whether a situation is classed as hard or soft is world view dependent, deriving from the weltanschauung of an inquirer and the paradigm that has been adopted. There are grades of hardness to softness, and these are normally seen to occur on a continuum that we say passes through relatively hard/soft.

4.3.2 Structure

Structure is related to the possibility of interrelationship among the elements of a situation. It is thus about the *relationships* between definable entities like roles, objects or processes. In ill-structured situations, the entities and their relationships are not well defined, whereas in well-structured ones they are. Dynamic well-structured situations link entities across time in causal relationships. As with softness, this is conceived as a continuum (Langley *et al.*, 1987, p. 15) which may be qualitatively divided. The simplest qualitative division is to use the term *semistructure* (or equivalently *partial structure*), which lies somewhere between well- and ill-structured situations.

A semistructured situation exists when neither a highly-structured nor an unstructured situation is found. Thus, a decision-making process involving well-known information about a manufacturing process and unpredetermined ideas about where the process should be directed would be semistructured. It may be noted that the concept of semistructured processes is important to the field of decision support systems (Alter, 1980; Keen and Scott Morton, 1978).

Structured situations may appear to be unstructured if they involve entities that have unpredeclared or even 'invisible' mutual relationships. Associated with the idea of seeing, the concept of distinguishing between visible and invisible structures also carries an implication that they are relative to the individual who is looking. It is more usual to refer to this concept as deep (or cognitive) and surface (manifest) structure. Situations that appear to be unstructured at a behavioural level when examined more closely or in a different way may be seen to have a conceptual relationship that is defined at a cognitive level and has not been manifested. This is referred to as deep structure (Chomsky, 1975; Keen and Scott Morton, 1978, p. 93). This idea also relates to the concept of relativity in that whether a situation is perceived to be well structured is determined by the context from which it is viewed.

The reason for this is as follows. Suppose that a group of manifest entities is defined to exist that appear to have no structural relationship with each other. They might still, however, be perceived by an inquirer to have a group coherence that gives meaning to the entities as a group. This meaning can still be transformed to generate a different kind of manifestation than that expected or able to be perceived. It can for instance create a purpose or set of purposes for the manifest entities of the group. It is at the surface level where the entities operate to carry out their purpose, and where this deep connection may be invisible. Whether a deep structure exists or not will depend upon how an inquirer sees, with what concepts, and what paradigm he or she uses in order to do the seeing.

4.3.3 Uncertainty

Uncertainty is spatially related to the possible knowledge available about a situation, or over time to any possible outcomes that derive from actions. For instance, certainty occurs when we know that each choice of action is linked with only one particular outcome. Uncertainty occurs where there is a plurality of possible outcomes resulting from one of many choices of action. We do not know which will result from a given action, and in any case we cannot assign probabilities to them, or even identify possibilities for them. It also relates to the technical nature of the situation, a term adopted by Habermas (1970) that relates to the control aspects of a situation and its future states or predictability.

We can therefore conceive of a certainty–uncertainty continuum defining an axis of variability, and we can differentiate between them with an intermediate graduation of relatively certain or relatively uncertain.

Minicase 4.2

Designing a hospital database

Consider a hospital in which it was seen to be necessary to create a database that would service the needs of the organisation to improve efficiency. Basically, it was identified that the hospital activities should be modelled as a system. In doing so it was recognised that the organisation implicitly operated through a number of entities, including staff (including doctors and nurses), patients, and wards and theatres. A simple view was taken of these operations so that each entity was developed totally independently of the others. This resulted in three separate non-interactive databases: one is used to generate staff payrolls, one is for clinical management, and one is connected to theatre and ward management. The design of this database system as it is implemented is shown in Fig. 4.2.

A systemic way of seeing would be to define each entity in relation to the others. Looking for direct interrelationships between each of the data files, we find that indeed they exist. Thus, for example:

● staff payroll will include information on staff name, address, job classification, grade, taxation number;
● clinical management data will include information on patients, the staff involved in the treatments and the wards in which the patients are housed;
● theatre and ward management involves information on wards and their specialism and address, the patients housed in them and the staff attached to them.

It is thus possible to build a common model linking the entities that define a deep structure. This differs from the original design, in which no attempt was made to examine the set of entities for deep structure at all. This results in an interactive system, the nature of interactions being shared information. From a practical perspective, this will function more efficiently, saving computer disk space, time for data entry and processing. It will also be more effective in that because the deep structure has been used at the surface implementation, it will be less prone to errors in data input.

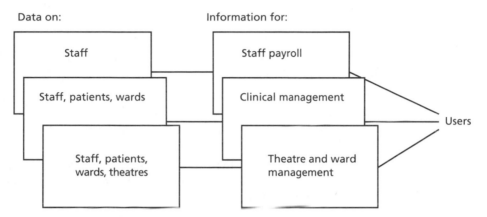

Fig. 4.2 Hospital database system not adopting deep structure

With the advantage of hindsight, the original model can been seen from the following perspective.

1 The distinct databases were not modelled as a single system, and thus no underlying relationship was conceived as a deep structure. This affected the prime purpose for the system, efficiency.

2 One could argue that at its inception it was designed as a hard system: people were not involved at the outset, though the meaning of the word Involvement will likely vary in different systems paradigms when the database is designed and built. We should note that in the current system, every time a member of the administrative staff wishes to put data into one of the databases about patients, he or she has to pass through seven screens; this causes frustration and stress, which could well impact in some ways on the operator. It could be argued that by involving staff to a sufficient degree, this could have been taken into account.

To obtain a better understanding of the situation, we could postulate how it might have been seen in terms of its modelling space.

Certainty

The database system was thought to be certain. This meant that it was thought that the computer system would ensure that the hospital would always know about the condition and location of patients, doctors and theatres. In other words, there would be full predictability. However:

1 doctors tend to be overworked and do not always put the correct data about patients into the system, who may therefore be misdiagnosed;

2 patients may not be where they should be when they need to be found, either because they disappear or are wrongly assigned to a ward;

3 it was thought that theatres could be assigned to patients for operations and patients tagged for theatres as a matter of routine – this is not always the case;

4 problems have been experienced because in some cases the wrong patients are operated on for the wrong problems.

The amount of mis-data is relatively small, and thus we shall suppose that the system is relatively certain.

Hardness

We consider here the need to take into account the subjective needs of stakeholders in the system. As an example of this:

1 Administrative staff make about two hundred entries per day. As functionaries at the sharp end, so to speak, their operational needs should be considered from their perspective in connection with system entries, and their ideas about what constitutes a user-friendly system should be considered.

2 Patients are individuals with their own motivations, purposes and perspectives, and should be involved in decisions about such consideration as their treatment and their redesignation to other wards.

In consequence, we would suggest that the influence of these human elements suggests that the system should have been considered as relatively hard, to enable at least some level of staff involvement to occur on a scale of no staff consultation at all, to total staff group decision making.

Structure

The system was seen to be simple with the parts considered independently without relation to the whole, and was envisaged to be well structured. Data about the entities patients, staff, wards and theatres were well defined in relation to one another.

To show this let us reconsider the categories involved. Staff and patients can be divided into the further groups: staff(nurses, doctors), patient_location(known, unknown) and patient_information (correct, incorrect). We know the purpose of each of the entities associated with patient_information and patient_location, their joint relationship and their relationship to the rest of the system. We can thus confirm our view that the situation can be modelled to be well structured.

The modelling space

To represent an event in this space we establish a set of coordinates (certainty, softness, structure) that defines a position as shown in Fig. 4.3. The space is a bounded cube with sides that can vary between a measurement of 0 and 1. These units are not intended to be indicative of a precise measurement scale, but are manifested from a qualitative evaluation that translates to a fuzzy point somewhere between these values. From the perspective taken here, we assign the values of (0.5, 0.5, 1) to the coordinates (certainty, hardness, structure). The methodology selected by this inquirer to undertake the information system design would have to take account of the evaluation of the situation in the modelling space.

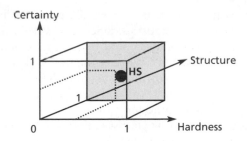

Fig. 4.3 Modelling space for the hospital problem situation (HS)

4.4 Changing paradigms to accommodate complexity

We have said that paradigms change as they mature, and other paradigms sometimes come to replace them. As an example of this, our interest in this section will be to illustrate changes in operational research paradigms, as provided by Yolles (1998).

4.4.1 The traditional operational research paradigm

Rosenhead (1989) discusses the recent history of operational research in terms of its changing paradigm. In its traditional light, a view of operational research is that it is a modelling process for problem solving that consists of the five steps:

1 identify objectives with weights;

2 identify alternative courses of action;

3 predict consequences of actions in terms of objectives, usually as a cause–effect relationship;

4 evaluate the consequences on a common scale of value;

5 select the alternative whose net benefit is highest, that is the optimal solution.

This approach was used for many years, until it was realised that while it was attractive because it created models of problems that could be solved, the solutions did not correspond with 'reality' except in very special cases. Difficulties with the traditional approach lay in the fact that the method:

1 was deterministic, which meant problems were assumed to be certain;

2 did not consider people as having subjective needs that should be individually explored, so that problems were assumed to be hard;

3 assumed that modelling relationships between entities in a situation were known, supposing that problems were well structured.

4.4.2 The dominant operational research paradigm

Determinism was shown to be inadequate in modelling situations when it was realised that the models were frequently far from complete explanations, and solutions were interesting rather than useful. Certainty was an assumption that was untenable in a world that seemed to be uncertain. One answer lay in a new approach through the application of Baysian statistics. Since it was seen that futures could not be foretold, the idea arose that probabilities could be used to generate future expectation. In this paradigm shift that Ackoff (1979) refers to as 'predict and prepare', existing certainties are replaced by probability estimations, and these are then assumed to be valid for future situations. Thus, certainty was replaced by relative certainty. With the addition of statistical theory, the new paradigm still maintained the traditional set of propositions. One of the difficulties with this view was that the modelling of futures in which the probabilities changed was not permitted, and it was therefore assumed that this did not happen. Rosenhead refers to this view as the dominant paradigm of operational research, the assumptions of which are identified in Table 4.1.

Table 4.1 Dominant paradigm for operational research

1 Problem formulation occurs in terms of a single objective that is optimisable; there may be multiple objectives that, if recognised, may be traded off one against the other on some form of common scale.

2 There are overwhelming data demands, with accompanying problems of data: distortion, availability and credibility.

3 Consensus is assumed possible, with the approach adopted assuming depoliticisation and scientificisation.

4 People are treated as passive rather than active participants in the situation.

5 There is an assumption of a single decision maker with abstract objectives from which concrete actions can be deduced for implementation through a hierarchical chain of command.

6 Attempts are made to abolish future uncertainty, and pre-take future decisions.

4.4.3 The need for a new paradigm in operational research

The difficulty with the dominant paradigm as discussed by Rosenhead still lay in its adherence to problems that were assumed to be hard and well structured, even though relative certainty was now a feature. For our purposes, explanation can best be presented by considering each of these dimensions in turn.

First, let us consider uncertainty. Data is needed to identify what is happening in situations, and this may be seen to be wrong or incomplete. There may be a problem with the relationship between data collection and problem location, and some dimensions of consideration will have intangible elements that are not quantifiable. Confidence over data collection may therefore be inappropriate. Without adequate information about a situation, it is not possible to formulate conclusions about the parts that make it up and the problems it has. Additionally, it is not possible for any objectives to be sensibly taken up in a course of action, nor is the easy identification of the probable consequences that might develop possible.

Uncertainty is an important consideration when evaluating situations and the way in which decision makers make decisions about them. Hopwood (1980) offers a typology from which we produce Table 4.2. This relates uncertainty to course of action in connection to both *goals* and *consequences*. Thus, the greater the uncertainty, the more decision makers rely on soft (human mentality and values) approaches rather than information in relating objectives for action with anticipated consequences.

Table 4.2 Typology for decision making under uncertainty, relating objectives for courses of action to consequences

Consequences of action	Goals for action	
	Certainty	Uncertainty
Certainty	Deterministic/probabilistic decisions	Decisions under bargaining
Uncertainty	Judgemental decisions	Decisions through inspiration

When considering the dimension of hardness, we see that people are involved in situations and directly influence how they change. As Rosenhead argues, 'an organisation is not an individual ... Decisions and actions emerge out of interactions between a variety of actors *internal* to the organisation. Each may indeed have an individual perspective or world view (weltanschauung) through which actions or statements of others are interpreted. What the constraints are, what the priorities should be, what the problem actually is, may be perceived quite differently ... A process of accommodation is necessary before a problem can emerge which can carry assent and commitment to consequential actions' (Rosenhead, 1989, p. 9).

The idea that participants to a situation are purposeful, and that decisions are a consequence of group processes in which conflicts sometimes have to be resolved, is a feature of modelling that should be addressed. This leads to the idea that different situations will be distinct from one another because they are composed of different groups of people. Situational uniqueness is therefore a consequence of softness, and this perspective abolishes a hard approach.

Having said this, it is appropriate to note that in organisational situations, we are normally concerned with situations involving small groups of people, hence the use of soft methodologies. In the social science literature where the modelling of these groups comes from, there is a difference between the interactive processes of large and small groups, the latter tending to be less predictable. In larger group situations, patterns of behaviour can develop, be recognised and sometimes be predicted with some degree of success. One example of this is represented by Hitler's ability to predict the responses of crowds and control them during the build-up to the Second World War. Another is the idea that the population's voting behaviour can be predicted because it is such a large-scale phenomenon. However, this is difficult to do because of the complexity of issues that can affect the value judgements of people. Situations involving large groups may therefore be considered to be less individualistic than small groups. This occurs when groups achieve what is referred to as 'critical mass', a term analogous to nuclear processes. It suggests that groups, having reached a particular threshold of size and therefore complexity, establish formalised patterns for classes of behaviour which to some extent and under certain reasonable conditions are predictable. Such situations may be considered to be classified as relatively soft.

To consider now the last dimension of interest, problems may not be well structured. To distinguish between well- and ill-structured problems, it is useful to introduce the terms *unitary* and *pluralistic*:

● a *unitary* situation consists of a set of identifiable parts that have a unique purpose and single set of objectives;

- a *pluralistic* situation occurs when there exists a set of parts that (a) represent different aspects that are not clearly definable or (b) have purposes that may be incommensurable and thus in conflict.

Pluralistic situations have goals that cannot easily be assigned to the parts in such a way that they do not clash. Modelling approaches that do not take account of pluralistic situations cannot work because courses of action cannot be defined for situations that are unclear. Such situations may thus be semistructured or unstructured, with some parts that cannot be clearly related one with another if, indeed, all parts are known.

In the event that parts to a situation are themselves well structured, their relationship to other parts may not be at all well structured. Well-structured problems are not only normally assumed to be unitary, but also to have firm constraints, and establishable time-related relationships between cause and effect.

4.4.4 The Rosenhead paradigm

The approach of the dominant paradigm in operational research contrasts with the thinking of Rosenhead, whose paradigm is sensitive to the needs of operational research as explained above, and is offered in Table 4.3. As a consequence, the modelling techniques and methodologies proposed by Rosenhead operate in a modelling space that is uncertain, soft and unstructured. While the dominant paradigm uses a calculus of probabilities, Rosenhead seeks rather a calculus of possibilities, which is able to reflect more of the complexity of situations. This is a requirement that presupposes unstructured or semistructured situations under uncertainty or relative uncertainty using methodologies that enable options to be defined and explored.

Table 4.3 Rosenhead (complexity) paradigm for operational research

1	Non-optimising, looking for alternative solutions acceptable on separate dimensions, without tradeoffs
2	Reduced data demands, achieved by greater integration of hard and soft data with social judgements
3	Simplicity and transparency, aimed at clarifying the terms of conflict
4	Conceptualise people as active subjects
5	Facilitating planning from bottom up
6	Accepts uncertainty, and aims to keep options open for later resolution

4.5 Mapping changing paradigms

It is possible to show that paradigms change. The traditional way (provided above for the operational research paradigm) is to verbally explore their features, and then provide an argument about how they have changed and what constitutes the important features of that change. From this approach, it would seem to be the case that the arguments that need to be generated would have to deal with the complexities of each paradigm. One way of dealing with this is to generate a complex argument that would deal with the details. This would leave open the possibility of peer disagreement with any parts of its particular detail. If we could find a way of collapsing the complexity of the argument, then the disagreement might less likely arise, and a demonstration that the paradigms do change would be less subject to detailed controversy.

Above, we have already provided one way of collapsing the complexity of situations, by introducing the idea of the modelling space. Whether the situation is appropriately placed in the modelling space may well be seen to be a function of perspectives. However it is done, it has generated some new conceptualisations that enable us to see the situations in a different and relative way.

To show that situations change, however, it is useful to take a further step. It draws on the work in artificial intelligence called landmark theory, which distinguishes between different qualities and allows inquirers to use them in a way that is normal for quantitative approaches. The approach is taken from Yolles (1998), and adopts numerical analysis techniques. Rather than simply explaining the approach, it will be more useful to illustrate it. This is done in Minicase 4.3, to show how the operational research paradigm has changed over recent decades.

Minicase 4.3

Logging changes in the operational research paradigm

It is possible to show that paradigms and the perception of situations do change in time graphically by attempting to estimate qualitative movements in quantitative terms. One way of doing this is shown here.

The appearance of a new paradigm must be able to be differentiated from an earlier paradigm in the modelling space. To do this for ease of modelling and comprehension we need to create an aggregate value that we propose to derive from the three dimensions of uncertainty, hardness and structure. If we can do this, then since the aggregate will repre sent the degree of involvement of each of the three characteristic variables, the resultant value will be an indicator of how well the paradigm is able to deal with complexity.

If we are able to find values that can be assigned to each paradigm for these three dimensions, then the aggregate value can be determined using a technique of numerical analysis referred to as the Euclidean norm (Wilkinson, 1965). This is equivalent to generating a mean vector in the modelling space of the movement, and taking its absolute size to be between (0,1). In doing this, the aggregate is obtained by squaring each term, and summing the result. This must be normalised to restrict it to its bounds, and this occurs by dividing by the maximum sum of the squares to bound the result. When plotted against time (decades), it should show how new paradigms are able to cope with complexity.

The first requirement in doing this lies in plotting paradigm positions in a fuzzy region as they occur in the modelling space. As a subject of this exercise, we choose the operational research paradigm that we have explored.

When we assign quantitative coordinate values to paradigm positions in the modelling space, they must be seen as representative of qualitative plateaus. They demonstrate a technique of assigning quantitative values to qualities typical of the approach taken in the domain of artificial intelligence to represent qualitative human thinking. In Table 4.4 we offer *landmark* values (Kuipers, 1986) that are intended to represent different qualitative descriptions through the creation of regions that we represent by a single landmark altitude.

Table 4.4 Assigning qualitative properties to regional landmark altitudes

Qualitative description	Landmark values
Certain, hard, well structured	1
Relatively certain/uncertain, relatively soft/hard, semi-structured	0.5
Uncertain, soft, ill structured	0

The traditional operational research paradigm is located in the modelling space with a coordinate landmark (certain, hard, structure) of (1, 1, 1); that is, the paradigm operates with situations that are certain, hard and well structured.

Some years after its use, a paradigm change occurred, and *certainty* was replaced by *probability* to be better able to predict events. We shall say that certainty was replaced by 'relative certainty'. Thus, the modelling space coordinate (certainty, harness, structure) becomes (1, 0.5, 1).

The Rosenhead paradigm shows a shift to give a new modelling space coordinate landmark vector in (certainty, hardness, structure) of (0, 0, 0).

For our purposes it would be useful to be able to identify at least one other paradigm. To do this we will interpolate, thus supposing the appearance of a paradigm not normally discussed in the literature. Prior to the Rosenhead paradigm a method existed that could deal with relative softness and semistructure, like the modelling technique of Fraser and Hipel (1984) called conflict analysis. Its coordinates of (certainty, hardness, structure) are (0, 0.5, 1) since it is supposed that (a) we are totally uncertain about the outcome of a conflict, (b) organisations are involved and their paradigms must be taken into consideration while still trying to address the situation and (c) it is known who the participants to the conflict are, and what their relationship is – that is, the situation is highly structured.

Four operational research paradigms are represented:

1 the traditional paradigm, which assumes situations to be certain and therefore purely deterministic, hard and well structured;

2 the dominant paradigm, which appends to the idea of certainty (that is, determinism) that of probability;

3 an interpolated Fraser and Hipel paradigm, which also supposes semistructure and the possibility of influence by groups of people (relatively soft);

4 the Rosenhead paradigm, which supposes uncertainty, softness and ill structure.

We can calculate aggregates for each paradigm coordinate in order to generate a mean value. This can be plotted across the decades to indicate that indeed, with respect to the generic characteristics of the modelling space, the paradigms do indicate movement. This has been done in Table 4.5 by adopting the Euclidean norm (the normalised sum of the squares of the coordinate values). The aggregate values are plotted in a modelling space in Fig. 4.4 that is intended to illustrate how the operational research paradigms have moved over a period of, say, four decades. They are also intended to illustrate the degree of complexity that a given paradigm is able to cope with. Highest levels of complexity occur when the aggregate value is at point 0, while lowest levels occur at an aggregate value of 1.

Table 4.5 Calculating modelling space aggregate values for operational research paradigms

Type of paradigm	Date period	Qualitative position of paradigm (certainty, hardness, structure)	Euclidean aggregate	Coordinate first difference	First difference aggregate
Traditional	1940s	(1, 1, 1)	1		
				(0, −0.5, 0)	0.08
Dominant 1	1950s	(1, 0.5, 1)	0.75		
				(−1, 0, 0)	0.30
Fraser and Hipel	1960s	(0, 0.5, 1)	0.42		
				(0, −0.5, −1)	0.42
Rosenhead	1980s	(0, 0, 0)	0		

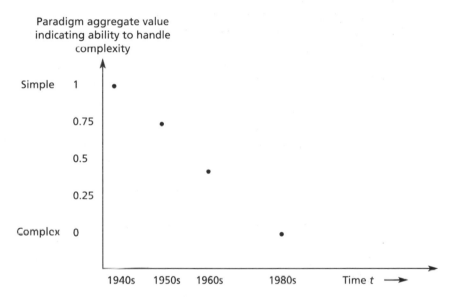

Fig. 4.4 Appearance of new operational research paradigm over the decades

We are also able to calculate first differences of the paradigm positions that are indicative of how the paradigms change. These are calculated in a standard way by subtracting one coordinate qualitative position from the next to illustrate the coordinate movement between the two. The aggregates are again generated using the Euclidean norm, and are indicative of the degree of change in dealing with simple and complex modelling processes. The result is shown in Fig. 4.5.

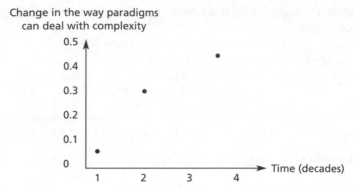

Fig. 4.5 Aggregate changes of paradigm in modelling space over the decades

4.6 Relating two forms of complexity

We have indicated here that complexity can be expressed in terms of the orthogonalities (certainty, hardness, structure). Yet in the last chapter we said that complexity could be expressed in terms of:

1 computational complexity, defined in terms of the (large) number of interactive parts;

2 technical complexity, occurring when a situation has a 'tangle' of control processes that are difficult to discern because they are numerous and highly interactive;

3 organisational complexity, defined by the rules that guide the interactions between a set of identifiable parts, or specifying the attributes;

4 personal complexity, defined by the subjective view of the situation;

5 emotional complexity, defined to occur when a 'tangle' of emotional vectors is projected into the situation by its participants.

It is reasonable to be able to relate these two expressions of complexity together. The correspondence will not necessarily be direct, and we leave as an exercise for the reader an exploration of the relationships that enable our modelling space to be defined in terms of these dimensions of complexity.

SUMMARY

Paradigms have a capacity to change, but they may be bounded by the very conceptualisations that at one time made them successful. As illustrated by operational research, in management systems there has been a continuous and seemingly crude linear movement from simple to complex paradigms, now capable of seeing situations as though they are complex. Soft systems thinking conceptualises that people and their subjectivities are important to situations. The involvement of the participants in a situation will offer a variety of views that will hopefully deal with complexity. Distinct from this, managerial cybernetics deals with complexity by seeing situations in terms of the relationships between a system and its metasystem.

REFERENCES

Alter, S.L. (1980) *Decision Support Systems: Current practices and continuing challenges.* Reading, MA: Addison-Wesley.

Ackoff , R.L. (1979) 'The future of operational research in the past', *Journal of the Operational Research Society,* 30, 93–104.

Argyle, M. (1957) *The Scientific Study of Social Behaviour.* London: Methuen.

Burnes, B. (1992) *Managing Change.* London: Pitman.

Checkland, P.B. (1995) 'Model validation in soft systems practice', *Systems Research,* 12(1), 47–54.

Checkland, P.B. and Scholes, J. (1990) *Soft Systems Methodology in Action.* Chichester: Wiley.

Chomsky, N. (1975) *Problems of Knowledge and Freedom.* New York: Pantheon.

Fraser, N.M. and Hipel, K.W. (1984) *Conflict Analysis, Models and Resolutions.* Amsterdam: North Holland.

Guastello, S.J. (1997) 'Science evolves: an introduction to nonlinear dynamics, psychology, and life sciences', *Nonlinear Dynamics, Psychology, and Life Sciences,* 1(1), 1–6.

Habermas, J. (1970) 'Knowledge and interest'. In Emmet, D. and MacIntyre, A. (eds) *Sociological Theory and Philosophical Analysis.* London: Macmillan.

Harry, M. (1994) *Information Systems in Business.* London: Pitman.

Hoffman, B. (1947) *The Strange Story of the Quantum.* Harmondsworth: Penguin.

Hopwood, A.G. (1980) 'The organisational behavioural aspects of budgeting and control'. In Arnold, J., Carsberg, B. and Scapens, R. (eds) *Topics in Management Accounting.* Deddington: Philip Allen, pp. 21–40.

Jackson, M.C. (1992) *Systems Methodologies for the Management Sciences.* New York: Plenum Press.

Keen, P.G.W. and Scott Morton, M.S. (1978) *Decision Support Systems: An organisational perspective.* Reading, MA: Addison-Wesley.

Kuipers, B. (1986) 'Qualitative simulation', *Artificial Intelligence,* 29.

Langley, P., Simon, H.A., Bradshaw, G.L. and Zytkow, J.M. (1987) *Scientific Discovery.* Boston, MA: MIT Press.

Mitchell, G.D. (1968) *A Dictionary of Sociology.* London: Routledge & Kegan Paul.

Patching, D. (1990) *Practical Soft Systems Analysis.* London: Pitman.

Rosenhead, J. (1989) *Rational Analysis for a Problematic World.* Chichester: Wiley.

Wilkinson, J.H. (1965) *The Algebraic Eigenvalue Problem.* Oxford: Oxford University Press.

Yolles, M.I. (1996) 'Critical systems thinking, paradigms, and the modelling space', *Systems Practice,* 9(3).

Yolles, M.I. (1998) 'Changing paradigms in operational research', *Cybernetics and Systems,* 29(2), 91, 112.

CHAPTER 5

Purposefulness, methods and purposeful intervention

OVERVIEW

Any purposeful activity system will have a culture within which cognitive models are created. These provide the framework that enables goals to be generated and sought. If goal-seeking behaviour becomes unstable, then methods are needed to find intervention strategies that can engineer stability. We can distinguish between simple methods – that is, those that have poor conceptual variety – and complex methods, which have rich conceptual variety. In simple situations with difficult problems, simple methods are satisfactory. In complex situations with messy problems a sufficiently complex method is required. Methodologies can be seen as complex methods. Methods can also be mixed and compared, while maintaining the truth of their paradigm incommensurability.

OBJECTIVES

This chapter will show:

- the nature of purposeful behaviour;
- the need for structured decision making;
- the need for complex methods to address complex situations.

5.1 Purposeful systems, behaviour and stability

5.1.1 Labelling situations as systems

Our interest here lies in describing organisations as purposeful adaptive activity systems; that is, metaphorical systems that can modify their behaviour in response to influences from the environment. We underscore the notion that the system is metaphorical because this reaffirms the idea that a systems model of a situation may:

1 break down when over-extended; that is, when aspects of the situation are seen not to be systemic;

2 change according to the world views that create it.

Consistent with this, Checkland and Scholes (1990) distinguish between what amounts for them to be a legitimate *abstract* way of using the term system, and a *practical* way that reflects world view. As an example of this within the context of this chapter, when they are in general referring to the purposeful activity that they perceive to be associated with a situation, they talk in terms of purposeful activity systems (p. 6) that seem to be *abstract labels* for parts of the situation that they are exploring. This is distinguished from the process of inquiry that defines the systems 'technically' or practically (i.e. in a non-abstract way) as particular perspective-dependent models.

Our approach will not differ distinctly from that of Checkland and Scholes in that when we talk of a system, we too will in general be labelling something in the abstract. If, however, we do begin to explore a system in a practical way (by creating particular models for a given situation), then it is because we have produced metaphorical systemic models that will be used according to some world-view criteria. Whether we are adopting a hard or soft approach does not really become significant unless one wishes to discuss how the models can be validated (for a discussion on model validation, *see* Checkland, 1995).

As a consequence, from here on when we talk of systems relating to a general situation, we shall be using the concept in the abstract. However, whenever we address particular case studies that we model systemically, we shall attempt to state the perspective taken. Part of this process will involve the creation of a case summary that is virtual paradigm dependent, and that in Part 3 is provided at the start of each case study in Chapters 10–15.

5.1.2 Purposefulness and goal seeking

Organisations are involved in *purposeful* behaviour. The concept of purposefulness comes from the idea that human beings attribute meaning to their experienced world, and take responsive action which has purpose. Von Bertalanffy (1968) attributed the idea of *purposefulness* to Aristotle, and its consequence *intention as conscious planning* to Allport (1961, p. 224). Purposefulness (Ackoff, 1981, p. 34) enables the selection of goals and aims and the means for pursuing them. Checkland and Scholes (1990, p. 2) tell us that human beings, whether as individuals or as groups, cannot help but attribute meaning to their experienced world, from which purposeful action follows. They, like Flood and Jackson (1991), also note that purposeful action is knowledge based. One would therefore expect that different knowledges are responsible for the creation of different purposeful behaviours. Consider now that purposeful behaviour is a property of an organisation that can be associated with its paradigms (and thus knowledges) and their associated cognitive models, processes and intentions. It is thinking as part of this (Levine *et al.*, 1986), that enables the creation of the goals and the taking of actions to achieve them. Goals provide a target towards which purposeful behaviour can occur.

The existence of cognitive processes also implies reasoning, and this can be defined in terms of goal formation and seeking. It can thus be seen as part of the rational or logical processes of any organisation. Purposeful adaptive organisations also have the ability to apply knowledge in any situation of interest, and to continually learn from new experiences in order to be able to respond to similar situations in the future.

Goals are determined by belief and occur through decision. Decisions are made in all organisational situations, though the goals associated with them may be ill-defined, fuzzy and uncertain, implicit and even inferred. They can be described in terms of the relative worth or penalty of each possible outcome or consequence of the decisions to be made. A goal is defined by Harry (1994, p. 54) as something we wish to achieve, where a choice of actions may have some effect on goal achievement. Goals can also be said to be a description of some desired future status of the system. Organisations come into existence because members that constitute them develop common goals. Now, in any organisation there will be a plurality of paradigms, each with its own culture and its associated values, propositions and conceptualisations. As a result there is a likelihood that a multiplicity of goals will develop, some of which will be in conflict. Multiple goals require discussion and bargaining, and conflict arises when their differences are contradictory. A political process is needed to settle these conflicts.

5.1.3 Stability in goal-seeking behaviour for learning organisations

The notion of the learning organisation is not new, and a useful introduction to this can be found in Johannessen (1995). Let us propose that purposeful systems are also learning organisations. We say this because if purposeful organisations survive, they normally do so because they are able to learn to survive in a changing and challenging environment.

Now, one way of exploring organisational stability is through inquiry into its learning process. Our interest points to two historical theories of learning that come from psychology, the stimulus–response (S–R) and cognitive theories. It will be helpful to our appreciation of the development of the notion of a learning organisation if we highlight them briefly before considering the nature of goals and goal-seeking behaviour.

In S–R theory, 'behaviour is seen as a transaction between the stimuli that impinge on an organism, and the resulting responses. Learning involves more or less lasting changes in the relationships between them' (Borger and Seaborne, 1966, p. 67). The organisms referred to act in an environment from which stimuli come, and to which responses are made. The theory proposes that the responses have a developing relationship to the stimuli. S–R theorists, particularly those following the Hull school of thought, are often seen to belong to the domain of *behaviourists*, whose fundamentally mechanistic psychology is decried by systemic thinkers (*see* Koestler, 1967).

Skinner had a variant of S–R theory. He proposed that respondent behaviour is produced or elicited by the input of particular completely predictable stimuli. Operant behaviour is seen to be 'emitted' by the organism, and it is pointless to look for detailed causal antecedents. The concept of 'operant' provides the basic feature of goal-directed behaviour, which may be brought under stimulus control by a reinforcing process. It is reinforcing that acts to enable the learning process to be seen as successful.

Another approach was that of the cognitive theorists, who have emphasised that learning behaviour is more complex than advocated by the simple S–R theories. Here, what some would argue is *appropriate behaviour* within a given situation may suddenly appear, as opposed to being an apparently simple developing response to determinable stimuli. Learning behaviour may also be seen to be goal directed or purposeful, 'where the result of learning seems not so much to be the creation of particular behaviour patterns as the establishment of a goal, towards which a variety of routes are available' (Borger and Seaborne, 1966, p. 70).

These conceptualisations of the last generation of thinkers can still be applied to the idea of organisational learning in such a way as to develop a new paradigm in the cybernetic tradition, connecting cognition and goal creation to stimuli and response. In creating such a view, the possible behavioural complexities of the cognitive theories of learning could be linked with those of stimulus–response theories. Our interest would also be to link in Ashby's notion that environments produce a variety of stimuli (called *environmental variety*) that perturb organisational processes, and to which an organisation will have to respond in a way that establishes *requisite* (or balancing) *variety*.

The relationship between stimuli and response may be expressed in terms of a simplistic stimulus–response cycle shown in Fig. 5.1. It is intended to illustrate that the way we react to our environment will be a function of our cognitive constructs that ultimately determines our behavioural strategies. Now, we perceive 'reality' through our cognitive models, and can define our organisation in an 'environment' in terms of that 'reality' through our systemic models. Consider that the environment provides the organisation with a variety of stimuli that act to perturb it and thus affect it in its behaviour. In order to ensure that it can maintain a stable pattern of behaviour, the organisation needs to respond to the stimuli, thereby maintaining what is perceived to be a balance with the environment. This response is (a) conditioned by the cognitive models that exist within the organisation and (b) manifested as goal formulation or modification.

Goals are belief based, derive from decision making and may change. The question arises: what is involved in goal formulation or modification? To answer this we must explore a little further what lies at the foundation of decision processes. Now, 'the only way to understand decision making in human systems is to understand the different appreciative systems that the decision makers bring to bear on a problem' (Jackson, 1992, p. 135, commenting on the work of Vickers, 1965). Vickers' notion of an *appreciative system* is an interconnected set of more or less tacit standards by which one can order and value experience, and represents a way of exploring situations that can provide us with either an approach that is alternative or an addition to goals analysis

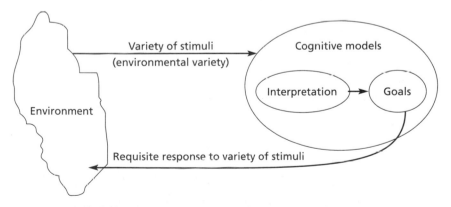

Fig. 5.1 Stimulus–response cycle model in goal-seeking behaviour

during the inquiry process. The appreciative system will determine the way the individual sees and values different situations, and how instrumental judgements are made and action is taken. How an organisation sees a situation is through its world view(s), and this depends upon shared understanding(s) and culture(s) that come from common cognitive models. It is this, then, that will determine the nature of the appreciative system.

A prerequisite for an organisation to maintain its stability is that the appreciative system must become a part of the world view. Without this, goal seeking will likely be fruitless. With it, common expectations can be generated and met. The appreciative system is itself derived from the shared standards or norms that define the purposeful behaviour of a group that is seen to represent the organisation. As we considered in Chapter 2, we see this as part of the organisation's paradigm(s). Following Checkland and Casar (1986) and their interest to put Vickers' work more simply, the norms can be defined in terms of (a) the *roles* of individuals in the organisation's social system and (b) the *values* attributed to them. Checkland and Casar see roles, values and *norms* to be analytically independent and established in interactive relationships. Since values and norms are part of world view, these relationships will more fundamentally be determined by the cognitive models within the organisation.

We have already explained that when a variety of stimuli affect the organisation from its environment, responses are manifested through cognitive models as goals that may either be spontaneously created or (in the case that the existing goals are seen to be still relevant) modified in some way. During this, stimuli may perturb roles, norms, values and their relationships, and changes in cognitive models will frequently be attributable to this. Since cognitive models involve beliefs, this is likely in turn to affect the belief-based goals, which will therefore also be subject to change. When this occurs we can say that the goals are dynamic. In complex situations, a variety of stimuli will affect the dynamic goals in ways that are different from simple cause–effect relationships. Rather, the changes can be related more appropriately to shifts in the cognitive models of the organisation that are themselves integral to world-view changes. It is not an easy process to inquire into these aspects of an organisation, particularly if they are unfamiliar to the inquirer, and especially if they are seen to be complex. Structured forms of inquiry can assist inquirers involved in this process.

5.2 Inquiry through method

In management systems, inquirers operating on behalf of management often wish to seek to find ways of maintaining stable organisations. An approach to this can be said to occur when goals have been defined, but in part it will also be that the goals must be seen to be achievable. If, because of changes in the environment, goals become seen to be unachievable, then adaptation may occur to enable the goals or their meanings to be altered. Part of adaptation is the ability for an organisation to be innovative, and so this may also be a requirement. Goals are defined through decision processes, but this may initially require a process of inquiry into the situation that is to be managed. We refer to such process as method. If the approach is such that systemic principles are adopted in the inquiry process, then the methods are systemic.

5.2.1 The concepts of method and methodology

According to Harry (1994, p. 20), the term methodology comes from the Greek *meta* (= along) and *odos* (= a way), which is the study of method or ways of doing things.

Olle *et al.* (1988, p. 1), writing on information systems, agree with this when they tell us that methodology *should* be used to mean the study of method, but that 'the common practice over the past decade has been to use "methodology" in place of "method"'. It would be interesting to explore this proposition for the field of management systems, and come to our own conclusions.

A dictionary definition (from the *Concise Oxford English Dictionary*, 1979) of method and methodology is as follows: methods are 'a special form of procedure', where we take procedure to be a set of behavioural rules. Methodology, however, may be seen to be 'an orderly arrangement of ideas', indicating that it relates to cognition (for ideas) and logical organisation (for orderly arrangement). This immediately suggests that we can relate method and methodology to our tri-domain model given in Fig. 2.5. However, before exploring this possibility further, let us first place modern use of the terms method and methodology into a historical context.

In 1906 Joseph produced the first edition of his book on logic within which he builds on the concepts of method by Kant and by John Stuart Mill. In the second edition published ten years later, he tells us that 'any rules for dealing with ... [inquiry into a given subject domain] will constitute rules of method, instructing us how to set about the task of singling out the laws of causal connections from amidst the particular tangle in which the facts are presented in such science. The consideration of such rules, as distinct from the use of them, is *methodology*; and so far as herein we consider how certain general logical requirements are to be satisfied in a particular case, it is sometimes called *Applied Logic*' (Joseph, 1946, p. 555). Thus, method can be seen as a practical rule-based tool for discovering knowledge, while methodology would seem to be used in two ways: (i) in the abstract as the study of the rules within method that enable the discovery of knowledge and (ii) in generalised practical terms of logic applied to a given situation. The second concept of methodology comes, for Joseph, from the notion that social situations involve complexities that make the use of method uncontrollable since the conditions within which it is used are always changing. Thus, it seems that the notions of uncertainty and complexity were affecting our view of the nature of method and methodology. Such ideas led to what may be seen as the start to a 'soft' physics that produced quantum mechanics. They may also be seen as an initiator of ideas that eventually developed 'soft' systems thinking. Let us suppose that method is a causal instrument that links cognitive purposes to inquiry behaviour. Then the practical definition of methodology implicitly introduces *inquirer indeterminism*. By this we mean that the inquiry process is affected by 'dissolving causality' (Hoffman, 1947, p. 50) due to the participation of the inquirer.

More recently Mitchell (1968, p. 118) tells us that *methodology* is used to refer to the *techniques* that a particular discipline uses to manipulate data and acquire knowledge. Now *technique* is 'mechanistic skill' (according to the *Oxford English Dictionary*), which can be related to procedure in that they are both behavioural. Mitchell further tells us that methodology is additionally concerned with the more abstract study of the logical basis of a discipline.

Seemingly developing on Joseph's notion that methodology can be a generalised practical tool involving applied logic, Checkland (1981) (following Atkinson, 1977) refers to his own inquiry approach as a methodology, not a method. Explaining this view, Checkland and Scholes (1990, p. 284) distinguish between method and methodology by telling us that (a) method is *technique* devoid of user influence, while (b) methodology involves 'principles of method' and is seen to be responsive to user influence.

Jackson (1992, p. 3) indicates that methodologies can be seen to refer to the procedures used by theorists in seeking to find out about social reality, though in any

91

particular instance reference is normally made to a set of theoretical assumptions that lie at the base of the methodology being examined. He further tells us that sometimes in the systems discipline, *methodology* is used to refer to *methods* for exploring and gaining knowledge about the discipline. His own use of the term methodology is to 'embrace both procedures for gaining knowledge about systems, and the structured processes involved in intervening in and changing systems' (p. 134).

Flood and Romm (1995, p. 378) tell us that 'methods have been understood to have a given and immediate purpose'. Such purpose derives from a cognitive domain. Flood develops this by saying that 'Methods are frequently presented as recipes. They describe what to do without explaining how the method works in terms of principles and purposes. It is essential, however, that an explanation is given and explored so that managers are able to understand the kind of changes that are supposed to occur' (Flood, 1995, p. 5). Flood appears to be using the term method generically for approaches to inquiry. In discussing method, he also appears to avoid the term methodology, despite (or perhaps because of) the strong arguments for the term by viewholders of soft systems. Thus, for instance, his own approach to inquiry (total systems intervention), which would seem to satisfy the definition of a methodology given by Checkland and Scholes, is referred to simply as a *problem solving system*.

Relating method and methodology within the tri-domain model

Let us now set the scene for our definition of method and methodology that is based on our tri-domain model (*see also* Yolles, 1998). Like Flood, we shall take *method* to be a generic term for an approach to inquiry used to explore and gain knowledge about a discipline. It may be seen to involve procedure (or technique) that occurs in the behavioural domain, but this derives from a cognitive model housed within its paradigm. Methods have logical processes that are strategic in their creation of behavioural schedules. These *may* be seen to be immune to the logical influence of an inquirer, but whether they are or are not will depend upon what we shall refer to as the 'quality of method', a term that we shall consider shortly. Partly accepting the definition given by Checkland and Scholes, methodology may be seen to be a form of method that is always susceptible to influence by an inquirer.

The logical processes of a method exist in the transmogrific domain. It involves transformation that harnesses cognitive ideas and sets them into the behavioural domain as procedure. We said previously (in Chapter 2) that a transformation has a property referred to as its *morphism*, and we have also distinguished between *isomorphic* and *homeomorphic* transmogrification. Applying this to method, a homeomorphic method is one that can meaningfully be applied to many different behavioural spaces. Simply, we shall call an isomorphic method one that is with meaning intended to be applied to only one distinct behavioural space. We also note from Chapter 2 that the behavioural domain can be seen as a continuum of changing social space. Now situations (a) are made up of groups of people, (b) have group composition that is defined by the individuals, (c) involve individuals who can leave and be replaced and (d) have individuals whose world views change over time. Then, in the behavioural domain, there are an innumerable variety of possibilities for manifest behaviour that defines situations.

As an example of an intended isomorphic method, we can construct a set of procedural rules to enable a manager to diagnose a problem for a given idiosyncratic computer package. As an example of a homeomorphic method, we see that soft systems methodology (Checkland and Scholes, 1990) can be applied to all classes of purposeful human activity situation. Change the composition of the groups that make up the situation, thus changing the social space, or the point in time when an inquiry is to be made, and the situation will likely alter.

When we referred just now to the classes of purposeful human activity, we did not intend to argue against the soft systems perspective that every situation is unique in itself because it is made up of people each of whom have distinct weltanschauung that form unique common cognitive models that can manifest themselves as organisations. This is clear from our own argument concerning situational variety in the behavioural domain.

Qualifying method

We have suggested that it will be possible to address a variety of views concerning the relationship between method and methodology by assigning qualities to the word method – that is, creating a qualifier. We suggest that such a qualifier is the notion that methods can have different degrees of complexity. The degree of complexity of a method can be determined from the *degrees of freedom* that it has assigned to it. The degrees of freedom will be related to the possibilities of variation in the way methods can be defined. From the tri-domain model, we can distinguish three classes of degree of freedom, one from each domain.

Degrees of freedom exist in the behavioural domain that relate to the way in which a schedule of behavioural elements is brought into existence. Typically one might refer to this schedule as a set of procedural steps. Like the methods of Simon (1960) and Kepner and Tregoe (1965), the schedule may be buried within a set of more macroscopic phases that can help us to understand the approach being followed.

Methods also have available to them possible degrees of freedom contained within the transmogrific domain. This idea relates in part to their cybernetic dimension, which determines if, and when, control processes can be implemented across elements of behaviour. Thus, Simon (1960) proposed a method that defines three phases: intelligence, design and choice; it has one single explicit control process that is intended to validate the design phase, to show that it has been satisfactorily completed according to effectiveness criteria that derive from the world view. The Kepner and Tregoe (1965) method also defines three phases: problem analysis, decision making and potential problem analysis. A fourth phase, 'direction and control,' evaluates the third. These controls enable the ordering of the behavioural elements to be adjusted, so that two applications of the method may be seen to be quite different in their process of behaviour scheduling. Another method is soft systems methodology, which like that of Kepner and Tregoe, has some control built into its behavioural elements. As with the Simon method, it also has additional control aspects that lie outside its behavioural schedule (*see* Chapter 13). However, it is more complicated than both of the above mentioned methods, not least because it does not compress its behavioural schedule into phases.

Degrees of freedom for a method also exist at the cognitive level, for instance through the creation of concepts. Concepts can become manifested as behavioural elements (e.g. procedural steps) or transmogrific elements (e.g. control specifications). For instance in soft systems methodology, the concepts used are that in any organisational inquiry one should be aware of not only the behavioural schedule (defined by the logical stream) of an inquiry process, but also its cultural stream, which explores the political and cultural aspects of the organisation. In contrast, organisational development (Chapter 12) is traditionally a methodology that centres on political culture (through inquiry into power relationships), social psychology (through inquiry into innate resistance to change) and cybernetics (through inquiry into organisational control processes).

The behavioural manifestation of concepts assigned to methods can be used to see complex situations more simply. Thus, for instance, in soft systems methodology the concept of a cultural stream can simplify the complex details of social interactions in one way. However, the viable system model (Espejo and Harnden, 1989) collapses complexity in a very different way by distinguishing between the system and its metasystem (Chapter 14).

Methods that can do this are phenomena that we might refer to as instruments of *complicity* that turn complexity into *simplexity*. These terms were briefly introduced in Chapter 3. We noted that simplexity was defined as a phenomenon of local systemic emergence, where a system's perceived pattern of behaviour could be described in terms of some large-scale emergent concept. Complicity, however, represents the notion of global systemic emergence, where distinct local systems can be related together across the perceived patterns of their behaviours. When we suggest that methods are instruments of complicity, we simply mean that while they can impose their conceptualisations at a local level of system examination, they can also in principle do so globally through their systemic instruments in order to identify the interconnectedness of the different systems. While we can distinguish between local systems and global ones in the abstract, there are many practical instances of situations where this is arbitrary: what constitutes local or global is simply a definition of the *focus* of examination created by an inquirer. We shall discuss this further in the next chapter.

When a method has available to it a degree of freedom in a given class, its viewholders are able to create variety in that class. If we can identify all of the degrees of freedom available to a method, then together they define what we would call its conceptual variety. A method that adopts more degrees of freedom has more conceptual variety than one that does not, and more conceptual variety is consistent with greater complexity of method. This leads us to the idea of at least distinguishing between two classes of method, *simple* and *complex*.

5.2.2 Simple methods

We say that a *simple* method has a poor level of conceptualisation in its paradigm. This leads to low levels of variety in the way that the method can deal with a situation. Simple methods are seen to be contextual procedures, and have limited ability to explain and verify a view of the nature of complex situations. Very simple methods are isomorphic, meaning that the paradigmatic conceptualisations can only be manifested behaviourally in one way, so that they are applicable to only one kind of situation. Less simple methods may be homeomorphic, enabling many different kinds of behavioural manifestation to occur from a given paradigm.

It is possible for us to define two types of simple method, and following Gore (1964) we shall refer to them as *rational* and *heuristic*. *Rational* methods are conscious, logical and planned, and testable, and are traditionally related to clear and quantifiable situations. They may be inadequate for complex situation inquiry in that they are not designed to disentangle problems and verify problem definitions. *Heuristic* methods are largely unconscious, intuitive, emotional and unplanned, and apply to intangible situations. They define a *bounded rationality* that represents a compromise between the demands of the problem situation and the capabilities and commitment of the inquirer (Keen and Scott Morton, 1978, p. 66). This view of inquiry and decision making processes assumes (Davis and Olson, 1984, p. 170) that a decision maker (a) does not know all alternatives and all outcomes, (b) makes a limited search to discover a few satisfactory alternatives and

(c) makes a decision which satisfies his or her aspirations. In complex situations the use of a heuristic method may be inadequate because of its degree of boundedness, and so unable to tackle all of the issues that need to be addressed.

5.2.3 Complex methods

Complex methods are homeomorphic, and have conceptually rich paradigms, providing more resources to generate variety and explore the intangibles of a complex situation. Attributes of complex methods can include an applied logic that is inquirer sensitive. One way that this can occur is through a well-defined transmogrification that uses feedback control loops to enable the inquirer to verify a set of steps or procedures and models according to criteria that have been predefined within its paradigm and interpreted by the inquirer. In the event that verification is not possible, a selection and rescheduling of the steps and a reformulation of the models can be made. While the logic derives from the paradigm, it is influenced by weltanschauung. One might also conceive of varying the very nature of the transmogrification by changing the paradigm-derived logical processes themselves. One could argue that examples of this can be represented by a mixing methods framework such as is proposed for total systems intervention (Flood, 1995), and possibly by the conflict modelling cycle (Chapter 15).

To satisfy the needs of complex situations, complex methods are needed to replace the limitations of simple methods. An example of such a method is soft systems methodology (Checkland and Scholes, 1990). Complex methods attempt to provide *satisfactory explanations* for situations according to criteria that are defined in their paradigms. According to Popper (1975, p. 191), an *explanation* means the set of statements by which one describes the state of affairs to be explained, and the explanations are satisfactory if evidence can be provided that they are true. This begs the question of what constitutes truth, and this must necessarily be belief based.

It will be useful to be consistent with the ideas promoted by Checkland since they have a relatively large following today. Hence, we shall say that very complex methods with a high level of conceptual variety that are sensitive to logical influence by an inquirer are called methodologies. We may suppose that methods lie on a simple–complex continuum that enables us to talk about *relative* simplicity or complexity. For instance if we refer to a simple methodology, then we will mean a relatively simple method that is able to deal with complex situations. If, however, we refer to a complex methodology, then we will mean a method able to deal with very complex situations involving the inquirer.

Fundamental to methodology is the ability for it to be influenced logically by an inquirer according to the demands of a given situation to which it is being applied, and from which a behavioural schedule arises. Methodologies are adaptable and can change both paradigmatically and behaviourally. Traditional methodological paradigms are hard, and see situations in terms of manipulable objects, and where 'better' models are sought. In more recent soft paradigms people are seen to have subjective significance. Their principles often include the notions that (a) the form of inquiry will provide insights concerning the perceived problems, which will lead to practical help in the situation, and (b) experiences using the form of inquiry will enable it to be gradually improved. Rosenhead (1989, p. 308) tells us that models created during methodological inquiry must be open to revision through a learning process. He also suggests that consideration of feasible/infeasible outcomes may lead one to redefine options to produce a *neater* model.

In order to make sure that the procedural steps of a method are carried out in a meaningful way, methodology applies strategic control processes that are paradigm determined. The strategy will determine the schedule of steps that define inquiry behaviour, and which may be related to inquiry style. Thus, we can distinguish between simple method and methodology in the following way.

1 Method is defined through a paradigm.
2 A conceptually poor paradigm provides little opportunity to generate variety in inquiry, and is associated with a simple method.
3 A conceptually rich paradigm provides great opportunity to generate variety in inquiry, and is associated with a complex method.
4 A manifestation of the paradigm defines a set of procedural steps that determine inquiry behaviour. Poorly conceptual paradigms concentrate on behaviour while richly conceptual paradigms balance behaviour with cognition.
5 The ability of an inquirer to influence strategically a logical inquiry process increases a method's complexity.
6 Methodologies are complex methods involving strategic control processes and strategic inquirer participation. This provides more variety by enabling the scheduling and rescheduling of the procedural steps used during inquiry.
7 Some methods can be classed as relatively complex when their paradigmatic conceptualisations are relatively rich. They are able to generate more variety than simple methods, but less than complex methods.
8 Methodologies should be able to produce neat models of situations.

Methods have a propositional base as part of their paradigms that defines the capabilities and constraints of the theory that develops (reflecting penchant), and provides the cognitive basis for modelling. They can be seen to operate in terms of different focuses of behaviour, such as phases and the steps that make them up, and can be seen as a network of cognitive purposes that make the method up. In management systems, complex methods should also by their very nature enable inquiry that can result in *intervention* into a situation.

5.3 The behavioural domain of systems methods

In the remainder of this chapter we shall consider two relatively complex methods that are in contrast to the five methodologies that we shall introduce in Part 3. The first derives from Simon (1960), and the second from Kepner and Tregoe (1965). They provide an introduction to the notion of structured systemic inquiry useful for messy situations.

We are only minimally interested in exploring their paradigms. Rather we wish to explore their complexities in terms of the systemic richness that is the manifestation of their paradigms, seen in terms of their procedural steps and control processes. The specialism of each illustrates the penchant of its paradigm, and their differences illustrate the notion of paradigm incommensurability. The methods have similar overall cognitive purposes. Our interest here, however, will be at a lower focus by examining the mission and goals of their phases. To appreciate how phases are used in behavioural inquiry, it will be useful to explore the behavioural domain a little further.

In contrast to these two methods, we shall introduce our own systemic approach that we call the framework method. We have called it this because we have not rested it upon a well-developed paradigm, but have rather been interested in establishing it as a vehicle for creating a comparative framework to which other methods can be related. The primitive paradigm that it is based on, however, is systemic. Systems methods are scientific and broadly seek to pursue the following *phases* of inquiry:

1 to build organised images (that are in essence systemic models of perceived reality) intended to represent a problem situation or aspects of it;

2 to create possible strategies that address the images, and that some may see as 'intervention strategies' and others as 'solution models' to those images;

3 to validate in some way the 'intervention strategies' or 'solution models'.

How one pursues each of these phases of building images, creating strategies and validating selected options will be substantially dependent upon the developed paradigm of each method. In order to implement each phase, it is normally composed of a set of procedural steps.

It is possible to interrelate the phases clearly through method, which enables us to develop a process of logical inquiry through our investigation of our images of the 'real world' situation under investigation. If the approach is systemic, then the images are explored through the use of a system metaphor. In management systems this can lead to a set of strategic model options that may possibly be used as intervention strategies. Selections can be made from these options based on an inquirer's world-view criteria. This is symbolised in Fig. 5.2 to indicate this nature of the inquiry process.

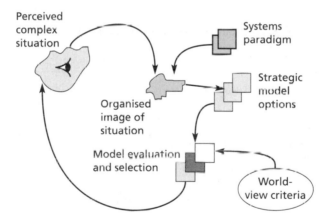

Fig. 5.2 The nature of inquiry

5.4 Simon's method of inquiry

Simon has defined a relatively complex method for decision making that is intended to disentangle problems. It defines the three purposeful phases (Fig. 5.3): intelligence, design and choice. Intelligence is information gathering and analysis, and involves problem definition. Design includes hypothesis making and model building to define problem solutions. Choice includes examination. Implementation follows choice. The phases, their individual mission and goals, and their composite steps are summarised in Table 5.1. A rationale for these steps is provided under the methods mission and goal statement that defines its cognitive purpose.

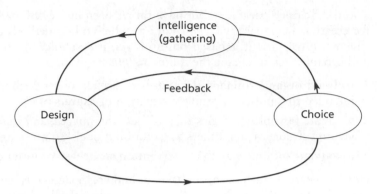

Fig. 5.3 Simon's modelling cycle

The Simon model has been used successfully as a basis for inquiry into semistructured decision making processes. The three-phased cycle of inquiry maintains implicit control and evaluation of the inquiry process. As we shall see much later on, these are inherent in the feedback and recycling capabilities of the approach. Recycling determines how frequently the method will be applied to a given situation, and feedback will determine the schedule of phases that will be selected.

Table 5.1 Steps in the phases of Simon's decision process cycle

Phase	Phase mission and goals	Step
Intelligence	Searching the space of inquiry for conditions calling for decisions; data inputs are obtained, processed, and examined for clues that may identify problems or opportunities. It involves (a) problem finding: finding a difference between an existing and desired state or goal, (b) problem formulation: making sure that you have the right problem. The complexity of a problem can mask this, and it may thus be necessary to reduce the complexity of a problem. This can be done by (i) determining the problem boundaries, (ii) examining the changes that may have precipitated the problem, (iii) factorising the problem into sub-problems and (iv) focusing on the controllable elements.	1 Gather data 2 Identify objectives 3 Diagnose problem 4 Validate data structure problem
Design	Inventing, developing, and analysing possible courses of action. Once the problems are understood, solution models are generated, and their feasibility tested. The development of alternatives requires an adequate knowledge of the problem area and an ability to generate feasible alternatives, the problem boundaries, and the motivation to solve the problem.	5 Gather data 6 Manipulate data 7 Quantify objectives 8 Generate reports 9 Generate alternatives 10 Assign risks or values to alternatives
Choice	Evaluating and selecting alternative course(s) of action from those available; a choice is made and implemented. This phase includes methods for analysing perceived and hypothetical situations, which should be involved as possible models for the future.	11 Generate statistics on alternatives 12 Simulate results of alternatives 13 Explain alternatives 14 Choose among alternatives 15 Explain choice

The ability to generate, manipulate and select the phases of Simon's method is explored through a generalisation of the ideas of Scott Morton (Keen and Scott Morton, 1978) in Table 5.2. We refer to these as the degrees of freedom in applying the method to a situation.

Table 5.2 Factors that determine degrees of freedom in applying the Simon phases

Characteristic	Analysis	Design	Choice
Generation	Size of data source. This may be both database and stakeholder sensitive.	Variety of concept emergence and its contextual applicability.	Alternative action strategies that need to be explored.
Manipulation	Processing capability, ability to generate information, and the ability to conceptualise variety.	Processing capability, and variety in conceptualisation.	Multiple criteria for comparing outcomes.
Selection	Criteria that may vary over time, and subject to cognitive limitations.	Selection of variables.	Comparison of multidimensional alternatives.

(*Source*: Adapted from Keen and Scott Morton, 1978, p. 21)

5.5 The Kepner–Tregoe method

The Kepner–Tregoe (Kepner and Tregoe, 1965) method is relatively close to that of Simon, but does provide some conceptual differences that are manifested in its procedural patterns, being directed at uncertain unstructured situations. As in all decision process approaches, decisions may be seen as interventions into a situation. In particular, a decision may take on the role of being 'interim, adaptive, or corrective action against a problem' (Kepner and Tregoe, 1965, p. 179). The method uses four phases for inquiry: problem analysis, decision making, potential problem analysis, and direction and control. It is illustrated in Fig. 5.4, and the steps involved are identified in Table 5.3. The mission and goals of each phase of the method are clearly defined, and are consistent with the method's overall cognitive purpose.

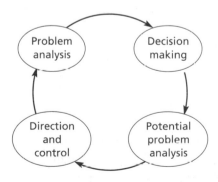

Fig. 5.4 The Kepner–Tregoe method for inquiry

Table 5.3 Steps within the Kepner–Tregoe method for inquiry

Phase	Phase mission and goals	Step
1 Problem analysis	Compare what is actually happening against what should be happening against standards. Deviations are located, trouble spots are studied. Any deviation considered to be important enough to require correction is a problem to be solved.	1 Recognise problems (should, actual) 2 Separate and set priority (urgency, seriousness, growth trend) 3 Specify deviation by developing distinctions and possible causes 4 Develop possible causes 5 Test for cause (explain, minimum assumption, verify)
2 Decision making	Choosing between various ways of getting a job done. Requires development of standards of comparison: the list of objectives to be achieved. Each alternative is measured against this standard. An alternative is chosen. Consequences are explored, balancing advantages and disadvantages.	6 Establish objectives (results produced, resources used) 7 Classify objectives (*musts*: limits, *wants*: weights) 8 Generate alternative actions 9 Compare and choose (*musts*: OK?, *wants*: relative fit) 10 Assess adverse consequences (minimise threat) 11 Make decision
3 Potential problem analysis	This solves problems in advance by either removing causes or minimising effects. Efficient direction and control depends on good potential problem analysis that sets the basis for preventative and contingency action.	12 Anticipate potential problems (should, could potential deviations) 13 Separate, set priority (probability, seriousness, invisibility) 14 Anticipate possible causes (assess probabilities) 15 Take preventive action (remove causes) 16 Set contingency actions (minimise problem effects)
4 Direction and control	Establish control processes that enable a decision to be implemented	17 Set controls (trigger contingency actions, progress versus plan) 18 Implement plan (new ways of operating)

Central to this approach is the idea that there are two types of goals that can result from a decision process. The *must* goals set limits that cannot be violated by any alternatives. They help a manager to recognise and screen out impossible alternatives at the outset. The *wants* do not set absolute limits, but express relative desirability. They are connected with relative advantages and disadvantages. The distinction between *musts* and *wants* avoids the need to settle for an alternative action, when it may later be discovered that it is inadequate because of missing attributes to the situation. The *wants* and *musts* become a set of specifications that enable alternative courses of action to be developed. These goals are individual statements of functions to be performed or fulfilled by the course of action. An inquirer now applies an intuitive approach to determine courses of action that balance the *wants*. In essence, a tangle of problems has now been untangled through the definition of *want* and *must* subgoals, and heuristic methods are now suitable.

5.6 Framework method

When building solutions for messy problems it is useful to stress the holistic view that enables the identifiable problems to be related to each other, and that is central to systems thinking. A holistic view can be achieved through making synthesis part of the inquiry process.

In reflection of our discussions above we introduce what we shall call a framework method (Fig. 5.5). It has three phases, beginning with analysis (breaking down of a problem situation), then synthesis (building up a whole solution) and choice (selection of alternatives). It is deliberate that no detail is provided for each of the phases, and this is why we have referred to the method as framework. The phases are related through the following linking processes.

- Analysis and synthesis are related by *conceptualisation,* which is connected to the knowledge responsible for the creation of models during synthesis. These models will act as options for action that determines an intervention for a given situation.
- The relationship between synthesis and choice is *constraint* since options that are generated within synthesis will then be constrained such that choices can be made.
- The output from choice is *action*, which may also be considered to represent an output from the method as a whole.

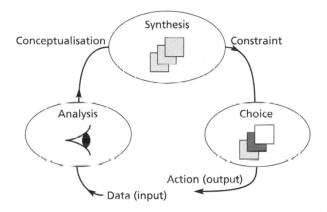

Fig. 5.5 Basic form of framework method

Thus, from Fig. 5.5:

 Analysis through action is essentially looking, perceiving, examining, seeing, finding out about and creating images of the real world through the application of systems techniques

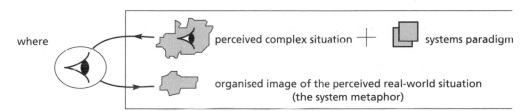

101

Synthesis through conceptualisation is the building of a set of strategic models some of which can, when validated, act as actions connected with possible intervention

Choice through constraint determined through validation is the selection of a set of the proposed model options for action in connection with possible intervention

Note that the *organised images of the real-world situations* of purposeful activity have *system representations* and are described as purposeful activity systems.

The images are metaphors, a function of the system paradigm, and lead to synthesised strategic models often constructed for the purpose of intervention. Thus:

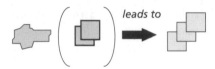

We may also say that:

In the same way we may say that constraint is determined by world-view criteria, and so:

5.6.1 Analysis

Analysis of a situation requires that it is examined and defined in terms of its perceived parts. At least two types of analysis may be identified: (a) behavioural and (b) cognitive.

Behavioural analysis is concerned with seeing the situation as a system, and differentiating it into a set of subsystems and their relationships with their environment. It is concerned with social aspects of the situation, including roles and their interactive relationships. It is also concerned with its political aspects, and power distribution. It explores the boundaries of the situation, each defining behavioural purposes or properties for the system. The creation of such boundaries can help with the process of problem definition. Clarity in behavioural analysis can be difficult when there is sufficient complexity. In reducing complexity one might:

1 examine the changes that may have invoked the problem situation;

2 identify the possible problem boundaries and associated parameters;

3 explore the complexity of the situation in terms of perceived problems definition.

Cognitive analysis may be seen as the process of inquiring into the set of paradigms and their stakeholders that make up the focuses of the situation. It therefore involves an examination of the culture, associated conceptualisations and other attributes of the paradigm. This can highlight some of the possible cognitive problems, and contribute to the formulation of perceived problem settlement options that are able to act as intervention strategies. Now, the paradigms within a situation may be unitary or pluralistic, depending upon recognition by the inquirer and the definition of boundaries to differentiate the paradigms one from the other. Unitary situations occur when only a single paradigm is recognised, either by the inquirer accepting a dominant one, say from the primary stakeholders or client, or from a consensus view. Pluralistic paradigm situations occur when more than one paradigm coexists. Plural paradigms may populate a situation in such a way that:

1 each paradigm is local to a given focus, referred to as *local unitary* situations;

2 each focus has a plurality of paradigms that can result in conflict.

Analysis is subject to the weltanschauung principle, where every inquirer will model a situation differently because his or her world view is unique. Thus, the nature of the problem situation will be dependent upon the weltanschauung of the inquirer, and since all weltanschauungen are different, we can expect there to be variation between the models that the inquirers produce as representations of the situation.

To undertake analysis, it is essential that participants in a situation and their influences are adequately defined. Actors are participants who tend to have trajectories, objectives, strategies, and they have an external environment with which they interact. They have internal constraints as well as external ones, variables, and cultural, social, and political attributes. This applies to all classes of actor, whether they are individuals, collections of individuals, enterprises, cultural groups, or nation states.

5.6.2 Synthesis

The idea of synthesis during inquiry is supported by such authors as Beer (1975) and Ackoff (1981). By synthesis we mean selecting, inventing, creating, designing or developing possible options or scenarios for use as strategies for action. It requires knowledge of the situation and an ability to generate feasible strategies for action.

Synthesis focuses on the functional necessities of a situation that will define an intervention strategy. It reveals why things operate as they do, and yields understanding that enables us to explain the situation. While analysis enables us to describe, synthesis permits us to explain. Synthesis is also the building up of a set of components into a coherent whole picture. It derives from the integration of analytic conceptualisations that define the prerequisites for model options.

Synthesis may also be thought of as the stage in which purposeful activity models are defined that hold within solutions to perceived problems. This phase of the method is susceptible to *preconscious* factors of inquiry. These are formally or informally defined ideology, norms and symbols that will usually be unconsciously applied to the modelling process. It is preconscious factors that are used by an inquirer in synthesis. Consider the case of two inquirers deriving from different backgrounds and who may be following the same method. The result of their independent creations during synthesis are likely to be different precisely because of their preconscious factors.

In general, this phase is concerned with the manipulation of data, evaluating or quantifying objectives, generating situation paradigms, creating alternative scenarios, forming individual or group simulations, establishing views about the form of a situation, creating agreement or generating reports. It will in essence establish a set of satisfying options (for the context of situation as seen from the perspective of the inquirer) that can be evaluated during the choice phase.

As we explained in the analysis phase, it may be perceived that a number of paradigms coexist. Such a situation can have immediate impact on the way synthesis is carried out (Table 5.4). Unitary situations occur when only a single paradigm is recognised, either from a dominant or a consensus view. The result is that options are more easily found since there is less complexity. Problems occur when this is not the case. In unitary situations, the need is simply to ensure that settlements are satisfying. In local unitary situations, it must be seen that settlement options are synergistic. In plural paradigm situations, it may be appropriate to inquire further through the use of pluralistic approaches like conflict theory.

Table 5.4 The possibilities that may occur in defining options for a situation during synthesis

Possibilities	Paradigm	Options for action
Unitary	A consensus or dominant paradigm can be identified for a situation. This often ignores the existence of other lesser paradigms.	A set of options is identified for a situation that forms a possible basis for a way forward through common agreement or acceptance.
Pluralistic	A set of paradigms may be maintained for a situation. These may each relate to independent local focuses of a system and are then unitary equivalent. If they are plural to a single focus, then they may coexist in balance or conflict.	Options arise from a plurality of paradigms. The difficulty is in attempting to ensure that the options are synergistic, and can therefore be seen to be for the benefit of the system as a whole.

5.6.3 Choice

Choices may involve identifying/selecting models or modes of implementation. These must be capable of representing feasible modes of action from those options defined in synthesis. This may involve:

1 consultation with the actors;

2 evaluation of the dynamic stability of options by comparing the models with the situation;

3 implementation into the situation.

One of the purposes of this phase is to produce an evaluation of model options and their ability to represent environments and decision scenarios, or to evaluate modes of implementation. Examination of the consequences of modelling options in a changing environment might also be appropriate. It would be necessary to activate these models as solutions to perceived problems to generate outcomes that may be applied to the situation. Choices involves setting up a modelling technique or mode of implementation. These models should be validated, examining the selected output or implementation, and this is related to observed events.

Consider the relatively hard approach to choice. A quantitative approach is used, and in the case of there being numerical outputs these must be interpreted qualitatively. Modelling results will be generated for evaluation. In the former of these, stochastic processes, Monte Carlo simulation, Markov processes or Weibull games (Yolles, 1985, 1987) can be used, and perhaps outcomes compared.

In a soft approach to choice, checking can occur so that the progress of individual or group experience is appropriate. A match between model outputs and paradigm perspectives will indicate the likelihood of the dynamic stability of the modelling approach. In a slightly harder paradigm, the simulating experiences through group participation games can be an effective way of highlighting implementation strategies that enable options to be selected.

This phase distinguishes the ability of each model to represent the situation and the constraints under which it operates. It is efficient for the validation of a model to be sought when modelling option evaluation has been successful.

5.7 Establishing controls

5.7.1 Feedback

Method complexification can occur through control and evaluation, and this involves feedback. Feedback occurs to either enhance the synthesis or modify it, either directly or by reformulating analysis. Negative feedback operates as a control, constraining the models created. It also operates when critical examination or testing of models causes difficulties. Positive feedback will encourage the further development of a model under synthesis, as in the case of generalisation. In Fig. 5.6 we show a number of possible ways for feedback between its phases to occur. It is possible to further complexify the method by introducing very different arrangements of feedback, but this is not the place to discuss these concepts. The purposes for any feedback processes would necessarily have to be paradigmatically defined, and this will assign meaning to such processes in the context of the method in its application to a situation.

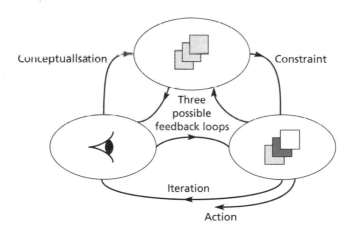

Fig. 5.6 Cycle of inquiry with feedback in framework method

5.7.2 Iteration

Figure 5.6 is iterative in that the method can be operated on over many consecutive reiterations. One way to use the iterative cycle of inquiry is as follows:

1 a problem situation is normally the catalyst for a method to be activated;

2 when we encounter the problem situation we do not know much about it; in the first iteration, we produce a simple model about it;

3 this is examined and criticised in order to understand more about the situation and its difficulties, and will hopefully lead to the synthesis of a set of possible intervention models;

4 we thus improve our definition of the problem, and improve our models;

5 we may also see any ramifications of the problem with other perhaps subsidiary or parallel problems.

The model may be applied to other related problems in order to explore its soundness. The growth through scientific method proceeds from old problems to new problems by means of conjectures and their adjustments.

An example of how the framework method and its iterative procedure might be applied is provided in Minicase 5.1.

Minicase 5.1

The case of the mouse in the house

You arrive home to find an uninvited mouse has joined your household, is eating the biscuits in your kitchen drawer, and offering you a potential health hazard. Your weltanschauung is that you do not wish to kill the mouse or risk maiming it to cause undue suffering, even though you define a human purpose to eliminate it since you cannot conceivably housetrain it. The paradigm legitimises a commonly agreed language that you can use to model the situation, which implicitly contains a set of underlying concepts and principles that enable you to describe your modelling ideas. It also points you towards the method that you wish to use. However, you are not yet sure of your paradigm, and thus not aware of your methodological approach, but this will become clear in due course. Rather than deciding on a particular way of tackling the situation, you wish to explore it through the more paradigmatically neutral framework cycle given in Fig. 5.6.

You analyse the situation, and find that the mouse is living in a place that you cannot reach. You want to eliminate this problem. You go to your local ironmonger, and ask for advice about catching the mouse. The manager assists you in synthesising a solution. Three solutions are offered: a traditional trap that is baited, and may kill or injure the mouse; poison bait that the mouse can eat; and a humane trap that will catch the mouse without hurting it. It is up to you to make the choice about which solution to adopt, and if you wish, to implement. There may be other options, but they are not presented to you. The ironmonger asks you to explain which option you would like to select so that he can help you engineer it. You decide upon a humane trap, which is consistent with your weltanschauung. You then find out that there are a variety of humane traps to choose from. The humane traps are more or less consistent with the purposes defined within the situation. Now, the way in which the humane traps should be used has been described, and you select one that is totally in keeping with your paradigm. It provides you with an ideal model of how the mouse will be caught. The tools of inquiry include bait and decisions about location. You bait the trap according to the instructions, position it, set it and wait.

The method that you wish to use is a humane mousetrap. It entails principles and purpose in the paradigm that exists for its use, and a behavioural manifestation that indicates how you use it. You have baited it, and return in the morning. Now you find that the mouse has not taken the bait. Why is this? What are the variables in the situation that have led to the mouse not being caught? To find out you guess that the mouse cannot smell the bait over and above the new plastic of the trap. In the synthesis phase, you decide to place extra bait where you can be sure that the mouse can smell it. In the choice phase you decide to place it at the mouth of the trap, hoping that the mouse will then be led into the catching zone.

The next morning, only the bait at the front of the trap is gone. Through the next cycle you place a trail of bait into the trap, hoping that the mouse will move into the catch zone. If not you can continue with another iteration. The saga continues, however, because the mouse eventually collects all the bait in the trail except one, that one which ensures that it triggers the trap mechanism. For the next cycle, the trap mechanism itself is altered to make it easier for the mouse to trigger it. A limited success occurs when the trap is triggered, but the mouse escapes because the trap door has not closed completely. Could this be because the length of the trap adjustment is such that now the length of the mouse becomes a critical factor? In case this is true, in the next cycle the trap is lengthened. However, now the mouse does not want to take the bait at all, perhaps because it was surprised by the trap door and does not want to chance its luck at present. Inquiry continues by reasoning and experimentation through analysis, synthesis and choice until either the mouse has been caught, or you seek an entirely different approach, or you give up altogether.

After a number of attempts to adjust the trap occurring over a two-week period, and failing to catch the mouse, you become frustrated because you are unable to encourage the mouse to trigger the trap and get caught. You are now becoming concerned with the continuing hygiene problem that the mouse is creating. It is clear that paradigmatic inquiry has failed, and that you must reconsider what to do. This means that you must reassess your perspective for the situation, and consider a new weltanschauung. So you shift your weltanschauung through the paradigm cycle. There has been a perspective that balances hygiene with mouse welfare, and until now this has favoured the mouse.

The time spent on unsuccessfully solving the problem has now placed the well-being of the mouse as a secondary importance to hygiene. Examining all other options, you discover a new one that you implement. There are a number of apertures at the back of the kitchen units and behind the wall skirting boards. The mouse may be using these as access points to and from the kitchen. You close up all apertures that might permit the mouse to enter the area that is showing signs of mouse activity. You hope that you have not sealed the mouse in. This move from option (a), the humane trap, to (b), sealing out the mouse, represents a sudden shift from one paradigm to another. The location of the situation in the modelling space now also shifts because the perspective of the problem is redefined.

The saga continues.

5.8 Method complementarism

The idea of complementarism may be seen to derive from the problem associated with the relative view of the inquirer. This has been the subject of debate in the development of quantum physics as discussed, for instance, by Niels Bohr in the late 1950s. In practice no view of reality can be complete (Weinberg, 1975, p. 116) since the weltanschauung of the inquirer is part of the process of inquiry. In particular, 'each view [of an inquirer], if constructed with a modicum of care, will contain some information about *what is really out there*, but they will never be completely reconcilable' (Weinberg, 1975, p. 120). As a result some methods seek as many stakeholder views as possible to define a situation. We have referred to this as the weltanschauung principle. Similarly, we can invent the paradigm principle to enable more variety in modelling.

Complementarism is concerned with the idea that different methods can be used coincidentally in application to a given situation. It recognises that they may each operate out of different paradigms, and have different rationalities stemming from alternative theoretical positions that they reflect. The idea that any one paradigm is the only legitimate one capable of absorbing all the others is problematic to complementarism. Rather, the different paradigms can operate in a way that are complementary to one another, each finding strength of examination and evaluation that others might not have in respect of different classes of situation.

Comparing and coordinating methods

There are ontological issues that create difficulties in the idea of comparing and coordinating methods. They suggest that it is problematic to even try to engineer the use of methods so that they become linked for a particular application. The issues centre on the idea of paradigm incommensurability, which tells us that different methods have at their base different paradigms, and thus cannot be used in a complementary way, let alone be coordinated.

One way of addressing the paradigm incommensurability argument is to create a new virtual paradigm that defines a cognitive basis for the integrated or coincident use of more than one method. This will clearly require some level of understanding of the paradigms that are to be associated within the virtual paradigm, and an ability to demonstrate that they can be connected in a satisfactory way. In this respect it is not an arbitrary process. That an inquirer is creating a virtual paradigm is not always clear, and one way of noting that this is happening is to examine the language that a methodologist is using. New language is indicative of a new paradigm being formulated.

As an example of this, Paton (1993) has proposed a way of linking two methodologies together. In doing so he would seem to be creating new terminology to describe the basis of each. He argues that part of the activity of soft systems methodology (SSM) is the creation of a primary task model (PTM) which addresses the situation through an identification of primary tasks. The PTM is used, it is said, by SSM inquirers as an analytic tool to enable understanding about the real world and inform debate about possible interventions within it. Paten suggests that rather than calling the model an analytical tool, it should be referred to as a *blueprint* for the real-world organisation. The blueprint, it is argued, then has the same ontological status as *system identification* in a viable system model (VSM) methodology described by Jackson (1993) or 'structuring the problem situation: naming organisations and issues' according to Espejo (1993). While we would not advocate this as an approach, it does now represent a new term that is used in neither VSM nor SSM, and consequently may be considered as language that now relates to a new virtual paradigm.

We can apply a different approach. To show how it operates we shall compare the Simon and Kepner–Tregoe methods, the paradigms of which are incommensurable. We propose to do this through the cognitive purposes at the phase level assigned to the framework method and consistent with Fig. 5.2. Our interest now will be to shift our focus of examination to see if we can find cognitive purposes that are conceptually comparable across the methods. This is possible since all of the three methods considered here are scientific and thus have common cognitive purposes approximately at the phase focus. We say approximately because the phase definitions vary slightly, but must have some level of commonality. The Simon and Kepner–Tregoe methods cannot be compared at the more detailed focus at the level of individual steps, because the details are manifestations of non-coextensive paradigmatic conceptualisations. In other words, each uses conceptualisations that the other does not have. Neither can our framework method be compared at this detailed focus, because it has not been created. In the same way, any science-based methods should be comparable at the phase level. Comparison of the three methods against a broad mission associated with the phases of the framework method is given in Table 5.5.

Table 5.5 The Simon, Kepner–Tregoe and framework methods compared at the phase focus

Mission associated with framework phases	Methods		
	Framework	*Simon*	*Kepner–Tregoe*
Model problem situation	Analysis	Intelligence	Problem analysis
Build intervention strategies	*Conceptualisation*	Design	Decision making
	Synthesis		
Evaluate, select and apply intervention strategies	*Constraint*	Choice	Potential problem analysis
	Choice		
	Action	*Implement*	Direction and control

SUMMARY

In general there has been some contradiction and confusion over the meaning of method and methodology that inhibits the development of a systemic view of systems. We have addressed this problem by defining a continuum for method, the poles of which are simple and complex. These terms are seen as qualifiers on the word method, and therefore enable people to maintain their current use and meaning of the word without difficulty. Thus, a user may talk of *method* and later relate it with terms *simple method* or *complex method*, depending upon the meaning intended. It also places the word *methodology* into context as *complex method*. Finally, it enables the word method to be used as a generic term, rather than simply referring to a procedure.

Two classes of method have been identified, simple and complex. It is also possible to identify the existence of intermediate relatively complex methods. Examples of simple methods are rational and heuristic. Complex methods are often called methodologies. In complex situations the use of complex methods is important since it enables the variety of a situation to be matched by the method. Two relatively complex methods are that of Simon and that of Kepner and Tregoe. A manifestation of their different paradigms is illustrated by their different sets of procedural steps. They cannot easily be compared at this level because their paradigms are incommensurable. Thus, comparison between different things has little meaning. However, the difference can be reduced by moving the focus of examination from the level of their individual steps to that of their phases. These have broadly similar cognitive purposes, enabling us to make meaningful comparison. Our framework method, which has been defined only in terms of the focus of their phases, is comparable, and illustrates some of the conceptual difference between the methods.

No exploration is made of the paradigms that lie at the basis of the methods explored. This is because our purpose was to explore the nature of method and to distinguish between simple and complex methods. Complex methods involve control processes that enable the schedule of simple ones. Both the Simon and the Kepner–Tregoe methods operate a single feedback process, while the framework method is defined to enable a variety of feedbacks. These methods are all scientifically based, and can each therefore be compared against the cognitive purposes assigned to the phases of scientific method.

REFERENCES

Ackoff, R.L. (1981) *Creating the Corporate Future*. New York: Wiley.

Allport, G.W. (1961) *Pattern and Growth in Personality*. London: Holt, Rinehart & Winston.

Atkinson, C.J. (1977) 'Towards a plurality of soft systems methodology', *Journal of Applied Systems Analysis*, 16, 43–53.

Beer, S. (1975) *Platform for Change*. Chichester: Wiley.

Borger, R. and Seaborne, A.E.M. (1966) *The Psychology of Learning*. Harmondsworth: Penguin.

Checkland, P.B. (1981) *Systems Thinking, Systems Practice*. Chichester: Wiley.

Checkland, P.B. (1995) 'Model validation in soft systems practice', *Systems Research*, 12(1), 47–54.

Checkland, P.B. and Casar, A. (1986) 'Vicker's concept of an appreciative system: a systemic account', *Journal of Applied Systems Analysis*, 13, 3–17.

Checkland, P.B. and Scholes, J. (1990) *Soft Systems Methodology in Action*. Chichester: Wiley.

Davis, G.B. and Olson, M.H. (1984) *Management Information Systems: Conceptual foundations, structure, and development*. New York: McGraw-Hill.

Espejo, R. (1993) 'Management of complexity in problem solving'. In Espejo, R. and Schwaninger, M. (eds) *Organisational Fitness: Corporate effectiveness through management cybernetics*. Frankfurt: Campus/Verlag.

Espejo, R. and Harnden, R. (1989) *The Viable System Model: Interpretations and applications of Stafford Beer's VSM*. Chichester: Wiley.

Flood, R.L. (1995) *Solving Problem Solving*. Chichester: Wiley.

Flood, R.L. and Jackson, M.C. (1991) *Creative Problem Solving: Total intervention strategy*. Chichester: Wiley.

Flood, R.L. and Romm, N.R.A. (1995) 'Enhancing the process of choice in TSI, and improving chances of tackling coercion', *Systems Practice*, 8, 377–408.

Gore, W.J. (1964) *Administrative Decision-Making: A heuristic model*. New York: Wiley.

Harry, M. (1994) *Information Systems in Business*. London: Pitman.

Hoffman, B. (1947) *The Strange Story of the Quantum*. Harmondsworth: Penguin.

Jackson, M.C. (1992) *Systems Methodologies for the Management Sciences*. New York: Plenum Press.

Jackson, M.C. (1993) 'Don't bite my finger: Haridimos Tsoukas' critical evaluation of Total Systems Intervention', *Systems Practice*, 6, 289–94.

Johannessen, J.A. (1995) 'Basic features of an information and communication system aimed at promoting organisational learning', *Systems Practice*, 8(2), 183–96.

Joseph, H.W.R. (1946) (reprint of second edition, 1916) *An Introduction to Logic*. Oxford: Clarendon Press.

Keen, P.G.W. and Scott Morton, M.S. (1978) *Decision Support Systems: An organisational perspective*. Reading, MA: Addison-Wesley.

Kepner, C.H. and Tregoe, B.B. (1965) *The Rational Decision Maker*. New York: McGraw-Hill.

Koestler, A. (1967) *The Ghost in the Machine*. London: Picador.

Levine, R.I., Drang, D.E. and Edelson, B. (1986) *A Comprehensive Guide to AI and Expert Systems*. New York: McGraw-Hill.

Mitchell, G.D. (1968) *A Dictionary of Sociology*. London: Routledge & Kegan Paul.

Olle, T.W., Hagelstein, J., Macdonald, I.G., Rolland, C., Henk, G.S., van Assche, F.J.M. and Verrijn-Stuart, A.A. (1988) *Information Systems Methodologies: A framework for understanding*. Wokingham: Addison-Wesley.

Popper, K. (1972) *Objective Knowledge: An evolutionary approach*. Oxford: Oxford University Press.

Rosenhead, J. (1989) *Rational Analysis for a Problematic World*. Chichester: Wiley.

Simon, H.A. (1960) *The New Science of Management Decisions*. New York: Harper & Brothers.

Vickers, G. (1965) *The Art of Judgement*. London: Chapman & Hall.

von Bertalanffy, L. (1968) *General Systems Theory*. Harmondsworth: Penguin.

Weinberg, G.M. (1975) *An Introduction to General Systems Thinking*. New York: Wiley.

Yolles, M.I. (1985) 'Simulating conflict using Weibull games'. In Javor, A. (ed.) *Modelling and Simulation*. Amsterdam: Elsevier.

Yolles, M.I. (1987) 'Modelling conflict with Weibull games'. In Bennett, J. (ed.) *Mathematical Modelling of Conflict and its Resolution*. London: Heinemann, pp. 113–34.

Yolles, M.I. (1998) 'A cybernetic exploration of methodological complementarism', *Kybernetes*, 27(4, 5), 527, 542.

PART 2

Viable systems and inquiry

INTRODUCTION TO PART 2

The intention in this part of the book is to provide a basis for the development of viable systems theory (VST) that, when directed towards inquiry, will lead to a theory of viable inquiry systems (VIS). Here interest in VST centres on complex purposeful adaptive activity systems that for economical convenience we refer to as actors or actors systems.

Such an actor can be seen as a 'whole' system (or holon) that exists with a network of other holons called a holarchy. Holons are defined in terms of system boundaries, as it is through their boundaries that systems are differentiated from or related to other systems. An actor system has a metasystem, its so-called cognitive consciousness, which directs the system and is responsible for decision making. In order to explore the features of a situation within which we define actors, it is essential to explore their social, cultural and political characteristics. It is through these that we will be able to understand how to define a situation, how to establish the boundaries of a holon, and how to formulate a holarchy (a network of holons). Only when this has been done will be able to determine effectively how intervention can occur. Part of this process will be to distinguish between local and regional focuses in a holarchy.

A holarchy has more traditionally been referred to as a system hierarchy, and is composed of a collection of focuses of bounded systems that define a situation. These are normally seen as autonomous systems that have the property of viability, which explains how and why they are able to survive under change. Viable systems theory is concerned with holons seen as semi-autonomous purposeful open systems that exist in a holarchy. The theory that develops centres on the ability of viable systems to maintain their stability through self-actuation, examples of which are self-regulation and self-organisation.

Viable systems can be said to maintain their existence and adapt through deterministic cognitive control, and sometimes despite it. The development of complexity theory has enabled us to extend our conceptions of the way in which viable systems are able to maintain their stability through processes of self-actuation. Applying these ideas to the process of inquiry, we will eventually be led to the idea that we might be more interested in the notion of viable inquiring systems rather than simply methods.

Complex adaptable purposeful activity systems can be viable. The activity that we are referring to may be inquiry, leading to the search for stable intervention strategies. The knowledge domain model distinguishes between a cognitive domain and a behavioural domain. Transmogrification has a very important role to play in linking the metasystem with the system. It is strategic, and supports logical, relational and cybernetic mechanisms, permitting inquiry to be controlled.

Viable systems can be classified in a variety of ways according to their cognitive purposes. Thus, we can for instance differentiate between the missions of public and commercial organisations, as we can with the mission of organisations of inquiry that relates to seeking strategic interventions in situations. The latter can be seen to involve method.

Methods can be seen as systems in their own right. They derive from a variety of interests, but inquirers often use them to seek to find a structured way of pursuing stability. Few methods deal with inquiry into dynamically non-equilibrium situations that pass through periods of change that are deterministically uncontrollable, chaotic and unstable. Applying the idea of viability to organised inquiry involving method brings us to the idea of viable inquiry systems. Like any variable system, it will also have a meta-system that derives from a set of world views. This implies that we see the process of inquiry as implicitly world-view plural. This is a proposition that defines the basic concepts of viable inquiry systems, and enables us to address the idea of paradigm incommensurability and methodological complementarism.

We have said that this part of the book centres on an introduction to viable systems theory. This relates in part to Schwarzian viable systems theory (SVST), which provides a cognitive basis for a paradigm of viability, and may be seen as a building block of holarchy theory that is distinct from other models of viable systems, but to which they also contribute. It is one that explains evolution of natural viable systems. Our developments also build on the work of Beer, as used for instance in his development of the viable system model (VSM), which seeks to be used as a conceptual tool to deal with complex problem situations involving purposeful adaptive activity systems. Beer has developed a way of looking at organisations and proposing interventions such that they can be made viable. The creation of our VST supports the fundamental conceptualisations upon which the VSM is based, rather than the VSM itself.

SVST is a modern theory that explains how viable systems undergo the processes of morphogenic change and the maintenance of stability in situations that may be chaotic. Through the work here it can link with VSM. Like all paradigms, the foundations of VSM, SVST, and our own models are all belief based and maintain their own logic. If we are prepared to accept the propositional base that is promoted within VST, then we are left to validate its conceptualisations empirically. The Western tradition of science has built into it the concepts of falsifiability and verification that stem from a propositonal logic that is believed to be true by those who adhere to the scientific paradigm.

As an illustration of the problem associated with this, Schwarz, in a letter to Yolles in 1996, explained a concern about this that is worthy of note: 'The other day I was talking about the [SVST] model with some bright but dualist people active in hard sciences and engineering. When somebody asked how one could put to the test such a proposal [as the SVST model] I had a hard time trying to answer. With the systematic–holistic paradigm we are really in a very uncomfortable position between logico-empirist science on the one hand, with its well known limitations but with the advantage of fallibilty, and verbose unfalsifiable religions and philosophies on the other hand. I think that one of the main visible manifestations of the pertinent non-duellist paradigm is that those who adopt it survive; but this takes time to verify and we may individually die before that paradigm changes! Unless the socio-economical situation collapses so quickly that we can see [or more aptly recognise] it. Pierre Thuillier, a notable French science philosopher, recently wrote a book entitled *The Big Implosion: Report on the Collapse of the Western World, 1999–2002*, supposedly written in 2077 by a "Research Group on the End of the Western Civilisation". The group tried to understand why nothing was done to prevent the collapse despite the fact that most symptoms were described in one book or another well before it happened. Believe it or not, Thuillier's book is almost not mediatised.'

CHAPTER 6

Systems as actors in networks

OVERVIEW

Purposeful adaptive activity systems can be represented as actors. As such, an actor is also a holon or 'whole' system that exists in a network of other holons called a holarchy. Holons are defined through their boundaries, as it is through their boundaries that they are differentiated from or related to other holons. Actor systems have a metasystem (its so-called cognitive consciousness) that enables it to make decisions. In order to explore the features of a situation within which actors are defined to act, it is essential to explore their social, cultural and political characteristics. It is through these that we will be able to understand how to define a situation, how to establish the boundaries of a holon and how to formulate a holarchy. Only when this has been done will we be able to determine effectively how intervention can occur. Part of this process will be to distinguish between local and regional focuses in a holarchy.

OBJECTIVES

This chapter will examine:

- the nature of system boundaries;
- the nature of a metasystem and its relationship with systems;
- the relationship between the system and the suprasystem;
- the connection between stability and security;
- the nature of holarchies and metaholarchies;
- social, cultural and political domains in connection with holarchies and metaholarchies.

6.1 System boundaries

It is normally possible to describe a situation in terms of a set of boundaries that break it down into a network of systems. All systems have, by their very nature, boundaries.

A boundary may best be seen as a *frame of reference* that is in transition (Minai, 1995). It is in transition because all phenomena are seen to be in a state of flux, and so the frame of reference continually changes. The nature of the frame of reference can vary. Holsti (1967) suggests that a boundary may also be seen as an issues line, beyond which actions and transactions between different systems have no direct effect on the environment, and where the events or conditions in the environment have no direct effect on the systems. Other ways of defining the frame of reference are through:

- purposes that generate patterns of behaviour
- behavioural patterns themselves
- properties (e.g. functional, learning)
- constraints on form
- constraints on behaviour
- degree of order and disorder
- regularity and irregularity
- contextuality.

Lack of clarity in the frame of reference (e.g. unclear purposes, constraints or properties) can lead to a fuzzy boundary, when differentiation between two boundaries becomes difficult. Boundary differentiation requires an ability to make comparison between frames of reference. To make a comparison between boundaries it is necessary to have a set of aims for a comparison (van der Leeuw, 1981, p. 235), and knowledge about the world views involved in defining them.

6.2 Systems hierarchies seen as holarchies

Systems are differentiated by their boundaries, and the nature of a boundary will vary according to who it is that is modelling it. Our purpose here is to discuss how we can see situations in terms of a set of boundaries that define our systems.

Systems are organised images of the real world that entail generic characteristics (as discussed in Chapters 1 and 5). We build system models because we can attribute to the perceived real-world situations that they are intended to represent these characteristics. We do this because we believe that this can reduce their complexity and help us describe and explain them. Koestler was so interested in seeing system as 'wholes' that he referred to them as *holons*. The real world can be modelled as a network of holons, some of which can be seen as sub-wholes (holons within holons). This is often referred to as the system hierarchy (Fig. 6.1), although it is perhaps simpler to refer to it as a *holarchy* (Schwarz, personal communication, 1996).

Since a holon is a 'whole', it must be seen to be in some way complete in itself and thus autonomous in that respect. The nature of autonomy is a 'relative concept' (Beer, 1979, p. 119), because even the natures and purposes of a system are subjective and a reflection of the weltanschauung principle. Schwarz (personal communication, 1996), rather than talking about autonomy as a relative concept, prefers to distinguish between

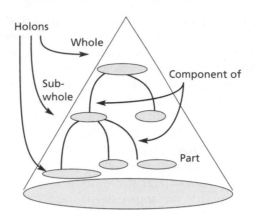

Fig. 6.1 Cone of three levels of focus in a system hierarchy.
A part may itself be a whole having its own parts. This illustration of a structured relationship between parts and wholes represents the idea of a system hierarchy.

fully and partially autonomous systems. Their distinction lies in that fully autonomous systems have no logical connection to their environment while semi-autonomous systems do. However, Schwarz also indicates that systems can be seen to have degrees of autonomy, and this is determined by the *intensity* of the influence on the system. The difficulty here is that except in some very special cases, there are no universal objective standards by which we can determine intensity of influence, and it is more likely to be a qualitative evaluation that derives from individual or group perspectives. This makes Schwarz's and Beer's views on autonomy equivalent. Thus the use of the word semi-autonomous therefore (a) acts simply as a stress on the relative nature of autonomy, and (b) indicates the possibility of logical system connections with the environment. When we discuss holons we may therefore be referring to either autonomous or semi-autonomous systems without ambiguity.

6.3 Focuses in a holarchy

6.3.1 A holon as a systemic actor with a metasystem

A holon can be defined to be a local focus in a holarchy. Let us suppose that the holon represents a purposeful adaptive activity system with normative processes that acts for some purpose, and that we refer to as an actor system (or, after Cornblis (1971, p. 226), a social actor). Each actor is a *local* focus in the holarchy, and the collection of all the actors in the total network of influences that defines a situation for an inquirer represents a *global* focus.

A focus is *regional* if it includes a set of actors in mutual interaction in a suprasystem (Fig. 6.2), the boundary of which is determined by the inquirer. As an example of such a regional focus, a given number of actor enterprises participate in a competitive market (the suprasystem), each vying for business. In the same way, actors may be individuals in a group activity, or nation states in an international situation.

119

Each actor system also has associated with it a metasystem (as shown in Fig. 6.2) from within which decision making processes occur. According to Beer (1975) *metasystems* exist wherever metalanguages do; if metalanguages are in operation, then somewhere you can find a metasystem. The term was originally used by Beer (1959, 1975) in cybernetics to represent 'a controller of internal relations between the variable subsystems and the relation of the whole environment' (Espejo and Schwaninger, 1993, p. 44), and 'as higher levels of management which define purpose for a system' (Flood and Jackson, 1991, p. 231). We do not have to restrict the definition to *management* purpose, noting that *cognitive purpose* is a generalisation of this. The metasystem can be seen to be part of any cognitive activity system.

We see the metasystem as the system's metaphorical 'cognitive consciousness'. Like any seat of cognitive consciousness, the metasystem is 'capable of deciding propositions, discussing criteria, or exercising regulation for systems that are themselves logically incapable of such decisions and discussions, or of self-regulation' (van Gigch, 1987). In particular, we note that:

1 the propositional logic of the metasystem is not accessible to that of the system (and vice versa);

2 the paradigmatic language (e.g. metalanguage) can generate statements the meaning of which is not mutually expressible (e.g. in the system's language);

3 the culture of the metasystem/system will not allow particular perspectives to develop.

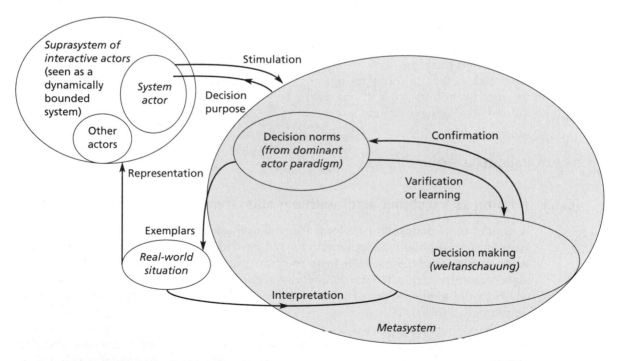

Fig. 6.2 A regional focus of a holarchy involving a suprasystem, its component actors and their decision making metasystem

6.3.2 The local actor focus

An actor is purposeful and has behaviour that is ultimately world view determined. It has a social structure that both facilitates and bounds behaviour. It *enables* behaviour by providing the support mechanisms that allow it to occur. We say that behaviour is structure determined because behaviour that cannot be facilitated by a structure is not possible.

The structure itself is a manifestation of the world views that the actor maintains. These world views not only generate the informal and formal perspectives, but are also responsible for the decision making processes that occur. We assign these aspects of an actor to its metasystem, which houses the world views that give its behaviour meaning.

The actor has behaviour when viewed from the perspective of its suprasystem, but internally it has social, cultural and political processes. It also has an economy that facilitates organised behaviour. In this way economic aspects can also be seen as part of the organising process and related to the political aspects of an actor.

The decision making processes for the actor system are assigned to its metasystem. With respect to interactive processes, the metasystem aspects that we are interested in can be said to relate to:

1 policy making, and the *paradigm* and *weltanschauung* of policy makers;
2 the *classes* of decision that can be made;
3 the *types* of decision making systems that can be developed.

These characteristics represent cognitive actor models equivalent to a cognitive consciousness that can be tied to belief and attitude. The manifestation of these characteristics defines the events that occur in conflict situations.

6.3.3 The suprasystem

The work of Holsti (1967, p. 28) in international politics provides a useful definition of the nature of a suprasystem. It is any collection of autonomous actors such as individuals, enterprises, tribes, nations or empires. They interact with considerable frequency and according to regularised processes that define a coherent situation. The inquirer is concerned with the typical or characteristic behaviour of these actors towards each other and their general interactive (policy) orientations. Actor characteristics are represented by the types or classes of administrations that an actor develops, the role of individuals in the actor system's external relations, and the methods by which actor resources are mobilised to achieve external objectives.

While inquirers into the interactive activities have traditionally explained the behaviour of the actors in terms of actor attributes, needs or the individual characteristics of policy makers, the external environment and particularly the structure of power and influence in a suprasystem may have profound effects on the general orientations of an actor towards the other actors in a global holarchy. Thus the major characteristics of any suprasystem can be used as one set of variables to help explain the typical actions of an actor.

The intergroup focus occurs by examining the suprasystem. A suprasystem may be regulated, and for Holsti this means that (a) it has explicit or implicit rules or customs, major assumptions or values upon which relations are based and (b) techniques and institutions are used to resolve major conflicts between the political actors. If regulation is in force, it is because the suprasystem will have at least a transient or virtual supra-metasystem. This may occur because of the 'big brother syndrome' where a comparatively powerful actor imposes regulatory constraints on the other actors in the suprasystem, or, in the case of a peer group of actors, a set of rudimentary agreements that constrain suprasystem behaviour are established. The creation of the suprameta-system may be seen to be a political process that enables the formation of agreements that hold for the suprasystem.

6.4 The notions of actor stability and security

We are aware that systems are continually seeking dynamic stability. This is an internal process that relates to its achievement of goals, and which is determined within its control processes. Stability is threatened when environmental perturbations affect the system and it cannot respond in such a way as to enable it to maintain control of its own processes.

Another related concept is that of security. While stability is an endogenous internalised concept, security is an exogenous externalised one. It often refers to a responsive position of the system that is not expressed in terms of control, but rather resource, strength or power, and can be defined in terms of perceived threat to the preservation of identity. Thus an actor under resource constraint in an environment that requires investment to achieve goals may be in danger of losing security, or perceiving the loss of security. Issues of security can also be expressed in terms of power and power relationships within the suprasystem. The difference between security and stability can also be seen as a shift of focus. What constitutes security for each of the actors in a suprasystem is a matter of stability for the suprasystem itself. Actors within a conflict suprasystem have power relationships that are continually under change as actors in a suprasystem see:

- new events occurring
- actor behaviour changing
- suprasystem political controls reaching their threshold
- suprasystem power instabilities occurring
- security becoming threatened.

While security relates to perceived threat and the preservation of group identity, we should realise that it may not be a tangible thing, but rather like many other aspects of conflict processes is rather something that might well be explored through social psychology. The group psychology associated with conflict can be a significant aspect. This has been shown in the Vietnam war as public opinion forced the US Government to final submission, and is also typical of terrorist conflicts whether they occur in social-scale or smaller-scale situations. The role of the mass media in this respect is also an important consideration (Weimann, 1996).

The nature of security will change according to the nature of the dominant perceived threat, and the perceived vulnerability of the system. Vogler (1993), for instance, discusses the idea that security is currently being determined by environmental issues. This poses a threat that is as real as any military threat has been in the past. However, it would appear to be more complex because there are not just two actors unable to impose control one over the other, but many more. Thus, power relationships would now relate to the ability of nations to involve themselves in some form of environmental normalisation.

We have already indicated that power and resources are linked. Consider, for instance, a market suprasystem of competitive enterprises. An enterprise can be seen as an actor that has economic power. Its economic security and very survival in the face of competition will also depend upon how it uses that economic power in relation to other competitive enterprises in the market suprasystem. The market may in this case be interpreted as the source for its economic power, and this may be represented by its share of the market. If such a thing as a balance of power were to occur, it would represent the proportional market share of each participating actor.

It is possible to distinguish between belief about security and security itself. In a complex world in which there are many organs of communication the perception of endangered security can be more potent than the possibility of a real threat to security occurring. Organisational control groups have often used this idea in order to control the organisations that they are part of for their own purposes. Two examples of such action are given in Minicase 6.1 within larger-scale (nation state) social organisations, though such actions can also be applied to small organisations like enterprises.

Minicase 6.1

Security and belief
The case of Soviet–American security

In international politics over the past few decades there has been an ideologically derived threat between different spheres of political thought that has established a conflict suprasystem. This operated through the creation of power relationships between the United States and the Soviet Union intended to enable the security of each system to be maintained, and its individual identity to be preserved. When power relationships have developed such that the nations in the suprasystem could feel secure, then the term 'balance of power' has been used. This means that the participant nations *felt* that the suprasystem had power relationships that were in an equilibrium condition. Since this is predicated on the *feeling* of security, it is not predicated on whether an objective notion of security could be identified and pursued.

During this period the paradigm that was responsible for Soviet–American conflict had its own special and restricted propositional logic that defined the nature of security and power. However, an alternative paradigm also existed. It said that the stockpiling of nuclear weaponry must implicitly threaten the preservation and thus the security of the nations within the suprasystem by its very existence. This was never politically acknowledged by the Soviet Union or the United States. We may conclude that this was because both the USSR and the USA were locked into their conflict, and were unable to accept the value of the alternative paradigm. With the demise of the Soviet Union as an ideological threat to the United States, the conflict became dissipated. A new paradigm has now arisen that recognises the danger of nuclear stockpiles.

The case of perceived security and terrorism

According to Dobson and Payne (1977, p. 206), in the summer of 1914 in Sarajevo, Archduke Franz Ferdinand, the Hapsburg heir to the throne of the Austro-Hungarian Empire, was assassinated by Gavrilo Princip. At his trial he explained why he had done so, saying that: 'I am a Slav nationalist. My aim is the union of all south Slavs, under whatever political regime, and their liberation from Austria.'

In response to questions about how he would accomplish his political aim, he replied: 'By terrorism'. He had chosen this particular form of warfare to achieve his aim because, he believed, it was practical and effective. What he succeeded in doing was to detonate the explosive charges of nationalism under an entire continent and to provoke the beginning of the First World War (Ibid., p. 206).

In nature, terrorism is intended to sow fear and to make heroes out of murderers. In so doing, it is intended to convince opponents that the cause of terrorism is just and that the authorities are wrong. During the last two decades, there have been a few cases where such tactics have been successful.

In the 1920s the southern Irish won their independence by terrorism that was embedded within a much stronger war. Terrorism differs from guerrilla warfare. The latter is conducted by unconventional means but with real military aims and targets. The former, however, is indiscriminate in both, and is planned for public effect rather than satisfying military objectives. The Black and Tan counter-insurgency force that fought against the rebels in Ireland was effective and successful. The Irish leader, Michael Collins, said to a British Official at the peace negotiations that they were finished, and could not have lasted another three weeks. It is clear that the conduct of the authorities is important to terrorist situations. In the Irish case the repressive methods used caused such an outcry in a free society that it was they who finally appeared as the villains.

'We believe that what brought about the success of the Irish at that time was not so much terrorism itself, but a symptom induced by terrorism that we call *fatigism*. Public opinion grows tired of endless news about killings and bombings, and eventually comes to believe that the nation is faced with an insoluble problem, and that struggle does not justify the bloodshed' (Ibid., p. 208).

However, perhaps it is not so much 'public opinion' that drives fatigism, but more the dynamics of the mass media that is supposed to be representative of it. This can provide an overwhelming view of structurally critical situations that influences the perspectives of the actors involved. It is not only the notion of stability that is involved here, but also that of perceived security.

6.5 Systems and metasystems

Consider the relationship between the cognitive and behavioural domains illustrated in Fig. 2.6 and its relation, Fig. 2.7. The tri-domain model can also be applied to the relationship between weltanschauung and the paradigm. A shared weltanschauung exists at a deep domain while the paradigm exists as a surface domain (Fig. 6.3). In this light, a paradigm can be seen as a system of 'truths' that, through its manifested behaviour, results in a production of knowledge. Transmogrification is always a potentially homeomorphic transformational process (subject to surprises) of organising behaviour that, relatively speaking, results in a formalisation of the shared attributes of weltanschauung. This means that they will become visible to others who may not be viewholders. We have already said that weltanschauungen can be classed as being informal world views, while paradigms are formal. A world view becomes formalised when a language has developed that enables a set of explicit statements to be made about the beliefs and propositions (and their corollaries) of a shared weltanschauung that enables everything that must be expressed to be expressed in a self-consistent way.

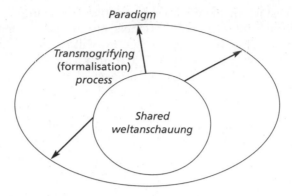

Fig. 6.3 Relationship between shared weltanschauung and paradigms

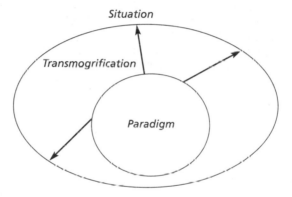

Fig. 6.4 Relationship between a paradigm and a coherent situation

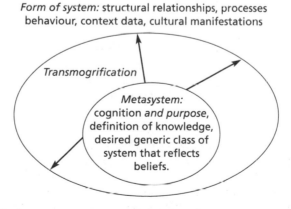

Fig. 6.5 Relationship between system and metasystem
(*Source*: Yolles, 1997)

Recursions of the model are possible. For example, a 'shared weltanschauung' is a result of the interaction of a number of individual weltanschauungen through transmogrification. Thus, each weltanschauung will be seen as an autonomous spar that extends deeper from the core of Fig. 6.3 to form a network. If these weltanschauungen are themselves seen as shared weltanschauungen that are each associated with smaller groups, then more recursions can occur to result in a complex web of weltanschauungen involving a number of focuses. The deepest focus is of course that of the individual.

We can also apply the knowledge domain model to the relationship between a paradigm and a situation, as illustrated in Fig. 6.4. We have said that if a shared weltanschauung becomes at least partly formalised through the development of language, then a paradigm (or virtual paradigm) will form. A paradigm is essential for the creation of a metasystem, which can be defined most easily as a system's metaphorical 'cognitive consciousness' (Yolles, 1996). While its role is important in the development of coherent groups, it is also important for coherent situations that occur when organisations arise and develop. Thus, for example, the cognitive consciousness of an organisation occurs through the strategic decisions made by senior management in an organisation.

Consider now an organisation seen as a system with a metasystem. The metasystem usually operates from a single dominant paradigm, but in some cases a plurality of dominant paradigms may be seen to coexist. If these are not balanced, then metasystemic schizophrenia is likely (we are adopting the original root meaning of the word schizophrenia – *schizo*, split and *phren*, mind – rather than the current clinical psychology meaning). The relationship between the metasystem and system is illustrated in Fig. 6.5. Recursive application of the generic domain model suggests that deeper metasystems exist, as explained through Fig. 6.1.

6.6 Metaholarchies

The idea of deep and surface knowledge provides an attractive representation of the way that systems operate. Deep knowledge is associated with cognitive organisation, and is world view based. Surface knowledge is seen as a manifestation of this, and is behavioural – being directly associated with the system structure. We can refer to this

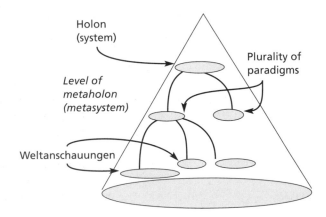

Fig. 6.6 Illustration of a metaholarchy

conceptualisation as the knowledge domain model. Within it the deep/surface model becomes a cognitive/behavioural or metasystem/system model.

The idea of there being a deep and surface domain is not absolute, however. It is recursive in that every deep domain may itself be seen as a surface domain with its own deep domain (*see* Minicase 6.2). In the same way that we have conceived of the idea of a holarchy, we can also conceive of a metaholarchy (Fig. 6.6); that is, a knowledge-based holarchy expressed in terms of world views, and associated with a given holon.

Minicase 6.2

Paradigms as bounded systems

Consider a paradigm as a bounded belief system that defines a framework of truths, which defines for a member of a group a frame of reference through which to view the world. The boundary of the paradigm will be determined by its properties, which distinguish it from, or make it similar to, other paradigms. From our earlier discussions, we are aware that these properties are expressed in terms of:

- conceptual extension
- the qualitative states of extensions
- the relationships that define paradigmatic truths.

The extensions are defined in terms of the concepts that result in a framework of logically consistent propositional truths. A qualitative state is a meaningful condition that can be assigned to a concept. The relationships define logical consistency within the framework of propositions. Extensions and qualities are identifiable in terms of the constraints that exclude other extensions and qualitative conditions, and this through constraint defines their boundaries. A paradigm's boundaries are ultimately, therefore, determined by constraint.

The idea that paradigms may be incommensurable now becomes a point of interest, where they cannot be compared or coordinated because of their differences in conceptual extension and qualitative state. Paradigm incommensurability can be expressed in terms of the degree of difference between two paradigms explored through their framework of propositions or sets of constraints. Alternatively, paradigm commensurability can be expressed in terms of the common or shared boundaries between them, and the similarity between their frameworks. The nature of the difference or similarity will be determined by an inquirer from a given world view, and this will affect the definition of this similarity or difference.

All organisations operate through their own paradigms. When two organisations wish to work together, then they do so by establishing a new virtual or transitory paradigm that entails shared conceptualisations that are common to each of the paradigms. When this occurs, it is essential that the qualitative states that are defined take on a similar meaning to both organisations, and that the logical relationships are well defined by both organisations.

In some cases of sudden change, like in company takeovers, a dominant paradigm is imposed upon another already existing paradigm. This results in conflict as the differences become suppressed, but do not die. The degree of conflict will be linked to the nature of the differences.

6.7 Domains of analysis during inquiry into situations

We are aware that the paradigms of an organisation entail cultural aspects that must be understood if we are to be able to appreciate the nature of the organisation, and what might work as an intervention. We shall refer to the cultural attributes that make up an organisation as its cultural domain that is centred in the metasystem. We can define two other domains, the social and the political, the former of which centres on the behavioural domain, and the latter on the transmogrific domain.

6.7.1 The social domain

The social domain of a situation defines structures and processes and makes up the nature of the system. It embeds the organisational aspects of the situation that have social connection. Checkland and Scholes (1990) refer to this as social system analysis, and it is seen to be concerned with *roles* and interactions within the situation under investigation. A *role* is a social position recognised as significant by people in the problem situation. It does not have to be a *formally* recognised position.

Social change is about how social structures and processes alter under the impact of environmental perturbations. It therefore affects, for example, role positions and processes, and group compositions and their associated processes and behaviours. While the structures of a social system enable actions and processes to occur, the actions and processes maintain the structures and their associated purposes. These purposes can often be seen in terms of the tasks of the system and the social issues that surround the mechanisms of production.

Purposes may also usefully be explored in terms of a distinction between superstructure and substructure as identified by Marx (Bottomore and Rubel, 1956). These can be distinguished in the following way.

1 *Substructure* defines the mode of production (e.g. craft or manufacturing) of an organisation including the means (technology) of production and the social relations that generated it. It can be related to the tasks of a system; that is, the identifiable activities and processes that are required to carry out the purposes of a situation. The resource or economic aspects that we associate with substructure can enable the development and maintenance of interactions between organisations.

2 *Superstructure*, to which all other aspects, such as institutional, political, religious and familial, relate. The normal occurrence of social change affects both individual experience and functional aspects of organisations. It can be related to the issues surrounding a problem situation that occur when events or conditions in the environment have no effect on the actors. These relate to the subsidiary activities that occur in a situation and are relevant to mental processes not embodied in formalised real-world situations. The superstructural aspect provides insights into the social context of interactions between organisations, particularly if the context of the interaction provides more definition for the interactive domain seen as a system; that is, a suprasystem.

While substructure relates to the *activity* of a purposeful actor system, superstructure relates to the frame of reference of the system, which in turn defines its boundaries. According to Marxian ideas, there is a dialectical relationship between substructure and superstructure that can be related to the relationship between the knowledge generated within a system and the manifested system itself that is its product (Berger and Luckman, 1966, p. 104 and p. 224). It is through the production of knowledge then, that frames of reference for systems and thus the systems themselves change.

Inquiry into the social systems of organisations in respect of, say, more efficient or effective production often leads us to having a primary interest in its substructure. However, the superstructure of the organisation is also of concern since this has an impact on such factors as performance.

6.7.2 The political domain

The view of politics adopted by Checkland and Scholes (1990, p. 50) relates to the work of Blondel (1978) and Crick (1962). For them, politics is taken to be a process by which differing interests reach accommodation through the dispositions of power.

Politics is concerned with power, elites and their membership, the manifestation and regulation of conflict, interest and political pressure groups, and the formation of stakeholder opinion. We can thus talk of the political structure of an organisation, in particular when we are interested in its political assignments.

Political structures exist through the distribution of power or authority, and are associated with social structures and the formal or informal role positions in an organisation. Blandier (1972) supposes that political power is seen in terms of the formal relations that express the *real* power relations between individuals. Thus, political structures, like social structures, can be seen as abstract systems that express the principles that make up concrete political organisations. However, these (dynamic) structures change over time through the development of incompatibilities, contradictions and tensions inherent in organisations.

Since politics is defined in terms of power, which is itself defined in terms of formal relations, we can adopt a view that politics centres the transmogrific domain that is involved in the manifest situation. It is concerned with facilitating the organising process that enables a system to become established, and it does this by distributing power to role positions that result in the making of judgements, dispensing of decisions, and in general facilitating formal action. Formal action is that action sanctioned by due process within the organisation.

More particularly, politics is concerned with causal relationships about behaviour that relates to 'having an organised *polity*'; that is, an organised 'condition of civil order; form, process, of civil government; organised society, state' (*Concise Oxford English Dictionary,* 1957). In its broadest terms, it is thus concerned with engineering the enablement of group form, condition of order and related processes.

Inquiry into the social aspects of political processes – that is, those processes that enable polity – is referred to as political sociology. This is the 'concrete political phenomena, influencing and influenced by the rest of the social structure and culture ... It treats political institutions, both formal or constitutional and informal, as parts of the social system, not self-subsistent but implicated in society. It concentrates attention to *elites* and their membership, on the manifestation and regulation of conflict, on interest groups and political pressure groups (which are often not self-aware) and formal pressure groups, on the formation of political opinion' (Mitchell, 1968, pp. 133–4).

Politics can also be related to the sociocultural attributes of organisations through the consideration of political ideology. This can be instrumental in defining (Holsti, 1967, p. 163):

1 an intellectual framework through which policy makers observe and interpret reality;

2 a politically correct ethical and moral orientation;

3 an image of the future that enables action through strategic policy;

4 stages of historical development in respect of interaction with the external environment.

When groups operate from a given paradigm they are often prone to particular orientations that (a) exclude other orientations and (b) predetermine ideology. When the groups operate in the political arena, this can be referred to as a political ideology. This can become a doctrine when it:

1 becomes a body of instruction about a specific set of beliefs which tends to explain reality;

2 prescribes goals for political action.

6.7.3 The cultural domain

The cultural domain is part of the metasystem and is concerned with paradigms. Cultural forms evolve and are transmitted as adaptive ways of making sense of shared existence. Culture changes through the importing of elements of a surrounding culture, and by internal innovations to meet new circumstances. In particular, in situations of conflict between groups, the cultural aspects can contribute to an understanding of the processes and motivations that cause or maintain it. Fundamental to this are the cognitive components that, together with elements of the social superstructure, can provide underlying explanations for conflict development and maintenance.

The basis for our view of culture comes from Kroeber and Kluckhohn (1952), and is also adhered to by Williams *et al.* (1993), who define it as follows:

> The explicit and implicit patterns of and for behaviour that are acquired and transmitted by symbols; this constitutes the distinctive achievement of human groups including their embodiment and artefacts. Its essential core consists of traditional ideas, and especially their attached values. It may be considered as both a product of action, and a conditioning element for action.

In Chapter 2 we considered the ideas of Rokeach concerning beliefs. He suggested that beliefs have three components: (a) cognitive, representing cognitive knowledge, (b) behavioural, since the consequence of a belief is action, and (c) affective, since a belief can arouse an affect centred around an object. It represents a deep/surface model that has been extended to paradigm-based culture, which is belief based. Following Nicholson (1993, p. 209) (referring to Pettigrew (1979) and Frost *et al.* (1985)), we can distinguish between *deep*, *surface* and *preconscious* components of culture:

1 *deep culture*: world views, basic assumptions and cognitive systems;

2 *surface culture*: values, rituals, myths, customs and forms of expression;

3 *preconscious culture*: ideology, symbols and norms.

Deep aspects of culture are paradigmatic, and thus relate to meaning, cognitive purpose and beliefs. The surface aspects represent *manifestations* of culture (Williams *et al.*, 1993, p. 14) which change as one moves from one cultural group to another. Examples of beliefs are *myths*, which are (Cohen, 1969, p. 337) erroneous beliefs clung to against evidence, which offer legitimacy for social practices, and which sustain values that underlie political interests. *Myth*, according to Pettigrew (1979), is often thought of as false belief, though it plays a crucial role in the continuous process of establishing and maintaining what is defined as legitimate and what is labelled unacceptable in a culture. An example of manifestations is *ritual* (Pettigrew, 1979). This is sometimes understood to be merely sequences of activity devoid of meaning to the actors in the ritual; it provides a shared experience of belonging and expresses what is valued.

The third category of culture, the *preconscious*, is the backcloth for the organising of beliefs and attitudes and their expression. The idea of the preconscious comes from the work of Freud (Hadfield, 1954, p. 23) in connection, for example, with the mechanism of dreams. In this work, the dream is seen as being used to try to express wishes of the unconscious that are incompatible with the self. They must therefore be transformed into a form approved by the self. This approval mechanism is primarily the work of the preconscious, which lies between the conscious and the unconscious. The unconscious, according to both Freud and Jung, 'consists of instinctual and other forces that have either been repressed or have never yet emerged into consciousness' (Hadfield, 1954, p. 116).

The preconscious class of culture, according to Nicholson, consists of *ideology*, *symbols* and *norms*. Ideology is 'an *organisation* of beliefs and attitudes ... that is more or less institutionalised or shared with others' (Rokeach, 1968, p. 123). This organisation of beliefs and attitudes may be religious, political or philosophical in nature, and it provides a total system of thought, emotion and attitude to the world. It refers to any conception of the world that goes beyond the ability of formal validation. Preconsciousness is also concerned with *symbols*; that is, arbitrary signs or emblems that are a representation of the beliefs of a group (Levi-Strauss, 1969). They are (Cohen, 1974, p. 23) objects, acts, relationships or linguistic formations that stand ambiguously for a multiplicity of meanings, evoke emotions and impel individuals to action. According to Pettigrew (1979, p. 574) symbol construction serves as a vehicle for group and organisational construction. The development process of a group or organisation involves a creation of structured images of itself and the outside world to which it attaches names, values and purpose. Symbols arise out of these processes, which include vocabulary, beliefs about the use and distribution of power and privilege, and rituals and myths that legitimate these distributions.

We are aware that the idea of the preconscious implies cognitive attribute, and suggests a hidden active process that operates from a deep cultural level. It contributes to active organising through the creation of cognitive and emotional constraints, and is thus involved in a transformational (or transmogrific) connection between cognition and behaviour. All human actor systems are constrained by cultural factors like ideology and norms that determine the bounds within which things can be done. We may note that these are bounds that also constrain inquiry processes, as they do in the synthesising of models (during an inquiry) intended to address a problem situation.

At this point it is useful to reconsider Nicholson's categorisation of surface aspects of a culture to include *values*. According to Rokeach, 'values are a type of belief, centrally located in one's belief system, about how one ought or ought not to behave, or about some end-state of existence worth or not worth attaining. Values are thus abstract ideals, positive or negative, not tied to any specific object or situation, representing a person's beliefs about ideal modes of conduct and ideal terminal goals' (Rokeach, 1968, p. 124). Since *values* are a type of *belief*, we should consider that they are part of the deep cognitive domain rather than the surface behavioural features, a view apparently not consistent with Nicholson's classification. This would seem to be supported by Rokeach, who considers beliefs, values and attitudes to be defined as cognitive organisation, and thus part of the cognitive system.

We are aware that culture changes with beliefs. Thus, while cultural forms evolve and are transmitted as adaptive ways of making sense of shared existence, changes occur through the importing of elements of a surrounding culture, and by internal innovations to meet new circumstances (Nicholson, 1993).

Large-scale cultures

Many social environments can be described in terms of a plurality of coexisting cultures. These can be differentiated through the creation of some generic emergent characteristics that have been provided by Sorokin (1937) through his research on large-scale cultures, and that Toynby has referred to as civilisations. His ideas, however, also have relevance to small-scale organisational cultures. Sorokin produced a theory of social and cultural change that explains how, through the definition of two cultural conditions, different patterns of culturally based behaviour can develop. The two cultural conditions identified are referred to as *sensate* and *ideational*. Sensate culture is to do with the senses, and can be seen to be utilitarian and materialistic. Ideational culture relates to ideas; an example might be the adherence to, say, spirituality. Every culture can be described in terms of its ideational and sensate content, and it provides the basis for the possible durable world views that are able to emerge.

When a culture has a balanced content of ideational and sensate cultural attributes, it is said to be *idealistic*. It is likely, however, that one cultural state predominates. During the early part of the industrial revolution, Western society was seen to have had a balanced mix of both sensate and ideational cultural states. Today it is seen as passing through a predominantly sensate state. The norms and belief system current to a culture will be broadly determined by its mix of sensate and ideational attributes. This will be reflected in turn by the way it responds to the views and behaviour of individuals or groups. It would be tempting to try to explore the ideas of Sorokin to changing culture through the normative approach taken in Minicase 4.3 in order to see if we could validate the reasonableness of his theories.

Postulating the existence of cultural personalities

It is tempting to elaborate on Sorokin's work by postulating that individuals have cultural personalities defined by a mindset of sensate/ideational attributes (Kemp, 1997; Yolles and Kaluza, 1997). We propose that the mindset of sensate people enables them to see the real world in terms of governing controls and constraints. Sensate people count the cost of invention and innovation, and disallow it if there is a danger that their arbitrarily defined constraints are exceeded. In so doing the possibilities that can be made available within our organisations are diminished. They destroy variety. Sensate policies provide an *apparently* safe environment because people actually believe that the constraints have some meaning.

Contrary to this, ideationists view the world through ideas. Kemp (personal communication, 1996) suggests that this relates to the *creation* of ideas rather than the idea itself. Ideationalists are unable to apply to the ideas created the practical or material governing controls necessary to manifest them as behavioural aspects of the system. People with a predominantly ideational mindset generate possibilities through the pursuit and maturation of a variety of ideas, though they tend not to know how to use them materially. They thus create variety, but they cannot harness and apply it.

The Western industrial revolution was built on a sensate–ideational mix that Sorokin referred to as *idealistic* culture, and that has enabled technological and commercial domination to occur. However, there is a view that ideational aspects of Western culture have now withered. This domination is being handed over to the Pacific Rim countries as their sensate–ideational leaders generate work opportunities. Thus, while Japan once had a reputation for copying products, it may now be more innovative than the Western non-Pacific Rim countries (Tatsuno, 1986). With this shift in culture the West finds itself in decline (Kemp and Yolles, 1992), as it reduces opportunity and imposes more constraints on its populations as a way of dealing with uncertainty. It is a curious time, which Ionescu (1975) identifies as operating centripetal politics, when corporate organisations accumulate power and make unrepresentative decisions in the stead of governments. This process is seen as a result of the industrial–technical revolution that we have passed through, and the resulting ineffectiveness of self-government is aggravated by a futile pursuit of autonomy in a highly interactive and interdependent environment.

Political states tends to change over the decades, while cultural states do so over very much longer time spans. Thus, for instance, the shift from mainstream Socialism to more ardent Conservative forms of political perspective has perhaps taken about 30 years, while the shift that some would argue has occurred from an idealist to sensate state of culture in the West has probably taken about ten times as long. This is because culture is handed on across generations while political perspective changes with shifts in opportunity.

Our cultural backcloth defines how able our corporate bodies are to respond to the surprises that our environment generates. If it is the case that Western culture is now predominantly sensate, it will therefore not validate mixed sensate–ideational thinking. It therefore accepts variety limitation that, during the recurrent periods of instability that we face, destroys variety generation and thus endangers our viability as a single cultural group with a single identity.

SUMMARY

A system can only exist because it has a boundary that differentiates it from other systems. The nature of that boundary may vary according to who sees and defines it. The boundary may better be seen as a frame of reference that is associated with the purposes that an inquirer has in defining that boundary.

Every actor system has associated with it a metasystem that can be seen as the system's 'cognitive consciousness'. It operates with a cultural perspective that derives from the dominant paradigm associated with system behaviour. System behaviour itself can be defined in terms of social structures and processes that can be seen as manifestations of the metasystem. These manifestations occur through a transformation process that we refer to as transmogrification, since the transformations may be subject to (chaotic) surprises. Consequently, the system and its associated metasystem can be explored totally in terms of the social, cultural and political characteristics.

Holons are 'whole' autonomous systems that exist as local focuses in a holarchy. The holarchy is itself a network of holons that interact with each other. Actor systems are a type of holon that we refer to as actors. An actor is a local focus in a holarchy. When a set of actors interact together in a suprasystem, then we refer to this as a regional focus of the holarchy. A global focus for the holarchy is the holarchy seen in a totality with all of its perceived focuses, which may itself be an actor in a suprasystem.

REFERENCES

Beer, S. (1959) *Cybernetics and Management*. London: English Universities Press.

Beer, S. (1975) *Platform for Change*. Chichester: Wiley.

Beer, S. (1979) *The Heart of Enterprise*. Chichester: Wiley.

Berger, P. and Luckman, T. (1966) *The Social Construction of Reality*. Harmondsworth: Penguin.

Blandier, G. (1972) *Political Anthropology*. Harmondsworth: Penguin.

Blondel, J. (1978) *Thinking Politically*. Harmondsworth: Pelican.

Bottomore, T.B. and Rubel, M. (1956) *Karl Marx: Selected writings in sociology and social philosophy*. London: Watts and Co.

Checkland, P.B. and Scholes, J. (1990) *Soft Systems Methodology in Action*. Chichester: Wiley.

Cohen, A. (1974) *Two Dimensional Man: An essay on the anthropology of power and symbolism in complex society*. London: Routledge & Kegan Paul.

Cohen, P.S. (1969) 'Theories of myth'. *Man* (new series), 4, 337–53.

Cornblis, O. (1971) 'Political coalitions and particular behaviour: a simulation model'. In Laponce, J.A. and Smoker, P. (eds) *Experimentation and Simulation in Political Science*. Toronto: University of Toronto Press.

Crick, B. (1962) *In Defence of Politics*. London: Weidenfeld and Nicolson.

Dobson, C. and Payne, R. (1977) *The Carlos Complex: A pattern of violence*. London: Book Club Associates.

Espejo, R. and Schwaninger, M. (1993) *Organisational Fitness: Corporate effectiveness through management cybernetics*. Frankfurt: Campus Verlag.

Flood, R.L. and Jackson, M.C. (1991) *Creative Problem Solving: Total systems intervention*. Chichester: Wiley.

Frost, P.J., Moore, L.F., Louis, M.R., Lundberg, C.C. and Martin, J. (eds) (1985) *Organisational Culture*. Beverly Hills, CA: Sage.

Hadfield, J.A. (1954) *Dreams and Nightmares*. Harmondsworth: Pelican.

Holsti, K.J. (1967) *International Politics: A framework for analysis*. Englewood Cliffs, NJ: Prentice Hall.

Kemp, G. (1997) 'Cultural implicit conflict: a re-examination of Sorokin's socio-cultural dynamics', *Journal of Conflict Processes*, 3(1), 15–24.

Kemp, G. and Yolles, M. (1992) 'Conflict through the rise of European culturalism', *Journal of Conflict Processes*, 1(1).

Kroeber, A.L. and Kluckhohn, C. (1952) 'Culture: a critical review of concepts and definitions', *Papers of the Peabody Museum of American Archaeology and Ethnology*, 47, 1.

Ionescu, G. (1975) *Centripetal Politics*. London: Hart-Davis, MacGibbon.

Levi-Strauss, C. (1969) *Totenism*. Harmondsworth: Penguin.

Minai, A.T. (1995) 'Emergence, a domain where the distinction between conception in arts and sciences is meaningless', *Cybernetics and Human Knowing*, 3(3), 25–51.

Mitchell, G.D. (1968) *A Dictionary of Sociology*. London: Routledge & Kegan Paul.

Nicholson, M. (1993) 'Organisational change'. In Mabey, C. and Mayon-White, B. (eds) *Managing Change*. London: Paul Chapman Publishing, pp. 207–11.

Pettigrew, A.M. (1979) 'On studying organisational cultures', *Administrative Science Quarterly*, 24, 570–81.

Rokeach, M. (1968) *Beliefs, Attitudes, and Values: A theory of organisational change*. San Francisco, CA: Jossey-Bass.

Sorokin, P.A. (1937) *Social and Cultural Dynamics.* New York: American Book Company.

Tatsuno, S. (1986) *The Technopolis Strategy.* New York: Prentice Hall.

van der Leeuw, S.E. (1981) 'Information flows, flow structures and the explanation of change in human institutions'. In *Archaeological Approaches to the Study of Complexity.* Amsterdam University.

van Gigch, J.P. (1987) *Decision Making about Decision Making.* Tunbridge Wells: Abacus.

Vogler, J. (1993) 'Security and global environment', *Journal of Conflict Processes,* 1(2), 16–24.

Weimann, G. (1996) 'Can the media mediate? Mass-mediated diplomacy in the Middle East', *Journal of Conflict Processes,* 2(1), 43–53.

Williams, A., Dobson, P. and Walters, M. (1993) *Organisational Culture: New organisational approaches.* London: IPM.

Yolles, M.I. (1996) 'Critical systems thinking, paradigms, and the modelling space', *Systems Practice,* 9(3).

Yolles, M.I. and Kaluza, J. (1997) 'Manifesting conflict from paradigm incommensurability', *Journal of Conflict Processes,* 3(1), 25–42.

CHAPTER 7

Viability and change in systems

OVERVIEW

Viable systems are complex actor systems that have a form and behaviour, a metasystem and a transformational process that links the two. Actor systems are autonomous, have the property of viability, and are able to survive under change through adaptation. Viable system theory centres on the ability of viable actor systems to maintain their stability through processes of self-actuation like self-regulation and self-organisation. Actor systems may change in different ways, and the degree of change possible is an indicator of their plasticity.

OBJECTIVES

This chapter will examine:

- the relationship between the form and behaviour of an actor system;
- the relationship between an actor system and its metasystem;
- how form and behaviour of the system relate;
- the dual nature of identity in an actor system;
- the nature of self-actuation.

7.1 Viable systems

In Chapter 5 we said that in general we will talk of purposeful adaptive activity systems in the abstract, while in the particular they can be practically referred to through a range of world views from the hard to the soft. Purposeful adaptive activity systems can also be examined in terms of their viability – that is, examined with respect to their survivability in situations of change. When we generally refer to systems as being viable, the term viable system is being used in the abstract. However, when exploring the particular survivability of a system, we will be referring to a definable systemic metaphor for the given situation being inquired into. Whether a soft or hard perspective is taken is primarily of practical interest. Viability, like hardness, structure and uncertainty (as discussed in Chapter 4), is an analytically and empirically independent dimension of consideration. All of these are facets of a picture that provides an abstract way of talking about complexity, and a practical way of dealing with it.

The notion of viability is to do with the ability of a system to maintain its existence, and as we shall see in due course this is integrally connected to the model that practically links its behaviour with its 'cognition' and culture. Equivalently we may say that it is dependent on the particularly defined relationship between the system and its metasystem. Thus, for example, it is a matter of inquirer commitment whether one sees the metasystem in terms of decision processes devoid of individual participation, or in terms of the people who make or take the decisions. The same is true for the way that a system and its dynamic processes are examined. In either case the world view of the situation will reflect how complex the situation is seen to be.

The nature of viable systems is that they are able to maintain an autonomous (separate) existence, and can be referred to as actor systems. They have a form that facilitates behaviour, and a metasystem that is responsible for the manifestation of that form.

Viable systems participate in the development of their own futures through self. They are therefore self-organising and adaptive. The idea of viability implies that the system must be able to maintain stability under conditions of change. Central to this is the viable system's ability to adapt to perturbations from its environment.

The theory of viable systems derives from general systems theory, which early on was equilibrium based. For instance, Ashby (1961) defined the concept of adaptability as follows: when a system is perturbed away from its equilibrium, it undergoes change through adaptation as its form passes through discrete sequential steps to new equilibria. Jantsch (1980) explains that the idea of stepwise adaptation through the establishment of new discrete equilibria is inadequate since it does not represent the usual evolutionary processes that occur, a consideration that we will explore further in Chapter 8.

A more appropriate way of explaining adaptation is through the idea of dynamic equilibrium, where a system that is changing is seen to do so in order to regain its balance with its environment, which it is being distinguished from. The concept of dynamic equilibrium can quite nicely be explained in terms of the idea of *variety*. The environment creates variety that perturbs the system, which may be seen as the manifestation of environmental states not previously encountered by the system. The system now generates responsive variety. The proposition of dynamic equilibrium is that the viable system will only seek a *requisite variety* that brings balance in the relationship between the viable system and its environment. Once balance has been achieved stability can be regained. The new stability will in general coincide with behavioural changes for the system that have occurred through morphogenesis.

It may be seen that the idea of dynamic equilibrium is not a necessary constraint on the system's response to the environment. It does not, for instance, explain responses that to another inquirer might be considered to be totally unexpected or 'out of context'. Explanations for system behaviour can also occur through the concepts of far-from-equilibrium so that we can link balance with evolution, and we shall consider these further in Chapter 8.

7.2 System form and behaviour

Any organised thing can be said to have *form*. This idea of form was considered by Plato as a representation of reality that will never actually be that reality. Reality, seen as an absolute, may be approached but not reached. Since the time of Aristotle form has been perceived as something that can be studied in the abstract through symbolic representation. The concept of form has played a part in all mathematical logic since then (Körner, 1960). According to Lee (1961, p. 13), form is taken to be an organisation of parts, to have pattern, structure and relationship, and is a general abstraction deriving from situations. Current common usage of the word form is an arrangement of parts, visible aspect, shape of body, conditions of the thing's existence (Baconian), the formative principles holding together the elements of the thing (Kantian), the mode in which the thing exists or by which it manifests itself. The study of form has become a branch of mathematical logic. A brief introduction to the logic of form can be found in Mingers (1995), where he refers to the work of Spenser Brown (1972). For our purpose we define the form of a system as follows. It:

1 comprises a set of parts definable by an inquirer to have a perceivable and purposeful relationship between them to create a *structure*, which enables desirable processes;

2 involves a set of *actions* or *processes* that operate in connection with the structure, and which maintain it dynamically through some 'formative principle' of the system;

3 has an *orientation* defined by a set of cognitive purposes, a *mode* that includes for instance its myths, rituals and customs, and *conditions* that enable behaviour organising to occur;

4 responds to the environmental *perturbation* in a way that is structure determined.

From points 1 and 2 we see that the form of a system is determined by the structural relationships that exist between its parts. The actions, processes or communications that relate to these parts enable the structure to be maintained. From point 3 we see that a system also has an *orientation* that will be determined by bringing it into clearly understood relations with respect to its external environment, and is derived from its cognitive purposes that come from the metasystem. The orientation will thus be influenced by the primary purpose of the system, the *conditions* under which it is enabled to operate, a *mode*, and *conditions* that derive from the cognitive knowledge of the metasystem that will be required for behaviour organising to operate. It can be responsible, for instance, for the identification of criteria that enable homeostasis to operate. Finally, from point 4 we are led to appreciate that a system will respond to changes that perturb it according to its own abilities of adaptation that are determined implicitly by its structure. The *condition* of a system is defined by the *circumstances* essential to its existence, though this may not always be known and cannot always be modelled. The *mode* of a system is culture determined, and is the manner in which it manifests its existence that defines the way in which it operates.

The parts of a situation each have a boundary that is capable of defining purpose. They can be related together *structurally*. The *orientation* of a system is derived from its cognitive purposes, which come from the metasystem. The formative principle of a system has *actions* or *processes* that enable it to retain that form and thus maintain structure. This formative principle may be described in terms of the assumptions and logic of a metasystem.

There is clearly a relationship between the concepts of form, organisation and structure. Suppose that we consider that an organisation has a set of roles with known relationships that determine structure. The actions or processes that enable the structure to be retained are the internal operational procedures of the organisation, which are a property of each role. The mode of these operational procedures will be directly related to the culture of the organisation.

The form of a viable system determines how it will behave within its environment. Behaviour is thus the response of the system to events that affect it. These responses are the manifest actions applied to the environment by the system. Since the behaviour and form of the organisation are linked, change in one is linked to the other. Noting the nature of the form of a system, we can say that:

- form determines *system behaviour*;
- the behaviour of a system is represented by the way in which it *responds* to its environment;
- a system responds to its environment through its *behavioural qualities* endowed by its structure.

When the steady state behaviour of a system changes coherently over time or social space, it shows a pattern of behaviour. These may change, and so the nature of the stabilities can change over both social space and time. If the nature of stability changes over time then we refer to it as *dynamic stability*. Weinberg (1975, p. 251) tells us through his *Law of Effect* that small changes in structure *usually* lead to small changes in behaviour. By *usually* we can understand the condition of dynamic stability. It is important, however, to realise that in connection with self-organisation in viable actor systems, our interest should be to encompass far-from-equilibrium situations that are implicitly unstable.

7.3 Actors as complex, adaptive and viable systems

Actor systems are complex, adaptive and thus implicitly viable. The idea of adaptation provides an explanation for the way in which systems change their form while maintaining a dynamic behavioural stability. A system is adaptive when it experiences a qualitative change in form at some level of consideration, and this is accompanied by a change in the patterns of its behaviour.

Consistent with the ideas of Fig. 6.2, but at a lower focus, we can think of an actor system not as a set of interactive *parts*, but rather as a set of interactive autonomous actor subsystems (or subactors) in an adaptive network. The subactors are arranged in intricate complicated networks so interconnected as to create a unity or organic whole with demonstrated capabilities to adjust behaviour to changing circumstances and to anticipate future events (*see* Wheelan, 1996, p. 57).

In other words, autonomous subactors in a network can create a global structure that is itself an autonomous actor system. Shifting focus and thus terminology, this is also saying that a set of actors interact not only with each other, but also with the suprasystem that they create. This is possible because the complexity of individual interactions generates patterns of behaviour that enable it to be seen as an autonomous actor system itself. These patterns are simpler than the complexity of interactions, and may be seen in terms of a relatively simple set of conceptualisations. They may also be expressed in terms of emergent properties of the suprasystem.

As an illustration of this explanation, consider a group of people who together form an actor suprasystem. The group is composed of autonomous individual actors in interaction. According to the work of people like Tuckman, all groups pass through a similar process of change that creates a global pattern. It is defined in terms of four stages (Wheelan, 1996, p. 61):

1 dependency
2 counterdependency and fight
3 trust and structure
4 work.

The pattern is dynamic, and changes for different groups according to their size or world-view make up. Thus, there will be variation across groups in the duration of each stage that they pass through, or the degree of intensity of each stage (e.g. more dependency or more conflict).

7.4 The metasystem and transmogrification

One of the fundamental features of a viable actor system is that it possesses a metasystem that is world-view based, and will determine the nature of the actor system. We can model coherent situations as though they are holarchies with different focuses, each focus having the possibility of a metasystem.

The metasystem operates through a cognitive model that defines its beliefs, knowledge and assumptions. It enables the creation of two types of identity that label *self*: (i) an *individual identity* enables system differentiation to occur, and is unitary since it is unique to a given actor system, and (ii) a *generic* identity that is pluralistic because it is shared with a number of other individual actor systems, and that it provides with a qualitative description, enabling it to be placed in a conceptual *class* that will provide a general expectation about its behavioural possibilities. It is thus to the metasystem that we must look if we wish to understand an organisation. Since all metasystems are world-view based, the holarchy may be populated by many paradigms that (a) operate individually across different parallel foci and (b) populate a single focus. In both cases there is a need to communicate across paradigms, and this can explain the conflictual and change processes that occur internally in an organisation.

The relationship between the actor system and its metasystem occurs through transmogrification, which operates as a behaviour organising process. Let us define a transmogrific domain as a field potential in which all behaviour organising processes are possible. We refer to it as *transmogrification* because the form of the actor system that becomes manifest may not be that which is expected or intended by the metasystem. Surprises can occur in particular when the system is seen as complex, implicitly unstable and structurally critical. It is in this case that perturbations can affect the domain of transmogrification such that the system manifestations that develop are unexpected.

Through behaviour organising, transmogrification can be defined to create and maintain:

- an *orderly structure* that occurs if the parts of a whole can be seen to have a relationship that has a meaning for the perceiver;
- a *working order* involving processes that enable purposes to be identified;
- an *organic* nature, defining a set of parts that comprise the whole and are coordinated within it.

Transmogrification will, through a process of organising, *usually* create or enable the maintenance of a system in accordance with the predetermined needs of the metasystem. The nature of the organising process will derive from its propositional logic, which identifies the way in which those involved in the metasystem think. Within transmogrification an arrangement of *processes* at one or more focuses of the system will occur. Each *process* is represented by a set of *activities* (each an application of effort) that causes a change or transformation of something within the system.

7.5 Viable systems and closure

We remind ourselves that the actor systems that we are interested in are conceived to form part of a holarchy that operates across a variety of focuses. In any analysis of a situation modelled as a holarchy, a number of coincident focuses will be considered at any one time. In the viable systems approach, each focus modelled by an inquirer is normally thought of in principle to be a unitary or plurality of autonomous systems. Now, active organising in autonomous systems involves self-actuation. This defines a set of boundaries against the environment that closes the system in respect of the particular actuation. The notion of self-actuation thus enables us to distinguish between a variety of dimensions of closure. This is consistent with the idea of Luhmann (1986), who identified that the main contribution of the notion that systems may be self-producing (a type of self-actuation) is that they can be seen as (recursively) closed.

We can identify a number of different dimensions of closure (based on Mingers, 1995, p. 83) that may be attributable to viable systems, each of which represents a characteristic of self-actuation, as shown in Table 7.1. We shall explore some of these in what follows.

7.6 Homeostasis in viable systems

Fundamental to viable systems is the idea that they involve self-regulatory processes. In cybernetic systems, homeostasis is used in order to explain how control and thus self-regulation of a process occurs. For example, the amount of water a horse will drink will normally be dependent upon the quality of its thirst. Self-regulation will ensure that the horse drinks no more than satisfies its thirst (providing of course that it is an uncomplicated, rational well-balanced horse that does not drink water for other reasons).

Table 7.1 Characteristics of self-actuation that define the possibilities of viable system closure

Characteristic of self-actuation	Explanation
Self-influencing	Circular causality and causal loops – patterns of causation or influence that become circular, such as large populations producing more offsprings.
Self-regulating	Maintenance of a particular variable – organised so as to keep essential variables within definable limits. It relies on negative feedback and specified limits.
Self-organising	The self-amplification of fluctuations generated in the system as a consequence of perturbations from the environment.
Self-sustaining	Self-sustaining operations are organisationally closed – when all possible states of activity must always lead to or generate further activity within itself. Once an organisationally closed process is started, it is self sustaining.
Self-producing	Autopoietic systems self-produce both their components and their boundary.
Self-referential	Symbolic reference to the self. These systems refer to themselves in terms of themselves or their components through image, expressed symbolically.
Self-conscious	Able to interact with descriptions of self.

The idea of homeostasis originates with Canon in 1937, and can be defined as follows:

> Those processes through which the material or energy of a system is maintained within predefined bounds. This occurs through feedback regulation that occurs such that the outputs from a process are monitored, and information about it is fed back to the input. This regulates the process through its stabilisation or direction action of the process (von Bertalanffy, 1973, p. 78).

Homeostasis is normally represented as a control loop, and involves a process that has inputs and outputs, an output monitor, a set of measures that relate to behavioural performance, a comparator against which standards, norms or goals can be compared, and an actuator that can take action to regulate the process. The monitor, comparator and actuator are active organisational processes that occur within transmogrification. The standards or norms and concepts that result in measures of behavioural performance are paradigm dependent. This is illustrated in Fig. 7.1 (on p. 144).

The components of the control loop can be expressed in terms of the systemic, meta-systemic and transmogrific domains. The components of the control loop are explained in Table 7.2.

Table 7.2 Characteristics of control

Characteristics	Nature of control characteristics
Input	In order to model it is essential to generate input information and materials about a situation. For instance, input information about the form of a situation and its cultural attributes are necessary in order for models to be built.
Process	The process is one which transforms something. In the case of model building, the input information is conceptually transformed into models.
Output	The output is the result of the process. In the case of a modelling process, a model or set of models is the output that can be used to represent and intervene in a situation.
Monitor	The monitor examines the model in the light of the output evaluations which explain it.
Output information	How the outputs are seen is dependent upon their contextual information. If the process is one of modelling, then the output is a set of models, and the model information will indicate the modelling context. Thus in a relatively hard situation, output evaluations may be facts and data, while in soft situations they may be qualitative evaluations of form determined by an inquirer in consultation with the participants of a situation. Sometimes output information is thought of as measures of performance. The need then is to determine measures that are representative indications of the output.
Real-world reference criteria	By the real world is meant a view of the reality of a situation. It is from this view that criteria of reference are obtained that can be used against which to make a comparison. The nature of reality will change according to the context of the situation being examined. For instance, a hard situation will normally require a reality that is defined paradigmatically by the group of inquirers. However, in a soft situation it may be considered that the paradigm belongs to the situation rather than to the inquirers. The nature of reality may also be seen to be a normative view. In this case reality is seen in terms of the norms that have been observed in the situation. They may be social and cultural norms, behavioural norms or standards. It is a normative view since the norms may be seen differently by different inquirers and participants of the situation under investigation. In some instances organisations may possess a number of conflicting norms that correspond to different minority groups, and it is important to know which group paradigm is being referred to.
Comparator	The comparator enables comparison between the output and the reality of a situation. The nature of this reality will be dependent upon the context of the inquiry and the way in which reality is perceived. Reality and the output are compared in the comparator, which enables an inquirer to perceive a deviation of the model from reality.
Actuator	The output can be adjusted by counteracting or amplifying the deviations through the actuator. Deviation–counteraction operates as a process that generates stability in the modelling process, which involves learning about a situation and adjusting the models in an appropriate way. In this case we can also talk of dynamic modelling processes.

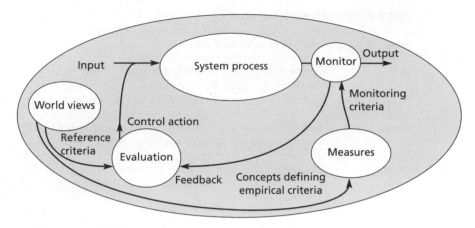

Fig. 7.1 Basic form of the control model

7.7 The nature of feedback

Control processes are normally thought of in terms of negative feedback. However, positive feedback can also be responsible for changes in the process. Negative feedback enables *deviation* of a processes to be *counteracted* so that predefined control criteria are maintained. These criteria can be seen as a set of control bounds that define *a threshold of stability*. If deviation is such that the bounds have been reached within the process, then the system is at the threshold of stability. Negative feedback is seen as a regulation process. When it is determined by the system itself, it is referred to as *self-regulation*. Successful regulation may be seen as a property of *robust* systems. To understand this term, if we see a system to be composed of a set of parts, then we would argue that a robust system as a whole is not vulnerable to changes in those parts. Referring to Thompson (1996, p. 152), we can distinguish between time- and structure-related dependencies within robust systems. We now say that a robust system has a frame of reference that enables changes in one part to be compensatable by those in another part to the homeostatic limits of the system. Dynamic systems may be robust in time or structure when vulnerability is minimised for time or structural perturbations. This means that as a whole either (a) the system has reduced sensitivity to any fluctuations in the parts, (b) the fluctuations are dampened down homeostatically or (c) the fluctuations compensate for any fluctuations by changes in other parts. Robust systems do not change their form, seek equilibrium conditions, and fail when they experience perturbations that take them beyond their homeostatic capabilities.

Positive feedback *amplifies* the *deviation* of system processes. This is a property of a system that is structurally critical, and results in a qualitative change in the form of the system, referred to as morphogenesis. As a consequence, the amplification of a 'successful' deviation is a continuing morphogenic process of evolution.

Let us consider an example of negative feedback. A bank informs an enterprise to which it is making loans that it will continue to service its needs only if long-term expenditure does not exceed long-term income. If by a given date expenditures continue to exceed income, then the control bounds will have been exceeded and the bank will refuse to continue to participate. The criteria for regulation are defined by the enterprise in conjunction with discussions with the bank. If the regulatory process of counteracting deviations to the agreement is carried out by the company, then self-regulation is occurring. However, consider that after repeated failures the bank loses confidence in the company's ability to self-regulate itself, then it may insist that external regulators are brought in to take charge of the enterprise debt.

As long as the metasystem and the system maintain their connection, qualitative change in form occurs through the metasystem, from which there is a consequential impact on the system. Let us look further at the possibilities open to the enterprise. The financial circumstances of the enterprise are traced to problems in a number of departments, which are unable to balance their budgets through their control processes. The reason, it is found, is that the financial structure of the departments is such that staff are not financially accountable. Senior management together with the manager of the worst offending department decide that the only way to resolve the problem is to introduce a new financial structure and associated processes to make staff accountable. After a year of trial, the change is so successful that it is copied in other departments with similar results. To do this the enterprise has passed through a cognitive learning process in which the metasystem has changed. Pringle (1968) explores the argument that cognitive learning is an evolutionary purpose that, like all types of positive feedback, increases complexity. After examining six types of learning originally identified by Thorp in 1950, he comes to the conclusion that learning can be considered to be a result of deviation–amplification.

In homeostasis it is necessary to have determinable *inputs* and *outputs*. The outputs must be meaningfully *monitorable*, and measures of performance must be definable and determinable. Information about the monitorable outputs can be used to define *measures of performance*. An *actuator* is well determined and it can act on the system *predictably* (so that input and output *relationships* must be known). *Standards*, *norms* and *objectives* that must be determinable and set against monitored outputs form *comparison*. From this we are able to differentiate between simple and complex homeostatic systems, as shown in Table 7.3.

Table 7.3 Distinguishing between simple and complex homeostasis

Simple homeostasis	Complex homeostasis
Homeostatic loops are likely to be linear and have a steady state behaviour with clear relationships between the inputs and outputs of a process. Indications of instability will probably be predeterminable and boundable. The actuator will be deterministic or involve rational expectation.	Homeostatic loops are likely to be nonlinear and far from a steady state behaviour. Instability may appear without prior indication. The relationships between inputs and outputs will in general not be strictly causal, but unclear. The effects of the actuator will be uncertain. It is not always the case that standards, norms and objectives will be well defined. It is not uncommon for them to be fuzzy, whether or not it *believed* that they are well defined, and it may be that such a belief can only be validated retrospectively; even if they *are* well defined, it may be that their definition entails some level of unrealised flexibility. Measures of performance may be inadequate to indicate the nature of the output.

In any system under control, a homeostatic bound may be reached and breached. This bound also represents the threshold of stability of the system. The threshold may not be a sharp bound, after which the system will fall away into instability and oscillate increasingly away from the desired or necessary states of behaviour to death. Rather, it can be a hazy region of bounded instability in which chaos rules.

At one time, systems involving homeostasis were conceived as operating such that state (or goal seeking) behaviour was maintained within bounds that defined equilibrium. These ideas were modified by looking at homeostasis as though it was a response to stimuli that created *tension*. Tension is seen as an inherent and essential feature of complex adaptive systems; it provides the 'go' of the system and the 'force' behind its ability to change (Buckley, 1968, p. 500). Through the work of authors like Bühler (1959) it was considered that homeostasis could represent a way of reducing these tensions.

In social actor systems regulatory control can operate as a negative feedback to limit any deviation from social norms. Under change, systems do not tend to try to manage tension, but rather to manage the situations interpreted as being responsible for the production of greater than normal tension. According to Thelen (1956), social life is a sequence of reactions to stress, and in stress energy is mobilised to produce a state of tension. This state of tension tends to be disturbing, and its reduction is sought through the taking of action.

7.8 Self-organisation

The concept of self-organisation was used by Ashby (1968) to explain how purposeful human systems are able to organise themselves and adapt. Ashby further tells us that a system under the impact of perturbation will adapt if it is to survive.

Jantsch (1980, p. 58) defines self-organisation as 'the self-amplification of fluctuations generated in the system'. It is clearly therefore connected to the equivalent ideas of positive feedback, deviation–amplification and morphogenesis. The fluctuations (or deviations) can be seen as perturbations that derive from the environment. This is consistent with the new systems paradigm that is concerned with non-linearity, instability and fluctuations, where inherently unstable systems have *dissipative processes* and are prone to large-scale perturbations that tend to emerge over the longer term (Prigogine and Stengers, 1984). This is as opposed to *equilibrium* or *steady state* processes that have an implicit order and are prone to relatively small, less significant perturbations because they are structurally robust. Biological or social systems are regarded by Buckley (1968) as examples of those whose dynamic stability can be retained only through the *adaptive* process of *structure elaboration* and *change* that is consistent with the idea of dissipative processes.

7.8.1 Self-organisation as a double feedback control loop

We can represent self-organisation as a double feedback loop control system. To understand this, consider the symbolic representation of a control process (shown in Fig. 7.1) as a single loop feeding back to a process (equivalent to the inner control shaded area in Fig. 7.2). Reference, monitoring and empirical criteria all derive from the world

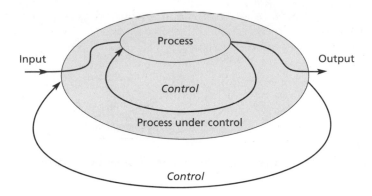

Fig. 7.2 Recursive representation of self-organisational control.
Deviation–counteraction represents structural preservation. Deviation–amplification represents morphogenic action, the constraints defined within a higher focus of metasystem.

views in the metasystemic domain. Consider now that the control process is recursive, so that all of the elements of control are implied again outside the inner control. The main difference between the two levels of control lies in the criteria against which comparison is made:

1 in the inner control, the criteria are defined *for the system* according to homeostatic requirements as determined by the metasystem;

2 in the outer control, the criteria are defined *for the metasystem* according to homeostatic requirements as determined from a meta-metasystem at a higher focus.

Let us suppose that there is a metasystem for the metasystem (a meta-metasystem). Let us suppose that the meta-metasystem is able to maintain its connection with the metasystem. It will provide some meta-criteria to guide the metasystem that operate bounds on its development, and within these it will be able to find its own stable states through a process of 'cognitive' learning. Suppose now that a break occurs between the meta-metasystem and the metasystem. In this case there will be no meta-criteria to guide the metasystem, which will now find its own arbitrary stable states through the learning process. In either case this can be seen as a morphogenic action on the cognitive model of the system contained within its metasystem. Repeated morphogenic action can accumulate as a process of evolution.

The discussions about the inputs, outputs, process, monitor, comparator and actuator that have occurred above are also relevant to the case of self-organisation. While standards, norms or objectives derive from the metasystem, changes within them may be seen as a consequence of cognitive learning that is a part of the self-organising process. According to Beer (1979), such learning results from an understanding of the interconnection between actuation for self-regulation and self-amplification. It explains how self-regulation can occur in implicitly unstable situations through self-organisation.

These ideas are consistent with the simpler ideas of Argyris (1990), who defines the concepts of single- and double-loop learning in terms of *actions* and *values*, as shown in Fig. 7.3. Single-loop learning is behavioural in that it enables actions and procedures to be adjusted, while double-loop learning is cognitive and can change meanings.

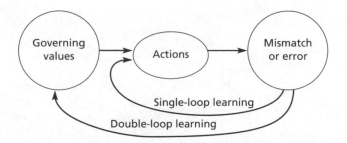

Fig. 7.3 The concepts of single- and double-loop learning
(*Source*: Argyris, 1990)

7.8.2 Self-regulation and self-organisation as a learning process

We can link these ideas together with the control loop of Fig. 7.1, the domain model of Fig. 6.5, and the notion that self-regulation and self-organisation are a result of learning, thus creating Fig. 7.4. Here we provide a control process in terms of materials and material flow in the systems domain, information processes of the transmogrific domain, and cognitive criteria from which goal evaluation criteria can be created. The learning activator feedback to the system is representative of behavioural change and consistent with homeostasis, while the feedback to the metasystem represents cognitive change that will result in structural/behavioural adaptation.

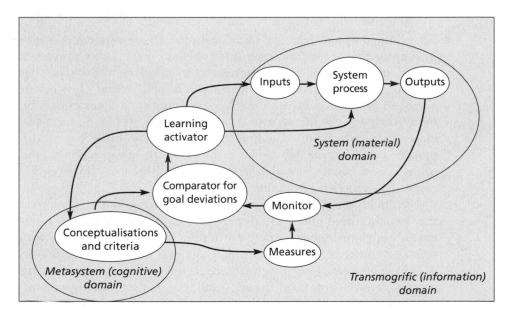

Fig. 7.4 Control model for adaptive actor system.
Feedback loops occur from the learning activator to the system and the metasystem.

7.9 Autopoiesis

Autopoiesis refers to self-producing systems. A useful definition of an autopoietic system is given by Jessop (1990, p. 320):

> A condition of radical autonomy ... [which] defines its own boundaries relative to its environment, develops its own unifying operational code, implements its own programmes, reproduces its own elements in a closed circuit, obeys its own laws of motion. When a system reaches what we might call 'autopoietic take-off', its operations can no longer be controlled from outside.

He continues by saying that thus autopoietic systems are 'not trivial input–output machines; they are not integrated into some broader control structure which determines their responses to environmental changes; and they are not pre-destined to perform a particular function for other systems. As most, the environment serves as a source for perturbing and/or potentially destructive changes to which they react, if at all, according to their own determined processes. Any internal operations or restructuring triggered in this way is always governed by efforts to maintain their own basic organisational forms – up to the point where any environmental changes are so perturbing that they overwhelm a system's capacities for self-preservation and it disintegrates ... there is no external control on their internal reorganisation and only internal constraint is the goal of self-reproduction'.

Another definition of autopoiesis is an interpretation of that given by Maturana (1980, pp. 15–16 and p. 29). Consider a dynamic system composed of a network of processes that generate outputs. It is autopoietic if it will:

1 generate outputs to that network of processes that are in part themselves the network of processes; this is a recursive definition;

2 define for the recursive network a set of boundaries that satisfy the manifestation of its cognitive purposes.

In the development of the idea of autopoiesis, Maturana and Varela (1979) use the two concepts structure and organisation. Mingers (1995, p. 15) indicates that their use of 'organisation' may be viewed as unobserved deeper forms of relationship that we may see as occurring within our domain of transmogrification (or behaviour organising), while 'structure' may be viewed as an empirical surface phenomenon. For us, then, autopoietic systems can be said to be closed at the organising level. Such *organisationally* closed systems are:

● systems not characterised as having inputs and outputs;
● systems that, once working, will continue to work through their own internal processes until an external force intervenes.

Schwarz (1996, personal communication) sees autopoietic systems as being logically closed. This means that they are closed with respect to the logical organising processes of transmogrification, and they therefore have no logical relationships with their environment. The exchanges with the environment will normally occur at the behavioural level, and be experienced as perturbations that affect the organising processes. Expectations of behaviour are evident during transmogrification, and behavioural perturbations will effect these. Homeostatic attempts will be made to adjust for the perturbations during transmogrification that will result in system regulatory changes. In the case that these fail, deeper cognitive learning occurs that will have an impact on transmogrification.

This in turn results in self-organisation at the physical level. In this way, autopoietic systems are able to respond to the environment and self-organise. However, there is slightly more to this argument.

Schwarz tells us that purely autonomous systems are logically closed (autopoietic). They also involve cybernetic positive (morphogenic) and negative (homeostatic) feedback loops, as well as being autopoietic. They react together through perturbations that derive from their environment. *Strictly speaking they do not adapt in this condition, but simply self-produce.* We are therefore forced to explain within this cognitive model how adaptation can occur.

According to the Schwarzian viable systems theory (Chapter 8), *total autonomy represents an ideal situation that does not exist in practice.* A holon exists with others as a partially autonomous viable system whose form has evolved together with all the others. This gives rise to Varela's idea of structural coupling (Varela, 1984), that is due to a shared history. We have already come across an idea associated with structural coupling, when we spoke of the change in systems being structure determined. Let us take a little time out to explore it further.

According to Mingers (1995, p. 35), the changes that an autopoietic system goes through are determined by its structure so long as autopoiesis is maintained. These changes may preserve the structure as it is, or in a plastic system they may radically alter it. The environment triggers the changes. It does not determine them. Only those changes can be triggered that are possible for the system at that time. When this occurs the system is said to become structurally coupled to its environment. It can similarly become structurally coupled to other systems within the environment. As a consequence, structural coupling is a reformulation of the idea of adaptation. Adaptation and structural coupling can be aligned with the proviso that we see that in an adapting system the environment cannot specify the adaptive changes that will occur. This is totally determined by the possibilities of the system itself.

Returning to Schwarz (1996, personal communication), it is because of this coupling that holons have developed conceptual devices that enable them to coexist. Each one has developed inside a map of the rest, and this enables coexistence and survival. A holon with a 'good' map can 'adapt' better than another with a 'poor' map. Thus the quality of the map is, in this conceptualisation, defined by the ability of the system to adapt. Now, within the context of this model, we define adaptation as a historical behavioural feature of a partially autonomous subsystem inside another one. Under certain condition, a cluster of holons may no longer be able to manage a situation. As a consequence of this, fluctuations, perturbation and randomness can all trigger a new phase of change in form. It is this condition that describes structurally critical systems that are prone to deviation–amplification.

Schwarz (1994) also adopts the notion that social systems are autopoietic if one considers them, as we would say, in terms of their metasystem and transmogrification. A social system must be able to regenerate its logical or organising networks that ultimately derive from its paradigms, through actor and institutional behaviour. Consider for example the *myth.* Myth regeneration and propagation occur through (for instance) story telling, cults, media, advertising and entertainment. They are enabled through:

1 pressure (like rituals, power, honour and money) applied by the system on mediators (like sovereigns, priests, presidents, leaders, owners, directors);

2 pressure of mediators on the masses (like faithfuls, slaves, taxpayers, electors, debtors, employees, consumers).

150

The boundaries of that network of myths can also be clearly defined because they are determined in transmogrific organising processes by the projected (mythical) 'truths' that define the paradigms. Paradigmatic 'truths' must be bounded, otherwise the problem of paradigm incommensurability would not be an issue. This evaluation would seem to satisfy Mingers' (1995) highlight that if sociocultural systems are to be seen as autopoietic, then they must be able to show that the outputs are themselves the network of processes, and the boundaries correctly define the system.

7.10 Self-referencing systems

Autopoietic systems are said to be capable of self-referencing. Self-referencing systems are open systems that refer only to themselves in terms of their intentioned purposeful organisational behaviour. This does not mean that they do not interact with the environment since it relates only to their purposefulness. Relations with the environment are determined from within the system. Morgan (1980) was interested in self-referential systems, with which he associated three features:

1 self-referencing closure – the attempt by organisations to interact with their environment as projections of themselves;

2 egocentrism – the attempt by organisations to try to maintain their own identity against a threatening outside world;

3 self-reflective evolution – the process of organisational change as an evolution of self-identity in relation to the wider world.

As Kickert (1993) suggests, organisational cultures that maximise their egocentric orientations may be successful in the short term, but often at the expense of their context, and they run the danger of destroying the whole. Morgan's motto for his approach is 'think and act more systematically: more self-reflection, less self-centredness'.

Minai (1995, p. 30) places autopoiesis in terms of self-reference, and self-reference in terms of information flow. From this perspective, self-reference means not 'a system such as self with top-down information flow, who makes judgements on its surrounding events independent of those events', but rather those that include mind and self, that 'are those systems which are interconnected to and an inseparable part of those events. Therefore any judgement on part of such a system is a two-way flow emerging from these interconnections'. Minai's idea of autopoietic systems refers to self-contained unities whose reference is not only to themselves, but also to their environment (p. 34).

7.11 Actor system identity

While self-referencing is essential to individual identity in actor systems, actors can also be attributed with having generic identity. We can distinguish between these as follows. Individual identity can be related to actors to enable them to be uniquely distinguishable. In doing this they establish for themselves the idea of a boundary from other perhaps similar actors that can be seen as a class of exclusive closure. All actor systems that have individual identity can thus be *differentiated* from one another at the individual level. Individual identity may also be seen as a property of actors that have self-reference, that is a symbolically defined reference to the self or components of self through image.

An actor normally connects its individual identity with its generic identity, which is not associated with self-reference. Unlike individual identity, the purpose is not to differentiate, but rather to qualitatively describe. The quality is defined through a set of normatively agreed characteristics that we call a *generic profile* that defines *class*, the general attributes of which are given in Table 7.4. An actor system will maintain a desired generic identity so long as its relationship with its metasystem is maintained. Shifts in generic identity are normally accompanied by shifts in cultural identity.

The relationship between identity and survival has been considered by Weinberg (1975, p. 240). He suggests that the maintenance of identity is closely bound up with that of survival with respect to the context of the situation. Thus, survival depends upon:

1 the nature of the environment;

2 how the system interprets the environment;

3 what constitutes the identity of the system;

4 how an inquirer interprets that which constitutes the identity of the system.

Table 7.4 Attributes of a generic profile of a system/holon

Attributes	Generic profile
Wholeness	Works as a whole and in connection with the cognitive purposes that derive from the metasystem.
Propositional	The characteristics of the profile are determined by metasystemic propositions.
Normative	The set of characteristics are normatively agreed to define distinct classes of behaviour.
Extension	The set of characteristics enable the similarity or commensurability between systems to be evaluated; this is because the characteristics establish a space of extension that identifies a system generically.
Qualities	Evaluation of qualities in a given extension will enable similarity between theoretical generic class and system classification. However, evaluation of similarities will be dependent upon inquirer perspective.
Identity loss	Hazy or loss of the generic identity implies that the generic characteristics have lost their normative coherence.

Change does not normally affect the individual identity of an actor unless it fails. However, it can affect the generic identity. In Table 7.5 we explore a set of possibilities in the relationship between individual and generic identity.

An example of the relationship between generic (or group) identity and individual identity is offered in Minicase 7.1.

Table 7.5 Options that can occur after systemic change

Identity		Possible outcomes		
Individual	Generic	Type of change	Evaluation	Consequence
Unchanged	Unchanged	Incremental	Unchanged cognitive purposes	Hidden cognitive purposes from uncovered beliefs
Unchanged	New	Dramatic	New cognitive purposes	New primary purposes and system behaviour
New	Unchanged	Radical	System failure	Similar new system
New	New	Dramatic	System failure	Dissimilar new system

Minicase 7.1

Group and individual identity

Peasant to farmer

Weinberg (1975, p. 248), in his consideration of identity, explores the situation of a peasant who trades his hoe for a tractor to become a farmer. While his considerations do not distinguish as we do between individual and generic identity, nor between the possible characteristics that differentiate generic classifications, the case provides a useful point of discussion.

Both the peasant and the farmer have different generic classifications. A characteristic that both the peasant and farmer have is that of working the land to produce food. Three other characteristics might be:

1 the area of land being worked

2 the methods of working the land

3 the use of technology.

Typically a peasant will be responsible for small parcels of land, while a farmer will farm a larger area. A peasant will typically use traditional and ineffectual methods of land management, while the farmer will have access to modern methods. While this will be a function of education, we shall ignore this for simplicity because we are then brought into contact with a whole further set of possible subsidiary characteristics to consider. Finally, a peasant uses a hoe and a farmer a tractor.

We could argue that as far as land area is concerned, this is a function of the efficiency of the land worker, and an efficient peasant may well be assigned land by his peer group in some cooperative agreement. In this role he might still be regarded as a peasant. Looking at technology, we should note that this tends to change, and the way it is used can also vary. Imagine a tractor being pulled by an ox. We might therefore wish to reject land and technology as characteristics of the occupations. Instead, working methods may be seen as a function of effectiveness, and land amount and technology a function of efficiency. Perhaps, then, it should be quantity of production that distinguishes the peasant from the farmer.

Suppose that the differences between the peasant and the farmer relate to the quantity of land produce that each outputs. There will be a fuzzy boundary that qualitatively distinguishes between the outputs produced by a peasant and a farmer. At some stage (and through normative peer group agreement) an inquirer will be able to say when the land worker has shifted occupation.

7.12 Actors, organisations and change

Typically, when we are interested in the endogenous processes of an actor system we refer to it as an organisation. We are aware that the organisation acts through its meta-system populated by at least one paradigm. We are also aware that the propositions of the paradigm provide the basic set of assumptions, logic and orientation for organised activity. Actor behaviour is predicted on the norms of its paradigm, and the language it uses to describe itself and its operations indicates the orientation that it has.

If it is possible to categorise classes of actor generically, then classification is determined through their paradigms. Thus, can we class an organisation as being in the public sector, and if so what are the characteristics that determine this? The same question can be put about organisations that are classed as being in the private sector. Paradigms offer a framework that determines how the organisation should operate, and what it considers to be important for its decision making and activities. An organisation develops structures and processes that enable it to operate according to a definable paradigm. This paradigm reflects the current propositions, beliefs, attitudes and views that define how it sees itself. This is in turn reflected in the organisation's behaviour.

Having said this, any organisation may have more than one paradigm. Organisations normally operate under a single power centre that is able to maintain the controls perceived to be necessary to it. A single power centre organisation will have a single dominant paradigm. In schizophrenic organisations there will be a plurality of dominant paradigms that may be non-cooperative. In either case there are likely to be alternative paradigms within organisational subgroups that represent other propositions and cultures, and they will manifest different patterns of behaviour. Many larger organisations have this paradigmatic pluralism that contributes to their complexity, though they may not be schizophrenic. Organisational schizophrenia usually occurs in cases when the organisation is passing through a period of chaos, when dominant paradigm oscillation occurs.

Organisations are also subject to change that may be incremental, radical or dramatic. Incremental change occurs as the system survives in an ever-changing environment. Radical change occurs as its core purposes alter in order to cope with an accumulation of change or with sudden change. Consequently, some of the processes and structures within the organisation will change. Dramatic change can be described as an organisational metamorphosis. This is because after it the global form of the organisation will have been qualitatively altered.

Organisations that can change in such ways are said to be plastic. Plastic organisations are thus able to redefine their structures or their structural relations to accommodate new processes under the pressure of their environment, while maintaining their individual behavioural stability.

7.12.1 Incremental change

In *incremental* change, organisations undergo continual morphogenic processes that can preserve their identity through evolution. In many situations an organisation is affected by changes that effect structures or processes *incrementally*. Thus, arguments of Darwinian evolutionary processes occur through the idea of continuous selection and incremental morphogenesis. As the system is perturbed, its form undergoes dynamic change. Incremental change only affects the metasystem in a piecemeal way.

All dynamic organisations have influences from the external environment. These influences *perturb* the organisation's structures and processes, interfering with its operations. If the perturbations cannot be controlled and the structure becomes critical, then the system may learn to adapt by introducing local qualitative changes into its structure. This in turn influences the system's behaviour towards and within its environment. We refer to these as qualitative incremental changes that define the process of morphogenesis.

7.12.2 Radical change

Radical change affects the primary purposes of an organisation, which are directly determined by its cognitive purposes. This in turn will effect the form, culture and behaviour of the system, but not sufficiently to change its generic classification. It will not be responsible for the generation of distinct morphogenic variety, i.e. new generic classifications. Behaviour will be affected, but not in a way that generically distinguishes it from its previous patterns of behaviour.

Radical change is 'far reaching for organisations and individuals' and impacts on 'the core [or primary] purpose of the organisation as related to the environment, and the core values as related internally to the ethos of the organisation' (Benjamin and Mabey, 1993, p. 182). This class of change creates 'a major alteration in strategic direction [that] inevitably implies a reassessment of an organisation's core purpose, [and] which in turn prompts individuals to question their work values, and the extent to which they are aligned with those of their employer' (Benjamin and Mabey, 1993, p. 183). It can affect an organisation's form and culture both locally and globally, and provides an impulse for change. As a consequence it will have an impact on the behaviour of the organisation.

The primary stimuli for change in organisations are the forces from the external environment (Benjamin and Mabey, 1993). It affects the purposes of the organisation, and causes the participants to examine it and its related objectives. In human organisations, the transformation of objectives and practices of working to meet new purposes is therefore a direct consequence of radical change.

Radical change is far reaching for both organisations and individuals, not only within the context of its primary purpose, but also with respect to its core cultural values. *Preconscious* cultural factors (e.g. ideology, symbols and norms) contribute to a basis of the social and political systems of an organisation, and these may also be affected by radical change.

7.12.3 Dramatic change

Dramatic change is a qualitative paradigm shift that relates directly to metamorphosis. It affects beliefs, culture and the propositional base, including the type of logic being used. Radical change is therefore an integral part of dramatic change. After a paradigm shift the generic classification of the system is changed. Even if the meta-purposes of the system are the same, they will have a new interpretation because of the new belief system, and thus radical change will be evident. Dramatic change will occur with the generation of distinct morphogenic variety, i.e. new generic classifications.

During dramatic change the whole propositional base that defines the nature of an organisation shifts. The inquirer's paradigm of inquiry classifies the system according to a set of *characteristics* within its propositional base. What differentiates between one generic classification and another is the set of characteristics that defines it. Questions can arise, then, about whether a particular system has these characteristics, or how a system that has been involved in a paradigm shift should be classified if it has some characteristics and not others.

Dramatic change impacts on the dominant paradigm of an organisation by shifting it, so that an *other* (rather than an observer) can see changes in the organisation's propositional base, culture and language. The sets of assumptions and logic that define the reasoning process of the organisation change dramatically, as will its beliefs, attitudes and values. So too will the language used to describe its structures and processes, and the exemplars that it holds up as successful representations of its paradigm. Since the propositions determine the way in which the purposes of the organisation are expressed, and the meaning that they hold, dramatic change can thus be seen as encompassing radical change. Like radical change, dramatic change impacts on organisational purposes, but it also has a global affect on form and culture that is consistent with a metamorphosis. Dramatic change will have a profound long-term impact on the future behaviour of the organisation, as it will on the *preconscious* cultural factors of an organisation.

After a dramatic change an *other* will be able to clearly distinguish the behaviour of an organisation before and after the event. Distinguishing between whether radical or dramatic change has occurred is a matter of distinguishing generic classes. Whether an organisation can be qualitatively assigned to one generic classification or another may not be a simple and clear-cut decision. It frequently requires a consensus view to assign membership of the organisation to a generic class.

An example of dramatic change occurs within a takeover in which a corporation has its board of directors replaced. The belief system of the new board will be different from that of its predecessor, and it is likely to interpret any core purposes it maintains in a different way from its predecessor. In a more specific example, the monopolistic UK telephone company has passed through a process of privatisation. Its belief system has been changed from a classification as a public domain organisation to one of private enterprise. It has thus passed through a paradigm shift. To demonstrate this we should define the paradigm extensions for each belief system and show that they are qualitatively different. The paradigm shift has impacted its internal structures and processes, and its culture. It has also affected its use of language, and the way in which it behaves in its environment towards its suppliers and customers.

7.12.4 The impact of change

Examples of dramatic change occur during revolutions, coups d'etat or takeovers. Metamorphosis has also been seen in the Central and East European countries, which have experienced two dramatic changes. One was when Communist rule transformed the market economy into a state owned one, the other when this regime suddenly collapsed and organisations become directed to the market economy. A much milder form of such change has occurred in Western Europe, first with nationalisation and now privatisation. Thus, a publicly owned organisation that has propositions that enable its members to talk of qualitative purposes for the organisation, would, after privatisation, have propositions that would instead enable talk about quantitative accountability. The two paradigms are clearly incommensurable, since talk of quantitative accountability in the early form of the organisation would be totally meaningless. This also suggests that situations that arise in connection with this organisation will have paradigms that are harder than those associated with the previous organisation.

Since the propositions and consequently the expression of the purposes of the two forms of organisation are generically different, it will be appropriate to see them as separate organisations. This is in the same way as one might examine a caterpillar and a butterfly that we might assign the same individual identity to, but which are generically different forms of animal. No confusion should therefore occur about the two organisations being the same thing, even though they might maintain the paperwork that shows them to have the same individual identity.

In purposeful systems, change impacts not only on social form, but also on culture (Nicholson, 1993). The argument for this is that change affects the internal innovations of an organisation that develop in order to meet new circumstances. If we refer to the socioculture of an organisation, it is this that we will mean. So distinct are the organisations *before* and *after* the *change*, that two cultural orientations can develop which relate respectively to the two different propositional frameworks. These sociocultural orientations determine the social and cultural values that are held by the segment of people who align themselves with that orientation.

The two sociocultural orientations may coexist in the same organisational space after the change, rather as in the case of two subcultural groups living together. Analogous to magnetic fields, it may be possible to postulate that socioculture can be viewed as a field encompassing the organisational environment that constrains the way in which events can be directed. After dramatic change the new organisation has two sociocultural fields originating from different sources, the old and the new. Two fields in a common area can, we hypothesise, create sociocultural perturbations or rifts that can interfere with the way in which the organisation operates, enabling conflict and confusion to arise.

Since organisations are actor systems, and their activities may relate only to inquiry, the concept of dramatic change may also be applied to an organisation that centres on inquiry. Inquiry is dependent upon the weltanschauung of an inquirer and the paradigm that is to be used to make the inquiry (Yolles, 1994). This is because the inquirer is able to shift the perspective of the situation being inquired into in accordance with his or her understanding of the purpose of the inquiry, and thus generate a system model that has a given form.

7.12.5 Organisational plasticity

We are aware that when organisations are plastic, they are able to support adaptability and change while maintaining their behavioural stability. An organisation that changes as a response to perturbation from its environment can be referred to as *plastic*. Every viable organisation has some degree of plasticity in that it is able to respond to perturbations from the environment. The limit of its plasticity is implicitly determined by its metasystem and reflected in its structure. When an organisation responds to perturbations through the inherent capability of its structure, then the response is said to be *structure determined* (Maturana, 1987, p. 336). The perturbations can now be seen as *catalysts for change* rather than instruments that create change. This is consistent with the way in which Maturana describes self-producing behaviour (autopoiesis) when he refers to perturbations *triggering* change that he sees as a process of system *compensation* (Mingers, 1995, p. 30). The triggering of change can also be seen as a process of activation that has a role in both self-regulation and self-organisation. In self-regulation it is seen to reduce environmental variety, thereby providing support for the system. Self-organisation is a morphogenic process and is seen to be able to induce variety into the system's regulatory process, thus becoming a learning device.

Both self-regulation and self-organisation may fail. Failure in self-regulation occurs when perturbations from the environment of the system arise that are not represented within feedback, or for which self-regulation cannot adjust. Failure in self-organisation occurs when perturbations are such that the system is unable to respond by inducing variety, then once more it cannot respond to the perturbations. When this happens the organisation has reached beyond its plastic limit. This explanation is fundamentally one of dynamic equilibrium, where perturbations are seen to be due to environmental variety, and the system must seek its own source of variety that is able to deal with this. The achievement of this variety balance is referred to as requisite variety.

Recognising whether an organisation has passed through plastic change requires a concept that is central to it, and we propose that such a concept is the idea of individual identity. It may be argued that as long as an organisation is able to maintain its individual identity as it changes morphogenically or metamorphically, then that change is plastic. To illustrate this, in Minicase 7.2 we offer example of plastic change in two very different situations. One of these represents a morphogenic situation as a child changes to an adult, compared to that of a metamorphic one as a caterpillar changes to a butterfly. The distinction between whether a change has been one or the other of these will very much be a function of scale of view (or depth of focus), and may therefore be seen as a matter of perspective. The second part of Minicase 7.2 argues that the UK National Health Service has passed through a metamorphic process of dramatic change. In doing this the opportunity is also taken to explore some of the other theoretical notions that we have already considered. We argue that the case of the National Health Service is more similar to change from the caterpillar to the butterfly rather than from a child to an adult, and that it and its purposes have been dramatically changed. In the same way that one would not expect the behaviour of a caterpillar to be the same as that of a butterfly, it highlights the notion that any expectations of change for a given situation may have no validity after it passes through a metamorphosis, especially if that change process is a complex one.

Minicase 7.2

Dramatic and radical change
Caterpillar to butterfly, child to adult

Like all insects, the butterfly passes through the stages of larva and pupa to reach adulthood. The larval stage, called a caterpillar, has a metabolism that is predestined to change. Certain conditions occurring within the caterpillar at a certain point in its lifecycle cause it to change its form from the crawling worm-like larva, which appears to be primarily concerned with eating, to a butterfly that flies and is concerned with reproduction. These specialisms have proved very successful in ensuring that this class of animal survives in an uncertain and often hostile world.

The caterpillar is hatched from an egg, and the butterfly develops out of the dormant caterpillar as it lies, metamorphosing, in the pupa that it has created for itself (Fig. 7.5). We suppose that the identity of the caterpillar is the same as that of the butterfly since the latter is built upon the foundation of the former.

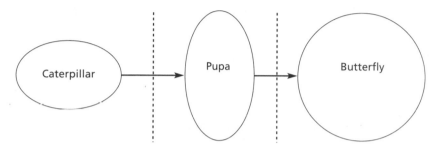

Fig. 7.5 Dramatic change from caterpillar to butterfly

Both forms of the insect have a metabolism that has been created according to what we shall refer to as a *propositional base*, the nature of which will be found encoded in the DNA (that is, the coded 'blueprint' that defines the way in which the butterfly lives, functions and changes). The caterpillar originally had a propositional base that enabled:

1 its primary purpose (we suppose this to be eating for growth) to be satisfied successfully;
2 its mode of existence, which we consider to be represented by its crawling form of mobility;
3 its orientation towards eating green leaves.

In order to reach the adult butterfly stage, the caterpillar has to pass through a dramatic change that alters its propositional base, enabling it to best satisfy a new primary purpose of reproduction. The propositional base will define the paradigm of the insect, and enables its structures and processes to be defined in a way that determines how it will exist and survive.

The transition through the pupa stage is a dramatic example of change. It is comparable to the radical change that one sees in humans as they pass through the teenager stage, to develop into adulthood (Fig. 7.6). There is a clear difference between the human transition from child to adult and that of the insect from caterpillar to butterfly. In humans the form of the animal is not qualitatively changed, though a continuous process of incremental change occurs at various physiological and mental levels, and the primary purpose may be thought to change.

The primary purpose that might be ascribed to a child form of a human being will depend upon the relevant system chosen. This is itself dependent upon the weltanschauung of the inquirer and the paradigm selected. However, it could be argued that it is the child's physical and educational development. The primary purpose of an adult might be considered to be reproduction (as viewed from a biological context), or mental and spiritual development (as seen from a spiritual paradigm). However we distinguish between the two classes of primary purpose, radical change occurs through change in the hormones which affect the biological processes at work. The consequences of this radically affect the structures and processes of an individual such that one can distinguish between children and adults.

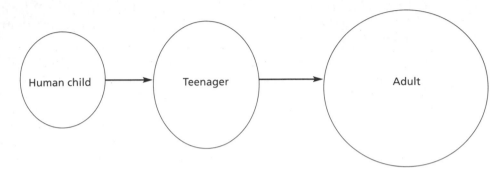

Fig. 7.6 Radical change in the human system during its development

Dramatic change and the National Health Service

Examining the consequence of UK Government policies over the past two decades shows that the National Health Service has passed through a metamorphosis. It was originally operated by Regional Health Authorities, which effectively defined policy criteria, controlled finance, and had a coordinating function, and District Health Authorities, which actually operated the service. Health policy normally related to the primary purpose of the Service, which was to manage health on behalf of the public. The criteria that determined the policy were determined from the propositional basis of the Authority. This was defined by the powers and constraints as engineered by Government. New policy initiatives directly affected the propositional base and influenced the organisational culture, and a paradigm shift occurred for the organisation. It has therefore passed through a dramatic change. It has moved from what we might refer to as a public sector organisation concerned with health in a cooperative environment, to a business sector one which must tender for its health care in a competitive 'market economy' environment. It must now satisfy its budgets in the same way as a commercial organisation before it can be considered to be operating successfully. Success is now judged on quantitative as well as qualitative criteria such as the number of patients seen or treated, and the minimisation of costs. Conflicts are now possible when attempts are made to balance qualities with quantities. The language of the new paradigm is also different from that of the old, when budgetary quantitative measures had little significance.

The change to the Health Service has occurred through the introduction of *Trusts* that are very much smaller than the Health Authorities, which in principle pseudo-privatise the service into a set of 'competing' organisations. This ensures that local Trust management occurs such that costs become a constraining influence on matters of health. In particular this is because the Trusts are required to 'sell' their packages of health care within the Region, and the optimal packages 'win'. Organisations like the District Health Authorities that originally controlled the health service prior to the change mutually cooperated unconditionally. In the new competitive form of the health service, cooperation between Trusts is more conditional since contracts with the Regional Health Authority, the purchasers of health provision, operate under competitive tender. This clearly has an impact on the way in which the health service operates.

The National Health Service can be seen as a *system* because it consists of a set of services that deal with different and distinct classifications of health evaluation, treatment and recovery. The very simple model is shown in Fig. 7.7. Each trust (Trust 1, Trust 2, ... , Trust n, Trust $n + 1$, ...) will belong to a sector. Each will also have a set of sections with medical specialisms or interests shown symbolically within Trust $n + 2$ in the figure. Some Trusts are able to cater for patients in a way that others cannot because of the specialist facilities of their sections. To enable this to occur patients are transferred between Trusts as outputs from one and inputs to another, in a form of cooperation. In the old form of the NHS, it was assumed that these exchanges, as we shall call them, were indirectly as frequent one way as another. Thus, Trust $n + 2$ may transfer to Trust $n + 1$, while Trust n transfers to Trust $n + 2$. The new form of the NHS makes each Trust undertake an accounting exercise so that patient transfers are accompanied by financially budgeted ones. Unlike in the old model for the health service, this cooperation process has now become conditional because Trusts are competitors in a Regional Health Authority marketplace, and constrained according to budgets. This can adversely affect the lives and potential of patients.

Two sociologically distinct groups of people can be associated with the trusts, and they hold distinct paradigms. One derives from the old form of the NHS, which was, one could argue, primarily concerned with quality and cooperation. The new dominant paradigm has an orientation that comes from those who believe in market economy principles, competition and quantitative (as well as qualitative) evaluation. It is within this cultural distinction that the possibilities of conflict occur.

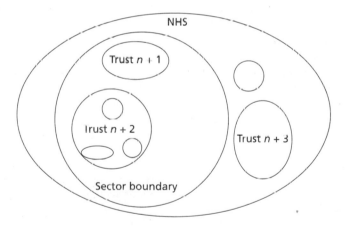

Fig. 7.7 System map indicating NHS is made up of Trusts

The shift in the dominant paradigm has created a new metasystem, the manifestation of which engenders new behaviour in medical practitioners. Within this process of dramatic change its cognitive interest moved from public to business. While its previous cognitive purposes have been retained, they have been subsumed within a new context of profitability and competition. This will necessarily change the way in which the Trusts behave.

Until the change, in the social context it could be argued that the NHS operated in a dynamic steady state situation, attending to social needs according to the perceived norms of health care. It could also be argued that through better education health care access to people was somewhat better than before. This hardly affects the Service since in terms of resources its operations are effectively running down because of Government cash restrictions. Consequently, the Service could be seen to be operating a deviance counteraction policy.

On the other hand, it might be argued that the NHS is in continual flux. As new medical developments occur its ability to treat new medical conditions increases. In consequence its requirement for Government resources has been increasing. This is seen as a condition of deviation–amplification. During this period of economic instability Government has continually been searching for ways of reducing a potentially unlimited drain. This has been without wishing to take on the political burden of being considered to be responsible for an increasing number of deaths each year because of financial cutbacks. The introduction of a paradigm shift for the NHS to the political right might well appear to have shifted responsibility from Government.

It is argued that the degree of qualitative change that has occurred represented a metamorphosis from one generic class of organisation to another. Since we are dealing with the form of the organisation, we select the characteristics and their qualitative evaluations as shown in Table 7.6.

Table 7.6 Characteristics of paradigm change in the UK National Health Service

Generic characteristic	Old NHS paradigm	New NHS paradigm
Cognitive interest	Public	Business
Structure of holarchy	Medical unit holons of the service are loosely structured into large autonomous regional bodies with a strong metasystem.	Medical unit holons (Trusts) of the service are small and autonomous, and are loosely allocated to a region. The holarchy works as a suprasystem with a minimal metasystem.
Mode	Holons operated *cooperatively* within and between regions.	Holons operate *competitively* within regions.
Decision making	Loosely structured consensus decisions between medical teams.	Tightly structured hierarchical management decision processes.
Primary orientation	Operated a *medical* accounting and management system. The only prerequisite is that of medical qualification. Funding derives from Government, assigned to Districts and allocated to Regions, which distribute it to medical units.	Operates a *financial* or *cost* accounting and management system that includes medical accounting. Budgeting processes are a prerequisite if a Trust is to be able to operate. Government allocated funds to Districts, which receive budget applications from individual trusts.
Relationship with public	Seen as potential patients.	Seen as potential clients and as a financial resource.
Funding control	Funding was bounded *globally* from a higher level of focus, thus making Government *directly* responsible for reduced spending.	Funding is bounded at a *local level* through competitive tendering and budget forecasting, thus making Government *indirectly* responsible for reduced spending.

One of the consequences of the change from the public to the private domain is as follows. In the old paradigm patients who wished or needed to see a consultant were informed that they would be put on the waiting list. However, they could be seen more quickly if their case was very urgent. In the new paradigm, patients (clients?) are often asked if they wish to go privately because of the long waiting lists. In this case they would see a consultant more quickly during his or her private practice. They would then have the opportunity of joining a new queue of patients currently being seen. The problem with this is that the two paradigms coexist, with resulting conflict of interests and professional confusion.

Despite the change, the NHS retains its individual identity. Its name, services, members of staff and legal identity remain more or less unchanged in comparison to movements in such areas prior to privatisation.

Consider now the following hypothetical extension of the above case. The new approach in Service management provided a success as far as the allocation of Government responsibility for short funding was concerned. In an attempt to extend the new NHS paradigm further, it was decided to fully privatise the Service. A conglomeration of privately-owned health insurance companies, headed by Blue Cross (an American-owned private health company that already operates many of its services in the UK), made a bid to the Government to take over and run the NHS. It was able to show its capability to continue the (currently reducing) level of treatments that the NHS is servicing. However, through staff reductions, lower salaries to nurses, and the hiring of more Third-World qualified practitioners from its foreign waiting lists, it can operate the Service at a very much reduced cost to that of the Government.

The possibility of National Health Service privatisation, where private organisations (e.g. supermarkets) set up their own trusts intended to service only their clientele, can lead to a further fractionation of the system as a whole, in particular because it will result in uneven local provision. More, it is likely that potential patients will receive superior or inferior medical attention as a function of their geographical location, customer loyalty or purchasing ability.

SUMMARY

The concepts presented here highlight the idea that the normal condition of systems is not equilibrium and stability, but rather bounded non-equilibrium and instability. This enables us to successfully explain their evolutionary processes.

Viable systems are self-regulating actors that attempt to maintain stability when there is a danger of passing beyond the threshold of control due to perturbation from the environment. In the event that this fails, they adopt self-organisational processes to enable themselves to regain stability, and this can emerge as morphogenesis. Holons are open system with respect to environmentally directed behaviour. They are also closed in respect of their self-actuation, for instance in respect of self-organisation and self-production.

REFERENCES

Argyris, C. (1990) *Overcoming Organisational Defenses*. New York: Allyn and Bacon.

Ashby, W.R. (1961) *An Introduction to Cybernetics*. New York: Wiley.

Ashby, W.R. (1968) 'Principles of self organising systems'. In Buckley, W. (ed.) *Modern Systems Approach for the Behavioural Scientist*. Chicago, IL: Aldine, pp. 108–18.

Beer, S. (1979) *The Heart of Enterprise*. Chichester: Wiley.

Benjamin, G. and Mabey, C. (1993) 'Facilitating radical change'. In Mabey, C. and Mayon-White, B. (eds) *Managing Change*. London: Paul Chapman.

Buckley, W. (1968) *Modern Systems Research for the Behavioural Scientist: A sourcebook*. Chicago, IL: Aldine.

Bühler, C. (1959) 'Theoretical observations about life's basic tendencies', *American Journal of Psychotherapy*, 13, 561–81.

Jantsch, E. (1980) *The Self-Organising Universe: Scientific and human implications of the emerging paradigm of evolution*. New York: Pergamon Press.

Jessop, B. (1990) *State Theory*. Cambridge: Polity Press.

Kickert, W.J.M. (1993) 'Autopoiesis and the science of (public) administration: essence, sence and nonsence', *Organisational Studies*, 14(2), 261–78.

Körner, S. (1960) *The Philosophy of Mathematics*. London: Hutchinson.

Lee, H. (1961) *Symbolic Logic*. New York: Random House.

Luhmann, N. (1986) 'The autopoiesis of social systems'. In Geyer, F. and van der Zouwen, J. (eds) *Sociocybernetic Paradoxes*. London: Sage.

Maturana, H. (1980) 'Man and society'. In Benseler, F., Hejl, P. and Kock, W. (eds) *Autopoietic Systems in the Social Sciences*. Frankfurt: Campus Verlag, pp. 11–31.

Maturana, H. (1987) 'The biological foundations of self-consciousness and the physical domain of existence'. In Cainiello, E. (ed.) *Physics of Cognitive Processes*. Singapore: World Scientific, pp. 324–79.

Maturana, H. and Varela, F.J. (1979) *Autopoiesis and Cognition*, Boston Studies in the Philosophy of Science, vol. 42. Dordrecht: Reidel.

Minai, A.T. (1995) 'Emergence, a domain where the distinction between conception in arts and sciences is meaningless', *Cybernetics and Human Knowing*, 3(3), 25–51.

Mingers, J. (1995) *Self-producing Systems*. New York: Plenum Press.

Morgan, C. (1980) *Future Man*. Newton Abbot: David & Charles.

Nicholson, M. (1993) 'Organisational change'. In Mabey, C. and Mayon-White, B. (eds) *Managing Change*. London: Paul Chapman, pp. 207–11.

Prigogine, I. and Stengers, I. (1984) *Order Out of Chaos: Man's new dialogue with nature*. London: Flamingo.

Pringle, J.W.S. (1968) 'On the parallel between learning theory and evolution'. In Buckley, W. (ed.) *Modern Systems Research for the Behavioural Scientist*. Chicago, IL: Aldine.

Schwarz, E. (1994) 'A trandisciplinary model for the emergence, self-organisation and evolution of viable systems'. Presented at the International Information, Systems Architecture and Technology Conference, Technical University of Wroclaw, Szklaska Poreba, Poland.

Spenser Brown, G. (1972) *Laws of Form*. London: Julian Press.

Thelen, H.A. (1956) 'Emotionality and work in groups'. In White, L.D. (ed.) *The State of the Social Sciences*. Chicago, IL: University of Chicago Press.

Thompson, D. (1996) 'A holistic approach to computer integrated manufacturing architecture and systems design', PhD dissertation, Plymouth University, UK.

Varela, F. (1984) 'Two principles for self-organisation'. In Ulrich, H. and Probst, G.J.B. (eds) *Self-Organisation and Management of Social Systems*. Berlin: Springer-Verlag, pp. 25–32.

von Bertalanffy, L. (1973) *General Systems Theory*. Harmondsworth: Penguin.

Weinberg, G.M. (1975) *An Introduction to General Systems Thinking*. New York: Wiley.

Wheelan, S.A. (1996) 'An initial exploration of the relevance of complexity theory to group research and practice', *Systems Practice*, 9(1), 49–70.

Yolles, M.I. (1994) 'Generic metamodelling', *Systemist*, 16(4).

CHAPTER 8

The dynamics of viable systems

OVERVIEW

Viable systems are often seen to be in dynamic equilibrium, but non-equilibrium theory provides an explanation of how they are able to evolve, as they pass through periods of change that are deterministically uncontrollable, chaotic and unstable. Viable systems exist in complex environments and survive through adaptation. This sometimes occurs through deterministic cognitive control, and sometimes despite it. The development of complexity theory has enabled us to extend our conceptions of the way in which viable systems are able to maintain their stability through processes of self-actuation. Schwarzian viable systems theory provides a broad explanation of how viable systems adapt and survive.

OBJECTIVES

This chapter will explore further:

- the impact of instability on organisations;
- the problem of complexity for the maintenance of stability;
- chaos and stability;
- viability through adaptation.

8.1 Abandoning equilibrium theory

Equilibrium theory has been effectively abandoned within a variety of disciplines, and a new paradigm has emerged that sees the universe as being fundamentally non-equilibrium. Equilibrium situations occur, but they tend not to be long-term tendencies. Ideas about dissipative processes (from people like Prigogine) and about chaos (from people like the physicist Feigenbaum in the 1970s) contributed to this evolution. The concept of self-organisation became important to this, and examination of self-organisation in non-equilibrium dynamics and non-deterministic situations developed.

Systems that are in equilibrium are not able to deal with fundamental change. In stable situations, the creation of new approaches is difficult. Structures, rules, procedures and plans need to be changed when shocks are encountered, but this is problematic because of the norms and cultural attributes of given systems. This difficulty disappears in complex situations in which chaotic behaviour occurs. In particular, consider dynamically unstable situations in viable systems. Here, new structures must be generated in order to develop new stable dynamic behaviour demanded by new conditions. It is important that organisations should *adapt* to new conditions.

8.2 Shifting paradigms: a business management perspective

Chaos theory is concerned with the development of situations away from cognitively (and deterministically) controlled stability. It reflects not only our theories about the viable system, but our perspective on commercial organisations.

Stacey (1993) is concerned with the new paradigm and organisational management. He tells us that the stable equilibrium sought by the predominant management paradigm is not appropriate. The ability of organisations to survive (to succeed, according to Stacey) should not be seen as being tied to stability, but rather by using *both* stability and instability. It assumes that the paradigm of stable equilibrium will enable a manager only to repeat the past, or imitate others who have already moved on. By shifting the management paradigm managers can harness creativity and control the future direction of the organisation. Ashby might have talked of this in terms of creating variety (and not just requisite variety). This would take into account a future that may be indeterminable because of the spontaneous interaction between people under conditions of uncertainty.

Western managers do not often see organisations as complex, dynamic and adaptive systems that are prone to uncertainty, non-equilibrium and a recurrent endangerment of instability. They tend to seek robust systems rather than plastic ones. They more often than not see situations in terms of sensate cultural perspectives devoid of ideational qualities. The consequence of new thinking can provide management approaches that might better be able to deal with problematic situations. They tell us that our organisations will in general best survive through proactive innovation instituted through malleable forms of organisation. In contrast, they normally only react to new situations through action that derives from equilibrium thinking. The occurrence of sporadic unpredictable perturbations from the environment offers a real danger of organisational failure. Our recent Western recessionary experiences tell us that organisations will only survive international commercial competition if they are creative and able to generate new strategic. The ability to generate these will be determined by the way in which they see their operations, and their ability to learn from what they see.

As a way of dealing with indeterministic futures we have in the past developed a calculus of probability. It has been argued (Rosenhead, 1989) that in order to deal with uncertainty we need a calculus that can identify *possibilities* rather than *outcomes*. It may be that the new paradigm of chaos and complexity is capable of providing this.

8.3 The dynamics of survival

Systems survive dynamically through maintaining stability. How they do this becomes the centre of the discussion of viability. Much of the theory today relates directly to the mathematics of dynamic systems that has previously been applied to the natural sciences. While it has also been applied to human behaviour, for instance in the 1960s through differential game theory as developed by Isaacs, this has been unable to characterise the complexities of situations involving purposeful activity.

The theory that has enabled us to develop our ideas about complex general systems and the way in which they respond to change centres around mathematical bifurcation theory. This describes *topological change* that occurs as discontinuities in systems. Topology relates to graphical form. By this we mean the discontinuities that can be described in the *form* and related *behaviour* of the system that we are observing when it changes spontaneously. If a system bifurcates, it can change in one or more possible ways, referred to as bifurcation branches.

Poincaré introduced the theory of bifurcations to explain such phenomena as the development of binary stars from a cloud of interstellar gas. Catastrophe theory was developed by Thom (1975) to investigate such phenomena as the division of one cell into two, and this involves bifurcations. Such inquiry is made in terms of dynamic mathematical theory that seeks stable regions (sometimes referred to as attractors) in a phase space of possibilities. A useful inquiry into this theory can be found in Nicolis and Prigogine (1989).

8.3.1 Conservative dynamic systems

All systems can be described in terms of energy content. There are traditionally two forms of energy – kinetic and potential. Kinetic energy relates to the energy of action of an object. Potential energy is the energy that is available to an object by virtue of the relative position or condition. In the physics of the 19th century, the concept of the conservation of energy was fundamental to its scientific development. The idea associated with this is that 'total energy is conserved while potential energy is converted into kinetic energy' (Prigogine and Stengers, 1984, p. 108). Different forms of energy are definable (like heat and light in physics), and it is seen to be possible to convert from one form to another. Systems that operate the principle of conservation of energy became known as *conservative systems*. In conservative systems, interaction with the environment involves a small or zero change in energy, and there is a tendency *towards* a steady state. This is because such systems have implicitly constrained properties that can be described in terms of a set of characteristics (variables) defined in a phase space (Nicolis and Prigogine, 1989, p. 80). When such a system is in equilibrium, the characteristics, and thus the properties of the system, do not change over time.

We are aware that under certain conditions a system can become structurally critical. When this occurs, the system is at the threshold of instability. Small perturbations in the system can affect it in a major way to create topological change. The result is metamorphosis. While the change in form is discontinuous, the theory explains how it derives from a continuous global relational representation.

We may wish to model a situation as a conservative system, and if we attempt to do so we shall need to define the system and its subsystem energy boundaries in such a way that we can convincingly show that we have a conservative system. We can often recognise conditions of structural criticality because the system is globally sensitive to small change.

As an example of the case of a structural criticality, in Minicase 8.1 we explore a hypothetical case for the way in which cultures can metamorphically change. The minicase adopts the ideas of Thom to illustrate how a macroscopic culture can change from one classification (sensate) to another (ideational). There are other examples of such change in more microcultures. As organisations get taken over by either new ideas or new management, new cultural perspectives can develop. This has occurred, it is postulated, within the context of European privatisation, in the same way as it has occurred through company mergers.

<hr>

Minicase 8.1

Cultural change

As introduced in Chapter 6, Sorokin (1937) produced a theory of social and cultural change that shows how cultures move between different sociocultural states. We have postulated that these can be seen to be the polar opposites in a cultural continuum of *cultural mindset*. The two states are sensate and ideational. They may be balanced, when the culture is said to be *idealistic*, but more often one cultural mindset is dominant. Western society has been passing through a predominantly sensate culture. In predominantly sensate cultures 'war, crime, and rising divorce rates are seen as phenomena inherent in an excessively sensate and materialistic culture' (Davis, 1963).

The concept of these macroscopic characteristics in a culture can be seen in terms of emergence, conceptually feasible because we can see cultures as highly complex. Sorokin would explain this differently since the paradigm of complexity was only starting at the end of his days, but his meaning is the same. 'Since in the total culture of any population there are millions of various cultural systems (and congeries), a study of small systems would give at best, only a knowledge of diverse, infinitesimal fragments of the total cultural universe. It never can give an essential knowledge of the basic structural and dynamic properties of this superorganic reality. As any nomothetic (generalising) science, sociology endeavours to overcome this bewildering diversity of the millions and millions of systems and congeries' (Sorokin, 1963).

It has been suggested that Western culture is passing through a condition of sociocultural decline (Kemp and Yolles, 1992), having moved from a sensate state that reached its height at the turn of the century, towards a more ideational direction. When this occurs, the society becomes socioculturally unstable so that its social and cultural values can lose direction and integration. The Western world is said to have taken about two thousand years to complete this cycle, since the fall of the Roman empire.

Many now talk about a shift of the centre of culture from the Atlantic to the Pacific. This occurs as the Western nations find it impossible to deal with their social and economic problems, perhaps because of their inability to see things ideationally. In their unstable cultural environment sensate thinking simply constrains what is seen as a way of addressing problems, and ideational goals are lost. However, the Pacific Rim countries continue to

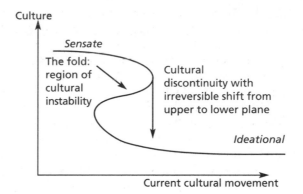

Fig. 8.1 Hypothesised 20th century shift in culture in Western Europe

The cultural discontinuity occurs as the culture shifts directly from the sensate (one topological condition) to the ideational state on the catastrophe curve.

develop their societies and economic systems and move towards eventual sociocultural domination. If we suppose Western culture to be a conservative system (perhaps meaning that it is not significantly influenced in its belief system by other cultures), then we can use catastrophe theory to present this shift through Fig. 8.1.

Such cultural shifts can be seen as fundamentally conservative. While all cultures have influences from other 'alien' cultures, in many instances these influences are not significant. While it may be argued that this was not the case of the American Indians or the Aztecs when they met Western culture, it could be argued that it is the case of the much more voluminous Western culture.

8.3.2 Dissipative structures and their systems

We are also aware that all systems can be described in terms of energy. All isolated systems conserve energy. In non-isolated systems, one can distinguish between systems in which the kinetic energy is conserved, and dissipative systems where the total (kinetic and potential) energy is conserved, but where part of the energy is changed in form and lost.

This is easily seen in a physical system like the bouncing of a tennis ball. Such a ball is a dissipative system because when it falls to the floor and bounces its kinetic and potential energy is converted to heat and dissipated to its environment. If dissipated systems are far from equilibrium they 'try' to recover equilibrium so quickly that they form dissipative structures to accelerate the process. Dissipative systems, in the process of globally increasing their entropy (as they move towards equilibrium), can create structured spots where entropy locally decreases and so negentropy locally increases to generate order and organisation.

Limited by our earlier mathematical techniques, the traditional way of modelling situations is with the assumption that they are conservative. Like conservative systems, dissipative systems have a definable form and a state of behaviour, though unlike conservative systems energy changes are large (Jantsch, 1980, p. 43). Prigogine and Stengers (1984) describe dissipative systems as those that have dissipative structures in which far from equilibrium process occur. For us dissipative systems are those systems that:

1 have *dissipative structures*;
2 are globally far from equilibrium;

169

3 are inherently dynamically unstable;

4 use energy to maintain order through negentropy beyond any thresholds of instability.

In other words, it is through the production of negentropy and thus the creation of order that structures with dissipative processes can survive.

Dissipative systems are in continual fluctuation, oscillating from one instability to another. These fluctuations occur in the mechanisms which result in the modifications of behaviour. The fluctuations may occur more or less randomly from the environment, but their effects can build up in the system through positive feedback. This can also be referred to as evolutionary feedback, and is consistent not only with the idea of the morphogenic development of systems, but also with that of learning systems (Deutsch, 1968; Pringle, 1968). Thus, new forms can occur spontaneously beyond a threshold of stability. When a system becomes structurally critical, then if it is to survive it will spontaneously shift to a new form. This occurs through the implicit production of negentropy; that is, the creation of order. It is because of the ability of such systems to change by generating negentropy that they are referred to as evolutionary. The cycle of change in dissipative structures occurs as depicted in Fig. 8.2.

In contrast to this, conservative systems that switch their form as a mechanism of survival do not need to produce negentropy to do this, and may therefore be considered not to participate in the modification of their form. They are not, therefore, normally considered to be evolutionary (Jantsch, 1980). This does not argue against the idea that conservative systems may also find themselves in a structurally critical condition and thus able to pass through a metamorphosis. Neither does it argue against the idea that conservative systems can develop dissipative systems within them that can differentially evolve.

Dissipative structures can also cease entropy and energy exchanges with the environment. They can thus develop the characteristics of closed or isolated systems by maximising their entropy, and hence achieve death through loss of order.

The fluctuations that dissipative structures experience can be seen as deviations that the system must deal with. The deviations can be either amplified or counteracted within mutual causal processes. In dissipative structures they are amplified (Maruyama, 1968). This so-called *deviation–amplification* is a positive feedback mechanism that represents the process of *morphogenesis*. It lies in contrast to the *deviation–counteraction* of negative feedback processes that represents *morphostasis*, which is typical of systems that adhere to steady state, like conservative systems.

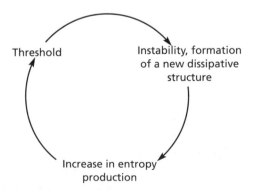

Fig. 8.2 The evolutionary cycle of dissipative structures
(*Source*: Jantsch, 1980, p. 43. Reprinted with permission of Butterworth-Heinemann, a division of Reed Educational and Professional Publishing)

A distinction between conservative and dissipative systems is given in Table 8.1, adapted from Jantsch (1980, p. 34). In conservative systems the preservation of states can under certain conditions be accompanied by qualitative changes in form. In dissipative systems the preservation of states is maintained through the creation and maintenance of order, or negentropy. There can be a close relationship between conservative and dissipative systems in that a conservative system can become dissipative, in the same way that a dissipative system can become conservative. Dissipative systems can be seen to occur as part of larger conservative systems, as explored through mathematical evolutionary game theory. When this occurs, it means that the relationship between the parts of a system may be continually evolving, while the system as a whole changes very gently through very small perturbations, always attempting to preserve its structure. In such situations, the form of a system may change dramatically in order to adjust to new conditions within which it finds itself. This is the situation in the theory of evolutionary games, where macroscopic systems are usually defined to be conservative, while subsystems can be described as having dissipative structures. This enables the subsystems to be evolutionary, or capable of learning, while the system as a whole is incapable of this.

Schwarz (1996, personal communication) distinguishes between different classes of dissipative system as in Table 8.2, aspects of which will be discussed in due course. In dissipative structures, self-organising behaviour occurs when systems evolve through a sequence of structures and processes that enables them to maintain the integrity of the system. A high degree of non-conservative behaviour maintains the self-organising mechanism through continuous exchanges of matter and energy with the environment. This represents a globally stable but never resting structure, which Jantsch considers to be representative of self-producing (autopoietic) systems. Self-organisation is a main phenomenon in systems maintaining their identity and autonomy. Hejl (1984) tells us that it causes processes that, due to certain initial and limiting conditions, arise spontaneously as specific states or as sequences of states. He does not, however, distinguish between systems that are conservative and dissipative. A problem faced by self-organising systems can be that they are not able to maintain themselves (Hejl, 1984), when their parts decompose or are consumed in the process and where there is no possibility of a resynthesis or replacement.

Table 8.1 Differences between conservative and dissipative systems

Characteristic	Conservative system	Dissipative systems
Structural orientation	Structure preserving	Structure changing (evolutionary)
Action towards deviation	Counteracting	Amplification
Dynamic	Close to zero energy changes and steady state with changes in time	Far from zero energy change with changes in time
Tendency of form	Morphostasis	Morphogenesis
Internal condition	Near to steady state	Far from steady state
Referent	Reference to steady state	Self-reference
Logical organisation	Irreversible process towards steady state	Cyclical irreversible process
System type	Open, with possible growth	Open, continuous, balanced energy exchange

Table 8.2 Classification of dissipative systems

System type	Proximity to equilibrium	Dynamic status	Behaviour	Evolutionary status
Conservative	–	Force field trajectory	Global laws of motion	Non-evolutionary, irreversible
Dissipative isolated	Equilibrium directed	Non-dynamic	Entropy maximising	Non-evolutionary, irreversible
Dissipative non-isolated	Near to equilibrium	Dynamic linear	Entropy minimising	Stationary flux (e.g. chemical reactions)
Dissipative non-isolated	Far from equilibrium	Dynamic nonlinear	Non-global (local)	Evolutionary
Dissipative non-isolated	Very far from equilibrium	Dynamic nonlinear	Non-global (local)	Chaotic flux (fractal)

(*Source*: Schwarz, personal communication, 1996)

Hejl also talks of self-maintaining systems. These may be seen as cyclical concatenations of self-organising behaviour: thus, the first self-organising system behaviour produces exactly the conditions for a second self-organising system behaviour, which in turn produces the starting conditions for a third process and so on, until one of the self-organising systems produces the initial conditions for the first system in the cycle. This system will belong to the same class as the first system which 'started' the cycle (Hejl, 1984, p. 63).

Self-maintaining systems are thus those in which self-organising systems regenerate and thus maintain each other. Self-maintaining systems are also self-referential systems, and these are open systems that refer only to themselves in terms of their intentioned purposeful organisational behaviour. This does not mean that they do not interact with the environment because it relates only to their purposefulness. While self-maintaining systems are self-referential, self-referential systems may not be self-maintaining. Self-organising systems which are self-maintaining and self-referential are said to be self-producing or autopoietic systems.

The creation of order consistent with self-organisation makes some theoretical demands on entropy. When a system develops entropy it moves towards disorder, so that any patterns of organisation that may exist become lost. The opposite process to this is the development of negentropy, which corresponds to the creation of patterns of order. Order can occur in any type of system, but self-organisation is needed in dissipative structures if they are to survive because of their implicit dynamic instability: order through negentropy is created to shift a dissipative structure from instability to stability.

8.3.3 Complexity theory

Complexity theory is derived from chaos theory and is concerned with complex systems. It is a unifying theory of organisations that focuses on the properties of complex adaptive systems. The composition of those systems is not a matter of consideration. All complex adaptive systems share common characteristics and operate in some ways that are similar.

Chaotic and self-organising behaviour of dynamic systems involves the theory of evolutionary or morphogenic systems of dissipative structures. Such systems involve complex adaptation. When the behaviour of a system reaches the threshold of its control, it enters a border area that we refer to as having bounded instability. It is non-equilibrium because behaviour patterns are continually fluctuating non-deterministically.

Fractals

Processes that are said to be recursive are self-similar. A self-similar object looks approximately like itself at different levels of inspection. Objects that are self-similar are called *fractals*. The term was coined by Mandelbrot (1982) in 1963 to describe the fine convoluted shapes found in nature in both the mathematical and natural worlds. A variety of graphic examples of fractals can be found in Pickover (1996, p. 198).

In dynamic systems, stability is characterised by attractors (Gleick, 1987, p. 138), patterns of stable dynamic pathways (said to be described in a phase space) that represent possible system changes. Systems in chaos not only have unpredictable behaviour, but also have fractal patterns that represent 'strange' attractors that embody self-organising principles. There may be a limited number of patterns possible, but within this the pattern that becomes manifest is unpredictable.

8.4 Schwarzian viable systems theory

A viable system is complex and adaptive, and is *able* to maintain a separate existence within the confines of its cultural or other constraints. The nature of viable systems is that they should have at least potential independence in their processes of regulation, organisation, production and cognition. The Schwarzian model provides a holistic relationship between the attributes that explain the nature of viable systems.

Schwarz proposes a generic model that addresses the emergence and possible evolution of organisations towards complexity and autonomy. In particular, it relates to self-organising systems that are far from equilibrium, and can refer to any domain of system (e.g. biological, social or cognitive). From these beginnings, Schwarz explains that all systems become viable when they develop:

1 patterns of self-organisation that lead to:
  a self-organisation through morphogenesis
  b complexity;
2 patterns for long-term evolution towards autonomy;
3 patterns that lead to the functioning of viable systems.

8.4.1 Objects, boundaries and events

Before exploring the ideas of Schwarz, it will be useful to consider the nature of systems in terms of their objects, events and boundaries.

Objects, events, and associations

According to Minai (1995) events can be defined in terms of 'bubbling nests of proximities' in a matrix of behavioural time and space. Any associations are by reference, and there are no actual localities. This suggests that the identification of localities is inquirer determined, and different inquirers see localities differently. Associations are information that results from the cross-referencing of objects and events in space–time. Guided by

Minai (1995, p. 37), we can differentiate between objects and events in the following way.

1 Objects are entities that have cognitively identified boundaries that may be expressed in terms of constraints on form and behaviour. They involve information generated from patterns and individual components that can be recognised through cognitive knowledge. They can be identified as vectors of concepts that are cognitively derived, and which may coincide with emergent properties. While an object may be a component of a system, it may itself have objects.

2 Events are energy patterns; they represent behaviour in the object world and their transformations. They can be represented as change that is attributed to the behavioural states of an object that may occur in either a random or a non-random way.

8.4.2 The conceptual planes

A system is seen as a non-separable entity that is composed of objects that are defined in mutual relation to each other. This entity is not reducible into a sum of its objects. The system exists in three distinct ontological planes:

1 the whole occurs in the existential plane;
2 relations occur in the logical plane;
3 objects occur in the physical (or behavioural) plane.

The existential plane

This is the plane of existing wholes (Fig. 8.3) that *is* identity. It symbolises the whole emerging from interacting objects. It is self-referential in nature thus making (a) the identity expressible by itself, without external reference, and (b) communication that occurs to itself. It is the domain of consciousness and meaning. It is the plane of cognitive 'truth' that defines what is valid. Validity itself is a logical entity that belongs to the relational plane. The existential plane defines epistemology, holds values, and is the place of the world view. Its holistic truths are paradigmatically determined, and can be referred to as *existential truth*; that is:

● the whole of all objects in relation;
● self-referentiality, or self-validated reality that is inexpressible in other terms;
● not separable into the objectal (or factual) truth of reality and logical (i.e. relational or validating) truth.

With respect to the last characteristic, holistic theories are said to make no distinction between objects and relations. Examples are quantum theory, Gödel's theory on completeness and consistency, and conscious systems. Philosophical holistic approaches are characterised by their indication of oneness, for example held by Schwarz (viability), D. Bohm, K. Pribram, R. Sheldrake, E. Laszlo and F. Valera (Buddhism) (Schwarz, 1994a).

The logical plane

The logical plane (Fig. 8.4) is that of relations and potential relations that identify associations. Thus realised interactions become manifest in the physical plane as structural relationships or energetic process. Potential relations are those that have not been physically manifested. They can, however, be described through logical propositions,

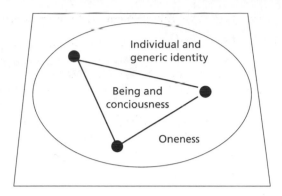

Fig. 8.3 The existential plane

mathematical expression and symbolic representations. This is the space in which symbols represent things, and of the abstract or potential relationship between such symbols. It is the place of organising information. It provides 'validity'. It is the place where methodological principles and theories exist. Within it there are images of self-organisation, autopoiesis and self-reference, though self-organisation is a physical process, autopoiesis an ontological feature so that it connects the physical plane and the logical plane, and self-reference is also an ontological feature – even more holistic.

We can speak of relational truth, by which we mean validity of relationships. For this Schwarz (1994a) identifies the following propositions:

- validity is an attribute of a relation;
- a relation is a constraint on the respective states of two symbols;
- a relation is valid if it is not contradictory with the rest of the causal network to which it is connected;
- a valid relation is an immaterial entity that can be symbolised by an algorithm;
- validity is influenced by states of objects changing randomly or ruled by other networks;
- validity can in general change with time;
- a network of valid relations at every instant represents the field of possible futures of a system.

Examples of relations in the logical plane are:

- holistic relations (non-local connections and correlations, semantic correlations, synchronicity);
- manifested actual relations or interactions (structural or energy relationships, light waves);
- potential relations (logical symbolic relationships, equations, networks of causal relations);
- non-random couples (states, parameters);
- philosophical (idealism, spiritualism, rationalism).

The physical plane

The physical plane (Fig. 8.5) is also an energy plane and the place of objects that have behavioural states. Objects are energetic and change over time. The physical plane is

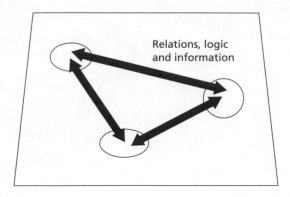

Fig. 8.4 The logical plane of relations

therefore the place of energy and material fluxes. It is the place where empirical form can be seen and examined. The physical plane is a manifestation that results from the other two planes. Now, the metamodel is a triad of objects, relations and the whole. These categories are untemporal, irreducible, inseparable and without priority. In contrast, reality appears to occur in the following time sequence:

1 differentiated parts (from a pre-existent medium)

2 interactions

3 coherence (the seven steps on the spiral; *see* Section 8.4.4).

It is therefore in this plane that 'reality' is identified. It is the place of systems manifestations, whether they are cognitive, social or natural. It is the place where interventions into the 'real world' occur. Thus, the physical plane is the plane of objectal reality; that is (Schwarz, 1994a):

● reality is an attribute of the objects (parts or components or sub-objects) of a system;
● the objects constituting reality can be perceived by our senses;
● reality is made of matter and energy stocks and fluxes in space and time;
● objects are distinguished by separation between subjects and objects.

Examples of objects in this plane are:

● inorganic objects (matter, energy, particles, minerals);
● living organisms (plants, humans, species);
● ecosystems (ant colonies, institutions, societies);
● artefacts (machines, motor cars, infrastructures, communications networks);
● philosophical (realism, materialism, empiricism, mechanism, modern positivist techno-science).

8.4.3 The principles of change

The traditional view of change relates to robust equilibrium systems, where the system as a whole is not vulnerable to changes in its parts, and where the sensitivity of the whole to fluctuations in the parts is minimised. Systems that are viable tend to show the characteristic of robustness.

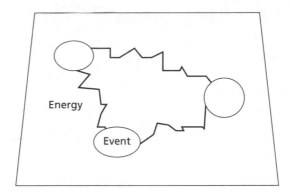

Fig. 8.5 The physical plane

In the thermodynamic theory of isolated systems, all events represent the universal trend towards the more probable. This trend is characterised by the spontaneous increase of entropy that leads to disorder, uniformity, to chaos and to death. However, viable systems exist by virtue of their ability to resist increases in entropy, to live, survive and reproduce, to increase their autonomy, to evolve and to complexify. Consistent with the cybernetic theory of Chapter 6, according to Schwarz they do this because of the logical plane (and in connection with the other two planes) through *operational closure*, that is the existence of closed loops in the network of its organisation. These loops are of two types:

1 self-stabilising (e.g. negative feedback)

2 self-organising (e.g. positive feedback).

The thesis of Schwarz is that the spontaneous and stochastic drift towards disorder and the emergence of order has a causal relationship. Within it lies a theory of generic patterns that enable us to:

- understand the origins of order;
- interpret the emergence and functioning of viable systems;
- identify the possible evolution of viable systems towards complexity and autonomy.

In the pursuit of a general explanation of this, Schwarz distinguishes between three types of thermodynamic system that we distinguish as the three classes i, ε, and f as depicted in Table 8.3. All material systems belong to one of these three classes.

Table 8.3 Three classes of system

Class	Nature of system	Explanation
i	Isolated equilibrium	Isolated equilibrium systems are characterised by having a maximal entropy and no energy changes. These systems do not evolve and are not time related.
ε	Conservative near equilibrium	Tend to be irreversible in their movement towards an unorganised state.
f	Non-isolated far from equilibrium systems	Characterised by feedback loops capable of (a) suppressing local fluctuations, (b) amplifying local fluctuations and (c) transforming fluctuations to macroscopic spatial and temporal dissipative structures. This usually results in a state of chaos. If the system can last long enough it may become involved in a spiral of self-organisation and complexification.

(*Source*: Schwarz, 1994)

8.4.4 The spiral of self-organisation

Self-organisation is seen to occur as a spiral pattern of stable behaviour. It has four successive recurrent phases (Table 8.4) that are shown graphically in Fig. 8.6.

Table 8.4 The phases of self-organisation

Phase	Steps	Explanation
1 Entropic drift (of which tropic drift is the general case)	1 Stability 2 Spontaneous entropic drift 3 Tropic drift 4 Increase in tensions	This leads to disorder or more generally to the more probable, to the actualisation of potentialities. It is often the coherent actualisation of the potentialities of the parts of the system that generates tensions and eventually breaks the global homeostatic or even autopoietic networks that hold all the social agents together.
2 Bifurcation (ALEA; i.e. crisis, randomness, hazard)	5 Fluctuations 6 Bifurcation 7.0 Option 0: decay 7.1 Option 1: type 1 (Watzlawick) change	Fluctuations occur internally, or in the environment as noise. Through amplification of fluctuations due to tensions following entropic drift, a discontinuity occurs in the causal sequence of events/behaviour. 'Stochastic' selection occurs, influenced by the tensions within a problem situation. The tensions correlate to the amplification of the fluctuations that occur. At this point three options are possible: 7.0, 7.1 or 7.2. Decay represents a process of either destructurising, disorganisation, regression or extinction of the system. This can be seen as the start of a catastrophe bifurcation. In type 1 the process of change begins with 'more of the same' small changes that maintain its current state. However, such changes, may be in some way bounded.
3 Metamorphosis	7.2 Option 2: type 2 change 8 Complexification	In type 2 change, metamorphosis begins as a local morphogenic event that is amplified within a critical structure to have a macroscopic effect. In the critical structure a new form can arise initiated by the nonlinear condition. It is one of many possible bifurcations that could have developed. Complexification can occur during iteration of spiral. Autonomy may develop.
4 Stability	9 Dynamic stability	Occurs through self-regulation and/or existential self-reference.

A system may drift away from stability by first losing its robustness. Tensions develop that make the system structurally critical, and thus macroscopically susceptible to small local perturbations. If these occur (as fluctuations), then either the system dies or becomes disorganised (the zero option), or self-organisation occurs and the system regains stability. This happens through morphogenesis that can be amplified. If type 1 change occurs, then the system is capable of further morphogenesis. With type 2 metamorphic change, then a spontaneous alteration in form happens. This occurs when the conditions within the system are such that the system has reached a bound in its ability to adapt morphogenically with respect to the perturbations from the environment. Thus, the six successive steps involved in the process of metamorphosis are:

1 differentiation as a response to tension;

2 communication/interaction between differentiated parts;

3 integration of the parts due to their interaction;

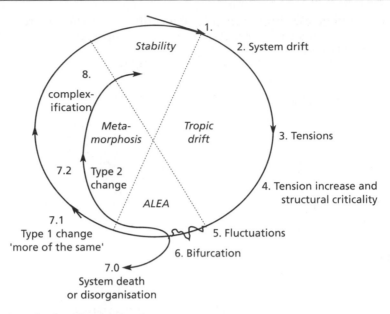

Fig. 8.6 The spiral of self-organisation

4 emergence of an encompassing common metalevel;

5 dynamical stabilisation of the whole;

6 recursion of above to result in more organisational metalevels and their integration (imbrication).

The creation of new systemic forms (step 6) is consistent with unexpected novelty. These are referred to as discontinuous bifurcations that derive from continuous relations. Embedded within the relations that connect with the new form are all the possibilities of innovation that might develop. Unexpected novelty occurs when these possibilities are not predeterminable. New forms are therefore not deterministically determinable, whether or not all the possibilities of form that might develop are known.

8.4.5 The ontological nature of viable systems

Any *viable system* can be characterised by two types of ontological cycle that connect between the physical, logical and existential planes: homogeneous and heterogeneous cycles (Table 8.5).

Table 8.5 The two types of ontological cycle

Homogeneous cycles	Heterogeneous cycles
Matter recycling between objects in the physical or event plane.	Morphogenic self-organising positive feedback loops between two different physical parameters.
Homeostatic loops in the logical or relational plane.	The autopoietic loop between the physical and logical planes.
Self-referential loops in the existential plane of wholeness or being.	The autogenetic metaloop between the autopoietic cycle and the system as a whole.

Within these cycles, we can also identify three dynamic processes involved in any viable system (Schwarz, 1994a), referred to as tropic drift, and stabilising and creative cycles (Table 8.6).

Table 8.6 Three dynamic processes

Tropic drift	Stabilising cycles	Creative cycles
Entropic drift towards uniformity	Vortices: matter recycling	Self-organisation: morphogenesis
Information (or negentropic) drift towards complexity	Self-regulation: homeostasis	Self-production: autopoiesis
Referential drift that intensifies self-reference and integrates differences. With the creation of identity and the emergence of consciousness, this results in existential drift towards being	Existential self-reference	Self-creation: autogenesis

These cycles and processes can be described in a generic metamodel that identifies the nature of viability. A viable system has the capability of self-regulation, self-organisation (including adaptation and evolution), self-production and self-reference. Evolution occurs when the spiral of self-organisation has occurred. The metamodel is explained in Table 8.7. Our view of the graphical representation of the metamodel created by Schwarz in the table is provided in Fig. 8.7.

In Table 8.8 we apply the model, explained in terms of its three ontological planes, to viable social systems (Schwarz, 1994).

8.5 A Schwarzian paradigm cycle model

8.5.1 Comparing Schwarz's planes to the paradigm-related domains

The approach adopted by us in this book centres on the paradigm cycle. It operates together with three ontological domains to provide a metamodel for methodological inquiry. We note that these domains are:

1 the surface manifestation of the system that entails behaviour;
2 the deep or cognitive metasystem;
3 the domain of transformation in which organising occurs.

There are similarities between our domains and the planes of Schwarz. The physical plane for Schwarz is 'reality'. For us reality is world view relative, and is thus a place where our models of reality exist that we represent as viable systems. In our terms, this is the place in which manifest behaviour is seen, and where empirical measurements are taken. It is the place of behavioural models. For us it would be the place of system manifestation, where events are defined in terms of their structures and energetic processes that are empirically examinable.

For Schwarz the existential plane would seem equivalent to our metasystemic domain. For us it is the place of cognition, where beliefs, attitudes and values are

Table 8.7 Schwarzian metamodel for the dynamics of self-organisation

Step	Movement towards evolution
1 Stability	The system starts in a non-isolated condition, with some degree of stability.
2 Tropic drift	Dissipative processes increase and the system is in danger of losing any robustness that it has. In complex systems the tropic drift enables potentials to be actualised. The drift takes the system away from its stable position and gives rise to tensions between the system and its parts and/or between the system and its environment.
3 ALEA (crisis)	The tensions, following the tropic drift that moved the system away from its stable domain, lead the system to a nonlinear condition of structural criticality. If the system loses robustness, fluctuations are amplified.
4 Metamorphosis	Morphogenic change is induced through amplification. This occurs through differentiation. While the steps 1–3 above occur in the event plane, here more relational processes appear in the system through positive and negative feedback, and integration.
5 Homeostasis	This slows down the morphogenesis of step 4, through the appearance of new integrative functional negative feedback loops. However, an unsuccessful result may produce regression, chaos or destruction.
6 Information drift and complexification	The above steps can be iterated, increasing the complexity of the system. This is represented in the logical plane.
7 Appearance of self-production cycles	When complexity reaches a very high level, a new kind of super-circularity can emerge: autopoiesis. This operates at the logical level of the system, reinforcing the network of production.
8 Autopoiesis	Complexification can continue in a safer way than in step 6. This is because there is an additional super-logical relation between the events that represent the system and its logical organisation. When this has happened, the system has increased its autonomy from the homeostatic steps of 5 and 6, to self-production.
9 Self-reference	Increase in autonomy and development of individual identity occurs with self-reference in the logical plane. In steps 5 and 6, the system could compensate for the unexpected variations in the environment through multiple homeostatic loops (steps 5 and 6). In steps 7 and 8 it developed the ability to increase its autonomy and complexification. Here it develops the ability to self-identify and dialogue with itself about matters that include its environment.
10 Self-referential drift	This represents an intensification of self-reference. This is accompanied by an increase in the qualitative and quantitative dialogue between the system and its image within the system. This increases autonomy, and elevates the level of consciousness in a living system. It therefore solidifies individual identity.
11 Autogenesis	This represents the self-production of the rules of production. It occurs in the existential plane. It defines the state of full autonomy, and is closed operationally. It defines being.

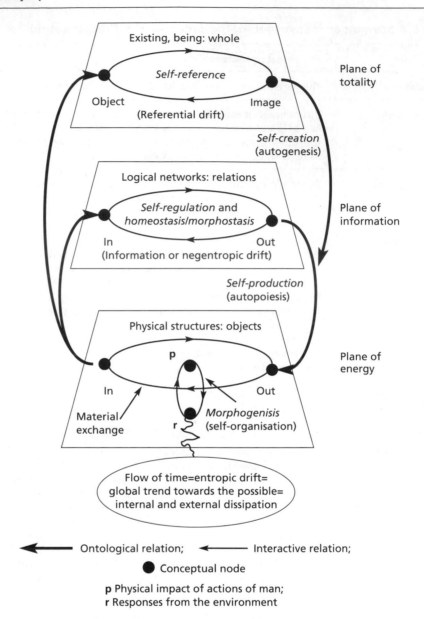

Fig. 8.7 Model explaining the nature of viable systems
(*Source*: Schwarz, 1994)

Table 8.8 The nature of viable natural social systems

Ontological plane	Action	Interpretation
1 Event	Structure	Social organisation produced through logical networks, individuals, groups, institutions, infrastructures, artefacts, natural movement, fluxes of energy-matter in space and time.
	Morphogenesis	Emergence, replication, regeneration, transformation, evolution or destruction of organic and artificial life forms, social structures. This is indicated by the autopoietic loop and within the energetic constraints. Positive feedback is especially important. Relationship between physical impact environmental responses highlighted. It connects to the flow of time, entropic drift, global trends toward the probable, and to internal and external dissipation.
	Material exchange recycling	This represents the social metabolism, energy fluxes, matter and signals ensuring physical processes, and social continuance and stability.
2 Ontological relation between event plane and logical plane	Downward autopoiesis	Production of individual and collective physical and psychic behaviour, from organisational networks, particularly the network of myths.
	Upward autopoiesis	Regeneration of the logical networks through actor and institutional behaviour. In particular, myth regeneration by (a) pressure (rituals, power, honour, money) of the system on mediators (sovereigns, priests, presidents, leaders, owners, director), (b) pressure of mediators on the masses (faithfuls, slaves, taxpayers, electors, debtors, employees, consumers). Myth regeneration and propagation through story telling, cults, media, advertising, entertainment.
3 Logical plane	Networks	Logical relations that determine society. Several levels of interaction with environment: for resource gathering, security, social organisation of the noosphere (e.g. networks of knowledge, myths, beliefs), and money.
	Homeostatic loops	Complex organisation of logical relations defining society as a functional unit. Globally homeostatic cycles and hypercycles resulting from the until recently viable co-evolution between actor behaviour and the corresponding logical network (in particular system of myths).
4 Ontological relation between existential plane and ontological relation 2	Downward autogenesis	Metacoupling between social groups as a whole and the autopoietic dialogue. Influence on social groups by its own rules of production. The intensity of this metacoupling is a measure of autonomy. Conflicts may arise between this social autogenesis and individual autogenesis.
	Upward autogenesis	Metacoupling between the autopoietic dialogue and the social entity emerging from the dialogue. Continuous creation, regeneration, evolution or transformation of society as an existing whole.
5 Existential plane	Being	Social group as an existing whole, including its holistic attributes. Its degrees of autonomy, coherence and identity (teleonomy) increase with its complexity.
	Auto-referential loop	Social entity emerging from the dialogue between itself and its own image. The closer the object is to the image, the greater its harmony and autonomy.

defined, and where understanding and meaning occur. It is where the weltanschauung and the paradigm coexist. Through the paradigm, it is where 'truths' of the metasystem are defined. For us, these 'truths' will determine logic.

The logical plane of Schwarz is similar to our domain of transmogrification. As in the work of Schwarz, it is the place of symbols and relationships that we see to be conceptualised in the metasystem. For us this is the place where logic is manifested. It is where the logic defined within the paradigm is harnessed and is then manifested as structures and processes in the physical plane. However, relations can also be seen as transformations in that they act on (and within) events and are responsible for events.

A relation is valid if it is not contradictory with the rest of the causal network to which it is connected. There is a complication with this proposition that closely relates to that of methodological complementarism and paradigm incommensurability. In answer to this Schwarz would say that there is a difference between giving a pure definition (here validity), in the symbolic (relational) world, and the description of a 'real' situation where the conditions admitted in the definition may not exist. Schwarz (1996, personal communication) tells us that the main difference between the dualist stance, the logico-materialistic science, and the holistic approach proposed here, is precisely that here we are able to apprehend paradoxical situations. In such situations a relation is not true or false (as in Aristotelian logic used in dualist science), but can oscillate as in self-contradictory self-referential sentences like 'this sentence is false'. Now validity is equivalent to non-contradiction. However, there may be real situations where (temporary) validity of a relation destroys its own validity, giving rise to ontological oscillations. This problem of distinction between definition and description of a global situation is also met in thermodynamics where one defines isolated systems knowing that there are no perfectly isolated systems. The cases of system incompatibility between the indications of the logical plane and the outcome of the object plane are the most interesting because they produce an endless dial which may be responsible (for example) for living, cognitive and eventually conscious organisms.

The ontological relationships that relate the three planes defined by Schwarz can be placed in terms of our own paradigm-based models. We identify the three domains of cognition, transmogrification and form that relate directly to the Schwarzian existential, logical and physical planes. We are now able to consider the ideas of action, conceptual node definition and drift as defined in Fig. 8.6.

Domain of behaviour

Most generally we define a manifest domain that is typically taken to be behaviour. Action (behaviour) occurs in the systemic domain that is directly related to system forms. A conceptual node in this domain may be determined by an event that can result in objects in some structural relationship. A change in their relationship is a morphogenic action that derives from the domain of transmogrification.

A node may also be an energy (or power) source, or an entropy source. Entropic drift can occur when the organisational process is weakened, and differentiation between the systemic parts becomes fuzzy. That is, the organisation starts to become disorganised.

Domain of transmogrification

Since this is the domain of ordering a node may be an input or output information or negentropy point, or a point of control decision or reference like a monitor. In the latter case, the relationship between a monitor and decided action for change through self-regulation can occur.

Negentropic drift can occur when the organisational process drifts away from that represented at the metasystemic level. This can occur because of a problem of perturbations or confusions during transmogrification. It can also occur when the ontological connection between the cognitive domain and that of transmogrification has either broken down or is subject to transcendental interference. As a result new structures and processes can arise which have little relationship to those represented by the belief system and from the metapurposes.

Cognitive domain

Generic identity is a classification that derives from the cognitive domain but is projected to the domain of form through transmogrification. In the cognitive domain a node may be a reflection or image of self that relates to existence. The relationship between the variety of reflections or images that an individual or group obtains from its ability to believe itself to be successful is a function of its self-reference. Thus, individual identity is a cognitive assignment of self-reference within the cognitive domain. Referential drift can be seen as the confirming development of identity as autonomy increases. We can also identify the idea of paradigmatic drift, meaning change in beliefs or purpose, or a shift from one dominant paradigm to another.

These ideas are summarised in Table 8.9. For each plane the nature, function, nature of node and nature of drift have been identified. The interaction between the three planes defines the nature of autopoiesis (or self-production) and autogenesis (self-creation). Thus autopoiesis defines the relationship between self-organisation and self-regulation, while autogenesis defines the relationship between self-reference and self-organisation.

8.5.2 Propositions of viable human activity systems

Complexity theory is built on chaos theory, which is itself built on the theory of dissipative systems. All of these have as their foundation the notion that viable systems are dynamic and frequently far from equilibrium. It explains how they change and still survive because they are able to maintain stability in their behaviour, even though finding themselves shifting between robustness and structurally critical conditions from time to time. These ideas have been integrated into systems theory and applied to social systems. It is now possible to propose a set of propositions (based on the work of Schwarz above, and that of other authors expressed earlier in this book) that tell us under what conditions a social system is viable.

1   A system is a unity of interactive objects each with its own frame of reference.

2   It is made up of *objects* that are composed of components that may themselves be seen as objects.

3   A viable social system is a self-organising group of individuals who maintain at least one paradigm.

4   The paradigm with its *logical* organising relationships and *manifest* consequences (like rituals and methods) represents the image of a social system.

5   The paradigms of a social system determine the *network* of beliefs, 'truths' about itself, and are responsible for myths and their manifestations like rituals; they will determine how the system will function.

Table 8.9 Classification of ontological relationship between system and metasystem

Domain	Nature	Function	Nature of node	Nature of drift
System	Self-organisation, deviation–amplification, morphogenesis	Action	Object, subject, thing, event	Entropic drift towards disorder
Transmogrification	Self-regulation, deviation–counteraction, homeostasis, morphostasis	Decision, negentropy, information, control	Point of: ordering, or negentropy, or information, or control decision	Negentropic drift towards unexpected forms
Metasystem	Self-reference	Belief, metapurpose	Point of: reflection, or belief, or purpose	Paradigmatic drift is a morphogenesis or metamorphosis of the cognitive organisation (beliefs, attitudes and values)

6   Viable social systems have operational closure through self-organisation, self-production or autopoiesis, self-reference and autogenesis.

7   Viable social systems involve dissipation (entropic drift towards disorder and uniformity) and teleonomy (degree of autonomy, coherence and identity) generated by operational closure. A viable social system has self-organisation if it has the ability to amplify unexpected fluctuations that occur within it. Fluctuations occur as a direct result of perturbations from its environment that affect its dynamic events.

8   A viable system may exist as a holon made up of networks of other holons in a system hierarchy (a holarchy), each a semi-autonomous cooperating entity. Such systems may adapt.

9   A viable system (according to Beer, 1975) is able to support adaptability and change while maintaining operational (or behavioural) stability. A system is adaptive when its form is maintained, elaborated or changed according to its self-organisational needs. Such adaptation is not determinable by its environment, but by its own possibilities. It is a complex adaptive system when it maintains complicated networks of independent components that are so interconnected as to form a unity or organic whole with demonstrated capabilities to adjust behaviour to changing circumstances and to anticipate future events.

10 Autopoiesis is the self-production of individual and collective physical and psychic behaviour that derives from its organisational networks. An autopoietic system defines its own boundaries relative to its environment, develops its own code of operations, implements its own programmes, reproduces its own elements in a closed circuit, and lives according to its own dominant paradigms. When a system reaches what we might call 'autopoietic take-off', its operations can no longer be controlled from outside. In general an autopoietic system will generate outputs to that network of processes that are in part themselves the network of processes.

11 According to Schwarz (1994) a viable social system is autopoietic. This can be shown because it can:

a Regenerate a social system's logical or organising networks that derive from its paradigms, through actor and institutional behaviour. Consider for example *myths,* that like other 'bubbles' participate in all of the three Schwarzian planes but start as existent 'truths'. They have manifestations that some refer to as rituals. Ritual regeneration and propagation occur through, for instance, story telling, cults, media, advertising and entertainment. They are enabled through:

   i pressure (like rituals, power, honour and money) applied by the system on mediators (like sovereigns, priests, presidents, leaders, owners, directors);

   ii pressure of mediators on the masses (like faithfuls, slaves, taxpayers, electors, debtors, employees, consumers);

b Define for itself the boundaries of that network, determined from paradigms.

12 Autopoiesis is essential to a viable social system since it enables it to 'digest' any unexpected fluctuation. It does this through entropic drift to regenerate the system's structure. We can thus say that such systems can become autopoietic by (a) modifying their structures and fluxes (social form and behaviour), and (b) changing the causal networks that derive from their paradigms and methods for achieving goals.

13 Self-reference occurs in open systems that refer only to themselves in terms of their intentioned purposeful organisational behaviour.

14 Autogenesis can be thought of as relating to coherence and oneness. It represents the influence it has on its own rules of production. It involves continuous creation, regeneration, evolution or transformation of society as an existing whole. The intensity of the influence is a measure of autonomy. In general autogenesis can also be related to 'consciousness'; in the context of a social system, such consciousness might be connected to what Jung refers to as the collective consciousness.

15 We are not alone in an environment of passive and controllable things; we are part of a network of teleonomic systems and subsystems; that is, complex active system with different degrees of autonomy in our economic, political, social and cultural parts, all striving for survival.

16 The paradigm of social systems should be compatible with their networks. This means that there should be consciousness of the self-producing dialogue between a system and its image.

17 In complex nonlinear networks of teleonomic subsystems, the drive for survival of each subsystem is no guarantee of the survival of the whole. The overall autopoietic logic has priority over the survival logic of the parts.

18 Viable social systems must be autopoietic, thus having compatibility and mutual production between their dynamic events and the networks that produce them. To survive in an organised way they must at least maintain compatibility between their events and the causal network of production.

SUMMARY

Complex environments can make it difficult for systems to maintain their stability. Equilibrium is not the normal condition for viable systems. Systems are more typically far from equilibrium. It is in far from equilibrium systems where self-organisation and evolution are natural processes. An understanding of evolution and the process of self-organisation is important for the viability. A good way of representing this is through the Schwarzian spiral of self-organisation, that clearly links together many of the concepts of viability. Applying these concepts to the domain of inquiry enables us to conceive of a viable inquiry system. This couples methodology to a target situation through an inquirer, and may be able to lead to methodologies capable of exploring the problem of chaos.

REFERENCES

Beer, S. (1975) 'Preface'. In Maturana, H.M. and Varela, F.G. (eds) *Autopoiesis and Cognition: The realisation of the living*. Dordrecht: Reidel.

Davis, A.K. (1963) 'Lessons from Sorokin'. In Tiryakian, E.A. (eds) *Sociological Theory, Values, and Sociocultural Change*. New York: Free Press, pp. 1–7.

Deutsch, K.W. (1968) 'Towards a cybernetic model of man and society'. In Buckley, W. (ed.) *Modern Systems Research for the Behavioural Scientist*. Chicago, IL: Aldine, pp. 387–400.

Gleick, J. (1987) *Chaos*. London: Sphere.

Hejl, P.M. (1984) 'Towards a theory of social systems: self-organisation and self-maintenance, self-reference and syn-reference'. In Ulrich, H. and Probst, G.J.B. (eds) *Self-Organisation and Management of Social Systems*. Berlin: Springer-Verlag, pp. 60–78.

Jantsch, E. (1980) *The Self-Organising Universe: Scientific and human implications of the emerging paradigm of evolution*. New York: Pergamon Press.

Kemp, G. and Yolles, M.I. (1992) Conflict through the rise of European culturalism. *Journal of Conflict Processes*, 1(1), 5–15.

Mandelbrot, B. (1982) *The Fractal Geometry of Nature*. New York: W. H. Freeman.

Maruyama, M. (1968) 'The second cybernetics: deviation-amplifying mutual causal processes'. In Buckley, W. (ed.) *Modern Systems Research for the Behaviour Scientist*. Chicago, IL: Aldine, pp. 304–13.

Minai, A.T. (1995) 'Emergence, a domain where the distinction between conception in arts and sciences is meaningless', *Cybernetics and Human Knowing*, 3(3), 25–51.

Nicolis, G. and Pigogine, I. (1989) *Exploring Complexity: An introduction*. New York: W.H. Freeman.

Pickover, C.A. (1996) *Keys to Infinity*. New York: Wiley.

Pribram, W.D. (1977) *Languages of the Brain*. Monterey, CA: Wadsworth.

Prigogine, I. and Stengers, I. (1984) *Order out of Chaos: Man's new dialogue with nature*. London: Flamingo.

Pringle, J.W.S. (1968) 'On the parallel between learning theory and evolution'. In Buckley, W. (ed.) *Modern Systems Research for the Behavioural Scientist*. Chicago, IL: Aldine, pp. 259–80.

Rosenhead, J. (1989) *Rational Analysis for a Problematic World: Problem structuring methods for complexity, uncertainty, and conflict*. New York: Wiley.

Schwarz, E. (1994) 'A trandisciplinary model for the emergence, self-organisation and evolution of viable systems'. Presented at the International Information, Systems Architecture and Technology Conference, Technical University of Wroclaw, Szklaska Poreba, Poland.

Schwarz, E. (1994a) 'A metamodel to interpret the emergence, evolution and functioning of viable natural systems'. In Trappl, R. (ed.) *Cybernetics and Systems '94*. Singapore: World Scientific, pp. 1579–86.

Sorokin, P.A. (1937) *Social and Cultural Dynamics*. New York: American Book Company.

Sorokin, P.A. (1963) 'Comments on Schneider's observations and criticisms'. In Zollschan, K.G. and Hirsch, W. (eds) *Explorations in Social Change*. London: Routledge & Kegan Paul.

Stacey, R. (1993) *Managing Chaos*. London: Kogan Page.

Thom, R. (1975) *Structural Stability and Morphogenesis*. Reading, MA: Benjamin Cummings.

CHAPTER 9

The nature of methodological inquiry

OVERVIEW

Methodologies may be seen as complex adaptable purposeful activity systems that can also be viable. The purposeful activity that we are referring to is inquiry, the purpose often being a search for stable intervention strategies in complex situations. The tri-domain model distinguishes between a cognitive domain and a behavioural domain. Transmogrification has a very important role to play in linking the metasystem with the system. It is strategic, and supports logical, relational and cybernetic mechanisms, permitting inquiry to be controlled. It is through cybernetic processes that we are able to define complex method, which, when added to a paradigm, defines methodology.

OBJECTIVES

This chapter will show:

- the nature of methodology;
- that a methodology can be seen as part of a purposeful system with cybernetic attributes;
- the distinction between cognitive and behavioural aspects of inquiry;
- the purpose and function of transmogrification during inquiry.

9.1 Seeing methods systemically

There is a systems perspective that methodologies should be seen to be a system of learning. It is, for instance, a proposition that is usually associated with soft systems thinking. This reminds us (Chapter 5) that learning systems can also be seen to be purposeful adaptable activity systems. Now, the nature of methodology is that it is an organisation of inquiring activities undertaken for some purpose – often to provide intervention strategies for a complex problematic situation. This suggests that it can be seen as a purposeful activity system involving *inquiry* as the *activity*. In this chapter we shall explore methodology within this context by assigning purposeful systemic attributes that include cybernetic principles.

In order to develop this approach, we will examine the nature of method. One introduction to this that we might refer to in these endeavours is the idea of Senge (1990) in his exploration of systems as the 'fifth discipline'. Part of his interest was in exploring the relationship in situations between fundamental change and action. His ideas are illustrated in Fig. 9.1, and we shall interpret them in our context. Let us consider first his *domain of action*. Behaviour is facilitated by infrastructure, and its innovative properties will enable behaviour to meet unexpected environmental perturbations. Behaviour is also formulated as a result of cognitively deriving ideas. In addition behaviour occurs through the use of theories, methods, and tools (i.e. procedures, techniques and other forms of situational knowledge). The *domain of enduring change* occurs through cognitive attitudes and beliefs, as well as awarenesses and sensibilities. In addition, skills and capabilities affect enduring change.

Broadly speaking there is some correspondence between Senge's model and ours, though this is certainly not linear. We distinguish between the behavioural (or systemic) and the cognitive (or metasystemic) domains that are more or less related to Senge's domains of action and enduring change. Our model assigns attributes to each domain, while that of Senge appears to indicate influences. Thus, one distinction is that skills are assigned to the system domain by arguing that they are situational phenomena that relate to surface knowledge defined in the behavioural system.

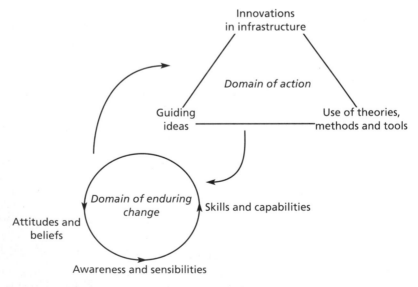

Fig. 9.1 Distinction between the deep and surface learning

Another distinction between Senge's model and ours is the introduction of a domain of transmogrification that connects the system and metasystem, and that enables us to represent cybernetic phenomena. It is not immediately clear how these phenomena would be expressed in terms of Senge's model. For our purposes the cybernetic domain is of some importance, and much of this chapter will be taken up in exploring aspects of it.

9.2 The cybernetics of method

Cybernetic phenomena occur in our domain of transmogrification. In part we can see this domain to be a potential field for control since it (a) defines a space that enables behaviour organising and (b) provides for all forms of possible behaviour to become manifested by creating an ordering process. It is also a field that defines behavioural strategy, involving the specification of logical and cybernetic relations that enable behaviour to be manifested according to *patterns of argument* that may otherwise be referred to as a field of *rationality*. The logical aspects are derived from the set of propositions that defines the conceptual theory of inquiry, and from which rise the paradigm and its tools of inquiry. The domain defines holistic and potential relations, conducts information, is constrained by ideology and normative standards, and defines the basis for symbols. It is also cybernetic in nature, extending logical projections to the environment of viable systems that are information sensitive.

The cybernetic nature of transmogrification therefore encompasses control essential to any activity system, and this includes inquiry. Control is 'the means by which a whole entity retains its identity and/or performance under changing circumstances' (Patching, 1990, p. 14). It ensures that a system can continue to accomplish a given purpose despite disturbances. The control actions in transmogrification enable systems to have:

- *intended definition* of form through its structural relationships and processes;
- *regulation* to ensure that the system operates in a way that is consistent with its intended purpose and the conditions under which it exists;
- *active organising* to ensure that the regulation processes are able to cope with the changing conditions of the system, and the facilitation of adjustments to form that enable it to adapt to new conditions.

If control is to occur, then we first need to establish an evaluation of goal deviations; that is, the deviation between an intended goal and our ability to achieve it. On exploring this further, we will recall that behaviour is a property of the system, while cognition is one of the metasystem. The relationship between the system and its metasystem in terms of the control field potential is depicted in Fig. 9.2, and as we are about to see now it can also be explained in terms of single- and double-loop learning (Chapter 7).

In the same way as used previously, in Fig. 9.2 the 'system' is defined in terms of form, contextual situation and manifest behaviour, and the metasystem in terms of the system's paradigmatic and cognitive exigencies. The system experiences empirical challenge that causes deviation in the control processes, and this can affect the metasystem. In single-loop learning the effect of empirical challenge is restricted to the system as its control mechanisms struggle to maintain order. Within double-loop learning there is a consequence of cognitive challenge that results from the system's inability to deal with the empirical challenge; the impact is that a demand is made on the metasystem to redefine any of its concepts, control criteria or meanings. Empirical challenge can thus result

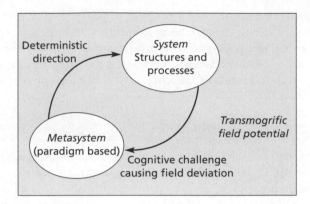

Fig. 9.2 Influence relationship between systems and metasystem

in transmogrific field turbulence, producing deviations that derive from the difference between a perceived goal state of the system, and some ideal or even abstract state as defined by the metasystem that is said to be *desirable*. Empirical challenge also has an impact on the deterministic direction offered by the metasystem. The purpose for exploring goal deviation is to determine the status of the system relative to the predefinable 'cognitive' characteristics defined by the metasystem that bounds the system's goal states. If behaviour is perceived to be so bounded, then it may be argued that we have achieved a desirable goal state.

9.3 Cognitive and situational inquiry

When one talks of a process of inquiry, one means a coherent set of inquiry *activities* that has meaning associated with it. A coherent or meaningful inquiry process may also be seen to be world view determined, thus having at its foundation cognitive knowledge-based models. Its projection into the situational space occurs through cognitive purposes that are interpreted in a situation, and describe the purposes of a set of inquiries relative to it. They are therefore placed within a situational context that orientates situational models (tools of inquiry). We can explore this further. In Chapter 7 we offered some attributes relating to the form of a system. Though unusual, there is no barrier to our saying that the metasystem can also have a form, and illustrating this by applying the same attributes. Thus, in Table 9.1 we offer attributes for the form of an inquiry system defined in terms of its situation knowledge, and this is related to the attributes of the form of its metasystem in terms of cognitive knowledge.

9.4 The nature of systemic methods

In management systems, it is sensible that the methods we use should be systemic. By this we mean that method has a form that might define a procedural schedule or ordered set of techniques to guide an inquirer's manifest behaviour, and this should be seen systemically. It also means that the contextual situation that a method is to deal with should also be explored from a systemic perspective, using for example systems

Table 9.1 Characteristics of an inquiry that relates to cognitive and situational knowledge

Characteristic	Cognitive inquiry	Situational inquiry
Structure	Propositional relationships between concepts subject to cognitive organisation.	A set of procedural steps manifested from paradigmatic principles.
Orientation	Also called a penchant. Defined by the cognitive knowledge that is produced from the propositional base, and that is distinct in every paradigm.	Defined through cognitive purposes that determine the direction that inquiry can take. It can be defined as the mission, goals. Inquiry effectiveness criteria can be defined in terms of inquirer aims.
Conditions	Defined through world views and cognitive knowledge, and results in inquiry criteria.	Defined for situations formulated through observation and empirical knowledge expressed as data and facts.
Dynamic actions and processes	Involves propositional issues that may evolve. They become manifested as inquiry behaviour.	The active organisation of the inquiry. May involve a changing structure for a given situation.
Mode	Defines generic classifications for inquiry to manifest itself as a system.	The way in which the steps of an inquiry are manifested for a given situation.

diagrams and perspectives. Metasystemic considerations should also be included. More clearly, it is appropriate to apply the generic characteristics of systems to methods. From Chapter 1 we note that methods should define:

- a set of connected parts (the procedural elements or individual techniques) for which purposefulness plays a part;
- a complex whole;
- a materially or immaterially organised body defined in terms of an orderly structure, a working order and an organic nature.

Now, in Chapter 4 we implicitly supported Flood in his argument that method cannot simply be assumed to be defined as a recipe of procedures that must be followed. To develop upon this we qualified *method* by referring to it as simple or complex. While some may wish to regard simple methods to be recipes dedicated to a single given area of application, complex methods, like methodologies, will be very different from this. As part of our study in managing complexity, our interest lies in complex methods (and in particular methodologies), and these should be seen to be systemic to enhance their ability to deal with complex situations.

We are aware that purposeful adaptable activity systems can be explored in terms of our tri-domain model, and that they have a metasystem, a system and cybernetic processes. Since methodology can be seen as a purposeful adaptive activity system, our intention now is to explore it in terms of these aspects.

An adaptable purposeful activity system can be seen as an organisation with a metasystem and a system. The system of a methodology has a form that is represented by its ordered procedures and their intimate relationships. Its metasystem is populated by world views that include its paradigm(s), and the world views of inquirers who operate it for the purpose of untangling the complexity of a problem situation. It is from its metasystem that we can understand the relationship between the world views involved, as well as between the position of the inquirer and any intervention strategy that might result from inquiry. By examining the metasystem, we are therefore examining the cognitive purposes of an inquiry. These can be manifested as the *mission* of an inquiry, and there will often be associated *goals* that relate directly to that mission. We are able to distinguish between two types of mission. These belong to a method in use, and an inquiring user. Associated with the mission we shall refer to a method's *goals*, and an inquirer's *aims*. In addition, there are effective criteria for a strategy of action that are determined by either a methodology or an inquirer, and will derive from the situation to which inquiry is directed. All are related to the orientation of an intervention intended for the situation being inquired into as determined by weltanschauungen and paradigms. Thus, we define the cognitive purposes of inquiry in Table 9.2.

Table 9.2 The cognitive purposes of inquiry

Method	Mission and goals (including criteria of effectiveness)	A *mission* that derives from the cognitive organisation of a paradigm as a set of cognitive purposes (also called meta-purposes). *Goals* that are expansions of the mission. Effectiveness criteria may be defined as goals.
Inquirer	Mission, aims, criteria of effectiveness	An inquirer's *mission* is identified by what are seen as the purposeful needs, and *inquiry aims* define in what way. Effectiveness criteria may be defined as aims.

While the inquirer's aims are determined through weltanschauung, the mission and goals of the method derive from a paradigm. This constrains the way the methods that derive from the paradigm are applied to the situation to be investigated.

Since the metasystem is bound up with paradigms and weltanschauungen, then these must be involved in the inquiry purpose. This relationship is shown in Fig. 9.3. The metasystem has previously been argued to be a result of world views. It is therefore belief based, and actions arise from beliefs. According to Jastrow (1927, p. 284) people are 'belief-seeking rather than fact-seeking'. This is because facts are what we *consider* to be true according to our beliefs. This is an idea that we explored earlier, when we referred to Beer's definition that facts are 'fantasies that you can trust'. We note that

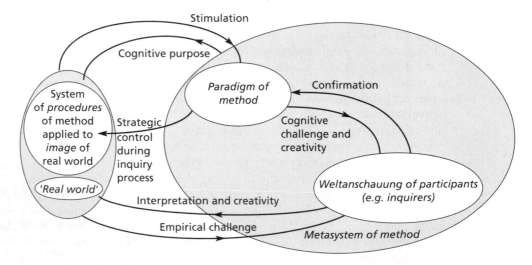

Fig. 9.3 Context diagram for method defined in terms of the tri-domain model

trust is dependent on belief, and what constitute facts can thus vary with weltanschauungen and paradigms. This has implications for the way we think about methods, and makes us think about what we are actually seeking when we make inquiries.

We have said that there is a relationship between a method's paradigm and the associated weltanschauungen of the participating individuals that can together be taken to define the basis for its metasystem. Identifying those individuals involved will be a function of the paradigm of the method: this will ultimately determine who is involved in establishing validation of the inquiry outcomes, and how it will occur. For instance, in a hard paradigm, the participants may be identified as solely the inquirer(s). In a softer paradigm, the participants might include the primary stakeholders seen (by either the inquirer or others) to be part of the situation.

Conceptualisations from a paradigm associated with a method are manifested behaviourally as a set of procedures or techniques that act on an image of the 'real world'. By referring to it as an image, we underscore the notion that we are examining that reality through a metaphor, and in particular from a systemic viewpoint. By writing 'real world' rather than real world, we highlight the notion that reality only exists through our perceptions. If, as supported by Talbot in Chapter 2, we suppose that the real world is holographic, then every view is a virtual image that has no physical extension in space. Thus, the tangible reality of our everyday lives is a kind of illusion. However, if each view of reality is taken to be a valid representation of the real world, a virtual part so to speak, then from a systemic perspective each part will maintain an implicit referencing to the whole. This is a perspective that supports the weltanschauung principle and which we may now refer to as being a 'virtual necessity'.

To develop the systemic view of a methodology further, we can draw on the idea espoused earlier that sees the procedural steps of a methodology as involving a strategic control process that defines a modifiable schedule for a set of procedural steps. We can identify a number of classes of concern that enable us to differentiate between the conceptual and procedural aspects of a methodology. A typology for this is given in Table 9.3.

Table 9.3 An exploration of the different conceptual uses of the metasystem and the system

| Class of concern | Metasystem deriving | | Procedural system deriving |
	Paradigm	Weltanschauung	
Aspect	Methodology	Purposeful inquiry	The perceived situation and its context, including roles, situation states, processes, controls and their relationships.
Action	What the methodology does: identifying orientation; propositional structure.	What the inquiry is intended to do: identifying the purposes for inquiry and for intervention.	What a system does and how it does it: its emergent properties and set of cognitive purposes.
Impact	Impact of cognition on methodology: identifying exemplars.	The impact of the inquirer and the inquiry; indeterminacy.	The impact of intervention; the change.
Form	The propositions that underwrite a methodology and determine its cultural style.	The informal view or personal approach that operates within inquiry and the inquirer.	Form of the system including structure and processes; consideration of participants and their roles, the inquirer.

9.5 The cybernetics of inquiry

A method can be seen as a cognitively defined process of inquiry that has an orientation defined by the penchant of the paradigm from which it derives. Methods can also be seen to involve a schedule of procedural steps that an inquirer will pass through, and that structures a pattern of inquiry behaviour. In complex method like methodologies, the patterns can be varied by introducing control processes that complexify the inquiry process and provide increased flexibility and the possibility of greater variety. A distinction between simple method and methodology is that the latter involves accessible transmogrification. If a methodology is to deliver a satisfactory proposed intervention strategy for a problem situation, then the inquiry itself must be a stable process. This means that their procedures, whether segmented into phases and subphases or not (*see* Chapter 5), should be evaluated for stability. It is here where the idea of strategic control comes in.

Consider any procedural step of a methodology. Within this an inquirer undertakes actions that result in outputs intended to achieve some local goal. Let us suppose that the inquirer has passed through the step, and achieved a result. It is now necessary to validate that this step is satisfactory according to some interpreted paradigmatic criteria. Let us suppose that the methodology under consideration has a soft paradigm. This means that validation must occur through a process of stakeholder participation. It may be useful to distinguish between at least two types of soft paradigm: that which seeks consensus and that which seeks dominant views to validate outputs.

If a consensus approach to validation is adopted, then the outputs that the inquirer participates in will be directed to the stakeholders for consensual evaluation. However, if the paradigm seeks a dominant view, then a reflection of the image will likely be directed only to the viewholders of the dominant paradigm for their evaluation. Here, possibly not all of the stakeholders will also be viewholders of the dominant paradigm in the organisation. In either case, part of the stability process must ensure that the nature of the validation process is cognitively sound, and that the meaning of the outputs is understood.

The creation of a strategy for intervention is only the final result of a whole set of steps that are embedded within the structured process of inquiry. If any of the intermediate steps towards the search for an intervention strategy are themselves unstable, then it is highly likely that the intervention strategy itself will not satisfy the purposes of the inquiry. The failure of stability at any point of the inquiry process can result in either negative feedback, or in the event of failure in self-regulation, positive feedback and cognitive learning by the inquirer (if not by the paradigm).

As an example of this, consider only evaluating the stability of the final stage of inquiry, the proposed intervention strategy that we refer to as action. For our purposes here, we are ignoring controls in all other phases except the result of choice. As a consequence of this, in Fig. 9.4 we have placed all three phases of our framework methodology from Chapter 5 under a single control loop, so that the whole structure is checked in respect of its outputs. The representation of this control on the overall inquiry process is simplified in Fig. 9.5, by using a simple return loop to represent the control details.

This diagram can be better represented as in Fig. 9.6. It suggests that through the introduction of a control process to evaluate proposed action, the structure is a meta-model that provides for models to be constructed, and that can be seen as a cycle of inquiry passing through analysis, synthesis and choice. An inquirer may need to pass through it more than once (iteratively) to maintain stability.

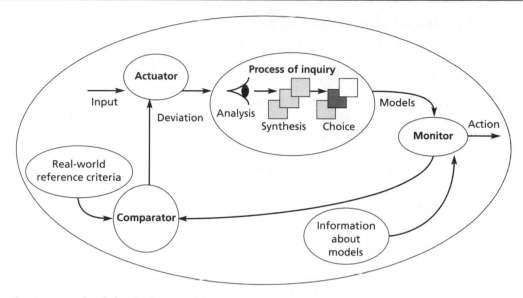

Fig. 9.4 Methodological control loop with phase options as process

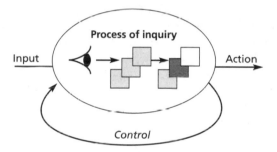

Fig. 9.5 Phases of the methodology, feedback representing a control loop

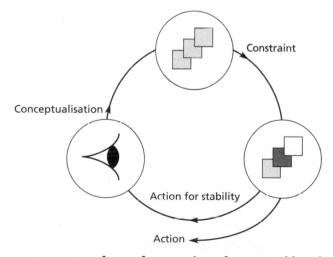

Fig. 9.6 The most common form of expression of structural inquiry, seen as a cycle

Thus, under the control loop we:

compare the form of the model that defines a proposed intervention
to our view of the real-world situation through predefined criteria
for confirmation that they are consistent.

Thus, proposed actions are tested against the real world. Application of the control loop to the proposed intervention from choice can show deviation, which can be either counteracted or amplified.

9.5.1 Extending the application of control

There are other ways of setting up the control loops within the methodology. Any two phases can be examined, any individual phases, or any steps within any of the phases. This enables cyclic metamodels to be seen to be nonlinear since the control loops can switch between non-sequential phases. When this occurs the methodology can be called 'flexible'. An example of one approach to control within our methodological approach is shown in Fig. 9.7. The controls introduced are explained as follows. In *analysis*, the systemic images that we create to represent real-world situations must be tested against the real world itself. This occurs, for instance, in the self-referencing control loop of Fig. 9.9 around analysis. Such testing is a verification of the systemic images according to some reference criteria. In soft method the criteria may be defined by the participants of a situation, while in hard methods they may be defined by an individual inquirer or group of inquirers. In *synthesis*, we can check that our models that are intended to represent possible strategies of intervention do relate to the conceptualisations that derive from the analysis. In *choice*, we can check that the model(s) that we choose does indeed

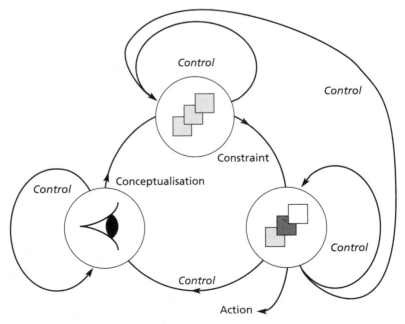

Fig. 9.7 Control arbitrarily applied to phases of the methodology involving strategic control

satisfy the constraints that, together with the model options from synthesis, act as inputs to choice. A control has also been placed across synthesis and choice.

Decision about how to apply control processes to the steps of a methodology tend to derive from its paradigm. However, the logical process including the associated control is always susceptible to the weltanschauung of an inquirer. This is not least because criteria that become involved in the validation of local goal outputs of a given procedural step will be determined by the inquirer. Thus, any intended logical process of a methodology always has the potentiality of uniqueness.

9.5.2 Recursion

The concept of recursion comes from mathematics (Kleene, 1952). In principle the idea of recursion is as follows. Consider that you are applying an *action* to an *object*, that is:

action = action(object)

or action *means* action *on* the object. An example of an action is the application of a *method*, and examples of an object are a *group of people, beliefs or issues* that make up a situation. It may be that if the same action can be applied to a different object at a hierarchically lower systemic level than the first action, then the action has been recursive. From a soft systems perspective, it will be possible to replace the notion of an *object* with that of a *situation* of subjective components (people). In this case there is no action *on* the *object*, but rather action *within* the *situation* that may be modelled as an *image* of the situation.

Consider the following as an illustration of recursion. We have all seen the effect of two mirrors facing one another at a slight angle. Since one mirror reflects the other (the action), each mirror shows the image of the other (the object). However, in the next 'inside' mirror reflection, the image of another mirror is shown. However, in the next 'inside' mirror reflection, the image of another mirror is shown. However, in the next 'inside' mirror reflection, the image of another mirror is shown ... This continues so that we can write the representation:

new image = reflection(image)

or:

$$image_1 = reflection(image_2)$$

where the subscripts indicate the hierarchic level at which the action reflection is occurring, 1 representing the top level. More generally, for any level of reflection n:

$$image_n = reflection(image_{n-1})$$

Having reflected on the concept of recursion, it would be of interest to look at it graphically in relation to a modelling cycle, since it more adequately demonstrates what we mean in connection with methodology.

In Fig. 9.8, we show how a single system model selected from a set of model possibilities for a given situation can be examined on its own by applying the whole modelling cycle to it. In this the relevant system that has been differentiated during synthesis is related back to the situation and examined on its own. This represents a shift in system hierarchy level from the unitary highest level, where only a single overall situation is identified, to the next pluralistic level, where a number of subsituations are seen. The evaluation of each subsituation, when compounded, will enable an integrated understanding of the situation to occur.

9.6 The evolution of methodologies

Consider a local process within a given focus of a system that is being controlled. The process has associated with it an identity. This can survive so long as control can be maintained. During negative feedback attempts are made to maintain the dynamic stability by comparing the outputs of a process to a goal, the shape of which is defined by a set of cognitive criteria. Successful negative feedback counteracts deviation. Thus the maintenance of stability can occur through *actions from within* the system, for instance by adjusting its processes or acceptance of inputs.

Negative feedback fails when the system finds itself with a point of structural criticality that makes it locally unstable. In this case, it is possible for the metasystem to alter the cognitive criteria through learning, thus attempting to regain stability locally. Here, changes *within the metasystem* result as *actions on* the system. In some cases the instability extends beyond the locality across more than one focus of the system. It may be regional, or even global. In either case, the relationship between the system and its metasystem breaks down. If the instability is seen to be regional, then a metasystem from a higher focus of the system may become involved in place of the system's own metasystem. In the case of global instability this is not possible, and any relationship between a metasystem and the system is totally severed. However, actions on the system may still occur chaotically. Both classes of change can be seen as morphogenic processes that relate to evolution and positive feedback. These stages of system stability maintenance are explained in Table 9.4.

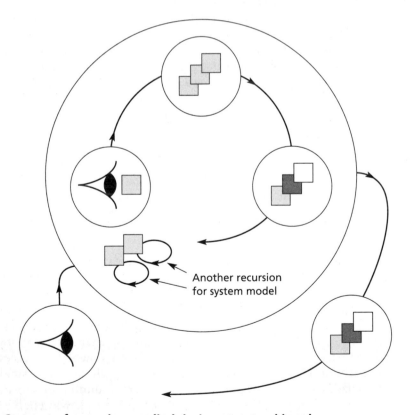

Another recursion
for system model

Fig. 9.8 Concept of recursion applied during structural inquiry

Evolutionary processes occur through a building up of morphogenic change so that steps 1–4 occur as a continuous cycle. Sometimes, morphogenic changes are not able to move the system back into a stable condition. Here, the system may still self-organise, but it is not in the controlled deterministic way that is seen to be required by a metasystem. Thus we can say that the relationship between the system and the metasystem breaks down, and self-organisation occurs without the benefit of cognitive decision making. This is typical of an evolutionary system that is said to pass through a process of global structural criticality and chaos.

Methodologies entail single-loop learning as part of their fundamental transmogrific mechanisms. They also pass through double-loop learning consistent with evolutionary processes. Two examples come to mind immediately. Soft systems methodology (SSM) (Checkland, 1980) was originally seen in terms of a logical process of inquiry that many interpreted as a relatively simple method, with control explicitly defined as prespecified procedural steps. Part of this logical process was to explore the culture of the organisational situation. In a renewed version of the methodology (Checkland and Scholes, 1990), it has been argued that situations should be seen in terms of (a) a stream of logical inquiry and (b) a stream of cultural inquiry. These streams may be seen as analytically independent and interactive. Effectively, the methodology has evolved from a single dimension of inquiry to a twin dimension, and this has an impact on the way that situations are addressed.

Table 9.4 Steps that a system can pass through as it attempts to maintain stability

Step	Process control
1	Perturbations from the environment of a system can make its control process fail as the threshold of stability is reached.
2	In order to regain stability, the system learns to introduce behavioural adjustments.
3	If stability still fails and a point of structural criticality exists that makes the structure susceptible to local change, then a different learning process occurs where the cognitive model is modified in an attempt to regain stability. Another way of saying this is that change occurs at the metasystemic level that is manifested as morphogenic change in the system. This process of morphogenesis can be seen as one of self-organisation that is directed from the metasystem (deterministically).
4	If stability is regained, continue process until step 1 reoccurs. As an iterative process, this represents an evolutionary process.
5	If stability is not successful, a regional structural criticality may have occurred so that the system's metasystem cannot learn because of the turbulence induced by perturbation. In this case a metasystem from a higher focus of the system may become involved. Morphogenesis may now have a regional rather than a local effect.
6	If stability cannot be re-achieved in the system (as it is cognitively understood) the process will fail. However, this may be replaced by other stable systems that have materialised through the chaos of non-deterministic self-organisation independent of metasystemic control. Generic identity typically changes.
7	Regaining stability through non-deterministic self-organisation may not enable the system to maintain its original individual identity.

Evolutionary development has also occurred in the method total systems intervention between its initial substantive appearance (Flood and Jackson, 1991) and its developed form (Flood, 1995). Its first version was based on Jackson's system of systems methodologies, that has now been abandoned and replaced by a new framework that has changed many of the propositions of its paradigm (Midgley, 1995).

9.7 Building a methodology

The above ideas taken together provide an approach that can be used to build and develop a methodology. It would be useful, therefore, to see how some of the ideas can be applied in the creation of a methodology. In order to address this suggestion, in Minicase 9.1 we shall develop a methodology to enable inquiry into situation that is directed towards building a decision support system (DSS). A DSS can be thought of as providing interactive support for decision makers in decision making. It can therefore be seen to be part of an inquiry system. In describing it we can with use differentiate between its cognitive and situational components.

Minicase 9.1

Designing a decision support methodology

DSSs take in data and facts from a system of operations and the environment. They require a situational model involving data in a database that describes the coherent situation being inquired into. The decision maker will be seen to be part of this. It involves situational knowledge of the system of operations (in relation to its environment) about which decisions are to be made. This will be a substantive part of the *knowledge base*. The knowledge is acquired through the collection of facts about the situation through sets of rules that determine the state of the processes, and measures of performance that evaluates the state of the processes. In order to assist this process of evaluation, models exist in a *model base*. The purpose of this is to provide models that can transform the data local to the situation into a form more appropriate to a decision context. This prepared data acts as an output from the DSS that will be used by the decision maker to make operational decisions.

The metasystem of the DSS contains a 'cognitive' domain that may also involve part of the knowledge base. This identifies the nature of the facts that are being collected: that is, what is meant by the facts of the situation. This is belief based and derives from the paradigm from which the system of operations derives. It also involves generic classifications for measures of performance that can operate as the basis for a control system. It may also be connected to the modelling base by providing a set of generic classifications to which the models can be assigned, and which can help decision makers identify how the data available is best able to be transformed in order to satisfy the perceived context of the decision. Sometimes these cognitive aspects of a DSS are not part of the physical components of a DSS, but belong rather to the stakeholders that are in some way associated with the situation.

The concept of decision support as illustrated in Fig. 9.9 derives from Sheehan (1996, personal communication). Decision support involves (a) access to databases, (b) access to model bases, (c) access to a knowledge base and (d) judgement by decision makers. Note that (a) and (b) are structured components of decision support, (c) may be experiential or structured transferable knowledge, and (d) is unstructured. Decision making is thus at best a semi-structured process.

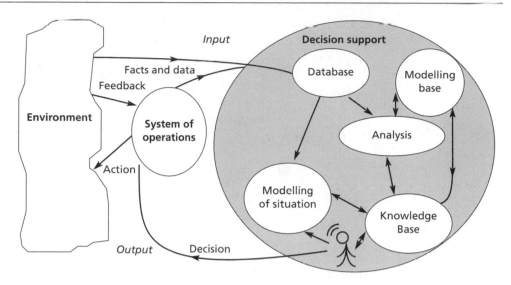

Fig. 9.9 Context diagram for a decision support system

Consider now the cognitive purposes of decision support systems. Discussion about structured decision making can be found in many texts on management decision processes, such as Simon (1960) or Keen and Scott Morton (1978). What constitutes the cognitive purpose of a DSS is dependent upon the paradigm of the organisation and the weltanschauung of an inquirer, though sometimes the latter is formalised as part of the paradigm. We propose the following cognitive purposes (illustrated in Fig. 9.10) of decision support:

- Mission of DSS methodology: the creation of stable decisions;
- Inquiry aims of DSS methodology: understanding of the system of operations and the impact of decisions, judgement that enables competent decisions.

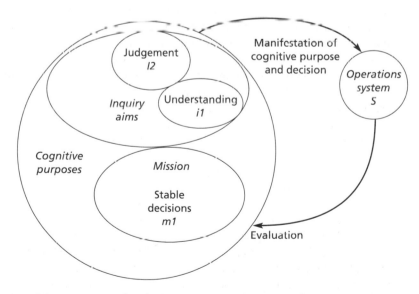

Fig. 9.10 Cognitive purposes for decision support shown to derive from the metasystem

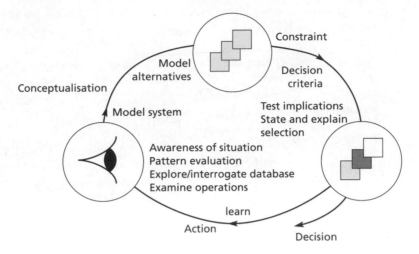

Fig. 9.11 Structured inquiry for decision support

Decision making (after Simon, 1960) can be structured, as can any form of inquiry. Decision inquiry within decision support systems is considered here according to the schema of Table 9.5 based on the work of Sheehan (1996, personal communication). This schema can be presented graphically in order to highlight the control processes of the methodology, as shown in Fig. 9.11. Only an overview control has been introduced here, but the methodology can easily be complexified with perceived cognitive needs with the introduction of more control loops. When the control loop operates without stability, single- or double-loop learning can occur.

It is also possible to explore the two qualities of learning process that occur within the decision support system: single- and double-loop learning. Single-loop learning is situational learning, while double-loop learning is cognitive learning. Situational learning has an impact on the situational models that define the operations of the system. It uses situational knowledge like database material, and operational procedures and rules. Cognitive learning, however, affects the cognitive model(s) associated with the system of operations. It uses deep knowledge like principles and basic concepts that contribute to the formation of beliefs, attitudes and values (the cognitive organisation) that go towards defining the basis of a decision. The Argyris view of double-loop learning can be put in terms of the theory that we have presented here, as shown in Fig. 9.12.

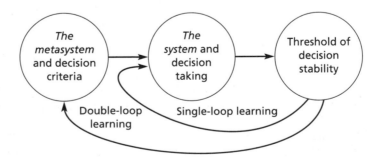

Fig. 9.12 Single- and double-loop learning seen in terms of the system and metasystem

Table 9.5 Steps in the cycle of inquiry for a decision support system

Phase/connection	Step	Purpose
Pre-evaluation	Discuss situation	Obtain initial model of situation
Analysis	Examine operations environment Explore company database: analysis monitoring through selected reports of type *standard* and *exception*	Problem identification
	User database interrogation Comparison analysis Pattern evaluation Awareness, understanding and knowledge of system	Checking/updating preliminary conceptual model of system
conceptualisation	*Model of system*	Define the relevant system including the tasks and issues that must be taken into account
Synthesis	Alternatives model options formed Examine implications	Identify alternatives Establish holistic options
constraint	*Decision making criteria defined* *Boundaries of options identified*	Define characteristics that must be addressed. Define feasible options
Choice	Test option implications Explore through *what-if* evaluation State and explain selection	Selection of preferred alternatives, with justification to enable decisions
control	Check that decision is consistent with intentions. If not examine why not and learn through the development of knowledge	Check on stability of chosen option. If stable undertake action, if not re-examine data or more seriously modify form of inquiry through behavioural organising, e.g. decision criteria
action	*Take decision or learn*	Make decision selection

SUMMARY

Extending from the knowledge domain model we can define three domains that relate to inquiry, the systemic and metasystemic domains, connected together through transmogrification. This is the domain of logic that defines relations and maintains information-based cybernetic mechanisms. It is this domain that is sensitive to perturbation from the environment. Under certain circumstances the perturbations can induce turbulence that results in a breakdown in the relationship between the system and its metasystem. In terms of inquiry this means that inquiry processes can lose track of the propositional base that guides it.

Cybernetic control enables us to distinguish between simple method and complex method (e.g. methodology). Simple method is defined in terms of a structured schedule of steps. Complex method enables logical adjustment that is inquirer influenced. In particular, control enables us to adjust this schedule according to the inquirer's perceived needs of an inquiry.

Cybernetic processes are also involved in a methodology's learning process. Two types of learning have been discussed. One is single-loop learning, which affects the behavioural domain, and the other is double-loop learning, which affects the cognitive domain. In terms of methodology, single-loop learning will have an influence on the scheduling of procedural steps that an inquirer must pass through during an inquiry. Double-loop learning has an impact on the metasystem of the methodology, and can lead to its evolving through a change in the criteria that dynamically determine the schedules of method. More significantly, double-loop learning can have an impact on a metasystem's very propositions.

REFERENCES

Checkland, P. (1980) *Soft Systems Methodology*. Chichester: Wiley.

Checkland, P.B. and Scholes, J. (1990) *Soft Systems Methodology in Action*. Chichester: Wiley.

Flood, R.L. (1995) *Solving Problem Solving*. Chichester: Wiley.

Flood, R.L. and Jackson, M.C. (1991) *Creative Problem Solving: Total systems intervention*. Chichester: Wiley.

Keen, P.G.W. and Scott Morton, M.S. (1978) *Decision Support Systems: An organisational perspective*. Reading, MA: Addison-Wesley.

Jastrow, J. (1927) 'The animus for psychical research'. In Murchison, C. (ed.) *The Case for and against Psychical Belief*. Worcester, MA: Clark University Press.

Kleene, S.C. (1952) *Introduction to Mathematics*. Amsterdam: Elsevier.

Midgley, G. (1995) 'Mixing methods: developing systemic intervention'. Research Memorandum No. 9, Centre for Systems, Hull University.

Patching, D. (1990) *Practical Soft Systems Analysis*. London: Pitman.

Senge, P. (1990) *The Fifth Discipline*. New York: Doubleday.

Simon, H. (1960) *The New Science of Management Decisions*. New York: Harper & Brothers.

CHAPTER 10

Viable inquiry systems

OVERVIEW

The process of inquiry is implicitly world-view plural. This proposition defines the basic concepts of viable inquiry systems, and enables us to address the idea of paradigm incommensurability and methodological complementarism. Its basis depends upon the notion that paradigm-based cognitive knowledge is independent from manifest cognitive purposes of a process of inquiry. A construction is also created that enables us to explain how, through the creation of a virtual paradigm that itself defines a frame of reference for an inquiry, methods can be used autonomously and 'mixed'.

OBJECTIVES

This chapter will show:

- that inquiry is implicitly world-view pluralistic;
- how we can deal with paradigm incommensurability;
- the nature of viable inquiry systems.

10.1 The who, what, why, how and when of inquiry

The concept of viability can be applied to any type of purposeful activity system. It is therefore tempting to extend viable systems theory to a variety of application domains. It has, for instance, been applied to the domain of learning (McClelland and Yolles, 1997; Yolles, 1996, 1997a, b; Yolles and McClelland, 1997). Here our interest is to apply it to the domain of inquiry that enables us to conceive of viable inquiry systems.

In order to claim that viable inquiry systems exist, we must show that the process of inquiry can be defined as a purposeful adaptable activity system. We shall argue that this comes from addressing the needs of an inquiry process through an exploration of the *who, what, why, how* and *when* of inquiry.

The *who* is the inquirer, and may be an individual operating under a weltanschauung or a group operating under a shared weltanschauung. The *what* concerns a complex problem situation that an organisation finds itself in. The *why* is finding ways of making the organisation deal with or adapt to change that impact on it from the environment causing the situation so that it can survive. While managerial heuristics can be used to inquire into the complex situation, the most satisfactory way of doing so is through method – the *how*. As a consequence methods should be seen to be part of the inquiry process. To make sure that the how is adaptable, we should be using complex methods such as methodologies. This is because methodologies involve organising processes that enable us to adapt our methods. Adaptation might further suggest that even the methodologies that we use should change, and this can mean that we might wish to adopt different methodologies for different situations. This suggests that we might be interested in methodological complementarism. Finally, since organisations are continuously being influenced by a changing environment, they should be associated with an approach to inquiry that is continually (*when*) exploring the changing situation that they find themselves, and to which they should adapt.

Our interest in this chapter is to explore under what conditions approaches to inquiry should be considered to be systemic, and when inquiry systems might be said to be viable. The work centres on the idea of world-view pluralism, and this reaches out to adoption of methodological pluralism through the creation of virtual or working paradigms. We shall therefore find it useful to explore ideas that enable methodological pluralism to occur. This will lead on to an approach that, by considering the *what, who* and *how* of inquiry, provides the basis of a viable inquiry system.

10.2 The paradigm principle

We are familiar with the weltanschauung principle that tells us that no view of reality can be complete, that each view will contain some information about reality, but that the views will never be completely reconcilable. The principle of finding a more representative picture of reality by involving as many weltanschauungen as possible generates variety through opening up more possibilities in the way situations can be seen. Those who adhere to this principle during an inquiry consequently regard weltanschauung pluralism as desirable.

We know that a plurality of weltanschauungen can form a shared weltanschauung, and that when this becomes formalised a paradigm appears. It is reasonable to consider, then, that there should also be a paradigm principle that might be expressed as follows. A paradigm defines a truth system that results in a logical process that determines behaviour. The truth system is also responsible for recognising and producing what its viewholders consider to be knowledge about reality. Since different paradigms have different truth systems, knowledge across paradigms will never be completely reconcilable. Formal models of reality are built from paradigms, and each model will contain some knowledge that guides behaviour.

Paradigms are created by groups of people, and a paradigm principle should be analogous to the weltanschauung principle. Thus, no formal model of reality can be complete, and finding a more representative picture of a given reality by involving a plurality of formal models generates variety through opening up more possibilities in the way situations can be addressed through action. To have paradigm pluralism, paradigm incommensurability must be addressed.

10.3 Methodological pluralism and paradigm incommensurability

'Some authors (e.g. Burrell and Morgan, 1979; Jackson and Carter, 1991) claim that philosophical paradigms are irrevocably incommensurable. This might lead one to suppose that methodological pluralism is a non-starter. Others claim that rational analysis may bridge the paradigm gap, allowing for a "unification" of paradigms (Reed, 1985), or that communication across paradigm boundaries is possible even if unification is neither feasible nor desirable (Willmott, 1993). Proponents of methodological pluralism claiming theoretical coherence must inevitably develop a position on the paradigm problem, otherwise they risk being accused of theoretically contradictory eclecticism' (Midgley, 1995, p. 9).

Various approaches that attempt to validate methodological pluralism in the face of paradigm incommensurability exist. Some of these are considered briefly below.

10.3.1 Habermas and cognitive interest

Several approaches to methodological pluralism (Jackson, 1993, pp. 201–2) occur through the selection of paradigms that are based on ideas within Habermas's theory of human interests (Habermas, 1970). It tells us that human beings possess two basic cognitive interests in acquiring knowledge: a *technical* interest relating to the human endeavour referred to as work, and a *practical* interest for interaction (Table 10.1). Another cognitive interest is *critical deconstraining* that results in the human endeavour emancipation, seen to be subordinate to work and interaction because it results from exploitation and distorted communication. Corresponding to these three classifications of human endeavour are three types of knowledge that can facilitate 'ideal' qualities of human situations, referred to as empirical analytical sciences, historical hermeneutic sciences and critical sciences.

Systems methodologies may be validly used in a complementary way when viewed in terms of Habermas's classifications (Jackson, 1993, pp. 290–1). To do this, we should see Habermas's horizontal distinctions as a way of differentiating between paradigms and their methodologies to form analytically independent domains. While paradigms guide knowledge production and therefore determine knowledge type, systems methodologies should be seen to serve cognitive interests. Most approaches would seem to follow this distinction.

Table 10.1 Relationship between human cognitive interests and their corresponding types of knowledge

	Technical	Practical	Critical deconstraining
Cognitive interests	Work. This enables people to achieve goals and generate material well-being. It involves technical ability to undertake action in the environment, and the ability to make prediction and establish control.	Interaction. This requires that people as individuals and groups in a social system gain and develop the possibilities of an understanding of each other's subjective views. It is consistent with a practical interest in mutual understanding that can address disagreements, which can be a threat to the social form of life.	Emancipation. This enables people to (i) liberate themselves from the constraints imposed by power structures and (ii) learn through precipitation in social and political processes to control their own destinies.
Knowledge type	Empirical analytical sciences, concerned with technical control of objectified processes.	Historical hermeneutic sciences, relating to practical interest. They can provide understanding of intersubjective life, and aim at maintaining and improving mutual understanding between people.	Critical sciences, which recognise the limitations and dangers of inappropriately applied empirical analytical and historical hermeneutic sciences. The attempt to synthesise and systemise them to enable people to reflect on situations and liberate themselves from domination by existing power structures and processes.

An example of this is the approach adopted by Flood and Jackson (1991) and Jackson (1992), referred to as a system of systems methodologies. Here methodologies are assigned to the domain of cognitive interest, and are seen in terms of a set of characteristics that correspond to Habermas's technical, practical and human deconstraining classifications. This results in a typology of methodologies. Methodologies that come from different cognitive interests can now legitimately be used together. This is because satisfying the needs of cognitive interests does not compromise any given paradigm from which a knowledge type comes.

Against this approach, Flood and Romm (1995) have argued that it is possible to use methods for a variety of purposes, some of which go beyond their original design. The system of systems methodologies approach does not recognise this in that it provides undue restrictions on the way in which methodologies are seen and evolve.

10.3.2 Paradigm evolution and revolution

For Midgley (1995, p. 13) methodological complementarism provides for methodologies being 'related together'. He explores this further by saying that the selection of methodologies within a plural framework involves issues of power that influence the way in which methodologies are chosen. Midgley believes that a contribution to addressing paradigm incommensurability occurs through the work of Gregory (1992), who argues that it is possible for paradigms to change through cognitive learning. This occurs through communications that enable one to appreciate other world views and thus transform one's own paradigm. This in turn can lead on to the cognitive development of paradigms. By connecting paradigms with their cognitive states under development, Midgley concludes that 'paradigms have infinite possibilities for evolution – if you include within your definition of evolution "revolution" too' (Midgley, 1995). While this forms the heart of the argument, he unfortunately does not tell us what he means by revolution, or indeed distinguish between that and evolution. It will be useful to consider this.

One of Kuhn's considerations is that paradigm development is bounded. If we think of a paradigm as being a shared weltanschauung manifested as a truth system, then like any system paradigms are susceptible to both morphogenesis and metamorphosis. Indeed, it would be of interest to see the development of a theory of viable truth systems following the propositions of viable systems theory. In particular, it would permit us to explore paradigms in the light of chaos theory and the generation of local stable nodes of knowledge (since what is recognised as knowledge is determined by a paradigm's 'truths').

This has relevance to Midgley's consideration of the relationship between evolution and revolution. To explore this a little more, let us consider a given paradigm p_0 to be a bounded system of truths defined in a global holarchy. *Each propositional truth* is a local focus in the paradigm, and a *logical set of truths* is a regional focus. The paradigm is evolving when it experiences a local or regional morphogenesis. When the morphogenesis is global, taking up all the truths within the holarchy, then we say that it is passing through a metamorphosis that many would refer to as a revolution. This means that the very nature of the paradigm is changed. In effect, p_0 is no more, being replaced by p_1. Thus, the original bounded paradigm has ceased to exist, having been replaced by another, new paradigm. If, however, p_0 is seen to be part of a larger paradigm, P, then what is a metamorphosis to an observer of p_0 is a morphogenesis to an observer of P. For example, suppose that we define all the set of system methodologies as P, and one of the members of that set is the paradigm p_0. Suppose that its truths are abandoned, and a new replacement paradigm p_1 is formed. While P has evolved, p_0 has been subject to revolution. It would therefore seem to be the case that the meaning of evolution and revolution will be dependent upon the frame of reference that we are using to define the boundary of the paradigm.

10.3.3 Total systems intervention

Another approach towards addressing methodological pluralism is that of Flood (1995), which has been referred to as both total systems intervention and, more recently, local systemic intervention. It has passed through a major change since its first significant appearance in 1991 (Flood and Jackson, 1991). It offers a cycle of inquiry that involves the three phases *creativity* (about the problem situation), *choice* (of methods) and *implementation* (producing change proposals). Its first version was based on Jackson's systems of systems methodologies, which has now been abandoned. It has been replaced by a framework that categorises four domains of inquiry that can be subject to intervention: organisational processes, organisational design, organisational culture and organisational politics. All of the domains need to be addressed, and the need then is to align systems methods to each domain in a way determined by the inquirer. Indeed, the inquirer may even wish to redefine the nature of the domains according to his or her own perspective.

Every method, according to Flood and Romm (1995), has a given and immediate purpose. While this may be the purpose that it was originally designed for, it may be used in other ways according to the perspective of the inquirer. This clearly draws on the idea of variety generated through adoption of the weltanschauung principle.

Flood (1995), in the development of his ideas, uses the work of Habermas and of Foucault. From Habermas (1970), the idea of emancipatory interest and power liberation is central. From Foucault (1980) power resides in knowledge, which is used to order social relationships. Power structures are a result of a process of knowledge formation that occurs when certain social practices become legitimated. Flood sees that Foucault's ideas enable the rationalities of methodological paradigms to be released, while Habermas's theory accepts openness and encourages diversity. The liberation of knowledges (Midgley, 1995) is achieved through the process of *creativity*, and the critique of these knowledges leads to *choice* between methods for *implementation*. In developing this approach, Flood and Romm (1995) acknowledge that an inquirer will have a perspective on a methodology that will be different from that of other inquirers in its application to a locally defined problem situation. Because of this, paradigm incommensurability is not an issue that they believe needs to be addressed.

Midgley (1995, p. 31) does not see that an integration of Habermas's and Foucault's work has been or is likely to be achieved. Rather, he sees that Flood has achieved a juxtaposition of their ideas that is in search of a new paradigm.

10.3.4 Midgley on methodological pluralism

Midgley's view about methodological pluralism develops out of the critical systems perspective. He believes that paradigms are commensurable in the sense that 'we can draw upon ideas from a variety of sources, but they are also incommensurable in the sense that we can never appreciate those ideas exactly as their original advocates do' (Midgley, 1995, pp. 34–5).

In order to address the problem of incommensurability, Midgley reconsiders the associated ideas of Habermas and Foucault, and refers to the power–knowledge formations that occur daily. This involves our making judgements about which forms of knowledge to promote, which identities to accept, and what to reject or challenge. The practice of this occurs in a three phase cycle of *critique* (revealing different possibilities of knowledge and identity), *judgement* (choosing between alternative knowledge and identities), and *action* (based on judgements already made). *Critique* centres on the nature of the boundaries of knowledge, and how those boundaries are able to change for different inquirers. It is quite consistent with the ideas of Minai (1995) on boundaries being fluctuating frames of reference. *Judgement* would seem to be concerned with an inquirer defining and matching knowledge boundaries with problem situation boundaries, which enables *action* to occur.

10.3.5 An alternative approach

Our interest lies in offering an alternative approach to those above. It is based on the notion that cognitive purpose has an autonomous status, in a similar way to cognitive interest. This will enable the creation of frames of reference that are cognitive purpose-related. To enable this, it will be neccessary to explore further the nature of cognitive purposes.

In pursuing this we will work through our cybernetic model introduced in Fig. 2.6 and developed in Chapter 6. It concerns viable systems that entail energetic purposeful activity or behaviour, and has associated with it facts (or surface knowledge). The (deep) knowledged based metasystem is the 'cognitive consciousness' of the system that operates from its paradigm(s). The two domains are connected together through an informational transmogrific domain that entails logical, relational and cybernetic processes, and is the place of strategy. In support of this the following propositions are adopted:

1 the metasystemic, systemic and transmogrific domains are analytically and empirically independent;

2 the metasystem works through a paradigm(s) that is itself populated by a belief system, standards or norms, and concepts bound into a set of propositions, all of which are communicated through language;

3 knowledges exist as part of paradigms, and are generated within them;

4 a paradigm has a penchant that is reflected in terms of the generation of a specialist type of knowledge;

5 specialist knowledge is connected to cognitive purposes;

6 the transmogrific domain is the place where systemic organising processes occur;

7 cognitive purposes are attached to the transmogrific domain, and can be seen in terms of mission and goals;

8 cybernetical, rational and ideological cognitive purposes attributes exist as part of the organising process of the system that contribute to systemic shaping;

9 cybernetical processes satisfy intention, and are concerned with control and communications that assist technical cognitive interests;

10 logico-relational processes define a rationality that is manifested in practical situations;

11 ideological processes define manner of thinking, have associated with them politics and ethics, and define a backcloth within which social structures and processes are facilitated.

These propositions can be formulated (Table 10.2) in a way not dissimilar to the way we have formulated the notions of Habermas (Table 10.1). A secondary issue that may be of interest is that while cognitive purposes are assigned to the transmogrific domain, cognitive interests would rather be seen to be assigned to the systemic domain. There is an explanation for this that comes from Chapter 8, and it relates to a well-known scientific approach that attempts to validate relationships by undertaking a unit analysis.

It will also be useful to show that cognitive interest has commodity units that are different from cognitive purpose. To do this we must first note that the distinction between our three domains is as follows: the commodity of the systemic domain is energy; that of the transmogrific domain is information; and that of the cognitive domain knowledge. Cognitive interests relate to the systemic domain since they operate through units of energy. Thus, 'work' has units of energy; 'interaction' is behavioural and thus energetic; and 'emancipation' can be seen in terms of the energetic potential for a system. In contrast, cognitive purposes operate through units of information: cybernetics is fundamentally informational in nature; rationality operates on a logico-relational basis that must ultimately be information-based; ideology can only be related to the view of a situation through an informational context.

10.4 Defining the basis for an inquiry system

In establishing a basis for dealing with paradigm incommensurability and methodological pluralism, we shall initially explore how the inquiry process normally works, since this presumably involves some form of world-view pluralism and incommensurability.

Consider an inquiry process that has a set of world views defined by an interaction between the *who* (the inquirer), the *what* (the complex problem situation) and the *how*

Table 10.2 Relationship between human cognitive purposes and the knowledge type

	Rational	Cybernetic	Ideological
Cognitive purpose	Logico-relational. Enables missions, goals and aims to be defined, and approached through planning. It involves logical, relational and rational abilities to organise thought and action and thus to define sets of systemic and behaviour possibilities.	Intention. This, through the creation and strategic pursuit of goals and aims that may change over time, enables people through control and communications processes, to redirect their futures.	Manner of thinking. An intellectual framework through which policy makers observe and interpret reality that has a politically correct ethical and moral orientation, provides an image of the future that enables action through politically correct strategic policy, and gives a politically correct view of stages of historical development in respect of interaction with the external environment.
Knowledge type	The science of reasoning. Logical processes derive from a belief and conceptual system that gives rise to a propositional basis. It involves a specialist type of knowledge that comes from a penchant that ultimately determines cognitive purposes.	The science of control and communications. It has associated with it goals that derive from a belief system and knowledge; knowledge of group norms and standards enable the organising nature of cybernetic processes to be defined or redefined.	The science of ideas. It is an organisation of beliefs and attitudes (religious, political or philosophical in nature) that is more or less institutionalised or shared with others. It provides a total system of thought, emotion and attitude to the world and is reflected in any organising process. It refers to any conception of the world that goes beyond the ability of formal validation.

(the methodology). Each component has an autonomous world view that is incommensurable with the other world views. The world views therefore cannot be sensibly combined, but they coexist independently while inquiry is manifested. To explain this we say that through communications, they can together form a metasystem that is manifested as a purposeful system of inquiry that must have a metasystem.

The question is now raised about how we can explain the formation of the metasystem. We propose that the way to do this is by *formally* differentiating between inquirers, situations and methodologies and their associated world views. This requires that we establish inquirers, situations and methodologies as a formal system, and this itself requires a set of propositions to be formulated that explains the relationship between them in a self-consistent way (having propositions that are not seen to be in contradiction to each other), and enables the possibility of manifesting a set of behavioural rules that defines form. To do this we shall begin by saying that inquiry into complex situations using any given methodology involves three classifications of world view:

1 *the who*: the world view of the inquirer I, also expressed as weltanschauung;

2 *the what*: the world view of the actors of a target situation S expressed in terms of a set of organisational paradigms and weltanschauungen;

3 *the how*: the world view of the methodology M, normally expressed as its paradigm.

The *who, what* and *how* create three dimensions of world view that are autonomous and that together form a triad of inquiry as illustrated in Fig. 10.1. We shall refer to inquiry bounded by the ISM triangle as *inquirism*. There are two purposes for *inquirism*:

1 to keep analytically apart the relationship between the target situation, the inquirer and the targeting methodology;

2 to clearly indicate the processes of inquiry and the mutual world-view inquiry influences.

Inquirism also highlights the idea that when methodologies are used:

- the world views of the actors in a situation are seen as an abstract property;
- an inquiry involves an inquirer with a world view (or world views for a plural inquirer);
- there is an interaction and influence between the formalised world view(s) of methodology and the world views of an inquirer and the situation through their cultures and 'truths'.

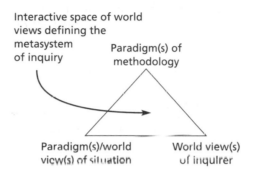

Interactive space of world views defining the metasystem of inquiry

Paradigm(s) of methodology

Paradigm(s)/world view(s) of situation

World view(s) of inquirer

Fig. 10.1 *Inquirism* **as an inquiry triad (ISM) defining an interactive space of world views and their knowledges**

10.5 Inquirism, the metasystem and the systemic inquiry

Part of our interest here is to argue that *inquirism* results in a viable inquiry system. This means that we must be able to argue that a metasystem can be formed that is manifested as a purposeful inquiry system that can evolve according to the principles of viable systems theory. The formation of a metasystem requires the creation of a shared world view through the establishment of a common cognitive model. This enables at least some of the knowledge of an inquirer to be used to apply at least some of the knowledge of a methodology to at least some of the knowledge of the paradigms that make up a situation. The selection of knowledge comes from the frame of reference that enables the metasystem to be defined.

The creation of the metasystem directs inquiry into complex target situations, and enables us to refer to a manifest purposeful inquiry system. If the three apexes of world view do not relate to each other in a common model, then *inquirism* is not seen to form a systemic process of inquiry. As a result the inquiry process will be seen to be composed of an arbitrary selection and application of methodology to the situation. Some might refer to it as illustrating a misunderstanding of the situation, of the methodology, or of the application of the latter to the former. Any intervention strategies that result will be meaningless and of little value.

When a process of inquiry falls into chaos, it loses its connection with the inquiry metasystem, and in response to environmental stimulus the inquiry process behaves spontaneously in a way that is structure determined. Thus, if a methodology's structure

215

is defined as an ordered set of procedural steps, then only these steps are available for selection in that order by an inquirer making an inquiry. How an inquirer understands those steps is another issue.

If a methodology is stable then its scheduling process of these steps is controlled. Contrary to this, under chaos the scheduling process will be arbitrary. Let us suppose that the inquiry system passes from a condition of stability to one of chaos, and then back to one of stability. As stability is regained, a new metasystem arises so that the system has passed through a metamorphosis. To understand the nature of the new metasystem, we must explore *inquirism* a little further.

In the formation of a viable inquiry system, the initial requirement of *inquirism* is that we have a set of parts – the situation, the inquirer and the methodology. Each has its world view, but together they do not define a whole metasystem. What functions as a metasystem is a disconnected and disjointed set of world views that simply contributes to the confusion of chaos. It is only when the parts come together by forming a whole metasystem that defines purpose that the system will be able to achieve and maintain that purpose. The emerging metasystem occurs through the formation of a virtual paradigm that may endure for the duration of the inquiry into the situation. Three functions of the metasystem are that it will:

1 define a shared world view that enables a methodology to be applied to a situation by an inquirer meaningfully;

2 constrain the inquirer by use of a methodology (the obverse of structuring an inquiry);

3 control the selection or use of the methodology to make it appropriate for the situation, having care in how the methodology is applied to the situation.

The first of these results comes through the creation of a virtual paradigm that formalises an inquirer's approach. Part of this process is to define the purposes of an inquiry. This comes from the inquirer's understanding of the actors' view(s) of the situation, the mission and goals of methodology, and his or her own purposes in applying the methodology to the situation.

In making an inquiry, the inquirer will adopt a set of propositions from the different world views that represents its 'truths' and enables knowledges to be recognised. This is guided by the selection of the methodologies and the impact of their paradigms, the situational paradigms that will constrain the possibilities of intervention strategy selection, and the inquirer's own propositions. This will create a virtual paradigm that makes the particular inquiry unique.

The idea that there are three autonomous world views in interaction is actually complexified because the world views attached to each autonomous apex of *inquirism* are themselves likely to be plural. This means that there may be many world views in a situation that must be addressed, that the inquirer may be a group that involves a number of world views, and that the methodology may also be pluralistic, being a coincidence of more than one methodology used in a complementary way.

Consider the plurality of inquirer world views. We know that people assemble into groups, and together form a set of common cognitive purposes within a single frame of reference defined within a virtual (or working) paradigm that enables them to work together as a team. Group behaviour is possible because of the formation of a shared weltanschauung. This occurs through a common cognitive model that enables meaning to be shared. Its boundaries are defined as a frame of reference for group behaviour. The individual weltanschauungen are maintained, though through association there may well be a learning process in which weltanschauungen are changed in some way. If failure of a group process occurs, then one explanation is through weltanschauung incommensurability.

In a situation world view plurality can occur with respect to both the informal and formal world views of an organisation. There is always an interaction between weltanschauungen and paradigms in the same way as there is between different weltanschauungen and different paradigms. The plurality of informal world views is often ignored by supposing that there is a consensus in a situation. Often, little is done to determine what the consensus actually means in a given context, and whether it has any value in respect of an intervention strategy. With respect to formal world views, it is normally the dominant paradigm that is referred to during an inquiry. This can also be seen as a supraparadigm of the organisation.

We should be able to deal with methodological pluralism in a way that is equivalent to the creation of a shared weltanschauung. Since a paradigm is a formalised weltanschauung, our need is to consider how to create a metaphorical shared paradigm – that is, a virtual paradigm with a common cognitive model that shares meaning that holds for the duration of an inquiry. For any inquirer, this must be seen to occur through the creation of a deep and critical understanding of the different views deriving from the individual paradigms being assembled, and must not be seen as a licence for 'anything goes'.

10.6 Inquirism through orthogonalities

In *inquirism*, we have already said that the three apexes of the inquiry triad are analytically independent. When manifested into the behavioural domain they are also empirically independent. Once they are established within a conceptual framework that explains their interrelationship, they may be seen as orthogonalities in association. This idea can be applied recursively to each apex in turn.

Let us first consider the case of a group inquirer with a shared weltanschauung. This is not a single common world view but rather one in which people retain their own world views and use common models to share meaning. Each weltanschauung is analytically independent, and manifests behaviour that is empirically independent. The manifestations of weltanschauungen are all relational within the group, however, so that the behaviour of one individual has an impact on that of the others. If the group is to be coherent and work together in an inquiry, it must establish a frame of reference that enables the weltanschauungen to be related to a common cognitive model. This will have associated with it purposes for inquiry that can be projected to the system. This enables us to see the behavioural manifestation of each weltanschauung as an orthogonality within the frame of reference. In other words, each individual and his or her behaviour can be considered separately and interactively.

Let us now consider a target situation. In general the organisation within which the situation is defined is paradigm plural (we have discussed this before, when we considered for example different departments in a division of an enterprise each operating from its own paradigms with its penchant). The paradigms are autonomous, but coexist in an interactive network of metasystems in what we may refer to as a metaholarchy. Each metasystem becomes manifested as a system with behaviour/action. The systems exist together in a holarchy that is itself a frame of reference within which the system boundaries are related to each other. The boundaries make the systems analytically and empirically independent.

Thus, within the context of the holarchy, each system may be seen as an orthogonality, and its behaviour can be considered separately and interactively.

Consider now targeting methodologies. Each methodology has its own independent paradigm, the penchant ultimately defining the mission and goals of inquiry that are interpreted by an inquirer for a given situation, and a set of aims that the inquirer should pursue as a personal purpose. Thus the particular purposes to which this penchant are put will be inquirer dependent. The manifestation of the paradigm provides a set of procedures and empirical processes that enables each methodology to be seen to be behaviourally autonomous. We can consider, then, that if it is possible to establish a frame of reference for each of the set of methodologies, then the methodologies involved can be seen as relational orthogonalities. The frame of reference is defined through a cognitive model within a virtual paradigm, itself satisfying the cognitive interests or purposes of an inquirer. One way of forming a frame of reference is by defining purpose that can be facilitated through the penchants of each methodology, making them purposefully orthogonal to each other. Clearly, if the methodologies are purposively orthogonal, they must be seen as analytically and empirically independent while maintaining a relational connection. It is a consequence of this connection that empirical results from the application of one methodology can be applied to another according to some predefined but perhaps adaptable inquiry procedures. The nature of the relational connection derives from the virtual paradigm that is formed to tie the methodologies together.

The virtual paradigm itself can be seen as a formalised weltanschauung that acts as the basis of an inquiry metasystem. It enables the establishment of inquiry purposes, goals and criteria. It is defined through an inquirer's understanding of the penchant-derived cognitive purposes of each methodology that have been assembled within a single frame of reference. The cognitive model that is established as the core of the virtual paradigm will be responsible for the logical associations between the methodologies that are defined for the transmogrific domain. Since the methodologies are each orthogonal, their individual paradigms do not have to be mutually related, and paradigm incommensurability becomes an issue of no operational concern.

Examples of possible logical associations for a given set of methodologies in a particular inquiry will be offered in Chapter 16. In the meantime, in Minicase 10.1 we offer a relatively simple example of how we can define a simple common situation in terms of a set of orthogonalities, and in so doing illustrate how the notion of orthogonalities might, if appropriately defined, help to simplify the way in which we explore complex situations.

Minicase 10.1

Laundering orthogonalities

In this minicase our interest lies in explaining how it is possible to launder one's clothes in order to get them clean. The intention is to use two tools behaviourally. One is a washing machine, and the other a spin dryer. Each class of machine has a paradigm associated with it, the theory of which validates the activities that each machine has. However, the two paradigms are incommensurable, and the knowledge each has respectively relates to the processes of washing and drying. Indeed, these very things are the cognitive purposes of each tool.

Now we claim that each tool is analytically and empirically independent. They are analytically independent because the conceptualisation and knowledge of washing does not require access to the conceptualisation and knowledge associated with the process of drying. They are empirically independent because we can observe the behaviour of clothes that have been placed within the machines, and any monitoring process will be independent for each machine. However, we are also aware that the focus of examination of the machines we are interested in must provide a naturally coincident level of the cognitive purposes. For instance, it is not feasible to look at the function of the washing machine as a whole, while examining the cognitive purposes of a part of the drying machine such as the electric motor, unless of course one's ingenuity can derive a relationship that is seen to sensibly relate.

In order to argue that the two machines can be used together, a virtual paradigm must be set up. This will enable the launderer to create a framework within which the relationship between the washer and dryer is clear. This relationship is expressed in terms of the cognitive purposes of each tool, and these must be linked with the cognitive purposes that project from the virtual paradigm. The simplest way of establishing the framework is to define a table (Table 10.3).

Table 10.3 Summary of inquiry

Activity	Description
Weltanschauung	There is a need to launder a set of clothes.
Inquirer's mission	To effectively launder a set of clothes.
Tools (method): *Washing machine* *Drying machine*	Mission to process clothes for the purpose of wet cleaning. Mission to process wet clothes for the purpose of drying.
Nature of operation	Goals of washer include detergent penetration and dirt removal. Goals of dryer include clothes separation and dehydration.
Nature of examination	The washer and dryer are orthogonal, connected through cognitive purpose. The washer is used first, and then the clean clothes are passed on to the dryer for processing.
Explanatory model	A strategy of clothing change is proposed. Both orthogonalities are required to be used in succession to succeed in this. However, they may also be used iteratively to improve the cleanliness of the clothes.
Options selection	Particular makes of machine are selected because they undertake the most satisfactory performance according to the criteria identified by the launderer.

10.7 Inquirism and ideology

Paradigms are defined through a cognitive model that involves beliefs, values, attitudes, norms, ideology, meanings and projected cognitive purposes. In particular, ideology is an organisation of beliefs and attitudes that is more or less institutionalised or shared with others, and is applied to the logical organising processes. It provides a total system of thought, emotion and attitude to the world. It refers to any conception of the world that goes beyond the ability of formal validation. It can also be referred to as a preconscious aspect of culture that can be seen as a way of expressing wishes of the belief system that may otherwise be seen as incompatible with the self. Like norms and symbols, ideology provides people who belong to a given culture with self-approval for their values and attitudes.

Methodologies, like situations, have embedded within them ideology. The common cognitive model that arises during *inquirism* through the relationship between the world views of an inquirer, methodology and the situation may or may not have ideology that is common to all world views. The likelihood is that the ideologies of each apex of the triad will not be common, and the cognitive model will as likely reflect the ideology of the inquirer over and above that of the methodology and the situation. The constraint on this is that the ideology that is applied in the inquiry process must result in a *culturally feasible* intervention strategy for the organisation involved in the situation.

An example of the problem of ideological autonomy is given in Minicase 10.2. This illustrates the relationship between two paradigms whose contrary conceptualisations mean that they are ideologically incommensurable.

Minicase 10.2

A case of ideological incommensurability

The idea of complementarism is important in principle, but can be prone to difficulty. How, for instance, does one relate two paradigms that are ideologically distinct unless one is forced to through a paradigmatic crisis?

Consider, for example, the domain of conflict processes. At least two different still developing paradigms exist. Neither has developed sufficiently to a point where paradoxes or exemplar contradictions exist between them. It is in the nature of such problems of contradiction that replacement paradigms are encouraged – or more, demanded – to emerge.

Of the two ideologically conflicting frames of reference that we shall consider, one derives from what is referred to as *peace studies* and the other from *war studies*. Peace studies is an eclectic and fundamentally humanistic approach that wishes to find explanations for complex situations that cause conflicts. On the other hand, war studies examines conflictual situations from the perspective of strategic processes and power relationships with the intention of finding strategic advantage. For peace studies, human value is important, and concepts used in war studies such as collateral damage (people killed by mistake) are anathema.

One of the simpler models of peace studies is that of Richardson, which tries to explain the processes and escalation of arms races. One of the simpler models of war studies is that of Lanchester, which tries to explain field strategies that can result in more or less war dead, which can define strategic advantage. The two paradigms are clearly ideologically orthogonal. While both deal with conflict processes, the paradigms from which they derive are incommensurable in that they use different sets of orthogonal concepts and different language. In those areas where coextension does exist, the scale of values tends to be qualitatively dissimilar.

Both peace and war studies are analytically and empirically independent, and have distinct penchants that can be expressed in terms of their cognitive purposes. However, it is feasible for a virtual paradigm to arise that defines a frame of reference that relates their penchants to enable them to be assembled as orthogonalities and used together.

10.8 Viable inquiry systems and autopoiesis

As we have discussed in an earlier chapter, viable systems are autopoietic. A viable inquiry system, then, must also be autopoietic, and *inquirism* enables this. It is through *inquirism* that a viable inquiry system will define its own boundaries of inquiry relative to its environment. Seen as a system of inquiry, it is autopoietic if it develops its own code of operations, implements its own programmes, reproduces its own elements in a closed circuit and lives according to its own dominant paradigms. When the inquiry system reaches its 'autopoietic take-off', its operations can no longer be controlled from outside.

In general an autopoietic system will generate outputs to that network of processes that are in part themselves the network of processes. Following the arguments of Schwarz (1994), this can be seen to occur when the inquiry system regenerates its logical or organising networks that derive from its virtual paradigms through actor behaviour, and when it defines for itself the boundaries of that network, determined from paradigms. Thus, autopoiesis occurs for instance when a viable inquiry process becomes recursive. Autopoiesis is essential to a viable inquiry system since it enables it to 'digest' any unexpected fluctuation. It does this through entropic drift to regenerate the system's structure. Viable inquiry systems become autopoietic by (a) modifying their structures and fluxes (form and behaviour) and (b) changing the causal networks that derive from their paradigms and methods for achieving goals.

Other considerations of Schwarzian viable systems theory concern self-reference and autogenesis. Self-reference occurs in viable inquiry systems when they refer only to themselves in terms of their intentioned purposeful organisational behaviour. This is self-evident since it is this that happens within the triad of inquiry world views. Autogenesis can be thought of as relating to coherence and oneness through *inquirism* and its integration into a metasystem. It represents the influence it has on its own rules of production. It involves continuous creation, regeneration, evolution or transformation of inquiry in (a) the way that methodologies are used and (b) how methodologies are applied to situations. The intensity of the influence is a measure of autonomy. Viable inquiry systems are part of a network of teleonomic systems and subsystems; that is, complex active systems with different degrees of autonomy in our economic, political, inquiry and cultural parts, all striving for survival. Methodologies and inquirers must be sensitive to this.

10.9 The propositions for viable inquiry systems

Based largely on the work of Schwarz and Beer, we can propose a set of propositions that define for us viable inquiry systems.

1 An *inquiry system* is composed of a unity of interactive formally or informally defined objects, each of which has its own frame of reference. The objects may be referred to as (a) methods, (b) situations and (c) systemic representations of a situation, and together with the behaviour of the inquirer they define a system of inquiry. These all interact with one another during inquiry.

2 The objects may be composed of parts that can themselves be seen as objects. In this way situations may be seen as a systemic hierarchy (or holarchy), methods may be composed of parts that are themselves methods, and an inquirer's behaviour is composed of behavioural subcomponents.

3 Objects in human activity systems derive from cognitive systems composed of inquirer weltanschauung, targeting methodology paradigms and target system paradigms.

4 Paradigms, with their cognitive models, lie at the basis of all organised human activity systems, whether they are target situations or targeting methodologies. In addition, inquirers approach inquiries with a weltanschauung that is cognitively based.

221

5 Methodological inquiry derives from a self-organising group of individuals who maintain at least one paradigm.

6 A paradigm that lies at the basis of a system methodology provides a propositional logic that enables (a) *logical* organising relationships that determine methodology and (b) *manifest* consequences called method.

7 A paradigm that lies at the basis of human activity systems provides a propositional logic that enables (a) the formulation of *logical* organising relationships and (b) *manifest* consequences that are seen as organisational form and behaviour.

8 A viable inquiry system may exist as a holon of inquirer, methodology and situation seen as a system. The holon may itself be made up of networks of other holons in a system hierarchy (a holarchy), each a semi-autonomous cooperating entity. Such systems may adapt.

9 The paradigm of a human activity system determines the *network* of beliefs and 'truths' that define itself, and it maintains its own myths. Rituals are manifestations of myths that will determine how the human activity system will function, though these may vary between groups distant from the centre of the system.

10 Viable inquiry systems have operational closure through self-organisation, autopoiesis, self-reference and autogenesis. This means that the inquirer is concerned only with inquiry into the situation once the human activity system for it has been defined, that the methodology will be adaptive to changing perspectives of the situation, and that the inquiry will be seen in terms of a systemic hierarchy (or holarchy).

11 Viable inquiry systems involve dissipation (entropic drift towards disorder and uniformity) and teleonomy (degree of autonomy, coherence and identity) generated by operational closure. This may operate for methodologies, target purposeful activity systems or the application of the former to the latter.

12 A viable inquiry system has self-organisation if it has the ability to amplify unexpected fluctuations that occur within it. Fluctuations occur as a direct result of perturbations from its environment that affect its dynamic events.

13 A viable inquiry system is able to support adaptability and change while maintaining behavioural stability in its methods. A system is adaptive when its form is maintained, elaborated or changed according to its self-organisational needs. It is a complex adaptive system when it maintains complicated networks of independent components that are so interconnected as to form a unity or organic whole with demonstrated capabilities to adjust behaviour to changing circumstances and to anticipate future events.

14 Autopoiesis is the self-production of individual and collective physical and psychic behaviour that derives from its organisational networks. An autopoietic inquiry system defines its own boundaries relative to its environment, develops its own code of operations, implements its own programmes, reproduces its own elements in a closed circuit and 'lives' according to its own dominant paradigms. When a system reaches what we might call 'autopoietic take-off', its operations can no longer be controlled from outside. In general an autopoietic system will generate outputs to that network of processes that are in part themselves the network of processes.

15 A viable inquiry system is autopoietic. This can be shown because it can:

a Regenerate an inquiry system's logical or organising networks that derive from its paradigms through actor and institutional behaviour. It is enabled through:
   i pressure on an inquirer applied by the stakeholders of a situation being examined,
   ii pressure of inquirers on the stakeholders of a situation.
b Define for itself the boundaries of that network, determined from paradigms.

16 Autopoiesis is essential to a viable inquiry system since it enables it to 'digest' any unexpected fluctuation. It does this through entropic drift to regenerate the system's structure. We can thus say that such systems can become autopoietic by (a) modifying their structures and fluxes (form of inquiry and behaviour) and (b) changing the causal networks that derive from their paradigms and methods for achieving goals.

17 Self-reference occurs in open inquiry systems that refer only to themselves in terms of their intentioned purposeful organisational behaviour.

18 Autogenesis can be thought of as relating to coherence and oneness. It represents the influence it has on its own rules of production. It involves continuous creation, regeneration, evolution or transformation of methodology and/or the situation as an existing whole. The intensity of the influence is a measure of autonomy.

19 We are not alone in an environment of passive and controllable things; we are part of a network of teleonomic systems and subsystems; that is, complex active system with different degrees of autonomy in our economic, political, inquiry and cultural parts, all striving for survival. Methodologies and inquirers must be sensitive to this.

20 The paradigm of inquiry systems should be compatible with that of the situation. This means that there should be consciousness of the self-producing dialogue between an inquiry system and the image it generates of the network of holons.

21 In complex nonlinear networks of teleonomic subsystems, the drive for 'survival' of each subsystem is no guarantee of the survival of the whole. The overall autopoietic logic has priority over the survival logic of the parts. In one example of this, a consensus methodology may provide a satisfying outcome when considered in terms of the dominant paradigm. However, if the subsidiary paradigms of the target situation are taken as subsystems, then the system may not survive as a whole. For further exploration of this, we should need to consult our earlier discussions about the nature of identity and survivability.

22 Viable inquiry systems must be autopoietic, thus having compatibility and mutual production between their dynamic events and the networks that produce them. To survive in an organised way they must at least maintain compatibility between their events and these causal networks of production.

10.10 Hard and soft methodologies from the perspective of viable inquiry systems

Methods exist as methodologies if they have associated with them organising and control processes. Thus, for example, homeostasis is fundamental to methodology. Morphogenesis and self-organisation can also be seen as a consequence of the inquiry process that can modify the way in which a methodology operates, the way in which a situation is perceived, or the relationship between the methodology and the situation. This model, then, should enable us to describe and explain what we would call the dramatic shifts in methodologies as has occurred in soft system methodology (from Checkland (1980, 1981) to Checkland and Scholes (1990)) and total systems intervention (from Flood and Jackson (1991) to Flood (1995)), and even the emergence of soft methodologies through the rise of action research in the 1960s. It should also enable us to understand paradigm shifts in our organisations, for instance as has occurred during the processes of nationalisation and more recently privatisation. Conceivably it might also contribute to an appreciation that there is an interrelationship between a methodology and a situation as well as that between a situation and an inquirer, a topic that has not very often been discussed. The model may also be able to explain how viable systems deal with chaos. We can now see three possibilities arise with respect to the model, which may:

1 direct our attention to the principles of how methodologies are able to respond to situations in chaos and evolve;

2 direct our attention to the principles of how situations are able to respond to chaos;

3 suggest that while a given situation may itself not be at a point of passing through morphogenesis, metamorphosis or chaos, the application of a methodology itself to it may (appropriately or inappropriately) result in these.

Hard methodologies are defined in terms of tangible things that tend to be seen as deterministic or adopt rational expectation. They usually assume that the situation being inquired into is well structured and certain. A hard approach can also represent a situation as a complex of systems, some of which may be perceived to be malfunctioning. In this case intervention strategies are often sought that can enable the malfunction to be dealt with. Strategic options for intervention are rationally determined according to the criteria that inquirers define within their approaches to inquiry. The selected strategies occur according to predefined criteria, and it is supposed that these criteria will hold in the future. Validation occurs through deterministic or rational logic.

Soft methodologies are people centred, and its inquirers tend to suppose that a situation is ill structured, uncertain and complex. The approach that soft viewholders take is to establish procedures of inquiry that involves the stakeholders. The degree of stakeholder involvement is indicated by the softness of the methodology. Soft methodologies tend to adopt degrees of consensus approach that feed the results of inquiry back to the stakeholders for validation. Having said this, the creation of 'consensus' may well evolve through accommodation or learning, which results from an inquiry process, when implicit world views that have been in conflict are addressed in some way.

In both hard and soft cases, the options generated are implemented while monitoring and evaluating progress homeostatically. There is also the possibility of behavioural or cognitive methodological change, while inquirers learn about the way in which inquiry and intervention have occurred.

While hard and soft methodologies thus derive from a base of different assumptions, they end up establishing implementation strategies that are quite similar in that they have an assumption of rational expectation. That is, they expect that if

1 their analysis and models are in some way validated;

2 they deduce an intervention strategy consistent with perspectives of the paradigm being used;

3 during implementation of the intervention strategy the specifications are honoured;

4 monitoring occurs to ensure that (2) and (3) are validated,

then the result will satisfy the perceived needs of the situation. In situations of chaos, it is this that establishes the weakness of both approaches. Cybernetic principles themselves fail during chaos when the relationship between metasystemic cognition and system behaviour breaks down. Here, the environment alone drives behaviour subject to Varela's idea that the possibility of change in a system is structure determined. Consensus approaches too may become volatile during this time, and shift along with situation contexts.

A counter argument to this is that the periods of stable equilibrium that we do experience may persist long enough for intervention strategies to be decided and implemented. However, this does not respond to the principle of the argument in the least. In particular, it does not address the problem of equilibrium thinking that Stacey (1993) decries.

Intervention strategies will introduce changes into the form and culture of an organisation to different degrees and over different durations. In organisations in which there is a structural criticality, the cost of a small failure can be very high, even to their survival. What is important, however, is the nature of the criticality. It may be a point criticality that affects only one focus of the organisation, or it might be regional and affect a number of foci, or global and affect the whole picture being seen.

This brings to mind the viable system model that is designed to tackle such situations. It will explore situations for the purpose of making them viable by correction of structural faults and ensuring that the relationship between the system and the metasystem is deterministic. For example, senior management must be able to generate policies, controls and coordination strategies that can deal with operational situations, and invest in the future. If they cannot, then the model tells us to move to a higher focus of inquiry, if one can be accessed. We could also approach the situation from a lower focus that works upwards. However such 'grass roots' approaches are normally difficult to implement, often require manipulation, and can be thought of as a (slow or fast) process of revolution that is a local metamorphosis, and that may or may not be part of a regional or global metamorphosis.

We are now led to the question of whether, in chaotic situations, it is even possible to implement intervention strategies at all. In concert with the principle of Stacey (1993), organisational structures should be highly plastic and able to adapt flexibly as new possibilities arise. Plasticity can occur through structures that release the potential of people, e.g. through those that have minimal structural violence (Galtung, 1972). They should be seen as *variety* generators, able to be proactive in creating potential solutions to problems not yet conceived.

One way of enabling variety generation is to invest in people, not structures. It suggests that organisations should be created as coordinated networks of small nodes capable of recognising and reacting quickly to new situations. In agreement with the principles of cybernetics, it is the nature of the interconnectivity between the nodes that is important, as well as the functionality of the nodes. Interconnectivity is normally expressed in terms of information exchanges, but it is also feasible to consider it in terms of social, cultural, power and even entropic and energy relationships. The existence of node-based plural paradigms should also be formally recognised. Now, the interaction between the nodes has to do with the structural and behavioural manifestation of each node, since it is this that determines its properties and capabilities. It has little to do directly with the paradigms that determine these manifestations. This idea applies not only to target situations, but also to targeting methodologies. Thus we are able to validate the complementary use of methodologies in a way that is independent of the idea of paradigm incommensurability.

Now, the weltanschauung principle tells us that there are as many weltanschauungen as there are individuals, or shared weltanschauungen as there are groups, and this validates the soft systems approach. Many soft approaches adopt consensus as a principle, however, which must place them in jeopardy because of the weltanschauung principle. It is because of the weltanschauung principle that in a network structure, one would expect the nature of the interconnectivity to be different and unique for every organisation and susceptible to change over time.

10.11 Methodology and viable inquiry

Our interest here has been in purposeful adaptable activity systems, which may also be seen as evolutionary systems that recurrently experience periods of chaos. The intention here is to identify some principles that a viable inquiry system might have to address if it is to deal with complex target situations that evolve. The principles that arise should be assignable to any of the parts of inquirism – that is, the inquirer, the targeting methodology or the target situation.

The holarchy of our society is composed of a network of autonomous focuses, some within others. It operates through competition in many of its aspects. Cohesion is maintained through the various infrastructures that support them. As such we are interested in inquiries that can result in intervention in evolutionary systems. Its cognitive purpose could be towards effecting a reduction in structural violence. It could draw on other approaches that are set up together in a framework of ideas to work in a complementary fashion. It would establish the following cognitive purposes that should be pursued during an analysis stage of inquiry, which derive from what we call the Kauffman (1993) caveats to inquiry:

1 organisations should be seen in terms of:
   a balance
   b collaboration

2 inquirers should identify:
   a sources of order
   b self-organising properties

3 inquirers should understand how efficacy can be permitted through self-ordered properties to:
   a permit
   b enable
   c limit

4 inquirers should understand which properties of complex systems:
   a confer on the system the capacity to adapt
   b indicate the nature of that adaptation.

The nature of the balance might be seen in terms of structural coupling to other organisations as well as the environment. The characteristics of the Kauffman caveats should be seen as local as well as regional or global phenomena. Global strategies are untenable unless they represent an appropriate cognitive ideational–sensate mix (Sorokin, 1937) to generate variety that deals with ideas (ideational) as well as more practical constraints, returns and resourced provision (sensate) for local evolution. An ideational mindset provides for variety, a sensate one for actuation. A network of evolutionary systems may develop unexpected forms of emergence, and it is in the interests of society to guide them in some way that minimises structural violence. The nature of structural violence is as follows:

1 structural violence is the passive violence that acts on one group through the structures established by another;

2 it can be seen as a suppressed form of conflict between the groups within a situation;

3 the conflict and its nature tends to be unclear and can be interpreted as generic in nature (thus distinguishing qualitatively between the different groups);

4 structural violence may not be acknowledged by either side;

5 an observer (or rather an *other*) can normally recognise structural violence to occur when one group is seen to be dominated by another, with subsequent exploitative practices;

6 the exploitation may be preconscious, and thus not recognised;

7 the exploitation may not be for the perceived benefit of the dominant group;

8 the structural violence may be institutionalised;

9 structural violence bounds the potential of individuals, thus constraining the variety that a system can generate;

10 structural violence thus limits the possibilities of the system that can be used to meet environmental challenges;

11 high levels of structural violence are therefore inconsistent with the plastic needs of social systems;

12 low levels of structural violence contribute to the maintenance of stable systems.

The use of the Kauffman caveats would enable inquirers to explore the possibilities that may develop in the shorter term for the implementation of intervention strategies. Various elements of the Kauffman caveats can be seen to be cybernetic in nature, and an appropriate methodology would need to be used. Synthesis would draw on the inquirer's perspectives and ideology to drive a direction for the intervention, influenced interactively by the stakeholders as part of the system. It would take into consideration the possibilities of evolutionary development as highlighted through Schwarzian viable systems theory. However, minimising structural violence could be central, provided that a virtual paradigm could emerge that recognised criteria that enabled a level of structural violence to be qualitatively estimated. Implementation and post-evaluation would monitor throughout using a form of the Kauffman caveats. Where possible, intervention strategies should be plastic, entailing as much variety as possible.

SUMMARY

Viable inquiry systems exist, based on the interrelationship between an inquirer, a target situation and a targeting methodology. The world views associated with each of these can form a cognitive model that acts as the basis of a metasystem from which a purposeful adaptive activity system is manifested. During the inquiry process, world-view pluralism occurs through the development of shared world views. In the case of an inquirer that may be a group, a shared weltanschauung develops that is intended to address the inquiry. In the case of the situation, a plurality of paradigms exist in the participant organisation(s) that interrelate, and come together through the pursuit of an agreed cognitive purpose defined within a supraparadigm. In the case of methodologies, the shared world views occur through the creation of a virtual paradigm that forms a frame of reference. This sees methodology as orthogonalities that have been relationally connected within the frame of reference. One way of making this connection is through relating the cognitive purposes of each methodology.

Another aspect of viable inquiry systems is that it is autopoietic. It has this property when it is for instance recursive in its inquiry processes, and when its organisational processes change or 'drift'. Also, self-reference occurs in viable inquiry systems since the inquiry process is concerned primarily with the situation in hand with respect to purposeful behaviour. Finally, viable inquiry systems involve autogenesis. In particular, through the metasystem it influences its own rules of production. It is involved in continuous creation, regeneration, evolution or transformation of the inquiry process in the way that methodologies are used, and how they are applied to situations.

REFERENCES

Burrell, G. and Morgan, G. (1979) *Sociological Paradigms and Organisational Analysis*. London: Heinemann.

Checkland, P. (1980) 'Are organisations machines?', *Futures,* 12, 421.

Checkland, P. (1981) *Systems Thinking, Systems Practice*. Chichester: Wiley.

Checkland, P. and Scholes, J. (1990) *Soft Systems Methodology in Action*. Chichester: Wiley.

Flood, R.L. (1995) *Solving Problem Solving*. Chichester: Wiley.

Flood, R.L. and Jackson, M. (1991) *Creative Problem Solving: Total intervention strategy*. Chichester: Wiley.

Flood, R.L. and Romm, N.R.A. (1995) 'Enhancing the process of choice in TSI, and improving chances of tackling coercion', *Systems Practice*, 8, 377–408.

Foucault, M. (1980) *Power/Knowledge: Selected interviews and other writings 1972–1977*. Brighton: Harvester Press.

Galtung, J. (1972) *Peace: Essays in peace research*, vol. 1. Copenhagen: Christian Ejlers.

Gregory, W.J. (1992) 'Critical systems thinking and pluralism: a new constellation'. PhD thesis, City University, London.

Habermas, J. (1970) 'Knowledge and interest'. In Emmet, D. and MacIntyre, A. (eds) *Sociological Theory and Philosophical Analysis*. London: Macmillan, pp. 36–54.

Jackson, M.C. (1992) *Systems Methodologies for the Management Sciences*. New York: Plenum Press.

Jackson, M.C. (1993) 'Don't bite my finger: Haridimos Tsoukas' critical evaluation of total systems intervention', *Systems Practice*, 6, 289–94.

Jackson, M.C. and Carter, P. (1991) 'In defence of paradigm incommensurability', *Organisational Studies*, 12, 109–27.

Kauffman, S.A. (1993) *The Origins of Order: Self-organisation and selection in evolution*. Oxford: Oxford University Press.

McClelland, B. and Yolles, M.I. (1997) 'Teaching and learning styles'. Presented at the conference on Educational Innovation in Economics and Business Administration, Orlando, USA.

Midgley, G. (1995) 'Mixing methods: developing systemic intervention'. Research Memorandum no. 9, Centre for Systems, University of Hull.

Minai, A.T. (1995) 'Emergence, a domain where the distinction between conception in arts and sciences is meaningless', *Cybernetics and Human Knowing*, 3(3), 25–51.

Reed, M. (1985) *Redirections in Organisational Analysis*. London: Tavistock.

Schwarz, E. (1994) 'A trandisciplinary model for the emergence, self-organisation and evolution of viable systems'. Presented at the International Information, Systems Architecture and Technology, Technical University of Wroclaw, Szklaska Poreba, Poland.

Sorokin, P.A. (1937) *Social and Cultural Dynamics*. New York: American Book Company.

Stacey, R. (1993) *Managing Chaos*. London: Kogan Page.

Willmot, H. (1993) 'Breaking the paradigm mentality', *Organisation Studies*, 14, 681–719.

Yolles, M.I. (1996) 'Critical systems thinking, paradigms, and the modelling space', *Journal of System Practice*, 9(3).

Yolles, M.I. (1997a) 'An introduction to the theory of viable learning'. Presented at the Third Panhellenic Conference on Didactics of Mathematics and Informatics in Science Teaching, Patras University, Greece.

Yolles, M.I. (1997b) 'Learning style and strategy, and the theory of viable learning'. Presented at the Third International Conference on Computer Based Learning in Science, De Montfort University, Leicester.

Yolles, M.I. and McClelland, B. (1997) 'Developing measures for learning strategy'. Presented at the CTI-AFM 8th annual conference, Bristol.

PART 3

Approaches to inquiry

INTRODUCTION TO PART 3

The objectives and contexts of the first five chapters of this section are all the same. The objectives are to show the nature of the given methodology, the purpose of the methodology, the form of the methodology, the way in which this methodology can relate to others through a doppelgänger paradigm, and how the methodology is used practically. The contexts reflect the same pattern in each chapter, and are essentially as follows: introduction, concepts of the method being considered, the nature of the doppelgänger paradigm – that is, the paradigm seen from another inquirer's perspective – a summary and their case study. The five methods and their case studies are summarised, and all are based on the idea of action research, which provides for the possibility of greater method complexification.

Action research

'Action research begins with a desire to be involved with the application of one's scientific interests and discoveries, but it goes much further ... the interests of action researchers are driven both by their intellectual pursuits and curiosities and by the interests and needs of the community of which it is part. Thus, action research is likely to be used to address needs that emerge as most important within communities rather than needs of small numbers of individuals' (Maruyama, 1996).

Action research is one foundation element of systems intervention strategy (SIS). It is also referred to as action learning, and was developed by Kurt Lewin in the 1940s. It can be described as follows:

> Action research is research on action with the goal of making that action more effective. Action refers to programmes and interventions designed to solve a problem or improve a condition ... action research is the process of systematically collecting research data about an ongoing system relative to some objective goal, or need of that system; feeding these ideas back into the system; taking action by altering selected variables within the system based both on the data and on hypotheses; and evaluating the results of actions by collecting more data (French and Bell, 1984, pp. 98–9).

It is based on 'the proposition that an effective approach to solving organisational problems must involve a rational, systematic analysis of the issues in question. It must be an approach which secures information, hypotheses and action from all parties involved, as well as evaluating the action taken towards the solution of the problem. It follows that the change process itself must become a learning situation; one in which the early participants learn not only from the actual research, the use of theory to investigate the problem and identify a solution, but also from the process of collaborative action itself' (Burnes, 1992, p. 160).

Action research programmes are normally composed of:

1 an organisation of individuals
2 the subject (of people who compose the change situation)
3 a change agent (a facilitator, initiator or coordinator).

These three components should be seen as subsystems of the problem solving system. The organisation is usually small, and defines 'the medium through which the problem situation may be changed, as well as providing a forum in which the interests and ethics of the various parties to this process may be developed. It is a cyclic process, whereby the group analyses and solves the problem through a succession of iterations. The change agent (consultant), through skills of coordination, links the different insights and activities within the group, so as to form a coherent chain of ideas and hypotheses' (Burnes, 1992, p. 161).

Action research is seen as a two-pronged process (Bennett, 1983; Burnes, 1992):

1 it emphasises that change requires action;

2 successful action is based on analysing the situation correctly, identifying all the possible alternative solutions, and choosing the one most appropriate to the situation at hand.

Action research thus suppose that the form of inquiry will provide insights concerning the perceived problems which will lead to practical help in the situation, and that experience of using the form of inquiry will enable it to be gradually improved.

The methodologies

Systems intervention strategy is a methodology that derives from the harder end of the soft–hard continuum of systems methodologies. It is designed to offer a straightforward and more familiar approach to the examination of messy and relatively soft situations, which novice inquirers can become familiar with quite quickly. In order to deal with complexity, the methodology conceptualises that three types of change should be addressed: technical, organisational and personal. The case study that has this methodology applied to it concerns a Liverpool City Council budget deficit that must be dealt with. It has been decided that service charging can help the situation, and a pilot project is applied to the Division of Social Services to change the way the issue of Disabled Car Badges occurs.

Organisational development is a soft methodology intended for use in complex situations, to enable intervention for change management. It approaches this from the perspective of individual and organisational inquiry. It adopts a systems approach by identifying a set of organisational entities which have functions the interactive effects of which require that the system is stable. In order to deal with complex situations, it conceptualises that they should be seen in terms of power relationships, control processes and innate resistance to change, all of which must be addressed through individuals and the culture to which they belong. The case study that has this methodology applied to it also concerns the Liverpool City Council, also in connection with its disabled car badge charging (DCBC). While SIS has been used principally to explore the technical aspects of the intervention strategy, OD is being used to explore its organisational culture, which does not historically admit such charging, and a cultural and organisational change will be required.

Soft systems methodology is a methodology for inquiry that is concerned with unstructured and uncertain situations. Like all dynamic methodologies, it creates dynamic methods through the control processes that it operates. Its dynamic aspect enables learning to occur that can manifest SSM as an infinite variety of simple methods. The broad conceptualisation that it adopts to deal with complexity is that change problem situations have to be addressed through an exploration of both the culture and the social structure of the organisation involved in the situation. The case study that has SSM concerns the Lancaster Priority Trust, which because of its status in a competitive market National Health Service and Government constraints on funding, needs to improve its efficiency in some way. The study by the way explores the effect that privatisation has had on the National Health Service.

The viable system model provides a powerful diagnostic approach to inquiry using a cybernetic approach. It has recently become quite popular as a 'technical' approach to the examination of complex situations, but must be seen to be much broader than this, particularly when embedded as a paradigm within an appropriate method. The conceptualisation that it adopts to deal with complexity centres on the notion that one can distinguish between a system and its metasystem. This enables decision processes to be drawn away from the behavioural processes of the situation under investigation. The case study that has the viable systems model methodology applied to it concerns further education in Liverpool, which has (it is perceived) passed through too many structural changes to give confidence that it is now viable. The methodology is applied to it in order to explore how it can be made viable.

Conflict situations are generated within or between organisations when the world views that are involved produce stable patterns of conflict that we call Moiré cognitive patterns. Conflict theory suggests ways of dealing with these patterns. The conflict modelling cycle can contribute to the exploration of the patterns, and to a realigning of world views to enable new stable Moiré patterns to emerge. Its cognitive model sees situations as being paradigm plural, an alternative to the premise of consensus approach. The cognitive model derives from the theory of conflict and its intended use is to identify intervention strategies that minimise violence. This is because in paradigm plural situations, it is either active or passive violence that sows the seeds for the future destabilisation of settlements and entry into structurally critical conditions. The methodology is also sensitive to the use of different paradigms through methodological complementarism, allowing it to explore a pluralism of modelling approaches and philosophies. It deals with complex situations by conceptualising that conflict, attitudes and behaviour are analytically and empirically independent, and can be addressed separately. Two case studies are addressed, the more significant of which is that of the Liverpool dock workers' conflictual situation with the Mersey Dock and Harbour Company, which had lasted for about two years at the time of writing. The second case study explores the demise of the Soviet Union.

Finally, in Chapter 16 a summary of the methodologies considered is given, and the way of comparing them identified in Chapter 5 is put to work. Methodologies of management systems can be seen as analytically and empirically independent orthogonalities established in a single frame of reference defined in terms of some cognitive purposes. This idea can be generalised in terms of conceptual domains that have a projected cognitive quality (like purposes, interests and influences). In this way we can see the principle to be recursive. For example, each methodology is itself composed of a set of conceptual domains that provide cognitive influences, and these may also be seen as orthogonalities within it. Such considerations enable us to provide additional ways of comparing and contrasting management systems methodologies. Illustrations of how this can occur are provided, and, as a backcloth to this, the methodologies considered here are characterised and a typology established for them. Methodologies can also be mixed, and examples of frameworks that enable this to occur are given.

The methodologies that we shall explore can all be defined to lie on the hard–soft continuum, some being relatively hard, and others soft. Whether it is useful to be concerned with the soft or hard nature of them has been questioned earlier. Such considerations are reflected in comments made by Mayon-White: 'the two extremes [of hard and soft approaches] reflect a reductionist view of the world, with positivism and a mechanistic view emerging in the "hard" paradigm, and the social sciences attempting to use the methods of the natural sciences to explain their objects of study' (Mayon-White, 1993, p. 141). In Fig. A we present a perception of the way in which hard and soft approaches have developed over time. They represent shifts in methodological paradigms. If the two extreme ends of the continuum are perceived to reflect the outlook of determinism, the central region can be seen to be phenomenological. Thus, the two extremes implicitly operate a similar outlook, while the relative central area represents contrasting paradigms. It is feasible, therefore, to consider that the extreme ends of the continuum can be formed into a circle; taking time as the vertical axis, we now find that we have a cylinder. In this way the continuum can be seen as lying on the surface of a cylinder in an 'evolutionary space' in which ideas and paradigms spiral through time.

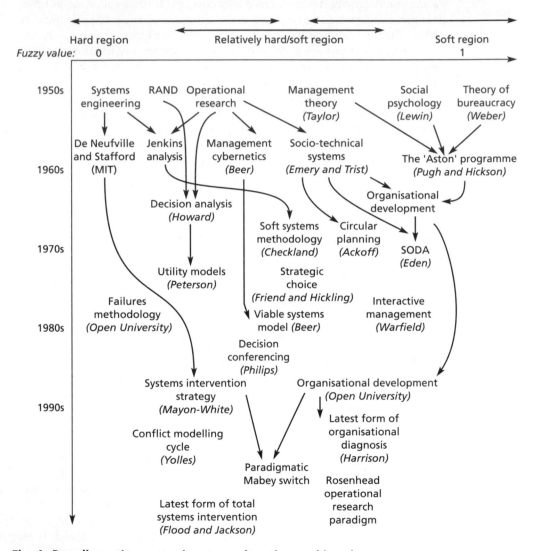

Fig. A Paradigmatic approaches to explanation and inquiry

The regions of softness/hardness are only approximations, and broad enough to enable the methodologies to be written. For comment on some of these approaches, see Jackson (1992). (*Source*: Based on Mayon-White, 1993, p.133)

Assignment

Each methodology operates its own particular style of system model varification that is a reflection of its paradigm, and connected to its position in Fig. A. Compare and contrast the different approaches to validation after reading through each methodology.

REFERENCES

Bennett, R. (1983) *Management Research*. Management Development Series No. 20. Geneva: International Labour Office.

Burnes, B. (1992) *Managing Change*. London: Pitman.

French, W.L. and Bell, C.H. (1984) *Organisational Development*. Englewood Cliffs, NJ: Prentice Hall.

Jackson, M.C. (1992) *Systems Methodologies for the Management Sciences*. New York: Plenum Press.

Maruyama, G. (1996) 'Application and transformation of action research in educational research and practice', *Systems Practice*, 9(1), 85–101.

Mayon-White, B. (1993), 'Problem-solving in small groups: team members as agents of change'. In Mabey, C. and Mayon-White (eds) *Managing Change*. London: Paul Chapman, pp. 132–42.

CHAPTER 11

Systems intervention strategy

OVERVIEW

Systems intervention strategy is a methodology that derives from the harder end of the soft–hard continuum of systems methodologies. It is designed to offer a straightforward and more familiar approach to the examination of messy and relatively soft situations, that novice inquirers can become familiar with quite quickly. In order to deal with complexity, the methodology conceptualises that three types of change should be addressed: technical, organisational and personal.

11.1 Introduction

Systems intervention strategy (SIS) is a development of Mayon-White (1986). It is intended as a structured approach for inquiry into messy situations that require change management. The methodology has its origins in systems engineering and operations research, but has been engineered to become softer to enable it to take people into account.

The development of SIS stems from the ideas of Churchman (1971) on inquiring systems, which examines ways in which inquiry might occur. Subjectivity, it is seen, must be embedded within the systems approach: the only way in which a whole system can be seen is from as many perspectives as possible. World views cannot be diminished by exposing them to 'facts'. Weltanschauung must therefore be seen as an important element in any inquiry that must be taken into account. The weltanschauungen of participants in a situation being inquired into will provide different partial views of a situation that contribute to the whole picture. Further, as an organisation evolves, it learns, and SIS operates in concert with the ideas of action research.

SIS is also seen as a team approach to learning. A new team attempting to manage change will be learning about the organisation, its environment and its own skills. During such a process, the team requires to develop human attributes such as confidence, rather than verifiable proofs that define a preferred course of action. It must also operate as an agent of change capable of structuring inquiry into complex situations. It must develop intervention strategies for change that satisfy the needs of the situation.

11.2 The paradigm of systems intervention strategy

11.2.1 Beliefs underlying the paradigm

The impact of change creates situations that may have, as one of their characteristics, intractable issues. Under conditions of change, it is often unclear about who is responsible for what. If causal relationships exist, it is frequently difficult to determine the nature of the relationships.

This leads Mayon-White to a concern that inquirers may use SIS incorrectly: as an algorithm, rather than as a means of generating learning and understanding about a set of changes for an organisation. If inquirers apply the former, then SIS is being used too restrictively. 'The good process consultant will take cues for moving to another stage in the analysis from the group and not from a table of instructions' (Mayon-White, 1993, p. 137). This means that the logical behavioural organising process of the methodology as a phased cycle of inquiry should *not* be considered as a set of linear steps, but rather as a set of nodes which should be accessible according to the changing needs or agenda of an inquirer.

SIS is a cyclic methodology that operates very clearly in unstructured and uncertain situations. It is intended that a team of inquirers will examine the various perspectives of a situation, and produce appropriate system models to act as an intervention strategy for change. It should be seen that such models may then become invalid when the situation that they are intending to represent is subject to environmental change.

SIS provides a cyclic structure for inquiry that uses the principle of iteration to deal with uncertainty. Inquirers should be able to model a situation as a system, and then confirm their belief that their models are appropriate to the situation. The cycle is intended to be iterated as many times as necessary in order to ensure that an intervention strategy, perceived to deal adequately with change, is suitable. Each iteration is a single pass through the cycle that in its early stages might operate in a linear way. However, the best use of SIS will not restrict users to its linear form.

In SIS inquirers seeking change in problem situations should:

1 be able to model a situation as a system;

2 be able to recognise that the situation is appropriate for SIS to be used.

The consequence of the first point is that a variety of systems tools can be used to explore the form of situations. The consequence of the second point is an attempt to ensure that the SIS human activity system paradigm is appropriate for the situation in terms of the degree of complexity of the problem. This questioning philosophy about the applicability of the methology is an important proposition of the SIS paradigm since it leads to the development of what we refer to as a *Mabey switch*. By this is meant a switch between SIS and the organisational development methology of the next chapter. It is discussed further in Chapter 16.

People with vested interests in a situation (its stakeholders) are important to SIS. In part this is because, for various reasons, stakeholders create resistance to change. Such resistance can be reduced by involving stakeholders in the change situation at an early stage. While resistance is seen to be inevitable, inquiry for change strategy can benefit from it.

Reducing options

At the start of an inquiry all options for change are perceived possible. The idea that there is a need to explore the wider aspects of a problem situation is often in conflict with that of needing to implement a set of changes. The overall challenge of change is to reduce the number of things that could be done to one set of things that should be done, as shown in Fig. 11.1 (Mayon-White, 1986), though the smooth curves should be seen as a tendency rather than an actuality. How we can define that subset of what should be done must be dependent upon both the paradigms from which the organisation operates and the weltanschauung of any decision makers involved.

The Eason model

Eason (1984) considered the way in which inquirers design new systems under the impetus of change. While it relates in particular to the introduction of information systems and new technology into organisations, it can as well be related to other forms of change. This is shown in Fig. 11.2. Here, the upper diagonal curve suggests that the methodological design process accelerates after a slow start and then slows down. During this process, an organisation learns slowly and gradually about the potential of a change (say, a new technology). The shape of the diagonal loop is sometimes referred to as a hysteresis loop, more usually found in physics to explain how magnetic materials achieve their magnetic condition suddenly when being subjected to a magnetic field. The actual explanation is 'the lagging of magnetic induction behind the magnetising force' (*Concise Oxford English Dictionary*), and by analogy the learning process lags behind the events that initiate it.

The dotted rectangle in Fig. 11.2 represents a *window of opportunity* in which it is appropriate to involve the potential users of a new system in the design process that results in the creation of implementable strategies for change. This occurs before all the flexibility of the design options is lost as the *degrees of freedom* in the design process. A totally open position permits unlimited design option freedom, while a closed position allows no design option freedom. The window should be as large as possible. Eason's model for change implies that sufficient time must be allowed for consultation and redesign.

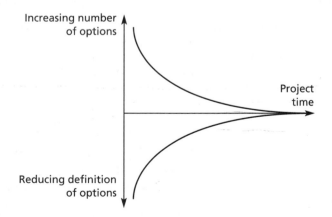

Fig. 11.1 Indication that option for action reduce in number with time. In addition, the definition for action should increase with time
(*Source*: Mayon-White, 1986)

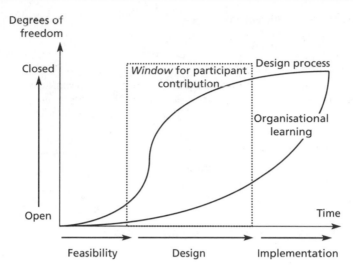

Fig. 11.2 Eason's model related to stakeholder involvement in design and implementation

From this, it is considered that change agents should take into consideration the stakeholders in the system. The involvement of stakeholders should be as great as possible. A change agent should identify all the stakeholders in a situation and their roles, in particular because they may be called in to assist the process. Strategies for change should have flexibility to permit adjustments that can suit the needs of the stakeholders to cope with environmental changes.

The impact of emotions

Any human activity situation that requires change involves people. Therefore, such a situation will have to address people-related issues. How one does this will very much depend upon the nature of the situation; for instance, whether it is emotionally charged or not. Evaluating such factors is important if an appropriate strategy for change is to be identified.

Emotions are associated with people-related soft perceptions of situations, while situations examined from a hard perspective will not include emotional considerations. In the same way, we can refer to situations being soft and having a high emotional charge, or hard with a low emotional charge. Emotion and computational complexity are analytically and empirically independent concepts that can be related together since they both affect situations. The relationship between increasing emotional involvement and computational difficulty in situations is illustrated in Fig. 11.3.

Mabey uses the technically complex emotional field introduced in Chapter 3 to identify the approaches that might be pursued for change management, by locating them graphically in different quadrants of the problem space (Fig. 11.4). Organisations facing change issues (representing intractable problem situations) in the top-right quadrant will often have more difficulties in setting objectives because of multiple stakeholders and conflicting agendas.

241

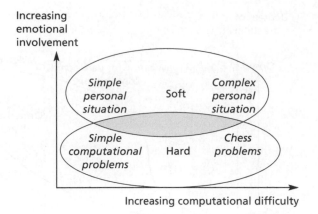

Fig. 11.3 Characteristics of hard–soft situations
(*Source*: Mabey, 1995)

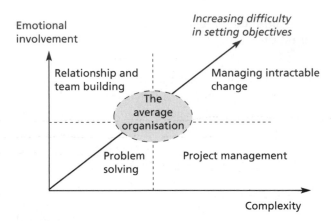

Fig. 11.4 Different approaches to change management in a complex emotional field
(*Source*: Adapted from Mabey, 1995, p. 61)

11.2.2 The cognitive model of systems intervention strategy

Change in order to generate a new environmental balance

SIS supposes that the human activity systems that it deals with are open. This means that a situation is modelled as a system in a way that allows it to be perturbed by its environment. The system continues to exist, to maintain its identity, because it manages to establish a balance of forces, an equilibrium in its relationship with its environment. Intervention for the creation of change in the *form* of an organisation is the process of establishing a new balance between the system and its environment. The process of change can thus be seen as a response of the system to pressures from its environment.

SIS can give insights into the form and behaviour of a situation seen as a system by examining its structure and processes. Since we suppose that we are dealing with an open system, indeterminable influences from an uncertain environment occur. A central idea in SIS is that strategy must be used for intervention to achieve change in a way that can enable uncertainty to be reduced.

After a change process, new pressures from the environment may develop that require a further change process. The change relationship between the environment and the system can be presented as in Fig. 11.5. Typical of the idea of open systems, three types of change can be identified – organisational, technical, and individual – where:

1 the development of an organisation is concerned with an organisation's structure (including roles) and processes;

2 technical development is concerned with control and predictability;

3 personal development reflects on cultural change and includes the adoption of new perspectives.

All three are analytically and empirically independent, mutually interactive, and individually directly influenced by the environment.

The change agent and the facilitator in SIS

In the terminology of this methodology, change in a problem situation is enabled by a change agent or facilitator. The situation is problematic because it is perceived to have problems that are unclear. It may be thought of as being 'owned' by an individual or group, the *problem owner* being a person or group seen by an inquirer as the *primary* stakeholder. We note that a *stakeholder* is a person who has a vested interest in the situation; that is, someone who is in some way involved and has something to gain or lose. A *primary stakeholder* is some person or group who has relatively more to lose or gain by a change.

An inquirer may be a problem owner, or a *client* that has initiated the inquiry, or both. When inquirers have purpose for intervention in order to initiate change, they are called *change agents*. A change agent may be an individual or a group of participants from the organisation, usually managers, who will act as a team. Inquiry by the change agent can be orchestrated through a facilitator, who may or may not come from the organisation itself. The change agent will be responsible for (a) the design of *robust change strategies* and (b) a risk or decision analysis, and (c) will work with the problem owner to reduce uncertainty. To understand the meaning of a robust strategy, let us define a strategy to be composed of subcomponents called goals. Noting the definition of a robust system in Chapter 7, a robust strategy can be identified as one that it is not vulnerable to changes in any of its goals.

The purpose of the change agent is to create a learning system in which more can be learned about the possibilities of change, until the organisation can become virtually independent of an 'expert'. It is thus through the use of a change agent that a problem owner can take responsibility for inquiry.

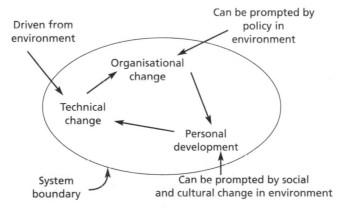

Fig. 11.5 The change process as a system
(*Source*: Mabey, 1995a)

A change agent may be defined in various ways, including as a facilitator, an initiator and a coordinator (Williams *et al.*, 1993, p. 112). As a facilitator the change agent role is intended to be a sounding board for ideas and a source of clarification. The role may be stronger in the early use of SIS where the team is learning about the methodology. The facilitator may play any of a number of roles, such as tutor, controller, counsellor, initiator, summariser or rapporteur. 'A skilled facilitator is able to manage status differentials between group members and elicit effective contributions from the most reticent, while containing the most extroverted members of the group' (Mayon-White, 1993, p. 134).

Facilitators may take on a relatively high profile early on in the study to achieve a 'parent role' (Harris, 1973), and ensure that the methodology is properly understood. As the inquiry develops, they may wish to reduce their profile to encourage the development of a change agent's creative thought. As the inquiry develops further, and strategies of intervention are defined, a sense of leadership is normally required. It is common for some form of leadership to emerge from the team, rather than being adopted by the facilitator. This derives from the self-organising nature of a maturing group as it develops its organisation, stability and cohesion. The nature of the leadership may vary according to the change agent, and can for instance take on the following forms: facilitator, rotating among other members, or pluralistic with different people taking on particular responsibilities.

The facilitator can be selected from the organisation, or be an external consultant. Sometimes, more than one facilitator may be needed, for instance one to act as team process manager and the other as content analysis manager. There are various views about whether a facilitator should be chosen externally or internally. These are summarised in Table 11.1.

Table 11.1 Characteristics associated with internal or external facilitators

Internal facilitator	External facilitator (consultant)
Can have knowledge of the organisation and its workings.	Brings an objective view to the organisation.
Can have knowledge of the personalities of the team members and of other personnel in the organisation.	Can avoid being labelled as having a political orientation to a situation that might bias the team.
Can become involved in arguments about content due to being seen as having a biased view of a situation.	Can avoid becoming enmeshed in arguments about content by focusing on process.
Can be used as a scapegoat when things do not work out as planned, but with possible internal consequences for the client.	Can be used as a scapegoat with impunity when things do not work out as planned, thus avoiding the need to allocate blame internally.
Can bias an inquiry by being seen as being aligned with a political or personal view of the situation.	Can bias an inquiry by *implicitly* pressing the political and personal views of the client in favour of a view of the problem and its solutions as seen by the team.
May not be sufficiently experienced as a facilitator to operate in an appropriate way.	Demands of a team 'process' associated with group working are so high that it requires a long apprenticeship to understand and cope with the pressures that this generates; typically only a consultant will have this background.

11.2.3 Rules and propositions appropriate to SIS

1 The methodology should be seen as a way of learning about change, not as an algorithmic approach to finding an intervention strategy for change.

2 The methodology should be seen as being appropriate for the situation in terms of (a) the time available for inquiry and (b) its degree of complexity.

3 A complex human activity change situation can normally be viewed as a system.

4 The perspective of the system will change according to the purpose for the inquiry and the weltanschauung of the inquirer.

5 Change should occur in a system to enable pressures from its environment to be balanced.

6 Pressures from a complex environment produce uncertainty.

7 The purpose of the change agent is to create a learning system in which more can be learned about the possibilities of change, until the organisation can become virtually independent of an 'expert'.

8 A change agent identifies change strategies for problem situations.

9 A change agent should derive from the participants in a problem situation.

10 The change agent is responsible for the design of robust strategies and risk or decision analysis.

11 It is through the use of a change agent that a problem owner can take responsibility for inquiry.

12 A problem owner is identified by a change agent as the most prominent stakeholder(s).

13 A change agent and problem owner are together responsible for dealing with uncertainty.

14 Strategy can enable uncertainty to be reduced.

15 Organisational change can be prompted by (a) environmental change and (b) technical change.

16 Technical change can be driven (a) from the environment and (b) by personal development.

17 Personal development can be prompted by social and cultural change, and by organisational change.

18 The three approaches to implementing change are (a) the big bang, (b) parallel running and (c) pilot running. The latter two are normally more expensive, but effective.

19 Complex systems require equally complex control systems, so that complex situations need complex responses.

20 Technology changes may (a) flatten the management hierarchy and skills, (b) de-skill craft and managerial roles and (c) produce new 'experts' or 'High Priests'.

21 'Experts' do not provide the best means by which problem situations can be changed.

22 The likelihood of resistance to change by stakeholders can be reduced if they are involved at an early stage of inquiry.

23 Failing to involve and inform stakeholders in advance of an intended intervention to introduce change is a sure way of starting a guerrilla war and sabotage.

24 Resistance to change is inevitable; some resistance is healthy; critics should be listened to and learned from.

25 Resistance to change is easy and can take many forms.

26 The more ambitious a design for change, the greater the risks of resistance (innate conservatism).

Generic nature

SIS operates more or less centrally within the hard–soft continuum. The approach has developed as a reaction to the difficulties associated with hard methods such as system engineering or operational research.

'Both "hard" and "soft" methods have their weaknesses that can be overcome by using methods that draw from both' (Mayon-White, 1993, p. 140). The basic structure of SIS reflects its origins in systems engineering. It uses three phases of work and iteration to refine and test the output of each stage.

'Superficially the early stages of description appear to match Checkland's rich picture construction. Both build models of the situation as perceived by the task force. However, SIS makes explicit use of systems concepts in this stage whereas the rich picture explicitly avoids using the concept of system. This is an important distinction. Checkland claims that his soft approach avoids the assumption that systems exist "out their" and await discovery by not using the terminology "system". SIS uses the concept of system to impose a shared structure on the problem setting and so makes the initial analysis possible' (Mayon-White, 1993). This establishes a reference point; the follow-on process is to modify or discard representations around this centre point. 'In its later stages SIS can make direct use of several well-known techniques such as brainstorming and objective setting. However, these techniques are used precisely because they are familiar and can thus be adopted and used efficiently by any task force' (Mayon-White, 1993).

SIS is intended to deal with situations that are relatively hard – that is, concerning both objective things and the involvement of people. It supposes that problem situations are unstructured and uncertain.

11.2.4 The language

The language used to explain and describe a methodological approach is necessarily a reflection of the propositional base of the paradigm. Table 11.2 lists the termination used in SIS.

11.3 Logical processes of SIS

11.3.1 The logic of SIS

The logic of SIS defines three phases in a cycle of inquiry. The behaviour of an inquirer need not be to select the phases sequentially, one after another. They can be chosen in a way that satisfies the needs of an inquirer. The phases of SIS are described in Fig. 11.6. It defines three phases of activity, diagnosis/description, design and implementation. These are defined as follows in Table 11.3.

11.3.2 The steps of the methodology

The steps that occur within the three phases are described in Table 11.4. They identify a confirmation process of the steps that make SIS a methodology rather than a method. If the

Table 11.2 The language of SIS

SIS terms	Meaning
Technical development	This relates to enabling change in the aspects of a situation that relate to prediction and control of both natural and social organisations.
Organisational development	This occurs through social change in an organisation involved in a situation. It is principally to do with structures.
Personal development	The development of new skills and new perspectives at the individual level. The perspectives will in part be cultural, relating to attitudes and values.
Inquirer	An individual or group that inquires. An inquirer may be a facilitator. When inquirers have a purpose of intervention in order to initiate change, they are called change agents.
Facilitator	An inquirer who facilitates change in any of a variety of facilitating roles, which may include tutor, controller, counsellor, initiator, summariser or rapporteur. Facilitation is the process of assisting a change agent to achieve the objectives, which in the case of SIS, are to seek a strategy for change. A facilitator manages status differentials between group members and elicits effective contributions from the most reticent, while containing the most extroverted members of the group.
Change agent	An individual or group that creates an intervention strategy for change. The purpose of the change agent is to create a learning system in which more can be learned about the possibilities of change.
Client	An individual or group that commissions an inquiry.
Problem owner	Defined by the change agent as a person or group that is the primary stakeholder. It is a plausible role from which the situation can be viewed.
Problem situation	A situation in which there are perceived problems that may be unclear.
Stakeholder	A participant in a change process who has a vested interest in the situation, who may have something (a stake, like a job, or an investment) to gain or lose. Groups and individuals affected by decisions or a project who seek to influence decisions in keeping with their own interests, goals, priorities and understandings.
Primary stakeholder	A person or group with relatively more to lose or gain than other stakeholders.
Relevant system	It is an inquirer's perception of the human activity system that is relevant to a problem situation.
Objective	A characteristic of a desired structure or behaviour of the system in its changed form.
Constraint	A form of behaviour or structure to be avoided in the changed system. Whether something is defined as a constraint or an objective may be a matter of weltanschauung.
Measure	A means of estimating or assessing the extent to which an option contributes towards the achievement of an objective. Objectives may be non-quantifiable (or soft). This may require qualitative comparisons like ranking or weighting.

Table 11.3 The phase of SIS

Phase	Meaning
Diagnosis	The process of developing a perspective from which to tackle a set of change problems
Design	Enables alternative methods or options for achieving change to be identified and explored
Implementation	Represents a commitment to a change, while developing a means for creating and developing a desired change

control checks show an instability in the inquiry, a logically previous step will be retaken. The logically previous step may not be the step immediately prior to the control check.

Step 0: Entry

The entry step 0 provides a pre-evaluation introduction to the situation to enable it to be classified as a mess or a difficulty, and so validates the use of SIS.

Step 1: Description

A description of the situation should occur in terms of:

- what people want;
- establishing a boundary around the mess;
- clarifying the relationships between the major subsystems;
- understanding the structure of the mess;
- deciding what objectives will be served by the change.

This step therefore involves an examination of the situation in order to understand the behaviour that occurs within it. Clarification of the interests of individuals within the situation should occur.

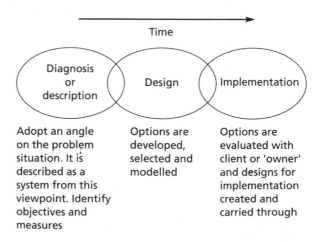

Fig. 11.6 Phases of SIS
(*Source*: Mabey, 1995, p. 9)

Table 11.4 Basic steps in SIS and the related actions

Phase	Step	Actions	Tools
Diagnosis	0 Entry	See change as a complex process	Identify situation as complex or difficult
	1 Description	Structure/understand change in systems terms Define problem owner Identify other perspectives of change problem or opportunity Select relevant systems	Use diagrams Set up special meetings Create models of reality
	2 Identify objectives and constraints	Confirm findings with problem owner Establish objectives for system under study Determine objectives of change	Create objective tree Prioritise objectives
	3 Formulate measures for objectives	Decide on ways of measuring achieved objectives	Quantify, scale or rank results from objectives
Design	4 Generate range of options	Develop any ideas for change as full options Look at wide range of possibilities Objectives may suggest new options Confirm with problem owner	Brainstorming Idea writing Interviews and surveys Comparisons with 'best practices'
	5 Model options selectively	Describe most promising options in some detail Ask of each option: what is involved? who is involved? how will it work?	Remember that diagrams are simple models. Model options include cost–benefit analysis, cash-flow models, computer simulations.
Implementation	6 Evaluate options against measures	Test performance of selected options against an agreed set of criteria	Set up simple matrix to compare performance of options Score each option against measures
	7 Design implementation strategies	Select preferred options and plan implementation	Look for reliable options Refer to problem owners Plan and allocate tasks
	8 Carry through planned changes	Bring together people and resources Manage process Monitor progress	Sort out who is involved Allocate responsibility Review and modify plans if necessary.

(*Source*: Based on Mayon-White, 1993, p. 136)

The problem owner should be clearly identified. This is a term adopted from Checkland, who used it in his methodological approach. The problem owner is a plausible role from which the situation can be viewed. The problem owner is chosen by the inquirer, who may be a facilitator or a change agent.

The situation should be represented as one of the 'relevant systems' selected. A relevant system is a term employed by Checkland in his methodology (Chapter 13). It is an inquirer's perception of the human activity system that is relevant to a problem situation. Any situation may have as many relevant systems views as perceived by an inquirer.

249

Simple systems models are used to represent this, such as:

- systems map
- influence diagram
- multiple cause diagram
- input–output model
- flow-block diagram.

Step 2: Identify objectives and constraints

The problem owner should be consulted about the current evaluation of the situation. The objectives, measures and constraints should also be clearly identified.

In the setting of objectives it may be seen that some are subordinate to others. An objective tree will help identify the list of objectives to be addressed. Some of the objectives can have quantitative measures assigned to them, while others may have to be evaluated qualitatively.

Step 3: Formulate measures for objectives

The design of strategies should involve an awareness of the forces at work within the situation that will bias intervention strategies. These should be avoided unless they appear as initial constraints established in step 2.

Step 4: Generate options

This is the inventive stage of the inquiry. A wide range of options should be generated without restriction. They will in due course be evaluated both logically and with the problem owner.

Step 5: Modelling options

Modelling options may sometimes involve physical representations of an idea. More typically in human activity systems they may involve such classes as:

- simulation model (e.g. computer based, stochastic, statistical)
- cashflow models
- cost–benefit analysis
- strategic models.

Step 6: Evaluation of options

The evaluation of options is often best undertaken through the use of a comparative matrix that operates as a decision table. This might take the following form:

Objectives/measures	Option 1	Option 2	...
Measure/quality ranking			
...			

Step 7: Design implementation strategies

Uncertainty may be generated by the potential users of any new systems that result from an intervention strategy. It is during this step that the whole of SIS can be re-applied recursively.

Step 8: Carry through

In this step the soft issues must necessarily be taken in hand, such as involving stake-holders at an early stage to reduce the likelihood of resistance to change.

11.3.3 The logical model

The formalised method is shown in Fig. 11.7. This highlights the idea that the design phase is considered distinctly from the diagnosis phase, and that the implementation phase follows through on design.

Implementation may feed back into diagnosis to start a new cycle. The iteration process, a repetitive cycle of the model, is used to improve understanding of the situation, and enables the various alternative models that can define an intervention for change to be debated and confirmed against the purposes for change. Such a change is perceived as a 'learning system' in which inquirers learn about change possibilities. In this way novice inquirers can become independent of a knowledgeable inquirer.

Step 7 of the cycle, the design implementation of strategy, is concerned with the development of strategies for implementing change. This can be viewed as a change process itself requiring intervention. Consequently, the whole of SIS can be applied within this phase, making the methodology explicitly recursive.

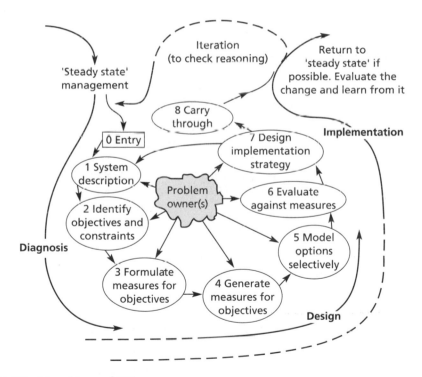

Fig. 11.7 Working form of SIS
Shows iteration to confirm modelling process of situation.
(*Source*: Mayon-White, 1986, pp. 2–8)

11.4 The doppelgänger paradigm

A view of SIS in terms of the metasystem

A real-world situation of human purposeful activity has occurred within which there appears to be a situation that requires improvement (a problem), and there is an intention to inquire into the situation so that it can be dealt with. The nature of the inquiry using SIS is represented in Fig. 11.8, and an explanation is given in Table 11.5.

Table 11.5 Definition of the system and metasystem for SIS

The system

S1 An appropriate *system* is determined by the inquirer.

Cognitive purposes

Methodology mission and goals

The methodological mission is to generate appropriate change to create a new balance with the environment. It is intended to deal with:

m1 technical development

m2 organisational development

m3 personal development

Inquiry aims for change

i1 Robust strategies

i2 Risk or decision analysis.

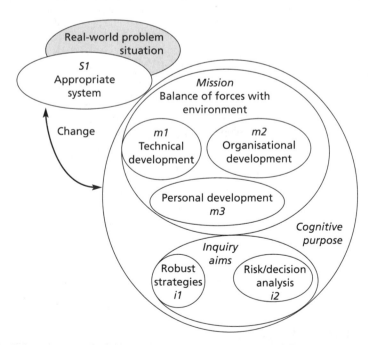

Fig. 11.8 Influence diagram for the cognitive purpose for SIS

In order to make an inquiry, an inquirer will have to build a systemic representation of a situation creating the appropriate *system* that is to be defined. Clearly, how you define a system is dependent upon the viewpoint of the inquirer who is inquiring into the situation. The appropriate systems model, referred to as *S1*, must be examined in terms of its methodology. There are two aspects of SIS:

1 A methodological mission is through change to create a new balance of forces with the environment. Goals that relate to the mission consist of establishing technical development, organisational development and personal development.

2 The inquiry aims are intended to ensure that strategies for change are robust and of known risk. Consequently, risk analysis and decision analysis should be undertaken.

SIS seen in terms of the framework method

Comparing the framework method of Fig. 5.2 to SIS enables a fulcrum of reference to be created that can enable methodological comparison to occur in terms of (a) structure, (b) methodological process and (c) methodological controls. Basic comparison of these entities occurs in Table 11.6.

Table 11.6 Relationship between SIS and doppelgänger paradigms

Doppelgänger paradigm Entity/process	SIS paradigm Explanation	Step
		Diagnosis
Pre-evaluation	Entry	S0
	System description/relevant system	S1
	Objectives and constraints	S2
Analysis	Measures for objectives	S3
Control	(Check with problem owner)	
Conceptualisation	Generate options	S4
		Design
Synthesis	Model options (selectively)	S5
		Implementation
Control	Evaluate against measures	S6
Constraint		
Choice	Design implementation strategies (possible recursion ®)	S7
Action	Carry through	S8
Control	Reiterate complete cycle for confirmation	
Control	Evaluate experiences from change implementation	

It can be seen that we are able to distinguish clearly between the cyclic actions of the methodology and the control processes that enable:

1 strategies of change to be re-evaluated;

2 a final overview of the methodology.

While point 1 offers a development of understanding of a situation, 2 offers a development of understanding of the application of the methodology.

The content of Table 11.6 can also be expressed as a graphical action cycle, as shown in Fig. 11.9. The dotted connecting arcs between the three phases of analysis, synthesis and choice indicate that the steps can be taken out of sequence by a problem owner, after the early stages of the inquiry.

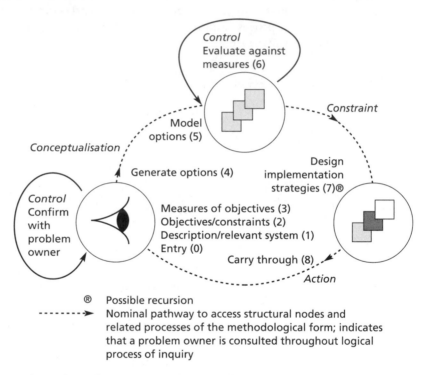

Fig. 11.9 A view of SIS through its controlled phases excluding the iterative post-evaluation cycles
The nominal pathway explains that nodes and methodological processes are accessible by an inquirer without having to pass along the pathways.

11.5 Summary of SIS

SIS is a simple methodology applicable to complex, uncertain situations in which sufficient time and intention exist to apply the methodology. It is a structured approach that is designed to enable development of a set of intervention strategies for change by a change agent. This development occurs through an iteration process that enables any strategies to be clarified and fully defined. Part of this process can be recursive, which can normally occur in the design of the implementation strategies.

The methodology is not intended as a linear cycle of structured examination, though this may be an attractive way of progressing though an inquiry for a novice inquirer. It is intended that the inquirer (who may be a stakeholder, the problem owner, or a person or group working on behalf of the problem owner) will be able to apply any of the steps of the methodology as necessary in order to satisfy the needs of inquiry.

11.6 The SIS case study

This case derives from the work of two of my 1996 students, Judy Brough and Nicola Magill, both on the final level of the part-time BA in Public Administration. It is a brief study concerned with the implementation of charging for the issue of Disabled Car Badges within the Liverpool City Council area. Though the students were not involved in the working committee that is exploring Disabled Car Badge Charging (DCBC), they examined it as a problem situation from the perspective of the working party. This case thus represents a hypothetical working party report that cannot comment on some of the aspects of the problem situation, nor on an implementation and post-evaluation. To help appreciate the process of inquiry here, we provide a case summary on p. 256 of how it will be addressed.

11.6.1 Pre-evaluation of the problem situation

In 1991 the Maastricht Treaty for European Union countries specified five control measures that a member country should abide by if it is to have membership of the currency union (Zis, 1995, p. 96):

1 its rate of inflation during the year immediately before its joining the union must not exceed by more than 1.5 per cent the three lowest rates of inflation in the Union;

2 the country's long-run interest rate during the year before its becoming a member of the Union must not exceed by more than 2 per cent the three lowest-run interest rates in the EU;

3 the country must have participated for at least two years in the 'normal' band of fluctuation of ERM without a devaluation of its currency;

4 its budget deficit must not exceed 3 per cent of its GDP;

5 the ratio of its national debt to GDP must not exceed 60 per cent.

Of these, only the last two are of relevance to our inquiry here. In order to enable it to address its national debt quickly, the Government would seem to have made the decision to reduce public spending dramatically. This is in line with its idea to control this area of expenditure. Prior to the Maastricht Treaty agreement, reduction in public spending amounted to £7 billion (1990–91) and £8 billion (1991–2) (Wilson, 1993, p. 10). After the

Case summary

Activity	Description
Weltanschauung	A Council budget deficit exists that must be dealt with. One way is service charging, to be applied to the Division of Social Services in its issue of Disabled Car Badges.
Inquirer's mission	To introduce service charging for Disabled Car Badge issue as a pilot action intended to recoup money, to be placed against Local Authority deficit.
Methodology: SIS	Mission to balance pressures from the Liverpool City Council environment on a proposed DCBC, that will in turn contribute to a balance of forces at a higher level of focus, between the Local Authority and its environment.
Goals and aims of inquiry	Methodological goals are to develop the situation in terms of its technical, organisational and personal attributes. It does this through the aim of creating robust strategies and risk/decision analysis.
Nature of examination	SIS is being used in order to explore the proposed introduction of DCBC, primarily centring on the technical change that will define an intervention strategy to enable DCBC to result.
Explanatory model	A focus of examination is created and the pressures that derive from the environment of the system at that focus are explored. Three focuses can be identified. One is defined by the Liverpool City Council, which defines the supersystem for the situation. The next focus is that of the Social Services Division, which sits inside the Council. Finally, there is the proposed DCBC system. The context for the situation as a whole will first be considered through pre-evaluation. The environmental pressures for the Council will be seen as becoming internalised, and as a consequence there will be pressures on the Social Service Division that will have to be balanced. These will be explored.
Options selection	Options chosen define technical, organisational, and personal features of strategy for the implementation of DCBC. Further work, however, has to be undertaken to ensure that the proposed strategy is implementable within the Social Service Division of the Liverpool City Council.

agreement, Government reduced public spending in 1992–3 by about three and a half times the previous figures, at £28 billion. An impact of this magnitude in spending cuts on public organisations like the National Health Service, the police force and Local Authorities must be severe. This also provides an insight into a main reason for the Government pressure for greater efficiency on organisations like Liverpool City Council to reduce spending. In addition to this, reductions on public expenditure are being forced by the continuing recession. The brunt of these cuts will be applied to Local Authorities, which consume about one-quarter of the public spending (Gardner, 1993, p. 171).

Step 0: Entry

The background

Liverpool is a European Community Objective 1 region, indicative of its poor economic condition after its historical decline as a major European port. It has a population of about half a million people. Like most major cities in the UK, it has suffered a population decline during the last generation. The causes for this predominantly include migration. Liverpool City Council's corporate strategy statement for 1995/6 predicts a further population change within the next decade because of a large fall in the number of pre-school children, a large increase in the number of residents aged 85 years and over, a very large reduction in the number of young adults, and an increase in the number of people aged from 45 years to retirement age.

As the population of Liverpool has declined, so too have its levels of employment, at about twice the 10 per cent level of other cities in the UK. Of this, nearly half are long-term unemployed, again almost twice the level of other UK cities. Many of the unemployed have never worked since leaving school except on Government schemes. Liverpool has nearly twice the 13 per cent national average of working age men either not working or looking for work. This has been due to increasing numbers of people classified as permanently sick or disabled and unable to work.

Unemployed people and their families thus represent a large proportion of the population living in poverty. Others vulnerable to poverty are the elderly, the sick and disabled, and single-parent families. In addition, part-time workers, who tend to be women, are low paid and susceptible to poverty. The black population is also prone to poverty because of higher than average unemployment, in part caused by racial discrimination (Pirani and Yolles, 1992).

The sectors of increasing unemployment include the manufacturing industries, where unemployment has risen by about 24 per cent in the last seven years, and service sector work. A decline in both skilled and semi-skilled work has similarly been significant. The result has been that employment in lower skilled work is more likely.

These perturbing effects on the city have had a significant impact on the demand for services and costs. The effect of a more dependent population will in the future place even more demands on local authority services, and on the caring sections of the population. As a result its infrastructure will have to be developed to satisfy the needs of an increased demand, while having an income that remains constrained.

Income derives predominantly from Council Tax paid by Liverpool residents. In recent years this has suffered considerably due to the Government's introduction of the Community Charge. This was abandoned because it was too costly to administer and to pursue outstanding income. It was also virtually impossible to collect overdue payments from the poor. In many cases the only recourse was to put people in prison for failure of payment. This was very expensive and contributed further to the overcrowding problem of prisons. Arrears to the city are over £100 000 million, over two-thirds of which are due to the Community Charge.

The Liverpool City Council (LCC) is responsible for the municipal services of the city. Its politics and culture determine the nature of these services. It has a core purpose defined as follows:

> The City Council exists for the benefit of, and is accountable to, all the people of Liverpool in providing high-quality services that meet people's needs and offer value for money.

257

In order to deliver the services of its mission, the Members and Officers of the Council have three overriding responsibilities that define the objectives of the Council:

1 planning what services to provide and how to provide them;

2 providing and overseeing delivery;

3 reviewing the performances achieved.

It is through performance review that the Council determines whether it is operating stably, and thus achieving its objectives. Pressures by Government on Liverpool have also directed its attention to its embracing a role as:

- a provider of those services the Council is best placed to deliver, to ensure a quality service, an efficient organisation and services which reflect the needs of all groups;
- a partner, advocate and enabler in relations to the community, the private sector and other agencies.

Local Authorities have always contracted out peripheral services activities under a policy of competitive tendering. Now, under the force of legislation, these objectives are impacting on their core purposes, and being directed at their primary tasks under the Government policy of Compulsory Competitive Tendering (CCT). Clearly the Councils are at least passing through radical change that is having a major impact on their form.

Central to the Government agenda is its concept of quality and quality assurance. This demands the codifying of policies, procedures and performance standards, and guarantees that these will be met. Quality assurance is connected to the idea of effectiveness, and is intended to establish measures for this. The ability of an organisation to introduce quality assurance policies will be bounded by the ability of its form and culture. The difficulty is that the form and culture of an organisation must be appropriate for quality assurance to work, and it may be rather difficult to achieve this. Newly acting quality insurance imperatives will impact on the core purposes of an organisation, and thus induce radical change. Legislated quality assurance was responsible for Liverpool City Council undertaking a reorganisation in its departmental structure in 1992.

We have talked about CCT. It is one of a series of measures introduced by Government and aimed at altering the power of the Local Authorities to organise and run local services. It demands that Councils put services out to tender, so that lowest tenders win out. While the basis of CCT is fundamentally ideological, its rational expectation is that competition will cut costs and make services more efficient.

CCT is now being extended from stage 1 and 2 services, to stage 3. Stage 1 services (1980) include new building (including renewal), building repair and maintenance, and highway construction and maintenance. Stage 2 services (1988) include refuse collection, street cleaning, building cleaning, school and welfare catering, other catering (e.g. town halls), vehicle maintenance, ground maintenance, and management of sport and leisure services. Stage 3 services include white-collar services – legal, information technology, finance, corporate administration, construction related – housing management and blue-collar services – on-street parking, security, vehicle fleet management. This whole process would seem to have the potential of diminishing Councils as local political opposition to Government. In terms of policy implications, a number of local political interests would seem to be becoming subsidiary to national ones.

There is debate about whether the policies of Government can work. For example, 'the Audit Commission, the government spending watchdog, said there was "little effective competition" in the market for local authority services, even after six years of compulsory tendering' (Rice, 1995). 'Only 30 per cent of local authorities make "positive efforts" to generate competition, while many deter small companies by only seeking tenders for large contracts, the local government watchdog says' (Authers, 1995). On the other hand, 'tougher competition from private contractors may squeeze council organisations out of the market for running local authority services, a report by the Joseph Rowntree Foundation says. A study by the social affairs think-tank found that companies in the UK and other European countries are increasingly interested in providing local authority services, seven years after the government forced councils to put work out to contract through compulsory competitive tendering' (Field, 1995). There are also arguments that CCT does little to encourage the economy of an area like Liverpool, with such high unemployment. According to Hartley (1987, p. 160), service providers manage to bid low tenders because they are (a) employing fewer people, (b) reducing pay and fringe benefits and (c) making more use of part-time staff. Unfortunately, socio-economic costs are not part of Government accounting processes.

The City has been attempting to balance the pressures (Fig. 11.10), identified as:

1 reduce spending while being forced to increase its administrative cost;

2 increasing service demands in the city, the majority of which are statutory;

3 a reduced income.

It has now found itself with a budget deficit. This pressure is occurring at a time when the organisation has passed through a dramatic change in form, and perceives itself to be experiencing a work overload. To deal with this it is seeking to find ways of raising income from its services. This problem has been handed to the Social Services Division, and one candidate for service charging is DCBC.

The purpose of the inquiry

The purpose of the study is to establish a strategy for the introduction of a DCBC system.

Difficulty or mess

Preliminary inquiry about whether the situation can be seen as a difficulty or a mess has resulted in Table 11.7.

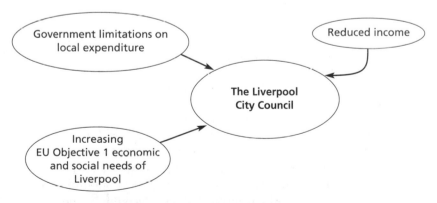

Fig. 11.10 Pressure from environment on the Authority

259

Table 11.7 Characteristics of difficulty or mess

Characteristics of difficulty/mess	Characteristic of situation
Certain/uncertain about:	
The problem	It is being proposed that disabled car badges should be a fund raising target. There is conflict about whether this is a valid target and uncertainty about how it should be implemented. Neither is it certain what the budget expectation for this would be.
Knowledge/information	Information is based on opinion rather than detailed evaluation of the situation. There is therefore insufficient information about the nature of the problem.
Solutions	Stakeholders include car badge users and Local Authority staff. Solutions should take into account the stakeholders, and there is no certainty about who to consult, and how a change in policy would be implemented. How an inquiry into this would occur is also uncertain.
Determinable/indeterminable:	
Implications	The issues are unclear. The policy would contribute further to a work overload and will result in extra pressure on staff. Unclear about the staff regrading requirements. Stakeholder resistance to change and indeterminable media attention that must be handled.
Timescales	There are no predetermined timescales. Implementation schedules are unclear.
Number of people involved	It is not immediately determinable how many car badge users will be affected. Staff levels may need to increase, and it is not sure to what extent. Management involvement is unclear. It may affect staff in a variety of departments including Finance, Personnel, Councillors, Complaints.
Clear/unclear priorities	It is unclear as to whether priorities exist to satisfy current workload commitments, or to engineer disabled car badge charging. They are two competing tasks.
Independence/interdependence of context	The task involves a complexity of interrelations between departments. It is not clear where the boundary of the task in the Local Authority Social Services Directorate would lie.

Many of the characteristics of the situation indicate a mess, suggesting the appropriate use of a structured methodology like SIS.

11.6.2 Analysing the SIS doppelgänger

Step 1: Description

The Local Authority

Liverpool City Council is the governing Local Authority for the city. It has a transparent political status showing clear political divisions through elected Councillors. Council work is divided into various committees covering major services, including Economic Development, Education, Environmental Services and Consumer Protection, Housing, Leisure and Tourism, Personnel, Planning and Resources, Social Services and the Contract Services Board. The estimated budget for 1996/7 for these services is about

£500 million. The proportion of this that accrues to the Social Services Division represents slightly more than £80 million.

The Authority provides most of the major services to the inhabitants of its domain through its Divisions such as education, engineering, housing and environmental protection, highways and building services and tourism, planning and economic development, and Social Services. Since 1979, they have been targets for Government cuts in spending. They have been under recurrent Government demands for greater efficiency. This has meant a policy of reducing staff levels.

The Liverpool City Council has a deficit of about one fifth of its budget due to the difficulty in collecting local contributions, most of which was due to the failed Community Charge system that was introduced earlier. Since there in no possibility of Government aid in this, there is a need to identify new sources of finance within its existing system. This means either reducing staff or introducing a policy for service charging. One way of balancing the budget is by raising funds through a charging policy. The issue of disabled car badges is the first target for this, and will operate as a pilot for service charging to identify the difficulties that will be encountered. It will not be expected to incur funds of any significant magnitude. Domiciliary changing will be the second and much more significant service to be charged for. Both services are operated by the Council's Social Services Directorate (Fig. 11.11).

The Social Services Division
Operations within the Social Services Directorate other than the issue of disabled car badges include day care services, domiciliary care, community care, children and family services, occupational therapy and mobile meals.

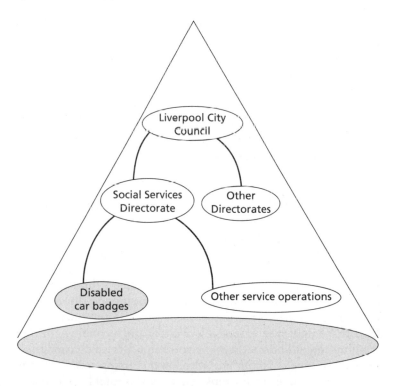

Fig. 11.11 System focus positions of the Liverpool City Council

Social roles

The working party have identified the roles listed in Table 11.8 in this inquiry.

Table 11.8 Social roles

Roles	Role takers
Client	Head of Resources
Problem owner	Area Resource Managers (ARM), Deputy Area Resource Management (DARM) and the Assistant ARM (AARM), Senior Clerical Officer Sc3 (SCO)
Stakeholders	Councillors, problem owner, management, all staff in area offices and headquarters, service users, agencies.
Change agent	Director of Liverpool City Council on behalf of City Councillors

There are a variety of views within the stakeholder community. The service providers are being forced to introduce the charging policy in order to satisfy the need of the budget deficit. In the local political arena, councillors are very divided about the introduction of the proposed charges. Service users are a vulnerable group, many of whom are on a low income or on DSS benefits and can therefore ill afford any of the extra expenditure. A consequence may be that service users cancel their subscription to the service, even though they have at one time been assessed and found to have met the criteria for that service. This will have implications for the financial return of DCBC. There is also the belief that such services have already been paid for within the Council Tax paid each year.

The staff involved are also very much divided over this issue. Many staff feel that their principles are being questioned in that they chose to work for the Local Authority in order to provide a caring service to people in need. On the other hand there is much pressure on managers to balance their budgets and find additional income from some source. One alternative suggestion to Disabled Car Badge Charging is to make staff redundancies. Obviously this raises staff concerns for their own futures. Ultimately they are governed by political party power, and the policies and budget allocations to Local Authorities. In many ways the public sector is entering into a market system that means that it has to be more accountable, competitive and 'on its toes', with the introduction of CCT.

Influences on DCBC

The pressures on the Council from its environment are being internalised. To see this it will be necessary to shift our focus of inquiry, so that we now see the Council as the environment for DCBC. The new perspective shows the external influences (Fig. 11.12) on DCBC that must be addressed during the inquiry.

There are a number of internal forces to the LCC that drive and restrain the introduction of DCBC. These are identified in the force field diagram shown in Fig. 11.13. DCBC could be more efficiently and effectively facilitated through the use of new technology. It enables efficient information storage, retrieval and operating procedures, as well as controls that might well be possible without the technology. It therefore has the potential of enabling the additional work involved in service charging to be undertaken within the existing volume of labour and with lower running costs than a purely manual system.

Further, systems of information networks enable information exchanges and security processes that back-up local procedures, which might otherwise be inappropriate, diffi-

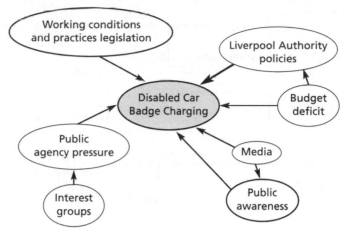

Note: strength of line indicates strength of influence

Fig. 11.12 Influence diagram on Disabled Car Badge Charging

cult or impracticable. Inadequate stationery provision means at least that effective operations are hindered. It can cause staff frustration, which itself may have impacts on performance or work attendance. As important, within the community it can displace official public relations policy.

In extension, we can think of this as part of the technical constraints on the situation, which include lack of information technology, outdated information systems, inadequate stationery provision and unsatisfied training needs.

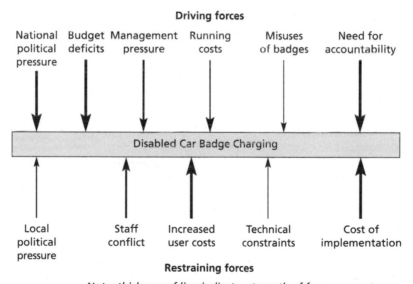

Note: thickness of line indicates strength of force

Fig. 11.13 Force field diagram

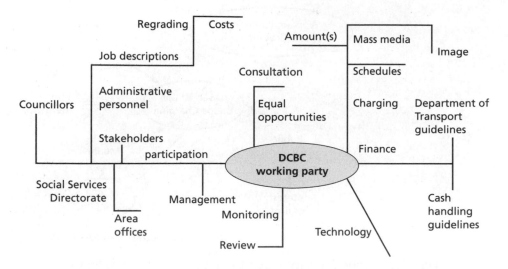

Fig. 11.14 Mind map to identify the possible working party considerations

In this problem situation we should also take into account the pressures that derive from the public agencies, from public awareness, from the media, and from working practices and legislation. A mind map (Fig. 11.14) provides a more detailed indication of many aspects of the situation.

The introduction of DCBC can also be seen in terms of a number of causative factors. In order to illustrate this, a multiple cause diagram is given in Fig. 11.15.

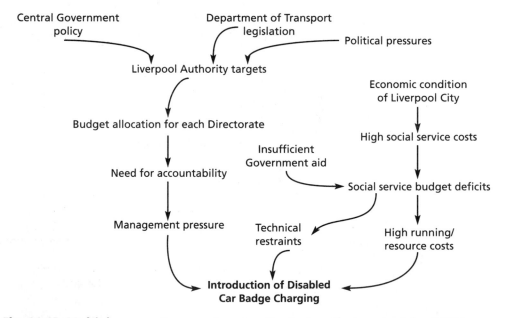

Fig. 11.15 Multiple cause diagram showing the factors that amount for DCBC

Step 2: Identify objectives and constraints

In consultation with the problem owners of the intended DCBC, a number of generalised objectives have been identified as shown in Fig. 11.16. The objectives have been classified according to three aspects of the situation: (a) through the creation of policy, the development of the organisation to deal with the DCBC implementation expressed in terms of operational structure and processes, (b) technical development to enable the DCBC system that is established to be controlled and predictable and (c) stakeholder support, which can be seen to operate through personal change including the adoption of new perspectives.

Step 3: Formulate measures for objectives

Our interest here will be to explore only some of the technical aspects of the objective tree in Fig. 11.16. In order to achieve an objective, we shall require measures of outputs against which the processes of achieving the objective can be compared. This will give us a way of identifying whether the system is stable in respect of the process under consideration. In service organisations, there tends to be a close relationship between process and administrative procedure, where the latter is supposed to be representative of the former. Indeed, the procedure becomes the process. It is not always clear to staff that this is the case, and in some instances procedures are performed without a real understanding of the processes that they are intended to represent. This can occur in particular when global procedures (say for quality assurance) are imposed. In such circumstances, it may be difficult to ensure the stability of the system.

An objective can usually be described in terms of criteria such as quantitative bounds or qualitative evaluations. These are used to judge the stability of the process. A measure is a means of evaluating the nature of the outputs from the process. Measures enable the output to be compared to the criteria. This is explained in Chapters 5 and 6.

Considering only the technical objective here, we can identify a number of both quantitative and qualitative characteristics to which we can attach criteria, standards or norms of judgement. Now we are aware that these criteria derive from cognitive models that come from belief systems, and which lie at the basis of an organisation's paradigm. In the case of Local Authorities, these paradigms are highly responsive to community demands through the local political process. By definition, all distinct Local Authority paradigms are incommensurable. This means that global criteria cannot be prescriptive if they are not to impose structural violence, with resulting consequences for operational performance, motivation etc.

Fig. 11.16 Objective tree for development of DCBC strategy

In Table 11.9 we have identified some quantitative characteristics against which we can form bounds that determine what is acceptable as an output, though it is for the implementation team to assign actual values to them. Against this we can formulate measures that contribute to a judgement about whether or not the technical operations are being undertaken effectively. So long as the measures fall within the bounds, then the process can be seen to be stable.

Table 11.9 Quantifiable criteria and measures

Some quantifiable criteria for effective financial control	Some quantifiable measures for effective financial control
Budgeted stationery running cost	Actual stationery running cost
Budgeted personnel running costs	Actual personnel running costs
Budgeted income accrued from DCBC	Actual income accrued from DCBC
Budgeted DCBC income	Actual DCBC income

Step 4: Generate options

In order to explore the options available to the working group, the working party had some brainstorming sessions. The mind map of Fig. 11.14 was used to help this process, and a variation capable of exploring options that should be considered for the implementation of DCBC is given in Fig. 11.17.

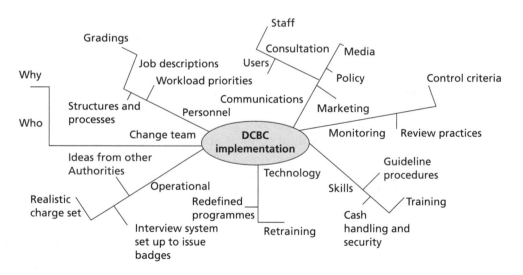

Fig. 11.17 Mind map to explore the range of options to be explored in DCBC

11.6.3 Synthesis

Step 5: Modelling options

In order to investigate how to tackle the issues represented by the introduction of DCBC, we must first identify the characteristics that need to be considered. These are as follows:

- role selection of change team;
- role assignment of staff (grading, justification of duties);
- marketing development and stakeholder profiles;
- design of consultation and communications processes.

The change team will be responsible for the design and implementation of the change. In Table 11.10 we have considered the roles of those to be included in the change team.

Table 11.10 Options and evaluations concerning membership of change team

Liverpool City Council (LCC)	Class	Purposes
Membership option available for change team		
Internal to LCC	Advisors, stakeholders	Those who have knowledge of (a) the LCC and its workings and (b) the personalities of personnel
External to LCC	Consultants	Those who can bring (a) an objective view to the inquiry and (b) an avoidance of becoming enmeshed in arguments about content by focusing on processes
Evaluation of possible implementation team		
Internal to LCC	Trainers	Those who have knowledge of the LCC and its workings
	Management	Knowledge of the personalities of personnel
External to LCC	Representative from other Authorities	Those who can bring an objective view to the inquiry
	Agency representatives, e.g. Department of Social Services	Those who can avoid becoming enmeshed in arguments about content by focusing on processes

Step 6: Evaluating options

A selection of options would have to be evaluated through some form of decision table or matrix. The options discussed above are now evaluated. Evaluation of roles to be included in the change team has been considered in Table 11.10. Questions of what is, and who are, involved should be put, as well as how the change will occur. These are considered in Table 11.11.

11.6.4 Choice

Step 7: Design implementation strategies

The above considerations should be addressed prior to implementation. A strategy for this based on the options in Table 11.11 is offered in Table 11.12.

Table 11.11 Most promising options for DCBC implementation

Option	What is involved?	Who is involved?	How will it work?
Establish change team	Define timescales Identify classification of participants Identify participants Identify venues Create agendas and guidelines	Participant from each stakeholder group (i.e. Sc3, ARM, AARM, DARM, management, services, users, agencies)	Regular formal monthly meetings scheduled Monitoring and review system established Minutes of meetings circulated Procedures decided in consultation
Appropriate regrading for senior clerical officers to justify cash handling and extra duties	Costing of eight staff (£10 000 approximately p.a.) Redefine job description Establish training programme	Staff: eight on scale 3 DARMs Personnel Head of Resources Assistant ARM Staff in area offices	Consultation with Sc3s Regrading presented in committee report; new duties outlined and to be approved Costing agreed Training courses established
Marketing	Define marketing policy Define marketing issues Define marketing strategy	External consultants to advise	Arrange press coverage and press releases Advertising Meetings
Consultation and communication with stakeholders	Define communications policy Establish schedules Define communications routes Communicate with service users	Service users Press All staff in area offices Management CCPI section	Positive action training on establishing communication policy Media coverage press release arranged by management in plenty of time Staff informed Consultation at each step

A more structured process to identify the design of implementation strategies can be enabled through a reapplication of SIS as a whole, which represents a recursive application of the methodology. As a tail or an alternative to this, it is also possible to introduce other methodologies provided that they can be validated as working together with SIS. This would require a virtual paradigm that explains the logic that validates their coordination.

In order to explore possible methodologies, we should be aware from stakeholder analysis that there are two classes of stakeholders: internal and external to the defined system.

In the next chapter we shall be using organisational development as a way of tailing an inquiry into how we can deal with the internal stakeholders to the Social Services Division of the Liverpool City Council with respect to the proposed implementation. The external stakeholders will maintain their own conflicting paradigms. To deal with this as a potential problem situation it would be appropriate to employ an alternative methodology such as the conflict modelling cycle, explored in a later chapter.

Table 11.12 Design implementation strategy for DCBC

Options	Implementation plan	Allocation tasks
Regrading for senior clerical officers Sc3 to Sc4	Consultation with Sc3s and justification to committee of regrading (costing provided) Consultation with other relevant staff; job description redefined and training provided Security issues addressed	Committee report by Head of Resources Consultation by ARMs to all staff Trainers involved in consultation Personnel to redefine job description
Set up change team	Participants visited from each stakeholder group Realistic timescales defined – formal monthly meetings scheduled Venues decided – minutes circulated	ARM coordination of stakeholder participation Responsibility circulated for chaining/ minuting meetings
Marketing	Implement marketing strategy Press release sent out Advertise benefits of DCBC	Marketing material designed and produced
Consultation with service users	Letters service users Define and schedule mechanisms for feedback	Councillors to agree on standard communications CCPI for press release
Operational guidelines	Badge issue days set Realistic charges set (and reviewed) Stationery implemented	Management to oversee
Consultation with all staff	Away days set up Training courses devised Team meeting arranged Speakers invited	Management ARMs, DARMs Change team
Monitoring	Change team to monitor/review Establish monitoring system Enable stakeholder feedback and complaints procedures	Change team
Training courses	Define skills Establish job rotation	Trainers, management

Step 8: Carry through

The softer issues should be taken into account during this step. If organisational development and/or the conflict modelling cycle are used in Step 7 above, then a summary could be formulated explaining how the soft issues that will have been explored should be addressed.

REFERENCES

Authers, J. (1995) 'Councils accused of failing to encourage competitive tenders', *Financial Times*, 2 March.

Churchman, C.W. (1971) *The Design of Inquiring Systems*. New York: Basic Books.

Eason, K.D. (1984) 'The process of introducing information technology'. In Paton, R. *et al.* (eds) *Organisations: Cases issues and concepts*. New York: Harper & Row, ch. 9.

Field, L. (1995) 'Council teams "face squeeze": contracting out', *Financial Times*, 14 August.

Gardner, D. (1993) 'Local government'. In Wilson, J. and Hinton, P. (eds) *Public Services and the 1990s*. Sevenoaks: Tudor Business Publishing, pp. 171–89.

Harris, T.A. (1973) *I'm OK, You're OK*. London: Pan.

Hartley, K. (1987) *Competitive Tendering. Public Domain: A yearbook for the public sector*. London: Public Financial Foundation; and London: Peat Marwick McLintock.

Mabey, C. (1995) *Managing Development and Change*, Open Business School course P751, unit 7. Milton Keynes: Open University Business School.

Mabey, C. (1995a) *Managing Development and Change*, Open Business School course P751, unit 9. Milton Keynes: Open University Business School.

Mayon-White, B. (1986) *Planning and Managing Change*. London: Paul Chapman.

Mayon-White, B. (1993) 'Problem-solving in small groups: team members as agents of change'. In Mabey, C. and Mayon-White, B. (eds) *Managing Change*. London: Paul Chapman, pp. 132–42.

Pirani, M. and Yolles, M.I. (1992) 'Ethnic pay differentials', *New Community*, 19(1), 31–42.

Rice, R. (1995) 'Business and the law: judges cook up confusion', *Financial Times*.

Williams, A., Dobson, P. and Walters, M. (1993) *Organisational Culture: New organisational approaches*. London: IPM.

Wilson, J. (1993) 'Public services in the UK'. In Wilson, J. and Hinton, P. (eds) *Public Services and the 1990s*. Sevenoaks: Tudor Business Publishing, pp. 1–21.

Zis, G. (1995) 'Whither European Monetary Union?'. In Healey, N.M. (ed.) *The Economics of the New Europe*. London: Routledge, pp. 83–102.

CHAPTER 12

Organisational development

OVERVIEW

Organisational development is a soft methodology intended for use in complex situations to provide intervention strategy for change management.

It approaches this from the perspective of individual and organisational inquiry. It adopts a systems approach by identifying a set of organisational entities that have functions, the interactive effects of which require that the system is stable. In order to deal with complex situations, it conceptualises that they should be seen in terms of power relationships, control processes and innate resistance to change, all of which must be tackled through addressing both individuals and the culture to which they belong.

12.1 Introduction

'OD was conceived as ... a strategy for large-scale cultural and/or systemic change ... [that] depends on many people accepting the need for change ... [and] until recently, was based on diagnosing gaps between what is and what ought to be' (Weisbord and Janoff, 1996).

Relating to the action research paradigm, organisational development (OD) is a consultant orientated people-centred and thus soft methodology. It is concerned with intervention into problem situations to achieve change management through individuals and their relationships. It arose from behavioural psychology, applying concepts to management that were formulated from a programme run by Pugh and Hickson, and has developed with work from people like Argyris (1970), Kotter and Schlesinger (1979) and Huse and Cummings (1985). Schein (1970) defined OD consultants as facilitators who assisted organisations to improve their inherent capacity to cope with problem situations by helping them to:

- diagnose themselves
- select their own responses
- determine their own progress.

Its intended use is 'to articulate a mode of organisational consultancy that paralleled the client-centred approach in counselling and contrasted with consultancy models that were centred on expertise' (Coghlan, 1993, p. 117). However, at its broadest, OD is concerned with 'boundaries and relationships at a number of different levels between enterprises, their stakeholders and society, and the way in which these relationships could change over time' (Pritchard, 1993, p. 132).

Harrison, in his discussion of traditional OD, explains that consultants involved with this methodology tend to assume that organisations are most effective when they 'reduce power differences, foster open communication, encourage cooperation and solidarity, and adopt policies that enhance the potential of employees' (Harrison, 1994, p. 8). To help assist organisational forms and cultures towards this ideal, consultants often use experienced small group training, feedback on interpersonal processes, participative decision making and build on strong cohesive organisational culture.

There is a belief that the OD tradition is based on a narrow view of organisational effectiveness, and that it is not able to deal with issues of politics and culture. It 'does not seem to work well in organisations that emphasise status and authority differences or in nations that do not share the values underlying development. Even where they are appropriate, traditional organisational development interventions usually yield minor, incremental improvements in organisational functioning, as opposed to the radical transformations needed for recovery from crises and decline' (Harrison, 1994, pp. 8–9). To make OD more flexible and broaden its ability to deal with organisational problems, it must be able to deal with:

- changes in organisational form, strategy and culture
- power alignments
- political bargaining
- cultural diversity at different levels of the organisation
- stability and instability.

Harrison would seem to come out of the *sociotechnical* school of OD thinking. In this, organisations are seen as 'pursuing primary tasks [that] can be best realised if their social, technological, and economic dimensions are jointly optimised, and if they are treated as open systems and fitted to their environments' (Jackson, 1992, p. 60).

12.2 The paradigm of organisational development

12.2.1 Beliefs underlying the paradigm

'It is a paradox that situations and problems which cry out most strongly for change are often the very ones which resist change most stubbornly ... On psychological grounds ... most individuals react to threats and unknown dangers by going rigid ... on organisational grounds, resistance to change can be understood when it is realised that from a behavioural point of view, organisations are coalitions or interest groups in tension ... the resulting organisation is a particular balance of forces which had been hammered out over a period of time and which is continually subject to minor modifications through hierarchically initiated adjustments and cross-group negotiations' (Pugh, 1993, pp. 108–9). Thus, if change is to occur in organisations, it must address both *psychological* and *organisational* grounds.

This represents the foundation of OD, and ensures its place at the soft end of the hard–soft continuum. According to Pugh, four principles can be identified that relate to both dimensions. They are the beliefs that:

1 organisations are organisms and changes require digestion;
2 organisations are occupational and political systems;

3 all members of an organisation operate simultaneously in the rational, occupational and political systems;

4 change is most likely to be acceptable and effective in those people or departments who are basically successful in their tasks but who are experiencing tension or failure in some particular part of their work.

Pritchard (1993) explains that OD is a methodology that involves both systemic and strategic principles:

> Social science models can help practitioners of OD to decide what to study, choose measures of organisational effectiveness, and identify conditions that promote or block effectiveness ... [They] can also obtain guidance from sets of models, theories, and empirical studies that serve as metaphors (Morgan, 1986) or frames (Bolman and Deal, 1991), in the sense that they lead us to look from some other perspective ... Forces for or against change can reflect a political frame of analysis (Harrison, 1999, p. 20).

As we attempt to better understand and explain the world we see around us, our beliefs change, as do our paradigms. In the case of OD, some of its ideas still remain embedded in concepts that were at one time prominent systems theory conceptualisations, but which have no place in modern paradigms. Two concepts that can be identified as having this status are based on the ideas of Ashby: stepwise change from one steady state to another, as used by Lewin, and ultrastability, as used by Pugh.

Pugh

In the 1950s, Pugh (1993), exploring an interest about the inability of organisations to respond to change, used the idea of their being *ultrastable*, an idea originally expressed by Ashby. An ultrastable system is one that 'will operate in the face of perturbations that have not been envisaged in advance' (Beer, 1979, p. 62). While this term is now rarely used in the context of explaining the survivability of an organisation, it is being used here by Pugh to indicate the *inertia* of an organisation to resist change by ignoring any influences that impact it. Thus, when an entity operates inertially, it does not enable variety to occur in respect of its behaviour, even if variety is called for. A more modern approach would therefore be to replace the proposition of *ultrastability* by that of *organisational inertia*.

Lewin

Lewin (1947) was a social psychologist who proposed the idea that change can be introduced into organisations by first unfreezing it, then, after change, refreezing it. The concept of *freezing* an organisation means that *it has established a set of structures and processes that have become institutionalised*. Unfreezing a pattern of behaviour requires action at the individual level (e.g. skill), the systemic level (e.g. reward systems, structures and processes), and in the climate or interpersonal style (e.g. decision making, conflict management). To understand the idea of unfreezing and refreezing expressed in terms of the institutionalisation, it is appropriate to realise what is meant by the concept of *institution* (Mitchell, 1968, p. 99). In the *First Principles* of Spencer an institution is described as the organs that perform the functions of societies. In 1906, Sumner, in his *Folkways*, argued that an institution consists of a concept (i.e. a notion, doctrine, interest) and a structure. Most institutions grow, according to Sumner, from folkways into customs, developing into mores and maturing when rules and acts become specified. It is then that a structure is established that enables the creation of an institution. *While folk-*

ways and mores are habitual unreasoned ways of acting, an institution can be seen as a 'superfolkway', relatively permanent because it is rationalised and conscious. Institutions are generally seen as complexes of norms formally established in an organisation to deal in a regularised way with a perception of its basic needs. They can also be seen as patterns of sanctioned or approved behaviour.

Lewin's conception, therefore, is that patterns of behaviour become regularised, and in order to introduce change they should be deregularised, or disturbed. The idea of *unfreezing* an organisation is that its behaviour should become de-institutionalised (that is, its *institutional behaviour* should be *deregularised*). To freeze an organisation means that its behaviour should be allowed to be re-institutionalised (that is, its *institutional behaviour* is allowed to become *regularised* once more).

Conceptually, this implies that new behaviour can only be successfully adopted and accepted if the old behaviour is discarded. 'Central to this approach is the belief that the will of the change adopter (the subject of the change) is important, both in discarding the old, "unfreezing", and "moving" to the new' (Burnes, 1992). This stresses the importance of 'felt-need', which relates directly to the concepts of action research.

Unfreezing normally involves reducing the forces maintaining the organisation's behaviour. It requires some form of confrontation or re-education process for those involved, perhaps through team building or related approaches (Rubin, 1988). In the language of Aam (1994), we might say that 'the group system [defining the organisation] must be perturbed sufficiently to free itself from this pattern. Perturbation for and the process of unfreezing ... are essentially synonymous terms' (Wheelan, 1996, p. 65).

The concept of refreezing can be tied into individual and group learning processes. 'For personal refreezing to occur, it is best to avoid identification and encourage scanning so that the learner will pick solutions that fit him or her. For relational refreezing to occur, it is best to train the entire group that holds the norms that support the old behaviour' (Schein, 1996, p. 34). Refreezing, then, is about attempting to stabilise a situation by establishing stable patterns of behaviour and desirable norms.

The concept of unfreezing was thus used to highlight the observation that the stability of human behaviour was based on 'quasi-stationary equilibria' (Schein, 1996, p. 28). Thus the terminology can be seen to be consistent in its implication with the old Ashby idea of organisations shifting from one steady state to another in evolutionary steps. Such shifts may operate under some conditions, in particular when steady-state organisations pass through a process of structural instability. An alternative way of expressing the ideas inherent within this might tend rather to support the idea of morphogenesis, where the form of organisations is in continual change as their environments change and they are forced to the threshold of their control processes. Perhaps rather than talking of unfreezing, it might be better to talk about *deregularising* patterns of behaviour through stakeholder participation in defining perspectives of the problem situation. Refreezing might be better referred to as *reinforcing* change in the organisation through the creation of new patterns (*reregularising*) with associated emergent norms.

The Schein (1996, pp. 29–34) classification (based on Lewin's work on change) explains the context of what we refer to as *deregularising* and *reregularising* behaviour as in Table 12.1.

Table 12.1 Schein classification explaining institutional *deregularising* and *reregularising*

Type of psychological change process	Meaning
Disconfirmation	Learning and change begin with dissatisfaction or frustration by data that deny our expectations/hopes. This process of denial must arouse 'survival anxiety' or the feeling that if we do not change, we shall fail to meet our needs or preset goals or ideas (survival guilt).
Induction of guilt or survival anxiety	Survival guilt requires that we accept denying data to be relevant and valid. Learning anxiety makes us react defensively because if we admit that something is wrong or imperfect we fear we will lose our effectiveness, self-esteem, or identity. Learning anxiety must be dealt with to produce change through the creation of 'psychological safety'.
Creation of psychological safety or overcoming learning anxiety	Psychological safety can enable the rejection of discomfirming data. Effective management requires that treatment from disconfirming data must be balanced by psychological safety. This can occur through group working, systems to provide work pressure relief, providing practice fields where errors provide a learning experience, breaking learning into manageable steps, and the adoption of other techniques to reduce anxiety and increase motivation.
Cognitive redefinition through behavioural deregularisation	Cognitive restructuring can assist motivation, but to do this existing patterns of behaviour must be deregularised through motivation to change and the freedom to accept new information. New information can be *semantically redefined* (to give words new meaning), *cognitively broadened* (to prove broader meaning than supposed), *new standards of judgement* or *evaluation* (shifting our criteria). This represents deep level learning processes, or, in terms of Argyris, double-loop learning.
Imitation and positive or defensive identification with role model	The learner becomes captive to a hostile environment that may not drive the learning process in a way that may be desirable according to some consensus. What new patterns of behaviour should be established through the change?
Insight scanning	A learner without role models scans the environment to seek role models to define a change target. Learners may attempt to learn things that may not survive because they do not fit the personality or culture of the learning system.
Personal and relational reregularisation	New behaviour should be congruent with the rest of the behaviour and personality of a learner if disconfirmation and thus unlearning is not to occur. In *personal regularisation* of patterns of behaviour, learners should not identify; they should scan to select appropriate solutions. *Relational regularisation* of patterns occurs through group processes that encourage the development of norms essential to group functioning.

12.2.2 The cognitive model of organisational development

Strategic management processes occur as a result of logical incrementalism. This may best be explained by the words of Quinn: 'Strategic managers follow a blend of formal analysis, behavioural techniques and power politics to bring about cohesive, step-by-step movement towards ends that are broadly conceived, but which are then constantly refined and reshaped as new information appears. Their integrating methodology can best be described as *logical incrementalism*' (Quinn, 1986, p. 67). Managers conciously and proactively apply logical incrementalism for the purposes shown in Table 12.2.

This view provides for a basis of OD, as we shall see in due course. From it will derive the ability of a consultant to be able to explore a client's problem situation, make appropriate evaluations and propose recommendations for intervention. The interventions occur through the use of conceptual tools that should be used to guide the development of a

Table 12.2 Relationship between contexts and needs

Context	Needs
Corporate strategic decision making	Improvement of information quality
Decision making in varying situations	Dealing with varying lead times; pacing parameters; sequencing needs of 'subsystems'
Strategic change encounters	Managing such factors as personal resistance and political pressures
Effective implementation of strategies	Building organisational awareness, understanding and psychological commitment
Strategic change during uncertainty	Allowing for interactive learning between the enterprise and its various impinging environments
Qualitative strategic decisions	Systematic involvement of knowledgeable persons; participation of those who carry out decisions; avoidance of premature momenta or closure that leads to deviation from ends

study through all of its stages. The tools include a set of rules, principles and points of consideration that should be explored, in particular, in the diagnosis stage.

The open system model

An organisation can be seen as a system, with a boundary and an environment. Changes in an organisation may be required because of environmental perturbations, such as new political ideologies that determine the way in which organisations can operate, new forms of competition due to technological developments, or the introduction of a new managing director with distinct views and orientation.

The typical way of explaining the systemic perspective in OD is illustrated by Nadler (1993). Seen as systems, organisations are composed of a set of parts that interrelate. Remove or change one part, and the whole system is affected. They can have the property of dynamic equilibrium, generating energy to achieve conditions of balance. As open systems, they are seen as needing to have 'favourable transactions of input and output with the environment in order to survive over time' (Nadler, 1993, p. 86). This is illustrated in Fig. 12.1 as a simple input/output diagram.

This model is referred to as the congruence model of organisational behaviour (Nadler and Tushman, 1977, 1979). It represents a general 'system' model of the organisation. The organisation is seen in cybernetic terms as a set of process having inputs and outputs that must be controlled. In Table 12.3 the meanings of the input, output and transformation process components are given.

As a result of the system process, Nadler takes *resistance, control* and *power* to represent three general problem areas that must be addressed when change is to be introduced. Resistance to change (Watson, 1969; Zaltman and Duncan, 1977) occurs by individuals when they are faced with change situations that affect their security or stability. It can generate anxiety, can affect their sense of autonomy and can make them alter the patterns of behaviour that have enabled them to cope with the management structures and processes. New patterns of behaviour must develop to accommodate change. Overcoming resistance to change can facilitate the change process.

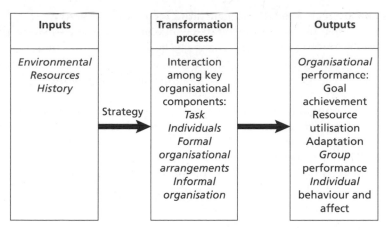

Fig. 12.1 Nadler's perception of the system model applied to organisational behaviour

Change also disturbs management control structures and processes, in particular with respect to the *formal organisation*. Change can affect the form of the organisation such that existing management controls can lose their meaning or usefulness, or controls that may be necessary can break down. Control requires known operational goals, measures of performance and organisational form for it to work.

An organisation is also a political system composed of individuals, groups and coalitions, that can be seen as competing for power (Tushman, 1977). New ideologies can also influence power positions. Balances of power exist within organisations, and

Table 12.3 A 'system' concept of an organisation

Feature	Nature	
Inputs	Environment provides constraints, demands and opportunities Resources facilitate the establishment and maintenance of structures, and activities of the organisation History provides a background that validates the organisation, its structures and activities Strategy is a set of key decisions about the match of the organisation's resources to the opportunities, constraints and demand in the environment within the context of history The effectiveness of the system's performance is consistent with the goals of strategy	
Outputs	Organisational performance indicates how well an organisation functions in comparison to predefined measures that relate to goals, resources and adaptation Group performance similarly indicates the ability of groups within the organisation to function Individual performance similarly indicates the ability of individuals within the organisation to function	
Transformation process	*OD system entity* 1 Task 2 Individuals 3 Formal organisation 4 Informal organisation	*Entity function* 1 Task redefinition 2 Resistance 3 Control 4 Power

changes can upset these, generating new political activity that forges stable power relationships. In order to facilitate change, it is necessary to shape the political dynamics of an organisation to enable change to be accepted rather than rejected.

According to Checkland and Scholes (1990) we can identify commodities of power (*see* Chapter 13). Examples of these are formal (role-based) authority, intellectual authority, personal charisma, participation in decision making bodies, external reputation, commanding access (or lack of access) to important information, membership or non-membership of various committees or less formal groups, and the authority to write the minutes of meetings.

The relationships between system components and function, as presented in the process component of Table 12.3, are intended to show the level of congruency between each sub-system, say between tasks and individuals, or between the formal organisation, its control structures and processes, and the informal power structures and processes that exist within the organisation. The basic hypothesis of the model is that an organisation will be most effective when all four components of the system are congruent to each another.

The simple input/output diagram of Fig. 12.1 is itself seen to operate within a control loop, with the inputs and outputs being subject to variation as long as the system is stable. In situations where it reaches the threshold of stability, changes in form may occur that we refer to as morphogenesis. Thus, tasks, individuals, and formal and informal organisation are subject to morphogenic processes.

The problems of resistance to change, control and power (Nadler, 1993) can be treated as shown in Table 12.4.

Table 12.4 Actions able to stabilise the relationship between resistance, control and power

Problem	Need	Action
Resistance	Motivate change	1 Assure support of key power groups 2 Use leader behaviour to generate energy in support of change 3 Use symbols and language 4 Build in stability
Control	Manage the transition	5 Surface dissatisfaction with present state 6 Participation in change 7 Rewards for behaviour in support of change 8 Time and opportunity to disengage from the present state
Power	Shape the political dynamics of change	9 Develop and communicate a clear image of the future 10 Use multiple and consistent leverage points 11 Develop organisational arrangements for the transition 12 Build in feedback mechanisms

(*Source*: Nadler, 1993)

Harrison (1994) has proposed a different version of Nadler's open system model. He identifies inputs, outputs and processes at three levels of focus: the organisation, the group and the individual. The transformation process is also identified in terms of a set of components that includes culture, process and behaviour. Here, the three-subsystem approach of Nadler is replaced by a more detailed approach, as shown in Table 12.5.

Table 12.5 Tabular representation of Harrison's open system model of organisational change

System focus	Inputs	Transformation process	Outputs
Organisational	Organisational resources	Goals, culture, technology, process, behaviour	Products, services, performance
Group	Group resources	Group composition, structure, technology; group behaviour process, culture	Products, services, performance
Individual	Human resources	Individual job, tasks; individual behaviour, attitudes, orientation	Products, services, ideas, performance; quality of work life; wellbeing

A matrix of organisational inquiry

The attributes of Harrison's open system model include the main elements: *form* (structure and process), *behaviour* and *context*. The processes represent an internal characteristic of the organisation that facilitates the maintenance of the structure, while the structure provides an accommodation to enable the processes to occur. The behaviour represents the activity manifestations of each level of focus as seen from its immediate environment. Context defines the setting of the situation being inquired into. We refer to Table 12.6 (based on the Pugh Matrix; Mabey, 1995) as a matrix of organisational inquiry. It operates as an OD tool that can be used recurrently throughout the process of inquiry as a centre of reference, and which can assist an inquirer in identifying:

- the level of inquiry appropriate to a problem situation;
- the possible point at which an intervention should occur;
- the degree of intervention that is likely to be required;
- the nature of the strategy that might be appropriate.

Employee participation

As referred to by Mabey, Lupton (1993) discusses the need to involve employees in the decision making process of organisations. 'The opening up of blocked communication channels in order to allow ordinary members of an organisation to contribute their knowledge and ideas which are different from, and often superior to, top managements' is a very typical aim of OD' (Mabey, 1995). This, it is argued, has a twofold effect:

1 introducing new information into the management structure to improve decision making;

2 improving the communication and participation process, and generating increased commitment and motivation.

Resistance to change

In 1975 Huse published a work concerned with reducing the resistance to change. The

Table 12.6 Organisation matrix

System focus	Behavioural manifestation	Process characteristics	Structure seen as a system	Context, the setting
Organisation	Generally poor morale, pressure, anxiety, suspicion, lack of awareness of or response to change in environment. *Survey feedback, organisational mirroring.*	Inadequacy of monitoring mechanisms. Form of governance: such as degree of bureaucratisation, centralisation, divisionalisation, standardisation. Stability, decline. *Change the processes.*	Purposes: system goals poorly defined or inappropriate; strategy inappropriate and misunderstood; organisational structure inappropriate. Stakeholder distribution and ownership. Size, complexity. *Change structure.*	Power distribution and alignments. Political orientation. Environment: geographical setting, market pressures, labour market, physical conditions, basic technology. *Change strategy, location, physical setup, culture.*
Group	Inappropriate working relationships, atmosphere, participation, poor understanding and acceptance of goals, avoidance; inappropriate leadership style, leader not trusted, respected; leader in conflict with superiors. *Team building.*	Task requirements poorly defined; inappropriate reporting procedures. *Process consultation.*	Role relationships unclear or inappropriate; leader's role overloaded. *Redesign work relationships (socio-technical systems), autonomous working groups.*	Insufficient resources, poor group composition for cohesion, inadequate physical setup, personality clashes. *Change technology, layout, group composition, culture.*
Individual	Failure to fulfil individual's needs; frustration responses; unwillingness to consider change, little chance of learning and development. *Counselling, role analysis.*	Tasks too easy or too difficult. Purpose of tasks poorly defined. Attitude and orientation problems. *Job modification/ enrichment.*	Poor job definition. *Job redefinition.*	Poor match of individual with job; poor selection or promotion. Poor incentives. *Personnel changes, improved selection and promotion procedures, improved training and education, recognition and remuneration alignment with objectives.*
Inter-relationship				
Intergroup	Lack of effective cooperation between subunits, conflict, excessive competition, limited war, failure to confront differences in priorities, unresolved feelings. *Intergroup confrontation (with consultant as third party), role negotiation.*	Exchanges between groups subject to chaos; inefficiencies. Required interactions difficult to achieve. Formalised competition versus cooperation. Poor communication. *Change reporting relationships, improve coordination and liaison.*	Relationships subject to chaos. Lack of integrated task perspective; subunit optimisation. Poor communication structures. *Redefine responsibilities.*	Locally distinct cultures (different values, attitudes, beliefs, behaviour in each subgroup). *Reduce psychological and physical distance; exchange roles, attachments, cross-functional social overlay.*

Two dimensions to the matrix are characteristic problems and typical remedies. The level of system focus identifies at what level examination is being made. Distinguishes diagnosis from remedy (in italics).
(*Source*: Derived from the Pugh Matrix, Mabey, 1995)

strategy intended to address this issue is expressed as a set of eight factors (Mabey, 1995):

1 account should be taken of needs, attitudes and beliefs of participant individuals, and personal benefits generated;

2 there should be adequate (official and unofficial) prestige, power and influence;

3 there should be appropriate information, which should be relevant and meaningful;

4 there should be shared perceptions of need for change, and involvement in information gathering and interpretation;

5 there should be a common sense of belonging, and an appropriate degree of participation;

6 the development of group cohesiveness reduces resistance;

7 leaders should be involved in the immediate situation;

8 communication channels should be opened, objective information shared, and the knowledge of the results of change made available.

Kotter and Schlesinger (1979) were also concerned with the reduction of resistance to change. Both *diagnosing* and *dealing* with resistance to change were considered, and the characteristics listed in Table 12.7 were identified. Where this strategy should be applied has been identified in Table 12.8 (Kotter and Schlesinger, 1979).

Table 12.7 Diagnosing and dealing with resistance to change

Diagnosing resistance	Dealing with resistance
Parochial self interest	Education and communication
Misunderstanding or lack of trust	Participation and involvement
Different assessments	Facilitation and support
Low tolerance for change	Negotiation and agreement
	Manipulation and cooptation
	Explicit and implicit coercion

Effectiveness

Harrison (1994) has provided a development of OD that he refers to as *diagnosis*. This is intended to broaden the ability of OD to diagnose and provide change strategies in complex organisational situations. It is built within the OD paradigm, though he extends it to include more comprehensive ways of examining the organisation.

The concept of effectiveness is important to *diagnosis*. 'To assess effectiveness and the feasibility of change, practitioners need to draw on an additional model that treats organisations as political arenas ... The political model of organisations draws attention to divergent stakeholders (or constituencies) in and around organisations. Stakeholders are groups and individuals affected by decisions or a project who seek to influence decisions in keeping with their own interests, goals, priorities, and understandings ... As a result their divergent interests and views, organisational subgroups from distinct fields, and ranks often advocate different ways of judging organisational success and effectiveness' (Harrison, 1994, p. 39).

Table 12.8 Use of methods to reduce resistance to change

Approach in dealing with resistance	Situational use
Education and communication	Where there is a lack of information or inaccurate information and analysis
Participation and involvement	Where the initiators do not have all the information they need to design the change. Where others have considerable power to resist
Facilitation and support	Where people are resisting because of adjustment problems
Negotiation and agreement	Where some individual or group will clearly lose out in a change Where the group has considerable power to resist
Manipulation and co-option	Where other tactics will not work Where other tactics are too expensive
Explicit and implicit coercion	Where speed is essential Where the change initiators possess considerable power

The characteristics that define effectiveness will therefore determine how an inquirer looks at and evaluates a situation. Characteristics of effectiveness operate as criteria or standards for control in evaluating the proposed programme of intervention. Sometimes the criteria relate to internal aspects of the organisational states and processes (e.g. cost of production, work and information flows adaptiveness), while in others they relate to conditions (e.g. employee welfare). More particularly, Harrison identifies three categories of effectiveness that correspond to the open systems model. These are:

1 output goals
2 internal system state
3 adaptation.

Based on these ideas (Harrison, 1994, pp. 40–1), in Table 12.9 we provide examples of operational definitions of effectiveness for each of these classes across a set of four characteristics.

The criteria for control can vary as organisations learn. It is also possible for different criteria to be conflictual, so that selecting a variety of characteristics to be used together can be problematic for consistency.

Effectiveness criteria are also relative to the organisation. In terms of our earlier theory, this is because the criteria derive from the dominant paradigm of the organisation, which will in general be unique to any given organisation. In situations where there exist a number of dominant paradigms that may operate at different levels of the organisation, then once again we may be facing the problem of conflict between the criteria selected.

In attempting to resolve any possible conflicts in the choice of effectiveness criteria, Harrison proposes solutions deriving from Cameron (1984), Campbell (1977), Connolly and Deutch (1980) and Goodman and Pennings (1980) in identifying them (Table 12.10).

Clients are those people who have responsibility for deciding what actions to take in response to a study. If different paradigms exist between clients and stakeholders, then

Table 12.9 Examples of effectiveness measures across a set of characteristics for the open system

Characteristic	Output goals	Internal system state	Adaptation
Attainment	Success/failure	Costs: efficiency, wastage, downtime Human: satisfaction of pay, working conditions, relations; motivation; work effort; absenteeism, lateness, turnover; health and safety.	Size of organisation; support and approval by community and public bodies; public image; compliance with standards in legal, regulatory, professional bodies; market share, ranking.
Flows	Productivity; returns; percentage of target group addressed.	Products, ideas, information; satisfactory communications; misunderstandings; accurate information analysis.	Resources; use of capacities to exploit external opportunities; ability to shape demand, government action, behaviour of others; control and learning processes with change; flexibility in handling crises and surprises.
Quality	Number of rejects, returns, complaints; clients, customer satisfaction; service rating, work performance; impacts on target population.	Goal agreement and procedures; group cohesion, cooperation; conflict as in strikes, stoppages, disputes. Trust; open communications and feelings; de-emphasis on status differences. Stakeholder decision participation; diffusion of power and authority. Compatibility of requirement to system.	Human capital; desirability of clients; reputation of staff; satisfying requirement; environmental constraints.
Innovation	New counting, evaluation or sampling methods; redefinition of meaning of attainment.	For development of human and group resources; structures and processes.	New products, services, procedures; management practices; new technologies

Table 12.10 Choosing effectiveness criteria

Class	Nature
Clients	Who are they? What preferred organisational states? What are criteria of preferred states? How do consultants facilitate resolution of conflicts/ambiguities?
Goals	Conditions and states to achieve goals as reflected in effectiveness criteria? How do consultants facilitate adoption of additional criteria?
Stakeholders	Favoured effectiveness criteria? Are there consensus criteria for powerful stakeholders?

there may well be inconsistencies and ambiguities in views between them in what constitutes effectiveness for the organisation, and thus in the criteria that define it. Consultants often encourage clients to develop a consensus about organisational priorities, thus enabling them to select effectiveness criteria. Alternatively, these may be dictated by the most powerful clients. They may then wish to use them as constraints while attempting to address the situation in other harmonic ways.

There may also be inconsistency between the stated priorities and those that are apparently in operation in decision making. In such situations, consultants are advised to confront clients with the inconsistencies.

In the case that appropriate effectiveness criteria cannot be found, ineffectiveness criteria may be discernible, and ways of combating them may be identified.

The language

The terminology used in OD is listed in Table 12.11. In the main the definitions that relate to Harrison's open system model are taken from his work, though some adjustment has been made in order to maintain consistency within this book. Two concepts in this position are *structure* and *process*. *Structure*, in Harrison's terms, includes elements of what we would regard as *process*; he also combines *process* and *behaviour*, which we differentiate.

We note that from our perspective the distinction between behaviour and process is determined by the boundary of the system: processes are seen by an observer to be internal to the boundary, while behaviour is seen to be representative of the way in which a system responds to it. In the end, the only distinction between behaviour and process will be made through the identity of the system that is being focused on.

Thus when discussing behavioural interactions, we can focus on the individual, the group or the organisation as a whole, each defining an appropriate boundary to the system that we are examining. Thus, an individual has a certain behaviour in connection with tasks, or interactive behaviour with his or her companions, determined in part by the individual's underlying psychological processes. In the same way, group behaviour is determined by the group's organisational processes and social psychology.

Rules and propositions of OD

According to Huse (1975) and others there are various assumptions (adapted from Mabey, 1995) underlying OD.

1 People have needs for personal growth and development which are most likely to be satisfied in a supportive and challenging environment.

2 Most workers are underutilised and are capable of taking on more responsibility for their own actions and of making a greater contribution to organisational goals than is permitted in most organisational environments. Therefore, the job design, managerial assumptions or other factors frequently 'demotivate' individuals in formal organisations.

3 In relations to groups:
   a groups are highly important to people, and most people satisfy their needs within groups, especially the work group;
   b work groups includes both peers and supervisors and are highly influential on the individuals in the group;

Table 12.11 The language of OD

OD terms	Meaning
Problem owner	Defined by the change agent as a person or group that is the primary stakeholder.
Problem situation	A situation in which there are perceived problems that may be unclear.
Stakeholder	A participant in a change process who has a vested interest in the situation, who may have something (a stake, like a job or an investment) to gain or lose. Groups and individuals affected by decisions or a project who seek to influence decisions in keeping with their own interests, goals, priorities and understandings.
Consultant	An individual who acts to 'reduce power differences, foster open communication, encourage cooperation and solidarity, and adopt policies that enhance the potential of employees' (Harrison, 1994, p. 8). To help assist organisational forms and cultures towards this ideal, consultants often use experienced small group training, feedback on interpersonal processes, participative decision making, and build on strong cohesive organisational culture. OD demands the ability of a consultant to be able to explore a client's problem situation, make appropriate evaluations, and propose recommendations for intervention.
Resources	These inputs to the system may include raw materials, money, human resources, equipment, information, knowledge and authority to undertake certain classes of potentially constrained actions.
Technology	Tools, machines, techniques for transforming resources that may be mental, social, physical, chemical, electronic, etc.
Goals and strategies	Goals (sometimes referred to as overall objectives) are desired future end states; objectives are specified targets and indicators of goal attainment; strategies are overall goal routes; plans specify courses of action towards end goals. Goals and strategies derive from conflicts and negotiations among powerful parties within the organisation and its environment.
Structure	Enduring relationships between individuals, groups and larger units (e.g. roles and their attributes such as authority, privilege, responsibility).
Processes	Operating procedures, mechanisms for handling key procedures (e.g. coordination of committees), human resource mechanisms, goal setting. Processes occur within system boundaries.
Behaviour	Action, representative of the way in which a system responds to its environment.
Culture	Shared norms, values, beliefs, assumptions, and the behaviour and symbols that express these. Includes belief of organisational identity, working practices, opportunities for innovation, role relationships.
Organisational performance	Depends on strategies, standards and goals that determine performance. Affects group and individual performance.
Group performance	Identify most important group products and in some way measure their quality/quantity over time
Individual performance	Includes the degree of quality of individual efforts, initiatives, cooperation, absenteeism, lateness, commitment to job; defined relative to the objectives of the group/organisation of the individual.
Environment	*Task environment:* all external organisations and conditions directly related to the system's main operations/technologies (e.g. sources, suppliers, distributors, unions, customers, clients, regulators, competitors, partners, markets, technical knowledge). *General environment:* institution and conditions having infrequent or long-term impacts on the organisation and task environment (e.g. economy, legal system, scientific knowledge, social institutions, culture).

  c work groups are essentially neutral, and they may be harmful or helpful to an organisation, depending upon their nature;

  d work groups can generally increase their effectiveness in attaining individual needs and organisational requirements by working together collaboratively;

  e for groups to increase their effectiveness, the formal leader cannot exercise all of the leadership functions at all times and in all circumstances;

  f group members can become more effective when assisting one another.

4 *Effectiveness* is seen (Harrison, 1994) to depend upon an organisation's:

  a output goals;

  b internal system state;

  c adaptation and resource position.

  Further, effectiveness may derive from criteria that:

  a are paradigmatically determined;

  b may have contradiction between their client and practice, when the client should be confronted;

  c may be in conflict when either:

   i consensus approaches may resolve them, or

   ii powerful clients will determine constraints.

5 An organisation is seen as a system, so that changes in one subsystem (social, technical or managerial) will affect other subsystems.

6 In relation to human feelings:

  a most people have feelings and attitudes that affect their behaviour, but the culture of the organisation tends to suppress the expression of these attributes;

  b when the feelings of people are suppressed, problem solving, job satisfaction and personal growth are adversely affected;

  c when an organisation accepts that feelings are important, greater access can occur to improved leadership, communications, goal setting, intergroup collaboration and job satisfaction.

7 In most organisations, the level of interpersonal support, trust and cooperation is much lower than is desirable and necessary.

8 Strategies that define winners and losers tend to be dysfunctional to both employees and the organisation.

9 If individual or group entities have clashes of 'personality', they tend to be a result of organisational design rather than the entities.

10 Confronting conflict in order to resolve it through open discussion of ideas facilitates both personal growth and the accomplishment of organisational goals.

11 Organisational structure and the design of jobs can be modified to meet more effectively the needs of the individual, the group and the organisation.

12 Institutional patterns of behaviour should be deregularised if change is to be introduced, and the change reinforced through the reregularisation of new patterns.

During the management of organisational change, Pugh (1993) proposes a number of general systems theory propositions. We express them as follows:

13 Organisations:

  a need to be under control;

  b are coalitions of interest groups in tension;

    c have organisation which represents a particular balance of forces;
    d experience change that represents a new balance of forces;
    e can be inertial in their behaviour.

14 When an entity operates inertially, it does not enable variety to occur in respect of its behaviour, even if variety is called for.

This introduces us to the idea of resistance to change:

15 Individuals in organisations need to feel that change is controlled. They react to change because (Nadler, 1993):
    a people have a need for some degree of stability and security;
    b change imposed on individuals reduces their sense of self-control or autonomy;
    c people typically develop patterns for coping with or managing the current situation and its structure;
    d change means that people will have to find new ways of managing their own environments;
    e change may affect people's position of power;
    f people may ideologically believe that organisation prior to the change is better.

Kotter and Schlesinger (Mayon-White, 1986) were concerned with ways of *reducing resistance to change*. For them:

16 Political power can emerge before and during organisational change efforts when (it is perceived that) what is in the best interests of one individual or group is not in the best interests of the total organisation or of other individuals and groups.

Power (Nadler, 1993) is seen as the reaction of the informal organisation to change, when:

17 Any organisation is a political system made up of different individuals, groups and coalitions competing for power.

18 During a change process, power relationships can become upset, creating uncertainty, ambiguity and thus increased political activity.

19 Individuals and groups engage in political activity because their ideological position on change may be inconsistent with their values or image of the organisation.

Kotter and Schlesinger (1979) identify an approach to reducing resistance to change. It defines a set of rules that identifies classes of situation, often under situations of power, and indicates a strategy that can reduce resistance to change. Thus:

20 In organisations in which there is a lack of information or inaccurate information and analysis, a process of education and communication should occur.

21 Where initiators of change do not have all the information they need to design change, and where others have considerable power to resist, people should participate and be involved in the change process.

22 Where people resist change because of adjustment problems, change should be facilitated by a supporting agency.

23 Where individuals or groups clearly lose out in a change, and where that group has considerable power to resist, negotiation and agreement should occur.

24 Where tactics will not work or are too expensive, people should be manipulated and co-opted.

25 Where speed is essential and change initiators possess considerable power, explicit or implicit coercion should occur.

From Pugh (1993) we have the following psychology propositions in respect of humans operating as managers:

26 In respect of human reaction to events:
    a individuals tend to react to threats and unknown dangers by going rigid;
    b managers under pressure tend to operate inertially;
    c inertial behaviour may be manifestly seen by others to be inadequate.

In respect of whether or not people can be effective in their behaviour as managers, Pugh (1993) identifies the following proposition that defines managerial effectiveness:

27 An effective manager:
- anticipates the need for change rather than reacting after the event of an emergency;
- diagnoses the nature of the change that is required;
- carefully considers a number of alternatives that might improve the organisation;
- manages a change process over a period of time rather than continually surmounting crises.

Pugh (1993) identified six rules about intervention in complex situations to create change strategy; the questions of who, what, where, when and how may be put for each of these:

28 Work hard at establishing the need for change.

29 Don't think out change, think it through.

30 Initiate change through informal discussion to get feedback and participation.

31 Positively encourage those concerned to give objections.

32 Be prepared to change yourself.

33 Monitor the change and reinforce it.

Price and Murphy (1993) identify the following rules about the way in which OD should be applied:

34 Think big (major change is possible).

35 Simplify and publicise.

36 Do not mystify change.

37 Do not rely on 'top-down' cascades to notify people about change.

38 Do not over-rely on consultants (their role can best be seen as catalytic).

39 Do not rely on groups (groups do nothing, participation as in group problem solving is beneficial, while group responsibility is not).

40 Where it occurs, regularised behaviour that might interfere with change should be identified and confronted in order to enable new processes and systems to become established.

41 A steering group can help time refreezing (when new structures and processes have been established).

42 Change requires time, energy and monitoring.

Generic nature

This section identifies the class of situations that OD is intended to deal with. It is concerned with psychological, social psychological and cultural organisational factors, and its exemplars provide the basic propositions that relate to the cultural norms found in Western society.

OD operates at the soft end of the hard–soft continuum. It deals with soft organisational issues; that is, those involving relationships between people. It also deals with group processes that are human related. Finally it deals with psychological and emotional issues that relate to the individual stakeholders.

It deals with situations that are ill structured, since the nature of the problem situation being tackled is initially unknown. Only then is it possible to identify elements and their relationships that define a structure for the situation.

Situations that OD typically addresses are uncertain, and it does so by identifying strategic approaches to intervention. Thus, causal relationships between definable elements in a situation will not be clear, nor whether predictions can be made concerning the outcome of strategies for change.

OD is very sensitive to the idea that inquirers can influence the situation itself, thus is high on the scale of indeterminacy. It is for this reason that consultants are often considered to best operate as facilitators, in an attempt to minimise their influence.

It is also a highly pragmatic methodology, enabling consultants to operate according to their own rule of thumb and interpret reality through the direct participation of stakeholders.

12.2.3 Logical processes of organisational development

According to Pugh (1993), an intention to manage organisational change can result in any of the following three unwanted pathways:

1 nothing happens

2 a cosmetic change occurs

3 unanticipated negative consequences of the change outweigh its benefits.

To deal with such possibilities it is useful to develop a structured methodology. We shall introduce two approaches, traditional OD and diagnosis, which are complementary.

A traditional OD cycle

A traditional OD sequential methodology has three phases that combine to produce seven stages as depicted in Table 12.12 (Mabey, 1995). The introductory and pre-evaluation (scouting) stage is identified by Harrison (1994).

More recently, Mabey (1995a) has proposed an alternative form to traditional organisational development, shown in Table 12.13. This sets up the phases in a new way, and establishes inquiry into the future state as the first step. This would in addition involve the initial step 0 as part of the pre-evaluation phase. The differences between the two styles of traditional OD lie in the idea that the new form should address the consultation process, which is perceived to lie at the centre of the methodology and is seen as a consensus building process. The contexts of step 2 relate to the work of Pettigrew (1988). Outer contexts relate to the sociopolitical, economic, legal, technological and business competitive factors in the external environment, through say a SWOT analysis. Inner

Table 12.12 The steps of the traditional organisational development cycle. Created in order to deal with possible unwanted pathways in development

Phases	Steps
0 Introduction and pre-evaluation (scouting)	0 Getting acquainted with clients; introduction to client organisation; introduction to problem situation; pre-analysis; client expectations defined; contract agreement
1 Diagnosis	1 Confrontation with environmental change, problems opportunities 2 Identification of implications for organisation
2 Involvement and detailed diagnosis	3 Education to obtain understanding of implications for organisation 4 Obtaining involvement in project 5 Identification of targets for change
3 Action evaluation and reinforcement	6 Change and development activities 7 Evaluation of project and programme in current environment and reinforcement

(*Source*: Mabey, 1995)

contexts relate to the internal capacity for change and include concepts of leadership, organisation structure and culture, personalities of key people, primary tasks and emergent technologies.

Table 12.13 New version of organisational development

Phases	Steps
1 Determine the future state (where do we want to be?)	1 Agree on organisational purpose/mission
2 Diagnose the present state (where are we now?)	2 Assess outer/inner contexts 3 Gather data 4 Gain involvement
3 Manage the transition	5 Set targets for change 6 Implement change and development activities 7 Evaluate and reinforce changes

(*Source*: Mabey, 1995a)

The conceptual theory already explored in practice outlines a set of OD methodological tools that can be used in order to inquire, model and take action for intervention to introduce change. These tools can be used according to the needs of the inquirer and the requirements of the situation. For instance, the Harrison model of Table 12.5 could be used during step 1 in order to contextualise the situation, noting all of the elements that should be taken into account, and exploring each element in relation to its context. The organisation matrix (Table 12.6) could be used in say steps 2, 3 and 5 of Table 12.13, depending upon the nature of the inquiry and the direction that the models for change are taking. It may also be used at step 7.

Diagnosis

Harrison (1994), in the exploration of how various conceptual tools can be used in his development of aspects of traditional OD, identifies what he refers to as *system fits*. Here, the open system model of Table 12.5 is fitted to the perceived reality of a situation. Thus, a system fit is a description of the situation and its context according to Harrison's system model.

System fit diagnosis, based on his open system model, represents the core of Harrison's theory. He defines an approach to inquiry shown in Table 12.14. It operates as a cycle of sequential stages that begins with inputs, involves a set of four phases, and then feeds back into the cycle.

Diagnosis involves more systems thinking than does traditional OD, in that not only does it adopt an open system model, but in addition explicitly highlights the focus of the system. In this sequence of stages, each of the dimensions of Table 12.6 can be considered in turn.

Various dimensions of system fit are explored. This includes power relations, identifying, for instance, who is powerful, where and how. It also deals with macro-level inquiry and environmental inquiry. Inquiry at the macro-level explores such issues as:

- customer/client relations
- performance in terms of sales and revenue
- reputation
- competition
- internal conflicts
- task failure
- problems in innovation
- recruitment problems
- project development capabilities
- communications faults.

Essentially, then, macro-level events are those that relate to the system in focus as a whole, and the relationship with its environment. The environment must also be explored. A client-centred approach to this by stakeholders is called open systems planning (OSP), and is concerned with external relations. It operates by conducting a series of workshops with members of an organisation or group who have responsibility or authority to engage in planning and to make decisions affecting the organisation's strategic relations to its environment. Participants explore their organisation's situation and model possible intervention strategies under the facilitating guidance of the consultant. OSP can be broadly broken down into the following stages of inquiry (Harrison, 1994, p. 120):

- analyse current environmental conditions
- analyse current responses to the environment
- analyse priorities and purpose
- predict trends and conditions
- define future idea
- compare future ideal with current states
- establish priorities
- action planning.

The stages of OSP can be used in phase 2 of the traditional OD cycle, as they can in phase 4 of diagnosis. It would, for instance, be appropriate to apply the organisation matrix (Table 12.6) at this stage of the cycle.

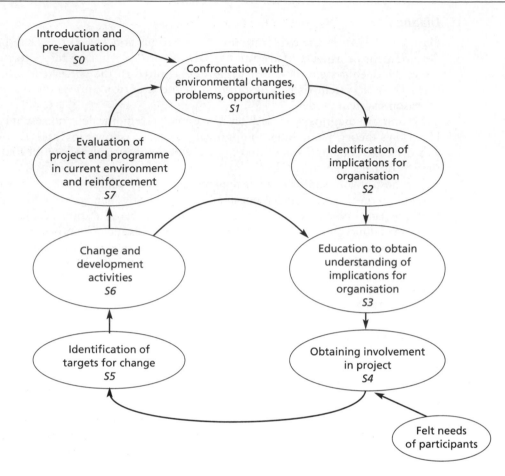

Fig. 12.2 The OD cycle
(*Source*: Based on Mabey, 1986)

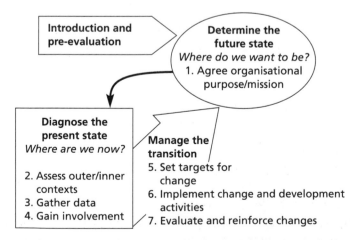

Fig. 12.3 More recent form of organisational development
(*Source*: Mabey, 1995a)

Table 12.14 The diagnosis phases of Harrison

Step	Attributes
1 Inputs	Problems Prior findings Models
2 Choose fits	Level System elements, subcomponents
3 Design study, gather data	Research design Methods Data collection
4 Assess degree of fit	Needs of units, system parts Conflicts, tensions Actual versus official practices Organisational design methods
5 Assess impacts	Negative Positive Loose coupling

The behavioural model of OD

The basic form of the traditional OD inquiry is shown in Fig. 12.2, based on the generalised description of the stages of the OD process (Mabey, 1995), and defined in Table 12.9. This is a sequential process that defines a cycle of inquiry. According to Harrison (1994), OD inquiry should begin with a prior introduction and pre-evaluation stage. It supposes a feedback between steps 6 to 3 in the event that the change and development activities are not seen to be satisfactory; that is, stable. The cycle then continues to step 4 and onwards.

The more recent form of the traditional OD cycle (from Table 12.12) is presented in Fig. 12.3 (Mabey, 1995, p. 335), and is loosely based on the work of Beckhard (1989) on transformational change. In any organisation there are perceived to be three 'states' – the future state, the present state and the transition state, which identifies how to move between the current and future states. We have amended Mabey's diagram by including the pre-evaluation step S0 and the link between steps 1 and 2 to ensure that this is seen as a cycle of inquiry. Comparing this to the original version of the traditional OD cycle, we note that stages S2 to S4 of the diagnosis phase have been redefined in Fig. 12.3 while steps 5–7 remains principally the same.

Another paradigmatically commensurable form of inquiry is that of Harrison's diagnosis, the form of which is identified in Fig. 12.4.

12.3 The doppelgänger paradigm

A view of OD in terms of the metasystem

OD is a soft methodology. Multiple and indeed contradictory views of reality are permitted and explored. The nature of the OD inquiry is represented in Fig. 12.5, and an explanation is given in Table 12.15.

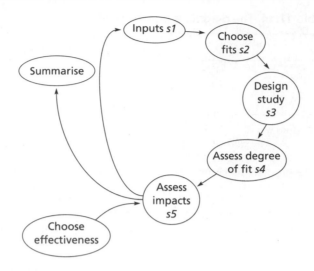

Fig. 12.4 Diagnosis cycle, that links with traditional OD

Table 12.15 Definition of the system and metasystem for OD

The system

S1 Three focuses of the system are considered; the organisational, the group and the individual. The system defined is not normally expressed in terms of relevant systems, but more with respect to the relative and sometimes contradictory views of stakeholders. Metapurposes will be determined by consensus view, or from the primary stakeholders/clients to whom the consultants have responsibility.

Cognitive purposes

Mission and goals

The overall methodological metapurpose is to manage a renewing balance of forces through cross-group negotiations. The mission-related *goals* determine what is meant and what the strategy for change is. These are:

m1 *Political power*, concerned with ensuring that an intervention strategy cannot be sabotaged through power conflicts.

m2 *Control*, which must be ensured if a strategy for intervention is to progress in the face of potential conflicts.

m3 *Resistance to change* must be addressed in order to ensure that stakeholders are able to accept change implementation.

Inquiry aims

i1 Determined by an inquirer in relation to the situation and relates to the creation of effective strategies for change. However, it takes into account many of the features characterised by the Harrison open system model, and thus provides creative constraints for inquiry.

The overall (methodological) purpose of inquiry is to introduce change to ensure a new balance with the environment of the system (*im1*). The nature of *im1* will depend upon the weltanschauung of an inquirer, and the stakeholders. No formalised system model is generally produced; models are normally informal. The impact of the real world on the informal system models produced is identified in terms of tasks and forces

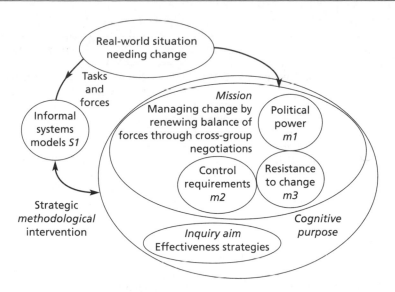

Fig. 12.5 Influence diagram cognitive purpose of OD

from the environment that generate the need for change. The system models are not separated out from the real world *s1*, but rather the models emerge from the human interactions that occur with the stakeholders.

Relating traditional OD with diagnosis

Two forms of traditional OD have been identified: Mabey (1995) and Mabey (1995a). The two forms differ in the first three steps and the way of presentation. We have taken the steps of the second to represent traditional OD. In addition, diagnosis is offered in Table 12.16. Since these two approaches are based on the same paradigm and are not incommensurable, they can be combined to generate a new specification which provides the basis of a new form of methodological cycle of inquiry that takes advantage of both approaches.

Table 12.16 Creating methodological inquiry by integrating traditional OD with diagnosis

Steps of traditional OD	Steps of diagnosis	Proposed steps
1 Agree organisational purposes, identifying environmental change, problems and opportunities	1 Inputs: problems, prior findings, models	1 Exploration of situation and define purposes
2 Gather information for organisational understanding	2 Choose fits: level, system elements, subcomponents	2 Define relevant system
3 Assess inner/outer contexts and identify meaning for organisation		3 Assess contexts
4 Gain involvement in project		4 Confirm stakeholder participation and relevant system

Continued overleaf

Table 12.16 (continued)

Steps of traditional OD	Steps of diagnosis	Proposed steps
5 Identification of targets for change	3 Design study, gather data: research design, methods, data collection 4 Assess degree of fit 5 Assess impacts	5 Identify targets and design models 6 Evaluation and selection of models
6 Change and development activities		7 Change and development activities
7 Evaluation of project and programme in current environment and reinforcement		8 Evaluation of project and programme in current environment and reinforcement

Clearly both methodologies can be linked to include the concepts of traditional OD with the broader advantages of diagnosis. It is thus possible to generate a combined form of traditional OD and diagnosis according to Table 12.12. This is given again in Table 12.17 with an explanation (that relates to Mabey, 1995) of what the steps involve, and the possible tools that can be used. These steps are shown graphically in Fig. 12.6.

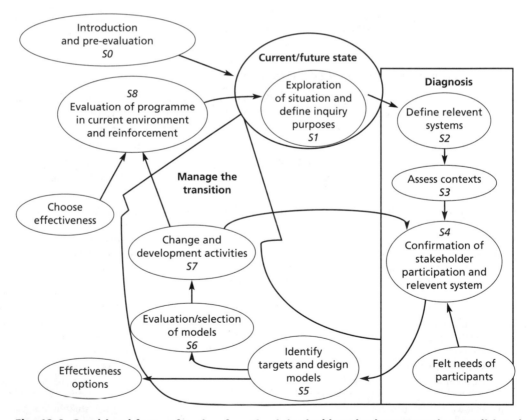

Fig. 12.6 Combined form of cycle of methodological inquiry incorporating traditional OD and Harrison's diagnosis

Table 12.17 A description of the steps of OD and their action

Phase	Step	Action and context	Explanation and tools
Current/ future state	1 Explore situation and purposes	Exploration of organisational mission. Consultation process, identifying where the organisation is going and what it wants to achieve.	Human interaction with clients. Throughout study, be aware of power, control and possible resistance to change aspects of situation.
Diagnosis	2 Define relevant system	Gather data. Identify stakeholders. Explore perspectives of the situation to create system representations. Identify structures and processes.	Interviews. Use of diagramming techniques like system maps, power context diagrams, activity sequence diagrams. Organisation matrix.
	3 Assess contexts	*Outer contexts* are sociopolitical, economic, legal, technological and competitive factors in environment. *Inner contexts* concerned with internal capacity for change. Identify commodities of power and control mechanisms. Identify input constraints.	Brainstorming, SWOT analysis, force field diagrams, mind maps, multiple cause diagrams.
	4 Confirmation of participation and relevant system	Strategic change requires different views to be heard as part of the process to win support and commitment. Ensure participation of appropriate stakeholders and confirm relevant systems.	Stakeholder consultation. Techniques to encourage participation. Explore resistance to change.
Manage change	5 Identify targets and design models	Change can cause confusion about roles, responsibilities and decision making channels. Public models of change can be instrumental in reducing this, and meaningful targets and reinforcing milestones derive from these. Explore designs for *deregularising* patterns of behaviour.	Scan for targets and milestones – you can refer to organisation matrix. Consider needs of components of system, evaluate conflicts and tensions, actual against official practices. Define effectiveness criteria. Use control diagrams. Refer to Schein classification.
	6 Evaluation/ selection of models	Evaluate the models and associated targets, and confirm selection with most important stakeholders/clients.	Consultation with major stakeholders/clients.
	7 Change and development activities	Reregularising patterns of behaviour to *reinforce* change if it is not to be defeated by history. This can help through (a) individuals should have a personal stake and be accountable for change; (b) new working relationships and boundaries between work groups to be negotiated; (c) find ways of recognising and rewarding desirable behaviours.	Refer to Schein classification. Work through a skeleton of the organisation matrix. Tabulate activities.

The characteristics of form

The doppelgänger structural model of OD

The structural inquiry represented in Table 12.18 is shown in Fig. 12.7 as a cycle. Here, control aspects of the cycle occur to determine the stability of the action stage. If this is not stable, re-education occurs and the cycle is continued from there.

OSP, considered earlier as a methodology used in the context of workshop client-centred activities, can also be put in terms of the OD cycle. This goes for any inquiry workshops, whether or not they are client-centred. Since workshops can be part of the OD process, for instance in steps S1, S3 and S5, the OD cycle with embedded themes can also be used, making OD a recursive methodology.

Table 12.18 The OD doppelgänger methodology

Doppelgänger paradigm Entity/process		OD paradigm Explanation	Step
Pre-anaylsis		Introductory and pre-evaluation	S0
			Current/future state
Analysis		Exploration of situation and define purposes	S1
			Diagnosis
		Defining relevant systems	·S2
		Assess inner/outer contexts	S3
Control		Confirmation of stakeholder participation and relevant system	S4
Conceptualisation			
Synthesis		Identify targets and design models	Manage transition S5
Constraint		Felt needs of participants Choose effectiveness	
Choice		Evaluation of models	S6
Action		Change and development activities	S7
Control		Evaluation if *action* is stable: *stable*: continue *unstable*: refer back to S4	
Control		Evaluation of project and programme	S8

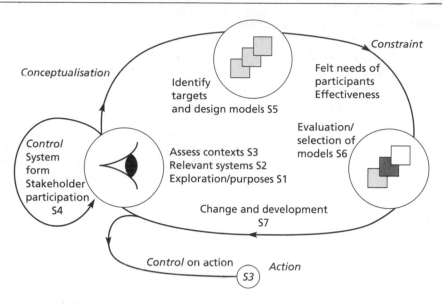

Fig. 12.7 Doppelgänger view of OD methodological inquiry

12.4 The OD case study

This case, like the one in Chapter 11, derives from the work of two of my students, Judy Brough and Nicola Magill, both on the 1996 final level of the part-time BA in Public Administration. It concerns Liverpool City Council's Social Services Directorate, which is to introduce charging for the first time through their issue of disabled car badges. As an aid to the way in which OD is being used, as before we provide a case summary. This, we recall, is a situation already defined and explored in Chapter 11 in order to examine how Disabled Car Badge Charging (DCBC) could be introduced. In this case study, we wish to explore the possible cultural reaction to the intervention, and whether it is such that it should be and can be addressed.

12.4.1 Pre-analysis

Introduction

In Chapter 7 we saw that Government, under pressure from the European Union to reduce its budget deficit, coupled with its own interests in controlling public spending, made very sudden severe cuts in the public domain. For example, of the £28 billion it cut from this budget in 1992–3 at a stroke (about £20 billion greater than for each of the two previous years), about one quarter was scheduled for Local Authorities. It was also explained that in Liverpool the City Council was under pressure because of (Fig. 12.8):

1 the UK Government demands for continuing efficiency;

2 a budget deficit substantially caused by a failed Government experiment in the collection of the local taxes.

Case summary

Activity	Description
Weltanschauung	The Liverpool City Council has decided to introduce Disabled Car Badge Charging (DCBC). This is because of continuing pressure from the government for efficiency cuts, and a budget deficit in attempting to satisfy the social needs of the community. The culture does not admit such charging, and a cultural and organisational change will be required.
Inquirer's mission	To find an effective way of introducing service charging within the Social Services Division of the Liverpool City Council through DCBC. This involves changing the culture of the Division as the consequences of change on its core purposes are accommodated.
Methodology: OD	Mission to balance the forces of the Liverpool City Council within its Social Services Division – that is, proposing DCBC.
Methodological inquiry	The inquiry does this with the aim of introducing an effective DCBC system. Part of this process will explore the organisation's internal politics and distribution of power, its control processes and resistance to the change identified by the proposal.
Nature of examination	OD is being used in order to explore the control and power attributes of the situation, as well as the likelihood of resistance to change with the introduction of the proposed DCBC system. As a result, a strategy for dealing with the human complexities of the organisation has resulted.
Explanatory model	Through the examination of the organisational and social psychological context of the Division, change is explored through a target focus. A strategy of change is proposed.
Options selection	Options chosen enable an effective introduction of DCBC while organisational and personal features address control and power. Through the examination of the organisational and social psychological context of the Division, change is explored through a target focus. A strategy of change is proposed. Resistance to change is identified.

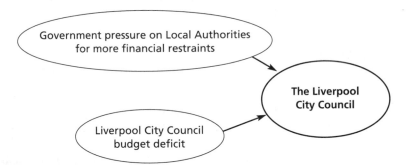

Fig. 12.8 Pressure from environment on the Authority

Since clearly no money was to be forthcoming from Government to cover the deficit, the least difficult solution for local government appeared to be to introduce a service charging policy. The first candidate for this is in the Social Services Division, and we refer to it as Disabled Car Badge Charging (DCBC). In Chapter 11 we briefly explored the technical aspects of a proposed DCBC operation, and the establishment of an effective form for the service charging unit. In addition, stakeholder support was broadly considered, in particular the generation of DCBC support from external stakeholders. In this chapter, our interests are more directed at the social and cultural system of the Social Services Division where the unit is to be set up.

The sociocultural background

The changes that are being forced on Local Authorities are particularly dramatic since as organisations they are quite inflexible. They are thus generally unable to respond adequately to such pressures from the environment. It is appropriate at this point to understand what we mean by this.

The Local Authority culture is broadly common with many other public and civil service organisations. While there will necessarily be local variations to the typical background that we shall highlight, and indeed there are some changes afoot that have in part been induced by actions of Government, we shall generate a scenario intended to generalise on such organisations. It should be realised that these generalisations do not in particular relate in all aspects to the Liverpool City Council Social Services Directorate, which is the centre of the case study. In particular, this Directorate would seem to have developed a more distributed organisation that is normal in such divisions.

Typically the social structure of such organisations is strongly hierarchical, and may not be seen as appropriate or systemically desirable for the tasks that need to be performed. Goals are frequently poorly defined or inappropriate, as is strategy, and there are often staff misunderstandings. There is little task ownership taken on by the staff in an organisation that is large and complex. Role relationships tend to be unclear or inappropriate, and leader's roles tend to be overloaded. There is often poor definition for the tasks that must be performed.

Processes tend to be highly bureaucratised, with a high degree of centralisation. Tasks are highly divisionalised so that those that require holistic integration may become problematic. There is little standardisation, recurrent problems matching the ill-defined goals to outcomes, and poorly defined procedures. This endangers the stability of the processes. There is also a problem with reporting procedures. Individual tasks tend to be either too easy or too difficult. Their purposes are often poorly defined, giving little guidance to implementing staff. This is particularly the case when tasks are directed down to Local Authorities by Government. There are often attitude problems with respect to work needs, and as a result work orientation is not achieved.

As a consequence, there is generally poor morale and a feeling of pressure. Along with this, there tends to be anxiety over performance, a distinct lack of awareness of changes in the environment, and consequently no response to such changes. Also, the working relationships between staff members tend to be poor. Goals are not well understood or readily accepted. There tends to be an inappropriate leadership style so that leaders are not trusted or respected. Group leaders may easily fall into conflict with superiors. There is also often failure to fulfil individual needs, resulting in frustration and unwillingness to consider change.

Mostly, the relationships between work groups are subject to chaos, as are their exchanges. No integrated task perspectives develop, and this lack of interconnectivity has a significant impact on the totality of the processes. This is aggravated by poor communications. This means that the quality of the interactions between groups is poor. Groups develop their own paradigms with distinct cognitive models and local cultures. The result is paradigm incommensurability so that groups can easily fall into conflict with each other. A consequence of this is a lack of effective cooperation between groups, limited war, a failure to confront differences in priorities and unresolved feelings.

Reorganisation

Two factors have influenced Local Authorities in recent years. One is the legislative demand that they pursue 'quality' through the principles of quality assurance (as discussed in Chapter 7), and the other is the introduction of Compulsory Competitive Tendering (CCT).

The Liverpool City Council, like other Local Authorities, was being directed towards a change in its mission. Its original mission was 'to exist for the benefit of, and be accountable to all the people of Liverpool in providing high quality services which meet people's needs and offer value for money'. This mission has now been qualified by the introduction of issues of quality that make it 'a provider of those services the Council is best placed to deliver, to ensure a quality service, an efficient organisation and services which reflect the needs of all groups; and a partner, advocate and enabler in relations to the community, the private sector and other agencies'.

The influence of these factors is identified in Table 12.19.

Table 12.19 The influence of quality and CCT

Factor	Influence
Quality	From 'providing a high quality service' the mission has been adjusted to 'ensure a quality service, an efficient organisation'. The enforceable requirement of efficiency and quality assurance has led to the need to change the Authority by defining for it a new structure and new processes that conform with quality assurance.
CCT	The 'provision' of services was constrained by 'best placed to deliver'. Curiously, it is Government that determines as an external global agency what this means (across the three stages of CCT). Through the introduction of CCT (see Chapter 11), many Local Authority departments are being hived off to an external environment, enabling them to compete in an apparently equal playing field with external enterprises.

It is interesting to consider whether these changes represent radical change where the core purposes alter, or a complete paradigm shift resulting in new belief systems and new metalanguage. Another indication of dramatic change occurs when the organisation's patterns of behaviour are seen to be sufficiently different from how they were previously for it to be classified as a different organisation. We shall suppose at this juncture that the Local Authorities have passed through radical, not dramatic, change.

With radical change being imposed on Liverpool City Council, there was a need to restructure. The major reorganisation of its departmental structure occurred in 1992. Previously there were 22 departments, and these were amalgamated into eight new directorates, plus a Central Policy Unit under the Assistant Chief Executive. The intention of providing a flatter structure was to break down the hierarchical/pyramid structure, so improving lines of communications and performance. There will likely be a consequence for the organisation culture that will have to be addressed.

As we have indicated previously, the budget for the Council's income is met by the residents in the city who use the services, and Government which makes contributions to the budget. This is discussed in Gardner (1993). The Government also has the power to constrain the budget. In Chapter 11, we explained why it is also keen to reduce its contribution and is therefore promoting more efficiency. The problem occurs that there will be a maximal efficiency from any organisational form at any given time, due to cognitive, cultural and technical limitations. A new form may exist that is more efficient, but shifting from one to the other can often require significant capital resourcing to develop a new infrastructure, provide training and facilitate cultural development.

The reorganisation that centres on quality assurance is a resource-intensive activity that involves fundamental changes to an organisation's system and culture. While there may be strengths in the new form of the organisation that develop through the partitioning of its processes, there are also weaknesses. These include (Magill, 1996) the realisation that:

- management skills are variable;
- personal rather than corporate agendas can be pursued;
- responsive rather than proactive approaches develop that reduce variety and limit possibilities;
- it is very costly on resources, and this is problematic in a highly constrained situation;
- there is an inherited workforce that requires training where previously the private sector has employed highly trained people, and this is problematic in a highly constrained situation;
- there is lack of motivation/incentive in comparison to the private sector.

12.4.2 Analysis

Step 1: Current and future state – exploration of situation

Our purpose here is to inquire into the internal consequences of the introduction of the DCBC system within the Social Services Division of the Liverpool City Council. The mission of the Social Services Division is to 'arrange, provide and regulate social services for the people of Liverpool, within the law'. It does this through the following four goals:

1 creating a care work and professional practice environment that promotes a high quality service, equality of opportunity, and political and public accountability;
2 making best use of money, people and other resources for and with the users of services to achieve the agreed objectives;
3 supporting best quality direct and public services;
4 giving clear messages to everybody about everything we do.

There is a view that argues that these goals are at odds with the idea of DCBC. For instance, with respect to the first goal the equality of opportunity can be question in this respect since services will be provided to those who can afford them, and not for those who need them most. With respect to the third goal, there is no guarantee that the quality of the service provided will be any better than before, although the service users will expect a high quality service if they are paying for it. They will also likely be less tolerant of minor mistakes or hold-ups.

Service charging, however, represents a major challenge to the culture of the City Council. Its custom and practice is that Council Tax is intended to pay for its services, and that no additional charges should therefore be seen to be necessary. The idea of charging for a deficit that is to no small degree caused by Government itself would seem to be asking its residents (many of whom are poor) to pay additional taxes to Government on top of their existing burdens.

Step 2: Define relevant system

The relevant system is seen to be as in Fig. 12.9. The stakeholders involved in this system are seen as:

- service users
- councillors
- agencies
- Area Resource Managers (ARM) (primary stakeholders)
- Deputy Area Resource Management (DARM) (primary stakeholders)
- Assistant ARM (AARM)
- Senior Clerical Officers Sc3 (SCO) (primary stakeholders)
- All staff in area offices and headquarters.

Since the DCBC is to be established within the Social Service Division of the Liverpool City Council, an exploration of both the Council and its Division (seen as the relevant system) will indicate a likelihood that similar attributes of the system will appear in the DCBC when it becomes established. These attributes are identified through the organisation matrix, as shown in Table 12.20.

Step 3: Contexts

Outer context

The Government is unwilling to help the Liverpool City Council out of its difficulties, and it is therefore attempting to find additional funds from within its own services in the community. The Local Authority is separated into a number of Divisions, one of which is the Social Service Division. Among the services performed is the issue of disabled car badges to those applicants classed as disabled, and one of the measures the Local Authority is taking is to introduce DCBC. The DCBC is to be established as an organisation that has a number of pressures upon it, as described in Fig. 12.10. Once in operation, these pressures will continue to affect it.

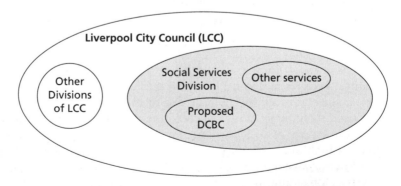

Fig. 12.9 System map for the Liverpool City Council and its Divisional Social Services
The shaded area represents the focus of interest.

Table 12.20 Organisation matrix for the Social Services Division of Liverpool City Council

System focus	Behavioural manifestation	Process characteristics	Structure seen as a system	Context, the setting
Organisation	Mixed morale issues, anxiety, suspicion, resistance to change, lack of awareness to change in environment. *Survey feedback from relevant sources.*	Lack of monitoring mechanisms. Bureaucratic, lack of standardisation. Decentralisation in progress. *Update new progress.*	Present systems and organisational structure inappropriate, computationally and technically complex. *Change structure.*	A political orientation. Uses basic technology. Distributed organisation. Inappropriate access points to organisation. *Change culture strategy, address buildings.*
Group	Poor understanding and acceptance of goals, setting up of new groups creates tension, leadership style addressed. *Team building, encourage participation.*	Task requirements poorly defined; inappropriate reporting procedures to management. *Improve consultation.*	Role relationships unclear, priorities not established. *Redesign work relationships and working groups.*	Insufficient resources, personality clashes. *Change technology, group composition, culture.*
Individual	Unwillingness to consider change; failure to fulfil individual needs. *Counselling, role analysis.*	Capacity for extra work; purpose of tasks poorly defined. *Job modification/enrichment.*	Inappropriate job description. *Job redefinition.*	Poor match of individual with job; poor selection or promotion. Poor incentives. *Personnel changes, improved training and education, recognition and remuneration alignment with objectives.*
Inter-relationship				
Intergroup	Lack of effective cooperation between area office and head office. Unresolved feelings. *Change cultural differences, encourage cooperation.*	Exchanges between groups subject to chaos. Inefficiencies exist. Required interactions difficult to achieve due. Poor communication. *Improve coordination and liaison.*	Lack of integrated task perspective. Poor communication structures. *Redefine responsibilities.*	Locally distinct cultures. *Exchange roles, cross-functional social overlay.*

Inner context

The inner context is ultimately concerned with the Nadler model, which stabilises the relationship between resistance to change, power and control. Part of the inner context relates to stakeholder commodities of power. These are listed in Table 12.21.

Inquiry into the inner contexts of the situation enable us to explore the possible strengths, weaknesses, opportunities and threats (SWOT) that the DCBC implementation is likely to induce. These are presented in Table 12.22.

A more compact way of presenting such perceptions is through a force field diagram, which can provide a comparison of attractive future opportunities against the current system restraints of the Social Services Division. This is shown in Fig. 12.11.

The power relationships between the stakeholders must be understood before any targets for change can be identified. These relationships are identified in the power diagram of Fig. 12.12. Here, the stakeholders internal and external to the Social Services Division are differentiated.

Note: Strength of line indicates strength of influence

Fig. 12.10 Pressures on DCBC that must be balanced

Table 12.21 Stakeholder commodities of power

Stakeholders	Power commodity
Service users	Complaint, media support
Agencies	Complaint; exceptionally: ministerial lobby
Councillors	Public (elected) authority
Area Resource Managers (ARM)	Role-based administrative authority
Deputy Area Resource Management (DARM)	Role-based administrative authority
Assistant ARM (AARM)	Role-based administrative authority
Senior Clerical Officers Sc3 (SCO)	Role-based administrative authority
All staff in area offices and headquarters	Formal and/or informal resistance

Table 12.22 SWOT analysis for implementation of DCBC

Analysis	Outcomes
Strengths	In-house training facilities developed
	Willingness by most to go forward
Weaknesses	Lack of communication policy
	Outdated procedures
	Inappropriate structures
	Inadequate technology
	Low level of involvement with stakeholders
Opportunities	Management/employee relations can be developed
	New (improved) structures can be defined
	Consultation can be improved
	Motivation can be improved
Threats	Resistance from staff likely
	Budget constraints exist
	Perceived likelihood of additional workload

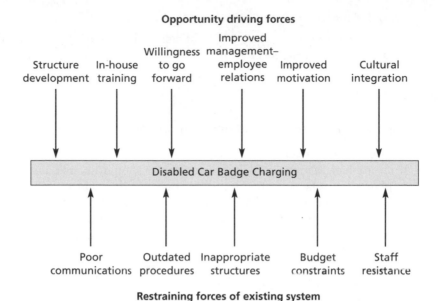

Fig. 12.11 Force field diagram showing pressures within the Social Services Division

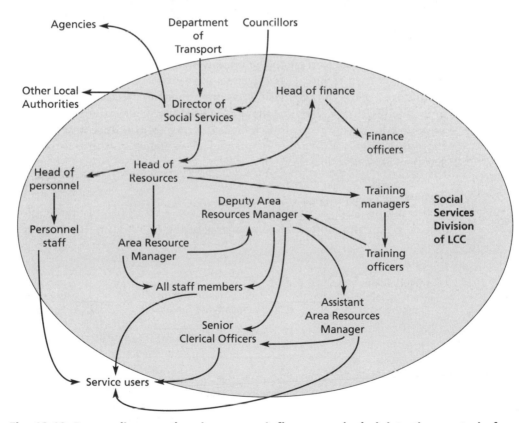

Fig. 12.12 Power diagram showing power influence and administrative control of one role over another

Step 4: Control action

Action process by inquirer for confirmation for participation and relevant system through stakeholder consultation.

12.4.3 Synthesis

Step 5: Identify targets and design models

Control and effectiveness

If an implementation of DCBC is to occur it should be effective and efficient. Effective implantation relates to the ability to satisfactorily perform its purpose (raising funds). Efficiency relates to the ability for it to operate with a minimum of resources.

Let us examine control for a DCBC implementation in terms of a control loop. In order for control to occur, two requirements exist. The first is that criteria exist against which outputs can be compared. The criteria are determined cognitively, and what constitutes acceptable criteria is culturally determined. The second requirement is that monitored outputs must be capable of being evaluated in some way, either quantitatively or qualitatively. The evaluation must be comparable to the cognitive criteria. The result of such a comparison can provide an evaluation of the effectiveness and efficiency of the process (Fig. 12.13). Examples of effectiveness were given in Table 12.9.

For effective DCBC implementation, the change process that we are interested in loosens the internal constraints of DCBC without interfering with the mission of the Division or its interrelationships with other divisions.

It is appropriate to refer to the organisation matrix for an exploration of the criteria that can be used to judge effectiveness in the case of the Social Services Division. The qualitative aspects of the Division are important for effectiveness. However, it should be embedded within a Division that recognises the values of an effective form, and this undoubtedly means a cultural change. In order to introduce an effective form requires that we account for a variety of changes, as explained in the multiple cause diagram in Fig. 12.14.

Targets

Following the lead of the organisation matrix, we can identify targets for the organisational, group and individual components of the organisation that must be addressed if

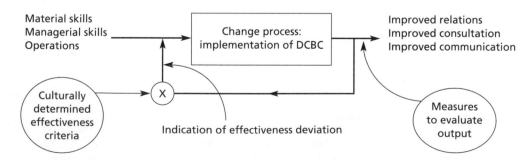

Fig. 12.13 Control loop showing a way of identifying effectiveness

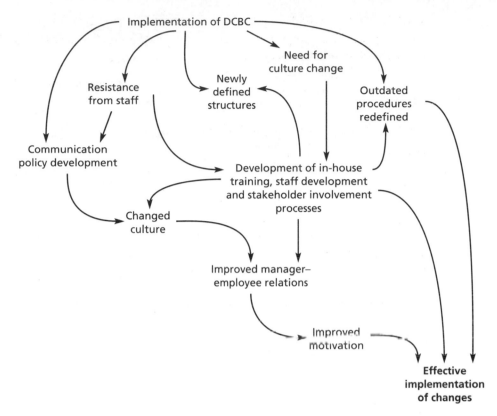

Fig. 12.14 Multiple cause diagram indicating the requirements of effectiveness

an effective implementation of DCBC is to occur. After discussing the needs of the system, a number of targets were identified. These are shown in a target focus map in Fig. 12.15.

Institutional deregularisation

If cultural change is to occur, then its formalised patterns of behaviour must be interrupted. That is, its institutionalised processes must first be deregularised, as explained through the Schein classification of Lewin's work (Table 12.1). Thus, for instance, we will need to include consideration of:

- change needed for preset goals or ideas;
- psychological safety needs to be addressed in setting solid structures and job enrichment;
- effective management needs to be balanced with psychological safety.

This can occur through the *change team*. It will establish systems to provide relief, enable learning experience, reduce anxiety and increase motivation. It will also introduce new standards, and key achievements will be addressed within adequate timescales. Staff should be able to fit to the culture of the learning system and adapt to new patterns of behaviour. Service users should be included in a new organisational culture, and standards should be achieved through consultation. There should be a perception of involvement.

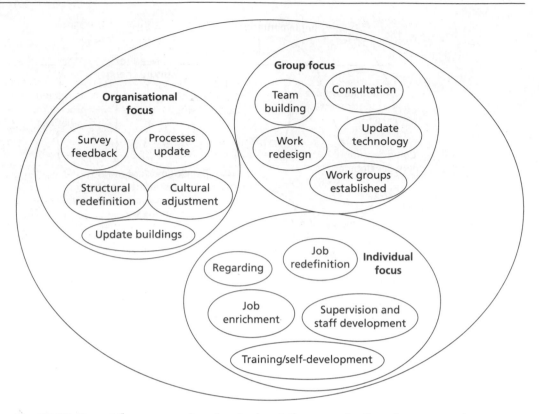

Fig. 12.15 Target focus map showing tasks at the organisational, group and individual focuses

Resistance to change

A model to deal with resistance to change is shown in Table 12.23.

Consulting with stakeholders will obtain some understanding of their felt needs, and enables effectiveness criteria to be chosen that can be used to monitor the implementation.

12.4.4 Choice

Step 6: Evaluation and selection of models

In Table 12.23 we deal with the Nadler attributes of resistance to change, control and power. In Table 12.24 we explain the action steps necessary to deal with the Nadler attributes.

In Table 12.25 we identify the strategy of change being proposed. It derives from the examination above, and considers changes that are required with respect to communications policy, stakeholder morale, consultation techniques, employee/managerial relations, organisational form, new technology, quality service and accountability, and working relationships across boundaries.

Step 7: Change and development

Since this programme is hypothetical and instituted by a working party not empowered to undertake change, no change and development activities have occurred. If change is to occur in the Social Services Division of the LCC, then it must address both psycholog-

Table 12.23 Explanation of how to deal with resistance to change

Characteristic of resistance	Dealing with resistance
Consultation and communication	Justify change to stakeholders. Generate valid information. Letters to service users and agencies indicating new terms. Implement marketing strategy involving mass media.
Participation and involvement	Implementation team to involve stakeholders. Provide free informed choice for participation. More emphasis on participation with service users and staff involvement in transition.
Negotiation and agreement	Create stakeholder commitment to choice of change. Power groups to resist change include other staff members and senior clerical officers. Regrading is to be negotiated and agreed tasks defined. Negotiation with working party in relation to management.
Explicit and implicit coercion	Timescales defined and adhered to. Ensure that management is in agreement with all that is involved. Working practices are defined.
Facilitation and support	Cultural change addressed. Retraining. Supervision and staff development provision. Communication policy to address role analysis. Structures set up to facilitate support mechanisms.
Re-educate to manage and accept change	Retraining to occur in relation to awareness of issues. Generate new culture.

Table 12.24 Examination of power, control and possible resistance to change

Attribute	Need	Action
Resistance	Motivate change	1 Gain support from management 2 Assure support from key players 3 Develop staff care and communication policy 4 Consultation with all involved 5 Regrading and job descriptions in place 6 New skills/training development
Control	Manage the transition	7 Present dissatisfaction addressed 8 Encourage participation in change 9 Recognition of positive behaviour 10 Time allowance to adjust
Power	Shape the political dynamics of change	11 Resourcing seminars to continue giving clear image of future 12 Mission statements addressed 13 Build in feedback mechanisms 14 Structures in place for transition

ical and organisational grounds. After deregularising its institutionalised processes, new processes must be regularised through the change and development.

This analysis would now be handed over to the change team for it to explore the recommended changes and their implementation for work processes and resourcing.

A reflection on the actual outcome

The implementation of DCBC occurred without the benefit of this study, which was an independent, unauthorised and parallel project. It will therefore be interesting to identify the outcome of the simple technical implementation of the change that occurred, and we base this report substantially on Magill (1996, personal communication).

Table 12.25 Strategy for change

Targets	Stakeholder involvement	Role responsibility	Decision making channels
Survey/feedback from relevant sources	Councillors, service users, head of resources, all staff, management	Relay information to constituents, complete survey, monitor progress, ensure quality service, collate information.	Councillors to head of resources to management to all staff
Update new processes	Head of resources, management, staff	Delegate to management – redefine budget and allocations, monitoring – consult staff and service users; similarly undertake participation and feedback.	Head of resources to management to all staff to service users to management
Change structures/ processes	Director, head of resources, management, service users	Consultation with all staff involved; develop proposed structures in line with resource allocation; participate and develop new skills	Head or resources to management to all staff
Adaptability of buildings and locations addressed	Director, head of resources, management, service users	Budget allocation; physical availability of access to users; working alongside users; feedback and participation	Director to head of resources to management to service users to head of resources
Supervision/ team building	Management, all staff	Community policy addressed – adopt appropriate leadership style; participate in community policy	All staff to management
Improve consultation	Councillors, director, head of resources, management, all staff, service users	Provide relevant information and accept feedback; visit to area offices and accept feedback and action; consult in area offices	As a network: councillors, director, head of resources, management, all staff, service users
Technology needs	Head of resources, management, all staff	Budget allocation and equipment defined; set up training programmes and consult with staff of new styles; participate in training and development of new skills	Director to head of resources to management to all staff
Job modification and enrichment	Head of resources, management	Attend committee cycle; consult with personnel management; consult with personnel/all staff to redefine job description; discuss new roles and accept new terms	Director to head of resources to management to senior clerical officers
Improved training	Head of resources, management, senior clerical officers, all staff	Consult with management and training section and produce costings; identify training needs and consult with all staff; participate in training	Head of resources to management to both senior clerical officers and all staff

Before DCBC, the same structure had been in place for about four years. A new pattern of behaviour had by this time been regularised. The introduction of DCBC required a new organisational form to enable the purposes of the service to be achieved. Thus, role structures were created, and money and badge handling processes were instituted. Now, the relevant staff needed recognition for their extra responsibility. However, the existing structures did not accommodate these provisions. The culture prior to the charges as far as the organisation was concerned was 'something for nothing'. That is, personnel were not used to having a set charge for individual services. This situation has little to do with the fact that other Councils have always had a culture for charging for these services. The service users who had to pay the charges had never been used to this, so there was apprehension on management's part about how much each badge would be. In Sefton the charge was set at £5 per badge. Management in Liverpool Social Services set it as £2 per badge.

Implementation of DCBC has had a significant impact on the organisation. At the individual level there were concerns about animosity from other members of staff as to why specific individuals had been targeted for regrading and not others. There was also a doubt from individuals with the new roles about whether they had the capacity to cope with the additional demands being placed on them. A working party group was set up to deal with all aspects of the new structures, individual views, etc.

The impact of the new proposals have therefore been significant, not only on the individuals carrying out the new roles, but on the organisation and other groups involved (i.e. service users and other colleagues). Measures had to be taken to ensure that the budget provision allowed for the regrading of nine staff across the city (one within each office), which was ironic because the reason for the introduction of the charges was to alleviate pressures on the budget.

The change has now been institutionally regularised, and the form has apparently been bedded in to the overall system. It has also acted as a pilot for a much larger change about to come into being – domiciliary care charging, due to be introduced in October 1996. Again, there are implications for organisational form and culture, in particular because it will happen on a much larger scale than DCBC because of the size of this service.

REFERENCES

Argyris, C. (1970) *Intervention Theory and Method*. Reading, MA: Addison-Wesley.

Beckhard, R. (1989) 'A model for the executive management of transformational change'. In *The 1989 Annual: Developing human resources*. University Associates.

Beer, S. (1979) *The Heart of the Enterprise*. New York: Wiley.

Bolman, L.G. and Deal, T. (1991) *Reframing Organisations: Artistry, choice, and leadership*. San Francisco, CA: Jossey-Bass.

Burnes, B. (1992) *Managing Change*. London: Pitman.

Cameron, K. (1984) 'The effectiveness of ineffectiveness', *Research in Organisational Behaviour*, 6, 235–85.

Campbell, D. (1977) 'On the nature of organisational effectiveness'. In Goodman, P. and Pennings, J. (eds) *New Perspectives on Organisational Effectiveness*. San Francisco, CA: Jossey-Bass, pp. 13–55.

Checkland, P. and Scholes, J. (1990) *Soft Systems Methodology in Action*. New York: Wiley.

Coghlan, D. (1993) 'In defence of process consultation'. In Mabey, C. and Mayon-White, B. (eds) *Managing Change*. London: Paul Chapman.

Connolly, E. and Deutch, S. (1980) 'Organisational effectiveness: a multi-consistency approach', *Academy of Management Review*, 5, 211–18.

Gardner, D. (1993) 'Local government'. In Wilson, J. and Hinton, P. (eds) *Public Services and the 1990s.* Sevenoaks: Tudor Business Publishing, pp. 171–89.

Goodman, P.S. and Pennings, J. (1980) 'Critical issues in assessing organisational effectiveness'. In Lawler, E., Nadler, D.A. and Cammann, C. (eds) *Organisational Assessment.* New York: Wiley, pp. 185–215.

Harrison, I.H. (1994) *Diagnosing Organizations: Methods, models and processes*, 2nd edn. Thousand Oaks, CA: Sage.

Huse, E. and Cummings, T. (1985) *Organisational Development and Change.* St Paul, MN: West.

Jackson, M.C. (1992) *Systems Methodology for the Management Sciences.* New York: Plenum Press.

Kotter, J.K. and Schlesinger, L.A. (1979) 'Choosing strategies for change'. *Harvard Business Review,* March/April.

Lewin, K. (1947) 'Frontiers of group dynamics', *Human Relations,* 1, 5–41.

Mabey, C. (1986) *Managing Change*, Open Business School Module for MBA. Milton Keynes: Open University Business School.

Mabey, C. (1995) *Managing Development and Change.* Open Business School course P751. Milton Keynes: Open University Business School.

Mabey, C. (1995a) 'Managing strategic change successfully', *Business, Growth and Profitability,* 1(4), 353–62.

Magill, N. (1996) 'The impact of quality in Local Authorities'. An assignment for the second year management module in the part-time degree in Public Administration, Liverpool John Moores University.

Mayon-White, B. (ed.) (1986) *Planning and Managing Change.* London: Harper & Row.

Mitchell, D. (ed.) (1968) *A Dictionary of Sociology.* London: Routledge & Kegan Paul.

Morgan, G. (1986) *Images of Organisations.* Newbury Park, CA: Sage.

Nadler, D.A. (1993) 'Concepts for the management of organisational change'. In Mayon-White, B. (ed.) *Planning and Managing Change.* London: Harper & Row.

Nadler, D.A. and Tushman, M.L. (1977) *Feedback and Organisation Development: Using data based on methods.* Reading, MA: Addison-Wesley.

Nadler, D.A. and Tushman, H.L. (1979) 'A congruence model for diagnosing organisational behaviour'. In Kolb, D., Rubin, I. and McIntyre, J. (eds) *Organisational Psychology: A Book of Readings,* 3rd edn. Englewood Cliffs, NJ: Prentice Hall.

Pettigrew, A. (ed.) (1988) *The Management of Strategic Change.* Oxford: Blackwell.

Price, C. and Murphy, E. (1993) 'Organisation development in British Telecom'. In Mabey, C. and Mayon-White, B. (eds) *Managing Change.* London: Paul Chapman.

Pritchard, W. (1993) 'What's new in organisational development'. In Mayon-White, B. (ed.) *Planning and Managing Change.* London: Harper & Row.

Pugh, D. (1993) 'Understanding, managing organisational change'. In Mabey, C. and Mayon-White, B. (eds) *Managing Change.* London: Paul Chapman, pp. 109–12.

Quinn, J. B. (1986) 'Managing strategic change'. In Mayon-White, B. (ed.) *Planning and Managing Change.* London: Harper & Row, pp. 67–6.

Rubin, I. (1988) 'Increasing self-acceptance: a means of reducing prejudices', *Journal of Personality and Social Psychology,* 5, 233–8.

Schein, E.H. (1970) *Organisational Psychology.* Englewood Cliffs, NJ: Prentice Hall.

Schein, E.H. (1996) 'Kurt Lewin's change theory in the field and in the classroom: notes toward a model of managed learning', *Systems Practice,* 9(1), 27–47.

Tushman, M. L. (1977) 'A political approach to organisations; a review and rationale', *Academy of Management Review,* 2, 206–16.

Watson, G. (1969) 'Resistance to Change'. In Bennis, W.G., Benne, K.F. and Chin, R. (eds) *The Planning of Change.* New York: Holt, Reinhart & Winston.

Weisbord, M.R. and Janoff, S. (1996) 'Future search: finding common ground in organisations and communities', *Systems Practice,* 9(1), 71–84.

Wheelan, S.A. (1996) 'An initial exploration of the relevance of complexity theory to group research and practice', *Systems Practice,* 9(1), 49–70.

Zaltman, G. and Duncan, R. (1977) *Strategies for Planned Change.* New York: Wiley.

CHAPTER 13

Soft systems methodology

OVERVIEW

Soft systems methodology is a methodology for inquiry that is concerned with unstructured and uncertain situations. Like all methodologies, it creates dynamic methods through the control processes that it operates. Its dynamic aspect enables learning to occur that can manifest SSM as an infinite variety of methods. The broad conceptualisation that it adopts to deal with complexity is that change problem situations have to be addressed through an exploration of both the culture and the social structure of the organisation involved in the situation.

13.1 Introduction

Gwilym Jenkins was one of those disenchanted with hard systems approaches because of their inability to tackle complex situations. An interest was *action research*, which he pursued within the postgraduate Department of Systems Engineering at Lancaster University that he started in the mid-1960s. Rather than differentiating theoretical research from practical situations, which was the typical approach of that time, it specified an interactive mode of behaviour, so that theory and practice were *balanced*. 'Action research requires involvement in a problem situation, and a readiness to use the experience itself as a research object about which lessons can be learned by conscious reflection' (Checkland and Scholes, 1990, p. 16). This means that the *form of inquiry* (defined by the structure and processes of the methodology that an inquirer applies to a situation as a set of procedures), or methods, must be adaptable to both different situations and inquirers.

The arrival of Peter Checkland from industry established a team that was able to look more carefully at where hard systems approaches were failing. These were the less-well-defined problems that peppered management situations. Checkland established a reputation that arose from his work in developing the particular approach referred to as soft systems methodology (SSM), and with it some epistemology that has today become part of what we shall refer to as the soft systems paradigm. The appearance of SSM in the mid-1970s represented a development of traditional inquiry consistent with the ideas of scientific inquiry typified by the work of Popper (1972). The form of SSM that initially appeared in the early 1980s in Checkland (1981) was what we may refer to as the *simple mode* in which the form of inquiry does not change.

During the 1980s, however, the *dynamic mode* of SSM arose, where the methods change according to the situation and the inquirer. This is due in principle to the use of controls that confirm or adjust the progress of the inquiry as it develops.

13.2 The paradigm of soft systems methodology

Checkland, the main developer and promoter of SSM, has produced a number of ideas that have been integrated into the domain of soft systems, and as such he may be considered to have been a significant influence in the field of systems within the past two decades. Much of the theory that lies at the bottom of his methodology has already been explored earlier in this book, and so a minimalist theoretical approach will be taken here.

13.2.1 Belief underlying the paradigm

SSM promotes itself as a systemic methodology, and its viewholders argue that its penchant is to establish a systemic view of the inquiry process rather than one of the world. It sees systems as relating to complex wholes that may be described in terms of emergent properties. The systems of interest involve purposeful activity, and these maintain their existence by *surviving*. Such a system can survive in a changing environment if it has processes of communication and control. This enables it to adapt in response to shocks from the environment. Together, these ideas generate the image or metaphor of the adaptive whole that can survive in a changing environment.

When SSM addresses a problem situation this is defined in terms of a user (possibly a participant) who will assume that there are some people in definable roles, some of whom 'have a concern for some aspects of their world seen to be problematical. They will share common concepts which enable issues to be explored; they will have some different perceptions of the world; and they will in principle remain, intellectually, free agents' (Checkland and Davies, 1986, p. 111). The use of SSM involves organised systemic thinking about the problem situation to enable purposeful action to occur. This represents an intervention that operates within and is part of social reality. Social reality is seen as a process in which participants are continually in renegotiation with others with respect to perceptions and world views.

World views are referred to as weltanschauung. This concept is central to SSM in more ways than one. Weltanschauung is seen to cover the idea of wide-scale images of the world, as well as the small-scale images that make sense of a situation, which Dilthy referred to as *weltanschauungslehre* (*see* Checkland and Davies, 1986).

Part of SSM is to distinguish between three classes of reality. These are (a) the real world, (b) systems thinking about the real world and (c) social reality. In order to distinguish between these different distinct classes, it is perceived that three types of weltanschauung are needed. These are referred to as W_1, W_2 and W_3. The first of these is the perception that helps build a system model. W_2 and W_3, however, relate directly to the real-world situation being examined. W_3 are the perceptions that hold in the real world about the situation. W_2 is concerned with the conceptualisations that make certain purposeful activities appear relevant to the situation that W_3 will have to make sense of. Thus, W_2 is similar to W_3, but is narrower in scope, and confined to the problem situation.

SSM is intended to deal with messy, ill-structured problem situations which are based on a goals-seeking model of human behaviour, and the notion that systems should be engineered to meet explicit objectives (Checkland and Davis, 1986, p. 109). It is a structured systemic methodology because 'the rich problematic pageant of human affairs can be improved by some structured thinking ... [and] can be developed around systems ideas' (p. 275). It should be perceived as 'a connected set of entities, not activities' (p. 291). It is not designed to solve problems, but to examine and intervene as appropriate in situations. This is because 'there are no problems, only problem situations' (p. 284).

The basic conceptual form of SSM is a linear process (Fig. 13.1), which:

1 connects the real world with *systemic images* of the real world called *relevant systems*;
2 models are created intended to represent an intervention into the situation;
3 the models are compared to the real-world situation through control loops;
4 a successful comparison according to criteria defined by the inquirer generates action to improve the situation;
5 the action is applied to the real-world situation of concern as an intervention;
6 an unsuccessful comparison enables the models to be reformulated.

SSM is concerned with purposeful action (Checkland, 1995), and its purposes are to produce simple models of pure purposeful systems. In real situations, autonomous individuals are seen to be free to establish their own constructions upon the purposefulness of action. These occur through the creation of models; each model created is seen as a 'pure weltanschauung'. They are also seen as 'epistemological devices' to coherently interrogate the real situation. In so doing they are used to structure debate with people having a concern for the problem situation. The structuring is to compare the models to the real world, and debate is intended to seek an accommodation (not necessarily through consensus) to enable action to occur and improve the situation. This action must be seen to be desirable with respect to the comparison between the models and the real world, and culturally feasible. What culturally feasible means is also open to debate, which occurs through another cycle of Fig. 13.1. Debate is seen to be essential to provide understanding of the situation, and new choices of what are seen to be relevant human activity systems.

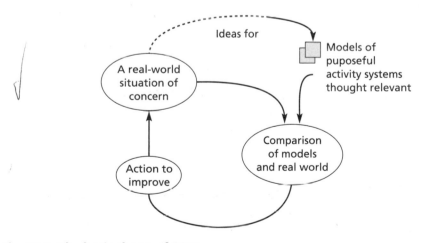

Fig. 13.1 The basic shape of SSM
(*Source*: Checkland and Scholes, 1995, p. 51)

317

The following question is now raised: can one – and if so, how does one – distinguish between what Checkland calls 'good' and 'bad' epistemological devices? The answer to this rests on two aspects. Firstly, it should be questioned whether the model is 'relevant', and secondly whether it is competently built. Checkland believes that it is the learning process that is responsible for determining this, and that the determination of whether a model is relevant occurs through a process of learning by cycling around the loop in Fig. 13.1. In creating models, Checkland used ideas from Churchman (1971) and Jenkins (1969), and assigned to models such attributes as systemic mission or purpose, measures of performance, resources and decision making procedures, boundary and a guarantee of continuity.

Fundamental to SSM is the idea that it should be possible to change the form of inquiry, thus enabling new methods to arise. This is different from many methodologies – and we have in mind those that derive from hard systems thinking – which consider learning not in respect of the methodology, but rather in respect of building 'better' models; that is, models that can optimally or better conform to a set of explicitly defined criteria. SSM philosophy derives from the principles of *action research*, which include:

1 the form of inquiry will provide insights concerning the perceived problems, which will lead to practical help in the situation;

2 experiences using the form of inquiry will enable it to be gradually improved.

The paradigm of SSM sees the relationship between the methodology and the real world in the way depicted in Fig. 13.2. Here, the real world may be viewed systemically, even though it may not be systemic.

13.2.2 The cognitive model of soft systems methodology

From time to time organisations experience problem situations. There is often an awareness by stakeholders that a problem situation exists, but how to deal with it is less than clear. At least as unclear is the need for an appreciation of *who* is to deal with it. Thus, the need for inquiring methodologies exists because problem situations that occur have not been clearly identified. Methodologies can help structure an unstructured problem, and indicate possible interventions that can 'improve' it.

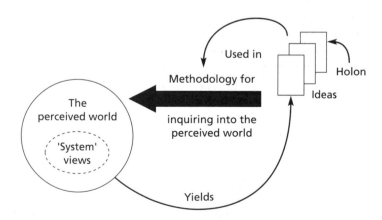

Fig. 13.2 A belief in SSM about the relationship between methodology and the real world
(*Source*: Checkland and Scholes, 1990, p. 23)

What defines 'improve' is determined by the intended improvers of the situation. These are one or more individuals who are motivated to do so. They may constitute the inquirer, or may simply work together in a collaborative way with an inquirer. Consequently, SSM must be seen as a collaborative approach to inquiry, so that sensible inquirers will involve other people in the inquiry process.

SSM supposes that in all human activity systems there are two streams of inquiry:

1 the stream of logical inquiry

2 the stream of cultural inquiry.

13.2.3 The stream of logical inquiry

The stream of logical inquiry defines the methodological process that an inquirer should take. In SSM, in order to make an inquiry an inquirer will have to build an image of the real-world situation creating the *relevant systems* that are to be defined. A *relevant system* derives from a viewpoint (Patching, 1990, p. 263) or weltanschauung that shows it to be relevant to an inquirer of the situation.

The logical stream of inquiry is responsible for:

1 exploring reality

2 creating relevant systems

3 creating the models to be built that can operate as mechanisms of improvement.

These each exist across two domains: the real world and the systems world. Exploring reality is a real-world phenomenon, the intention of which is to:

- identify the nature of the problem situation;
- express clearly the nature of the problem situation.

Once a situation is deemed to be problematic, it must also be determined that it can be changed in a beneficial way. The situation is expressed clearly through graphical illustrations that are called rich pictures. In order to create these pictures, data must be collected about the situation, a view taken and the rich pictures generated. It should be noted that these pictures may always be subject to modification in the future.

The creation of relevant systems occurs by moving into the systems world. The relevant systems that can be defined are of two generic types: the *primary task* system and the *issue*-based system. 'The distinction between primary tasks and issues based relevant systems is not sharp or absolute, rather these are ends of a spectrum' (Checkland and Scholes, 1990, p. 32). We can thus conceive of the task/issue relevant systems as a continuum with issue and task poles.

Primary task systems are those systems in which there is a visible real-world purposeful action that could be reflected in a 'notional human activity system whose boundary would coincide with the real world manifestation' (Checkland and Scholes, 1990, p. 31). 'They are those immediately related to the processes for which an organisation exists' (Harry, 1992, p. 268). At the extreme of the task/issue continuum, primary task systems project on to institutionalised arrangements.

Issues, however, tend to be less direct, and relate to the subsidiary activities that occur in a situation. They are 'relevant to mental processes not embodied in formalised real world arrangements' (Checkland and Scholes, 1990, p. 32). 'Issue based themes relate to the concerns which are generated in wider activities surrounding the primary task' (Harry, 1992, p. 267), and relate to the *identifiable activities and processes* that are required to carry out the core purposes of a situation.

Having defined relevant systems, it is necessary to name them. The name is referred to as a *root definition*, because it is intended to express an ontological relationship to the object of perception that is being modelled. It thus expresses the core purpose of the purposeful activity system that is concerned with transforming expected inputs into intended outputs. Thus, the following intentions now exist:

- create a root definition of the situation
- develop conceptual models that address the situation.

The root definition is a systems representation of the situation indicated within the rich pictures. It defines the purposes that will lead onto the creation of a set of possible intervention strategies that are referred to as the conceptual models. Root definitions derive in SSM from:

C customers – the victims or beneficiaries of a transformation T;
A actors – those who would do T;
T transformation process – the conversion of input to output;
W weltanschauung – the world view which makes this T meaningful in this context;
O owner(s) – those who could stop T;
E environmental constraints – elements outside the system, which are taken as given.

To make the transformation process meaningful it must be paired to weltanschauung. 'For any relevant purposeful activity there will always be a number of different transformations by means of which it can be expressed, these deriving from different interpretations of its purpose' (Checkland and Scholes, 1990, p. 35).

Exploring weltanschauungen is also referred to as 'finding out'. It uses such techniques as interviewing and reading, and links to the cultural stream of inquiry that will be considered shortly.

Root definitions are based on purposeful holons called human activity systems. Thus, a holon is a systems representation of a real situation. The model that is constructed for this is intended to address the problems within the holon. The modelling process involves assembling and structuring the minimum necessary activities that are needed to enable the transformation process, having explored CATWOE.

The models will entail within them the methods by which a perceived situation can be improved. Back now in the real world, these models will be validated, confirmed as desirable and feasible intervention strategies, and then implemented. Validating the models is a process of comparing them with reality. The model itself will be used to define a framework of validating inquiry, and will work through a process of stakeholder debate. Four ways of undertaking this comparative process (Checkland, 1980) are:

1 informal discussion

2 formal questioning

3 scenario writing based on 'operating' (or simulating) the models

4 trying to model the real world in the same structure as the conceptual model.

The formal questioning option (2) tends to be the most common. What we refer to as the simulation option (3) is the second most common, and may consist of a conceptual or paper-based 'dry run' of the model to see the results that emerge. As a result of this a written scenario is produced. Answering questions begins a process of debate that is facilitated and guided by the inquirer. It may occur at an individual or a group focus level.

While situations are perceived to be improved in SSM, the models that can represent an intervention strategy are not intended to be 'improved'. This is because such a conception would suggest that a best or better model may exist. This approach is representative of an optimisation philosophy, which supposes that it is often possible to identify criteria that enable a best solution to a problem to be found. However, the difficulty comes when we are examining not problems but problem situations that are unbounded and messy, and that may vary in definition according to the weltanschauung of an inquirer. Because *improving a situation* very much involves weltanschauungen, what constitutes 'better' can vary from individual to individual, many of whom may be stakeholders in the situation. Rather, it is intended that an accommodation between different interests should occur in the situation that can be construed as constituting an improvement to the initial problem situation.

Achieving this improvement is not a concern of the logical stream of inquiry, however. It entails an appreciation of the cultural aspects of the organisation.

The logical stream of inquiry is not a linear process, however. Rather it is dynamic, involving switching non-sequentially from one step of the methodology to another to confirm evaluations and proposals.

13.2.4 The stream of cultural inquiry

It is important to find out about the culture of the organisation with which problem situations are associated. This is not restricted to an initial inquiry into a situation. Rather it is an important and recurrent process, just as important as the logical stream of inquiry. Checkland has developed a tool that contributes to the expression of the culture of a situation, referred to as the rich picture. It represents a set of entities identified to be of interest in a situation, and their relationships. In the sense that it represents a structural picture of the situation, it shows its social dimension, which must be a contributory aspect to culture.

Initial structuring of the situation

The nature of the situation is initially identified through rich pictures in an attempt to determine its structure and context. Initial identification of relationships occurs, value judgements are made, and a 'feel' of the situation develops. A clarification that the many relationships preclude instant solutions occurs. Rich pictures represent a compact way of expressing relationships.

Social system analysis

Social system analysis is concerned with roles and interactions within the situation. It is through this that the form of the social 'system' of the situation is identified, determining structures and management processes.

'The first model built in SSM is often a model of the structured set of activities which the problem solver(s) hope to turn into a real world action in doing the study' (Checkland and Scholes, 1990, p. 48). Inquirers are part of the situation that is to be studied, and should be seen as such by taking role positions in the situation. Any situation is seen to involve three roles:

1 the *client* – the person or persons who caused an inquiry to take place;

2 the *problem owner* – who may or may not be the client, but who wishes to do something about the situation of interest;

3 the *problem solver* – who must decide who to take as possible problem owners.

Social analysis was originally referred to by Checkland and Scholes as role analysis, but is now referred to as *analysis 1*. It lists the client(s) and the possible problem owners. Rich pictures are repeatedly drawn or amended within an SSM inquiry. This is in order to ensure that any changes in the roles of problem solver and owner are acknowledged.

The cultural dimension

The social and cultural aspect of the inquiry is also prevalent. A model that explores the structural definition of the sociocultural dimension derives from the work of Vickers (1965) referred to as 'an appreciative system'. Checkland and Casar (1986) provided a simpler version. It *assumes* that a social system is in continual change as the three entities, *roles*, *norms* and *values*, interact, as shown in Fig. 13.3.

A *role* is a social position recognised as significant by people in the problem situation. It may be institutionally defined (e.g. a manager or minister) or behaviourally defined, enabling it to be used, for instance, as a metaphor to describe an individual (i.e. a 'comic' or 'just' person). A role has associated with it *norms*, and role performance will be determined by *values* held by stakeholders. Values are *beliefs* about what good and bad performance means in relation to a given role.

An adequate understanding of a social system will not in general be derived by asking direct questions. This is because replies will often be the 'official myths' of a situation. Rather, an *analysis 2* is required, which is conducted through such mechanisms as informal conversation, interviews and reading around.

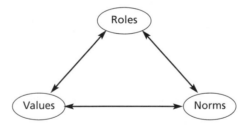

Fig. 13.3 Interactive relationship between roles, values and norms

The political dimension

Analysis 3 explores the political dimension of the situation being inquired into. Politics is taken to be 'a process by which differing interests reach accommodation' (Checkland and Scholes, 1990, p. 50), a view derived from the work, for instance, of Blondel (1978), Dahl (1970) or Crick (1962). The accommodation of interests is a political process, and rests on the dispositions of power. Thus, politics is seen as a power-related activity concerned with managing relations between different interests.

Analysis 3 is a political analysis that occurs by asking how power is expressed in a situation, and what its commodities are. Examples of commodities of power suggested by Checkland and Scholes are:

- formal (role-based) authority
- intellectual authority
- personal charisma
- participation in decision making bodies
- external reputation
- commanding access (or lack of access) to important information
- membership or non-membership of various committees or less formal groups
- the authority to write the minutes of meetings.

Questions may be put about these commodities, such as how, and through what mechanisms, they are:

- obtained
- used
- protected
- preserved
- passed on
- relinquished.

A summary of the way in which the cognitive space of SSM is explored is provided in Table 13.1.

Table 13.1 Summary of exploring the cognitive space of SSM

Dimension	Analysis	Purpose
Social structure/roles	1	Identifies client(s), possible problem owners, role of problem solver, organisational form through rich pictures within an SSM inquiry
Cultural dimension	2	Explores the relationships between social roles, behavioural norms and cultural values within an organisation
Political dimension	3	Explores the power relationships, the commodities through which power is represented and how these commodities are obtained

Desirable and feasible changes

A cultural stream of inquiry thus includes social and political affairs. Mutual reference between these streams occurs in order to check the relationship between the modelling process and perceived reality. The intention of the methodology is to seek *culturally feasible* intervention. This means that an intervention is consistent with the cultural and social norms, and is permissible through the political tensions of an organisation associated with the situation. An intervention should also be *systemically desirable*. This means that it should be appropriate to the organisation considered as a whole.

The possible implementation of changes will be determined by several relevant weltanschauungen. What constitutes implementation possibilities are thus *systemically desirable* and *culturally feasible* changes. Changes are systemically desirable if the relevant systems are perceived to be relevant, and they must be seen as culturally meaningful.

13.3 Propositions, identity and language of SSM

13.3.1 Propositions and rules

General propositions

1 The cultural stream of inquiry includes the social and political system of an organisation.

2 The social system is in continual change.

3 A social system reflects cultural aspects of an organisation, including myths and values.

4 A social system involves three independent entities (*roles*, *norms* and *values*), which interact.

5 A political system is concerned with power-related activity concerned with managing relations between different interests.

6 Power is expressed through a set of formal or informal commodities.

7 Changes in a complex situation should be *culturally feasible*.

8 A situation may be seen in terms of *relevant systems* (systems representations of the situation), which are defined through the weltanschauung of a problem solver.

9 Relevant systems are deduced through consultative processes with the stakeholders of the situation.

10 Intervention strategies should be seen as *systemically desirable* through consultation.

Constitutive rules of SSM

The following form the set of rules that constitute SSM (Checkland and Scholes, 1990, p. 286).

1 Structured thinking:
   a SSM focuses on real-world situations;
   b SSM aims to bring about improvements in a situation.

2 Explicit epistemology:
   a SSM must be expressed in terms of the epistemology which defines its paradigm;
   b the language of SSM does not have to be used;
   c whatever is done in SSM must be expressible in terms of its language regardless of the scope of study (making point b trivial).

3 Guidelines for SSM:
   a there is no automatic assumption that the real world is systemic;
   b if part of the real world is taken to be a system to be engineered, then that is done by conscious choice;
   c careful distinction is made between unreflected involvement in the everyday world, and conscious systems thinking about the real world;
   d the SSM user is always conscious of moving from one world to another, and will do so many times in using the approach;
   e in systems thinking phases holons are constructed;

   f holons are normally seen as human activity systems that embody emergent properties, layered structure, process, communications and control.

4 Relativity of SSM:

   a SSM can be used in different ways in different situations;

   b SSM will be interpreted differently by each user;

   c use of SSM is characterised by conscious thought about how to adapt it to a particular situation.

5 SSM as methodology:

   a every use of SSM will potentially hold methodological lessons additional to those about the situation of concern;

   b methodological lessons may include SSM's framework of ideas, processes and way of use;

   c potential lessons will always be there, awaiting extraction by conscious reflection on the experience of use.

Systems thinking propositions

A summary of the systems thinking that SSM adheres to (Checkland and Scholes, 1990, p. 25) adopts the following systems propositions.

1 Systems thinking takes seriously the idea of a whole entity which may exhibit properties as a single whole ('emergent properties'), properties which have no meaning in terms of the parts of the whole.

2 To do systems is to set some constructed or system models (seen as abstract wholes) against the perceived real world in order to learn about it. The purpose of doing this may range from engineering some part of the world perceived as a system, to seeking insight or illumination.

3 Within systems thinking there are two complementary traditions. The 'hard' tradition takes the world as being systemic; the 'soft' tradition creates the process of inquiry as a system.

4 SSM is a systemic process of inquiry that also happens to make use of systems models. It thus subsumes the hard approach, which is a special case of it, one arising when there is local agreement on some system to be engineered.

5 To make the above clear it would be better to use the word 'holon' for the constructed wholes, conceding the word 'system' to everyday language and not trying to use it as a general term.

6 SSM uses a particular kind of holon, namely a so-called 'human activity system'. This is a set of activities so connected as to make a purposeful whole, constructed to meet the requirements of the core image (emergent properties, layered structure, process of communications and control).

7 In examining real-world situations characterised by purposeful action, there will never be only one relevant holon, given the human ability to interpret the world in different ways. It is necessary to create several models of human activity systems and to debate and learn their relevance to real life.

13.3.2 Generic nature

SSM is primarily intended for situations that are complex and messy. It is therefore directed at problem situations that are uncertain, ill structured and soft, and its basic philosophy has grown in order to address such situations. However, the proponents of its paradigm have the belief that SSM can also be applied to other simpler situations such as those that are perceived to be certain, structured and hard. In other words, the methodology can be tailored to suit the generic nature of the situation being inquired into.

13.3.3 The language

The language of SSM and its meaning is given in Table 13.2.

Table 13.2 Metalanguage and epistemological elements of SSM

Metaword	Meaning
Real world	The unfolding interactive flux of events and ideas experienced as everyday life.
Systems thinking	The world in which conscious reflections on the 'real world' using systems ideas take place.
Problem situation	A real-world situation in which there is a sense of unease, a feeling that things could be better than they are, or some perceived problem requiring attention.
Root definition	Concise verbal definitions expressing the nature of purposeful activity systems regarded as relevant to exploring the problem situation. A full root definition would take the form: do X by Y in order to achieve Z. It expresses the core purposes of purposeful activity systems. The root definition is a model that relates directly to a relevant system.
Relevant system	An inquirer's perception of the human activity system that is relevant to a problem situation. Any situation may have as many relevant systems views as perceived by an inquirer. Two kinds of relevant system are possible: primary task and issue-based.
Primary tasks	These relate to the identifiable activities and processes that are required to carry out the core purposes of a situation. They map on to institutionalised arrangements.
Issues	These relate to the subsidiary activities that occur in a situation. They are relevant to mental processes not embodied in formalised real-world situations.
Transformation T	The core purpose is always expressed as a transformation process in which some entity, the 'input', is changed or transformed into some new form of the same entity, the 'output'.
Role	Social position recognised as significant by people in a problem situation. Such a position may be institutionally defined, or behaviourally defined.
Norm	Expected behaviours of those who have roles.
Values	Beliefs about what is humanly 'good' or 'bad' performance by role holders.
Client	The individual or group that caused the study to take place.
Problem solver	An individual or group that undertakes the inquiry. An inquirer. It can be whoever wishes to do something about the situation in question; the intervention should be defined in terms of their perceptions, knowledge and readiness to make resources available.

Problem owner	Plausible roles from which the situation can be viewed. They are chosen by the problem solver. The problem solver must decide who the possible problem owners are. It may or may not be the client. It may or may not be the problem solver. If the problem solver is chosen, then this may mean that the first relevant system looked at is 'a system to do the study'. The first problem solver(s) hope to turn into real world action in doing the study. Thus, the problem solving system becomes part of the problem content.
Analysis 1	Originally called role analysis, and also called social system analysis. It structures the situation and provides an examination of interaction or possible intervention in terms of roles, including client(s), problem owner(s) and problem solver(s).
Analysis 2	Examination of the social and cultural characteristics of the problem situation via interacting roles (social positions), norms (expected behaviour in roles) and values (by which role-holders are judged).
Analysis 3	Examination of the power-related (political) aspects of the problem situation via elucidation of the 'commodities' of power in the situation.
Rich pictures	Pictorial/diagrammatic representation of the situation's entities (structures), processes, relationships and issues.
CATWOE	Elements considered in formulating root definitions. The core is expressed in T (transformation of some entity into a changed form of that entity) according to a declared weltanschauung (W). Customers (C) are: victims or beneficiaries of T. Actors (A) are those who carry out the activities. Owners (O) are individuals or a group who could abolish the system. The environment (E) establishes a set of constraints that the system accepts as given.
The 5E criteria by which a transformation (T) would be judged	Efficacy (do the means work?); Efficiency (are minimum resources used?); Effectiveness (does the T help the attainment of longer-term goals related to the owner's (O) expectations?); Ethicality (is T a moral thing to do?); Elegance (is T aesthetically pleasing?).
Conceptual model	The structured set of activities necessary to realise the root definition and CATWOE, consisting of an operational subsystem based on the 5Es.
Comparison	Setting the conceptual models against the perceived real world in order to generate debate about perceptions of it and changes to it that would be regarded as beneficial.
Desirable and feasible changes	Possible changes that are (systemically) desirable on the basis of the learned relevance of the relevant system, and (culturally) feasible for the people in the situation at this time.
Action	Real world action (as opposed to activity in conceptual models) to improve the problem as a result of operational of the learning cycle for which this epistemology provides a language.
Weltanschauung	World view that relates to a transformation T [by an inquirer]. There is a distinction between the three types of weltanschauung. W1, W2, W3.
W1	A world view that determines model building of relevant systems and the conceptual models of CATWOE.
W2	The world view for which in a particular situation certain notional systems are seen as relevant; involves sociocultural analysis.
W3	The world view behind the perceived social reality of the situation in which the study is made.

13.4 Logical processes of soft systems methodology

SSM organises the behaviour of inquiry as shown in Fig. 13.4. The cultural and logical streams of inquiry can be mutually related through the organising process to help ensure that intervention strategies are both feasible and consistent.

The methods of SSM

The simple mode of SSM (Fig. 13.5) has a form that is represented by its seven steps and their relationships. It was seen by many as a method that defined a simple sequential cycle of inquiry. However, at its inception it was intended that the principles of action research should be embedded within it. This meant that it should not be seen as a method, but as an infinite variety of methods. Each method would be determined uniquely by the learning process of an inquirer passing through the methodology.

The new expression of SSM changed in the 1980s. In Checkland and Scholes (1990) it was explained that the simple mode of SSM was not able to address many of the complex situations that were found to arise. The new version of the methodology that appeared was referred to as its dynamic version, and we have referred to it as its *dynamic mode*.

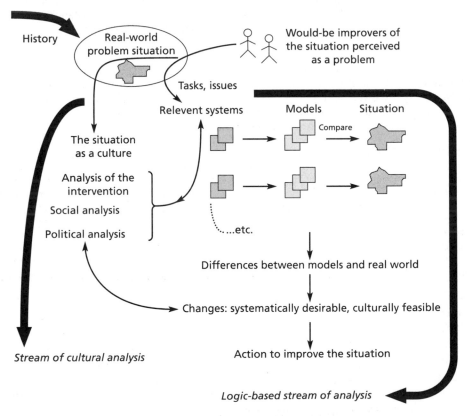

Fig. 13.4 The conceptual idea of the dynamic mode of SSM
(*Source*: Checkland and Scholes, 1990, p. 29)

The form of the dynamic mode is given in Fig. 13.6. It highlights that the methodology is capable of adapting to new situations as its practitioners learn about its failures. The step numbers of the simple mode are placed against equivalent steps in the dynamic mode (in brackets).

Assignment

Do you think that the change from the simple to the dynamic mode of SSM was: (a) dramatic, (b) radical or (c) gradual?

Explain why you believe this to be the case.

Hint: This relates to the ideas explored earlier about dramatic and radical change. To consider whether the methodology has changed through (a), we will need to examine its paradigm to see if it has passed through a shift. If you are not able to argue that it has passed through dramatic change, can you show that it has passed through radical change (that is, the core purposes of the simple mode have altered)?

13.5 The doppelgänger paradigm

As usual, we adopt an image of SSM that derives from our own world view and language. It is thus our interpretation of SSM rather than an expression from the SSM paradigm.

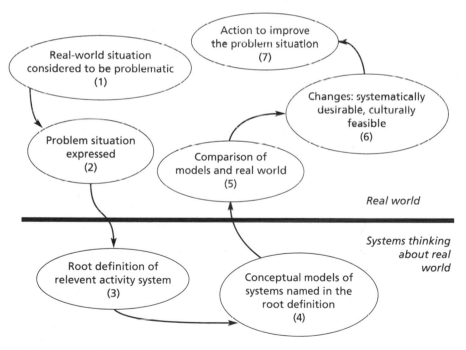

Fig. 13.5 Simple mode of SSM

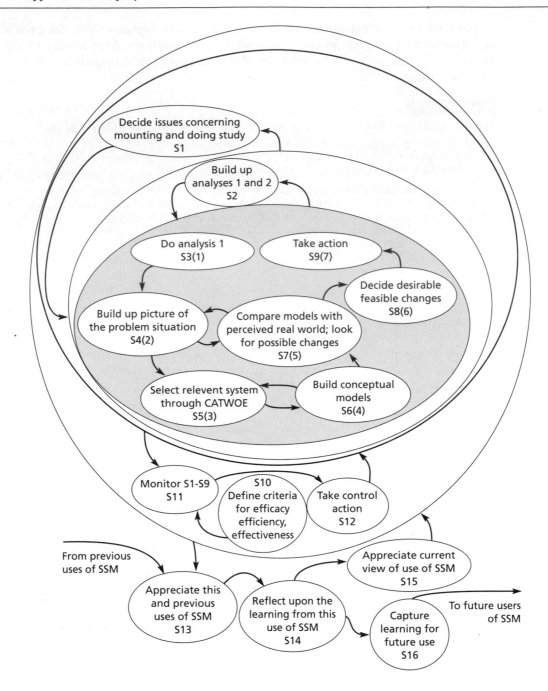

Fig. 13.6 The current form of inquiry of SSM

Examining weltanschauung

It was Checkland who was primarily responsible for the promotion of the word weltanschauung into the systems language. During this development Checkland and Davies

(1986) found themselves in a position of defending a plurality of ways of using the word that some feared caused confusion. In the current work, three classes of weltanschauung (Table 13.2) remain a conceptual part of the methodology. A single class of weltanschauung would be useful, especially for a novice user. Here we shall briefly explore the possibility of this.

The original definition of weltanschauung is clear. It represents a view of perceived reality that is particular to an actor, who may be an individual or a social (group) actor. Now, weltanschauung is related to the concept of paradigm, which can be considered to be a *formalised weltanschauung*. The two differ in that the paradigm requires some explicit formalised definition through propositions and associated epistemology and logic, while weltanschauung does not.

In Chapter 2 we introduced the concept of the virtual paradigm, explaining that it is a link between weltanschauung and paradigm. In particular, the *virtual paradigm* can be a *weltanschauung* or *shared weltanschauung* with *weak formalisation*. By differentiating between weltanschauung and shared weltanschauung, we are explicitly indicating that so long as the virtual paradigm has some level of formalisation, it may be simply that of an individual or of a group. The formalisation may be a statement of logic and propositions, or it may be more than this.

Virtual paradigms are often transient things that change according to weltanschauung or shared weltanschauung with time or with the composition of the group. In some cases, however, they can develop into paradigms (group phenomena) that clearly define the way in which groups perceive and deal with 'reality'.

In Table 13.3 we explain how the 3W approach can be reconsidered in terms of the virtual paradigm, and why the term weltanschauung can therefore be considered to have a unique class.

Table 13.3 Examining the 3Ws of SSM

Ws	Checkland's view	Alternative view
W_1	Determines the *model building* of relevant systems and the *conceptual models* of CATWOE	The model building activity might better be seen as due to a virtual paradigm in which group/individual propositions are explicitly defined. This also applies to the creation of images of reality through the construction of relevant systems. The same virtual paradigm is capable of constructing the conceptual models of CATWOE.
W_2	Determines which *systems* are seen as *relevant*	This must be due to weltanschauung as we know it. It cannot be a group phenomenon in the first instance, though a group can agree on what constitutes a set of relevant systems through a *shared weltanschauung*.
W_3	A view of the *social reality* of a *situation*	Each situation has potentially at least two views: that of the participants and that of the inquirers. Typically, participants will have one paradigm, while an inquirer will have another. In addition, a W_1 virtual paradigm may be used by the inquirers. A good application of methodology will find that the two paradigms are commensurable.

A view of the SSM metasystem

A real-world situation of human purposeful activity has occurred within which there appears to be a situation that requires improvement (of a problem situation), and there is an intention to inquire into the situation so that it can be dealt with. The cognitive purposes embedded in the metasystem for the methodology are its *mission* and *inquiry goals*, which are represented in Fig. 13.7. An explanation is given in Table 13.4.

We have said that in order to make an inquiry, an inquirer will have to build an image of the real-world situation creating the *relevant systems* that are to be defined. The relevant systems model, referred to as *S1*, must be examined in terms of its methodologically defined sociological context, and this involves culture (*m1*), and social system (*m2*) and political (*m3*) contexts. These issues have been discussed earlier. Consequently, there are two aspects of SSM:

1 inquiry goals that are variable (undefined) and dependent upon the weltanschauung of individual inquirers providing unconstrained flexibility;

2 a mission of the methodology is for situational *improvement*.

The mission that derives cognitively from the paradigm is to improve the situation. The aims of inquiry *a1* will depend upon the weltanschauung of an inquirer. The impact of the real world on the model that is produced as a possible intervention strategy is identified in terms of tasks and issues that relate to the situation and evaluation of the real-world response to the *S1* that occurs.

Table 13.4 Definition of the system and cognitive purposes for SSM

The system

S1 The *relevant system* is determined *flexibly* from the viewpoint of the inquirer; there may be any number of relevant systems determined by the inquiring metapurposes.

Cognitive purpose

Mission and goals

The overall methodological metapurpose is to generate improvement; the cognitive goals that determine what is meant by improvement are informed by ensuring whatever intervention occurs, cultural integrity, social conformity and political consistency have been adhered to.

m1 *Cultural feasibility* is concerned with ensuring that any intervention in the situation is consistent with the cultural values (and meanings) possessed by an individual, and addresses actor roles appropriately.

m2 *Social system desirability* is concerned with ensuring that any intervention that occurs is consistent with the social norms that are part of a situation.

m3 *Political feasibility* is concerned with ensuring that any intervention that occurs is politically appropriate so as to ensure that power relationships are not interfered with.

Aims

The aims of the methodology are variable, but there are secondary level aims that determine whether a decided intervention strategy satisfies the following properties: *Efficacy* (do the means work?); *Efficiency* (are minimum resources used?); *Intervention effectiveness* (does the intervention strategy help achieve expectation stability?); *Ethicality* (is the intervention strategy moral?); *Elegance* (is the intervention strategy aesthetically pleasing?).

Definition of terms

We note that while analysis, synthesis and choice are not technical SSM terms, we are again using a doppelgänger paradigm which allows us to use our own terms. In doing so we relate SSM to the generic metamodel (Fig. 5.2) in Table 13.5. This occurs through the coupling of Figs 13.5 and 13.6 which defines the form of inquiry of SSM.

Table 13.5 Relationship between SSM and doppelgänger paradigms

Doppelgänger paradigm Entity/process	SSM paradigm Explanation	Step
Pre-evaluation	Issues of mounting and doing study	S1
	Build up analyses 2 and 3 (sociocultural)	S2
Analysis	Real-world analysis 1	S3
	Build up pictures of situation	S4
	Relevant systems	S5
Control	Compare form of relevant system to real world	
	stability: continue; *instability*: reframe relevant systems	
Conceptualisation		
Synthesis	Build conceptual models	S6
Control	Compare sociocultural aspects of models with relevant system for stability	
	stability: continue; *instability*: redefine model in S6 or fail	
Control	Compare form of models with perceived reality	S7
	Involve cultural stream of inquiry	
	stability: continue; *instability*: go to S3	
Constraint		
Choice	Decide desirable, feasible changes	S8
Control	Compare models with perceived reality; involve cultural stream of inquiry	
	stability: continue; *instability*: accept model or fail	
Action	Action	S9
Post-evaluation controls: Control	Relate S9 to efficacy, efficiency, effectiveness	S10–12
	stability: continue; *instability*: reconsider	
Control	Overview of form of inquiry	S13,14
	stability: appreciate application	S15
	instability: learn about inadequacy	S16

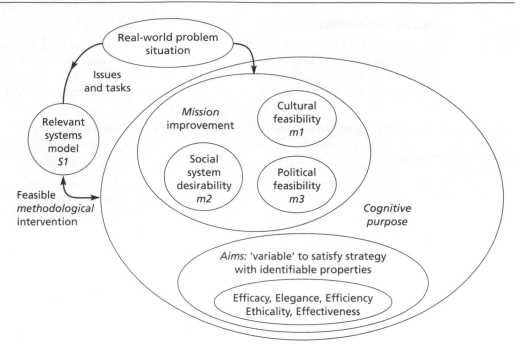

Fig. 13.7 Context diagram for the metasystem and the system for SSM

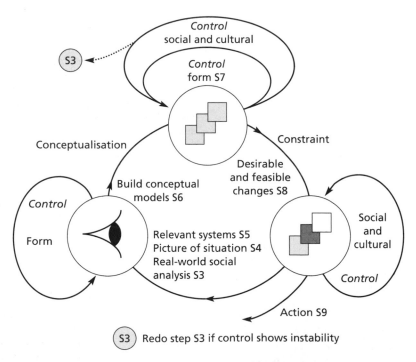

Fig. 13.8 A view of SSM through the phase controlled generic metamodel excluding the pre-evaluation phase

Application of the principle of control to the methodology

SSM as defined in Table 13.4 has been presented in terms of the generic metamodel with controls. A graphical form is produced in Fig. 13.8 in a way consistent with the ideas of Chapter 5. The synthesis phase involves two control loops: one relates directly to the form of the situation (S7) as perceived by the inquirers and referred back in some way to the participants, and the other is social and cultural. The two are independent. From this it would seem appropriate to propose not two streams of inquiry as currently defined in SSM, but in addition a third that relates to the form of a situation as perceived by the participants.

From Fig. 13.8 it can be seen that SSM can be viewed as a five-entity simple metamodel (S3–6, S8) that is made dynamic through the introduction of control loops. S9 (action) is an activity or process rather than an entity and S7 (comparison) is a control.

It is of interest from this description that SSM is vary carefully controlled locally – that is, around each stage of the logical process of inquiry. Thus, for example, if during synthesis the social and cultural control loop does not enable an inquirer to confirm that a model is culturally feasible, then new models can be built and evaluated. It is also globally controlled around the whole cycle to ensure that it has dealt suitably with efficacy, efficiency and effectiveness, and is generally stable. Global control is shown through the action link entering the analysis phase. This global control can be thought of as a post-evaluative phase of the methodology.

The characteristics of form

The form of SSM can be produced graphically as above. However, it can also be defined in terms of the characteristics established and applied in earlier chapters. These characteristics are explored in Table 13.6.

Table 13.6 The characteristics of form for SSM

Characteristic	Simple mode of SSM	Morphogenic mode of SSM
Structure	Defines a set of linearly related entities that direct an inquirer towards action	Defines a set of entities that relate to one another according to a set of control loops
Orientation	In terms of the modelling space, the generic orientation is relative softness, uncertainty and semistructure	In terms of the modelling space, the generic orientation is softness, uncertainty and ill structure
Conditions	Defined by the form of the situation, and the needs of SSM for inquirers to be interactive with participants	Defined by the form of the situation, its socioculture, and the needs of SSM to be interactive
Dynamic actions and processes	Processes defined within each entity, and only implied between them	Processes defined within each entity and within the controls, and only implied between entities
Mode	Principally linear	Nonlinear and dynamic through use of control loops. Can operate as a cyclic methodology though is cyclic through its controls. Also operates a pre- and post-evaluation process

13.6 Summary of SSM

SSM is a powerful consensus methodology that has become a cornerstone approach for inquiring into complex situations. It generates dynamic methods that offer a people-centred way of examining complex situations. Its purpose is to intervene in a situation in order to improve it. What constitutes improvement is determined by the stakeholders of the situation.

The methodology recommends a pattern of behaviour by an inquirer that explores two streams of inquiry, the logical and the cultural. The logical stream of inquiry involves a set of nine sequential steps that was at one time taken by many readers of SSM as a simple sequential methodology. The referencing between the two streams of inquiry is a very useful way of describing the methodology in action. The introduction of controls on the organisational behaviour of SSM has enabled the formulation of a dynamic method, which changes as it is applied to complex situations.

To satisfy the cognitive needs of the methodology, three classes of analysis have been proposed for SSM. The first is *analysis 1*, which is concerned with the social and contextual aspects of the situation. *Analysis 2* is concerned with organisational culture, and *analysis 3* with the politics and power relationships with the situation.

13.7 The SSM case study

This case is a study of the UK National Health Service after the dramatic change that it has recently passed through. As resource material, it uses a study undertaken by Raymond Turner, a 1996 final year student on the BA in Business Information Systems at Liverpool Business School, investigating human resource management in the National Health Service (NHS). In addition, it draws on the final year 1996 student project of Mark Muirhead, concerned with National Health Service information networking. Both apply SSM to their respective study areas. It briefly draws on a secondary source, a study presented by Checkland and Scholes (1990, pp. 89–114), and on a confidential study by another final year student at Liverpool on the part-time degree in Business Studies. The latter two are useful to us only for their contextual information about the NHS, though the Checkland and Scholes case similarly applies SSM to a problem situation that concerns community health care. Finally, it draws on primary evaluative research.

A dramatic change in the National Health Service has shifted it from a cooperative publicly managed homogeneity operated across management regions, into a competitive market of Trusts with bounded cooperation and business practices and purposes. Since a significant intention of Government in introducing a competitive system into the National Health Service is to draw out economies, Trusts are obliged to seek efficient ways of operating, especially because of the additional load of management that they have. The purpose of this study, therefore, is to inquire whether it is possible to improve the ability of the Lancaster Priority Trust to do this, and if so how. Particular reference is given to the provision of information for human resource management. The conclusions of the study do not, however, have implementable detail. Rather, they have a set of recommendations that can be examined in more detail through a further recursive application of SSM. As a consequence, no post-evaluation of the methodology to the situation has been undertaken. For the sake of clarity, we shall initially present a case summary.

Case summary

Activity	Description
Weltanschauung	The Lancaster Priority Trust, because of its status in a competitive market National Health Service and Government constraints on funding, needs to improve its efficiency in some way.
Inquirer's mission	To identify the areas that should be tackled in order to improve the efficiency of the Trust, and in particular service the needs of the head of the Manpower Information and Planning (MIAP) department.
Methodology: SSM	Mission to improve the situation, while ensuring cultural and political feasibility and social systemic desirability.
Methodological inquiry	Inquiry goal is to improve the situation, by first improving the goal specification of the inquiry.
Nature of examination	In order to understand how to improve the situation, an examination was required of the stakeholder perceptions while bearing in mind the need to tease out the particular goal specifications. The needs of the client (MIAP) were respected in this, and in particular related to the needs of local information provision. Part of the awareness in the study was to identify the cultural and political constraints on the organisation.
Explanatory model	Improvement of the situation occurred by defining a goal specification for the Trust that satisfied the needs of the client (MIAP). These needs identified the orientation (towards information system provision) that the study would take.
Options selection	The following areas need to be addressed specifically, through the recursive action of the methodology: (a) new personnel system, (b) user needs specification, (c) information technology support for operations, (d) executive/management information systems needs specification and (e) quality control systems.

13.7.1 Pre-evaluation

The context of the National Health Service prior to the change

The UK's National Health Service was established as a free publicly funded service. Prior to 1990 it was the largest employer in the UK, with almost half a million staff. Its budget in the 1980s was around £20 000 million.

The 1970s and 1980s saw major restructuring. Prior to 1983 the NHS operated through consensus management. Decision making occurred within professional teams of medical consultants, doctors and nursing staff. Constraints on operational activities were defined through medical accounting boundaries, i.e. what was medically feasible. As a result of a report under Sir Roy Griffiths (who had experience in the retail industry) on management restructuring, the Government instituted a change in management practice in 1984. The approach adopted was general management, which introduced a business style operation into the health service for the first time. General managers were to be appointed at all tiers in the organisational hierarchy. They were to be invested with general management functions and overall responsibility for managerial performance.

A hierarchical structure was adopted that descended principally from the NHS Board down to about 20 Regional Health Authorities, and then down to 192 District Health Authorities. This shift was intended to provide efficiencies that would seem unlikely to materialise through adjusting management processes without addressing NHS structures or culture. At district level a District General Manager would be responsible for the quality and range of services that the professionals of his district provided. A district might have a variety of units, such as a department of occupational health, the chronic unit and the community services unit.

The National Health Service as a competitive market

The next stage of the changes to the NHS occurred in 1991, with the introduction of internal market reforms. It was in fundamental conflict with the 1984 move to generalised management, both strategically and operationally. However, these reforms were a prerequisite for the 1991 change since the culture of consensus management would not easily have permitted the intended reforms. The introduction of this new change was also responsible for a more fragmented approach to health care. It divided the NHS into two, with one section that does not participate in an internal market, and one section that does. In the market section, districts are divided into smaller independently managed units, so that entire tiers of the structure have become virtually redundant.

The function of the Regional Authorities was to arrange the distribution of the regions' health resources throughout the district. Regional Authority planning is composed of (a) service planning and (b) capital planning. Funding was calculated according to the statistics of the population, taking account of such variables as age, gender and mortality. The reforms altered the method of allocation by introducing market disciplines, and encouraging trade between districts and trust status institutions. This led to the accusation that those organisations that had opted out of achieving trust status were resource disadvantaged since they could not engage in such trade.

District Health Authorities have largely ceased to be in charge of the operational aspects of health care. They have been effectively replaced by numerous smaller Trusts that now individually take on this mantle of responsibility. However, districts are still able to purchase health care from the suppliers – the Trusts. The generalised responsibilities of the Trusts are as follows:

- to ensure that the health needs of the given population are met;
- to ensure effective health promotion and disease prevention policies;
- to provide comprehensive health care;
- to operate targets and performance monitoring.

To gain trust status an intentioned organisation must demonstrate financial health now and in the foreseeable future. This requires forward budgeting, and shifts priority from traditional medical to financial budgeting. A Trust has the status of a public corporation, is placed under the jurisdiction of the District Health Authority, and is directly responsible to the Government Health Secretary. Funding also comes directly from the Department of Health, and is allocated through a core grant. All other income is secured through competition for contracts.

A key intention within the market reform in the National Health Service was to distinguish between health care purchasers and providers. These functions were originally carried out together by the District Health Authorities.

Purchasers included District Health Authorities, General Practitioner Fundholders and private patients. Purchase contracts are based on costs incurred to the provider for the previous financial year's service activity levels. In the case of General Practitioner

Fundholders, they individually enter into contract negotiations with Trusts on behalf of the patients of their practice. The District Health Authority budgets are reduced to take account of this. Finally, private patients can opt to purchase health services of their choice, within medical ethical limits, from any providers.

Providers include secondary care units (hospitals) managed by District Health Authorities, Trust hospitals and private sector units. Non-Trust NHS hospitals are known as District General Hospitals, still part of the structure, but directly managed by the Districts. Private hospitals such as those owned by BUPA can also compete for contracts for NHS patients if they wish.

The budgeting of fundholders is limited to spending of on average £500 per patient per year. As an unforeseen consequence of this, particular patients who are more expensive treatment cases may be rejected as patients by the Trust. This is a most curious situation, since it (a) establishes the basis of a culture in which costs take precedence over care within the Trusts, seemingly an adjustment of the mission of the NHS, and (b) accentuates the potential vulnerability of medical cases.

As the piecemeal creation of new Trusts occurs, funding is continually being taken away from the intermediate District Health Authorities. It is now moving directly to the local level through District and Regional Health Authorities to secondary care units. One of the consequences of the internal market is that Trusts publish prices for particular treatments. Variations in price can occur between hospitals. Thus, for example, in the London area a rectal excision can vary between £3768 in Croydon to £2638 in East Surrey. This leads one to consider issues of quality differentiation and professional service charging. It also leads to the possibility of staff pay differentiation. The Government would applaud this as a competitive device, while the nurses' union would decry it by arguing that geography or social condition has nothing to do with given levels of staff skill and qualification.

Another difficulty with the internal market is that Trust casualties can occur. Particular projects must come out of internal budgeting, and Trusts that have particular needs and are not competitive may find themselves being continually more disadvantaged.

The quality of Trusts

A highly competitive market of Trusts in the NHS is computationally complex, and in comparison to the old structure one might expect there to be some difficulty in ensuring NHS quality. Service audit would be able to determine whether this is the case. We have indicated that the quality of NHS information is inadequate because of computational complexity, a problem that can only be solved by an interconnectivity that is lacking. However, there is also a problem with the quality of basic services. Thus, for instance, some Trust hospitals have relatively low success rates in certain types of surgical operation. Reasons for this include pressures of time on surgeons performing operations caused by competing commitments under constrained budgets, and lack of investment in specialist training.

However, an example of a perhaps more serious nature (because of its implications across the whole of the NHS for inadequate administrative processes) is shown by an audit of blood handling services in one Trust. In testing and classifying blood, the audit highlighted problems that included:

- documentation for blood samples had no space for patient identification labels required for case note retrieval;

- complex information was produced that was not specifically document orientated, and consequently the results would not indicate the current standards of clinical practice;
- certain documents were found to be missing at the point of audit;
- certain patients were prescribed so many drugs that to record them all was impracticable and deemed to be a less significant factor of the audit;
- signatures of doctors/nurses often required time consuming effort to decipher for audit purposes.

Such problems are relatively easily solvable given proper audit procedures, adequate resources and sufficient time to identify and correct them. However, the efficiency drives that are encouraged by Government provide a financially tight environment for any of this to occur.

The NHS as a global enterprise

While it is tempting to think of the NHS as a global business enterprise, doing so has associated with it a number of management problems (Checkland and Scholes, 1990, p. 93). We can identify the following in this respect:

- the NHS is not a single entity, and health workers do not think of themselves as working *for* the NHS, but *within* it;
- the parts of the NHS are locked into a complicated network of autonomous and semi-autonomous groups concerned with health care matters;
- the NHS network includes local authority social services departments with geographical boundaries that do not coincide with those of the Regions, and voluntary and charitable organisations, which have diverse forms, purposes and cultures;
- there are multiple perspectives within the NHS that derive from its network nature and the tasks it is required to perform;
- conflict has developed between the new managers and their cultural values and attitudes, and those of many health care professionals, who regard their primary duty as servicing the needs of health care;
- there is no demonstration of a global unitary power structure in the NHS as a whole;
- the Trusts have been able to institute local unitary power structures, but this has fragmented the service;
- health care provision emerges from the professional activity of its autonomous and semi-autonomous groups;
- delivery of health care provision lies in the hands of clinical professionals rightly concerned to protect their autonomy as professionals. Cost accounting methods in undertaking surgical procedures must not be a factor;
- cost accounting is the major constraining factor on Trusts, followed by medical accounting. While this should not affect medical and surgical practice, it is not clear that this is the case.

Trust classifications

Trusts would usually be classified as Community and/or Acute. Community Trusts operate Community Units such as:

- adult mental health
- rehabilitation
- child, adolescent and forensic psychiatry
- learning disability services
- child disability services
- psychiatric hospitals.

The Community Trusts are involved in a form of health care with a tradition that is at least a century old. It is concerned with public as opposed to individual health care. Prior to the shift to a business enterprise culture, community health care was not highly regarded, even though it was encouraged because of its implicit efficiencies in Government spending. Even where it represented a high quality service, it has failed to win a perception of credibility by District General Managers (Checkland and Scholes, 1990, p. 96).

Acute Trusts provide the Primary Care Units and facilities that include:

- conventional hospitals
- pathology laboratories
- radiology laboratories
- accident and emergency facilities
- specialist units such as neurology, microbiology, etc.

National Health Service information interconnectivity

Prior to the shift, information flow between districts was centralised and uncomplicated. However, now individual Trusts have had to adapt to changes in the way in which they control resources. This has led to a complexity of departments that each control aspects of resources such as contracting and tendering. Thus, essential to the new competitive and fragmented NHS is the need to establish a high level of effective global information interconnectivity between its parts. This in particular satisfies the need to provide accurate and timely information about service exchanges between Trusts. The NHS executive instructed its Information Management Group to develop a portfolio of projects that would use modern information technology to gather information where and when it was needed. As the result of a study by Muirhead (1996), it was found that there were a number of technical problems surrounding the introduction of an information interconnectivity group, as well as security problems that had not been addressed.

The problem of global information interconnectivity is, however, exacerbated because local information sources, the Trusts themselves, are not always aware of the information needs that they have, or at least the contextual issues that might be making competitive demands on such a system. An example of such a local problem is that of the Lancaster Priority Trust.

Impact on drug companies

An interesting consequence of the metamorphosis of the NHS has been in relation to the drug companies. In the past they have, as a representative indicated, been the 'fat cats' of the Health Service environment, producing what we shall call designer drugs targeted on medical conditions, and charging high prices for them. They have now become the 'lean cats' of the environment. The Family Health Service Authority recommends that General Practitioners prescribe generic drugs to patients. These are no-name drugs that are not sold under a company label. These drugs are, according to the company representatives, not necessarily quality controlled, having consequences after administration that might be unexpected. With the developments in the NHS, it would also seem that medical practitioners are less willing or able to meet with representatives, and this has in the past provided a good source for supplying information about new drugs.

This is having an impact on the drug companies. They are finding it difficult to fund the research needed to put a designer drug on the market. An immediate consequence of the NHS transformation has been the number of mergers between the larger drug companies. Representatives from the companies feel that there will be a consequence of limiting the research and development of new drugs for new conditions, or better drugs for existing conditions.

13.7.2 Analysis

Real-world social analysis for the Lancaster Priority Trust

Lancaster Priority Trust has recently become a part of the internal market structure of the NHS. It is required to undergo a change in form that can accommodate Government directives to transfer priority services away from institutionalised care into a predominantly community-based care service (Turner, 1996). It is generally aware that in order to undertake its activities most efficiently and effectively, it must introduce an information system that can assist with human resource management. Present provisions demonstrate that the end result will be to replace the existing integrated personnel system with one that will improve staff record maintenance. It will also provide a basic reporting mechanism to the Trust. In order to determine a specification for the intended system, the project has been set up without a project manager, with no budget, no resources, no timescales, and without ends on which to base the means of development. Unfortunately, management seems to be unaware of the more global demands of information interconnectivity. Even if it was, this would be a less significant issue for it than internal optimisation on a zero budget. A representative structure of the Lancaster Priority Trust (LPT) is described in the hierarchical chart of Fig. 13.9.

The primary activities of LPT are (a) the provision of core health care services as stated by the Department of Health, (b) competition for contracts from District Health Authorities and from General Practitioner Fundholders, (c) community care activities, (d) institutional care, (e) development of facilities and skills and (f) direct treatment of patients. From (a), the LPT is responsible for providing the priority health care services for its catchment population. 'Priority services' include:

- mental health care
- learning disabilities
- provision of care for drug- and alcohol-related problems
- community care (e.g. physiotherapy, midwifery, occupational therapy).

LPT operates two hospitals (both to be closed in 1997), a community unit and a large number of smaller units deployed around the region. The staff employed by the Trust number about 2000.

Interest lies in particular in the Manpower Information and Planning (MIAP) department within which the information system is designated. A system hierarchy chart (Fig. 13.9) shows the structure of the organisation and shows the position of MIAP. The pri-

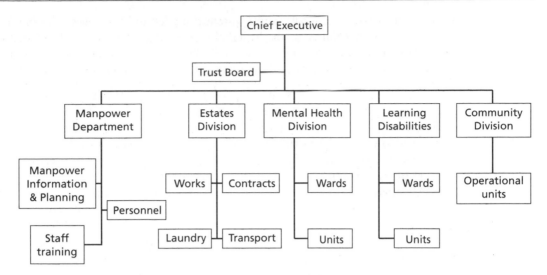

Fig. 13.9 Organisational structure of Lancaster Priority Trust

mary purpose of MIAP is to provide management information for the Trust. It is responsible, among other things, for standard customer reports on operations on a weekly, monthly and yearly basis. It is also responsible for the compilation of manpower reports for the Regional Health Authority on request. Examples of the type of report information that MIAP requires access to are:

- ethnic information
- age and gender information
- staff details and distribution by division
- new starters and leavers
- staffing skills levels.

MIAP is faced by many constraints, not least from the Department of Finance. The personnel computer system and the finance computer system operate independently without common information. This is problematic for the development of manpower projects, for example because staff rota codes and pay scales will be needed for the financial computer system.

Within the next year the computer services contract will run out, and will not be renewed. Thus at present there is nothing in place that is able to maintain the system after 1997. With the removal of the Computer Services Department, the building that the Manpower Department currently occupies is to be shut down.

In relation to manpower issues within the Trust, the following were identified as being relevant to the development of a manpower information system:

- unit managers are mostly unable to generate reports on their own information requirements due to current system shortfalls and their own technical inexperience, leading them to rely heavily on MIAP;
- lead times for manpower reports to divisions or departments are lengthy due to complicated procedures for generating acceptable reports and the smaller number of staff available with the technical experience;

- the current executive information system provided to Trust managers is not used and has not been distributed to the 'right' managers. The system was developed by a separate organisation called Professional Data Care, which would seem to have undertaken little research analysis on health service management needs.

The Integrated Personnel System (IPS) is an old mainframe system that is intended to provide information to Manpower. There is no confidence in its ability to satisfy information needs; neither is it a user-friendly system. Only MIAP staff would seem capable of using it to generate reports. Since information outputs from IPS are transferred to a Windows environment for further processing to satisfy given purposes, reports tend to be quite time consuming for the three members of staff involved.

MIAP services the needs of 50 distributed departments. Requests for advice on generating their own information using their dumb mainframe terminals are made on a daily basis. MIAP generates a comprehensive monthly spreadsheet model for personnel management, plus it responds to *ad hoc* requests. There are about two of the latter per month, but this is increasing because staffing breakdowns are becoming significant to the organisation as (a) it heads towards hospital closures, (b) it requires to relocate the 2000 employees, (c) it becomes more directed to community-based health care provision and (d) it becomes more directed towards limiting and balancing budgets.

There is a need to provide information to Trust managers on human resources. The information is required by the users according to their specifications. MIAP provides consultation about available information, its form of storage, the principles of its change and the dynamics of its access. The standard of service is impaired by poor communications between customers/users and the department, with the latter frequently ignorant about their needs and accessible information. The large lead time between information requests and delivery provides a degrading influence on the quality of the information.

Relevant systems

The tasks and issues of the situation

The intention of the Lancaster Priority Trust is to use information to improve its services. An example of this is the provision of patient waiting list information. It is passing through a radical change through redirecting its purposes away from large-scale institution-based care to community-based care. The effective utilisation of human resource information is essential for this to be successful, due to large-scale redeployment of staff into new areas. It is the role of the information systems strategy to create the necessary infrastructure in line with the business plan. If the strategy is to meet the needs of the human resource function, then the information system strategy should be a direct continuation of the business strategy.

The Trust's information strategy is divided. At present there are no links between the business strategy and the information technology strategy. There is little hope of tackling the issues that need to be addressed to satisfy manpower information needs. Another consequence of the fragmented strategic position will be that securing cooperation with other departments for the development of the systems will be made more difficult.

The strategic plan for LPT has been developed through a planning process that involves five areas of consideration: (1) mission, (2) strategies, (3) policies, (4) decisions and (5) actions. Applying the five areas to LPT enables us to produce a set of planning purposes (Table 13.7).

Table 13.7 Matching planning areas with planning purposes

Planning area	Purpose
Mission	To provide the best possible health care to the catchment population, while becoming increasingly competitive in the health service internal market
Strategies	To transfer the Trust's primary functions from an institution-based care system to a community-based care system, shifting operations to smaller units, while maintaining administration and management as a centrally coordinated body
Policies	Give patients easy access to 'drop-in' centres, while transferring ward-based health workers to a more mobile role
Decisions	Closure of the Trust's remaining hospitals
Action	Instigation of large-scale planning, investigating new sites, redeployment of staff with minimal redundancies (incorporating natural wastage), transfer of long-stay patients into the community, transferring sectioned patients into new units

The information technology strategy has in part evolved through the recognition that the organisation is passing through a period of change. The strategy is defined as follows:

> To investigate provisions for a new personnel system to serve the priority health service trust. The aim is to implement new systems providing the organisation with the ability to maintain the capture of essential manpower information after the loss of computer services, since after this IPS will be non-maintainable. The provision of manpower information will remain with the central office (MIAP).

This strategy aims to develop an information system structure to aid the overall business plan. It is one of the many elements in the Trust's overall information technology strategy, which should form an integrated and coherent whole. This is not the case at present because different information technology strategies that exist are not connected with one another and are without a central development focus.

In the case of MIAP, the overriding business strategy is to transfer its business away from institutionalised base care to community care. The divisional strategy for Manpower should be to provide support to the overall business strategy, by providing human resource management for the massive relocation of staff. This in turn needs the information systems provided by MIAP to manage the overall transformation. MIAP's information technology and system strategy is to develop a new system to replace the outmoded IPS and to continue providing human resource information to the Trust. However, this is a local strategy that is not globally incorporated into LPT as a whole. This lack of interconnection between local and global strategies is likely to result in a conflict of strategic policy outcomes.

Without globally-linked information technology systems, the management of human resources needed to accomplish the mission will be difficult, and the organisation's policies for change will be impeded. Although the personnel system has proved to be adequate in the past, it is clear that the existing system is not sufficient when the present (and increasingly) competitive environment is taken into account. The future planned system development will affect many stakeholders. The MIAP department provides a service for two health service Trusts, with over 15 divisions, and over 200 operational units involving more than 4000 staff.

Developing an information technology strategy incorporating new systems will incur some level of business process refinement. This will require cooperation from other departments. Although these departments are members of the same overall objective, many will see no direct benefits to their departments for a global system, and this will constrain their cooperation. This problem of ensuring cooperation for manpower systems development is a concerning factor. The management of these organisational and political issues should become a prime concern for development, if the resulting systems are to serve the business needs of the organisation as a whole.

The organisation is immature in its information system development. The general manager of Manpower is an expert on personnel matters, but has little appreciation of the role that information technology has to play in the organisation. Similarly, other staff, who will be the key to the project, have no information technology knowledge. If an information system strategy is be fully incorporated into the business strategy then there will be a need for action to be taken by the organisation to upgrade the knowledge of its senior managers.

Educating top-level executives in information technology must be a prime objective. This is because they will be involved in policy formation and implementation, and information access and handing must be a major factor of consideration.

Stakeholder analysis

The stakeholder definition (Table 13.8) identifies who is concerned with the problem situation as we see it. Prior to an exploration of this, however, it is appropriate to define three roles: the problem owner, the problem solver and the client:

- the client is the general manager of MIAP, who is responsible for the employment of the inquirer and provided authorisation for the inquiry to occur;
- the problem solver is Anthony Turner, a student on placement during his third academic year at Liverpool John Moores University Business School, and well versed in the use of SSM;
- the problem owners, as identified by the inquirer, are taken as the primary stakeholders. These are the managing directors of MIAP, Finance and Personnel.

Table 13.8 Stakeholder identification

Stakeholder type	Name
Internal stakeholders	Manpower (MIAP personnel)
	Financial accounting and payroll
	Hospital units (radiography, nursing, laundry, etc.)
	Board and general managers
	Staff on record
	Computer services
	Users of the personnel system
External stakeholders	Department of Health
	Regional Health Authority

Manpower department

Manpower Information and Planning

MIAP is currently the personnel system coordinator. Current provisions for manpower information are satisfied by this central office, operated with three staff members. The department is a primary source for technical knowledge. It is also likely that the MIAP manager will hold a key position in the development with the two assistants providing technical support. With no provision already made as to how new structures will incorporate the MIAP into the function of manpower information provision, it may be deemed necessary to change the overall function of the office as well as staffing levels due to the departure of the Computer Services Department.

The Personnel Department

The Personnel Department will be using any new personnel system in an operational role; as it will be the prime user of the new system in this context a level of cooperation in the system development is essential. This department will provide operational and tactical expertise in areas affecting the personnel function. The Personnel Department also has the role of maintaining staff files updated on the system. This information is to be used in the strategic context, and the department should play a key role in the development of any systems to serve this function.

The Board and general managers

The Board and general managers will provide the strategic context for the system, incorporating it into the overall business plan. The power they exercise over the different divisions is of primary concern as divisional cooperation will be essential to gain full support for the project. They also hold the power over the budget for the project, appointing the project manager as well as providing the role of project sponsor. The role of project sponsor has been identified as holding a substantial weighting in determining the chances of success of any development project. Success can be described as completing the project to schedule, satisfying the expectations of the users and meeting limited budgets. The project sponsor helps to ensure success by using political power to give full support to the project manager, as well as ensuring support for the project throughout the organisation. Without a project sponsor holding considerable power, the project manager cannot hope to gain the support needed for the system development to be successful. The hope would be that the project sponsor would either be the chief executive, thereby ensuring the credibility of the project, or the general manager of the Manpower department, who has good connections throughout the organisation.

Regional Health Authority

The Regional Health Authority requires that the Trust provides it with manpower information on a regular basis. If this is impaired due to some aspect of the new system, then it may become a political power within the Trust in order to guarantee the provision of this information.

Financial accounting and payroll

Finance owns the financial information that the system will need to access to provide accurate staffing cost breakdown and analysis. It is also a requirement to feed the financial system with staff rota codes that identify the working hours of staff and pay scales. Finance must be involved in the project from the beginning to ensure that this system requirement is met.

Hospital units

Individual hospital units are at present responsible for inputting a large part of the data to the IPS. They are also MIAP's primary user of tactical and operational level information. The units will be required to work closely with new systems as well as being major consumers of its information. They should therefore have an involvement in the project development.

The Department of Health

Seen as a remote stakeholder, the Department of Health is a primary revenue source for the project, as it is for the LPT budgeted grant. It will receive aggregated information from the system as provided by the Regional Health Authorities.

Computer Services

The Computer Services department is currently responsible for maintaining all the hardware operated by Manpower and both the acute and priority Trusts, as well as providing technical support. During the next year its contract runs out and the department switches location to Acute buildings and ends its support to priority services. While its contract remains, the department could be an invaluable source of expertise in constructing the support structures that the Trust requires for its systems.

System users

The system users must be taken into consideration. These include MIAP, personnel records, hospital units, VDU clerks, managers and executives. Many systems have failed in the past even though they worked technically, as a result of their user-unfriendly natures. During systems design and analysis, the users' needs must be continually monitored. They must be involved in all stages of development as this will give users a feeling of control over their own designs, as well as providing essential information to the system developers on what is needed.

Staff on record

The use of the data held on the system must be in accordance with the Data Protection Act of 1984. If the system steps outside the boundary defined by this the Trust could encounter problems with legal bodies as well as with health service unions. The staff must have the confidence in the organisation that records held on them are being used in accordance with the stated function.

Analysis of political power

A stakeholder analysis matrix provides a view of where power is invested within the Trust. This is provided in Fig. 13.10. This mapping provides a clear picture of who holds the greatest power and has a key interest in the system. It has for simplicity been divided into four sections, A, B, C and D, each of which has had attributes assigned to it. Those stakeholders falling into segment D are in demand of a high level of management during the development. Those in A are of less concern to the success of the project. The distribution of the stakeholders within the analysis matrix is given in Table 13.9.

Table 13.9 Stakeholders' power properties

Stakeholder	Power of: interest/dynamism
MIAP	D/C
Board and general management	C/C
Finance	B/B
Hospital units	A/B
Computer Services	B/D
System users	A/A
Staff on record	D/B
Regional Health Authority (RHA)	C/C
Department of Health (DoH)	C/C

The Board and general managers, and Computer Services have been identified as the biggest threats or opportunities to the project. As of yet, full support from the Board has not been established. It will thus be a prime concern to Manpower, and an area of further investigation. While Computer Services is the largest centre of knowledge with respect to information technology, its position within the organisation is very unstable. Its involvement could save a considerable amount of money, avoiding external subcontracting for technical assistance.

A number of attributes have been identified that would probably be derived from a new system. Table 13.10 reports on an examination of the positions that each of the stakeholders takes over these.

Table 13.10 Political positions on a selection of possible attributes of a new information system

	Board and general managers	Finance	Hospital units	Computer Services	System users	Manpower	RHA	DoH
New personnel system		N	N	P	?	P		
Different reporting style	P		P	N	P	P	?	
Loss of existing system	P	N	P	?	P	P		
Complete change in working practices	?	N	?	?	?	?	?	
Smaller budget due to IT investment	N	N				P	N	
MIAP managers' increase in power through system ownership	N	N				?		

N = negative support; P = positive support; ? = divided; blank = neutral.

349

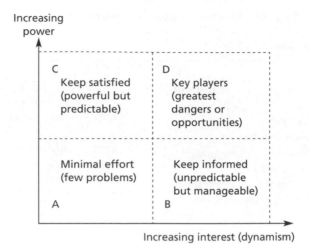

Fig. 13.10 Stakeholder analysis matrix

Summary of the situation

This summary will identify many of the characteristics already discussed, but in the specific terms that are recommended within SSM. This is done in Table 13.11.

Table 13.11 Summary in SSM terms

Characteristics of SSM	Explanation
Boundary	The Manpower department, sitting in an environment
Interactions with respect to the boundary	These represent the provisions for the manpower management function, with interactions from the environment (Fig. 13.11)
Activities within the boundary	Personnel function, management information in MIAP, staff training

Identifying a relevant system

The relevant system that we are interested in is represented in the influence diagram of Fig. 13.12. It centres on MIAP, the role of which is to provide the Trust's manpower information. The relationships are interdependent, and the elements of form are those features connected to physical layout, power hierarchy, reporting structures, and formal and informal communications.

Root definitions for the relevant systems

The CATWOE is as follows

- *customers/users*: these are represented by the managers of other departments, and are coordinators of human resources;
- *actors*: system users (units, departments/divisions and MIAP);
- *transformation process*: Trust pre-designated process capturing information which is transformed into resource reports;
- *weltanschauung*: the capture of human resource information for the management of staffing levels;

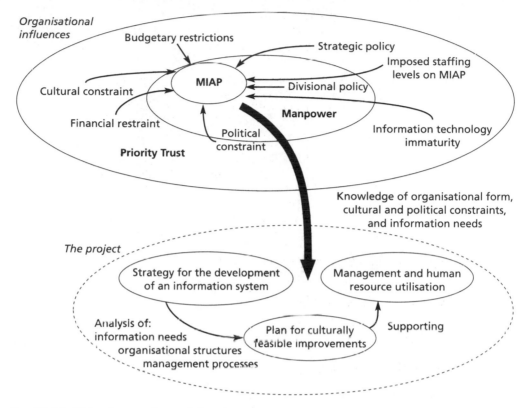

Fig. 13.11 Rich picture view of the situation

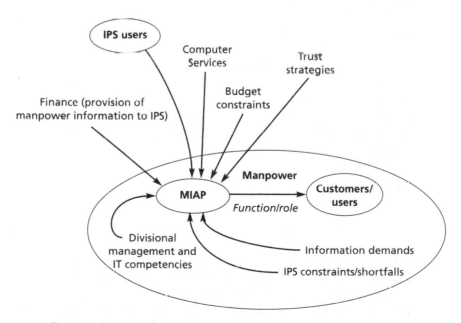

Fig. 13.12 Influence diagram for relevant system of situation

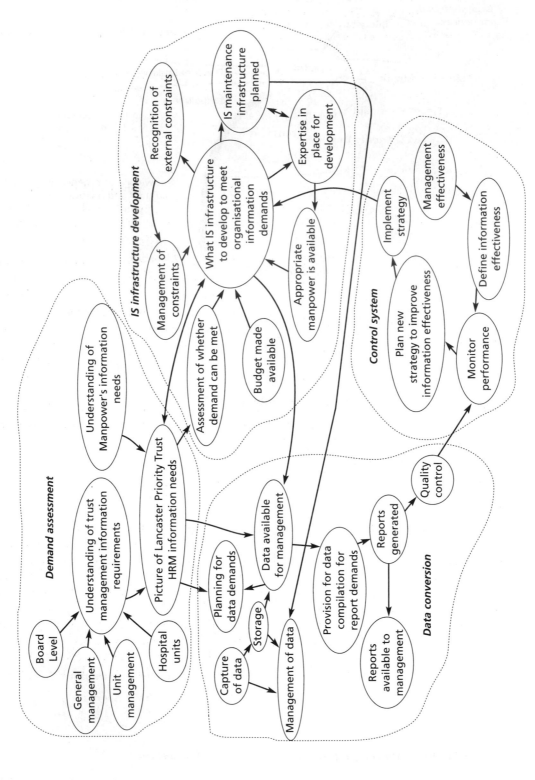

Fig. 13.13 Influence diagram highlighting the relationship between the four aspects of the root definition

- *owner*: the Manpower division, part of Lancaster Priority Trust;
- *environmental constraint*: the provision of health care.

Four aspects of the root definition can be identified that are relevant to the system development:

1 demand assessment (identify information needs for human resources)

2 information system infrastructure development

3 data conversion

4 control.

An influence diagram explains these aspects of the root definition in relation to one another (Fig. 13.13).

The conceptual model provides the base from which we can further explore the situation by testing the weltanschauungen of others in the situation. It is treated as a learning phase for the inquirer. As a result of this, three root definitions are identified, RD1–RD3, which each involves the aspects identified above. These are as follows:

- *RD1*: a Manpower-owned system with the function of capturing data from the personnel function. This information then responds to organisational demand and is used to provide management insight into current human resources. It operates within the constraints of the software, the users, and Trust and Government legislation.
- *RD2*: a Manpower-owned system which aims to establish the provision of manpower resource information for all levels of the Trust to maximise the effectiveness of the organisation in terms of its productivity, while maintaining the interests of the Finance department, staff, users, Board and managers, and serving the users of the Trust.
- *RD3*: a Manpower-owned system with the purpose of providing an information system infrastructure to the Trust. It is to serve the human resource function of an organisation competing within a wider NHS internal market.

13.7.3 Synthesis

Build up conceptual models

Each conceptual model that we synthesise derives from one of the root definitions. These are given in Figs 13.14–13.16. Figure 13.14 is the conceptual model (M1) that serves the basic function of the system needs. Figure 13.15 is the conceptual model that takes into account the wider organisational issues and constraints. Here, the wider organisational issues are the effective human resource information functions necessary to the Trust. These use CM1 as a base component. The model tackles the issues of organisational information needs as well as the process that this information is to serve. Issues that should be considered are where information is produced, by whom, on what architecture and in what dynamic environment Figure 13.16 is the final conceptual model. It contains the inquirer's perception of a sufficient set of activities needed for the present resolution of the system.

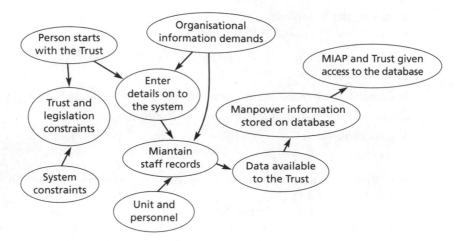

Fig. 13.14 Conceptual model CM1

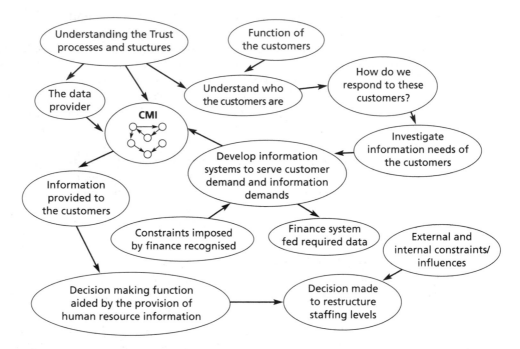

Fig. 13.15 Conceptual model CM2

Model comparison with perceived reality

Comparison was made with the models that derived from the root definition with stakeholder perceptions, examining the data conversion, control, demand and development systems. Questions related to the desirability, feasibility and possible action of different aspects of the proposed system models. These questions included gathering information on:

● user information requirements
● data capture points

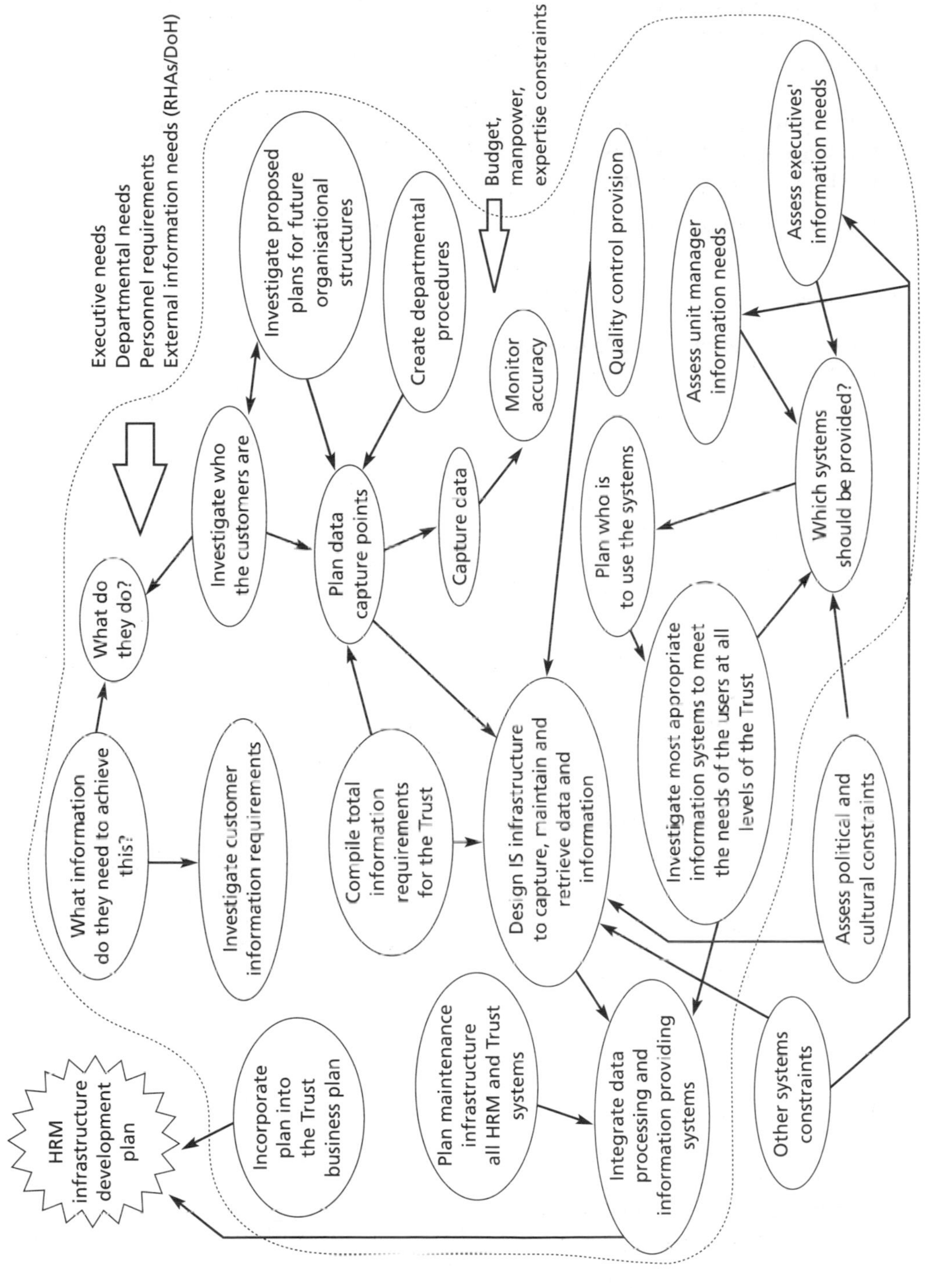
Executive needs
Departmental needs
Personnel requirements
External information needs (RHAs/DoH)
Budget,
manpower,
expertise constraints
HRM infrastructure development plan
Incorporate plan into the Trust business plan
Plan maintenance infrastructure all HRM and Trust systems
Integrate data processing and information providing systems
Other systems constraints
What information do they need to achieve this?
Investigate customer information requirements
Compile total information requirements for the Trust
Design IS infrastructure to capture, maintain and retrieve data and information
Investigate most appropriate information systems to meet the needs of the users at all levels of the Trust
Assess political and cultural constraints
What do they do?
Investigate who the customers are
Plan data capture points
Capture data
Plan who is to use the systems
Which systems should be provided?
Investigate proposed plans for future organisational structures
Create departmental procedures
Monitor accuracy
Quality control provision
Assess unit manager information needs
Assess executives' information needs

Fig. 13.16 Conceptual model CM3

- proposed future plans
- monitoring
- infrastructure design
- quality control
- political and cultural constraints
- system integration
- integration of information system into Trust business plan
- other system constraints
- who is to use the system.

This inquiry would inform the next choices phase of the methodology.

13.7.4 Choice

Decide desirable, feasible models

We have explored the total organisation, and identified the nature of the extensive service to it. The need is now to define the options that can be selected, and make choice according to their systemic desirability and cultural feasibility. As indicated in the introduction to this case, these options have not been adequately defined to date, and require a recursive application of the methodology to make specific recommendations, and cost–benefit analysis, which can now be explored for desirability and feasibility. We can, however, summarise the generalities that should be considered. The options that are defined so far for development within LPT for MIAP are as follows.

1 The analysis and design of options for a new personnel system to be owned by the Manpower department. The system will be designed to be compatible with the standard payroll system, and will, first, feed the system with staff data and, second, provide the provision of costing by staff information to the Trust.

2 Identification of system customers with detailed investigation into their information requirements. The analysis could be carried out using a variety of methods, such as business process investigation, critical success factors and means–ends analysis.

3 Design options for a central information technology support agency to maintain all LPT information systems. The agency can be implemented either using internal expertise and resources or through contracting-out. The role of the agency will be:
   a provision of technical support to the development of an information technology structure;
   b maintenance of systems already in place;
   c technical support to the Trust on information technology;
   d providing help desk support to users who have technical problems.

4 Options to be identified for executive and management information needs from Trust-wide systems, not just newly designed human resource management systems. Finance permitting, analysis might be better carried out by external consultants to maintain a neutral standpoint, and supported by the chief executive of the Trust.

5 The provision of a quality control system to monitor the system's effectiveness, likely to be carried out by (a) the Trust's audit department or (b) regular routine checks by MIAP and the information technology support agency.

These are information provision options that derive from the main study undertaken above. Another option that could be explored, and which has been mentioned in the larger context but not as part of the LPT study, is the broader issue of interconnectivity. Specific provisions that could be explored, though they would come out during the recursion, are (a) the definition and costings for quality services options and (b) audit procedures and specifications that could ensure operational control and standards within LPT.

REFERENCES

Blondel, J. (1978) *Thinking Politically*. Harmondsworth: Pelican.

Checkland, P.B. (1980) 'Are organisations machines?', *Futures*, 12, 421.

Checkland, P.B. (1981) *Systems Thinking, Systems Practice*. Chichester: Wiley.

Checkland, P.B. (1995) 'Model validation in soft systems practice', *Systems Research*, 12(1), 47–54.

Checkland, P.B. and Casar, A. (1986) 'Vickers' concept of an appreciative system: a systemic account', *Journal of Applied Analysis*, 13, 3–17.

Checkland, P.B. and Davis, L. (1986) 'The use of the term Weltanschauung in soft systems methodology', *Journal of Applied Systems Analysis*, 13, 109–15.

Checkland, P.B. and Scholes, J. (1990) *Soft Systems Methodology in Action*. New York: Wiley.

Churchman, C.W. (1971) *The Design of Inquiring Systems*. New York: Basic Books.

Crick, B. (1962) *In Defence of Politics*. London: Weidenfeld & Nicolson.

Dahl, R.A. (1970) *Modern Political Analysis*, 2nd edn. Englewood Cliffs, NJ: Prentice Hall.

Harry, M. (1992) *Information Systems in Business*. London: Pitman.

Jenkins, G.M. (1969) 'The systems approach', *Journal of Systems Engineering*, 1(1), 3–49.

Muirhead, M. (1996) 'NHS-wide networking: information through inter-connectivity'. Final year dissertation for the BA in Business Information Systems, Liverpool Business School, Liverpool John Moores University.

Patching, D. (1990) *Soft Systems Methodology*. London: Pitman.

Popper, K. (1972) *Objective Knowledge: An evolutionary approach*. Oxford: Oxford University Press.

Turner, A.R. (1996) 'A project on the supervision of IT to support the human resource management function'. Final year dissertation for the BA in Business Information Systems, Liverpool Business School, Liverpool John Moores University.

Vickers, G. (1965) *The Art of Judgement*. London: Chapman & Hall.

CHAPTER 14

Viable system model methodology

OVERVIEW

The viable system model provides a powerful diagnostic way of exploring organisations using a cybernetic approach. It has recently become popular as a 'technical' approach to the examination of complex situations, but must be seen to be much broader than this, particularly when embedded as a paradigm within its own logical propositions. The conceptualisation that it adopts to deal with complexity centres on the notion that one can distinguish between a system and its metasystem. This enables decision processes to be drawn away from the behavioural processes of the situation under investigation.

14.1 Introduction

The viable system model methodology (VSMM) that we shall introduce has at its core a well-developed conceptual cybernetic model called the viable system model (VSM). Like all viable system approaches, it stands on the ideas of general systems theory and is connected to purposeful adaptive activity systems. It incorporates, for instance, the concepts of self-regulation, self-organisation and self-production, all of which have been discussed at some length.

The idea of *requisite variety* (Ashby, 1956) has been extremely important to cybernetics, the domain with which VSM is associated. Stafford Beer (1979), a good friend of Ashby, developed his viable system model to satisfy the needs of *variety engineering*. VSM has its origins in neurophysiology as a means of handling variety (Beer, 1981). Discussion of VSM and its applications can be found in Espejo and Harnden (1989), Flood and Jackson (1991) and Jackson (1992). VSM attempts to enable organisations, of any size and level of complexity, to improve the control mechanisms proposed to be essential for that organisation to be viable.

VSM is a formalised cognitive model that can be adopted into a variety of methodological approaches. Its intention is to diagnose a situation seen as a system, and identify and correct its faults of form that stop it being viable. VSM is sometimes called a technical approach to inquiry that deals with control and prediction. While this is seen by some inquirers as being powerful, it is also viewed by some as being *devoid* of ideological, moral or cultural principles. We would suggest that this latter perspective derives from a misunderstanding about the nature of VSM as we have considered it in Chapter 10. Observers of its applications should not see it just as the cognitive part of a methodology, but rather as part of an *inquiry system* in which the inquirer is as important as the variable targeting methodology and variable target situation. These 'devoid' aspects of the cognitive model should be seen to derive from the variable inquirer and the nature of the situation, both of which are integral to the inquiry system.

14.2 The paradigm of viable system model methodology

14.2.1 Beliefs about the metasystem

The VSM paradigm

VSM can be seen to derive from a paradigm that involves:

1 a set of purposeful problem solving systems that Ulrich (1977) refers to as a *hierarchy of problem solving systems;*
2 an epistemology that enables the belief that metasystems exist, where the cybernetic principles that are associated with it operate through a relationship between the system and its metasystem.

The set of purposeful problem solving systems will perform three basic kinds of complementary processes (Ulrich, 1983):

1 *inquiry*, producing meaningful knowledge with respect to its purpose;
2 *action*, securing the purposeful use of knowledge gained during inquiry;
3 *valuation*, responsibly evaluating the production and use of knowledge from the perspectives of those whom it serves positively and negatively.

Epistemologically, this paradigm includes (van Gigch, 1989, p. 30):

● a hierarchy of problem solving levels in which higher level systems can judge and rate solutions for lower level systems;
● a framework to provide evaluation criteria in metalanguage terms using a language appropriate to judge lower system solutions;
● a guarantor of 'truth' at each system level.

We see van Gigch in his reference to 'truth' as pointing to the paradigms that each level operates, and highlighting the idea that every system is paradigm plural. When we speak of something that is true, we say that it is in accordance with 'fact' or 'reality', with reason or 'correct' principles or a received standard that is 'accurately' confirming (*Concise Oxford English Dictionary*, 1959). Leonard (1996, personal communication) sees 'truth' as a *tricky* concept that perhaps can be described at best by providing reliable evidence according to an agreed set of criteria. Like criteria, 'truth' is belief based and *defined* within the paradigm of a given system focus. We can try to *evaluate* it, but to do so we need criteria for judgement. If the 'truths' of a metasystem are being used to explore a lower system focus, then the criteria derive from its own propositions, not from those of the lower focus. Another way of saying this is that we can only use our own criteria to judge others. This must apply to ethical as well as technical criteria in systems design.

14.2.2 Beliefs about the hierarchy of problem solving systems

We have considered at some length that when systems can be described in terms of subsystems that themselves have subsystems in interaction, then we can talk about a holarchy, which can as well be expressed in terms of suprasystems embedded in suprasystems.

If we are able to examine each systemic level separately, then we say we can focus in on it. We have previously considered the nature of recursion, and this is central to VSM, whose concepts can be used recursively at many levels of focus. Holistic evaluation of the system as a whole means considering the results of all recursions together.

A VSM analysis normally begins by identifying a situation that can be seen as a system. It:

1 involves a set of distinct but systemically interrelated hierarchic levels;
2 has hierarchic levels that can each have a VSM model applied;
3 has hierarchic levels that can each be seen as a level of recursion since VSM can be applied to it in its entirety;
4 has system levels that each have their own metasystem;
5 has a focus that defines the hierarchic level being modelled by VSM.

Thus, part of VSM includes the definition of a metasystem, the function of which is to 'design other system levels' (van Gigch, 1989, p. 28). The metasystem operates from a paradigm which is concerned with 'the design of a paradigm by which other paradigms are designed' (van Gigch, 1989). Such an approach is 'not problem orientated, but constitutes an inquiring system by which methodologies for solving problems are designed' (van Gigch, 1989).

In applying these ideas, note should be made of the work of such authors as Ulrich (1977) illustrating that problem solving methodologies can be integrated into a hierarchy of problem solving systems. 'This is a general system model of design. It is devoid of content in the sense that it can be applied to all systems. It can be constrained as the conceptualisation of Beer's idea of the metasystem which can be used to design other systems' (van Gigch, 1989, p. 28).

The purpose of the metasystem

The VSM paradigm operates a methodology that conceives that every human activity system has associated with it a metasystem. A system is perceived as an organisation of operations, and a metasystem is represented by 'higher levels of management that define purpose for a system' (Flood and Jackson, 1991, p. 231). According to van Gigch (1989) a metasystem can also be defined as a system over and above a system of lower logical order.

We have previously referred to a metasystem as the metaphorical 'cognitive consciousness' of a system. Like every system, every system focus has its own 'cognitive consciousness'. If we can identify the boundaries of a human activity system (focus) that we perceive as being capable of acting semi-autonomously, then we can find a cognitive consciousness for that system (focus). If we can find a holarchy, then we can also find a metaholarchy that will complexify the nature of the situation under inquiry.

Like any seat of cognitive consciousness, the metasystem is 'capable of deciding propositions, discussing criteria, or exercising regulation for systems that are themselves logically incapable of such decisions and discussions, or of self-regulation' (van Gigch, 1989). Further, it can do anything that might be expected from a cognitive consciousness.

Consider now that in an organisation a system has a formalised metasystem from which institutionally acceptable decisions are made with respect to the needs of the organisation. This formalised metasystem may itself have a metasystem (or meta-metasystem). We are aware from earlier work that a metasystem is manifested through a paradigm that controls it. Thus, the system and its formalised metasystem are each controlled by their own different (and therefore incommensurable) paradigms, with their own inherent attitudes, beliefs, values and conceptualisations. In such a relationship any of the following may occur:

1 the propositional logic of the metasystem is not accessible to that of the system (and vice versa), or
2 the paradigmatic language (e.g. metalanguage) can generate statements the meaning of which is not mutually expressible (e.g. in the system's language), or
3 the culture of the metasystem/system will not allow particular perspectives.

Since cybernetics is concerned with control, and VSM is a cybernetic model, it is clear that control must play a significant part in its beliefs. A useful approach to describing this is offered by Kickert and van Gigch (1989, pp. 37–55) in which the relationship between system control and the metasystem is examined. Given a set of objectives within a situation, the latter is controlled in order to maintain stability by a controller. These objectives apply to the operations of the system, which may be seen as the object of control.

However, the controller is not alone. The controller is also controlled by a controller at a different level of hierarchy. This higher-level controller operates from the metasystem, and exercises metacontrol. To the metacontroller, however, controlling the controller is an operational activity, and may also have its own metacontroller. Consequently, it is possible to move the view of that which defines an object of consideration either up or down the hierarchic level. Moving the view can also be called moving the focus of the system.

The VSM can also be seen as a model that balances system autonomy and control according to the purposes of the system (Leonard, 1996, personal communication). By autonomy we mean the freedom to be self-directed or self-governed.

A system is often defined in management contexts in terms of a set of operations and its immediate management. However, the metasystem is 'something logically beyond ... the logic of the operational elements combined. In ordinary managerial parlance, the metasystem thus defined is called "senior management"; and this carries the connotation that it is superior to a "junior management". But that is only to invoke the language of command, which we have forsworn' (Beer, 1979, p. 116). Such a notion of the metasystem is illustrated in Minicase 14.1.

14.2.3 Beliefs underlying the viable system model

Variety

The variety of an environment is determined by the more or less distinguishable entities (elements, events or states) that occur within it, and can be expressed in terms of time, space or purpose. The distinguishable entities:

- may be constrained through relatively stable causal relationships between them in time and space;
- may appear to have a lack of constraint or be chaotic, when they appear to be loosely related such that one event or state cannot be clearly associated with another.

Minicase 14.1

Manufacturing the metasystem

In the same way that the system can have many hierarchic levels, so too can the metasystem. The relationship between the system and metasystem in VSM is that every hierarchic level of system has associated with it a hierarchic level of metasystem.

Thus, consider the following example. An organisation is seen to have a manufacturing system with its own management team. This system has within it two subsystems, production and distribution, each with its own management, and each of which is potentially viable in its own right. In respect of the two subsystems, the manufacturing management team (a) is senior and (b) undertakes control and evaluation of the operations in production and storage. This situation is shown in Fig. 14.1. Senior management therefore constitutes the formalised metasystem.

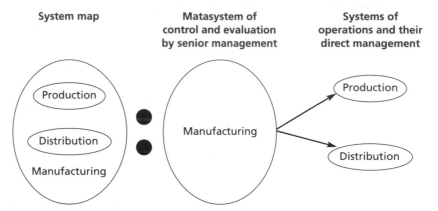

Fig. 14.1 Relationship between system and metasystem in terms of control
Note that the metasystem can be seen in terms of senior management.

The idea of variety is central to VSM. The *variety* of a system can be defined (Beer, 1979, p. 3) as the number of possible states that the system is capable of exhibiting. The basic condition of the complexity of a system is determined by its variety. Variety can therefore be seen to act as a measure of complexity. As environmental variety changes, so will environmental complexity. Organisational and social problem situations are often seen to arise with changes in complexity. We often see this as a natural development with, for example, the rise of new technologies and their consequences for existing labour mechanisms.

The context of a situation that exhibits variety is important when discussing complexity. Thus, what we mean by variety will be dependent upon the context within which the system is placed by an inquirer. In this light we can say that when we talk of the number of possible states in a situation that defines variety, then we are also talking about the weltanschauung of an inquirer.

Requisite variety is the variety that a system must have in order to deal with environmental variety. The VSM paradigm is perceived to have three requirements that are needed to achieve requisite variety (Jackson, 1992, p. 102). These can be expressed as follows:

1 the organisation should have the best possible model of the environment relevant to its form;

2 the organisation's information flows should reflect the nature of that environment so that the organisation is responsive to it;

3 communications that link different functions within an organisation are important.

An illustration of the idea of requisite variety is given in Minicase 14.2.

Minicase 14.2

A triumph of requisite variety

According to Ashby, variety can destroy variety. Thus, to place a system under control, there must be as much variety available as is exhibited by the system.

A Triumph Spitfire has entered in an old sports car race. Information has come to the waystation in Preston that it has broken down on the road to Lancaster, its next destination. Now, there are two roads by which the city can be reached from Preston, and there is a need to reach the car urgently in order to bring it in for repair. This must be done as soon as possible. Since there are two roads, this represents the environmental variety that affects the race organisation.

The most obvious option is that both roads should be searched simultaneously, thus representing the requisite variety of the situation. To do this two breakdown vehicles should be sent out to search and retrieve, representing the variety in the solution needed to destroy the variety of the problem situation

Viability

A system is viable if it can respond to changes regardless of whether they have been foreseen – that is, if it can respond to the environment with *requisite variety*. 'In order to become or remain viable it must be able to achieve requisite variety with the complex environment with which it is faced. It must be able to respond appropriately to the various threats and opportunities presented by its environment. The exact level at which the balance of varieties should be achieved is determined by the purpose that the system is pursuing' (Jackson, 1992, p. 105).

A viable system is one that can be seen to be self-dependent, and thus take on an independent existence. Now, a system can be viewed as a set of hierarchies that together form a complex whole. In the same way as it is possible to explore the viability of an organisation as a whole, the viability of each hierarchic level can also be explored as a part of the system.

This leads on to a question posed by Beer: 'If a viable system is one "able to maintain a separate existence", how is it that a viable system *contains* viable systems which are clearly *not* separate from the viable system in which they are contained?' (Beer, 1979, p. 118). The answer is that often parts of the system that might be identifiable as self-standing viable systems have other social, cultural, propositional, operational or human constraints that do not enable them to be separated out to work as independent viable systems.

A system that is viable is self-contained in its ability to survive. This can be seen as meaning that the nature of a viable system is that it is *autopoietic*, and able to support adaptability and change while maintaining its operational or behavioural stability.

Behavioural stability

Now, the *form* of an organisation is determined by (a) its structure, which can facilitate desirable processes, and (b) its processes, which enable that structure to be maintained. Behaviour is the response of the organisation to events that impact on it (the environmental variety) – that is, it is the manifest actions applied to the environment by the system. Since the behaviour and form of the organisation are linked, change in one can affect the other.

The behaviour of a system can be defined in terms of the *key operations* that enable the organisation to *achieve its objectives*. Thus the tendency towards achieving a set of goals (if that tendency can be evaluated adequately) is indicative of stable behaviour.

These goals will have a tendency to change. Systems that are organised to continually review their goals do so because they are aware of the propensity of complex environments sometimes to change rapidly. As a consequence there will often be a need to change the goals in order to satisfy requisite variety. The creation and examination of future scenarios is one way of dealing with this.

VSMM is used to maintain behavioural stability while supporting adaptability. One of its basic tenets is that the behaviour of an organisation can be stabilised by improving its communication and control system. Communication and control have both structural and process aspects in an organisation. We note that the purpose of control is to generate either:

1 negative feedback (homeostatic action) to damp down unwanted deviations from a required norm; or

2 positive feedback (morphogenic action) to amplify deviations to create adaptation.

The purpose of communication is to facilitate processes that are necessary to maintain:

1 organisational form

2 requisite variety.

Autopoiesis

When we consider the nature of a viable system, we should also consider autopoiesis (self-production). 'Viable organisations produce themselves. This is something different from self-reproduction, which involves changing the level of recursion' (Beer, 1979, p. 405). Thus, 'the viable system is autopoietic: it produces itself. Thereby it maintains its living identity. It preserves its own organisation' (Beer, 1979, p. 408). As a consequence, in Beer's view, organisations that are viable are necessarily autopoietic.

Now, there is a logical relationship between the total operational system and its metasystem, of which the sociocultural values are not necessarily part of the consideration. The idea that we are dealing with a logical relationship between the system and metasystem is central, for instance, to the related Schwarzian viable systems theory considered in Part 2. It is also implicit to our core model, in which the cognitive and behavioural aspects of a system are linked through a process of logical organising. Beer's proposition of autopoiesis can now be seen to imply that the connection between the system and the metasystem is logically closed. We can also say that the organising relationships that enable the form of a system to be established are closed.

This brings us to Beer's view of closure in the organisation. 'Closure turns the system back into itself, to satisfy the criteria of viability at its own level of recursion. Closure is the talisman of *identity* ... by "closure" I mean a self-referential process, and not the isolation of the system within an adiabatic shell' (Beer, 1979, p. 260). This does not mean that closure is self-reference, but that closure enables self-reference.

The autopoietic nature of an organisation should relate to system focuses and the organisation as a whole. It should not apply only to the metasystem. An example of when this might occur is when the metasystem attempts to control for the sake of control. Seeing control as a product of the organisation destroys the viability and autonomy of the broader system. In Beer's terms, a system in this condition can be described as *pathologically autopoietic* (Beer, 1979, pp. 408–12). Ultimately, the pathology of a viable system concerns the failure of its cohesiveness.

Adaptive systems

Systems that exist in complex environments must be able to *adapt* to the variety that confronts them. A system that is capable of adapting to variety is referred to as an *adaptive system*. To adapt, an adaptive system must have an appropriate *internal organisation*.

The internal organisation of an adaptive system can acquire features that permit it to:

- discriminate
- act upon
- respond to

aspects of the environmental variety and its constraints.

When this happens then the system has adapted by *mapping aspects of the environmental variety and constraint* to achieve requisite variety. This occurs through channels of communication. We can say that when a system has adapted it becomes *selectively matched* to its environment, both physiologically and psychologically.

We can also talk of adaptability in terms of the management of variety. In situations in which the variety is either unlimited or very large, it is appropriate to attempt to reduce variety through control. Managing variety is usually called *variety engineering* (Beer, 1979; Jackson, 1992, p. 102). It can occur through changing the form or behaviour of an organisation through:

1 *Reducing variety* impinging on a situation from an environment; this can occur, for instance, through structural change (e.g. relationships between roles, departments) and related process changes (e.g. expected role behaviour, work practices, management style). Variety reduction strategy indicates a selection of what variety must be handled and what can be safely ignored through the use of what can be referred to as data filters;

2 *Increasing variety* available to a situation; this can occur, for instance, through changes in information and communications, and through behavioural change (in the case of managers demonstrating behaviour to amplify their variety as controllers).

14.2.4 The cognitive model of VSMM

The principle of VSM is to propose axiomatically that any organisation able to be modelled as a viable system can also be modelled as a set of five subsystems. These represent five interactive cybernetic functions that act together as a filter between the environment and the organisation's management hierarchy, and connect management processes and their communications channels. The filter is sophisticated because it *attenuates* (reduces the importance of) some data while simultaneously *amplifying* other data. The filtered data is converted into information that is relevant to different levels of management within the organisation. A final control element addressed in the model offers auditing tools to make sure that the correct data is being collated. The audit channel mops up variety by sporadic or periodic checks. However, making sure that the appropriate data is assembled is only one of its functions. The VSM is composed of five entities, referred to as system one (S1) to system five (S5), and their direct relationship is shown in Fig. 14.2. Using the theory developed earlier in this book, we can assign the 'S's to the system and metasystem domains. To do this we place S1 in the system domain, and S4 and S5 in that of the metasystem. Not usual to VSM is our introduction of a transmogrific domain, which we have identified in the diagram, and to which we assign S2, S3 and S3*. Each of the 'S's has a designation that is explained below.

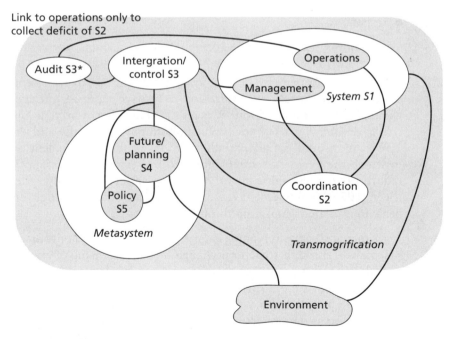

Fig. 14.2 Relationship diagram showing the online concept of the viable system model
The subsystem entities in S1 (management and operations) are implicitly interconnected.

System(s) 1 (S1): Operations

This may be seen as a single or multiple system. The interconnections from each of S2–S5 occur to any one S1. Thus, if there is a multiple S1, each can therefore be seen as being linked between audit and coordination separately. S1 is concerned with the *system in focus* ('the system') and its behaviour. The system in focus can alternatively be referred to as *the relevant system and its defined purposes*. Operations provides a representation of what the system does and produces; it is usually broken down into functional units, and interacts with the environment through futures/planning. It is the system that is itself the subject of control. S1 interacts with the environment directly and through S4. There may be a number of perspectives from which to see S1, and it may be seen from more than one by an organisation. 'For instance S1 could be seen in terms of product line, technology used, location, cycle time of products, customers, distribution channels, etc.' (Leonard, 1996, personal communication).

System 2 (S2): Coordination

The cybernetic function can provide effective control. It concerns aspects of culture and is interested in limited synergy across divisions of an organisation. It tries to harmonise the culture and structure of the enterprise while also trying to reduce chaos and introduce order. It amplifies the control capability to try to induce self-regulation into its behaviour; that is, in the implementation of operations. It can be seen as predominantly anti-oscillatory. 'It implements non-executive decisions like schedules, personnel and accounting policies and other areas governed by (legal and other) protocol. The aspect of culture it addresses is that of house style rather than the values/identity questions of S5. It is interested in achieving smoothness across divisions – not synergy across which deals with the view from the perspective of the system as a whole which is S3's job' (Leonard, 1996, personal communication).

System 3 (S3): Integration/control

The cybernetic function is concerned with effective regulation of the dynamic internal to the organisation. Integration/control is in charge of the functional units of the system. It controls and monitors what is going on. It is responsible for the implementation of policies, resource allocation, and the control and monitoring of the implementation activities. It determines information needs. It is involved in synergy related tasks. 'S3 is more likely to be dominant over S4 as it is line [management] and S4 may be staff [management]. They should be equal' (Leonard, 1996, personal communication).

System 4 (S4): Future/planning

This cybernetic function is important to the identity of the organisation. Future/planning involves issues of development and strategic planning. It macromonitors, observing the enterprise from both an internal and an external view, gathering information from the environment and the system itself. 'It does all the future orientated tasks: research and development, training (except the orientation and maintaining skills at S2), recruitment, public relations, and market research' (Leonard, 1996, personal communication).

System 5 (S5): Policy

This cybernetic function is concerned with the establishment and maintenance of a coherent context for the processes of the organisation. It relates to what the organisation sets out to do. It defines the direction of the organisation. 'From the perspective of VSM, ... this function is realistically embedded in lower level processes' (Harnden *et al.*, 1995). It requires an accurate overview that represents the various dimensions of activity. Policy provides the systematic capability to choose from the different problem situations or opportunities thrown up by the environment. 'S5 is concerned with identity and cohesion and with monitoring the balance between emphasis on S3 and S4' (Leonard, 1996, personal communication).

Relationship between the metasystem entities

Like any metaphorical cognitive consciousness, among other things the metasystem controls and evaluates the system and its behaviour. The system (of operations and its direct management, referred to as S1) is variable. It is treated as a *black box* so that interest lies in its inputs and outputs rather than its internal processes.

Within the metasystem there are five generic subsystems that represent management functions. Coordination (S2) is intended to dampen down any unstable oscillations that might develop within the system. This represents an attempt to reduce the likelihood of moving into instability. Integration/control (S3) in connection with the system contributes (with S2, S4 and S5) to requisite variety. The true role of S3 in terms of viability is to look after the synergy of the system (S1). Future/planning (S4) provides insight into weaknesses within the internal structure of the metasystem, and focuses mostly on the outside rather than on activities. Policy (S5) is needed to monitor the operation of balancing operations that occur between S3 and S4.

There is thus a relationship between each of the elements S2–S5 and the system. The relationship between S4 (future/planning) and S3 (integration/control) is intended to generate variety. S3 originates messages (which it seeks to amplify) to S4. S4 originates (and amplifies) messages from S3, which places into context future prospects. S5 is designed to monitor the interaction between S3 and S4, and to generate policy that will enable requisite variety to be generated. It thus enables closure to occur at the local hierarchic level that is being considered. The relationship between the different metasystemic elements is shown in Fig. 14.3, which illustrates how some aspects of homeostasis occur within the organisation, as well as self-reference, self-organisation and closure.

14.2.5 Rules and propositions appropriate to VSMM

Complex environments contain variety to which systems must adapt if they are to survive. Complex adaptive systems exist in potentially changing environments. Different classes of adaptive systems may generate patterns that can often be described as similar, or that have comparable emergent properties. In relation to human groups, a complex adaptive system will have the following characteristics:

1 a group must be a network of independent agents;

2 an agent is not only a part of an adaptive system, but is in itself an adaptive system;

3 local interactions of group members generate global patterns or emergent properties;

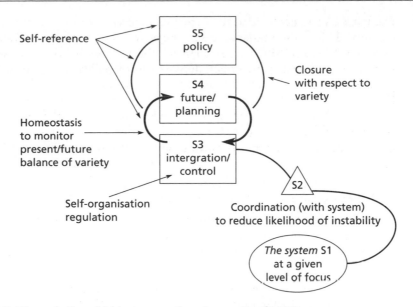

Fig. 14.3 The relationship between the elements of VSM
S3 and S4 enable requisite variety, which is generated by S5, while S2 recommends regulation.

4 the patterns that emerge are independent of the characteristics of the members that compose the system;

5 similar patterns, or emergent properties, should arise in different groups;

6 similar patterns, or emergent properties, should occur in systems other than groups;

7 a complex adaptive system will adapt to changing circumstances.

Such a system must have:

8 plasticity and irritability (causing tension) such that it carries on a constant interchange with environmental events acting on it and reacting to it (and to potential events);

9 source of variety, to act as a potential pool of adaptive variability;

10 a set of selective criteria which may be selected from the 'variety pool';

11 an arrangement for preserving and/or propagating successful adaptability.

These propositions of adaptability depend upon the ideas that:

12 information is available that can provide meaning about a given situation;

13 communication can occur.

The purpose for communication is contextually related to the adaptive system to:

14 aid adaptation

15 learn.

The use of VSM is intended to correct control and communications processes to ensure viability. This is the fundamental proposition of the approach. Referring to Flood and Jackson (1991, p. 89), we can identify the following principles of the methodology associated with VSM, and which may be considered to represent its propositions. Thus:

16 recommendations endorsed by VSMM do not prescribe a specific organisational form, rather they are concerned with the essentials of organisation and maintenance of identity;

17 the notion of recursion is fundamental so that vertical interdependence can be dealt with;

18 in any viable unit, horizontally interdependent subsystems are integrated and guided by metasystemic higher management levels;

19 sources of command and control are of particular concern and are spread throughout the architecture of the viable system; this enhances the self-organisation and localised management of perceived problem situations;

20 emphasis is placed on the relationship between the viable unit and its environment in terms of influencing and being influenced by it; this relationship is in particular used to promote learning.

For Beer it is *axiomatic* that:

21 a viable system is also autopoietic.

Such a system will have:

22 closure with respect to its requisite variety;

23 self-reference.

Both closure and self-reference occur in the metasystem rather than the system. This is axiomatic in the VSM paradigm, and independently argued in Chapter 6. While (14) and (15) provide a necessary condition for autopoiesis, they are not sufficient. To show that a system is autopoietic, we note the discussion in Chapter 6, and see our system as (a) dynamic and (b) composed of a network of processes that generates outputs. The system is autopoietic if it can:

24 generate outputs to that network of processes that are in part themselves the network of processes (a recursive definition);

25 define (for the recursive network) a set of boundaries that correctly defines the system and satisfies its cognitive purposes that in the content of a metasystem can also be called metapurpose.

In systems approaches an inquirer defines a situation which, when viewed as a system, can normally be seen to have distinct subsystem levels. Each level can then:

26 represent a level of system hierarchy (or focus of inquiry);

27 be considered independently;

28 be seen to be viable.

An organisation as a whole can be seen as viable if all of its hierarchic levels are viable.

In VSM the system in focus is a given level of operations. VSMM can be applied to any higher or lower levels than those in focus; that is, the focus can be moved up or down. When applied to different levels, VSMM is being used recursively, when we can talk of levels of recursion.

14.2.6 Generic nature

VSMM is a versatile cybernetic approach directed towards system intervention, and defines the domain that most refer to as managerial cybernetics, but which Jackson calls organisational cybernetics in an attempt to highlight its orientation towards soft and uncertain situations. Thus, people are important to it, and are very much part of the inquiry process.

The methodology is concerned with complex situations. It assumes that situations are very uncertain, that problem situations are ill structured. It is sensitive to the principle of indeterminacy, and is thus concerned not only with what is often seen as mechanical control processes, but with the role and influence of an inquirer. The approach is also pragmatic, enabling a great deal of freedom to the inquirer in the way VSM is interpreted within a situation.

14.2.7 The language

Table 14.1 The language of VSMM

VSMM terms	Meaning
System in focus	The relevant system and its defined purposes.
Viability	The ability to cope with unpredictable futures.
Viable system	A viable system is one that survives, that can respond to changes regardless of whether they have been foreseen, that can achieve requisite variety, and that is able to support adaptability and change while maintaining the stability in its behaviour. A viable system is also defined to be autopoietic.
Variety	Measure of the number of possible states.
Requisite variety	The required number of states that enables environmental variety to be balanced by system variety relating to a purposeful activity.
Metasystem	The higher level system that acts as a controller of a lower level.
Adaptive system	A system that can adapt to the variety of its environment by in some way adopting that variety into its organisational form and information content.
Self-organisation	This occurs when deviations from a normal or expected situation are amplified such that a change in the form of the organisation occurs.
Self-reference	This occurs when a system refers only to itself in terms of its internal actions or processes.
Autopoiesis	Autopoietic systems are self-organising, produce and eventually change their own structures, are self-referencing, and are self-producing in that they produce the network of processes that enables them to produce their own components.

Continued overleaf

Table 14.1 (continued)

VSMM terms	Meaning
Algedonic filter	An algedonic filter is an alerting mechanism for problem situations.
Algedonic system	A system that generates alerting mechanisms for problem situations.
Recursion	The application of a whole concept or set of actions that occurs at one level of consideration can also be applied at a lower logical level of consideration.
Suprasystem	A system that is at a higher hierarchic level than the one under consideration.
Subsystem	A system that is at a lower hierarchic level than the one under consideration.
Closure	This refers to a system being logically closed such that it is able to undertake self-reference.
Identity	In the VSM paradigm identity refers to the *individual* identity of a system that uniquely distinguishes it from other systems. There is no differentiation between class identity as used in autopoiesis and individual identity.
Homeostasis	A process of negative feedback control, also referred to as deviation-counteraction.
Attenuation	Reducing the importance of something.
Amplification	This refers to deviation-amplification, and indicates that certain data which is important to the organisation should have its importance highlighted.

14.2.8 Logical processes of VSMM

One principle of VSM is that the model can be applied to different levels of systemic hierarchy in exactly the same way. This is referred to as the principle of recursion. Flood and Jackson (1991, p. 90) define recursion as occurring when the whole system is replicated in the parts so that the same viable system principles may be used to model a subsystem in an organisation, the organisation itself, and the suprasystem of which the organisation forms a part. The directly connected hierarchical levels that define the system, the subsystem and the suprasystem can also be seen in terms of connected environments. Thus the suprasystem may be seen as an external environment, and relative to this there is a system environment and a subsystem environment.

When talking of the application of the model to different focuses (F), let us arbitrarily define a top level of consideration (F0), which includes an environment in which the system as a whole is embedded. This, then, will represent the highest systemic level of interest. Within this at F1 is a focus on the potentially viable relevant system that enables the purpose of an inquiry to be facilitated. The next focus below this is F2.

Jackson (1992) has identified three phases in his approach to the application of VSM: system identification, system diagnosis, and evaluating and correcting structural faults cybernetically (we would rather talk of diagnosing and correcting faults of form). These are defined in Table 14.2.

According to the paradigm operated in some VSM groups, the set of phases is used within a continuous cycle through which iteration occurs in order to ensure that the system in focus has been satisfactorily identified, cybernetic faults correctly diagnosed, and intervention strategies to correct the faults appropriately defined.

Table 14.2 The phases of VSMM

System identification (System 1)

Identify/determine purposes to be pursued

Determine the system in focus (F1)

Specify viable parts of system (F2)

Specify the viable system as a whole (F0)

System diagnosis

S1: The system

- study the parts of the system (S1) in terms of its environment, operations, local management
- constraints
- accountability, indicators of performance
- establish the VSM model

S2: Coordination

- list possible sources of conflict between the parts of the system and their environments
- identify the elements of the system that have a harmonising or dampening effect on behaviour
- consult to find status of S2 (threatening or facilitating)

S3: Integration/control

- list elements involved in integration/control
- consult to find how S3 authority is exercised
- determine process of resource bargaining in system parts (S1)
- consult to find out responsibility for system performance
- identify audit (S3*) inquiries in S3
- Sociopolitical aspects: what is relationship between S3 and system (S1) elements (i.e. degree of freedom, autocratic, democratic, etc.)

S4: Future/planning

- list S4 activities
- identify length of future consideration
- how do activities guarantee adaptation to future?
- is macromonitoring occurring to assess trends and the environment?
- is the system open to novelty through S4?
- does a management centre exist to integrate internal/external information for decisions?
- can urgent developments be flagged (in S5)?

S5: Policy

- identify who is involved, and S5 behaviour
- does S5 define a suitable identity for the system?
- how does the ethos of policy (S5) affect future/planning (S4)?
- how does the ethos of policy (S5) affect the relationship between integration/control (S3) and futures/planning (S4) – is stability or change emphasised?
- does policy (S5) share an identity with the system (S1)?
- confirm that information channels, processes, and controls are suitable

Continued overleaf

Table 14.2 (continued)

Evaluating and correcting faults of form cybernetically

- Confirm recursion has been adequately identified at each level of operation
- confirm that appropriate operational parts at a given hierarchic level and lower hierarchic levels are considered as viable systems
- organisational features may be additional and irrelevant to viability, which may interfere with a search for effectiveness and survivability. These should be dispensed with. This can be seen as *correcting* the non-viable aspects
- S2–S5 serve the system (S1), and should not be pathologically autopoietic: that is, they should not be concerned with their own self-production at the expense of the system, and should not become independently viable system since this will be at the expense of the system as a whole
- ensure that all key elements defined by VSM exist in the system and operate correctly
- confirm that S5 (policy) represents the wider system to better ensure viability
- confirm that the communication channels are appropriate for rapid transmission of information between the environment and the organisation. It may involve such ideas as lag, transduction, variety handling capability/channel capacity etc.

14.2.9 The behavioural model of VSM methodology

It is normally the VSM rather than the phases of inquiry of VSM methodology (VSMM) that is stressed in the literature. We can present the phases in a cyclic fashion as in Fig. 14.4. The conceptualisation is that once the three phases of inquiry have been undertaken, a correct application followed through with an appropriate intervention will ensure that the system is viable.

However, after passing through each of the three phases, the cycle of inquiry must be continually reapplied in order to ensure that the system remains viable. This is because systems can drift organisationally and cybernetically. We say this noting that the condition of viability normally focuses on monitoring the environment and the system's response to change.

Central to this is a formalised cybernetic map of the organisation resulting from system diagnosis, referred to as the VSM.

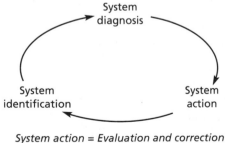

*System action = Evaluation and correction
of structural faults*

Fig. 14.4 Basic form of VSMM

This shows the recurrent cycle of inquiry intended to ensure that once a system being inquired into is viable, it is able to maintain its viability.

Characteristic problems of VSM

VSM is used in a variety of situations concerned with an understanding of the cybernetic and adaptive nature of an organisation. Thus, for example, inquirers may be interested in:

- the possibilities that may exist for an organisation's adaptation to changes;
- the possibilities for defining appropriate policy;
- how policy communicates to and can affect the system;
- the possibilities for synergy within the system as a whole;
- a variety of soft elements such as the sociopolitical factors of a situation.

During diagnosis it is appropriate to identify the characteristics that are problematic in situations. A number of such weaknesses have been identified as typically occurring. These are highlighted in Table 14.3 (Harnden *et al.*, 1995).

Table 14.3 Typical weakness found in organisations

System	Typical problem situation
1 The system	Failure to identify S1 manifests itself by such symptoms as mismatch between formalised job description and actual skill requirements, inoperative resource allocation, inaccurate planning criteria, inappropriate assessment of information needs, ineffective specification of criteria of performance, and faulty design of information systems, through inaccurate identification of key variables.
2 Coordination	Weak S2 can be indicated by problems of queuing and log-jams, whether in production, service to clients, distribution or information dissemination; oscillations and violent fluctuations; inconsistent responses to customer queries; unhappy workforce due to uncoordinated wage policy; fortress mentality – 'us versus them'; uncoordinated regulation leading to confusion and mistakes; lagged or inconsistent performance appraisal standards.
3 Integration/control	Ineffective S3 can be represented by over-involvement of top management in low-level tasks, lack of mechanisms in place to permit sporadic audits of operations, failure to appreciate, trust and build on self-organising potential of an enterprise, over-reliance on rules and interference, demands between autonomy and cohesion generating conflict, alienation and resentment because of interference from more senior management.
4 Future/planning	Ineffective S4 can be seen as policies taking little account of external threats and opportunities, over-reliance on short-term issues of control and performance, the efficient dinosaur, little market research, limited encouragement of novelty, reluctance to consider structural changes.
5 Policy	Ineffective S5 can cause use of unrealistic criteria in forming policy, policy directives out of step with expectations of workforce, policy emerges in isolation, over-reliance on either external and long-term or internal and short-term issues, failure to take effective action in response to alerts and alarms, hazy or incompatible notions of core purpose of organisation from different perspectives in it, inconsistent guidelines for such things as quality, effectiveness, leadership, team, responsibility.

The formalised map of VSM

Unusually for inquiring methodologies, the form of inquiry centres on the core model, and the phases of the methodology follow. The usual presentation for VSM is given in Fig. 14.5. This has been developed in order to ensure that the holistic principles of the five VSM cybernetic functions are implemented, that the model can be appropriately mapped on to a situation, and that evaluation is possible.

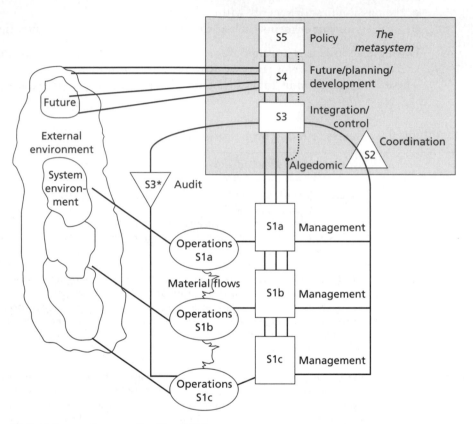

Fig. 14.5 Cybernetic map for the VSM

Within each system environment there may also be local environments that can be seen as a lower level of focus.

The formalised map of VSM can be applied to a higher level of system focus, as it can to a lower one. When lower levels of focus can be defined such that VSM can be applied, then it is said to be used *recursively*. The reason is that an organisation tends to have many levels of focus, each of which may itself be capable of being viable. 'In a recursive organisational structure, any viable system contains, and is contained in, a viable system' (Beer, 1979, p. 118).

If we envisage a System 1 with only one managed operational unit, then Fig. 14.5 can be simplified, as shown in Fig. 14.6. Management interactions operate on the operation through an effector, while a sensor reports back from operations to management.

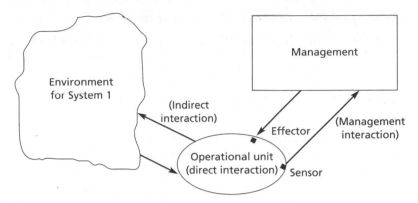

Fig. 14.6 The System 1 (operational unity and its direct management) an interaction with environment

14.3 The doppelgänger paradigm

The VSM paradigm supposes that organisations have a metasystem that is defined in terms of a higher level of recursion. While the concept of the metasystem as defined in Chapters 5 and 6 is consistent with this, it has rather been defined in terms of both individual and group world views; that is, the weltanschauung and the paradigm.

To see how the two concepts relate, we can consider the VSM metasystem in terms of senior management. Here, there will be an organisational paradigm within which a set of propositions defines the organisation, for example in terms of its group identity. It also determines the organisation's culture in terms of its normative attitudes, values, beliefs and behaviour. Thus, individuals in an organisation behave in a way which is culturally determined, for instance, with respect to one another, towards their customers, or within their roles.

While we might talk of a paradigm that relates to the organisation as a whole, we can more profitably talk of each level of recursion having its own individual paradigm. It is clear that each group world view at each level of system hierarchy can be different. It is not unusual to find that different groups operating at either different hierarchical levels or at the same level on a different organisational parallel have differentiable paradigms.

If we relate the metasystem to senior management, then not only will the managers operate as a group within an organisational paradigm, but the individual managers' weltanschauungen will also be involved. This will clearly determine how they behave individually.

In the same way that one can talk of the metasystem associated with an organisation, one can talk of the metasystem associated with inquiry, as discussed in Chapter 5. The VSMM metasystem, like all other methodological approaches, can also be defined in terms of the paradigm with its methodological definition, and the weltanschauung determining its individual approach to inquiry. The paradigm defines a number of metapurposes (the cognitive purposes that relate to the metasystem) designed to ensure that the system is seen to operate viably; that is, being adaptable to change while being able to ensure that the organisation has dynamically stable operations.

In Chapter 5 we introduced two components of the metasystem for VSMM. These are:

1 a well-defined and fixed individual purpose of inquiry that must be transformed through the weltanschauungen of individuals through the process of inquiry;

2 a methodological purpose referred to as organisational viability, defined by the paradigm.

VSM is composed of system S1, overall methodological metapurposes m1 and m2, and inquiry metapurposes S2–S5. These are explained in Table 14.4.

The inquiry metapurposes all relate to the overall methodological purposes that ensure system viability, and are thus contingent to it. The metapurposes can become an intervention into the system through the methodology to ensure that it does function viably.

When the system is monitored and its evaluations are fed back to the metasystem, the senior management team can reinterpret and affirm that their interventions satisfy their perceived metapurposes; that is, that they are dynamically stable. An influence diagram defining the cognitive purposes for the system is given in Fig. 14.7.

The doppelgänger form of VSM

There are probably as many ways of applying VSM as there are inquirers. This is because it is traditionally seen that the power of VSMM lies in the cybernetic definition of VSM, rather than the methodological approach to its application. While the cycle of phased inquiry explained by Jackson does provide the basis of the approach, different inquirers and groups of inquirers are able to apply approaches that show some variation.

While VSM is fundamentally an approach that highlights comparison and control, its methodological vehicles sometimes seem to suffer from the problem of the shoemaker with no shoes. By this we mean that forms of methodological inquiry using VSM do not

Table 14.4 Definition of system and cognitive purposes for VSM

The system

S1 Operations, as represented by what the systems do and produce

Cognitive purpose

Mission and goals

The overall mission is to generate viability through correcting faults of form in an organisation under inquiry; the goals of VSM that satisfy this are to ensure that the organisation is adaptable and dynamically stable.

m1 Dynamic stability explores the purposes that are part of the system model, and evaluates whether or not the objectives that are derived from them are being achieved.

m2 Adaptability requires the ability of responding to change.

Inquiry aims

i1 Coordination, the nature of which is to try to harmonise the culture and form of the system while also trying to reduce chaos and induce order.

i2 Integration introduces control and monitoring of the system's functions while ensuring the implementation of policies and resource allocation. It harmonises behaviour.

i3 Futures development gathers information from the environment and the system.

i4 Policy selection provides the ability to choose systematically from the different problem situations or opportunities imposed on the system by the environment.

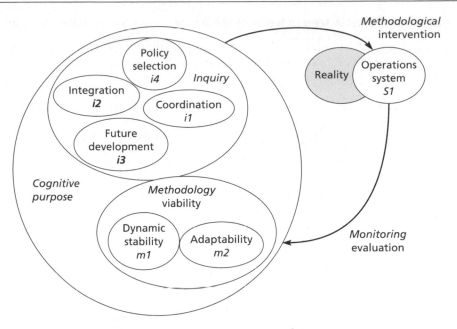

Fig. 14.7 Influence diagram for cognitive purposes of VSM

often in themselves formally propose many of the controls that could be applied to ensure that each phase in a VSMM has been properly undertaken. As a result of inquiry, controls are proposed if the diagnosis suggests them. In Table 14.5 we adjust our view of the Jackson explanation of phased inquiry by adding our own control loop to the

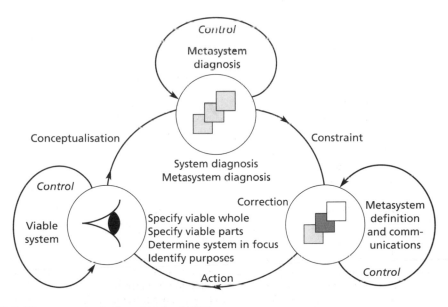

Fig. 14.8 Phase control diagram for VSM

Table 14.5 The VSM cycle seen in terms of the generic metamodel doppelgänger

Doppelgänger paradigm *Entity/process*	*VSM paradigm* *Explanation*	*Step*
Pre-evaluation		
	Identify/determine purposes of inquiry	1
	Determine system in focus	2
Analysis to specify	Specify viable parts of system	3
viable system	Specify viable system as a whole	4
Control confirm viable system definition		
Conceptualisation		
Synthesis system and metasystem diagnosis	System diagnosis: study the parts of the system in terms of its environment, operations, local management; constraints; accountability, indicators of performance; establish the VSM model	5
	Metasystem diagnosis	6
Control check synthesis of the system in focus		
Constraint		
Choice on cybernetic model	Correction of non-viable aspects of system	7
Control confirm metasystem definition	Confirm non-autopoietic nature of S2–S5 Confirm existence/operation of key VSM elements Confirm S5 represents wider system Confirm appropriate communications channels	
Action	Consult with participants or their representatives Recommend changes in organisational form After changes, enter new cycle of inquiry	

phased loop of inquiry immediately after the analysis phase. Other control loop options might also be appropriate, but they have not been considered here.

Finally, we transform Table 14.5 into a cyclic of inquiry consistent with that of Jackson. This is shown in Fig. 14.8.

14.4 Summary of VSMM

VSM is a powerful cybernetic approach that can define intervention in organisations that show faults of form. The methodology in which it is embedded offers logical relationships within a set of constructs that are supposed to represent the organisation in a general way. The logical relationships are not embroidered with a view that examines the cultural, social, political or individual aspects of individuals.

VSMM is able to examine a situation in order to make it viable if it is not already. This may involve making changes to information and communications processes, for example by amplifying certain information while attenuating other information. Change may also occur to the form of the situation such that its behaviour is adapted in ways that enable it to become selectively matched with its environment. This can bound the environmental variety, and enable the situation to generate requisite variety.

14.5 The VSMM case study

This case study derives from a student project completed by Terry Ashford in April 1993 for the completion of his MBA at Liverpool Business School. It explores the impact of then recent structural changes in the Liverpool further education system and its effects upon the inquirer's perception of its operations. In particular it diagnoses the viability of the School of Transport (within the City of Liverpool Community College) with the aid of the viable system model. As a consequence it identifies a number of measures that are seen to correct its faults of form. Ashford acted as an informal facilitator within the School of Transport, and the study shows how inquiry can, on its own, become an informal intervention strategy that can initiate changes. It thus implicitly stresses the concept of indeterminism. Since this study was not formally instituted by the college system, we are unable to explore the implementation of fault correction and post-evaluative exploration.

Ashford's original study explores three levels of focus, the College, Faculty and School. In a final summary he explores the correction of faults, and in doing so allows the different levels of focus to interplay. Unfortunately, a full study of all levels of focus is beyond the limited space available to this chapter. As a consequence only the School level will be examined. A reader wishing to explore this case further is recommended to refer to the source.

In order to enable the use of VSM to be followed more easily, a summary of its processes is given here.

14.5.1 Pre-evaluation

The Riverside College of Technology was opened in 1952 as the Riverside Technical College. It was established in South Liverpool on a 30-acre site near Aigburth. It was Liverpool Education Committee's first post-war technical education project. Due to a heavy demand for its educational provision, it opened an extension for automobile

Case summary

Activity	Description
Weltanschauung	Further education in Liverpool has passed through too many structural changes to give confidence that it is now viable.
Inquirer's mission	To explore the impact of structural changes in the Liverpool further education system on the Liverpool City School of Transport (within the City of Liverpool Community College). In particular, the intention is to establish the adequacy of the strategies used by the Liverpool City to cope with the complexity of tasks of further education in Liverpool, and its ability to deal with the influences from its environment. It will look at the college as a system with a set of embedded subsystems, and will address the question of whether the three focuses, College, the Faculty and the School of Transport, are viable.
Methodology: VSMM	The mission is to examine the structural condition of the City of Liverpool Community College, and in particular the lower focus of the School of Transport, and thus to examine its ability to operate as a semi-autonomous system. Such an exploration of its viability will enable an evaluation to occur as to whether it has any faults of form and what they are. This will enable the policy formation to correct these faults.
Goals and aims of inquiry	Methodological goals are to explore the dynamic stability of the City of Liverpool Community College seen as a system. This means that the objectives of the system will be examined in terms of its mission, and an evaluation will occur to see if the objectives are being achieved. In addition, the adaptability of the system will be explored to inquire into the system's ability to respond to change. The study does this through exploring the system in its interrelationship to the metasystem. The metasystem consists of the four cognitive functions generally taken to be coordination, integration, futures and policy. By coordination we are referring to a cognitive function that will harmonise the culture and form of the system while also trying to reduce chaos and induce order. By integration we mean introducing control and monitoring of the system's functions while ensuring the implementation of policies and resource allocation. Integration harmonises behaviour. Futures and development gathers information from the environment and the system. Finally, policy provides the ability to choose systematically from the different problem situations or opportunities imposed on the system by the environment.
Nature of examination	The methodology is being used to explore the relationship between the system and the metasystem. This relationship should be stable and able to withstand a variety of impacts from its environment.
Explanatory model	Three focuses of the target situation seen as a system will be defined. These are the College, the Faculty and the School. In each system focus the metasystem will be defined and explored to identify whether there are any faults of form, and whether it is capable of generating the variety required to manage the changes in its environment.
Options selection	A set of recommendations is proposed that may be regarded as options available to be implemented.

engineering in 1960. The was enlarged within two years. There was steady growth in all of its departments towards the close of 1970. These departments were:

1 construction
2 electronic and radio engineering
3 general and automobile engineering
4 marine engineering
5 navigation
6 scientific, general and communication studies.

The sixth department also undertook a servicing role for the other five.

At this time eight further education organisations were being maintained by the Liverpool Authority. These were:

1 Riverside College of Technology
2 Old Swan Technical College
3 North East Liverpool Technical College
4 Millbrook College of Commerce
5 Mable Fletcher Technical College
6 Ciluith Technical and Nautical Catering College
7 Childwall Hall College of Further Education
8 Central Liverpool College of Further Education.

These colleges provided some nationally marketable courses, but they predominantly serviced the needs of the local community. As a consequence, they were vulnerable to the social condition of the city. As Liverpool declined, so too did the colleges. Reasons for this decline include:

- the city's inability to attract industry;
- the decline of the British merchant fleet and use of the Liverpool Port;
- growing concentrations of:
  - unemployed people
  - one-parent families
  - pensioners
  - ethnic minorities.

The first reorganisation (1986–88)

In 1983, Her Majesty's Inspectors and the District Audit Service each undertook a complementary study of the further education college in Liverpool (HMI, 1983). The following conclusions resulted:

1 the Education Authority should review the roles of:
  - its colleges
  - their departmental structures
  - the reallocation of accommodation
  - the replacement of physical resources;

2 academic staff levels were too high in some areas of work;

3 some accommodation was under-utilised while other colleges were experiencing shortages;

4 capital investment was required in all colleges to update equipment;

5 high rates of student loss required investigation;

6 the presentation of examination results needed to be made more meaningful;

7 courses between colleges were duplicated; individual instances that were uneconomical could be consolidated;

8 there was confusion over class sizes;

9 there was a total under-utilisation of lecturing staff while overtime and additional duty claims were being met.

A reorganisation was instigated in 1986, and the South Mersey College was established through the amalgamation of Riverside College and Childwall Hall College. The integration policy that arose during this period resulted in four institutions:

1 City College (from Central and Ciluith)

2 Millbrook College (Millbank and North East Liverpool)

3 Sandown College (Old Swan and Mable Flecher)

4 South Mersey College (Riverside and Childwall Hall).

However, there was no coordination and harmonisation over course provision between these colleges, enabling duplication and possible course redundancy to occur.

As an example of the consequences of the reorganisation, the management of South Mersey College through its Principal introduced a simple technical way of looking at further education as an input/output system under control. It identified (a) input as finance, equipment and labour, (b) outputs as trained and qualified students and (c) a transformation process that involved the interaction between the formal educational system, the social system and technology. This enabled a visible control procedure to be implemented. As a result of this thinking, a new structure of faculties emerged:

● automobile and general engineering
● construction
● general studies
● maritime studies.

As a result of this rationalisation, a number of early retirements occurred and staff redeployments also became part of the agenda. In the faculty of automobile and general engineering, general engineering shrank in size, and staff were moved to the automobile section. Further, the college's vocational provision maintained its orientation to technology, and recurrent capital reinvestment occurred with technology development. A marketing team and an intelligence team were created, in which the automobile section had strong representation.

A second reorganisation (1988)

In 1988, more reorganisation occurred, and the vehicle body trades were transferred from City College to South Mersey College. This resulted in structural and human relationship problems, in particular between the vehicle and maritime workshops.

The third reorganisation (1989–91)

In 1989 the Faculty of Transport was announced, which was to integrate the shrinking faculty of maritime studies. Childwall campus was also closed and all of its courses and staff were moved to the Riverside site, despite strong resistance. This, it seems, led directly to a confrontation between management and staff.

Despite this, the faculty of transport continued to prosper, conflict subsided, and an important link with Honda established a motorcycle division. However, while the motor vehicle division was recruiting well by the academic year 1990/91, this was not the case for the marine division. As a result these courses were phased out, and now all transport-related courses were delivered on one site.

The fourth reorganisation (1991)

The Education Committee in Liverpool, made up of seconded representatives from the existing four colleges covering a variety of disciplines, established a rationalisation policy to integrate the four colleges into one. In 1991 the four colleges that represented further education in Liverpool were reorganised into a single college called City of Liverpool College. It opened in April of that year. This was a shock to both staff and students. It was also a shock to the new governing bodies, which would have to be disbanded after being set up after the 1988 Education Reform Act.

The City of Liverpool college was now one of the largest in the country. It had 30 000 students, more than 1500 staff, and a revenue budget of about £30 million. It had also passed through a number of reforms that had probably established a fragmented, conflictual and destabilised cultural environment. Its new structure is shown in Table 14.6.

The Principal has below him a Deputy Principal for Resources in charge of the resource departments and a Deputy Principal with responsibility for the curriculum, in charge of the faculties. The deputy for resources also has charge of the college management information system. Subsidiary to them both is the College Registrar. Each resource department has its own director, and the faculties each have a head.

Table 14.6 Structure of City Community College, indicating levels of focus

Principalship				
Faculties	Resources			Registrar
Vocational: ● Business studies ● Technology ● Creative and performing arts ● Science, health and service industries Non-vocational: ● ACE Central ● ACE East ● ACE North ● ACE South Curriculum Support Unit	Finance	Personnel	Premises management	

14.5.2 Analysis

Identify purposes of inquiry

The purpose of the inquiry was to explore the impact of structural changes in further education in Liverpool seen as a system in its provision of education through the City of Liverpool Community College. In particular, the intention was to establish the adequacy of the strategies used by the Liverpool City to cope with the complexity of tasks of further education in Liverpool, and its ability to deal with the influences from its environment. Looking at the college as a system with a set of embedded subsystems, the study also addressed the question of whether the three focuses – College, the Faculty and the School of Transport – are viable.

System in focus (F1)

The focus of the system that we are interested in is the Liverpool City Community College at focus F1. The viable parts of the system 'produce' it. It has its own mission, parts and stakeholders, as listed in Table 14.7.

Table 14.7 Focus F1: City Community College

Mission statement

To provide quality, equity and value in programmes offering access to and progression within education, training, employment and personnel development

System 1 parts	Stakeholders
Board of governors	Governors
Principalship	Principal
Faculties: Business Studies, Technology, Creative	Deputy Principals
and Performing Arts, Science, Health and Service	Faculty Heads
Industries, ACE Central, ACE East, ACE North,	Directors of Finance
ACE South, Curriculum Support Unit.	Director of Personnel
Unions	Director of Premises Management
Education Councils	College Registrar
Administration	MIS Manager
Registration	
College Management Information System (MIS)	
The Technical Education Colleges (TECs)	

Specify viable parts of system (F2)

Within the Liverpool City Community College lie the faculties at focus F2. The viable parts of the faculty system 'produce' it. Each faculty has its own mission, parts and stakeholders, listed in Table 14.8.

Table 14.8 Focus F2: City Community College, faculty focus

Mission statement

Developing and promoting technological knowledge and skills as a means of contributing to the prosperity and well-being of the individuals, organisations and communities of the area and nation

System 1 parts	Stakeholders
Schools	Senior heads/managers including heads
Courses	of faculty and heads of school
Library	Employees
Unions	Technicians
Management information system (MIS)	Students
Examining bodies	Administrative staff
Administration	

Specify viable parts of system (F3)

Within the Faculty of Technology lie the schools at focus F3. The viable parts of the school system 'produce' it. They have their own mission, parts and stakeholders, listed in Table 14.9.

It is traditional to distinguish between two types of operations that have different purposes, academic and administrative. While they are closely interactive, and thus influence each other, our interest for this study lies only within the academic area since it is this domain that has been subject to destabilising variety from the environment.

Specify viable system as a whole

The school system sits inside a faculty system that itself sits in the Liverpool City Community College. They are all open systems and have influences from not only their higher-level system, but also from the wider environment. The Liverpool City

Table 14.9 Focus F3: City Community College, school focus

Mission statement

To develop and deliver quality courses of a transport related nature, either in-house or at the customer's venue, and to market those courses to the widest possible audience

System 1 parts	Stakeholders
Courses	Head of school
Library	Senior lecturers/course team leaders
Stores	Course teams
Office of student registration	Course tutors
Administration	Class tutors
Audio visual aids	Students
Transport institutes	Potential students
Rooms	Technical staff
	Stores personnel
	Room allocations

Table 14.10 Focus F0: Liverpool City Community College, environmental influences.

System 1 parts	Stakeholders
Liverpool Education Authority	Liverpool Education Authority Committee
National unions	Members
Further education colleges	Unions representatives
Principals forum	Principals of other colleges of further education
The FEFC	Principals of TECs
The Technology Education Colleges (TECs)	Senior industrial managers
Industry	Training provider managers
Public sector training providers	

Community College as a system and its environment are described as the F0 focus. The environmental influences and relevant stakeholders are listed in Table 14.10.

In addition, it will be of use for later analysis to describe in particular the environments that are particular to the F3 (school) and F2 (faculty) levels of focus (Tables 14.11 and 14.12).

Table 14.11 Focus F1: Faculty of Technology, environmental influences

System 1 parts	Stakeholders
Industry and commerce	Captains of industry and commerce
Industry lead bodies	The senior management of City College
The City College	Heads of faculties
Other college faculties	Heads of schools
Schools in other colleges	Managers of employment centres
Other faculty schools	Managers of trade institutes
Employment centres	Controllers of funding and resource mechanisms
Trade institutes	Members of examining bodies
Funding and resource mechanisms	Staff in City Community College
Examining bodies	Institute committee members
	Examiners

Table 14.12 Focus F2: School of Transport, environmental influences

System 1 parts	Stakeholders
Industry lead bodies	Managers of lead industry bodies
Other further education facilities	Heads of other college schools
Other higher education colleges	Heads of City College schools
Employment centres	Managers of employment centres
Trade institutes	Managers of trade institutes
The motor industry	Controllers of funding and resource mechanisms
Examining bodies	Members of examining bodies
Schools	Staff in City Community College
	Institute committee members
	Examiners
	Children
	Heads of schools

14.5.3 Synthesis

This phase of the methodology highlights the importance of the inquirer's weltanschauung, and the related cognitive map that enables VSM to be placed, for instance, in a sociocultural context. In this respect the reader might wish to compare this study with, for instance, that of Wooliston (1994) concerning the South West Region Political Economy.

System diagnosis
School focus of system 1 specification

The operations of system 1 at the school focus are comprised of its courses and teams of staff members who compile and deliver them. The school has six client-based courses. Some of these are independent. Others interrelate and can act as feeders to student enhancement. System 1 at this level of recursion is shown in Fig. 14.9. We shall now inquire into the metasystem at focus F3 by examining systems 2 to 5.

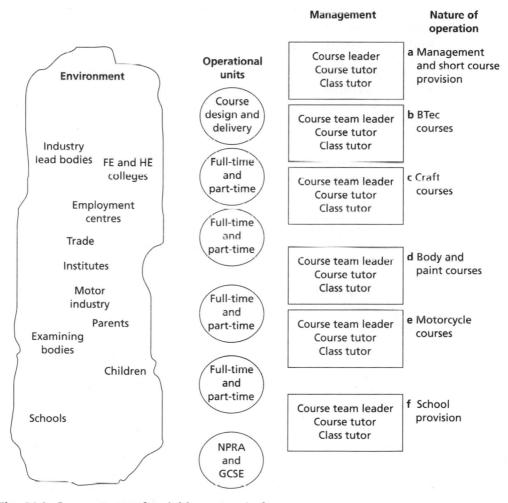

Fig. 14.9 Components of a viable system in focus

Metasystem and transmogrific diagnosis

School focus of system 2

System 2 is the cognitive coordinator of the system. Compatible instructions should derive from metasystem agents like senior management. We will therefore seek to explore the cognitive coordination centres that deal with homeostasis. In exploring system 2 we therefore extract from the complex situation that we are faced with a set of cognitive coordination problems that we seek *solutions* for. A *solution* is a strategy that can harmonise the regulatory components of the system. System 2 identification occurs in Table 14.13.

School focus of system 3

This is concerned with control of the system. It oversees implementation policy and resource distribution, and monitors operations. It is connected with the audit channel (system 3*) that enables direct access to operations. It is concerned with synergy, with 'improving' operational performance. As a consequence of the principles of control, system 3 must be aware of the cognitive conditions that bound homeostasis, and the nature of behavioural and cognitive learning. As a consequence, it may be involved in negotiations that define cognitive bounds, for instance with unions about pay scales and with the Director of Finance about applicable funding. It must also be aware of organisational issues like working practices and quality. Operations must also be accountable to system 3, and they must be able to initiate the processes for behavioural or cognitive changes. To enable this it will provide resources where it identifies that they are needed. In the School of Transport, system 3 is identified according to Fig. 14.10 by defining the appropriate stakeholders.

Table 14.13 System 2 coordinating activities

Conflict of interest or potential instability	Solutions
1 To ensure right student for right course, and no 'poaching' occurs	1 Pre-testing, meetings, regular evaluation, profiling
2 Funding arrangements for the various courses	2 Meetings, formula based on full-time equivalent student numbers, variance based on type of course, safety 'pot'
3 Staff teaching duties	3 Fair and flexible timetabler ensures all have larger percentage of what they want, and are capable of teaching same
4 Teaching space	4 Regular meetings to slot right group in right room
5 Teaching aids	5 Booking to ensure equipment is distributed relative to needs
6 Distribution of technical staff	6 Staff delegated to specific groups in relation to work being done and grade of staff
7 Contact with Industry for students, placements, technical advice, equipment	7 Booking system to ensure regular contact, non-duplication, no 'poaching'
8 Delegation of other duties	8 Based on negotiation related to skills, position, time available, workload, ability, interests
9 Workshop store facility and distribution of equipment	9 A combination of workshop loading and syllabus movement

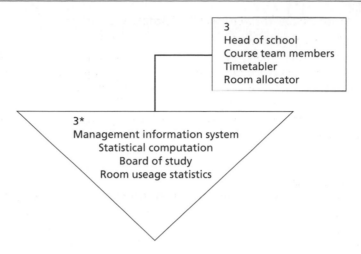

Fig. 14.10 Identification of system 3 for control and its audit channel (system 3*)

Thus, as part of this, fortnightly meetings are arranged between the head of school, course team leaders and the timetabler. They discuss funding, operations and staffing requirements, and address problem areas.

School focus of system 4

This is the future/planning part of the metasystem. It must link information from the system itself with its environment. Adopting the strategy of Beer (1985), Ashford follows the approach that we identify as future TRAP: an exploration of Timescale (the current or future date stamped future activity), Responsibility (who has to do it), Activity (what sort of planning to do) and Priority (what priority should be given on a scale of, say, 1 to n where n may be the lowest priority, and where $1 - n$ represents unassigned priority). A system 4 TRAP exploration for the School is given in Table 14.14. The interrelationship between these activities is defined in Fig. 14.11.

Table 14.14 TRAP analysis for system 4 evaluation of future activities

Timescale	Responsible unit		Activity	Priority
Current	All	1	Updating of staff skill	$1-n$
Current	All + marking team	2	Marketing courses	1
Current	Workshop team	3	Redefining workshop of equipment	1
Current	Workshop team	4	Replacement of equipment	2
Current	Head of course team leaders, all in interest areas	5	Maintaining links with industry to identify their changes	2
Current	All	6	Maintaining links with institute and examination bodies and other transport colleges	$1-n$
Current	Team leaders	7	Investigation into new courses	2

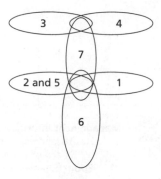

Fig. 14.11 Interrelationship between future activities of system 4 (Table 14.13)

Finally, the stakeholders who are the 'experts' that compose system 4 are:

- head of school
- staff marketeer
- course leaders
- board of studies.

School focus (F3) of system 5

This has responsibility for the whole system. It is the thinking or cognition processing part of the metasystem. It concerns itself with the complex interactions between systems 3 and 4. It is constrained by policy while monitoring the whole organisation and its operations. Taking the brain as a metaphor, system 5 stakeholders might well be arranged as a neural network of individuals. In the case of the School of Transport, system 5 is:

- faculty head
- school manager.

The system 1–5 components that have now been considered are integrated into the formalised VSM control diagram given in Fig. 14.12.

Exploration and evaluation in the School of Transport

This phase of the methodology is important because during it the situation is explored and models are built that determine intervention strategies. This will depend not only upon the situation, but also upon the inquirer. The inquirer may be a facilitating part of the organisation or a consultant (or team of consultants) brought in from the outside. In the former case the inquirer will have a view of the situation; in the latter case he will have to obtaining a view. He will also determine what methods to adopt within this phase to gain an insight into a situation. Some inquirers may decide on using relatively hard approaches, while others may adopt soft approaches. The inquirer in the case of this study is a facilitator who has applied questionnaires and informal discussion to make inquiry.

It is during this stage of VSMM that other methodologies can be implemented. A given fault of form may be perceived to occur, and the inquirer may wish to determine how to correct it. This may require the application of approaches like organisational development (Chapter 12), soft systems methodology (Chapter 13), or the conflict modelling cycle (Chapter 15). The inquiry purpose will be determined by the nature of the fault found. It is at this point that constraints on weltanschauung can be introduced.

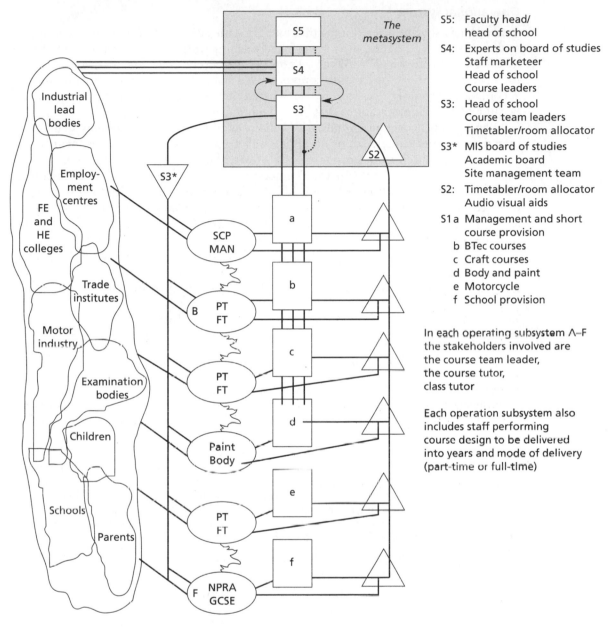

Fig. 14.12 Cybernetic map for focus of the School of Transport in its environment

Thus, cultural and political constraints could be used, or constraints on resistance to change, or constraints on conflict in a paradigm plural situation. However this is done, it is essential first to establish a virtual paradigm, perhaps in a form similar to that in Section 14.5.

Operational system 1

System 1 has six operational units that interact with one another, with the environment and with system 3. At the next lower focus each operational unit in turn contains its own subsystems to which VSM can be applied recursively. New courses can be added to the operational units, or existing courses moved from one operational area to another according to arbitrary decision criteria. These criteria may change as the system learns because of changing conditions that the system finds itself in.

In an attempt to obtain an indicative consensus of the level of autonomy that the six operational units have, a set of questions was prepared for their management teams. They were intended to inquire into a set of attributes that defined the issues of the situation, identified in Table 14.15. The questions concerned (1) the view of each team about day to day operations, (2) the value of its contribution by the school, (3) the value of its contribution by the faculty, (4) efficient use of the teams' skills by the school, (5) as previous, but 'perceived', (6) sufficient opportunities for training, (7) need for further training, (8) opportunities for progression, (9) adequacy of performance measurement, (10) adequacy of accountability, (11) whether there is a received upward flow of information, (12) whether this information has any effect, (13) as (11) and (12) but at faculty level, (14) extent of autonomy of the unit, (15) degree of self-management, (16) quality

Table 14.15 Attributes of the operational units at school focus

Attribute of operational units	Outcome of School of Transport inquiry
1 **Operational autonomy**	The consensus was that autonomy is high, and that roles were valued. Units felt they understood their role in the school, were achieving goals, and considered the environment. The picture was felt to be known, agreed and valued by the management teams.
2 **Training**	Knowledge, skill and ability are training dependent. In general, inadequate training facilities for retraining basic skills and management skills. Currently uses training by experience. Should be a rolling training programme including staff placements in working environments. Skill levels unknown (implications for quality). Implications for interaction, flexibility, working environment. Reasons identified were that other schools had lower running costs thus making them more popular.
3 **Budget**	Budgets were inadequate, though allocations to operational units fair. Inadequacies due to a higher focus.
4 **Performance and accountability**	Mechanisms for this needed since operational units are fundamentally autonomous while having funding needs. Partially achieved: communications faults and also some lack of real support for this attribute.
5 **Communications**	Faults cause time lags and delays in making changes. Blame was put at a higher level of focus, and operational units worked within predefined constraints.
6 **Quality**	Maintained through monitoring resources and standards. Constraints on course operation are student numbers. Issues concerning student/college attendance and level of drop-out rate less significant. Control information about students from trades and examining bodies available. Control action possible.
7 **Strain**	Contributions felt not to be recognised or valued, and no future progression in school.

of interaction with environment, (17) as (16) but for faculty, (18) adequacy of funding by school management, (19) adequacy of school funding and (20) relative value of school by faculty. Each team within the six units was provided with opportunities to respond to the questions. The answers could be given as a variable grading between a low and high bound, for instance between 1 and 10.

The answers to these questions could be placed with the context of the choice phase since they indicate faults of form. However, we shall rather formulate a summary of the evaluations that follow, and place these under choice. An analysis resulted in Table 14.15.

The Metasystem

Examination of the metasystem (S4 and S5) is facilitated by an appreciation of the S1 analysis and the transmogrific elements S2, S3 and S3*.

Systems 1, 2 and 3

The interaction between systems 1, 2 and 3 is represented by Fig. 14.13. It models the system as six vertical channels that interconnect through operations. The channels are:

- C1: environmental intersects
- C2: audits and surveys (system 3*)
- C3: operational interactions
- C4: mandatory system 3 information
- C5: negotiated system 3 information
- C6: System 2 (stability) information.

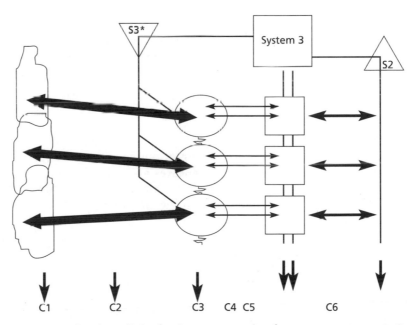

Fig. 14.13 Communications links for interconnection between systems 1, 2 and 3

An evaluation of the relationships exposes a number of characteristics of the form of the system. These are summarised in Table 14.16.

Table 14.16 Characteristics of the form of the system

Characteristics of form	Explanation
Conflict with environment	The college environment has a customer base that is influenced by schools, the motor industry and unemployment seen as a system. Overlaps can generate internal conflict between the unit groups and the environment. This has already been addressed through unit leaders, who manage unit agreements that enable identification of who goes where and for what purposes. Newly introduced features include maintaining a school diary of visits to include who, where, when and why, and the outcomes. This has been enhanced now by operational units having set up an inter-unit card system to pass on details or requirements that did not refer to the visitors units, but required specialist input.
Information flow	Informally delivered information occurs through casual meetings. Formal information flows are also seen as adequate, as is regulation by the class tutor system and requisite documentation.
Stability (system 2)	Operational units are not always staffed by lecturers with the 'right' specialisms; school not permitted to replace leaving staff; school infills with staff from redundant areas; rooms withdrawn from pool by college; rooms mostly in poor condition; averaging and overtime cause for concern.
Optimisation (system 3)	Information about the operational units considered on a fortnightly basis by school manager and his team of leaders. This is normally seen positively. Constraint is lack of funds allocation, which is calculated per student capita. Audit (system 3*) assist in allocation through information. System 3 appears to operate well without blockage. School will operate semi-autonomously soon, but lacks performance indicators for this within systems 1, 2 and 3. Insufficient quality measurement.

System 4

This evaluation develops, from the previous section, and in particular from Table 14.14 and Fig. 14.13. Responsible for futures and planning, system 4 must have access to external and internal information. It balances the operational units of the system in focus with the variety coming from the environment. It is responsible for adaptation, and must therefore be sensitive to the organisational culture, knowledge, potential and interests of stakeholders. An examination of system 4 at the school focus for information gathering revealed the information listed in Table 14.17.

Table 14.17 System 4 at the school focus

Attribute	Explanation
External communications	School manager and team leaders are normally in contact from day to day with industry, trade institutes and other colleges.
External validation	A board of studies provides a validating mechanism for the school system, comprising external and operational unit experts, the school manager and examination board representatives.
External marketing	The marketing officer visits actors in the external environment as perceived necessary. He sources information from his connections and so enhances the viability of the school.
Internal capabilities	Operational unit capabilities and their constraints must be known. Planning new courses with insufficient resources is inappropriate system 4 behaviour.

System 5

System 5 is the cognitive driver for the system. It makes investment decisions at policy level that must be responsive to environment variation. Thus, the school must be able to respond to change in the environment, and system 5 oversees the relationship between system 3 and system 4. Policy is decided for the school between the faculty head and the school manager, based on the internal and external information they are supplied with.

Summary of the school focus

In summary of the above, in this section we explore the whole metasystem as a consequence of the previous modelling (Table 14.18). The whole system is balanced through the primarily internal actions of systems 1, 2 and 3, and the primarily external actions of systems 3, 4 and 5.

Table 14.18 The metasystem

Attribute	Explanation
System 2: Coordination	
Timetable	Timetabling demands timely information about needs, and accurate knowledge about staff, skills and rooms characteristics that define their potential use. This includes specialist rooms like laboratories. Strain is due to external operational units (other schools) taking rooms out of allocation. It requires constant meetings with room allocations in other school systems. A room audit (system 3*) is essential, and is being implemented.
Staff shortage strain	Stability need in non-replacement of staff, and appointment of part-time replacements. Can cause instability if staff do not 'fit in'. Induction periods for new staff.

Continued overleaf

Table 14.18 (continued)

Attribute	Explanation
System 3: Control	
Resource constraints	This will be discussed under choice since it connects with higher levels of focus.
System 4: Future/development	
Information	Future planning is seen as well. A problem might have occurred with the demise of the Labour Market Intelligence Unit within the school. However, it has become an informal and unresourced unit. At present this is not seen as a problem.
Various	School manager operates this. Well respected. His major problems relate to time away from the system, inability to control earned funds, and the constant need to consult with the head of faculty.

This summary represents the results of the VSM study for the school level of focus. Before we can pass through to the next phase of the inquiry, it will be essential to explore the higher levels of focus. While we are looking for viability in the school system, it is recognised to be a semi-autonomous open system, influenced directly by the faculty and the college levels of focus.

We do not have the space here to initiate a higher-level recursion of VSM at the faculty and college levels (*see* Ashford, 1993). Rather, we shall pass directly on to a specification of the faults of form, which includes these other explorations.

14.5.4 Choice

Correction of non-viable aspects of system

This evaluation summarises and, where appropriate, interrelates the results of each focus of inquiry at the school, faculty and college levels of inquiry. It thus represents a holistic evaluation of the system.

An important aspect of fault correction is variety generation. Brainstorming can generate good ideas that can contribute to this. Other approaches may also be appropriate.

The school focus

Correction of non-viable aspects of the school system occurs through identifying the faults in its form and correcting them (Table 14.19). Form is made up of structure and process. We will recall that structures enable management processes, while processes maintain structures. Thus, faults of form may be diagnosed for both structures and processes. It will be useful to take note at this point of an impending event (for 1993) discussed at the college focus of the Ashford study – college incorporation. This loosens the administrative and constraining connection between the Local Authority and the college, and impacts all focuses of the organisation.

Table 14.19 Identifying and correcting faults of form

Attribute	Explanation	Correcting faults of form
System 1: Operations		
Autonomy	A consensus was that operational units had autonomy, and their objectives are achievable and attainable. Some strain/tension was apparent.	Staff development can help to alleviate strain. A programme of training can give staff in the faculty greater flexibility. This can be enhanced with a staff appraisal system that is to be introduced in the college. However, this very much depends upon the nature of the appraisal, the quality of its results, and perception that staff have about it.
Staff levels	These affect course provision, management, and operational performance.	This is uncertain and thus future orientated. It is a structural fault that cannot easily be tackled except through income generating activities to secure autonomous finance.
Resource allocation	A fair way of allocating resources can reduce strain in a system.	Each school is being seen as a cost centre by the finance director. This will be regressed to the next focus down, to make operational units cost centres. Local accounting can then act as a detailed audit mechanism.
Time allowances	Fair allocation of allowances reduces strain. Adequate time should be made available for this process.	With systems 2 and 3, one half day per week will be free from staff teaching, when team meetings can occur. Individual workloads will be reviewed.
System 2: Coordination		
Staff as a requisite variety resource	Knowledge/information about staff skills and abilities, course needs, student numbers, and room availability and room characteristics can make requisite variety generation easier.	A knowledge/information bank is being established. This could be coupled with a decision support system, development funding permitting.
Room allocation	Difficult to manage because rooms are a college, not a school, resource (excluding specialist rooms).	School currently uses a computer-based room allocation system. This could be college networked for wider access to enable open visibility of room availability, and room audit.
System 3: Control		
Materials	Teaching materials are centred with individuals, staff newly delivering courses may need to develop materials newly when they exist elsewhere.	Despite recommendations, staff do not bank materials. Assigning organisational unit's responsibility for its behaviour might help this. A further inquiry to this, identifying benefits and rewards for staff, may be useful. Internal publishing of materials for student purchasing that can reward staff may be a solution to inquire into.

Continued overleaf

Table 14.19 (continued)

Attribute	Explanation	Correcting faults of form
Information	Indicators (preferably in real time) provide information about the operational units.	Additional indicators, including finance, will be necessary. This should be explored further.
Training	Members of system 3 require appropriate training.	School heads will attend a three-day programme on management topics.

System 4: Futures/planning/development

Attribute	Explanation	Correcting faults of form
Turbulence	National Vocational Qualifications (NVQs) are affecting training provision. They affect curriculum development and delivery. (Note: it may be that NVQs are one manifestation of a chaotic environment; if so there will be others.)	Methodologies and outcomes will be more rigidly inspected. Testing requirements will have to occur in the workplace. Deliverers of prescribed course units will be needed to train as both assessors and external verifiers. Vigilance of the environment can help. A 'better' organised and documented visiting schedule may maintain a high school profile in the minds of employees. This requires further exploration.
Perspective	System 4 must identify the perspective believed to be appropriate to the situation it finds itself in, and define and operate its strategic models.	Define perspectives that enable strategies for staff training and related facilities, maintain and encourage staff in generating variety in work, particularly those that may be charged at full cost while providing equipment funding.
Marketing	The college was (in 1993) facing incorporation. This set a new priority for school viability and the generation of a high profile. Dangers facing the college can easily affect the school.	Marketing can provide a high profile. It requires a budget for this, and a strategy. This links closely with system 3.

System 5: Policy

Attribute	Explanation	Correcting faults of form
Training	There are needs for metasystemic managers to understand the management implications and impacts of incorporation.	School managers training in management skills and financial methodology are planned, intended to enable the system to cope with change.
Finance	Finances for continuance and growth of the school are essential.	One way of seeing this is that school managers will be competing with one another for funds. This will require criteria to be established for such competition, which may be consensual or dissensual. This requires further investigation.
Autonomy	Autonomy is encouraged if the schools are empowered to control their own finances.	Make schools cost centres that are accountable and auditable.

Continuation

The choice phase has not been completed in the Ashford case work. It was an informally introduced study that has itself had an impact on the organisation. Had a formalised study been commissioned, it would have passed through the following further steps:

- consultation with participants or their representatives
- recommendation of changes in organisational form
- after changes, enter new cycle of inquiry.

REFERENCES

Ashby, W.R. (1956) *An Introduction to Cybernetics*. London: Methuen.

Ashford, T.A. (1993) 'The School of Transport – a viable system?', MBA research dissertation, Liverpool Business School, Liverpool John Moores University.

Beer, S. (1979) *The Heart of the Enterprise*. New York: Wiley.

Beer, S. (1981) *Brain of the Firm*, 2nd edn. New York: Wiley.

Beer, S. (1985) *Diagnosing the System for Organisations*. New York: Wiley.

Espejo, R. and Harnden, R. (1989) *The Viable System Model: Interpretations and applications of Stafford Beer's VSM*. New York: Wiley.

Flood, R.L and Jackson, M.C. (1991) *Creative Problem Solving: Total systems intervention*. Chichester: Wiley.

Harnden, R., Adams, D., Haynes, D., Bryde, D., Davies, P., Tutcher, G. and Leonard, A. (1995) 'The system management of quality: a new cybernetic tool'. Working paper series no. 4(1994/5), Liverpool Business School, Liverpool John Moores University.

HMI (1983) 'Further education provision in Liverpool District Audit Services'.

Jackson, M.C. (1992) *Systems Methodology for the Management Sciences*. New York: Plenum Press.

Kickert, W.J.M. and van Gigch, J.P. (1989) 'A metasystem approach to organisational decision making'. In van Gigch, J.P. (ed.) *Decision Making about Decision Making*. Tunbridge Wells: Abacus Press, pp. 37–55.

Ulrich, W. (1977) 'The design of problem-solving system', *Management Science*, 23, 1099–1108.

Ulrich, W. (1983) *Critical Heuristics of Social Planning: A reconstruction of Kantan A-Priori Science for Planners and Practical Philosophers*. Berne: Paul Haupt.

van Gigch, J.P. (1989) *Decision Making about Decision Making*. Tunbridge Wells: Abacus Press.

Wooliston, G. (1994) 'A cybernetic analysis of the south west region political economy'. Institut d'Economie Regionale du Sud-Ouest, Bordeaux, France.

CHAPTER 15

Conflict modelling cycle

OVERVIEW

Conflict situations are generated within or between actors as a manifestation of *contesting differences*. They occur when the world views that are involved collide to produce cognitive turbulence, which can result in stable patterns of conflict behaviour. Conflict theory suggests ways of dealing with these patterns. The conflict modelling cycle (CMC) can contribute to the exploration of the patterns, and to a realigning of world views to enable different patterns to emerge. Its cognitive model sees situations as being paradigm plural, an alternative to the premise of consensus approach. The cognitive model of CMC derives from the theory of conflict and its intended use is to identify intervention strategies that minimise active or passive violence and equivalently maximise individual potential. The methodology is also sensitive to the use of different paradigms through methodological complementarism, allowing it to explore a pluralism of modelling approaches and philosophies. It deals with complex situations by conceptualising that conflict, attitudes and behaviour are analytically and empirically independent, and can be addressed separately.

15.1 Introduction

The conflict modelling cycle (CMC) began its life in discussion with Graham Kemp, arising out of our common interest in examining in a structured way the probable conflicts that were expected to develop during the reformation of the Soviet Union (Kemp and Yolles, 1992; Yolles, 1992). Conflicts are seen as primarily sociopolitical phenomena that occur between actor systems, but cultural and social actor characteristics are also of great significance.

Most inquiring methodologies are interested in unitary complex problem situations. These occur *within* an actor system, which we might alternatively refer to as an intra-actor or organisational situation that derives from environmental perturbations. Consensus methodologies are unitary complex since they assume a single (consensus) paradigm in a complex situation. Most methodologies that can be broadly identified as operating within the softer systems domain adopt the consensus principle when seeking intervention strategies (*see* Jackson, 1992), and therefore do not recognise cultural or paradigmatic pluralism. Even the viable system model methodologies that can be found are invariably unitary complex.

Another possible way of viewing a situation is to see it as plural complex, examining *between* (or inter-) actor systems in a suprasystem. To find explicitly pluralistic approaches other than CMC one must move out of management systems, perhaps to game theory or macroeconomics. However, the models that are used in these domains tend to be hard and deal with probability and risk rather than addressing softer, human-related situations that relate to uncertainty.

Broadly, the suprasystem in the plural complex view and the organisation of the unitary complex view can be seen as equivalent in that they relate to a similar focus of examination. The essential difference between the two views is that within the organisation the intra-actors must be said to be autonomous, while in a suprasystem the actors are assumed to be. International trading or conflict situations, competitive market situations, and rivalries that occur at departmental levels within corporations are all examples of what we are referring to. Since each actor system is seen as autonomous, it will have its own paradigm that will be analytically and empirically independent from the others. The conceptualisation of a suprasystem is synonymous with the creation of a framework that enables actor interaction and the paradigms to be related to one another. It also enables us to postulate the possibility of the formation of common cognitive models that can operate as a rudimentary metasystem, sometimes through the aid of facilitators.

To inquire into pluralistic complex situations, it is also useful to have access to a plurality of ways of seeing, an idea that calls on the paradigm principle. This is not the traditional management systems view, neither is it the traditional view of social science, from which much of management systems springs. This is not least because social science tends to be reductionist in that it examines only that part of a social situation that is of interest.

A plurality of ways of seeing situations leads us to an interest in the different paradigms that generate them. These may vary from relatively hard modelling approaches, applying, for instance, hypergame methodologies (Fraser and Hipel, 1984) or statistical (Ruloff, 1975) or stochastic (Petersen, 1992) models to situations. Others are soft, inquiry being a process of interaction with individuals (Crawley, 1992). Consistent with the systems viewpoint, our proposition is that all of these approaches have a potential value that can conjointly contribute towards an understanding of group conflict and its settlement, one of the purposes of CMC. Each of the modelling approaches described above derives from its own distinct paradigm. CMC was intended to be responsive to different paradigms, and should therefore be seen as a complementarist approach that is intended to tackle modelling pluralism.

15.2 The paradigm of the conflict modelling cycle

15.2.1 Types of conflict situation

Three classes of conflict situations are (Holsti, 1967; Galtung, 1975):

1 *tensions* that may have no discernible cause

2 *disputes* caused by accidents and minor provocations

3 *conflicts* represented as a manifestation of differences.

Tensions, disputes and conflicts are all destabilising influences on a system. This is especially seen to be the case if one considers that they are all manifestations of degrees of cognitive turbulence. In complex situations that involve emotions, conflicts (because of their turbulent nature) cannot be implicitly controlled. Rather, homeostatic processes are replaced by self-organisation as systems may be forced to learn, forms change through morphogenesis and evolutionary processes take effect.

Tension

Two forms of *tension* may be identified. *Consensual tension* can define the conditions for change in a system that enable change to occur, resulting in *achievement* and defining it to be constructive. By *achievement* we will understand the development of a consensus view about the change that is *satisfying* to the group members. When there is dissent within the group about whether achievement can occur, then the tension may be seen as dissensual. *Dissensual tension* is harmful in that it can predefine the conditions for system breakdown. Consensual and dissensual tensions are obverse qualities that can occur simultaneously, and are identifiable from different perspectives, which may be incommensurable and contradictory. In international political terms, tensions 'arise from a juxtaposition of historical, economic, religious, or ethnic conditions, and are perpetuated by widespread public attitudes of hostility' (Holsti, 1967, p. 443) between two or more groups. Tensions may involve *conflicts* 'but by themselves do not give rise to, or perpetuate, all of the forms of hostile behaviour ... Since tensions have no single source, they are more difficult to resolve than those conflicts whose origins lie in expansive demands and in the incompatibility of recognisable objectives' (Holsti, 1967). They can involve irrational fears and traditional hatreds. In addition, they can involve 'distorted' perceptions by inquirers, defined as the perception of purposes assigned to the perpetrators of events without reference to the beliefs of those perpetrators.

Disputes

Disputes grow out of accidents or minor provocations. They happen when events occur so that the participants become aggrieved. This can occur when a participant intends to operate within an agreed convention, but may not realise that a particular action contravenes it in some way that is important to the world view of another participant. Typically this type of situation arises when the world views of the participants have meaning and generate knowledge that is not common to their different cultures.

Conflict

Conflict can be seen as the development of instability in the interactions between a group of entities. In human situations it can be seen as a challenge that is potentially constructive (Crawley, 1992, p. 11) when it acts as a catalyst for action that results in individual or group achievement. In cases where there is a consensus that such achievement has occurred we will talk of *consensual* conflict. When there is dissent within the group about such achievement having occurred, then we refer to it as *dissensual*. Dissensual conflict is disruptive without achievement, and is responsible for destruction. Due to the changing nature of consensus in unstable situations and the involvement of irreconcilable individual perspectives, conflict situations will have a fuzzy boundary that distinguishes whether they are seen as consensual or dissensual. Indeed, there may be aspects of a conflict that involve both of these, depending upon the perspectives of those who are perceiving.

In the end, in an attempt to distinguish whether a conflict situation is consensual or dissensual, it may be appropriate to try to couple it with principles that cut across all world views. Later we will talk about the idea of structural violence, which for the moment we can define as the passive violence that acts on one group through the inactions or structures established by another. The minimisation of both active and passive violence represents for us a proposition that attempts to secure consensual rather than dissensual conflicts. Violence minimisation and the maximisation of individual potential are coincident conceptualisations: violence by its very nature inhibits the development and manifestation of potential. Thus within this context, we consider equivalent the minimising of violence and the maximisation of potential. Like all other 'common' concepts, maximising of potential can be subject to interpretation within different paradigms. In particular, what constitutes violence minimisation or potential maximisation will also tend to be an issue of balance within the differentiable groups in an organisation and across time. For instance, might it be possible for short-term violence minimisation to create greater violence in the longer term? In examining such issues, it is essential for the systemic view to be taken of a situation. Finally, the idea of active or passive violence minimisation may be in conflict with predominant ideologies in some paradigms, or the emotional and intellectual pursuits of those in power.

The causes of conflict

Conflict is caused by the recognisable occurrence of incompatible goal states (Galtung, 1975, p. 78) between actor systems that together form a conflictual suprasystem. A realisation of one goal will exclude, wholly or partly, the realisation of others. If the goals are held by different actors in the suprasystem, then we have what is called an *inter-actor* conflict. If they are held by a given actor independent of the suprasystem, then we have an *intra-actor* conflict, which is referred to as a *dilemma*. Dilemmas are therefore a problem of choice. However, the distinction between an inter-actor conflict and a dilemma is a relative one determined by the depth of focus of an inquiry.

A broader explanation for the rise of conflict that subsumes Galtung's has already been introduced earlier as a manifestation of differences. It is more aptly defined by Crawley as 'a manifestation of differences working against one another' (Crawley, 1992, p. 10). More succinctly, we prefer to define conflict as a manifestation of *contesting differences*.

The question now to be put is: why do contesting differences develop and why are they elaborated so that the conflict is developed? An explanation comes from Krishnamurti in his conversations with Bohm, when they discuss the roots of psychological conflict. He adopts an Eastern tradition of thought to explain why this can occur when he says that 'the origin [of conflict] is ego, the "I" and the "me" ... If there is no ego, there are no problems, there is no conflict, there is no time, time in the sense of "becoming"' (Krishnamurti and Bohm, 1996, p. 14). From this we can deduce that a fundamental cause for conflict derives from ego and a related cognitive desire for *becoming* that manifests contesting differences over time and encourages their elaboration.

These comments are in line with the ideas proposed by Chorpa when he discusses the notion of Maya, as introduced in Chapter 2. 'Maya is the illusion of boundaries, the creation of mind that has lost the cosmic perspective. It comes from seeing a million things "out there" and missing one thing, the invisible field that is the origin of the universe...Maya [is] a poor substitute for the cosmic perspective' Chorpa (1990, p. 205). While ego may be defined by Maya, its nature is 'the conscious thinking subject' (*Concise English Oxford Dictionary*, 1957) or 'the conscious part of our personality'

(Eysenck, 1957, p. 153), or the 'self' (Brown, 1961, p. 28). Ego has a 'pure' form that is apodictic or absolutely indubitable (*see* Mingers, 1995, on Husserl, 1979). The 'pure' form is detached from the world-view belief system. However, when ego connects itself to world-view beliefs it identifies with them and therefore creates its own boundaries (Ventura, 1997, personal communication). World views are producers of knowledge (Chapter 2), and so ego must also identify with that knowledge. To explore the relationship between ego and world view, we are thus led to examining world view in terms of its knowledge attributes. Two of these are (a) its belief deriving constituent knowledges and (b) the nature of its frames of reference and boundaries, which enables recognition or provides response to other knowledges from other world views. To explore this further we posit the following propositions:

1 world views are local generators of knowledge;

2 world-view knowledge can be partitioned into 'referential areas';

3 a world view has a boundary that can also be seen as a frame of reference that may be subject to change;

4 a frame of reference indicates the inclusiveness of the knowledge-producing truth system of a world view, while a boundary constrains it;

5 a world-view frame of reference can be defined in terms of its ability to *respond* to other world views, while a boundary can be defined in terms of its ability to *recognise* other world views;

6 world views can collide, when their frames of reference/boundaries may be influenced, and knowledge of one may perturb that of another;

7 when knowledge perturbation occurs to affect a partition of knowledge, the belief system of a world view will be disturbed in some way.

These propositions have either been explored previously, or may be seen as axiomatic. They can be used to distinguish between four 'ideal' types of world view that we shall call closed, semiclosed (or partially closed), open and centrifugal, and which we say have the following characteristics.

● Closed world views cannot relate their frames of reference to those of other world views, and are totally self-referring, egocentric and directed towards 'becoming'. A closed world view is one whose boundary enables no recognition of the existence of other world views. It has a *rigid* frame of reference that cannot be influenced by the knowledges that other world views generate: knowledge perturbation (of its own knowledge) in any one referential area may damage the frame of reference.

● Like closed world views, semiclosed world views cannot relate their frames of reference to those of other world views, and are totally self-referring, egocentric and directed towards 'becoming'. A partially closed or semiclosed world view has a boundary that enables recognition of the existence of other world views while diminishing them. It has a *robust* frame of reference that can only be partially influenced by the knowledges that other world views produce: it may be possible to compensate for knowledge perturbation in any one referential area from other areas to the homeostatic limits of the world view, after which the frame of reference suffers damage.

● Open world views are capable of developing referents beyond self, though they retain self-referential ego. An open world view is one whose boundary enables the recognition of other world views and their validity within the worlds from which they derive. It has an *adaptable* frame of reference that can be influenced by knowledges generated by other world views: knowledge perturbation can result in cognitive redefinition through world-view morphogenesis to the plastic limit of the world view, after which the frame of reference suffers damage. Since it can respond to other knowledges, an open world view provides for the possibility of greater development and growth than closed or partially closed world views.

- A centrifugal world view is one that moves away from the centre of self and is therefore ego reducing. This is distinct from the centripetal world view that we see as fundamentally ego increasing. According to Ventura, the expansive boundary of a centrifugal world view enables recognition, acceptance and constructive interaction with other world views: knowledge perturbation does not occur since the world view is directed towards the processes of change and growth rather than the achievement of goals. It has a *self-actualising* (*see* Maslow, 1954) frame of reference that accepts the existence of other knowledges generated by other world views without interpretation or judgement.

While Maya is the illusion of boundaries, it is ego that is responsible for maintaining them. 'Ordinarily, the ego has no chance but to spend life desperately erecting one boundary after another. It does this for ... protection. The ego finds the world a dangerous, hostile place, because everything that exists is separate from "I". This is the condition known as duality, and it is a great source of fear' (Chorpa, 1990, p. 212).

To enable the reduction of ego we note the notion of the Eastern concept of 'awareness' seen as a state of cognition that enables an actor to transgress its world-view boundary. It can occur through reflection on self, and through meditation that is said to enable one to pass from consciousness to a paraconsciousness through a transcendental state. As in the case of the centrifugal world view, in so doing the actor expands its frame of reference. As a result, the significance of self-reference is reduced, and a path is defined (where knowledge is not locally relative to world views) that mystics might say can lead to 'enlightenment'. This path clearly enables contesting differences to be diminished together with ego since differences are neither further contested nor elaborated.

Pirani (1997, personal communication) has suggested that these concepts can be formulated into a typology that proposes how people are able to deal with conflict situations. We offer his proposal in Fig. 15.1, for the purpose of distinguishing between the types of world views involved in conflicts. The conflict situations can be seen to range between (static, dynamic), and (simple, complex). As in the modelling space (Chapter 4), we can represent this as a world-view space that has been relatively normalised according to the perspectives of those in the suprasystem so that dimensions range between (0,1). Figure 15.1 is shown as a plane, but it can be set up as an *n*-space to represent the world views in a supersystem of *n* actors, where each actor has a plane assigned. Relative to the set of actors, an inquirer may plot in the space the way that each actor sees a particular conflict situation according to some predefined criteria. At the same time, the associated world views of the actors should be identified according to predefined criteria, and this should be indicative of the possibility of addressing the conflict situation.

The plot is undertaken according to the following notion: a value of 0 represents a very simple situation, and 1 a highly complex one; 0 represents a static situation, and 1 a very dynamic one. We note, however, that both dynamics and complexity are relative phenomena to inquirers that depend upon the focus of examination and the conceptuali-

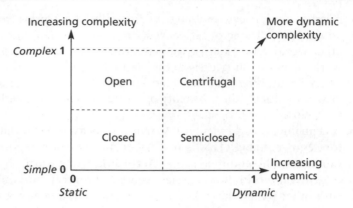

Fig. 15.1 Typology of world views and their ability to deal with complex and dynamic conflict situations

sations used. The typology suggests that closed world views are able to deal with relatively simple static conflict situations, partially closed world views with relatively simple dynamic conflict situations, open world views with relatively complex static conflict situations, and centrifugal world views with complex dynamic ones.

If a conflict situation is seen to be very dynamic and complex, then it can in principle be addressed by those involved adopting a self-actualising frame of reference. However, it can alternatively be addressed by changing the conceptualisation of the nature of the conflict to take it from being, say, highly complex-dynamic, to perhaps relatively simple-dynamic or simple-static. The value of this is that there is now the possibility that it can be addressed by actors with closed or semiclosed world views and rigid or robust frames of reference. To appreciate how we can diminish the complexity of the conflict situation, we refer to Chapter 3, when we discussed the different types of complexity that can occur. If, for instance, we suppose that the complexity of a situation is influenced by emotional involvement, then a de-emotionalising process will reduce complexity. Such de-emotionalising can also reduce the speed at which events take place.

A suggestion by Pirani is that in the 'real' suprasystem world the actors may not always articulate within their individual frameworks whether the 'context' is simple or complex or static or dynamic. The actors may actually adapt dysfunctional strategies that are unaligned to the situation.

Seen in the light of the proposition formulated earlier, this may be seen as a lack of understanding that comes from world-view incommensurability. This arises because each actor has its own world view (which may be a shared world view) with its individual cultural organisation and truth system. Consequently, each actor has its own distinct knowledge. Since different knowledge leads to distinct understandings, it is clear that the strategies that each actor adopts in viewing the conflictual situation and dealing with it will in general be different. If each actor identifies with its individual knowledge through its ego, then this could be a cause for the raising of further conflict.

The notion of contesting differences in a unitary suprasystem

The notion of manifest contesting differences normally relates to a plurality of two or more actors with their own world views in a suprasystem. Thus, the now historical international conflicts of the two superpowers, the United States and the Soviet Union, have provided a representative example of 'national security' related conflicts in a suprasystem in which settlements occurred through the accommodation of behavioural threat. It involved tensions, disputes and conflicts.

However, actors can also be seen to be in conflict with an innate situation, as for instance occurs when an actor defines a unitary suprasystem attempting to achieve goals that are being perturbed by an uncontrollable environment. Here, the environment is credited as being a metaphorical actor, resulting in contesting differences because the *expected* and *actual* goal trajectories are different. As an example of this, Vogler (1993) explains that with the demise of the Soviet Union, there is now a new concern in the international system that also relates to national security. It centres not on the threat of behaviour from other actors, but on the threat of the environment. Here, we can see two focuses of conflict suprasystem. We can look at the international community as an actor, interacting with the natural environment in the suprasystem. Shifting the level of focus downwards, we see nations adopting different shorter term objectives to satisfy the perceived economic and social needs of their populations. The suprasystem is then defined by the nation actors in conflict about how their individual objectives or contesting difference relate to the longer-term goals of environmental balance that can ensure human security.

15.2.2 Contesting difference and cognitive turbulence

We have indicated that contesting difference can be explained in terms of cognitive turbulence, which derives from the relationship between a plurality of world views. We are aware of the nature of world views, and of the idea that individuals or groups create shared world views through the formation of common cognitive models. We are also aware that the sharing process will not include the whole of each world involved. Thus, we have the notion that outside the common model, world-view incommensurability is preserved.

In exploring the consequence of this idea, it will be useful to restrict ourselves to paradigmatic world views, only because paradigms are formalised and therefore more clearly visible than are informal weltanschauungen. Let us envisage that any organisation is composed of a metaholarchy defined by a network of metasystems that are themselves paradigmatically defined. All the paradigms are, by definition, incommensurable and have different degrees of conceptual similarity or qualitative differentiation. The beliefs held by their stakeholders are therefore always to some extent in conflict. During interactions between two groups of stakeholders, we can envisage a process in which the paradigms are superimposed to produce some form of cognitive alignment. If this is done in an arbitrary way, as is often the case, then a partially arbitrary common cognitive model is likely to develop. We say partially because it is subject to paradigm penchants that may define an overall interactive pattern.

We can compare this process metaphorically to an idea in physics that explains the curious patterns that occur when light waves interfere with each other under particular circumstances. Take two pieces of fine net curtain and place one arbitrarily over the other so that the lines of each are in some way orientated one to the other. Unless the lines are particularly aligned, a pattern will appear that is dependent upon both the form that the net curtains take and their relative orientation. Now shift one of the pieces in any arbitrary way and you will see a change in pattern results, though its basic form may remain, depending upon the degree of shift. Shift the piece a little more, and the pattern changes again. This is the result of light interference between the two pieces of net curtain, and is referred to as a Moiré pattern.

We can argue that by analogy Moiré cognitive patterns exist. These, we propose, are patterns of cognitive turbulence that results from the interactive coincidence of two paradigms (or, more generally, world views) when attempts are made for meaning to be shared between their stakeholders. They derive from differences in beliefs, attitudes or values, and may be ideologically connected and emotionally enhanced. They are responsible for arbitrary stable processes of understanding and misunderstandings, and communication and miscommunication, that become institutionalised in organisations. When the differences are contested within a behavioural domain, they are also responsible for the manifest conflictual behaviour that occurs, which in many cases can be described as having an arbitrary (as opposed to a logical) origin due to the way in which the cognitive turbulence has arisen. The degree of turbulence may be thought of as being a potential for conflict development. Greater potential allows for a larger degree of conflict.

Metaphorically speaking, if an organisation finds itself with an internally generated problem situation that needs to be changed, the paradigms will need to be realigned to enable new Moiré cognitive patterns to emerge. In this way the nature of understanding or misunderstanding will shift, perhaps by the creation of new arbitrary stabilities. It may be that a new pattern may not be any more suitable for the organisation, but it may be possible for pattern variations to emerge such that the conflicts are less eventful. This can be assisted when the conflict has associated with it some form of facilitation that acts as a remedial metasystem. Part of this process may be that the paradigms involved can be adjusted in some way, as may occur when the culture and penchant of the local stakeholder group change through a process of learning.

15.2.3 Conflict, competition and cooperation

A form of consensual or dissensual conflict is *competition*. 'When two individuals compete peacefully for the control of limited resources we speak of competition rather than conflict and when two individuals with conflicting interests haggle over the terms of an exchange we speak of bargaining. Where there is bargaining and free competition at the same time we speak of a market situation. But a market situation may break down if there is a restriction on competition and the parties to the market-bargain seek to compel compliance with their own interests by deploying sanctions. In these circumstances the market-situation gives way to a conflict situation which is resolved on the basis of a balance of power' (Mitchell, 1968, p. 39). If we maintain that conflict is the ultimate result of cognitive turbulence, then competition is thus similarly derived and may be difficult to constrain.

There is a view that competition can enhance the *efficiency* and *effectiveness* of organisational processes. Competition may sometimes be a sufficient condition for such enhancement to occur, but it is not a necessary one. There are also the dangers of uncontrollable cognitive turbulence in establishing a competitive system in a situation if one is simply seeking efficiency and effectiveness. This would seem to be the case within the political conceptualisation of privatisation as it occurred as a Government policy in the UK during the 1980s and early 1990s, when the social infrastructure was shifted from public service to a competitive situation in a market suprasystem. The result was that organisational missions changed to reflect new interests. The resulting cognitive turbulence has been elaborated as differences as competition has influenced cooperation.

The notion of competition is exclusive to that of *cooperation* (*see* Minicase 15.1). Thus more of one in any classification of activity means less of the other. If one sees conflict and cooperation as two poles of a continuum, more competition can mean less cooperation, and still higher levels of competition can mean dissensual conflict. Guha (1993) talks of competition generating rivalry and hatred, while cooperation creates tolerance, rationality and good neighbourhood. Attempts to justify or legitimise the motivations of conflicts themselves will contribute to the institutionalisation of the conflict. In his explorations of these two concepts, Guha identifies a typology (Table 15.1) that distinguishes between competitive and cooperative processes in terms of a set of characteristics. These represent the attributes of systems in conflict situations.

Conflict may be seen as a political situation between groups, though it may have a basis elsewhere, for instance in the cultural, social or economic areas. It is inappropriate to consider any complex situation merely in terms of a simple balance of power (Smoker, 1972). Political situations can change, as can the nature of conflicts. The relative nature of a political development can therefore be reflected in the state of a given conflictual situation, which may occur at any level of focus. For instance 'the concept of political development is as applicable to the global system or to a single urban region as it is to the national society' (Singer, 1978, p. 5).

Table 15.1 Characteristics and conceptual framework of conflict resolution comparing the cooperative to the competitive approach

Characteristics	Cooperative process	Competitive process
Properties of system	Has horizontal nature, more stable	Has vertical nature, and is not lasting
Perceptive, cognitive processes	Sensitivity to commonness and similarity	Sensitivity development to differences and distrust
Attributive psychological mode	Confidence (mutual/common), friendliness and helpfulness	Suspicion, aggressiveness (enmity), hegemonistic dominance and coercion
Communications intent	Accuracy, tolerance and openness	Misrepresentation, wrong interpretation, half-truth and concealment
Intended goal achievement	Solution with mutual/common consent and conscience	Solution through pressure and coercion, escalation and prolongation

(*Source:* Adapted from Guha, 1993)

15.2.4 Generic types of conflict suprasystem

Galtung classifies conflict situations generically through a typology (an adaptation is given in Table 15.2) that distinguishes between symmetric and asymmetric classification within a dyadic conflict suprasystem.

Symmetric conflict occurs between two actors of roughly the same level. Galtung refers to them as topdog/topdog and underdog/underdog situations. This implies that they are of the same political class (e.g. both nations or both ethnic groups), and will also have roughly comparable properties and resources available to them.

Minicase 15.1

Pseudo-privatisation in the UK National Health Service

During the recent recessionary period in the Western world the introduction of competition into our infrastructural organisations has been engineering primarily through privatisation. In the UK, privatisation has occurred in the nationalised industries like British Telecom, the bus and rail networks, and the National Health Service. There are at least two difficulties with this idea.

1 When you change the way in which an organisation operates you may be changing its primary purposes, and its paradigm may shift. If this occurs then it must be realised that the generic classification of the organisation has changed. The organisation is thus likely to respond to situations in new ways or create new situations that may not be consistent with previous experiences and expectations.

2 It is often not possible to control whether competition will be consensual or dissensual. This is particularly the case in structurally critical suprasystems. Thus, rather than offering the opportunity of producing efficient and effective organisations, you are changing the organisational structures and processes in a way that may well be destructive overall when viewed from the perspective of the original purposes.

Consider the case of the paradigm shift of the National Health Service in the UK, which moved it from a cooperative public domain, where the structures and processes were more or less dependent upon locally perceived needs and District and Regional Health Authority policies, to a pseudo-privatisation domain that was intended to operate a competitive mechanism depending on market principles for achievement and survival, and where some medical facilities in one locality were advantaged above others through a process of tender failure rather than considered needs for a locality or specialism. The purpose for this change was to make the service into a more flexible organisation that, through competition, would be able to provide a more efficient service. It would also disguise the idea that the responsibility for financial constraints on health spending was due to Government. It did this by assigning it to the Trusts, who would either succeed or fail in their tendering and/or cost management processes.

Prior to the change the NHS had an uncompromising process of cooperation between the different districts. The current situation is that cooperation has been compromised because of the tension generated by a conflict of interests between the competing Trusts in a health market defined by its new paradigm.

Asymmetric conflict occurs between actors of different political class, so that they do not have similar resources available to them (e.g. a superpower nation in conflict with a lesser nation, or a nation in conflict with a cultural minority group). Galtung refers to them as topdog/underdog situations.

Most conflict theory (Galtung, 1975, p. 79) is developed on the assumption of symmetric conflict. This explains how conflicts (like wars between nations, or intrafamily wars) develop, are perpetuated and decline. It connects conflictual tensions with physical and psychological violence at the social level. Asymmetric conflict frequently results in the development of *structural violence* – that is, the dominance of one group over another, with subsequent exploitative practices. While the exploitation may be obvious as in a master–slave situation, it may be much more subtle, and may even operate preconsciously and thus

Table 15.2 Typology of conflict: whether we are talking of exogenous or endogenous derivation of conflict is a matter of level of focus and how we wish to see the situation

Conflict type	Symmetric (topdog/topdog or underdog/underdog)	Asymmetric (topdog/underdog)
Endogenous: conflict that derives from within the system	Leads to conflict resulting in physical or psychological violence, and which can be destructive to the system; can also lead to diversionary exogenous symmetric conflict.	Leads to conquest that can lead to *structural violence*; this can in turn result in physical and psychological violence, as occurs in terrorism.
Exogenous: conflict that derives outside the system, in the suprasystem	Leads to conflict that can result in physical or psychological violence; it can change power balances and suprasystem interaction, and be contagious.	Can lead directly to *structural violence*, which occurs as an exploitation that develops within a suprasystem, so that implicit conflicts occur between the topdog and the underdog. This can result in physical and psychological deviance.

be unrecognised by either group. Neither may it be for the perceived benefit of the dominant group. It bounds the potential of individuals, thus constraining the variety that a system can generate (*see* Minicase 15.2). It thus limits the possibilities of a situation that can be used to meet environmental challenges. High levels of structural violence are therefore inconsistent with the plastic needs of social systems. Low levels contribute to the maintenance of dynamic stability. Whether structural violence is in operation may not be directly obvious.

The development of conflicts can have two origins, referred to as exogenous and endogenous. Endogenous conflict is that which develops within a social actor, while exogenous conflict derives from outside, from the suprasystem. Thus, discussing either of these is in effect shifting the point of reference for a given focus. They can also be used to refer more easily to the involvement and organisational role of third parties to a conflict.

Examples of exogenous asymmetric conflict occur when a feudal interaction pattern occurs; that is, where there is a tightly integrated topdog group (e.g. social security administrators), and a highly atomised underdog group (e.g. social security recipients).

15.2.5 The conflict triangle

According to Galtung, one basic tool for the discussion of conflict is the ABC triangle as shown in Fig. 15.2. It has two purposes:

1 to keep analytically apart the relationship between attitude, behaviour and conflict;

2 to indicate processes of conflict escalation and de-escalation.

It highlights the ideas that:

● conflict is seen as an abstract property of an action system;
● parties to a conflict are seen to have an attitude (towards themselves in an intra-conflict, to others in an inter-conflict);
● parties to a conflict have patterns of behaviour or emergent properties.

Minicase 15.2

Examples of structural violence in asymmetric conflict

An example of an implicitly structurally violent situation is provided by earlier case studies concerning public service organisations. In this illustration staff potentials are suppressed because of the form of the organisation. The distinction between the topdog and under-dog groups will be determinable through the different paradigms that each group maintains as stakeholders. The implicit conflict between the groups is suppressed, unclear and unrecognised by either side. It rarely occurs through overt behaviour, being mani-fested virtually entirely through the structure of the organisation. It is thus contributing further to the structural violence. As an example of this, reward systems for each of the two groups will be highly differentiated, and there will be very limited opportunity for underdog staff to achieve the relatively high levels of reward available to the topdogs. One result of the structural violence is that there is a relatively high level of staff frustra-tion and lack of motivation. The organisation is consequently neither efficient nor effective. Since the structural violence has been institutionalised, the topdog group may be as helpless as the underdogs to introduce changes in form, and both may be contributors to its perpetuation through the myth that it maintains organisational stability. The topdog metasystem (the Home Office component of Government) would need to take ultimate responsibility for this situation.

This type of situation is explored by Wilkinson (1996) in his study of the British Civil Service, commented on in a newspaper article in the *Observer* (7 October 1996) entitled 'Inequality kills'. It explores situations in which there is a high level of role differentiation in power and financial returns. It discovers that there is more ill health, sickness and absen-teeism at the lower levels of power than the higher levels, and that life expectancy is lower at the lower levels. This relates not to better diet or other trapping of position or power, but rather to the levels of stress and frustration that underdog participants experi-ence in contrast to topdog participants.

Some of these characteristics would also seem to be appearing in privatised infrastructural organisations like the water authorities and British Gas. A manifestation of this would appear to be the relatively enormous level of pensionable and non-pensionable income increases being gained by topdog senior managers while underdog staff maintain similar income levels. Such characteristics contribute to the realisation that there is a form of institu-tionalised structural violence that is fundamentally sensate, and highly constraining for the underdogs. It can be indicative of fundamental organisational problems. If it is also indicative of a lack of ideational components of the organisations, then this contributes to their reduced plasticity. It also indicates the possibility of their implicit inability to therefore create variety that can be used to establish requisite variety to maintain dynamic equilibrium with the environment in the face of either problems or potential open playing field competition.

The corners of the triangle represent orthogonal concepts, having analytical and empiri-cal independence from each other. All three are mutually interactive, one influencing the other. Thus, conflicts may, for instance, develop through a perceived negative attitude, or a perceived bad behaviour. Changing behaviour or attitudes will thus affect a conflict.

Conflict also leads to frustration, which leads to aggressive attitudes, which become acted out as aggressive behaviour. Such conflicts may also be ended by:

Fig. 15.2 ABC triangle of Galtung, differentiating between attitude, behaviour and conflict

- settling the cognitive turbulence that manifests conflict;
- controlling the attitude;
- controlling the behaviour.

The converse of the conflict frustration proposition is the Ruloff (1975, p. 37) deprivation–frustration–conflict proposition. It proposes that deprivation – or shall we say, at least, perceived deprivation – causes conflict through frustration. Such perceived deprivation, we note, may occur in the social, political or economic level of consideration. Ruloff shows that as well as frustration, there are other elements that contribute to aggression, including psychological factors, uncertainty and inter-actor tensions.

The conflict triangle provides an important way of exploring situations. This is because the three orthogonal dimensions of consideration can provide three modelling approaches to explore a situation. The nature of the conflict can be explored *technically* (Habermas, 1970) through conflict models such as that of conflict analysis (Fraser and Hipel, 1984). Actor attitudes can also be explored, through the work of, say, Rokeach (1968), though such a study would have to involve *cultural* considerations. In principle, 'an attitude is seen as a relatively enduring organisation of beliefs about an object or situation predisposing one to respond in some preferential manner' (Rokeach, 1968, p. 134). *Attitude change* would then be a change in *predisposition* – that change in a hypothetical state of an actor which, when activated by stimulus, causes a selective, affective or preferential response. This change will occur in either the organisation or structure of beliefs, or in the content of one or more beliefs entering into the attitude organisation.

Behaviour is a manifestation of attitude. As discussed in Chapter 2, attitude may be focused on either an object or a situation, and behaviour is a manifestation of the difference between the two types of attitude. The expression of behaviour will vary according to the attitude towards a situation, which facilitates or inhibits the expression of attitude towards an object, and vice versa. 'It is not merely enough to assert that social behaviour is a function of two attitudes. To predict behavioural outcome requires a model about the manner in which the two attitudes will cognitively interact with one another. Such a model, the belief–congruence model ... was originally formulated to deal with various issues raised by the Osgood and Tannenbaum congruity model (1955), with only minor modifications it can be more generally employed to predict the behavioural outcome of cognitive interaction between the two attitudes' (Rokeach, 1968, p. 136).

Yet another approach towards behavioural adjustment comes from power political situations, as, for instance, can be identified with the work of Guha, and which will be discussed below. It is typical of both *conflict management* and *institutionalisation and control*, and at least in part *conflict resolution* approaches.

15.2.6 Conflict settlement

Conflict settlement is the process of realigning Moiré cognitive patterns, and its approach will depend upon the type and nature of a conflict situation. Power is required to make a realignment. Guha (1993) identifies three types of power that can enable conflict settlement to be approached:

- structural: a controlling and dominating power;
- bargaining: the power of being placed at a superior position;
- compromising: the power of acceptable understandability.

These may occur within different approaches towards the settlement of the conflict, which can be identified as (Galtung, 1975, p. 85):

- conflict engineering through management;
- conflict de-escalation through institutionalised control;
- conflict resolution.

Ackoff (1979) suggests that conflicts can sometimes be addressed by *dissolving* them. This involves 'changing the system and/or the environment in which the ... set of interrelated problems ... is imbedded so that "problems" simply disappear' (Flood and Jackson, 1991, p. 147). It is often not possible to redesign a conflict suprasystem, making dissolution in Ackoff's sense impossible. However, a form of dissolution (we shall call it logical dissolution) can occur when the actors in a situation see it from a different perspective that changes the meaning of what is happening. That is, by looking at a problem situation in a different way, it vanishes. Unlike Ackoff who distinguishes between dissolution and resolution, we consider that *logical dissolution is part of resolution*.

15.2.7 A technical approach to conflict settlement

A technical approach to the search for settlement of conflict suprasystem problem situations is also possible, and that given here derives from a game theoretical tradition. While it may not generate settlement outcomes that can be used directly in a conflict situation, it will contribute to the exploration of possible outcomes and in this way contribute to the search for settlement.

An actor in a conflict situation, seen as one system among others in a conflict suprasystem, can be explored in terms of (a) its properties, (b) its short-term political aims and (c) its longer-term goals.

1 *Properties* form the current characteristics of an actor, and relate to its power base over social, political, economic and cultural processes. The properties of each actor very much relate to the framework of perception of self that it has, and provide the foundation from which a set of objectives is defined. As the nature of the set of perceptions changes, so will both the framework and the objectives. Adjust the framework of perception of an actor, and you adjust the perception of self.

2 *Goals* are the objects of effort or ambition that each actor intends to achieve. There may be a distinction between expressed goals, real goals, and achievable goals. In game theory (Fundenberg and Tirole, 1991), for instance, much work has been done in exploring the relationships between actors in, say, a bargaining situation, that have different qualities of information about the goals of the other actors. Thus, for

instance, identification of a 'wrong' goal set in a conflict situation can be misleading in terms of the framework of perception and the degree to which apparent choices are feasible. These choices can be expressed in terms of the selection of objectives.

3 *Needs/aims* form the set of possible options available to each actor in the conflict suprasystem that are perceived by an actor to be required in order to meet his goals. If it was possible to express as a table the needs of the set of actors in the suprasystem, then an interactive *conflict tableau* could be created that generates interactive conflict scenarios. As the framework of perception changes, so do the needs that an actor deems necessary to achieve a set of goals. This in turn influences the definition of the objectives table and consequently the way in which conflicts develop.

An actor tableau is offered in Table 15.3 and an illustration of its reduced use in Minicase 15.3. It identifies actor properties that operate in relation to the needs of the other actor to provide a position of relative power. The ranking process enables an evaluation to occur of the relative importance that any power attributes, goal options of needs have in connection to the conflict situation.

Table 15.3 Actor tableau proposed for two actors in a conflict situation

Actor attributes	Actor 1	Actor 1 rank	Actor 2	Actor 2 rank
Properties				
Goal options				
Needs/aims				

Needs are often seen tactically, and relate to negotiating, bargaining and associated processes that result in decision making. The relationship between the aims and the decision outcomes is subject to the structural criticality of the suprasystem. The decision process derives from the metasystem of an actor. In the case that this is robust, then an actor's dominant paradigm is not susceptible to perturbations from its internal or suprasystemic environment. As a result, the aims pursued by the actor can be maintained and form a stable decision making process.

The set of actor goals may be achievable only under the condition that they are feasible within the conflict suprasystem. The achievement of a future for the suprasystem that conforms to the set of goals of the system will only occur in dynamically stable situations. Conflicts arise from incompatible goals that contribute to the creation of a structurally critical situation. This is in part because each actor is pursuing its own goals independently of others, and the conflict suprasystem has no homogeneity in terms of its overall goals, let alone approaches by which it is capable of implementing control procedures.

An actor system has a set of properties that support its behaviour. Since the properties of a system determine its behavioural possibilities, this must necessarily be directly related to its power. In particular, and expressed in cybernetic terminology, it will have domains of power that provide the strength to adapt to certain classes of variety that the suprasystem throws up.

Seeing the actor as a political system, the relationships between its needs, goals, properties and power are shown in Fig. 15.3.

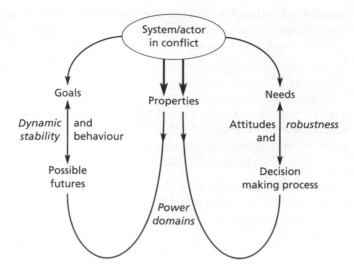

Fig. 15.3 Relationship between the system/actor and its power in the conflict suprasystem

Part of the process of identifying the possible settlement of a conflict suprasystem is to explore the perceived outcomes that may be common to all the actors, each of which has its own needs and goals. One logical approach to this is *conflict analysis* (Fraser and Hipel, 1984). This is a sophisticated form of decision table evaluation based on metagame theory (Howard, 1971). It is an approach that depends upon the intervention of an inquirer, who will determine what is considered to be a feasible set of options, and operates in conditions of uncertainty. This approach within the context of CMC has been considered by Yolles (1992). However, for it to operate successfully, it must be able to change with the situation, as feasible options described as scenarios become infeasible, and new options appear. Another approach intended to rank characteristics of conflict potentials, due to Gass (1994), uses a multicriteria decision analysis methodology.

The impact of perturbations from the conflict suprasystem may affect actors so that they destabilise. This clearly endangers the internal decision making process of actors, as it does the possible futures that are available. This has immediate impact on the conflict suprasystem and the possibility of conflict settlement.

Minicase 15.3

Actor tableau for Scottish independence

As we write this chapter, Scottish independence is shifting from a desire by a significantly large group of Scots, to a likely position as the current UK Government is drafting a referendum and legislation to enable this to occur partially.

Mitchell (1993) has explored the issue of Scottish independence from the UK, and from this we can see a situation that could relate to the case of a cultural minority group (the Scots) wishing autonomy from its host nation (the UK). A single-actor tableau for the Scots might in this case take the form shown in Table 15.4.

Table 15.4 Example of a possible actor tableau for a coherent minority group seeking independence

Actor attributes	Condition; date
Actor properties	
economic power	No
essential infrastructure	Yes
critical mass of commerce	Yes
critical mass of public support	Yes
Actor goals	
economic autonomy	Yes
currency control	No
Actor needs/aims	
local income accrues to actor	Yes
control of natural resources	No
control of public expenditure	No
control of currency	No
control of employment policies	No
control of education policies	No
control of taxation	No

15.2.8 Conflict management

This is the domain of the management of change, and can here be related to other methodologies such as organisational development. Conflict management intends to decrease conflict or maintain it at a given level. It promotes the idea of there being a controller (rather than a control process). It is often associated with structural violence (passive violence created by social structures) in asymmetric conflicts. While structural violence may not be easily recognisable, there are often indications of it, such as the occurrence of relatively high levels of types of 'deviance' (e.g. mental, social, political or legal) from a social norm.

Within conflict management, it is possible to undertake both conflict regulation and creation. Galtung has developed a typology of conflict management that relates to behaviour and attitude (Table 15.5) in the ABC triangle of Fig. 15.2.

Table 15.5 Typology for conflict, behaviour, attitude

Major purpose for conflict management	Conflict purpose	Attitudinal and behavioural manifestations of conflict	Latent incompatibility of goals leading to conflict
Regulation	Decrease	De-escalation or control	Resolution
Regulation /creation	Maintain	Stabilisation or institutionalisation	Protraction
Creation	Increase	Escalation or manifestation	Consciousness

The typology of conflict offered previously is redrafted in Table 15.6 in relation to conflict management.

Table 15.6 Typology of conflict relating to management

Conflict type	Symmetric (topdog/topdog, underdog/underdog)	Asymmetric (topdog/underdog)
Endogenous organisation: conflict management organised from outside the conflict	Typically with both parties being topdogs, and without upper topdog power to draw on.	Typically where the topdog demands that everyone else stays out.
Exogenous organisation: conflict management organised by the parties to the conflict themselves	Typically both parties being underdog and intervention by topdog.	Typically where the topdog requests assistance from outside.

15.2.9 Institutionalisation and control

The principle way of controlling conflict involving attitudinal or behavioural manifestations is through polarisation, as shown in Table 15.7.

Conflict polarisation is a dangerous approach since it can escalate conflict as well as reduce it. Depolarisation is an alternative to this. However, this is better undertaken prior to conflict manifestation, or after its institutionalisation. Institutionalisation makes the conflict into an equilibrium situation; in an international conflict this can often take about three years of hostilities.

Table 15.7 Controlling conflict through polarisation

Origin of institutional organisation	Polarisation (creating conflictual distance)	Possible consequence
Endogenous	A self-protective mechanism for the total conflict suprasystem.	Can escalate conflict by providing enough distance to organise and deal with antagonists in a highly violent way. Can de-escalate conflict by reducing the surface contact to a minimum.
Exogenous	Typically a freezing of the conflict by a third-party intervention, (often through topdog action in an underdog/underdog conflict).	From a history of violent exchanges, can result in mutual hatred and distaste; it may (a) escalate violence or (b) be a forceful way of keeping parties apart.

15.2.10 Conflict resolution

In social circumstances where the parties to a conflict cannot be managed (as in the case where the parties are all topdogs), the most appropriate to deal with the conflict is through *resolving* it. Resolving problem situations is, according to Ackoff, an approach that 'is a "satisficing", trial and error, approach based on a mixture of experience and common sense' (Flood and Jackson, 1991, p. 147). However, for our purposes this is not a sufficient definition. Resolution is concerned with settling a conflict (problem situation) through action at its causes. It thus represents a holistic approach. A typology of conflict resolution based on Galtung (1972, p. 86) is offered in Table 15.8. We have said that conflicts arise as a manifestation of difference through cognitive distinctions that are paradigm derivative. These can require (a) empirical adjustment, as in the case of dividing up resources according to new share divisions (which will complexify a situation), (b) logical reinterpretation of goals through trading-off one goal against another or (c) logical dissolving of a situation through the parties redefining the way in which they see the situation. The latter situation is more appropriate for conflicts at the level of the individual, since they have no group reinforcing support for their views.

Table 15.8 Options for action to resolve conflicts

Resolving action on conflict suprasystem	Eliminate cognitive distinction	Preserve cognitive distinction
Preserve suprasystem		
1 Empirically (e.g. changing shares)	1 Compromise	1 Protraction
2 Logically reinterpret	2 Tradeoff	2 Increase frustration
3 Logically dissolve	3 Redefining	3 Entrenchment
Change suprasystem by		
1 Increasing pluralisation	1 By multilateralisation	1 By absorption
2 Unitarising situation	2 By participant	2 By incapacitation that is:
	a integration to one party	a social
	b decoupling to restrict interaction	b physical

Guha is also interested in identifying the when and how of conflict resolution. To do this he defines a set of possible stages that can be used (Table 15.9) in settling conflict situations through the process of mediation.

15.3 The paradigm of CMC

15.3.1 The language

In Table 15.10, the ideas used within this paradigm reflect the idea that virtually any situation can be seen to involve conflict, either between actors, or between an actor and its environment. It can thus be seen as a relatively broad way of examining problem situations that need to be settled from a political perspective. This does not, of course, restrict the logical mechanism of the methodology to the conflict domain.

Table 15.9 Stages and steps for conflict resolution

	Stages of conflict resolution through mediation		
Steps	Primary	Secondary	Final
1	Creation of atmosphere for negotiation	Consultation	Cooperation
2	Understanding the conflict situation	Mediation	De-escalation (status quo and non-spread of aggression)
3	Bringing the parties to the stage of discussion and the table of and for evaluation	Re-consultation and clarification loss and gain or give and take strategies and tactics	Evaluation of positive and negative aspects or gains and sacrifice of points
4		Conciliation at the point and stage of confrontation	Compromise and final understanding and conclusion of final agreement

Table 15.10 The language of CMC

Term	Meaning
Actor	A set of individuals functioning as a group, an institution, or any social unit considered to be relevant for the interpretation and explanation of events. The actor is seen as the system of interest operating within a suprasystem. In the context of conflict processes actors can be thought of as being political units that have social and cultural motivating positions. The examination of power relationships is therefore necessary, but must be seen as only part of an inquiry. The settlement of conflict situations can in part be seen as a political process.
Actor properties	The characteristics of a given actor. This is often seen in terms of the intragroup decision making process that establishes political action.
Actor relations	Different types of dyadic relations between actors.
Suprasystem	Can be seen as a system defined by a set of actors. If each system is a coherent group, the suprasystem is seen as the set of the intragroup (or between group) processes. A conflict suprasystem involves only those actors mutually engaged in conflict.
Boundaries	The line between interaction and environment, for example: geographic, cultural, issues.
Political	Types of governments/managements, administrations of political units, the roles of individuals or subjects in the political unit's external relations, and the methods by which resources of the units are mobilised to achieve external objectives.
Structure	A characteristic configuration of power and influence or persisting forms of dominant and substrate relationships. It includes identification of major subsystems enabling us to inquire into the important rivalries, issues, alliances, blocks or international organisations.
Interaction	Interchange between entities. In political terms, the entities are individuals and groups that establish diplomatic contacts, trade, types of rivalries and organised violence.

Table 15.10 (continued)

Term	Meaning
Regulation	Explicit or Implicit rules or customs, major assumptions or values upon which relations are based; the techniques and institutions used to resolve major conflicts between the actors.
Issues	Lines beyond which actions and transactions between the actors in a suprasystem have no effect on the environment, and where events or conditions in the environment have no effect on the actors.
Social superstructure	The broader social domain of an actor to which institutionalised political and cultural aspects relates. An examination of these factors can highlight a basis for the motivations of a conflict.
Social substructure	The social domain that includes mode and means of production and the social relations that accompany them. This can provide some insight into the resource nature that enables a conflict to occur or be maintained.
Orthogonality	Analytically and empirically independent entities that have their own set of characteristics that operate together with others as distinct conceptual planes within a framework of thought.
Conflict situation	Can involve tensions, disputes caused by accidents or minor provocations, or conflicts seen as manifest contesting differences. Tensions and conflicts may be consensual (when they are of benefit to an actor) or dissensual (when they are harmful). Conflict may be seen as being part of a conflict–cooperation continuum, where competition lies somewhere between the poles. When referring to conflict situations, we normally mean those involving dissensual processes.
Asymmetric conflict	In terms of resource capability and power, where two different classes of actor are engaged in a conflict.
Symmetric conflict	In terms of resource capability and power, where two actors of the same class are engaged in a conflict.
Endogenous	That which derives from inside the system. This may be the conflict situation itself, or the intervention.
Exogenous	That which derives from outside the system. This may be the conflict situation itself, or the intervention.
Security	Relates to perceived threat and the preservation of actor identity.
Structural power	A controlling and dominating power.
Bargaining power	The power of being placed in a superior position.
Compromising power	The power of acceptable understandability.
Conflict settlement	The settlement of conflict situations either through its management, institutionalised control or resolution.
Conflict management	The control of conflict situations through a controller (not necessarily a control process), which is intended to maintain or decrease conflict.
Institutionalised control of conflict	The principle of controlling conflict that operates through the process of polarisation or depolarisation. It can work better if conflicts are addressed prior to their manifestation.
Conflict resolution	The settlement of conflict through action at its causes.
Moiré cognitive patterns	The stable patterns of turbulent interaction that occur between world views that become the basis for conflict situations and are the cause for miscommunication.

15.3.2 Rules and propositions of CMC

The purposes

The purposes of CMC are:
1 from the perspective of the methodology:
   a to provide a structured inquiry into situations through a metamodel;
   b by predefining a purpose for inquiry and a context, to construct a virtual paradigm within which orthogonal models can coexist either in a composite way, or by association through their inputs and outputs;
2 from the perspective of the inquirer, to define a virtual paradigm that can enable exploration to occur of (a) the cultural related attitudes of the group decision making process, (b) the coherent group behaviour that is associated with conflict resolution, management or control processes and (c) the intragroup political power aspects of a situation;
3 from the perspective of the participants of a situation, to provide an explicit opportunity to examine an organisation's paradigm;
4 from the joint perspective, to provide a way of confirming that the paradigms of inquiry and of the organisation are commensurable; that is, an inquiry is applied to the situation in a way that is not incompatible with its events.

System concepts

1 Seeing conflict situations as human activity systems enables one to:
   a give a *description* of regular patterns of interaction among independent political units;
   b see systems as variables that help *explain* the behaviour of the units comprising the system.
2 The system concept provides an abstract way (Spanier, 1972) of looking at:
   a part of reality for the purposes of analysis;
   b the level of exploration of the conflictual system that is often put in terms of the focus of the system level.
3 A conflict situation can be seen as a political system that is influenced by social, cultural and economic factors.
4 Three levels of focus that are useful to conflict situations are:
   a the intragroup suprasystem;
   b the group as an actor itself seen as a system and participant in the suprasystem;
   c the actor decision making level seen as occurring in a metasystem.
5 The actor system is the centre of focus, which can change.
6 Actor systems have characteristics that include perception and cognitive processes, attributive psychological orientation, communications intent and goals.

The conceptual model

7 Three orthogonal dimensions of interest that contribute to an understanding of conflict processes are social, political and cultural.
8 Conflict systems can be seen from the perspective of a political situation with other causes.

9 At the suprasystem level, conflict involves power relationships that are continually under change as:
   a new events occur
   b system behaviour changes
   c systems behaviour is perceived to change
   d political controls reach their threshold
   e power instabilities occur.

10 Actors acting in a suprasystem are concerned with their feeling of security, which relates to perceived threats to (a) power and (b) the preservation of group identity.

11 What is perceived to relate to security is dependent upon the dominant threat defined by a given paradigm.

12 Suprasystem paradigms can shift.

13 Political processes can be susceptible to popular beliefs within the system.

14 Conflict situations are determined by
   a *tensions* that may have no discernible cause
   b *disputes* caused by accidents and minor provocations
   c *conflicts* represented as manifest contesting differences.

15 Conflict situations may have elements that are consensual or dissensual.

16 Conflict and cooperation can be seen as opposite ends of a continuum, with competition residing somewhere along it.

17 Competitive processes are vertical in nature and not very long lasting, while cooperative processes are horizontal and more stable.

18 Conflict situations may be symmetric or asymmetric.

19 Conflicts and their settlement may be endogenous or exogenous.

20 Conflict, attitude and behaviour can be considered as independent orthogonal dimensions.

21 Perceived deprivation can be responsible for frustration.

22 Conflict can lead to frustration, and frustration can create conflict and aggression.

23 Uncertainty and inter-actor tensions can contribute to conflict and aggression.

24 Three ways of settling conflict situations are through management, institutionalised control and resolution.

25 Conflict regulation can either decrease or increase conflict.

26 Conflict situations can be institutionally controlled through polarising or depolarising them.

27 Conflict resolution provides the most holistic way of settling conflicts.

15.3.3 Behaviour organising and model of the conflict modelling cycle

The phased model is suitable for a variety of modelling situations that require inquiry, whether they have a hard orientation towards seeing situations as things, or a soft one involving people and their personal relationships. It includes the three phases *analysis, options synthesis* and *choice*. This can be preceded with a pre-analysis stage that defines the overall context of the situation (Table 15.11).

To undertake *analysis*, it is essential that actors and their influences are adequately understood. Actors have goals, objectives, strategies and an external environment with which they interact. They have internal constraints as well as external ones, and variables that include general cultural attributes. This suggests the need for a pre-evaluation stage in CMC. Analysis, like each of the other phases, is itself seen as a cycle. Options synthesis provides the opportunity to create modelling options that are capable of addressing the conflictual situation. Iteration through this subcycle can occur to enable, for example, a developing explanation of a situation, and comparison between old and new situations during change. This can, for example, enable different purposes or paradigms to be distinguished. It will also enable either or both additional options for the situation to be sought, which may themselves be evaluated, and greater detail.

There are a variety of ways of addressing this methodology. For instance, the analysis phase can be iterated. For example, it can be applied to an inquirer to explore a situation in general terms, and to each actor to clarify individual paradigms. After repeating the analysis phase for each actor the paradigms can be compared in terms of their cognitive organisation (attitudes, beliefs, values). Also, options synthesis may be iterative. A first iteration could explore an intervention strategy, and a second might explore the turbulence caused by a clash in paradigms. There are alternative ways of using the methodology.

The choice phase provides for the examination and selection of implementation strategies to deal with the situation, and can be iterated. For example, a first iteration might confirm that selections were satisfactory, and a second iteration might enable implementation of an option.

These stages are quite consistent with those of Guha described in Table 15.9, and the latter can quite easily be explained in terms of the former.

15.3.4 CMC as a modelling inquiry metamodel

Preliminary modelling inquiry can occur with CMC to enable different models of inquiry to be assembled and used conjointly. It can do this through the creation of a virtual paradigm that is created (Fig. 15.4) within the paradigm cycle originally given in Chapter 2.

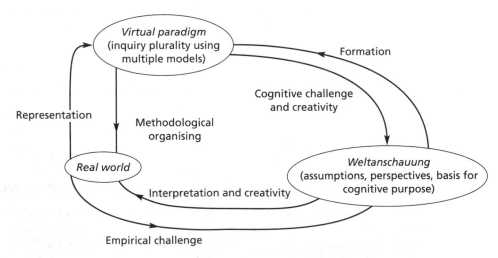

Fig. 15.4 The paradigm cycle to identify and link candidate models in inquiry plurality modelling

Table 15.11 Phases and steps of CMC

Phase	Step	Meaning
Pre-analysis	P0	Explore the context of the situation in order to identify its nature.
Analysis Conceptual dismantling of a situation into a set of component parts. Assumes sociological understanding of situation, so that an appropriate context can be defined, and an examination of distinct paradigms.	P1.1 Context	P1.1 Examine the nature and context of the situation, and the environment in which it operates. The context will initially be tied to the cultural dimension of the situation being inquired into. It will also indicate paradigm associated with the situation.
	P1.2 Problem definition	P1.2 Examine the changes that may have invoked the problem; identify the problem boundaries, parameters; examine problem plurality, and the existence of sub-problems; explore cultural attributes that enable conflictual turbulences to occur.
	P1.3 Form and Influence	P1.3 The form of the situation is defined through a stakeholder analysis. Realise that there may be a plurality of situations or perceptions of a situation. Also identify the influences on the situation. Establish relationship between entities within the situation and outside it.
	P1.4 Trajectory	P1.4 Actors in a situation involving conflict have a trajectory or pathway intended to lead to achievable goals. In general the goals are egocentric and have little to do with those of other actors. Trajectories may not lead to a given goal. The difference between an intended and an actual trajectory is an indicator of dynamic stability in the situation.
Options synthesis Defining and selecting appropriate options according to holistic principles.	P2.1 Paradigm	P2.1 Define the different paradigms that will enable the generation of a range of options. This involves the modelling of interactive actor relationships as definitive scenario possibilities. The models should represent holistic forms that represent solutions to conflictual problems as identified in analysis.
	P2.2 Options	P2.2 Define the options that will form the basis of the settlement.
	P2.3 Pruning	P2.3 The purpose of pruning is to seek paradigm commensurably with the situation, and it represents the reduction of the alternatives to a core set of options (CSO). Since options represent solutions to the set of problems, these should be sociologically appropriate so that they satisfy the cultural and social attributes identified in the situation. It is essential that the paradigm associated with the synthesised options is commensurable with that of the problem situation, otherwise they will either be rejected, or they will not work.
Choice Distinguishes the ability of each option model to represent the situation and the constraints under which it operates. Validation of an option only occurs if an evaluation has been successful.	P3.1 Selection	P3.1 Provide the choice of *selecting options*. Identify option demands, constraints, perspectives and implications explicitly, and criteria of selection. Identify commensurability between the modelling paradigm and the paradigm believed to be associated with the real-world situation. This step might also include identifying methods of prediction, or, perhaps more realistically for complex situations, anticipation based on cognitive belief.
	P3.2 Activation	P3.2 This enables the *option evaluation*. The tools for this should be defined, as should be the assumptions on which they are based. The propositional base of a tool should be commensurable with that of an option. Thus, in a soft modelling environment, a tool might be group discussion or groupthink, or a game. In a hard modelling environment it might involve testing against simulations whose propositions will also have to be examined (e.g. Gaussian distribution models that assume randomness). Options may be activated either for implementation, or by analogue simulations or games, etc.
	P3.3 Outcome	P3.3 Comparison of option outcomes or expected outcomes will *validate option selections*. This occurs by examining the results of activated options by identifying their consequences in comparison to events identified in the situation. In soft situations, the approach might be to determine through feedback from the actors the utility of the model as a way of thinking about the situation (an analytic tool). In hard models, a match between model outputs and perceived real-world events might indicate how 'good' the option is.
	P3.4 Stability	P3.4 Investigate dynamic and structural stability of the synthesised system. In a soft approach this might mean evaluating options against their intended or expected purposes. This could occur through a report back from a groupthink or game. In hard situations prediction could indicate whether predefined goals were achievable.

The purpose of conjoining models of inquiry derives from the cognitive purpose, which will change according to the nature of the inquiry being undertaken. This also provides the context within which model selection will occur. The creation of a virtual paradigm will enable the basic logic and assumptions to be established for the linking of candidate inquiry models.

Typically, CMC is used recursively to create model plurality through a set of candidate models. The candidate models themselves will be identified during the recursive analysis phase. They will be linked together through the propositions set up in the virtual paradigm during the synthesis phase. In the case that the models have associated with them independent ideologies, these will also be linked logically according to a set of propositions. Choice will enable a selection according to the context defined during analysis.

The cognitive model has at its base Galtung's conflict triangle as a way of exploring a conflict situation. One dimension of this has been suggested as conflict analysis, a *technical* approach (in the sense of Habermas, 1970) through the methodology of Fraser and Hipel (1984), which inquires into the feasible options available in settlement of a conflict suprasystem. Another is the orthogonal approach of Rokeach (1968) concerned with attitude, which is a development of the belief-congruence model that requires *cultural awareness* of the actors. Yet a further approach is that of *power political* models that are intended to induce behavioural differences. In developing this way of exploring a situation, it is possible to attempt to accommodate such approaches into a complementary holistic view of a situation by addressing attitudes (in a culturally sensitive way) and behaviours while at the same time addressing the *technical* aspects of the conflict. Each modelling approach can occur through an individual cycle of CMC, producing results that can be identified as potentially contributing to an overall understanding of the situation, and which can contribute towards the development of an intervention that can settle the conflict.

A summary of the approach to conjoint modelling is provided by Table 15.12. The recursive nature of CMC will be clear from this table. The whole of CMC can be reapplied to the situation within the synthesis phase in order to identify an appropriate virtual paradigm for the methodology to define an appropriate domain framework. It can also be recursive in the choice phase in step P3.2, activating each model as required in a separate cycle.

Table 15.12 A summary of the approach to conjoint modelling

Phase	Activity	Description
Analysis	Weltanschauung	Inquirer's perception of needs
	Inquirer's methodological purpose	Purposes for establishing conjoint modelling approach
Synthesis	Paradigm	Basic logic and assumption of conjoint action
	Paradigmatic inquiry	This is simply an identification of the modelling needs at the propositional level
	Examination	Characteristics of models needed to be matched in candidate models
	Explanatory model	Rationale for needs
Choice	Model options selected	Define the models selected

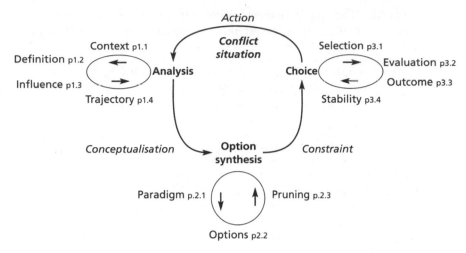

Fig. 15.5 The basic form of CMC

Preliminary model inquiry must work hand in hand with a pre-evaluation of the situation being inquired into. Model selection is therefore an interactive process with the perception of change in the situation. This takes place through the implicit control mechanisms that operate within the methodology, as shown in Fig. 15.5, which operate in terms of the social, cultural and political dimensions of the situation. They also ensure that CMC is not seen as a simple sequential method.

15.3.5 The behavioural model of the conflict modelling cycle

The form of inquiry is shown in Fig. 15.5. It offers three phases that normally operate sequentially. It is possible to introduce controls to adjust this. Each phase is itself cyclic, with the controls embedded. Analysis is used to understand the situation of interest. Typically analysis can be used in a first iteration as a pre-evaluative study of the situation. Further iterations will develop and consolidate any views formed.

The process of conceptualisation will establish a relevant system view of the situation, for which options will be identified. These will be explicitly explored and non-feasible options pruned out. Identification of constraints and possible measures will determine the criteria that enable the choice phase to be implemented.

15.3.6 Cognitive purposes of CMC

Inquiry into conflict situations for the purpose of conflict settlement will be impossible without a sensitivity to the social, cultural and political aspects of a situation. However, principle attention must be paid to the politics and the associated power relationships of a situation because it is this that drives conflicts.

A real-world conflict has occurred that should be settled in some way. The nature of the inquiry using CMC is represented in Fig. 15.6, and an explanation is given in Table 15.13.

In order to make an inquiry, an inquirer will have to build a systemic representation of a situation creating the appropriate *system* that is to be defined. Clearly, how you define a system is dependent upon the viewpoint of an inquirer who is inquiring into the situation. The cultural aspects of the system, seen to be in political interaction with the other systems in the suprasystem, must be examined in terms of the methodology. There are two aspects of CMC:

1 purposes of inquiry are dependent upon the individual inquirers but require that an inquirer explores attitudes, power relationships and behaviour within a situation; this means that they are also required to explore the sociocultural conditions of groups that

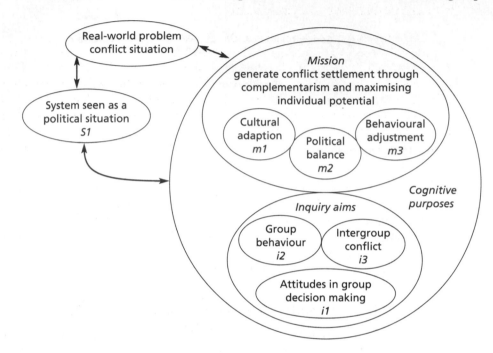

Fig. 15.6 Influence diagram for cognitive purposes of CMC

Table 15.13 Definition of the system and cognitive purposes for CMC

The system

S1 A political *system* with social and cultural attributes is identified by the inquirer.

Cognitive purposes

Mission

The mission is to generate conflict settlement by generating new Moiré cognitive patterns, through complementarism and maximising individual potential. The mission-related goals are:

m1 Cultural adaptation

m2 Political balance

m3 Socio-behavioural adjustment

Inquiry aims

i1–3 Undefined approach to (a) exploring the conflictual suprasystem by exploring Moiré cognitive patterns, (b) addressing actor behaviour and (c) exploring actor attitudes in decision making structures and processes, as determined by the inquirer and the nature of the situation. A virtual paradigm can be identified that can explain the conflict situation intended to determine intervention strategies intended to affect power relationships, and attitudinal and behavioural conditions.

define attitudes, the sociopolitical aspects of the intragroup relationships that define the conflict and produce power structures for the conflict processes, and group behaviour;

2 a methodological purpose is of inquiring into the intergroup, group and intragroup decision making processes.

15.4 The doppelgänger paradigm

CMC enables methodological comparison to occur in terms of (a) structure, (b) methodological process and (c) methodological controls. Basic comparison of these entities occurs in Table 15.14. A control cycle results, as shown in Fig. 15.7.

The creation of systems models can occur during the analysis stage. However, implicit to the methodology is the idea that this, like all phases, can have a first cycle of iteration to provide pre-evaluation. Thus, analysis will involve a pre-evaluation of the situation in its first cycle, and only after that will it attempt to establish a relevant system view. Systems modelling can be constructed during a further cycle. How this occurs very much depends on the needs and intention of the inquirer.

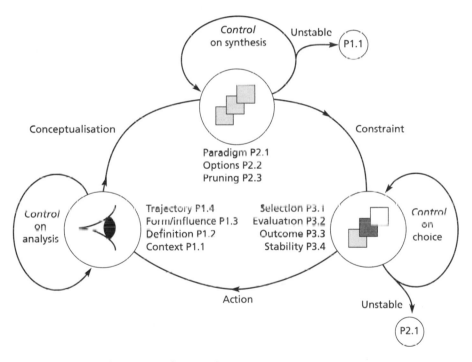

Fig. 15.7 CMC seen in terms of control processes

15.5 The CMC case studies

Two case studies will be introduced. The first is concerned with the Liverpool dock strike, which began in 1995, and was resolved only recently. The second case study is concerned with the changes in Central and Eastern Europe with the demise of the Soviet Union.

Table 15.14 CMC seen in terms of the generic metamodel

Doppelgänger paradigm Entity/process		CMC paradigm Explanation	Step
Pre-evaluation			P0
		Context	P1.2
		Definition of situation	P1.1
Analysis		Form and influence	P1.3
		Trajectory	P1.4
Control		Recycle P1 for exploring alternative views or for configuration of views *unstable*: iterate again or fail	
Conceptualisation		Assemble concepts for option modelling	
		Paradigm	P2.1
Synthesis		Options	P2.2
		Pruning	P2.3
Control		Recycle P2 for confirmation or recursion *unstable:* return to P1.1	
Constraint		Define constraints and evaluate measures	
		Selection	P3.1
Choice		Evaluation	P3.2
		Outcome	P3.3
		Stability	P3.4
Control		Recycle P3 for confirmation or recursion *unstable*: return to P2.1	
Action		Action in situation, or action of re-evaluation	
Control		Reiterate complete cycle if required	

Like the other cases associated with other methodologies in this part of the book, these case studies are intended to be illustrative of the use of the CMC methodology, and do not seek an intervention strategy to the problem situations examined. The methodology is capable of defining a basis for the tandem use of a variety of models and methods through the creation of a virtual paradigm. As in other cases, a rudimentary paradigm is given with the case summary, explaining what models and methods are to be used together, to satisfy what needs, and according to what legitimate purposes as far as the inquiry is concerned.

15.6 Case study 1: The Liverpool dock strike of 1995

This case study is based on a study undertaken in the summer of 1997 by Kathy Ricketts, a student completing the final part of her degree in public administration. It is concerned with the long-standing dispute that was current at that time between a group of 329 dismissed dock workers (DDW) and their former employer, Mersey Docks and Harbour Company (MDHC). In pressing the dispute, the DDW are taking direct action in a brave attempt to obtain what they consider to be justice and their rights within a situation that they see to have been engineered against them. Indeed, they would seem to be the casualties of a continuing promotion of anti-union legislation that was pursued by the previous UK Government. MDHC does not recognise the legitimacy of the claims that the group makes against it, while at the same time making attempts to eliminate the problem, which is likely to be causing it some discomfort.

The exploration shows two world views that exist within the conflict situation. Two very different perspectives in this dispute are seen, which derive from each of the two principal actors, the MDHC and the DDW. The DDW are no longer seen by the MDHC as part of a legitimate employer/employee relationship, and there is no formal structure that connects them there. The MDHC recognises the existence of the DDW as a disenfranchised group, which has a misguided perspective. MDHC maintains that the present situation on Merseyside involving the DDW and their quest for reinstatement has occurred as a result of an issue that had nothing to do with it, and it sees the continuing action by the DDW as a tactical move to reinvent the National Dock Labour Scheme. The DDW believe the MDHC to be operating in an unprincipled way that involves profiteering and an attempt to circumvent Government provision and introduce low pay mechanisms for dockers in an area of high unemployment. The intractable situation has developed into a stand-off between the two groups.

An application of the theory considered above will provide the following insights. An inquirer will explore the relative properties and needs of the two primary actors involved, and thus represent a third view in the situation that may well itself be seen to be distinct. The two actors form a suprasystem, the structure of which is determined by empirical circumstance. While it may have involved cognitive design on the part of one of the actors, it has resulted in cognitive turbulence and a manifestation of contesting differences. Settlement would appear to require conflict resolution, and a compromise will have to be sought. The conflict situation is seen to be asymmetric, and thus care should be taken about the creation of a structurally violent settlement. Settlement options include suprasystem preservation or change. We shall see that one option for preservation is the proposal of a workers' cooperative. One change situation might be the creation of a labour pool, while another could be to unitarise the suprasystem by in some way subsuming DDW into MDHC.

15.6.1 Pre-evaluation: The situation

In 1989 the National Dock Labour Scheme was abolished by the Government and in July of that year a new severance scheme for redundant dock workers was announced. This was followed by a national dock strike. By the end of the year 343 redundant dock workers in Liverpool had taken the severance scheme. MDHC then employed 1927 dock workers.

Case summary

Activity	Description
Weltanschauung	MDHC dismissed 329 employees (DDW) for breach of employment contract, resulting in ongoing conflict between the two parties that appears to be intractable.
Inquirer's mission	To seek to identify an intervention strategy for settlement of conflict between the two parties, MDHC and DDW.
Methodology: CMC	Mission to explore possible settlement of conflict through exploring cognitive turbulence caused by the clash of two paradigms.
Goals and aims of inquiry	To establish the nature of the conflictual turbulences caused by clashing paradigms, and seek resolution by empirical compromise either through eliminating or preserving the conflict suprasystem.
Nature of examination	To explore the situation to seek an implementable resolution for all stakeholders involved that maximises individual potential.
Explanatory model	Examination is focused on two key actors, MDHC and the dismissed employees, DDW, which together define the supersystem. Both employer and ex-employees are the subject of environmental pressures and share a common mission for resolution. It is their behavioural response to the situation that forms the basis for exploration and analysis.
Options selection	To generate a range of options that represent solutions to the conflict problem identified in the analysis.

The abolition of the Scheme meant that in the event of a closure of a company employing port workers there was no longer any guarantee or commitment for other employers at the same port to provide employment for those losing their jobs, which in effect meant cancelling the accepted 'job for life' policy. The discontinuance of the scheme also meant that employers were no longer obliged to recognise union representation, although MDHC was one of the employers who continued to do so.

The Port of Liverpool is owned and operated by the MDHC, though there is a 14 per cent holding by the UK Government. The company is ranked among the top 250 UK companies by the *Financial Times*, and is the UK's second largest port operator, encompassing a broad spectrum of subsidiaries, all related to the Group's core business. In 1995 the MDHC made a pre-tax profit of £31.7 million on a turnover of £138 million. It operates Britain's largest and most successful freeport, handling £1 million worth of goods a day, and has now established a similar trade on the Medway.

MDHC is both a shipping line operator and a ship owner, with terminals in Belfast, Dublin and Cardiff. Through ownership of Coastal Container Line and through its long tradition in the ports industry, it provides expert guidance through its subsidiary Portia Management Services, the UK's largest port management consultancy. Other commercial interests include a travel agency and Mediafine Ltd, publisher of specialist handbooks and yearbooks for the ports and airports industries.

It has a green light from the Secretary of State for Transport for the go-ahead of a £20 million plan to expand by 70 acres the Port of Liverpool and Liverpool free-port, which could also create 500 new jobs. The plan to extend the dock estate, thereby creating a dynamic new warehousing and industrial zone, is a vital factor in fulfilling the aspirations of Bootle Maritime City Challenge in creating future long-term prosperity for the area and was developed in close consultation with Sefton Borough Council and Merseyside Corporation Development.

Since the 1980s Liverpool dock workers have been considered by MDHC and the shipping world in general to be the most productive, flexible and efficient dock labour force. This was reflected in record tonnages and record performances, marking a leap forward for the Port of Liverpool, with cargo volumes and customer confidence at a premium. In September 1995 Liverpool dockers were praised as 'best in Europe' by Lloyd's influential shipping journal.

In September 1995 80 port workers employed by Torside, an independent stevedoring company in the Port of Liverpool, lost their jobs after taking unofficial industrial action over a demand for extra overtime pay (action which, it is claimed, eventually resulted in the company going out of business). The former eighty employees established an unofficial picket line at the gates of the Royal Seaforth Docks, headquarters of MDHC, with demands that MDHC take them onto their books.

Of the 1200 people employed by MDHC some 900 crossed the picket line but 329 port workers with whom the company had no disagreement refused to do so. Their refusal to report to work over an issue that was unofficial and not recognised by their union, the Transport and General Workers' Union, brought activity at the Royal Seaforth container and timber terminals to a virtual standstill. The rest of the Port continued to work normally.

The company sent letters on 28 September 1995 to the home of each port worker who had not turned in for work, warning that he was in breach of his contract and would be dismissed if he did not return to work the next day. The men did not return and were dismissed on 29 September 1995. New contracts offering nearly 200 of the men their jobs at the same rates of pay and on the same terms were delivered by hand to their homes within 24 hours. Only a limited number signed them and returned to work by the deadline of 2 October 1995.

An advertisement offering permanent jobs at the port published in the local press generated nearly 1000 applications, with MDHC reiterating that if any of the dismissed men wanted a job in the port, they should apply as individuals and would be considered. The company announced that it had retained Drake Ports Distribution Services, a division of Drake International, to provide a permanent workforce for cargo handling operations at the Royal Seaforth container terminal.

Many talks involving the union and Advisory Conciliation and Arbitration Service (ACAS) representatives followed, together with an offer by MDHC for former dismissed employees to apply for a job at the port. Those candidates who were unsuccessful and men who chose not to return to the industry were offered ex-gratia payments of £10 000. This, with commuted pension, could have given many of the men who were in their mid-50s a lump sum of £40 000 and a £150 a week pension.

A mass meeting on 20 October 1995 rejected the offer, whereupon MDHC withdrew the offer, which it claimed it had made purely as a gesture of compassion in a situation where former employees had caused their own dismissal and had no legal right to receive any offer. However, other financial settlements and incentives have been offered, with payments to unsuccessful job applicants and men choosing not to apply being raised to £25 000. Deadlines for these offers have come and gone, with even the Bishop of Liverpool, the Right Reverend David Sheppard, intervening for further extensions of offers and continued talks.

At the time of writing both parties were continuing to disagree about how they had found themselves in the situation, and with no trusted common ground talks were becoming increasingly difficult. After 21 months of dispute, hopes of a mutually amicable agreement were fading, yet nevertheless both parties were adamant about continuing to seek resolution.

15.6.2 Analysis

First iteration: The MDHC perspective

1P1.1 The context
This is defined in the pre-evaluation.

1P1.2 Definition
MDHC sees the situation as the culmination of more than 12 months of unofficial industrial action by a small group who sought to turn the clock back by reimposing constrictions similar to those that applied before the abolition of the National Dock Labour Scheme.

MDHC affirms that it was justified in dismissing the 329 dock workers for breach of contract when they failed to turn up for work on 29 September 1995. It maintains that the dock workers, whose reason for not returning to work was because they felt unable to cross a picket line set up by previously dismissed Torside employees, was irrelevant because that issue had nothing to do with MDHC or its employees. MDHC views the establishment of the picket line by the 80 dismissed Torside workers outside its premises as being incidental and the action taken by the 329 MDHC men put them in breach of their employment contract in a strike that was not recognised as official by their union, the TGWU.

Despite much publicity being given to the number of employees dismissed as being 500, MDHC reiterates that the only figure it recognises is that of 329 dismissed employees. It feels that the figure of 500 is a gross misrepresentation and assumptions are made that publicity or tactics on behalf of the dockers have incorrectly included the 80 dismissed Torside workers and miscellaneous others in the claim of 500 dismissed workers.

Within the dispute negotiations, MDHC sees its financial offer of a settlement in December 1996, which remains on the 'negotiation table', of £28 000 per man and the restarting of 40 of the dismissed workers as fair and final. It is adamant that it will not reinstate the 329 dismissed workers in total for several reasons:

- the action taken by the dismissed men was as a result of an issue not involving MDHC or its employees, and the men were given an opportunity to return to work at the time of the initial incident;
- MDHC is in no way liable to reinstate the dismissed workers, who in effect dismissed themselves by breaching their employment contracts;
- the strike action was unofficial and has never been recognised by the official union representing the men in its chosen course of action;
- it is not practical to engage 329 dismissed employees because the majority of those vacant positions have now been filled with other skilled men.

MDHC recognises the hardship and suffering by the majority of the 329 men involved in the dispute and puts the blame and responsibility for the incident on bad leadership locally. The company claims it is only because it wishes to recognise those men who have had long service and good employee contracts that negotiations and offers of settlement exist at all. However, it also points out that, at a final cost of £9 million, this settlement is already being wondered at by some shareholders when there is no legal requirement to make it, and its withdrawal at any stage would be feasible.

MDHC points out that any involvement by the Government in the company is through historical reasons. In the 1960s the Mersey Docks and Harbour Board Trust got into financial difficulties and the Government intervened with financial help. A financial reconstruction began, resulting in the formation of MDHC. Initially the Government held a 20 per cent share, which has now been reduced to 14 per cent. MDHC sees the Government as a silent shareholder, which plays no active role in the running of the company and which has declared in the past that it will relinquish its shareholding when the time is right.

Before the general election of May 1997 that saw the Labour Party brought to power, Margaret Beckett, then a senior member of the Opposition, intimated that if the Labour Party were to win the election it had no plans for intervening in the dispute at the docks on Merseyside. In contradistinction, the Government shareholding is viewed by many dock workers as an opportunity for the Government to manipulate and exert undue pressure on management to enforce further changes in the present system of hiring and firing the workforce, the ultimate goal being a casual labour workforce.

MDHC repudiates any claim by the dismissed dockers that their action has caused serious disruption to the running of the company or the port. While it acknowledges that support from the Longshaw workers in the USA for the dismissed dockers caused the withdrawal of Atlantic Container Ltd, it insists that this only existed for one month before ACL returned to normal operatations at the Port of Liverpool. It affirms that the port continues to operate both normally and successfully, with increased cargo handling tonnages, and points out that the token number of protesters and demonstrators at the gates of the port in support of the dismissed dockers' claims for reinstatement in no way disrupts the normal everyday routine of the port.

The company further claims that it has been accused of attempting to de-unionise the workforce but maintains that the majority of its employees are still union members and the company honours all official union procedures although it is no longer required to do so.

It also reiterates quite strongly that it does not, and never has, employed casual labour at the port. The company does, however, use the services of Drake International, a professional company that must only engage workers who meet the criteria set out by MDHC and who are offered the same commercial terms and conditions of employment as other port workers.

MDHC sees that within the dispute it is the only party willing to compromise, and that it is not obliged to do this in the first place. It also sees that a small nucleus of the DDW have their own agenda that drives the conflict towards their own ends. What these ends are can only be surmised, but they include the demand for the reinstatement of all the dismissed port workers by MDHC – and this will never happen.

1P1.3 Form and influences

The form of the conflict situation is seen by MDHC to define a suprasystem that includes itself and the DDW as the principal actors, and the TGWU and international parties as secondary. The influences that affect the situation as seen from the perspective of MDHC are illustrated in Fig. 15.8.

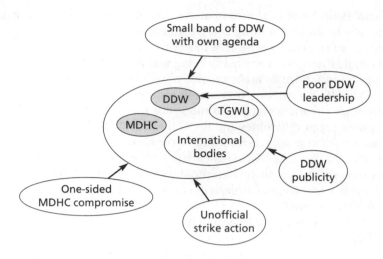

Fig. 15.8 MDHC perception of the influences on the situation and participating actors
Shaded areas are principals.

2P1.4 Trajectory

For practical reasons MDHC says it would be impossible to employ casual labour because it must have a skilled workforce to operate, among other things, expensive heavy equipment such as straddle carriers costing £40 000 each and gantry cranes costing £500 000 each. MDHC sees Liverpool Port as having one of the best safety records in the UK – a record that has improved over the past 18 months, not deteriorated as claimed by some.

MDHC wants an end to the dispute quickly. Its final offer of settlement is subject to withdrawal at any time with no future date set to resume talks.

Its latest move to help ease the settlement was the encouragement to produce a plan for the supply of labour to the port of Liverpool, which it funded jointly with the TGWU and commissioned through KPMG Peat Marwick financial consultants.

Recognition of a workers' cooperative, to operate under strict commercial terms, for the supply of port labour has also been considered by MDHC.

MDHC sees the only way forward being for the dismissed dock workers to be allowed to hold a secret ballot to decide on their options. It claims to have had many telephone calls from the wives and families of some of the dismissed workers who would welcome and support this move. It also feels that if the leaders of the dispute were as confident of the result as they suggest then they should not be afraid to conduct a secret ballot.

Second iteration: The DDW perspective

2P1.1 Context

This is defined in the pre-evaluation.

2P1.2 Definition

Torside shop stewards' chairman Jimmy Nolan goes back to the origin of the dispute in his claims (Dockers Charter, March 1997) that the MDHC operation was brought in to circumvent Government provisions for the abolition of the Dock Labour Scheme. Prevented from employing ex-dockers who had taken severance money, the MDHC helped to set up an 'independent' stevedoring company, which became a tool for introducing part-time, casual labour on much reduced rates of pay. The picket line that the Torside employees established at Seaforth was judged to be illegal – Torside was supposedly a separate company from the MDHC. By refusing to cross a picket line, Seaforth dockers were held to be in breach of their contracts of employment by their employer, MDHC.

Local support for the dismissed dock workers has been demonstrated in fundraising events, marches and rallies, with local comedians and other celebrities giving their time free to boost the occasions. The community of Merseyside has continued non-stop with morale-boosting efforts of food, clothes and finance for the dismissed workers and their families.

As a demonstration of support for the dismissed workers, non-casualisation of port labour and union solidarity, a call to undermine the economic base of MDHC resulted in dockers in 27 countries, affecting 100 ports and cities, being involved in some form of direct action on 27 January 1997.

The dockers are greatly disappointed by the lack of support from their union, the TGWU, which feels unable to support the men in their unofficial strike action for fear of breaking the law, which could result in union funds being seized.

A report by David Osler of Lloyd's List quoted a key passage from a TGWU document of 10 February 1997, which envisaged a cooperative with an employee share ownership plan to provide a permanent workforce for MDHC, from which the following extract has been taken.

> The TGWU seeks a job for those who wish it and a voluntary retirement package for those who wish it. It has been a principle of ours that such a job should be with MDHC. As a result of the company's declared change of policy, whereby it now contracts out all dock labour, the situation has changed fundamentally. MDHC has adopted as a policy that it will no longer be a direct employer of labour itself. It is this policy – and the resolve of the sacked dockers to obtain dock work jobs – which stands in the way of a settlement.

This is seen as a climb-down from the shop stewards' earlier stand that all 329 dockers sacked in September 1995 and around 180 others be given their old jobs back.

Central to the campaign of the dismissed dockers is the issue of casual/'scab' labour which they claim is being used by MDHC. They feel that until this is resolved, no agreement between the parties can be reached. However, this is not an issue that Bill Morris, general secretary of the TGWU, acknowledges. Instead, the official position of the TGWU has two priorities:

1 to alleviate the hardship of the dockers' families;

2 to seek a negotiated settlement.

Dismissed dockers claim that accidents are occurring on the docks caused by inexperienced casual labour, and random checking for drug and alcohol abuse has also been introduced for the first time on the docks of Merseyside.

The dismissed dockers' support group has consistently maintained that its public meetings are peaceful, orderly and without incident. Violent scenes and actions published in the papers always involved fringe groups of activists with other causes, such as the environmental protesters 'Reclaim the Streets', who caused an affray at the March for Social Justice in London in April organised in support of the dismissed dockers.

It is felt necessary here to include the connection that dismissed dock workers make between MDHC and KPMG Peat Marwick, financial consultants, which they feel is crucial for an appreciation of the full facts of the situation. The inclusion also helps to explain the origins of the conflict which first began to model the world views and mission of the group of the DDW and their members, and which have fostered the beliefs, attitudes and suspicions that have influenced their actions. KPMG Peat Marwick not only acts for MDHC but was also the company involved in the Medway Port shares scandal.

Briefly, 300 Medway dockers were dismissed – deemed to have 'sacked themselves' – when they refused the 'downsizing' of their agreed contract presented by Medway Ports managing director, Peter Vincent. Any new contract involved the introduction of casual working, extended 12-hour shifts and wage cuts of several thousand pounds per annum. When the dismissed Medway dockers were forced to sell their shares back to management in March 1993, these shares they were valued at £2.50 by KPMG Peat Marwick. Six months later, in what became known as the 'Medway Deal', Director, Peter Vincent made £12 million virtually overnight when MDHC cashed in 7 per cent of government shareholdings and bought Medway Ports for £102.7 million based on a new valuation by KPMG Peat Marwick of the very same shares at £37.25 each.

At the same time, Liverpool dockers were being served with an ultimatum: accept radical changes in their contracts – 12-hour shifts and wage cuts – or be sacked. A two-and-a-half year legal action by the sacked Medway dockers against KPMG Peat Marwick ended with an out-of-court settlement on 5 July 1996.

When the dismissed dockers of Liverpool refused to cross the picket line mounted by dockers employed by MDHC's client Torside Ltd, MDHC diverted shipping from Liverpool to its new port of Medway. The Liverpool dockers called for a public inquiry into the industrial and financial actions of MDHC and its consultants, in particular its purchase of the port of Medway and the sacking of its 300 dockers. Unfortunately, the previous out-of-court settlement prevented the public examination of the facts of this case being disclosed.

The dismissed dockers are disappointed at the general lack of media support in what they feel could be the start of national casualisation of labour and the total erosion of the union influence, which had helped to create a better standard of living, improved safety at work and increased rates of pay.

2P1.3 Form and influences
The form of the situation as seen by the DDW is a suprasystem that includes DDW and MDHC as the principal actors, and the TGWU, Drake International, and the Government as secondary actors. The influences on this suprasystem are illustrated in Fig. 15.9. The abolition of the National Dock Labour Scheme as part of Government policy is felt strongly by the dismissed dockers to be the catalyst for the conflict situation.

2P1.4 Trajectory
Reinstatement of DDW participants with normalisation of contracts.

Third iteration: The inquirer's perspective

3P1.1 Context
This is defined in the pre-evaluation.

3P1.2 Definition
After detailed inquiry, the schedule of events listed in Table 15.15 was identified.

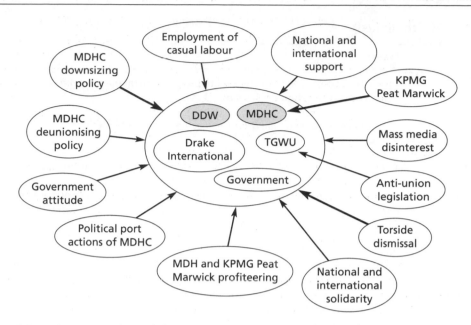

Fig. 15.9 DDW perception of the participating actors and influences on the situation
Shaded areas are principals.

Table 15.15 Schedule of significant events that relate to the conflict situation

Date	Event
26/9/95	80 port workers employed at the independent Torside company in the port of Liverpool lost their jobs after taking unofficial action over a demand for overtime pay.
28/9/95	The 80 former employees established an unofficial picket line at the gates of the Royal Seaforth Docks, with demands that MDHC employ them under the old National Labour Scheme. Of the MDHC employees, around 900 crossed the picket line, but 329 refused to do so. Refusal to work was seen as an unofficial action by the TGWU.
28/9/95	Letters were sent to DDW about breach of contract and requesting that they return to work the following day.
29/9/95	The men who had not returned to work were dismissed.
2/10/95	Deadline of an offer of new contracts at the same rates of pay and terms and conditions made to 200 DDW members, some of whom accepted. Shortly after this, an advertisement appeared in the local press offering permanent dock work jobs,resulting in 1000 applications.
12/10/95	Talks involving the TGWU, ACAS and MDHC resulted in the sacked workers being offered the opportunity to reapply for their previous jobs. Ex-gratia payments of £10 000 per person were offered to those not willing to do so, which would result in a £40 000 payment and £150 per week pension.
20/10/95	A mass meeting rejected the offer, which MDHC then withdrew.

Continued overleaf

Table 15.15 (continued)

Date	Event
23/10/95	Drake Ports Distribution Services was to provide a permanent workforce for MDHC. The first employee was recruited on this date.
19/12/95	TGWU general secretary Bill Morris and senior representatives of MDHC met to seek a resolution to the situation.
09/01/96	A second meeting of these two parties was described by both as 'constructive'.
24/01/96	After a further meeting between the same two parties MDHC announced an offer of 40 port worker jobs still available in the Port of Liverpool and ex-gratia payments of between £20 000 and £25 000 for the remaining 289 men in recognition of their past service. The offer would cost MDHC between £7 million and £8 million, and TGWU general secretary Bill Morris described it as 'the best deal possible'.
08/02/96	Offer substantially rejected by the men in a postal ballot announced on this date.
06/03/96	Meeting between MDHC, national officials of the TGWU and for the first time representatives of the DDW.
02/04/96	A second meeting of the same parties broke up after four hours when representatives of the dismissed men refused to talk further unless MDHC sacked the 150 new container terminal recruits and reinstated all 329 dismissed port workers, plus the men from other companies. MDHC left the offer of 40 jobs and ex-gratia payments of £25 000 per man on the table but warned that this would be withdrawn if the call by the DDW for overseas action against Liverpool ships succeeded in driving away trade.
22/05/96	At the instigation of ACAS, MDHC, the TGWU and representatives of the DDW met in London for further talks.
04/06/96	The parties met again at ACAS in London, when MDHC presented its final offer to the national officials of the TGWU. The final offer was conditional on a private postal ballot.
18/06/96	Deadline of 5 p.m. for a commitment to such a ballot after which the offer would be withdrawn. The offer was rejected by the DDW on a show of hands at a mass meeting. The Right Reverend David Sheppard intervened on behalf of church leaders to request a two-week postponement of the offer deadline to allow every avenue to be explored. MDHC agreed to this request.
20/06/96	Atlantic Container Line announced its withdrawal of its service from Liverpool because of threats of action against its ships by the International Longshoremen's Association in America, promoted by demands of support from the DDW. MDHC announced the same day that its final offer had been withdrawn, reiterating that the £8 million package could only be afforded if established revenue was maintained.
21/06/96	MDHC announced the loss of 80 jobs across the company and the implementation of a voluntary severance scheme together with a warning that hundreds of jobs could be lost among the many companies that provided services to ACL.
24/07/96	Atlantic Container Line returned to the Port of Liverpool and now maintains its normal service.

Table 15.15 (continued)

Date	Event
08/96	Leaders of the DDW declined an invitation to meet for fresh talks with MDHC and TGWU general secretary Bill Morris until 11/96.
16/12/96	Talks held between MDHC, national officials of the TGWU and representatives of the DDW resulted in MDHC making its ultimate, closing offer to its 329 port workers of: (a) £25 000 severance payment or (b) the opportunity to apply for one of the 40 jobs in the Port of Liverpool. In addition an offer was made of a special 12-week fixed contract of employment which would not require the men to report for work but would give each man £3000 in pay for the period. This period of fixed-term contract would be to enable severance applications to be processed and applicants for re-employment assessed. MDHC stated that the offer would remain open until 31/12/96.
23/12/96	Bill Morris, general secretary of the TGWU, wrote to MDHC requesting more time to allow the offer to be put to the men in a secret ballot. MDHC agreed to the extension. At a mass meeting attended by the DDW and the former employees of Torside Ltd and others, the leaders of the DDW called for a rejection of a secret ballot on the MDHC's offer. A show of hands supported the proposition. MDHC had announced previously that if this revised ultimate offer was rejected, no further offer would be made by the company.
24/01/97	DDW announced a proposal to resolve the situation by establishing a workers' cooperative of former Mersey docks and Torside men, to provide stevedoring manpower in the Port of Liverpool with the following proposals: (a) sack the Drake workforce at the Royal Seaforth Container terminal, (b) finance the launch of the cooperative at £0.5 million and (c) take a 55 per cent share in the company. In response, MDHC indicated that a workers' cooperative had previously been discussed in negotiations and the company would support such an establishment provided it operated on a fully commercial basis. However, the proposal to replace the Drake workforce was totally unacceptable to the company. MDHC felt that the suggestion should not distract attention from the fact that the unofficial leaders continued to refuse to hold a secret ballot on its final offer.
24/06/97	A report in the *Liverpool Echo* stated that MDHC was poised to make a fresh offer to the DDW in a bid to end the 21-month dispute. The package could support a proposed workers' cooperative with the creation of 30–40 general cargo-handling jobs, around 60 possible jobs at MDHC's new ferry terminal at Trafalgar Dock, and the DDW would be invited to apply for 41 ancillary jobs made in an earlier offer, taking the total jobs package to around 150. The remaining 180 DDW would get cash pay-offs in the region of £28 000 each plus pensions. In the event of a new offer, TGWU general secretary, Bill Morris, may impose a postal ballot on the DDW.

1P1.3 Forms and influences

The forms and influences are embedded within the mind map shown in Fig. 15.10. Other diagramming approaches, such as a multiple cause diagram, that might be indicative of a direction for synthesising a resolution to the conflict situation would be useful here.

The activity influence diagram in Fig. 15.11 indicates the sequence of events that has led to the situation, and this illustrates the influential factors.

1P1.4 Trajectory

It is evident from the perceptions of both actors involved that many changes have occurred to both trigger off and further influence this problem situation.

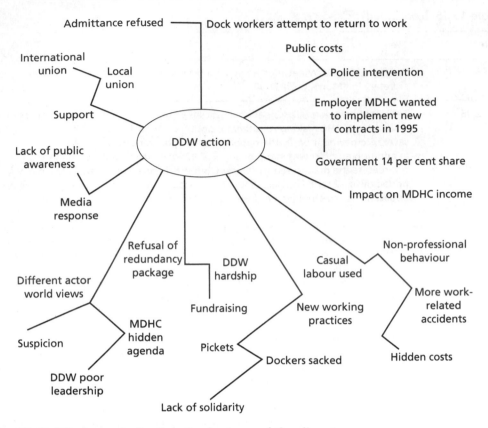

Fig. 15.10 Mind map indicating the features of the dispute causes

Within this complex situation of distinct views and claims, a pattern is seen to form within the activity influence diagram of Fig. 15.11. There would seem to be a deliberate strategy to create a new national dock labour force employed on new contracts with new working practices. These new practices might well include new technical opportunities and training that could enhance the industry and improve productivity and pay schemes. However, the strategy has harboured the fear of more introductions of change with fewer union safeguards and the ultimate threat of the casualisation of the entire dock labour force.

It is also apparent that if MDHC were to reinstate the 329 dismissed employees and be in a position to offer employment to the dismissed Torside workers they would be in danger of once again initiating the Dock Labour Scheme policy 'jobs for life', which would have serious ramifications for other port employers and be deemed unacceptable politically.

The reduction in power and influence by the unions is a cultural shock that the dismissed employees and their colleagues are having to deal with. Union discipline and support is a way of life for many of them and they are witnessing the erosion of that control through the power of legislation.

Government legislation has provided the initial power of direction for increased employer power and influence and reduced union activity and strength.

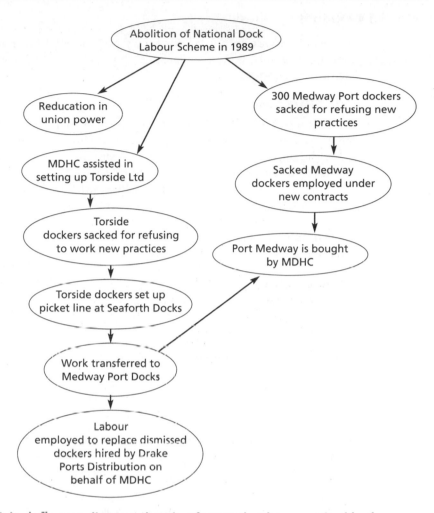

Fig. 15.11 Activity influence diagram showing factors that have resulted in the deadlock position between MDHC and DDW

MDHC has an attitude of justification in imposing the rules of the organisation and dismissal for breach of employment contract in the first instance. However, since that incident it is evident that it has now changed a fundamental management policy by choosing to disassociate itself from the task of recruiting replacement and new labour and dischargement of labour. By engaging another company to fulfil this duty it has thereby released itself from the employer's role in the recruitment of human resources within the company and any future similar incidents that may occur as a result.

15.6.3 Conceptualisation

Here, ideas are generated that enable solutions to be created. Techniques may include brainstorming with participants.

445

15.6.4 Options synthesis

In this phase our purpose is not to explore options fully, but rather to indicate possible options. Possibly, a more exhaustive approach is required with more primary data and actor participation.

1P2.1 Paradigm

The dismissed dock workers hold the attitude that it is their heritage to continue to be employed at the docks in Liverpool and it should be their legacy to their children to have the opportunity to carry on the tradition in the years to come. The different perspective are illustrated through a comparison of the paradigms of the two actors in this dispute that identifies some of the beliefs, attitudes, values and conceptualisations of both actors (Table 15.16).

It is clear that the paradigms generate cognitive turbulence that is manifested in the behavioural conflict situation. A settlement requires a set of options to be identified and possible options selected.

1P2.2 Options

MDHC wants a resolution, and is prepared to finance the means for a resolution, but will not recognise the reinstatement of the 329 dismissed dock workers as that resolution.

Table 15.16 Illustration of the different paradigms of the two actors in dispute

Characteristics	MDHC	DDW
Rights	Have the right to choose who, how, when and why they employ in their company	Have the right to expect a guarantee of employment in the industry they have cultivated
Leadership	Belief that local bad leadership has caused the ongoing conflict	Disappointed that local union leadership has not been supported nationally
Safety	Safety record has improved during dispute to be one of the best in UK ports	Replacement casual labour has increased accident rate at Port of Liverpool
MDHC business practice	Financial consultants KPMG Peat Marwick provide sound business advice	KPMG Peat Marwick in conjunction with MDHC share dubious business transactions
Business success in face of conflict	The port is operating successfully and achieving record cargo tonnage movements and high customer satisfaction	The dismissed workers have succeeded in effecting a boycott of MDHC and the Port of Liverpool, resulting in loss of income and contracts to MDHC
MDHC conflict mission	The desire for a multi-skilled competitive Dock Labour Scheme	Casualisation of all dock labour is the ultimate scheme of things
MDHC conflict goal	MDHC sees its gesture of a financial settlement as fair since no legal commitment binds it to any offer.	Offers of financial settlements are attempts to divide the solidarity of the strikers and 'sell-out' their right to reinstatement
Success of DDW goal	MDHC says that the demonstrations by DDW have almost disappeared from the docks in the port	Dismissed dock workers continue to display solidarity and demonstrate at Seaforth Docks on Merseyside

DDW, however, want the only resolution to be reinstatement of all dismissed workers with no compromise.

Options for the DDW

Clearly the dismissed dock workers do not have a great deal of options to choose from. They have no power, and have probably brought to bear all the supportive influence they are able to, therefore their options are limited.

In such a long-drawn-out conflict they are using up both their personal and financial resources, leaving themselves susceptible to weakness in their ranks. Their options would probably be:

1 continue to lobby their ex-employers and remain unemployed, enduring more hardship;

2 accept financial offer of settlement on negotiation table, with at least 40 employees gaining their employment back;

3 continue to lobby Parliament for the reintroduction of the National Dock Labour Scheme (NDLS), thereby justifying the origins of the dispute and requirement of their reinstatement – while this is desirable, it is extremely difficult to reverse legislative powers;

4 support the plan instigated by MDHC and TGWU for a labour pool and hope to seek employment under this scheme if it is adopted.

If they were to choose to accept option 2 it is likely that they would have to hold a secret ballot to support this move and this type of action still remains unacceptable to the leaders of the dispute, thereby reducing their options still further.

Options for MDHC

MDHC has the power, influence and finance to make and instigate changes and choose between multiple options. These could be to:

1 reinstate the dismissed dock workers without disciplinary action – though feasible, highly improbable;

2 dismiss the employees engaged by Drake International Services and replace with the dismissed dock workers on new contracts of employment – once again, though feasible, highly improbable since MDHC maintains that it does not engage its own labour any more;

3 support the reintroduction of the National Dock Labour Scheme (NDLS) and lobby Parliament in this respect, thereby acknowledging the actions of the origins of the dispute to be true and founded and requiring the immediate reinstatement of the dismissed dock workers – an almost impossible course of action for any port employer to be engaged in;

4 increase the number of offers of re-employment to the dismissed dock workers – feasible but the offer of re-employment has already fallen from 180 to 60 to the present 40, and as the dispute carries on presumably those positions will continue to be filled;

5 develop an aim for a philosophy of negotiation that includes a constructive deadline – the offer on the negotiation table is said by MDHC to be the final one so perhaps a deadline has already been agreed upon;

6 investigate the feasibility of the proposals for a workers' cooperative put forward by the Mersey Port Shop Stewards Committee for a labour supply/hiring hall plan with its primary function being a totally professional workforce trained and experienced to deal with all cargo-handling equipment in the port of Liverpool – having already instigated and jointly funded a survey to be carried out on a similar scheme for port labour by its own financial advisors KPMG Peat Marwick, it is highly likely that MDHC will follow KPMG's advice and await the outcome of the survey.

7 To satisfy shareholders and pull out of negotiations completely.

15.6.5 Constraint

Here, constraints are defined that act to diminish the possibility of certain options. Some of the options available may not be appropriate in combination because of either cultural or systemic reasons. We can reduce the options that we can consider possibilities for settlement from this. Part of the process is also to establish a ranking on the existing possible option outcomes.

The scenario possibilities discussed above and that relate to the actor paradigm Table 15.16 are definable as shown in Table 15.17 through an actor tableau that summarises the options information. The ranking has occurred informally by an examination of the actor paradigms, though it might have been better, in addition, to have consulted the actors directly and then compared with the paradigms to seek contradiction. Within this summary and its ranking lies the possibility of a settlement. We note the relationships between the actor properties and needs, which operate as a source of power for each actor in the situation that maintains the conflict process.

Table 15.17 Comparative actor tableau indicating possible actor ranking. Note that properties of one actor relates to needs of other

Actor attributes	DDW	DDW rank	MDHC	MDHC rank
Properties	Solidarism in embargo action	1	Shareholder support	1
	Public support	3	Financial strength	2
	Mass media support	2	Employment opportunities	3
	International support	4		
Goal options	Reintroduction of NDLS	1	Reinstate DDW:	
	Support plan for a workers cooperative	2	a directly	5
			b through Drake International	3
	Accept existing offer	3	Support reintroduction of NDLS	6
	Pull out of negotiations	4	Increase number of DDW job offers	1
			Introduce labour pool with DDW employment possibilities	2
			Pull out of negotiations	4
Needs	Long-term settlement	1	Normalisation of business:	
	Opportunities for employment	2	a processes	1
	Relief of individual hardship	3	b opportunities	2
			c workforce balance	3

15.6.6 Choice

In the above phase we have explored the conflict informally through an inquirer's perspective. We shall continue this below by considering only the selection step. Other steps in this phase will be appropriate in the case that a formal exploration of synthesis has occurred.

1P3.1 Selection

The selected choice of options for both principal actors to sustain the least structural damage would involve some form of compromise. For example if MDHC were to once again increase the number of job offers, perhaps the leaders of the action could be persuaded to hold a ballot to decide on the offer.

Any of the options generated for both actors would still need to have a consensus taken, and once again as far as the dismissed dockers are concerned we return to the question of a ballot.

Ballot is an emotive word for some which seems unacceptable at this present time. However, if it is the case that attrition has played a role in dramatically altering DDW weltanschauungen that is not yet represented in their manifest paradigm, then a secret ballot for the acceptance of a financial settlement with some job offers would appear to be the choice of option for solution.

This and only this will prove conclusively if the structural damage sustained has advanced beyond a critical impasse. If voting independently without pressure still records a call for continued action by the dismissed dockers, then MDHC must reconsider its options. This might well be to pull out of negotiations completely and satisfy its shareholders.

Iterations or recursions

Formal approaches to this conflict situation could also be developed. For instance, the actor tableau could be further explored by a recursive application of CMC, perhaps applying only the outline phase description of analysis, synthesis and choice. Either soft or hard approaches are applicable here, which would have to be tied together within a virtual paradigm to ensure that their basic propositions are themselves not contradictory.

A soft approach would take the paradigms and the actor tableau to the stakeholders (DDW and MDHC or their representatives) and enable them to resolve the issues through a process of facilitation. A harder approach that is also useful for a comparative pre-emptive analysis is that of Fraser and Hipel (1984), the conflict analysis model, which extends Table 15.17. This would enable us to explore the relationships between the goal options elements already defined, and would seek stable goal possibilities by attempting to maximise the ranking of each possible outcome for the actors involved. Part of this process might be to set up games that are capable of exposing the myths of each actor, which often contribute to the continuance of a conflict situation, and examining in further detail the exposed attitudes and beliefs of those involved.

Another, perhaps related, approach is the Petersen (1992) stochastic model of the data collected in the 3P1.2 step. This would occur through yet another independent recursion. In this, we would have to rework the data in order to express the events as a Weibull frequency distribution that is capable of identifying changes in the structural relationships of the sequence of events. This could expose whether circumstances have developed in which the structural relationship between the two principal actors has changed around specific dates. This could provide deep insights into the decision processes of each actor that would contribute to an understanding of the formal hard approach, or of the facilitation in the formal soft approach.

15.6.7 Conclusion for the Liverpool dock study

The Liverpool dock conflict situation can be seen as an asymmetric conflict situation with an exogenous conflict situation and topdog/underdog actors. If this is the case then there is a danger that any settlements may lead directly to structural violence, which in turn will reduce individual potential. The options suggested above would have to be examined with this in mind, and it would be up to each actor to evaluate their position to see if this was developing. Structural violence results in a continuing unsettled relationship between management and the workforce. A settlement that leads to the situation becoming an endogenous conflict if the DDW become subsumed within the MDHC may in addition lead to a form of terrorism developing that is a direct result of the structural violence imposed within the settlement. However, such an end result would seem to be unlikely in this particular situation. In any case, structural violence minimisation would seem to provide the safest longer-term settlement.

15.7 Case study 2: The fall of the Soviet empire

In this case study, taken from Yolles (1996), our intention is simply to examine the sociopolitical paradigm shift experienced by the Soviet Union as it passed through a dramatic change. The exploration of possible intervention strategies as models within a synthesis phase that could lead to a stable sociopolitical situation in Russia alone would require a very long answer, and it is not at all clear that such strategies exist. At least, we shall be able to show how it is possible to examine organisations that pass through paradigm shifts.

We remind ourselves that, simply expressed, the paradigm (Yolles, 1996a) represents a way of representing culture, assumptions and logic, and language that explains their behaviour. While we cannot explore the impact of the dramatic change on the market economy of Central and Eastern Europe in any detail, our intention is simply to indicate the nature of the paradigms, and to show how viewing situations in terms of paradigm shifts and through the conflict modelling cycle can help understand situations such as this and possibly anticipate problems to understanding.

As an introduction to the case study, we as usual produce a case summary.

15.7.1 Pre-evaluation for the case study

The rise of Communism has historically been a brief respite in the development of Central and Eastern Europe. Many of the pressures and conflicts that existed prior to the rise to power of the groups operating this political ideology have been submerged by autocratic rule. They have now reappeared as though the Communist empire had not existed (Kemp and Yolles, 1992). The Yugoslavian problem is a severe example of this (Katunaric, 1993), and the problems of a search for state (rather than 'underworld') structural stability within the Russian Federation is another.

The changes that have occurred since the demise of the Communist bloc, and in particular of the USSR, have held the attention of the world media. It has moved dramatically towards a market economy, causing a great deal of uncertainty, insecurity and individual hardship. Industries previously supported by the state now find that they must adjust from production quotas to economic targets. What does this mean, not only

Case summary

Activity	Description
Weltanschauung	The Soviet Union has collapsed as a political unit and empire. It has shifted from one ideology to another.
Inquirer's mission	To explore the basis of the paradigm shift that has occurred in what was the Soviet Union.
Methodology: CMC	To examine the nature of the change that occurred in what was the Soviet Union, and the possible consequences.
Goals and aims of inquiry	No intervention strategy is being sought, and so the goals and aims of the methodology are not being harnessed.
Nature of examination	The nature of the old paradigm of the Soviet Union is explored in terms of ideology and behaviour, and this is compared to the new paradigm of Central and Eastern Europe.
Explanatory model	The Soviet Union held a Communist ideology operated as an authoritarian structurally violent regime. However, it was still broadly part of Western culture and part of its industrial revolution. Its ideology might therefore be seen as an extreme version of that in other parts of Europe and the United States. Like the whole of the West, the Soviet Union was experiencing the impact of a recession that might best be explained macroscopically in terms of Sorokin's theory about cultural change. Like the Western countries, the Soviet bloc has passed through a new paradigm of privatisation with an impact that has been more compressed and thus extreme.
Options selection	No options have been intended for selection, since the complexity of situation has not been completely explored.

to the problems of enterprise management in these countries, but also in terms of governmental policies in dealing with the future?

The sociocultural context

Sorokin (1937) produced an empirical work that attempted to show how cultures change over the millennia because of their internal dynamics. These operate through the theoretical idea that societies have two opposing cultural forces at work, the *sensate* (i.e. through the senses, consistent with utilitarianism and materialism), and the *ideational* (relating to the idea). These forces are in opposition, and as their balance within a culture shifts, so does the nature of the culture. So, a period which was highly indicative of an ideational period began during the Christian era two thousand years ago, an insight supported by the examination of various cultural attributes like architecture, the arts and science. At the turn of the twentieth century, Western culture would seem to have shifted its orientation to the sensate.

Dramatic change in Central and Eastern Europe

In the examination of this situation, it is appropriate to identify the nature of the paradigm shift within analysis. As a result, two iterations will be undertaken, one for the pre-change situation, and the other through a second iteration to define the nature of the shift. The shape of the change may have some impact on the synthesis stage. There is no space here to do more than a cursory examination of the change through these two iterations. Synthesis would follow on by looking at solutions to the change and examining the relationship between the two paradigms, and the perceived needs of the different groups (government, enterprise, individual) that should be met.

1P1.1 and 1P1.2 Context and definition

In Europe, it has been said that governments operate oligarchically (a country run by the state), rather than democratically (government by the people directly or by representation). This is supported by the idea that government makes decisions about social issues in general without reference to the population it rules, and is only called to account periodically after a number of years. In this sense, the difference between governments of the old Communist states of Europe and those of the West can be seen as a distinction in respect of factors like the degree of coercion (and terrorism; Ionescu, 1975, p. 210) within their instruments of rule. Despite this, the two spheres of ideology represent a similar form of society in that they represent different 'species' of the same genus (Ionescu, 1975, p. 14).

The European recession has led to a search for economic stability by the voting public. As a result, voting behaviour has sought what may appear to be stability through the success of parties operating in such a way that they appear to *know*. This situation is exacerbated by the consideration that both Communist and non-Communist Europe faced the same problem: the incompatibility of their respective degrees of centralism with post-industrial society (Ionescu, 1975, p. 16).

In the implementation of policies governing Central and Eastern European countries, various instruments were used which satisfied Soviet ideology. One was based on the proposition that individual interest was seen as secondary to the social interest, which was itself seen to be representative of the individual interest. The economy was planned, and organisations knew what was expected of them, even if they found difficulty in satisfying those expectations.

Thus, one of these instruments concerned the use of labour. In theory, individuals owned their own force of labour, and could use it according to their wishes. However, under Communist Party policy implementation, the state, using a variety of legal and other procedures, was able to limit the way in which that right was exercised. Consequently, processes of employment became centrally controlled.

To many observers, Communist regimes in Central and Eastern Europe were essentially not prone to inflation or industrial unrest, primarily because the population tended to be under less freedom of expression than in other forms of European political regime. In Central and Eastern European countries, a centralist dependency occurred during Communist rule towards the Soviet Union, as also occurred, for instance, for Iceland, Finland, Egypt and Afghanistan (Holsti, 1967).

The Soviet paradigm includes consideration of its cultural attributes and its propositions. Its ideology relates to its cultural attributes, and its mode of operations concerning 'strong' centralised government define its paradigm. The propositions will include responsibility for labour (including its state management and assuring full employment), responsibility for the economy (for instance, no inflation), and ways of ensuring these, such as the use of coercion.

1P1.3 Form and influences

The form of the Central and Eastern European countries under Soviet domination relates to the nature of their structures, and the way in which the underlying processes occurred which supported these structures. Thus the history of the rise of Communism resulted in an autocratic ideology that demanded rigid structures with role and departmental processes that were highly defined. In effect, the structure was totally incapable of adaptability to new environmental pressures.

While there was committed trade between the Communist bloc countries and the USSR, there was still an interdependency with the West, for example in the need to purchase high technology products and grain. Having a controlled economy did not therefore insulate Central and Eastern Europe from the effects of a major recession in the West.

1P1.4 Trajectory

The problems associated with Central and Eastern Europe related to a stationary political regime and economy, and neither was flexible enough to deal with the impact of recessionary influences.

2P1.1 and 2P1.2 Context and definition

The dramatic change in Central and Eastern Europe occurred because of the socio-economic pressures that arose, in a similar way to the change that occurred in Western countries like the UK. It is possible to debate whether the ensuing political change was inevitable, but this is not a purpose of this case study. If the ideas of Sorokin are valid and correctly applied to Europe, and if they represent a situation of structural instability, then relatively small changes in the social fabric of Central and Eastern Europe could have had an affect on its whole sociopolitical structure.

The international recession has had an impact on Central and Eastern Europe, as can be seen in the changes in policy that have occurred in the various countries during the past two decades, and this culminated in the shift to a market economy. This change, and the consequential expected individual freedom and wealth, was a spring of joy for the populations of the countries of Central and Eastern Europe that were loosened from the USSR. Visions of a market economy, freedom of choice and action, and prosperity abounded. In due course, the realities of a market economy would come to be a socio-economic shock.

The new market economy paradigm was centred around principles of competition, which apply not only to sales of products, but also to payments to the labour force. In Germany, for instance, this resulted in structural violence (damage caused to the potential of individuals because of the social structures set up around them) to the East Germans, who saw that they were getting paid significantly less than their West German co-workers in the same company. There were also problems in defining and achieving production, now that quotas were no longer defined. Social problems arose, for instance in Russia and Poland, as the expectations of the market economy were not shown to realise the promise. Neither were expectations fulfilled that the new economies could be well managed, as illustrated by the effective devaluation of the Czech economy in 1997.

Not only were there difficulties at the governmental and the individual levels, but also at the company level. One of these is Vitcovice, with about 20 000 employees, operating from Ostrava in the Czech Republic. It is involved in the manufacture of many types of steel, rubber and associated engineering products.

The company was committed to producing quotas for the USSR, and financially supported to do this by the Czech state instruments under encouragement by the USSR itself. It was the major employer in its region. Vitcovice, like many other companies in its position, found itself in a social dilemma. It could no longer sell its products to the bankrupt Soviets, nor with ease in the West, which was experiencing its own problems of recession. The company had absolutely no marketing expertise, nor an understanding of the market economy in anything more than a theoretical way. More importantly, there were significant implications of changes in business for these companies, especially for management unused to the dynamics of a market economy. With losses of significant markets in the East, the company was going through a period of retrenchment. Management training was an essential requirement. Senior posts were filled by staff whose background was in science or engineering. There were very small budgets for management training and these tended to be spent on update courses when needs were pressing rather than on widespread management development programmes. University curricula had in the past provided a good grounding, whether in economic or technological disciplines, though not in market economy principles. The retrenchment meant, however, that graduate recruitment was likely to be stalled. One solution was to change the management to enable the company to operate under the market economy paradigm. However, this required that suitable management staff were available in the market, and early on in the change this was not the case. This situation has now changed, and many of the staff have been replaced.

2P1.3 Form and influences

Typically in Central and Eastern European countries undergoing change, two centres of powers existed, the central government and the popular movement. The two centres had to accommodate each other. Their interplay generated anomalies, however. For example, in Romania after December 1989, a variety of measures were initiated by government representation, and through the popularist movement of change. The number of working hours was officially reduced to six hours, though it remained between eight and ten hours.

The international community provided a small amount of funding to the countries of Central and Eastern Europe in order to assist them in developing the market economy organisation. Much of this, however, was fed through existing organisations in the West that had their own commercial interests to cater for. They brought their own paradigms with them, which influenced the view of their partners. However, this influence was a two-way process as companies learned what could and could not be done, and a mode of operations and communications process that enabled partial implementation of activities.

1P1.4 Trajectory

The propositional base of the market economy was different from that expected or understood by government, individuals or industry. A clear theoretical knowledge of the principles was present, but there was little practical experience except by a few individuals who had been exposed previously. Without an ability to match expectation with practical matters, there was bound to be some social unrest. New social problems would also be met as the new paradigm would impact society. Difficulties in Russia with a new power class represented by the Russian mafia was one more graphic example.

15.7.2 Conclusion for the Soviet study

Central and Eastern European countries have looked towards the West in order to help them develop their market economies. Problems in these countries were appearing at all levels of society. Few systemic modelling instruments were apparently constructed to enable probing into the uncertain waters of a possible future stability. Negative feedback seemed to be the main mechanisms to be used, as the progression into the market economy occurred.

The way it has been applied in the case is discursive, but this is needed in order to provide a basis for understanding the approach to the case. It is also because of the limitation of space. If one examines the change as though it represents a paradigm shift, then some of the consequences that have been seen are subject to anticipation, and policy can be initiated to respond to such anticipation. The idea that the dramatic and apparently discontinuous change can be viewed as catastrophic change is interesting in as far as it offers the idea that more dramatic change is possible, if only we knew the significance of small parametric changes, and, indeed, could identify the parameters that we refer to. The use of CMC as one of the many systems methodologies available is appropriate because it is, as far as this author is aware, the only cyclic inquiring methodology that is intended to address large-scale situations.

REFERENCES

Ackoff, R.L. (1979) 'The future of operational research in the past', *Journal of the Operational Research Society*, 30, 93–104.

Brown, J.A.C. (1961) *Freud and the Post-Freudians*. Harmondsworth: Pelican.

Chorpa, D. (1990) *Quantum Healing: Exploring the frontiers of mind/body medicine*. New York: Bantam Books.

Crawley, J. (1992) *Conflict: Managing to make a difference*. London: Nicholas Brealey.

Eysenck, H.J. (1957) *Sense and Nonsense in Psychology*. Harmondsworth: Penguin.

Flood, R.L. and Jackson, M.C. (1991) *Creative Problem Solving: Total systems intervention*. Chichester: Wiley.

Fraser, N.M. and Hipel, K.W. (1984) *Conflict Analysis: Models and resolutions*. Amsterdam: North-Holland.

Fudenberg, D. and Tirole, J. (1991) *Game Theory*. Cambridge, MA: MIT Press.

Galtung, J. (1975) *Peace: Essays in peace research*, vol. 1. Copenhagen: Christian Ejlers.

Gass, N. (1994) 'Conflict analysis in the politico-military environment of a new world order', *Journal of the Operational Research Society*, 45(2), 133–42.

Guha, A. (1993) 'From continuing conflict to peace'. *Journal of Conflict Processes*, 1(2), 36–43.

Habermas, J. (1970) *Knowledge and Interest in Sociological Theory and Philosophical Analysis*. London: Macmillan, pp. 36–54.

Holsti, K.J. (1967) *International Politics*. Englewood Cliffs, NJ: Prentice Hall.

Howard, N. (1971) *Paradoxes of Rationality*. Cambridge, MA: MIT Press.

Husserl, E. (1977) *Cartesian Meditations*. The Hague: Martinus Nijhoff.

Ionescu, G. (1975) *Centripetal Politics*. London: Hart-Davis, MacGibbon.

Jackson, M.C. (1992) *Systems Methodology for the Management Sciences*. London: Plenum Press.

Katunaric, V. (1993) 'The conflicts in ex-Yugoslavia/Croatia in the light of the ethnic competitive model', *Journal of Conflict Processes*, 1(2), 2–14.

Kemp, G. and Yolles, M. (1992) 'Conflict through the rise of European culturalism'. *Journal of Conflict Processes*, 1(1).

Krishnamurti and Bohm, D. (1996) *Más Allá del Tiempo*. Barcelona: Kairós. Originally translated from 'The Ending of Time', Krishnamurti Foundation Trust Ltd. London: Bramdean.

Maslow, A. (1954) *Motivation and Personality*. New York: Harper and Row.

Mingers, J. (1995) *Self-Producing Systems*. New York: Plenum Press.

Mitchell, G.D. (1968) *A Dictionary of Sociology*. London: Routlege & Kegan Paul.

Mitchell, J. (1993) 'State formation and minority nationalism: Scotland's demand for self-government', *Journal of Conflict Processes*, 1(2), 26–34.

Osgood, C.E. and Tannenbaum, P.H. (1955) 'The principles of congruity in the predication of attitude change', *Psychological Review*, 62, 42–55.

Petersen, I. (1992) 'Modelling international wars', *Journal of Conflict Processes*, 1(1), 57–73.

Rokeach, M. (1968) Beliefs, Attitudes, and Values: A theory of organisational change. San Francisco, CA: Jossey-Bass.

Ruloff, D. (1975) *Konflictlosung durch Vermittlung: computersimulation zwischenstaatlicher Krisen*. Basel: Berkhauser Verlag.

Singer, J.D. (1978) *The Correlates of War*. London: Collier Macmillan.

Smoker, P. (1972) 'International process simulation'. In Laponce, J.A. and Smoker, P. (eds) *Experimentation and Simulation in Political Science*. Toronto: University of Toronto Press.

Sorokin, P.A. (1937) *Social and Cultural Dynamics*. New York: American Book Company.

Spanier, J.W. (1972) *Games Nations Play*. London: Thomas Nelson & Son.

Vogler, J. (1993) 'Security and global environment', *Journal of Conflict Processes*, 1(2), 16–24.

Wilkinson, J.H. (1996) 'Inequality kills', *Observer*, 7 October.

Yolles, M.I. (1992) 'The conflict modelling cycle', *Journal of Conflict Processes*, 1(1), 39–56.

Yolles, M.I. (1996) 'Modelling the consequences of the Soviet fall', *Systemist*, February.

Yolles, M.I.(1996a) 'Critical systems thinking, paradigms, and the modelling space', *Practical Systems*, 9(5).

CHAPTER 16

Exploring the practice of mixing methods

OVERVIEW

Methodologies of management systems can be seen as analytically and empirically independent orthogonalities established in a single frame of reference defined in term of some cognitive purposes. This idea can be generalised in terms of conceptual domains that have a projected cognitive quality (like purposes, interests and influences). In this way we can see the principle to be recursive. For example, each methodology is itself composed of a set of conceptual domains that provide cognitive influences, and these may also be seen as orthogonalities within it. Such considerations enable us to provide additional ways of comparing and contrasting management systems methodologies. Illustrations of how this can occur are provided, and as a backcloth to this, the methodologies considered here are characterised, and a typology established for them. Methodologies can also be mixed, and examples of frameworks that enable this to occur are given.

OBJECTIVES

This chapter will show:

- the domain composition of methodologies through an example;
- how different methodologies differ;
- the main conceptualisations of each methodology;
- how the methodologies can be compared;
- how to define a framework for mixing methods.

457

16.1 Partitioning methodologies

In Chapter 10 we argued that methodologies can themselves be seen as orthogonalities when they are:

1 analytically and empirically independent;
2 established in a framework that relates their cognitive purposes together.

We can generalise this idea by conceiving of conceptual analytically and empirically independent domains established as orthogonalities. These occur because they are established in a single frame of reference through some cognitive quality. In the work of Habermas this quality is 'interest' at the systemic or behavioural level, while in our work it has been 'purpose' at the organising or transmogrific level. We can use this idea at the metasystemic level taking the quality as 'influences'. Let us consider an example of such an idea by examining the cognitive influences on organisational development (OD).

OD has a core of ideas that derive from systems that centre on the simple open system model (Fig. 16.1). Many of its ideas also derive from the relationships that have been identified to occur in Western society from theory coming from social psychology, politics and organisational culture.

The domain of social psychology deals with considerations such as social factors in perception–cognitive processes, social influence process, group structure process, the individual and the process of socialisation. Politics is concerned with engineering the enablement of group form, condition of group order, and related processes. It is through politics that differing interests reach accommodation, and it rests on the dispositions of power. Thus politics is seen as a power-related activity concerned with managing relations between different interests. Finally, organisational culture is concerned with values, attitudes and beliefs, and it relates to the roles of personnel.

Each of these domains is analytically and empirically independent, and is seen to provide a cognitive influence on the OD paradigm. This has the same status as Habermas's cognitive interests and our cognitive purposes, both explored in Chapter 10. The OD paradigm is effectively a frame of reference that enables each domain to be established

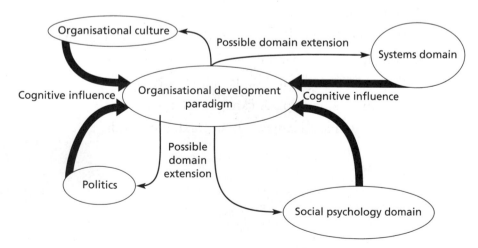

Fig. 16.1 Cognitive influences on organisational development

as an orthogonality. It is used in a way that Midgley might refer to as 'mixed', and enables domain 'coordination' to occur through domain cognitive influences without encountering the danger of paradigm incommensurability.

The cognitive purposes of the OD paradigm are expressed in terms of its methodological mission (to seek a balance of forces with the environment) and goals (resistance to change, political power, control). Resistance to change involves aspects of social psychology, organisational culture and politics, while control is more seen from the perspective of social psychology. These domains are analytically and empirically independent, and have been established in a broad framework to explain the type of situation being inquired into. We refer to such domains as *orthogonalities* that are tied together in a domain framework created through a paradigm.

Since a domain may be seen to be an independent part of the conceptual whole of a methodology, it will have a propositional sub-base within a partition of the paradigm that will be responsible for the generation of part of the knowledge of the methodology. In conjunction with the other domains, a unique whole propositional base is developed for the methodology. The relationship of the propositional sub-bases (and thus the domains) may be nonlinear, and will together be responsible for the generation of a plurality of knowledges. This nonlinearity suggests that manifest domain missions may not contribute to the overall mission of the methodology in a way that may be seen to be linearly differentiable.

16.2 Summarising methodologies

We have considered the cognitive aspects of methodological complementarism, have discussed the possibilities of comparing and coordinating methodologies and methods, and are now in a position to look more to the practical matters of actually comparing and mixing methodologies.

The methodologies considered here are systems intervention strategy (SIS), organisational development (OD), soft systems methodology (SSM), viable systems model methodology (VSMM) and the conflict modelling cycle (CMC). As a start to making comparison between the methodologies, we shall provide a summary overview about each of them. Direct comparison will then be made in terms of their cognitive purposes. Since cognitive purpose is analytically independent of the knowledge generated by the paradigm, the problem of paradigm incommensurability does not arise.

A comparator of methodologies might well also be interested in relating the methodologies cybernetically. The basis of this has been established in each of the other chapters of Section 3, and it has not been seen to be necessary to develop this further here.

16.2.1 Systems intervention strategy

In order to deal with complexity, SIS conceptualises that three types of change should be addressed: technical, organisational and personal. It is a relatively simple but useful methodology that adopts two orthogonalities in its cognitive space: human needs and technical organisation. It has a mission to provide a strategy for intervention intended to balance the forces from the environment. It does this through three goals during intervention, to achieve (a) technical development, (b) organisational change and (c) personal development of the participants within the situation. The aims embedded in the methodology are that an inquirer should attempt to ensure that intervention strategies are robust, and to enhance this a risk and/or decision analysis should be undertaken.

SIS is particularly useful for situations in which definable objects of attention can be identified. Unlike some hard methodologies, its practitioners become involved in consulting the participants of a situation, thus attempting to identify their needs. It is a straightforward methodology, which therefore holds a great deal of power.

The methodology seeks to introduce steady state changes that enable new balances with the environment to occur. This in essence derives from the perception that there should be equilibrium between the system and its environment. In many situations that are continually under environmental flux and shifting beyond the threshold of control, balances are continually being disturbed. The problem of seeing the nature of the disturbance in order to reapply the methodology may be problematic.

SIS recognises the distinction between the real world and the system model by permitting the idea of a relative perspective. This is equivalent to Checkland's idea of a relevant system that is dependent upon the purpose for an inquiry and the weltanschauung of an inquirer. However, SIS recommends little to explore this. Once a system has been defined, the various models can be explored through a process of methodological iteration that enables inquirer learning to occur. Thus, a dominant perspective sought through SIS may be inappropriate. SIS can also be used to create models that formulate strategies for intervention to produce change that relates to a problem situation that does not exist. Human considerations for the possible feasibility of implementing a strategy are not adopted. Consistent with its hard origins, SIS is mostly used such that situations are considered in terms of organisational objects that may not see human mental attributes as anything but constraints to object-related intervention strategies. SIS is also devoid of any organisational theory, and this can make the search for intervention strategies more difficult.

The methodology may be seen to be used linearly in its early stages. However, its intention is that the steps should be used according to inquirer need rather than procedural definition. The control aspects of SIS are undeveloped, explicitly enabling control to originate from an inquirer.

16.2.2 Organisational development

Unlike SIS, OD provides a systemic foundation for a theoretical base of organisational theory. In order to deal with complex situations, OD conceptualises that situations should be seen in terms of power relationships, control processes and innate resistance to change, all of which must be dealt with by addressing both individuals and the culture to which they belong. It adopts three orthogonalities as part of its cognitive space. These are social psychology, politics and culture. It may be thought that culture might be a part of social psychology. However, as indicated by Secord and Backman (1964) (in the preface to their book), culture and personality 'appears to have become a distinctive field in itself rather than an integral part of social psychology'. Indeed, books on organisational culture and change (like that of Williams *et al.*, 1989) do not appear to associate themselves with social psychology.

The mission of OD is to establish a balance of forces with the environment of the system. To do this its goals are to provide intervention strategies that are sensitive to political power, resistance to change and control. An inquirer, when exploring a situation, should be able to define characteristics of effectiveness that will be used as reference criteria in controlling the application of the methodology.

The OD tradition is based on a narrow view of organisational effectiveness, and it is not able to deal with issues of politics and culture. It 'does not seem to work well in organisations that emphasise status and authority differences or in nations that do not share the values underlying development. Even where they are appropriate, traditional organisational development interventions usually yield minor, incremental improvements in organisational functioning, as opposed to the radical transformations needed for recovery from crises and decline' (Harrison, 1994, pp. 8–9). Harrison's developments address this situation by concentrating on effectiveness criteria to be used as reference criteria during the control processes of the methodology.

OD is very distinctly a soft methodology. Soft and hard methodologies have distinct orientations, and each is susceptible to its own set of generic criticisms. Criticism of hard paradigms is that they see situations as a set of 'entities with an objective existence in the world', and of soft paradigms because they see situations as a set of 'mental constructs of observers ... and systemicity is transferred from the world to the process of inquiry into the world' (Jackson, 1992, p. 6). Different soft methodologies also have distinct criticisms that are unique to them because of their different propositional bases.

OD is a consultant-orientated methodology. Consequently, an OD consultant may have a weltanschauung that biases the facilitating role being played in an indeterminable way. While the bias may be consultant led, it may also be client led, thus destroying consensus approaches to inquiry. This is interesting since OD, like many soft approaches, is a consensus methodology that is intended to adopt consensus views about situations. It requires that stakeholder participation occurs during diagnosis such that situations can be explored. 'Participation is essential to soft systems thinking, philosophically because it provides the justification for the objectivity of the results and practically because it generates creativity and ensures implementation' (Jackson, 1992, p. 163). It is assumed that active participation will occur, though this may not be the case in coercive or fragmented situations, or more generally where there is no motivation for participation.

As with SIS, those who see situations in terms of dissipative structures have a further problem with OD. It is an equilibrium methodology that attempts to maintain a balance of forces with their environment. In the longer term this probably cannot be maintained because of the inherent instabilities that will continually manifest themselves. OD is normally intended to address problem situations caused by identifiable change rather than to establish proactive approaches that can respond to it dynamically. The circumstances of an inquiry into a situation may 'permit' social engineering that appears to resolve social conflicts, but do not 'permit' analyses or acts that challenge clients' interests (Rosenhead, 1976). As an additional note, OD is based on a social theory that defines a set of rules according to which psychological and social psychological processes operate. This theory is based on experiences with Western culture, and proposed individual and group action may be inappropriate for very diverse culturally plural situations.

16.2.3 Soft systems methodology

SSM deals with complexity by differentiating between a logical and a cultural stream of inquiry. It can be seen as having two orthogonal dimensions within its cognitive space. Its cultural stream is conceived to be composed of culture (including politics), and social or technical organisation. Its mission is for improvement of the situation, and to do this its goals are to produce an intervention strategy that has cultural feasibility and social (system) desirability. Its inquirer aims are variable, determinable through weltanschauung.

It is a versatile methodology because of its concept of streams of inquiry, and the related control loops that operate between the streams in an attempt to ensure modelling commensurability with a situation. However, as a soft methodology it is not without its criticisms. Two useful summaries of these exist in the works of Jackson (1992) and Flood and Jackson (1991), and centre around the nature of soft methodologies themselves, of which SSM is an example. SSM is a consensus methodology (Thomas and Lockett, 1979), obtaining consensus opinion about situations, and consensus may not highlight conflictual profiles. This is normally the case even though Checkland and Scholes (1990) say it need not be. Thus, SSM plays down conflicts of real interest. It can be characterised by asymmetry of power, structural conflict, contradiction and cultural dominance.

The involvement of stakeholders from a situation being inquired into is essential for SSM to work. It is assumed that this is possible, though this may not be the case in coercive or fragmented situations. It believes that any conflicts that do exist can be resolved at least temporarily. It does this through structured debate around root definitions and conceptual models. Conflict is always seen as a clash of values and not as a difference in material interest (Burrell, 1983). Power can shape which weltanschauung influences change (Thomas and Lockett, 1979). Stages 5 and 6 of SSM will be critically inhibited by power imbalances deriving from the structure of the organisations and society. Consequently the results will favour the powerful. This is only sustained because SSM inquirers artificially limit the scope of their inquiry so as not to challenge their clients' or sponsors' fundamental interests.

SSM rarely finds itself with incommensurable weltanschauungen because it works with a community (managers) that shares similar interests (Burrell, 1983). Powerful clients can restrict the emergence of alternative, radical weltanschauungen and lead to reformist recommendations for change (Thomas and Lockett, 1979). The client can restrict the information available to an inquirer at the analysis stage. Radical culturally feasible root definitions may not be permitted by clients in client dominant situations. The circumstances of an inquiry into a situation may 'permit' social engineering that appears to resolve social conflicts, but do not 'permit' analyses or acts that challenge clients' interests (Rosenhead, 1976). SSM is seen as a subjective and idealistic methodology (Mingers, 1984). It fails to find structural features of social reality such as conflict and power. Organisations are created by people who may have conflicting aims and intentions, and who may not know what they are creating. They will involve different resources when social construction is taking place. The social world that is created constrains its individual membership within its complexity.

Too much attention is paid to power. Thus a function of SSM is idealism (Rosenhead, 1984) since inquirers ascribe prime motive power to the force of ideas. Idealism also limits the ability of soft systems inquirers to understand how change comes about. This impacts on their ability to promote change. Like SIS and unlike OD, SSM lacks a social theory capable of accounting for why particular sets or perceptions of reality emerge, and why some perceptions are found to be more plausible than others (Willmott, 1993). Neither does it recommend through theory how perceptions that may be seen to be problematic may be addressed through organisational theory. SSM has a practical weakness of being unable to take into account the possibility of systemically distorted communications (Jackson, 1992). Weltanschauungen are not very easily changed

(Mingers, 1984). In order to improve some situations, change in the weltanschauungen of participants is essential.

As Jackson argues in a summary about SSM criticism, 'if it is impossible to achieve consensus through open and free participation, if there is fundamental conflict, if weltanschauungen refuse to change, if power determines the outcome of debate, then soft systems methodologies cannot be properly employed in many situations' (Jackson, 1992, p. 166).

16.2.4 Viable systems model methodology

The viable systems model (VSM) deals with complexity through the notion that one can distinguish between a system and its metasystem, enabling decision processes to be drawn away from the behavioural processes of the situation under investigation. There are a variety of methodologies associated with the VSM. They necessarily all distinguish between the system and metasystem in effect as behavioural and 'cognitive' domains, and often adopt *technical organisation* and *cultural behaviour* as orthogonalities. Their mission is to generate viability, and to do this they have goals that are to generate dynamic stability and adaptability. Inquirer aims are to explore policy, coordination, integration and future. The VSM is a powerful approach intended to correct the faults of form in an organisation that interfere with its viability.

In the VSM identity is secured when a system becomes viable. However, is there more than one type of identity? Following Mingers, we can talk about autopoietic systems having class identity. The next stage is a self-referencing system that defines individual identity. Suppose we say that a caterpillar is an autopoietic system. When it changes to a butterfly it also changes its (class) identity (Mingers, 1995). However, it could be argued that the individual identity does not change after the caterpillar metamorphoses. If viability is not related to class identity, then a change in an organisation from one generic class to another cannot be recognised methodologically. Indeed, the question now arises: can VSM operate as a methodology within a situation in which class identity changes? If VSM is used to heal the faults that appear in structurally critical systems, then can inquirers recognise if the system has shifted class through a dramatic change? This may in the end be determined by the relationship between the ideology attributable to the weltanschauung of an inquirer and that of the paradigm of the system.

However, both individual and class identity are implicit to VSM, which deals with the former as it relates to survival, and with the latter in the metasystem if only to ensure that the organisation is holistic. Thus, the question could be put 'to what extent you think that the people who constitute the senior management team share a picture of what it is that they manage' (Beer, 1979, p. 420). Beer's work with the rudimentary form of VSM in Chile, in which a democratically elected Marxist government led by Allende metamorphosed into a despotic one with the arrival of Pinochet, is an example of an organisation that we can argue had an unchanging individual identity (Chile remained Chile), but a changing generic identity (from democracy to totalitarianism). In cases where the inquirer is not part of the generic shift, an inquirer's aim may well be to check on the class status of an organisation being inquired into. This would enable verification that the organisation and the inquirer are not in ideological conflict.

VSM is a cybernetic model that has at its base general systems theory. An antecedent is Ashby's idea that systems should be ultrastable. Since the 1960s this term has rarely been used. Instead, the idea of morphogenesis has replaced it. VSM is designed to generate an ultrastable world, where control from a metasystem can always operate. However, in more modern theory, in environments involving chaos, control systems break down in the nether region between stability and instability (referred to as bounded stability), and self-organisation takes on a new meaning. This is the region in which chaos operates, when new organisations develop from old ones through meta-morphosis. This process has been going on all around us as old organisations die or are transformed. In situations such as this the relationship between the system and the meta-system breaks down, as does metasystem control. It may be recognised that this has occurred. If so, then the use of VSM can be applied to a different level of system focus, where there is a deterministic (or at least rational expectation) connection between cog-nition and behaviour. However, the situation may not be addressable because either chaos runs through the whole organisation or some essential levels of the organisation are inaccessible to the VSM inquirer. In this case, self-organisation cannot be controlled from a metasystem.

The difference between self-organisation involving or not involving a metasystem is that in the former case the systems evolve according to the deterministic cognitive processes of a metasystem, while in the latter they evolve spontaneously according to undeterminable criteria that may or may not be related to the goals of a higher focus. Consider the case where the individual identity of an organisation continues to exist, but where the organisation has passed through a dramatic change. It can now be seen as a different organisation. If a VSM methodology is applied to make the organisation viable across the period of dramatic change, it must be realised that the original conceptualisa-tions may no longer be valid.

There are arguments that while VSM defines a logical stream of inquiry, it is not generically sensitive to social or cultural dimensions. It means that cultural and political aspects are not required to be taken into account.

VSM deals with logical relationships which (a) may break down in the chaotic region beyond system stability or (b) do not take into account authoritarian use. Some would argue that VSM can be misused by powerful groups. This can happen in the first case when the groups might wish to take advantage of the lack of metasystem if it occurs. In the second case such comments would derive from ethical judgements by others. Let us explore these ideas a little further.

It has been said that there is an inability in VSM to cater for the purposeful role of individuals. 'The model suggests that it is to the advantage of organisations to grant maximum autonomy to individuals' (Jackson, 1992, p. 122). However, it is said, this may not and often does not happen. According to Checkland (1980), VSM misses the human meaning aspects of individuals. Ulrich (1981) suggests that tools of inquiry should have an ethical dimension. It may be said, however, that 'it has never been claimed that VSM is all that is needed, or that sociocultural and sociopolitical aspects should not be addressed as well as structure, nor that VSM is rascal-proof, although its emphasis on devolving autonomy down to the lowest possible level is not popular with autocrats' (Leonard, 1996, personal communication). This clearly encourages one to con-sider the possibility of using VSM together with other methodologies that can address situations in ways that VSM is not directed towards. OD might well be one of these.

Some of the issues highlighted above can be addressed by noting that VSM provides a pragmatic approach towards inquiry. This is because mostly in the literature the cogni-tive model rather than the methodology is explored. This gives the inquirer a great deal of freedom to adjust the interpretation of VSMM to include, say, a cultural stream in the sense of Checkland's SSM. It is quite easy to develop a methodology that integrates VSM with other softer approaches of inquiry, as shown, for instance, by the work of Flood (1995) in total systems intervention. It is dependent upon weltanschauung, from which inquiry is occurring. The difficulty with such a powerful approach as VSM that we always come back to is that it is not a methodology, and inquirers may therefore not be guided according to ethical or ideological principles.

16.2.5 Conflict modelling cycle

The conflict modelling cycle deals with complex situations by conceptualising that conflict, attitudes and behaviour are analytically and empirically independent, and can be addressed separately. It explores situations through the orthogonalities of technical organisation (which relates to conflict process adjustment), culture, politics and social psychology. It is concerned with both conflict settlement and complementarism through addressing the conflicts that emerge from the paradigm pluralities of a situation.

The ideas embedded in the conflict settlement approach derive from conflict theory. It thus supports the concept that situations should be examined from a paradigm plural position as opposed to the more usual soft systems position of consensus intervention strategies. In order to facilitate settlements that do not invest in future problem situations, a fundamental proposition is that strategies for intervention should minimise structural violence. Also deriving from conflict theory are the goals that organisations should be able to adapt socioculturally, involve sociopolitical reorientation, and should be able to involve themselves in behavioural adjustment. The aims of an inquirer are to explore and engineer attitudes in group decision making, intragroup power and group behaviour.

Its approach towards complementarism comes from the idea that it needs to explore models that derive from different paradigms in order to satisfy the multidisciplinary needs of conflict settlement. An inquirer using CMC may adopt a mixed approach to inquiry. Circumstances and weltanschauung will determine the approaches selected on the soft–hard continuum. It should be determined by a knowledgeable inquirer in a well-defined inquiry space established through a virtual paradigm.

16.3 Comparing methodologies

A summary of each of the cognitive purposes of each of the methodologies considered in this section is given in Table 16.1.

If we are interested in mixing methods, then we may talk of their *congruence*. By this we mean agreement and consistency between two or more methodologies defined through cognitive purpose. Methodological congruence can work by selecting methodologies to work together, to be coordinated in a sequential and iterative way according to some predefined purpose that has been constructed in a virtual paradigm. The approach can be similar to the way that in OD the current and future state of a situation is to be decided. Equivalently, methodological congruence occurs by exploration of the methodological mission, and through an inquiry into the goals and aims of the methodology that determines where it is going and what it is intended to achieve.

The idea of congruence is thus that methodologies are selected to work together according to locally defined criteria. If this happens by respecting paradigm incommensurability, then their cognitive models should be kept distinct. This implies that the methodologies can be in some way coordinated by sequential working. We can thus see complementarism as acting through a sequence of locally defined *orthogonal inquiries* that together establish a space of inquiry. An inquiry space is therefore seen as a set of methodologies, each of which are orthogonalities tied together by a set of propositions and with given cognitive purposes. There might be a variety of alternative regimes for working in this space of inquiry that are defined by the set of propositions. For instance, the inputs for any one inquiry might include elements of the outputs from others. Prior to implementation of any strategy, outputs might be compared one to another, rationalised according to some local criteria, and then processed again through each methodology to ensure consistency.

Table 16.1 Comparison of different methodological and individual cognitive purposes for inquiry

Methodology		Cognitive purpose		
Name	*Cognitive influence orthogonalities*	*Methodological mission*	*Methodological goals*	*Inquirer aims*
Systems intervention strategy	Human needs, Technical organisation	Balance forces with environment	Technical development, Organisational change (in form), personal development	Robust strategies, Risk/decision analysis
Organisational development	Social psychology, Culture, Politics	Manage a renewing balance of forces through internal group and individual processes	Addressing resistance to change, political power, control	Effectiveness
Soft systems methodology	Culture, Politics, Technical organisation	Improvement	Cultural feasibility, social system desirability, political feasibility	Variable
Viable systems model methodology	Technical organisation, Cultural behaviour	Viability	Dynamic stability, adaptability	Policy selection, coordination, integration, future development
Conflict modelling cycle	Technical, through conflict resolution institutionalisation and control, or management Culture Politics Social psychology	Conflict settlement, complementarism	Cultural adaptation, political reorientation, behavioural adjustment	Attitude change, power adjustment, group behaviour modification

16.4 A framework for mixing methods

As an illustration of defining a framework for mixing methods, we shall explore the relationship between SIS and OD. To do so we shall refer to the cases of Chapters 11 and 12 of the budget deficit of the Liverpool City Council, which it wishes to address through service charging, the pilot example of which is the introduction of Disabled Car Badge Charging (DCBC). A case summary is provided below, giving a transparent specification of the nature of the problem, the inquirer's mission, and the methodologies that are to be adopted. It also gives a reasoning process for the linking of the two methodologies, and in so doing provides a propositional basis that acts as a rudimentary virtual paradigm. It may be noted that completion of this table may be an iterative process, occurring after the inquiry has been started, once the inquirer has achieved a sufficient level of understanding about the nature of the problem situation.

To begin with we will have in mind a situation from which the inquirer draws a mission. Normally a pre-evaluation of the situation will occur, and it is then that an idea of what method(s) is (are) to be chosen develops.

SIS is a methodology the mission of which is to establish a balance between an organisation and its environment. It does this from a relatively hard perspective, being successful in its examination of the more technical aspects of a situation and tending to define entities objectively. However, it also enables the exploration of situations in terms of mental perspectives, and thus takes on board soft aspects of a situation.

Case summary

Activity	Description
Weltanschauung	A council budget deficit exists that must be dealt with. One way is service charging, to be applied to the Division of Social Services in its issue of disabled car badges.
Inquirer's mission	To introduce service charging for disabled car badge issue as a pilot action intended to recoup money to be placed against Local Authority deficit.
Methodology: SIS	Mission to balance pressures from the Liverpool City Council environment on a proposed DCBC that will in turn contribute to a balance of forces between the Local Authority and its environment, by identifying a strategy that can implement the inquiry mission.
OD	Mission to balance the forces of the Liverpool City Council within its Social Services Division (that is proposing DCBC), thus ensuring that an SIS strategy is implementable.
Goals and aims of inquiry	SIS goals are to explore the technical, organisational and personal attributes of the situation to enable change to occur. It does this through the aim of creating a desirable robust strategy and evaluating it through a risk/decision analysis. OD goals address issues of resistance to change, political power, and control that may inhibit a change strategy from being feasibly implemented.
Nature of examination	SIS is being used to explore the complexity of a proposed introduction of DCBC, and, as a result, a strategy for DCBC implementation has resulted that looked primarily at the technical aspects of the situation. The strategy now becomes an input to OD to explore the internal nature of the organisation to see what needs to be done to enable the changes to the organisation to be acceptable. As a result, a strategy for dealing with the human complexities of the organisation results. The outputs from OD can be used as a constraining input for SIS.
Explanatory model	In SIS a focus of examination is created and the pressures that derive from the environment of the system at that focus are explored. In OD, a focus of examination is the organisational and social psychological context of the Division.
Options selection	In SIS options chosen define technical, organisational and personal features to be constructed for the implementation of DCBC. Further work, however, has to be undertaken to ensure that the proposed strategy is implementable within the Social Services Division of the Liverpool City Council. In OD options chosen the organisation's politics, control and resistance to change are explored.

OD is a soft methodology whose mission is to manage a renewing balance of forces within an organisation, through individuals, group involvement and cross-group negotiations. It does this through examining political power interests and an exploration of cultural form. It is a people-related process, and is therefore classed as a soft methodology. It is not traditional to produce a formalised system model as occurs with SIS. The impact of the real world on the informal system models produced is identified in terms of tasks and forces from the environment that generate the need for change. The system models are not separated out from the real world, but rather the models emerge from the human interactions that occur with the stakeholders.

SIS and OD have been used together in the exploration of a single situation in the pragmatic *Mabey switch*. This acknowledges that the SIS paradigm does not have a penchant directed towards soft situations and in particular is devoid of the organisational theory possessed by OD. The penchant of SIS is directed towards relatively hard situations in which 'objective' aspects of a situation are identifiable by the team of participants who are involved in the inquiry. It recognises that once SIS has been able to address a situation, and come up with possible intervention strategies for change, then it must be determined whether or not this solution is implementable within the situation under consideration and with the people involved. No matter how good a possible intervention strategy, it will only work if the people who are in some way involved, the stakeholders, are able to accommodate it, either because of their biases or prejudices, or because of conflicts embedded in relationships. The Mabey switch is what we may refer to as a *complementary action* between two or more methods, by which we mean that the inputs and outputs of two or more methodologies are mutually interactive.

The mission, goals and aims of a methodology represent a cognitive projection to the behavioural domain that enables the nature of congruence to be decided locally. SIS has a mission of maintaining a balance of forces between the defined system and its environment. It takes a principally technical approach to formulate change strategies, and has consequences that relate to organisational change and personal development. In particular, it engenders inquirers to explore robust strategies, and undertake risk and decision analysis that represents a relatively hard way of exploring situations. OD can be taken to be concerned with the internal balance of forces that result from a disturbance, and can be used to determine whether the intervention strategy derived from SIS is implementable in the situation being inquired into. OD is directed towards the perspective of power, resistance to change and control. It encourages inquirers to explore change from the perspective of the effectiveness of intervention strategies. As a whole, this represents a softer approach to inquiry.

Used in this way the two approaches are congruent even though they have incommensurable paradigms. SIS generates an output of a selected strategy suitable for a situation. This can now be considered as an input to OD that it must balance with a strategy of implementation. In the case that OD determines that the SIS strategy is not implementable because of certain organisational conditions, then a paradigm switch back to SIS occurs. Here the outputs from OD could be used as a new input to SIS. It is the switching back and forth that we refer to as a *Mabey switch*.

In Chapters 11 and 12 we provided the case studies on the Liverpool City Council. One is concerned with identifying a strategy for intervention using SIS, and the other with testing it through OD. These two cases are not accidental in their association. They have been offered to illustrate that the two methodologies can indeed be used together. However, to 'mix' them requires that a virtual paradigm is formulated, which enables a common frame of reference to be created. The creation of the virtual paradigm requires, however, a deep understanding (that comes from an appreciation of the meaning of their propositions) of the principles of each methodology to be harnessed in a 'mix'. The purposes of the two methodologies are seen to be analytically and empirically independent. This means that the methodologies can be taken as orthogonalities in an empirical space, and the output of one provides for an input to the other as defined within a virtual paradigm. Thus, the output of SIS is an intervention strategy. Let us now formulate a basic proposition that defines a virtual paradigm enabling us to mix the two methodologies. We propose that the penchant of SIS is basically systemic desirability, and while it addresses cultural feasibility it is not sensitive to it in the same way that OD is. If we take the strategy created as an output of SIS, then we may see it as an input of OD. In this way the behavioural aspects of each methodology are sequentially mixed while still maintaining their separateness. If we examine the paradigms of each methodology, it will be to ensure consistency or lack of propositional contradiction.

It is worth noting at this point that by adopting the Mabey switch neither the whole cycle of SIS nor many of the knowledge facets of OD are used. It therefore represents knowledge selection in Midgley's sense (Sections 10.3.2 and 10.3.4). To operate the mixed method strategy, we have therefore been selective about the knowledge that we adopt as part of our virtual paradigm. In order to see how we can do this, it is appropriate to pursue an epistemological argument.

Now, we have also argued in Chapter 5 that a scientific methodology can be subdivided into three time phases, and, like the methodology as a whole, each will have its own mission and goals. However, as also argued in Section 16.1 for the case example of OD, there are other ways of partitioning a methodology into orthogonal subsidiary domains that each have associated with them their own independent knowledge, and which contribute to the knowledges of the whole methodology. In the case summary we formulate a set of propositions and missions to enable a Mabey switch to occur. To do this means that we must be able to partition the cognitive purposes of SIS and OD, and use them selectively in a new virtual paradigm. Thus, the case summary can be taken as a basic representation of a virtual paradigm. This creates a common cognitive model that shares the world views of the methodologies, the inquirer and the situation, and applies the knowledges that have been accepted within that model.

If we return to the metaphor offered in Chapter 4 that a paradigm can be seen as a map, then its domains are autonomous regions of knowledge that can be selected and used to satisfy some purpose.

SUMMARY

Since methodologies with different **paradigms** have different cognitive purposes and attributes, they can in principle be selected to establish them as analytically and empirically independent orthogonalities in a single frame of reference, and related together in terms of some consistent cognitive purposes. In this way they can be mixed. Mixing methods does not mix together the knowledges of the different paradigms. Rather, the methodologies are used individually to satisfy defined intentions through selection and appropriate coordination to satisfy an inquirer's aim. The knowledges that are associated with these cognitive purposes are applied in a way determined by the inquirer according to his or her understanding, and these are established within an elementary virtual paradigm to provide an opportunity for their transparency to others.

REFERENCES

Beer, S. (1979) *The Heart of Enterprise*. Chichester: Wiley.

Burrell, G. (1983) 'Systems thinking, systems practice. A review', *Journal of Applied Systems Analysis*, 10, 121.

Checkland, P. (1980) 'Are organisations machines?' *Futures*, 12, 421.

Checkland, P.B. and Scholes, J. (1990) *Soft Systems Methodology in Action*. Chichester: Wiley.

Flood, R.L. (1995) *Solving Problem Solving*. Chichester: Wiley.

Flood, R.L. and Jackson, M. (1991) *Creative Problem Solving: Total Intervention Strategy*. Chichester: Wiley.

Habermas, J. (1979) *Communication and the Evolution of Society*. London: Heinemann.

Harrison, I.H. (1994) *Diagnosing Organisations: Methods, Models and Processes*. Thousand Oaks, CA: Sage.

Jackson, M.C. (1992) *Systems Methodologies for the Management Sciences*. New York: Plenum Press.

Mingers, J. (1984) 'Subjectivism and soft systems methodology – a critique', *Journal of Applied Systems Analysis*, 7, 41.

Mingers, J. (1995) *Self Producing Systems*. New York: Academic Press.

Rosenhead, J. (1976) 'Some further comments on "The Social Responsibility of OR"', *ORQ*, 17, 265.

Rosenhead, J. (1984) 'Debating systems methodology: conflicting ideas about conflict and ideas', *Journal of Applied Systems Analysis*, 11, 79.

Secord, P.F. and Backman, C.W. (1964) *Social Psychology*. New York: McGraw-Hill.

Thomas, A. and Lockett, M. (1979) 'Marxism and systems research: values in practical action'. In Ericson, R.F. (ed.) *Improving the Human Condition*. Louisville: SGSR, pp. 284–93.

Ulrich, W. (1981) 'A critique of pure cybernetic reason: the Chilean experience with cybernetics', *Journal of Applied Systems Analysis*, 8, 33.

Williams, A., Dobson, P. and Walters, M. (1989) *Changing Culture: New organisational approaches*. London: Institute of Personnel Management.

Willmott, H. (1993) 'Breaking the paradigm mentality', *Organisation Studies*, 14, 681–719.

INDEX